The Writer's Craft

THE McDOUGAL, LITTELL STUDENT BOARD

Song of a Clown

Laughing eyes behind white paint,
Painted smile on a silly face,
With curly wig and giant feet,
You bring joy to all you meet.

(Chorus)
Nothing beats the roar of the crowd,
playing fun and being loud,
Who wouldn't want to be a clown?
Until the circus tent comes down.

The Writer's Craft

SENIOR AUTHOR

SHERIDAN BLAU
University of California at Santa Barbara

CONSULTING AUTHOR

PETER ELBOW
University of Massachusetts at Amherst

SPECIAL CONTRIBUTING AUTHORS

Don Killgallon
Baltimore County Public Schools

Rebekah Caplan
Oakland Unified School District

SENIOR CONSULTANTS

Arthur Applebee
State University of New York at Albany

Judith Langer
State University of New York at Albany

McDougal Littell Inc.
A Houghton Mifflin Company
Evanston, Illinois   Boston Dallas Phoenix

SENIOR AUTHOR

Sheridan Blau, Senior Lecturer in English and Education and former Director of Composition, University of California at Santa Barbara; Director, South Coast Writing Project; Director, Literature Institute for Teachers

The Senior Author, in collaboration with the Consulting Author, helped establish the theoretical framework of the program and the pedagogical design of the Workshop prototype. In addition, he guided the development of the spiral of writing assignments, served as author of the literary Workshops, and reviewed completed Writer's Workshops to ensure consistency with current research and the philosophy of the series.

CONSULTING AUTHOR

Peter Elbow, Professor of English, University of Massachusetts at Amherst; Fellow, Bard Center for Writing and Thinking

The Consulting Author, in collaboration with the Senior Author, helped establish the theoretical framework for the series and the pedagogical design of the Writer's Workshops. He also reviewed Writer's Workshops and designated Writing Handbook lessons for consistency with current research and the philosophy of the series.

SPECIAL CONTRIBUTING AUTHORS

Don Killgallon, English Chairman, Educational Consultant, Baltimore County Public Schools. Mr. Killgallon conceptualized, designed, and wrote all of the features on sentence composing.

Rebekah Caplan, Coordinator, English Language Arts K-12, Oakland Unified School District, Oakland, CA; Teacher-Consultant, Bay Area Writing Project, University of California at Berkeley. Ms. Caplan developed the strategy of "Show, Don't Tell," first introduced in the book *Writers in Training,* published by Dale Seymour Publications. She also wrote the Handbook lessons and Sketchbook features for this series that deal with that concept.

SENIOR CONSULTANTS

These consultants reviewed the completed prototype to ensure consistency with current research and continuity within the series.

Arthur N. Applebee, Professor of Education, State University of New York at Albany; Director, Center for the Learning and Teaching of Literature; Senior Fellow, Center for Writing and Literacy

Judith A. Langer, Professor of Education, State University of New York at Albany; Co-director, Center for the Learning and Teaching of Literature; Senior Fellow, Center for Writing and Literacy

MULTICULTURAL ADVISORS

The multicultural advisors reviewed the literary selections for appropriate content and made suggestions for teaching lessons in a multicultural classroom.

Andrea B. Bermúdez, Professor of Multicultural Education; Director, Research Center for Language and Culture, University of Houston—Clear Lake

Alice A. Kawazoe, Director of Curriculum and Staff Development, Oakland Unified School District, Oakland, CA

Sandra Mehojah, Project Coordinator, Office of Indian Education, Omaha Public Schools, Omaha, NE

Alexs D. Pate, Writer, Consultant, Lecturer, Macalester College and the University of Minnesota

STUDENT CONTRIBUTORS

The following students contributed their writing.

Amity Baca, Denver, CO; Mousumi Behari, Aurora, CO; Mark Blatchford, Grand Rapids, MI; Regina Bly, Atco, NJ; Chakkarin Burudpakdee, Clementon, NJ; Stacy Smith, Kenosha, WI; Rene Froehmer, Clovis, CA; Matthew D. Jackson, Clarksville, TN; Ashley Kuhlman, Lansing, MI; Jamie Lentz, Hamilton, OH; Annie Maxwell, Santa Barbara, CA; Jim McConnell, York, PA; Utica Miller, Evanston, IL; David Norr, Evanston, IL; Nina Ramundo, Hamilton, OH; Trang Phan, York, PA; Luziris Pineda, Houston, TX; Tiffany Shue, York, PA; Jennica Thuet, Las Vegas, NV; Brook Volle, Las Vegas, NV; Jennifer Wilson, Mount Clemens, MI

The following students reviewed selections to assess their appeal.

Meghan Dwyer, Chicago, IL; Jason Greer, Evanston, IL; DeDe Heuerman, Effingham, IL; Adam Hooks, Mason, IL; Lucy Luevano, Chicago, IL; David Moo, Gurnee, IL; Katie Schnepf, Barrington, IL

TEACHER CONSULTANTS

The following teachers served as advisors on the development of the Workshop prototype and/or reviewed completed Workshops.

Wanda Bamberg, Aldine Independent School District, Houston, TX

Karen Bollinger, Tower Heights Middle School, Centerville, OH

Barbara Ann Boulden, Issaquah Middle School, Issaquah, WA

Loutish Burns, M. Lamar High School, Houston, TX

Christine Bustle, Elmbrook Middle School, Elm Grove, WI

Denise M. Campbell, Eaglecrest School, Cherry Creek School District, Aurora, CO

Cheryl Cherry, Haven Middle School, Evanston, IL

Gracie Garza, L.B.J. Junior High School, Pharr, TX

Patricia Fitzsimmons Hunter, John F. Kennedy Middle School, Springfield, MA

Mary F. La Lane, Driftwood Middle School, Hollywood, FL

Barbara Lang, South Junior High School, Arlington Heights, IL

Harry Laub, Newark Board of Education, Newark, NJ

Sister Loretta Josepha, S.C., Sts. Peter and Paul School, Bronx, NY

Jacqueline McWilliams, Carnegie School, Chicago, IL

Joanna Martin, Thompson Junior High School, St. Charles, IL

Karen Perry, Kennedy Junior High School, Lisle, IL

Patricia A. Richardson, Resident Teacher-Trainer, Harold A. Wilson Professional Development School, Newark, NJ

Pauline Sahakian, Clovis Unified School District, Clovis, CA

Elaine Sherman, Curriculum Director, Clark County, Las Vegas, NV

Richard Wagner, Language Arts Curriculum Coordinator, Paradise Valley School District, Phoenix, AZ

Beth Yeager, McKinley Elementary School, Santa Barbara, CA

ISBN 0-8123-8666-3
Copyright © 1995 by McDougal Littell Inc.
Box 1667, Evanston, Illinois 60204
All rights reserved. Printed in the United States of America.

3 4 5 6 7 8 9 10 – VJM – 99 98 97 96 95

Table of Contents

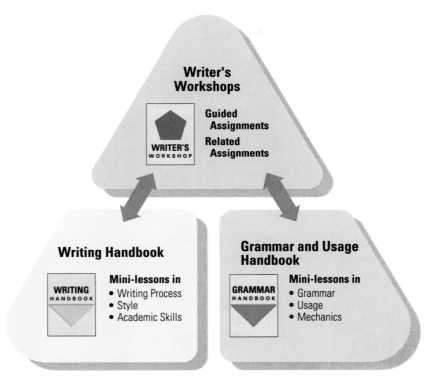

Writer's Workshops

WRITER'S WORKSHOP

Guided Assignments

Related Assignments

Writing Handbook

WRITING HANDBOOK

Mini-lessons in
- Writing Process
- Style
- Academic Skills

Grammar and Usage Handbook

GRAMMAR HANDBOOK

Mini-lessons in
- Grammar
- Usage
- Mechanics

You are special. You think and act in ways that are uniquely your own. This book recognizes the fact that you are an individual. On every page you will be encouraged to discover techniques best suited to your own personal writing style. Just as important, you will learn to think your way through every writing task.

In each of the Writer's Workshops, you will experiment with ideas and approaches as you are guided through a complete piece of writing. Cross-references to the Handbooks will allow you to find additional help when you need it. Then, as you write, you will discover what you think about yourself—and about the world around you.

Starting Points

For more in-depth treatment of each stage of the writing process, see the Writing Handbook Mini-lessons on pages 215–375.

Writer's Workshops

WRITER'S WORKSHOP 1

Personal and Expressive Writing

Narrative and Literary Writing

Informative Writing: Explaining *How*

Informative Writing: Explaining *What*

WRITER'S WORKSHOP 6

Persuasion

WRITER'S WORKSHOP 8

Informative Writing: Reports

Writing Handbook

MINI-LESSONS

Sketchbook

Grammar and Usage Handbook

MINI-LESSONS

xxi

(Clockwise from top left) "Mother Bear and Cub," Greg Colfax; "Welcome Drum," Spencer McCarty; "Raven Eating Salmon Eggs" and "Whale," Greg Colfax. The Makah are a Native American people of northwestern Washington. Colorful storytelling drums play an important part in their culture. Makah stories often tell about the figures represented such as the whale, a symbol of bravery, or the raven, a symbol of trickery.

Starting Points

Suppose you were asked to list your favorite activities. What would you include? Would listening to music, playing a sport, or watching TV make your list? Would you include talking on the phone, going to the movies, or taking care of a pet? Would *writing* appear on your list of favorite things to do? If not, you're not alone.

Many people don't write unless they have to. They would rather speak with another person face-to-face or talk on the telephone. For some people—and perhaps for you too—writing is difficult and boring, something to avoid as much as possible.

Writing doesn't have to be that way, however. Writing can be exciting, satisfying, even fun! This book can help you find the fun in writing. Perhaps one day soon, writing *will* appear on your list of favorite pastimes.

Getting Ready

WHY WRITE?

Try to remember what you were like two or three years ago. What did you like to do after school? What were you interested in? Who were your friends?

Now think about who you are today. How is your life different than it was back then? What has changed? Has anything stayed the same? Is making and keeping friends as easy as it was? Maybe you have more independence. How does that feel?

You're not the only one growing and changing—so are your family, your school, your neighborhood, and the rest of the world. Do you find that you're more concerned about what's going on in the world than you were a few years ago? Does what you see interest you, or excite you, or worry you? What can you do to make sense of it all?

You may be surprised to learn that the writing you do for yourself and the writing you plan to share with others are terrific ways to make sense of your past and your present—to sort through your feelings and your ideas. The process of writing can help you discover more about who you are, what you think, and why you think the way you do.

MAKING WRITING MEANINGFUL

WRITER TO WRITER

I often use writing to contact my emotions.

Mousumi Behari, student, Aurora, Colorado

Take a few minutes to think about what writing means to you. Perhaps your teachers have told you what a powerful tool writing can be. Have you ever experienced that power? Has your writing ever made someone laugh or cry? Has it ever persuaded someone to do something or to feel the same way you do?

Perhaps you've read about how rewarding it can be to write for yourself. Have you ever used writing to help you "contact your emotions," understand how you feel, or figure something out? If your answer was *yes* to any of these questions, then this book will help you go on using writing as a tool for discovery. If writing has been dry and boring for you up until now, however, then get ready—you'll soon discover how to make your own writing important to you.

Make It Your Own

Writing is more rewarding when you focus on topics and issues you think really matter. When you explore what is important to you, you may find that your ideas—and your words—will flow faster than you can write or type them.

Even when you're writing for school, you can find a way to care about each topic you explore. You might even be able to turn a topic you don't particularly care about into one you do. As you'll see in the Discovery Workshop that follows, every topic can be looked at and written about from many different angles. Your writing will always be unique because no one else sees things in quite the same way you do.

Freewrite

What's the best way to discover what's on your mind or what you care most about? Freewriting is a simple but very useful writing technique that allows you to explore your thinking. When you freewrite, you just start writing and keep on writing, even when you're not sure you have anything to say. Start anywhere and let one idea flow into the next. Don't stop to worry about how you sound or whether you've remembered all your commas. Like a doodle that turns into an amazing design, your freewriting can start small and turn into something special and unique as you write.

Focused freewriting is a kind of freewriting that can help you discover what you think about something. Instead of writing about anything that comes to mind, however, you begin with a specific subject and go from there. If your subject is allergies, for example, you might freewrite what you know about them, then write about what you don't know. What do you want to know? What do you need to find out? Freewrite the answers, and you're on your way.

Write for Yourself

Have you ever wanted to say something but no one was there to listen? Do you have a secret you could never tell anyone but that you still want to express? When you write for yourself, you can explore your innermost thoughts and feelings without worrying about what someone else will think or say. Private writing is for your eyes only, so feel free to take risks and write about anything that's on your mind. Even if you're writing something you want to share with others, you can keep early drafts private. Take chances when you write for yourself—you have nothing to lose!

Write with Others

Most writers—including novelists, journalists, poets, songwriters, and technical writers—think of themselves as part of a community of writers. They read and respond to each other's work, offer advice and encouragement, and share frustration and inspiration.

You too belong to a community of writers—when you work with your peers on writing projects, when you write for yourself, and when you publish or present your writing to a wider audience.

Even though there will be times when you'll want to write on your own and keep your writing strictly private, at other times it can be fun and helpful to show your writing to other people. In *The Writer's Craft,* you'll be encouraged not only to share the final products of your writing but also to share your writing process with your peers at several steps along the way.

Getting Started

UNDERSTANDING THE WRITING PROCESS

When you write to a friend, do you plan your letter first, or do you just sit down and start writing? Do you read the letter over for spelling and punctuation when you're finished? Now think about a school assignment. Do you write a report the same way?

Writing is a process, a group of related activities that you can use in any order or way that is helpful. The following activities are all part of the writing process:

- prewriting and exploring
- drafting and discovering
- sharing and getting responses
- revising
- proofreading
- publishing and presenting
- reflecting on your writing

The way you write will depend on what and why you're writing. In some situations, you might ask someone else what he or she thinks of your topic before you begin to explore it for yourself on paper. Sometimes, you might need to repeat a prewriting activity. Revising your writing may mean changing the form of your work. You can create and re-create your own writing process each time you write.

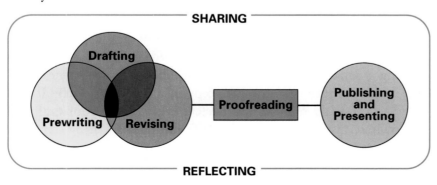

PREWRITE AND EXPLORE

Think of prewriting as exploring what you already know and discovering what you need to find out. At this stage you may also gather material that you may or may not use later in your writing.

To help you explore ideas, you might try a variety of prewriting activities, such as freewriting, talking to friends, reading, or even drawing pictures. Handbooks 1–5, pages 218–235, will help you learn more about prewriting. Remember that this is a time to experiment, so let your imagination roam as far and wide as it will go.

DRAFT AND DISCOVER

Drafting is a stage of discovery where you put your thoughts on paper and see where they lead. Let your thinking be your guide, but allow your ideas to develop and change as you write.

When you draft, don't worry about whether or not you're saying exactly what you thought you would say before you began. You also don't need to worry about getting your ideas in the right order or about choosing just the right words. Like a dancer who is creating a dance, a writer will take a number of steps in one direction and then turn and try the steps in a different order. If you spend too much time trying to perfect every detail, your draft will go nowhere fast. The very process of drafting, of writing out your ideas, may surprise you and help you discover exactly what you're thinking and how you might express those ideas.

After you've completed a first draft, set it aside for a while. Then review your draft and think about how it strikes you. Do you like what you read? Your writing may look like a complete mess, but that's OK—you're not done yet.

At this stage, you might want to go back and work on your draft some more, clarifying your ideas or adding more information. However, you may wish to share your writing with others first. Hearing what your writing sounds like and finding out how it strikes others early in your writing process can help you see what in your draft is working and what is not. The responses of other students—peer readers—can help you get even closer to what *you* want to say. Handbooks 6–18, pages 236–286, give you the specific help you'll need as you draft.

REVISE YOUR WRITING

WRITER TO WRITER

Sometimes you just can't get everything in your head on that little piece of lined paper.

Mark Blatchford, student, Grand Rapids, Michigan

Your first drafts are almost never what you want your finished piece of writing to be. That's because it's nearly impossible to get all of what you wanted to say onto your paper the first time around. Revising is a stage of thought and change. It is much more than making corrections—touching things up and fixing mistakes. When you revise, you have a chance to rethink and rearrange what you have written. Revising may mean replacing ideas. It may even mean creating a whole new draft. See Handbook 19, pages 287–289, for more information about revising and making your writing as good as it can be.

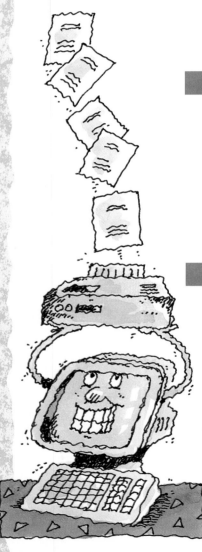

PROOFREAD

Proofreading is the stage where you correct errors in grammar, capitalization, spelling, and punctuation and get your writing ready for your teacher, your classmates, or a wider audience. Use the symbols in the box on page 20 to help you mark changes in your draft. After you've proofread your writing, you can make a final copy. Handbook 20, pages 290–292, contains more information about proofreading.

PUBLISH AND PRESENT

Although you may have shared your writing process with peer readers, now is the time to share your finished piece with a larger audience. You may choose to present your work orally, to display it on a bulletin board in your classroom or in a school corridor, or to submit it for publication in a class, school, or community newspaper or magazine. Handbook 21, page 293, has more information about how to share and publish your writing.

REFLECT ON YOUR WRITING

When you have finished a piece of writing, take some time to think about your writing process. Reflecting on your writing experience can help you gain new insights about writing and about yourself. You may want to ask yourself questions like these.

- What new things did I learn about myself—and about my subject—through writing?
- Which parts of the writing process were easiest for me? Which parts were most difficult?
- What was the biggest problem I faced as I wrote? How did I solve it?
- What have I learned that I can apply to my future writing?

Your reflections may take the form of a journal entry or a note to your fellow writers or your teacher. Attach your reflections to your writing, and add your work to your writing portfolio.

Using This Book

You have seen how writing is a process of discovery. You discover what you want to say and the best way to say it in each writing situation. Since there is no "right" way to complete a piece of writing, *The Writer's Craft* shows you what your choices are and offers directions and suggestions so you can choose what's best for you each time you write.

The Writer's Craft has three sections: Writer's Workshops, a Writing Handbook, and a Grammar and Usage Handbook.

WRITER'S WORKSHOPS

Each Writer's Workshop focuses on a specific kind of writing. You'll explore each writing type in a guided assignment, in a related assignment, and through additional writing opportunities.

Guided Assignments

In each guided assignment, you'll have the opportunity to write on your own and to discover writing strategies that will help you achieve your goals and create something uniquely your own. You'll also see how a professional writer and another student approached the same kind of writing activity. As you work through each guided assignment, you can turn to the Handbooks for assistance or practice with certain skills.

Related Assignments

A related assignment follows each guided assignment and helps you build on the skills you've developed. While the guided assignment offers detailed writing options, the related assignment gives you greater freedom to explore independently and to solve your own writing problems.

Additional Writing Opportunities

Throughout *The Writer's Craft*, you will find feature pages that provide further opportunities for you to practice your writing skills. **Sketchbooks** give you a chance to be creative and try out writing

ideas just for fun. **Springboards** offer suggestions for applying writing skills to other subjects, such as science, art, or history. Finally, **Sentence Composing** activities give you the chance to develop your writing style by studying and imitating sentences written by professional writers.

HANDBOOKS

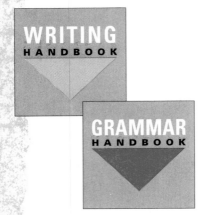

The Writing Handbook and the Grammar and Usage Handbook give you the help you need when you need it most. These Handbooks contain mini-lessons that allow you to develop new skills or give you extra practice with skills you already have.

The **Writing Handbook** lessons cover the writing process, writing techniques and style, and skills you need to succeed in school. The **Grammar and Usage Handbook** lessons cover the essentials of good grammar, usage, and mechanics.

Throughout the Workshops, **Problem Solving** notes direct you to particular Handbooks for help and explanation. You'll also want to explore the Handbooks on your own, especially when you need to find answers to questions that arise as you write.

USING WRITING FOLDERS AND PORTFOLIOS

As you work on a piece of writing, keep all your drafts and notes in a writing folder. You may need to go back to your prewriting notes or an earlier draft to get more ideas or to check how your thinking has progressed.

You may wish to put the finished piece in a portfolio, just as an artist does. Your portfolio might contain the pieces you're proudest of, and it might also include your reflections—your thoughts and feelings about each piece.

Now that you've read about the writing process and about how *The Writer's Craft* is organized, you're ready to discover what writing can mean to you. In the Discovery Workshop that follows, you'll see how *The Writer's Craft* can be your guide to writing something special, something uniquely your own.

Discovery Workshop

Each Writer's Workshop in *The Writer's Craft* tells you what form your writing will take—for example, an autobiographical incident, a report, or a poem. Sometimes, though, writers have no idea where their writing will lead. They begin with what's important to them—an incident (a friend moves away), a feeling (jealousy), or an issue (racism). They write to explore what they think.

The Discovery Workshop will give you a chance to see what this kind of writing surprise feels like. You'll write about something that matters to you and gain a better understanding of how your own writing process works. You'll also see how you can use this book to help you grow as a writer and accomplish your writing goals.

11

Writing to Discover

Starting from LITERATURE

Ashley Kuhlman, a Korean girl whose name was Kim Jin-hee before she was adopted by a family in Michigan, wanted to write about an issue that was very important to her. Ashley tried writing about her topic in different ways until she found what she really wanted to say, as well as how she wanted to say it. As you read her work on these pages, think about how the pieces are alike. How are they different?

The *Starting from Literature* and *Reading a Student Model* boxes give you important information about the professional and student models.

Ashley Kuhlman
Eighth Grade

People adopt children for different reas
A couple may not have been able to have
children of their own for health reasons.
Sometimes relatives adopt children from
another side of the family if something
happens to the children's parents. People also
adopt children from other countries who are
homeless and parentless. This was the case
with me.
Social service agencies arrange most of the
adoptions in the United States. Doctors and
lawyers are sometimes also involved.
Unfortunately (for both the children and the
people often have to wait for years
before they adopt a child.

Adopted and Satisfied

I guess I'm lucky to be adopted.
Think of all the kids who spend
Their whole lives in the orphanage,
Maybe never knowing a family.

I'm glad I have a family.
People who care for me mean so much.
It's nice to know someone loves you.
Caring is such an important thing.

I came to them when I was a baby,
They're the family I have, and I'm glad.
They're a special part of me.
I'm happy with life as it is.

By Ashley Kuhlman, 5th grade.

June 17

Fourteen years ago she gave me up for adoption, a baby she would never know, a teen-ager she could never imagine. Who is my mother? In Korean, I would call her Omoni, a soft beautiful name for mother, a person I always imagined to be young and beautiful herself, never changing. But fourteen years is a long time. Does she still have the smooth face of a child or does she look old and wrinkled? I have so many questions about her life. Why did she give me up? Did she [...]? Did she just not want me?

Did she love me? Does she now? Does she ever think about me? Does she want to remember? Sometimes I [...] I want to go back [...] But would [...] Would [...]

Dear Omoni,

I am now your grown-up daughter, not the fat, bald Korean baby that you gave up fourteen years ago. What are you like now? Are you beautiful, young like new leaves, tender and sweet like a strawberry as I always imagined you? Or are you old, [...] roughly by time and tears? Do you [...] in the morning and see [...] old woman's wri[...]

Sometimes [...] san?" and yo[...] asking ques[...] let me go? [...] baby? Or [...] me? Do [...] want t[...]

Be[...] be s[...]

he room was cold and musty, lit only [by] a pair of greasy red candles. Like slabs [of ce]metery stone, the four walls loomed, [closi]ng in on the woman lying on the narrow [bed.] She knew that she could not recover from [her] illness; but she rested hope in the promise [that] her child would be adopted, and have a [hap]pier life than she had known.

A baby's cry spread through the dark

Think & Respond

What feelings does Ashley Kuhlman seem to be trying to work out in her writing? How have Ashley's ideas and the form of her writing changed as she explored her topic? Which version affects you the most?

Think and Respond questions like these help you reflect on what you read.

INVITATION
— TO —
Write

Ashley Kuhlman's writing process was one of exploration
and discovery; she learned what she wanted to say by trying
out different ways of saying it. In this workshop, you too
will have the chance to explore your ideas in writing—without requirements or restrictions. You will write simply to
discover what you want to say and how you can say it best.

**Explore some ideas that really matter to you, ideas
that you care about. Then begin writing to see
where your ideas lead you and what form they take.**

PREWRITE AND EXPLORE

1. Find an idea to explore. The best writing ideas come from
events, memories, or feelings that are important to you. Try these
activities to find an idea or incident that makes you *want* to write.

Exploring Topics

- **Freewriting**   What's on your mind? Is there a particular
  incident or conversation that you can't seem to forget? What
  people or issues are you thinking about? Make a list of possible topics for writing, then do some freewriting about one or
  two of them and see what you have to say. Begin anywhere
  you want and let each idea flow into the next.

- **Instant replay**   Rewind the events of the last few days in
  your mind. Did anything happen that took you by surprise or
  that made you feel particularly happy, disappointed, or confused? Did you have any conversations that you wished afterwards had never happened—or that you wished had happened a lot sooner? Get together with some of your friends
  and talk about what's happened lately and what's on your
  mind right now. Together you may find ideas you want to
  explore in writing.

2. Share your ideas. After you come up with some writing ideas, you may wish to discuss them with others. Listen carefully—one of your classmate's ideas may spark a memory, lead you to a new topic, or help you look at your idea from a new perspective.

One Student's Process

Ashley Kuhlman talked to her friends about their family histories. The conversation turned to adoption when Ashley spoke of her family's past. After the conversation, Ashley did some freewriting to help her clear her mind and sort through her feelings.

> Talked to Nora, Greg, and Amanda today—about our parents, grandparents, how we came to live in Lansing, etc. We talked about my family too. They all knew I was adopted, and they asked the same questions I get all the time— how does it feel? (fine) Do you talk to your parents about it? (yes) Would you want to meet your mother if you knew where to find her? (I don't know.) I wrote a poem in 5th grade about being adopted. I should try to find that—it really said a lot about how I felt then and still do feel about my family, my real family here in Lansing. That question about meeting my mother is tough. It's weird to think that somewhere out there is a person who was once your mother—that a stranger might be thinking about you sometimes. Does my other mother think about me? I wonder if she thinks about me as much as I think about her.

In *One Student's Process,* you'll follow the thinking, writing, and revising done by student writers just like you. Your own writing process may be similar—or it may be very different.

Problem Solving features help you find answers to your writing questions. When you feel stuck, these features will direct you to the Writing Handbook and to the Grammar and Usage Handbook for help.

PROBLEM SOLVING

"I'm not sure what form I want my writing to take later on. What are my options?"

For more information about various writing forms, see

- Handbook 7, "Forms of Writing," page 238

3. Imagine possibilities. Think about what kind of writing you might work on. Do you, for example, see the beginnings of a short story in your freewriting? Perhaps you think a poem or song lyrics would best express your feelings or experiences. Maybe you want to share your ideas in a letter to a friend. It's all right if you're not sure you'll continue with a choice you make now. Remember, you are free to change your mind about your topic or your form at any time during your writing process.

1. Start writing.   Try drafting one of the writing ideas you came up with during prewriting. Remember, drafting can be an adventure in which you uncover unexpected ideas. You don't need to know where you'll go with your writing when you begin. Just trust that your writing will lead you to a place you'll want to explore further.

One Student's Process

Ashley reread her freewriting and thought she might like to write an informative report about adoption. She had done some reading on the topic, and she knew she could include her own experiences.

> People adopt children for different reasons. A couple may not have been able to have children of their own for health reasons. Sometimes relatives adopt children from another side of the family if something happens to the children's parents. People also adopt children from other countries who are homeless and parentless. This was the case with me.
>
> Social service agencies arrange most of the adoptions in the United States. Doctors and lawyers are sometimes also involved. Unfortunately (for both the children and the adults), people often have to wait for years before they can adopt a child.

2. Write some more.   As you continue to write, you may find your words flowing faster and faster. Don't stop if the writing is going well. If you do pause to review your writing, ask yourself some of these questions. Your answers may help guide you.

- What do I want this piece of writing to accomplish?
- Do I like the direction I'm going in?
- Am I saying what I want to say? What else do I want to say?
- What's the best part of what I've written so far? Will my readers think my draft is interesting or meaningful?
- Do I like the form I'm using? Should I try a different form?

Writing
TIP

Some people like to write with music playing in the background; others need absolute quiet. Find the working style that's best for you.

Writer's Choice   What form has your writing taken so far? Does it feel right? Ask yourself if another form would better suit your ideas. For example, would a personal narrative work better for you than a report?

You can tailor the writing process to suit yourself each time you write. The *Writer's Choice* feature gives you options and allows you to select what's right for you.

One Student's Process

Ashley was frustrated with the draft of her report on adoption. She wasn't saying what was really on her mind. What she really kept thinking about was her birth mother and what might have happened to her. She thought the short story format would better suit this topic, so she invented this story about her birth.

> The room was cold and musty, lit only with a pair of greasy red candles. Like slabs of cemetery stone, the four walls loomed, closing in on the woman lying on the narrow cot. She knew that she could not recover from her illness; but she rested hope in the promise that her child would be adopted, and have a happier life than she had known.
>
> A baby's cry spread through the dark room, and a sigh escaped the woman's lips. An old woman, her only friend, cradled the baby girl in one wrinkled arm, and the dying woman breathed her last, supported by the old woman's other arm.

3. Find your focus.   Has your drafting led you to some conclusions about your personal goals, your content, or your organization? Jot down some responses to these questions.

Personal Goals
- Will this writing be for my eyes only or will I share it?
- If I share it, what effect do I want this piece to have?
- What do I want to learn from this writing experience?

Content and Development
- Have I gotten to the heart of what I want to say?

Form and Organization
- Are my ideas in an order that makes sense?
- Has my draft led me to a specific form of writing?

Writing
══ TIP ══

Keep the answers to these questions in mind as you work on your draft. See Handbook 12, "Methods of Elaboration," pages 255–261, for more information on how to develop your ideas.

PROBLEM SOLVING

"How can readers help?"

For information about peer response, see

• Handbook 18, "Peer Response," pages 284–286

4. Decide about feedback. Sometimes you don't want any-one's opinion but your own. At other times, you may want to see how others respond to your writing. Are you ready to share your draft with peers? You may simply want to read your draft aloud to them to hear how it sounds. On the other hand, you may want someone to read your draft closely and offer reactions and sugges-tions. Try asking your peer readers questions like these:

• What do you think my piece is really about?
• Which part did you like best? How did it make you feel?
• What do you want to know more about?

Peer Reader Comments show you the responses and suggestions that one student gave to another.

Peer Reader Comments

I'd be asking myself this question too.

I like this line about Omoni.

So many questions only Omoni could answer. . . . What if you tried writing her a letter?

I know what you mean— you want to know and not know at the same time.

One Student's Process

After writing the beginning of her story, Ashley found that she was still thinking about her friends' question: Would she want to meet the mother who gave birth to her? Ashley knew that going ahead with her short story wouldn't bring her any closer to the answer. She did some more writing and then shared it with a close friend, whose responses appear in the margin.

Fourteen years ago she gave me up for adoption, a baby she would never know, a teenager she could never imagine. Who is my mother? In Korean, I would call her Omoni, a soft beautiful name for mother, a person I always imagined to be young and beautiful herself, never changing. But fourteen years is a long time. Does she still have the smooth face of a child or does she look old and wrinkled? I have so many questions about her life. Why did she give me up? Did she die? Did she just not want me? Did she love me? Does she now? Does she ever think about me? Does she want to remember? Sometimes I think I want to go back to her. But would she want me? Would she take my love? I want to know the answers, but then again, maybe I don't.

REVISE YOUR WRITING

1. Consider your readers' comments. How did your draft strike your readers? What can you learn from their responses? Think about what your readers said—and what you yourself think about your draft—and decide what changes you want to make. Remember that this is your writing, and whether or not you take the advice of others is completely up to you.

2. Think about your goals. Have you said what you most wanted to say when you began? Have your writing goals changed now that you've written a draft? Check to see if you need to add more information to make your writing clear and complete.

3. Check your organization. You might want to read your draft aloud to see if your writing flows smoothly from beginning to end. Is anything out of place?

In this section, you'll learn strategies for reworking your writing and making it as good as it can be.

COMPUTER
━ TIP ━

Make a copy of your original document on your disk. Then, experiment with your organization by moving blocks of copy around. You'll always be able to return to the original.

One Student's Process

Ashley thought her friend's suggestion to write a letter was a great one. Here is a piece of her next draft and some changes she made by hand. She would make even more changes later.

Dear Omoni,

I am now your grown-up daughter, not the baby you gave up fourteen years ago. What are you like now? Are you beautiful, young, tender and sweet *like new leaves   like a strawberry* as I always imagined you? Do you look in the mirror in the morning and see a child or an old woman? *smooth   's face   's wrinkles*

Sometimes I talk to you, asking questions about your life. Why did you let me go? Did you die? Did you not plan for a baby? Or did you just plain not want to take me? Do you love me? ~~Do I~~ *at all* ~~even want to know?~~ I don't think I really want to find out.

PROOFREAD

Before you prepare a final copy of your writing, check for errors in grammar, capitalization, punctuation, and spelling. These errors can distract your readers and make your writing hard to follow. Ask yourself the questions in the Proofreading Checklist below, and mark corrections on your draft using the proofreading symbols shown.

Proofreading Checklist

Step 1: Check the forms of words.
- Did I use correct verb tenses?
- Did I use any adjectives where I should have used adverbs?
- Did I use *-er/-est* and *more/most* correctly in comparisons?
- Did I use all forms of *be* and other irregular verbs correctly?
- Did I use the correct forms of pronouns?

Step 2: Check sentence structure and agreement.
- Are there any run-on sentences or sentence fragments?
- Do all verbs agree with their subjects?
- Do all pronouns agree with their antecedents?
- Did I keep all verb tenses consistent?

Step 3: Check capitalization, punctuation, and spelling.
- Did I use the correct form for every plural noun?
- Did I capitalize the first word of each sentence?
- Did I capitalize all proper nouns and proper adjectives?
- Is any punctuation mark missing or not needed?
- Did I spell all words, including possessive forms, correctly?

Proofreading Symbols

∧ Add letters or words.

⊙ Add a period.

≡ Capitalize a letter.

⌣ Close up space.

⊸ Add a comma.

／ Make a capital letter lowercase.

⌗ Begin a new paragraph.

∿ Switch the positions of letters or words.

— or ℒ Take out letters or words.

PUBLISH AND PRESENT

You can share your writing with other people—your classmates, your teacher, or even a public audience outside of school—in a variety of ways. Here are a few of your options.

Each workshop suggests a variety of ideas for sharing your writing with a wide audience.

- **Give an oral reading.**   Get together with a small group of your classmates and take turns reading your works aloud. After each piece is read, discuss the thoughts and feelings the writing inspired.

- **Make a poster for your classroom or school hallway.** Try illustrating your writing with drawings, photos, or pictures from magazines. You might even assemble a collage to go with your writing. Display your work on a bulletin board.

- **Send it off.**   Submit your writing to your school or community newspaper, to a magazine, or to a writing contest.

REFLECT ON YOUR WRITING

You can learn a lot about yourself as a writer by reflecting on your writing process. As you look back over your prewriting notes and your drafts, you can see changes in your thinking and patterns in your writing.

You'll have the opportunity to reflect on what you've learned about writing and about yourself after you've completed each piece of writing.

Take some time to think about the writing you just completed. You may wish to do some freewriting or write a note and attach it to your final draft. The following questions can help you get started. Then attach your reflections to your finished piece and put your work in your portfolio.

- How did I discover my topic? How did I know it was what I wanted to focus on?

- What surprised me most about this piece of writing?

- Did I share my drafts with others? How did I feel about their responses? Did I make any changes they suggested? Why?

- How do I feel about the final piece?

- What part do I like best? What, if anything, would I change?

- Did I write differently from the way I usually write? How? Why?

One Student's Writing

Dear Omoni,

I am now your grown-up daughter, not the fat, bald Korean baby that you gave up fourteen years ago. What are you like now? Are you beautiful, young like new leaves, tender and sweet like a strawberry as I always imagined you? Or are you old, handled roughly by time and tears? Do you look in the mirror in the morning and see a smooth child's face or an old woman's wrinkles?

Sometimes I miss you, I call out, "Omoni-san?" and you don't come. But I talk to you, asking questions about your life. Why did you let me go? Did you die? Did you not plan for a baby? Or did you just plain not want to take me? Do you love me at all? I don't think I really want to find out.

Because I don't want my dreams of you to be shattered. I want to believe that you were poor, or already had several children, and most of all that you <u>did</u> want to keep me. Maybe I'm fooling myself, but if I am—if you know I am— keep it to yourself. I don't want to hear it.

Omoni, do you remember me? Do you want to? I want to wrap my love around you. I want to come back to you like a pigeon goes home. But do you want my love, would you take it? And do I want to be tied to you?

Do I want to know you and belong to you? Or will I be happier depending on myself? You see, I think we'd both be expecting too much of each other—you'd be expecting an innocent child, I an angel who can do no wrong. I think I'd rather keep my illusions of you and let you keep yours.

I used to dream that one day we would get a <u>very long</u> distance call, and it would be you. And we would talk, and I used to think this is what you'd say:

"Hello, Jin-hee. I'm sorry if you wondered about me and never got any answers. I had to finish school and get a good job before I could come back for you. Then I spent years trying to trace you. But now everything is fine. Will you come back and live with us?"

Yes, Omoni, I would always say. And so we'd live happily ever after. But, Omoni, I was a child then. I was the innocent child that you probably want me to be, and you were the cherry blossoms at Halla and Paektu. I do not believe in the innocence of spring anymore. I am too old for a child's fantasies. And . . . I guess . . . Omoni, you do not make the same magic in my heart.

Your daughter,

Kim Jin-hee
Ashley Kuhlman

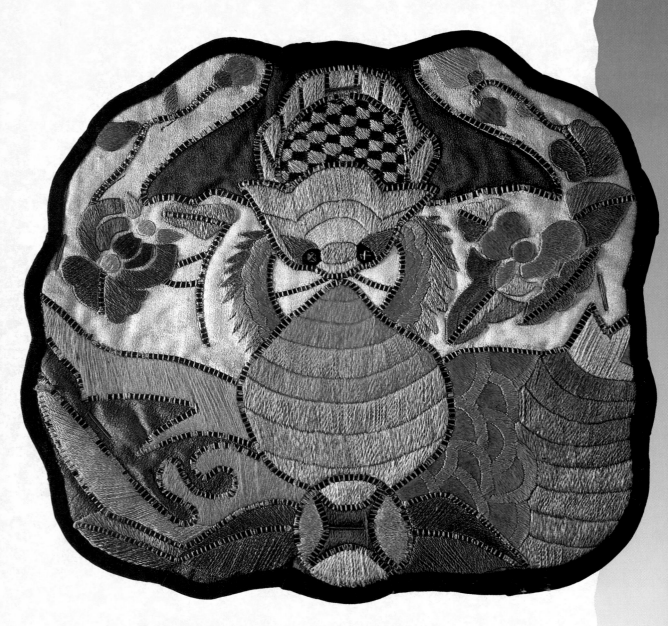

The design of this embroidered pillow contains several symbols often used in Chinese folk art and stories. The bat represents good luck, the peach stands for long life, and the coin symbolizes prosperity.

Writer's Workshops

To be nobody-but-yourself—in a world which is doing its best, night and day, to make you everybody else—means to fight the hardest battle which any human being can fight; and never stop fighting.

E. E. Cummings
A POET'S ADVICE TO STUDENTS

- What is special about you? What makes you who you are? Jot down some of your thoughts.
- Think about something you did that made you proud. Write about the experience.

Show, Don't Tell

When you write about personal experiences, you re-create the events so that readers feel what you felt. By using examples and details, or anecdotes and descriptions, you show what happened rather than just tell about it. Turn one of the *telling* sentences below into a *showing* paragraph.

- It was one of the best moments of my life.
- I had to make a difficult decision.

1

Personal and Expressive Writing

Guided Assignment
Autobiographical Incident

Related Assignment
Song

Autobiograpical writing is special. Only you can see the world through your eyes. Only you know what it's like to be you. In personal and expressive writing, you draw upon your own thoughts, memories, and feelings to create something no one else in the world could have produced.

This workshop will give you a chance to do this special kind of writing. It will guide you in describing an incident out of your own life. In the related assignment, you'll be able to capture a special feeling or insight and put it into a song.

Autobiographical Incident

Starting from LITERATURE

Have you ever felt as if you didn't quite fit in? Growing up can be difficult, as you discover who you are—and who you're not. Leo F. Buscaglia learned an important part of this lesson when he was just about your age. This experience had such an impact on him that he wrote about it years later. As you read this excerpt from his autobiography, try to put yourself in his place. What feelings would you have had? How would you have acted?

from

PAPA WAS AN AMERICAN

by **LEO F. BUSCAGLIA**

AS I ENTERED JUNIOR HIGH, Papa and Mama, whom I had loved without question, suddenly became an embarrassment. Why couldn't they be like other parents? Why didn't they speak without accents? Why couldn't I take peanut-butter-and-jelly sandwiches in my school lunches, rather than calamari? (Yuck, the other kids said, he eats squid legs!) There seemed no escape from the painful stigma I felt in being Italian, the son of Tulio and Rosa. "Buscaglia"—even my name became a source of distress.

One day, as I left school, I found myself surrounded by a group of boys. "Dirty dago!" they shouted. "Your mom's a garlic licker. . . . Go back where you came from!"

It seemed an eternity before I was released from the circle of pushes, punches, and taunts. I wasn't really certain what the epithets meant, but I felt their sting. Humiliated and in tears, I broke free and dashed home. I locked myself in the bathroom, but I couldn't stop the tears. What had happened seemed so wrong, yet I felt helpless to do anything about it.

Papa knocked on the door. "What's the matter?" he asked. "What is it?"

I unlatched the door, and he took me in his arms. Then he sat on the edge of the bathtub with me. "Now tell," he said.

When I finished the story, I waited. I guess I expected Papa to immediately set off in search of the bullies or at least find their parents and demand retribution. But Papa didn't move.

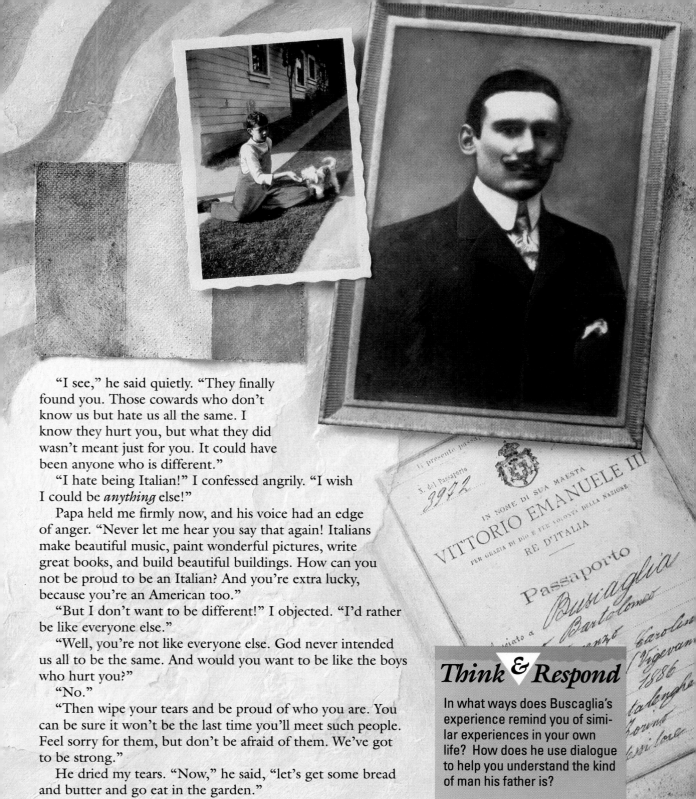

"I see," he said quietly. "They finally found you. Those cowards who don't know us but hate us all the same. I know they hurt you, but what they did wasn't meant just for you. It could have been anyone who is different."

"I hate being Italian!" I confessed angrily. "I wish I could be *anything* else!"

Papa held me firmly now, and his voice had an edge of anger. "Never let me hear you say that again! Italians make beautiful music, paint wonderful pictures, write great books, and build beautiful buildings. How can you not be proud to be an Italian? And you're extra lucky, because you're an American too."

"But I don't want to be different!" I objected. "I'd rather be like everyone else."

"Well, you're not like everyone else. God never intended us all to be the same. And would you want to be like the boys who hurt you?"

"No."

"Then wipe your tears and be proud of who you are. You can be sure it won't be the last time you'll meet such people. Feel sorry for them, but don't be afraid of them. We've got to be strong."

He dried my tears. "Now," he said, "let's get some bread and butter and go eat in the garden."

Think & Respond

In what ways does Buscaglia's experience remind you of similar experiences in your own life? How does he use dialogue to help you understand the kind of man his father is?

One Student's Writing

A Lesson Learned Well
Brook Volle

It was a Wednesday night in mid-June when I first met Jorgina. My youth group was having an activity to prepare us for camp. My leader started calling out names for the tent assignments.

Just as I thought my name would never be called, I heard it, along with Kari's, Cynthia's, and Jorgina's. I didn't know Kari very well, but I knew I could probably get along with her. Cynthia I knew was very quiet and shy. Then there was Jorgina. Wasn't she the new girl all the boys were drooling over?

At that moment I glanced up at the door and saw a girl who was probably no older than myself. She reminded me of a princess in a fairy tale. I immediately assumed she was Jorgina—perfect in every way. Not one hair on her head was out of place. Her face looked like that of a porcelain doll. Her clothes were immaculate. Her whole appearance made me think of a future Miss Universe.

"How am I going to spend a whole week in the mountains with a girl who will probably faint every time she cracks a nail?" I questioned myself.

Our leader brought Jorgina over to our group.

"Girls, this is Jorgina Jorgenson. She just moved to Las Vegas from a small town in Utah. I'm sure you'll all become good friends," my leader exclaimed with a false smile.

"Hi ya, girls," Jorgina said with too much enthusiasm. We all just stared at her like she was an alien invading our private space. "So, what's it like in Las Vegas?" she asked nervously.

"It's ok," I commented, trying to avoid eye contact. "What's it like where you came from?" I asked.

Dear Brook
Hi! I'm sorry I had to leave camp in such a rush. How was the last night's bonfire? I really wanted to be there.

We went to Cedar Breaks on the way home — it's even more beautiful than the picture on the front. How was the rest of your summer? Write soon and tell me what you did.

—Jorgina

POST CARD

Brook Volk
182 Mockingbird Lane
Apt. 2 E
Las Vegas, NV 8?108

"It's just great!" she said with a smile. "I lived on a farm. We had a river and a pond in our back yard!"

"What did you do for entertainment?" I questioned. I was more interested in her than I had hoped to be.

"Oh, we would always go exploring through the woods. Plus, there was a mall. I also spent a lot of time at gymnastics," she replied.

"So maybe she's not such a snob after all," I thought to myself.

I decided to give her a chance to prove what she was really like instead of just making judgments about her. We talked the rest of the evening, and I got to know her quite well.

The next two weeks slipped by, and before we knew it, we were in camp at Beaver High Adventure Base in Utah. Jorgina and I became very trusting and dependent on each other. Whenever she had a problem, I tried to help her solve it. When my ankle started to give me problems, she let me use her as a crutch. When I wanted to go tromping through the woods, she always came with me. She quickly became the best friend I had.

On the last day of camp, tragedy struck. A car pulled into our campsite, and out stepped Jorgina's mom.

"Jorgina," she said, "you need to get your stuff, 'cause we're movin' back home tonight."

I went with Jorgina to our tent and helped her pack. Then we said our goodbyes and she left.

We still keep in touch, and every once in a while, she comes to visit. Jorgina made a great impression on my life and taught me a very important lesson. Because of her I've promised myself never again to judge people because of their appearance.

Think & Respond

Respond as a Reader
▶ How would you have first reacted to Jorgina?

▶ Why do you think Brook's feelings changed?

Respond as a Writer
▶ What descriptive details help you understand Brook's initial reaction?

▶ How does she show the reader her own changes in attitude?

INVITATION
═ TO ═
Write

Leo F. Buscaglia and Brook Volle both had experiences that changed the way they think. Both writers gained a greater understanding of themselves and of their experiences after writing about them.

Write about an incident in your life that stands out in your memory or has special meaning for you. Help your readers understand why you wanted to write about the experience.

P REWRITE AND EXPLORE

PROBLEM
S O L V I N G

"How can I find an incident to write about?"

For help finding ideas, see

• Sketchbook, page 26

• Springboards, page 45

• Handbook 1, "Discovering Writing Ideas," pages 218–223

1. Look for an incident.   Look back through your life for a special moment. It might be funny or frightening, sad or embarrassing—maybe something you learned from. It could be moving into a new neighborhood, feeling close to a grandparent, or losing a pet. Here are strategies for finding a special memory to write about.

Exploring Topics

• **Categories**   Jot down terms like "summertime," "holidays," "accidents," "moving," "grandparents," and "pets." Maybe, like Leo Buscaglia, you'll find a term like "Papa" that brings back a powerful memory. **Brainstorm** to find memories that you associate with these terms.

• **Snapshots**   Browse through personal or family photo albums. Try freewriting about the pictures to see where your thoughts lead. Use a **cluster diagram** to follow up on any promising topics.

• **Famous firsts**   Do you remember your first bicycle, ice skates, or skateboard or your first teacher, friend, or pet? How about your first job, your first painful loss, your first vacation, or your first dance? Choose one and **freewrite** about it.

One Student's Process

Brook Volle started with the idea of summer and used a clustering technique to look for memories and associations of summer. Her cluster looked like this:

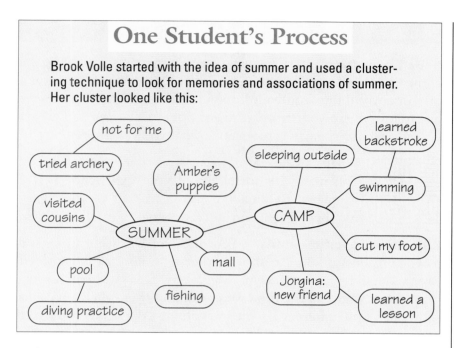

not for me

tried archery

Amber's puppies

sleeping outside

learned backstroke

swimming

visited cousins

SUMMER

CAMP

cut my foot

pool

mall

fishing

Jorgina: new friend

learned a lesson

diving practice

COMPUTER TIP

If you tend to slow down during freewriting, always correcting what you write, try writing at a computer with the screen turned off. Turn it on sometimes to see what you've written.

2. Select an idea and begin exploring it. Try one or more of the following ideas to help get you started.

- **Sharing with others** Jot down four or five incidents that stand out in your memory as special—even if you don't know why. Then briefly describe each of them to a small group of classmates. Which incident seems most important, powerful, or puzzling—something the others would like to know more about?

- **Jumping in** If you like, just begin writing about the experience. Go back to it in your mind and start at whatever point seems most interesting. As you write, look for meaning in the incident, the reason you care about it.

- **Mental snapshot** Imagine a snapshot of the most important moment of your experience. Hold that picture in your mind and quickly make some notes. What do you see—what people, objects, scenery? What do you smell and hear? How are you feeling, physically and emotionally? What is the story you can't see, the story behind the snapshot? Try to capture on paper as many sensory details as you can.

Autobiographical Incident

1. Begin drafting. Try focusing on that mental snapshot of the event you chose to write about, and start there. As you write, you may discover things you hadn't remembered earlier. That's fine— just follow where your words and memories lead. You can always go back later to change or reorganize what you've written.

Writer's Choice Is your story a very personal one? You may wish to tell about your experience as if it happened to someone else instead of to you. If so, use the third person and have a narrator tell the story.

2. Include specific details. Your incident will seem more real to your readers if you can show, rather than just tell, your story. Brook doesn't say that Jorgina was pretty. She says that Jorgina was "the new girl all the boys were drooling over." Leo Buscaglia shows just how different he felt by writing, "Why couldn't I take peanut-butter-and-jelly sandwiches in my school lunches, rather than calamari? (Yuck, the other kids said, he eats squid legs!)"

Paragraphs at Work In autobiographical writing, a paragraph might not need a topic sentence. Make sure, however, that all the sentences in a paragraph contribute to a main idea or focus. Look, for example, at Brook's third paragraph. All of its details have the same focus: Jorgina's hair, face, and clothes; fairy-tale princess; Miss Universe. The reader gets a unified impression of Jorgina as Brook saw her. Remember these tips.

- Not every paragraph has a topic sentence.
- Every paragraph should have a single main idea or focus.

3. Conclude your draft. How do you know when to stop writing? You can end after you've fully described what happened, or you can summarize what you learned or tell why the incident is important to you.

4. Reflect on your writing. Decide whether you'd like to show your draft to a reader now or work on it some more first. If you do want to make changes at this time, read over the questions for yourself under "Review Your Writing."

Questions for Yourself
- What part of this incident do I care most about?
- What details can I add so that I show instead of tell?
- How have I made clear where and when the events took place?
- Have I shown why the experience is important to me?
- Is my order of events clear? Does the piece make sense from beginning to end?

Questions for Your Peer Readers
- How did you react to the experience I wrote about?
- What parts helped you really feel or understand what I was describing?
- What would you like to know more about?
- Which passages seemed most memorable or striking?

One Student's Process

Here is part of Brook's first draft. She asked a classmate to read it and offer some reactions. How would you have responded?

My leader said she knew we would all become good friends, but I wasn't sure she meant it. When Jorgina said hi, we all just stared at her like she was an alien invading our private space. Finally she asked us what Las Vegas is like.

"It's ok," I commented, trying to avoid eye contact. She looked so neat and clean. I was wondering if she had a ton of friends at home and if she would fit in here. I asked her what it was like where she came from.

"It's just great," she said with a smile. "I lived on a farm. We had a river and a pond in our back yard!"

Peer Reader Comments

Why weren't you sure?

I like the alien part. What was Jorgina really saying and doing?

The eye contact part works for me—really shows your feelings.

This really gets across an idea of her personality.

Autobiographical
Incident   **35**

1. Review the responses of your readers. Look over the responses to the questions you asked yourself and your peer readers. Remember that you get to decide which changes you would like to make.

2. Check your organization. Whether you start your story at the beginning, the middle, or the end, you'll need to make clear the order of the events. Brook tells her story in chronological order—that is, she begins on the Wednesday night she first met Jorgina, and she winds up in the present.

Making a time line or storyboard may help you plan the sequence of events in your story. Here is a storyboard for Brook's autobiographical incident.

Writing
— **TIP** —

You may want to use a flashback, pausing in your story to tell about an earlier event.

1. MEET JORGINA — THINK SHE MIGHT BE A SNOB

2. BEGIN TO LIKE HER

3. SHARE CAMP EXPERIENCES

4. BECOME GOOD FRIENDS

5. JORGINA LEAVES

6. LEARN NOT TO PREJUDGE

One Student's Process

Brook considered her classmate's reactions. She decided to add details to make the behavior of the characters clearer and to help readers see and experience what happened. She made even more changes later.

¶ "Hi ya, girls," Jorgina said with too much enthusiasm.

~~My leader said she knew we would~~ "I'm sure you'll all become good friends, ~~but I wasn't sure she meant it.~~" my leader exclaimed with a false smile.

~~When Jorgina said hi,~~ we all just stared at her like she was an alien invading our private space. ~~Finally she asked us what~~ "So, what's it like in ____?" she asked nervously. Las Vegas ~~is like.~~

"It's ok," I commented, trying to avoid eye contact. She looked so neat and clean. I was wondering if she had a ton of friends at home and if she would fit in here. I asked her "what's it ~~was~~ like where ~~she~~ you came from?"

"It's just great," she said with a smile. "I lived on a farm. We had a river and a pond in our back yard!"

¶ "What did you do for entertainment?" I questioned. I was more interested in her than I had hoped to be. "So maybe she's not such a snob after all," I thought to myself.

1. Proofread your work. Check your work for errors in grammar, capitalization, punctuation, and spelling.

L I N K I N G
MECHANICS AND WRITING

Punctuating Dialogue

If you divide a quotation with a phrase such as "he said," don't capitalize the first word of the second part unless it begins a new sentence. Any comma or period at the end of a quotation goes inside the closing quotation marks. Notice how Brook followed these rules.

Original

"Jorgina," she said, "You need to get your stuff 'cause we're movin' back home tonight."

Revised

"Jorgina," she said, "you need to get your stuff 'cause we're movin' back home tonight."

For more information about punctuating dialogue, see Handbook 49, "Punctuation," pages 651, 664, and 665.

2. Make a clean copy of your writing. Are you satisfied with your work? Give your piece a final check, using the Standards for Evaluation listed in the margin. Make any additional changes you feel are necessary and make a final copy.

- **Share your experience.** Send your writing to friends, relatives, or other people involved in your experience. Ask for responses.
- **Have a readers' theater.** In a performance for the class, different class members can read or act out their stories.

Standards for Evaluation

PERSONAL
W R I T I N G

An autobiographical incident

- explores an experience important to the writer and shows why it was important
- draws the reader in at the beginning and concludes in a satis–fying way
- makes the setting clear—where things happen
- gives a good sense of time, place, and character through vivid sensory details and possibly dialogue
- helps readers follow the order of events in time

- **Publish your story.** Print your class's stories in a class magazine or submit them to a schoolwide literary magazine.
- **Display your story.** Make a class bulletin-board display, including any drawings or photographs that could illustrate the stories.

WRITER TO WRITER

Good writers write to find out about themselves.
Gloria Steinem, writer

1. Add your writing to your portfolio. Now that you have written about an autobiographical incident and have read two others, think about your writing process. Jot down answers to some or all of the following questions, and attach your answers to your piece when it goes into your portfolio.

- How did I decide what to write about?
- What kinds of changes did I make after my first draft?
- What could I learn about myself from my story?
- What did I most enjoy about this assignment? What didn't I like?
- What writing techniques from my own piece or from the autobiographical incidents I read did I especially like? Which ones could I try again in another piece of writing?

2. Explore additional writing ideas. See the suggestions for writing a song on pages 42–44 and Springboards on page 45.

FOR YOUR
PORTFOLIO

Autobiographical
Incident
39

Song

Ever since human beings first began to speak, they expressed themselves by singing. A song is a poem you can sing. Usually short and simple, a song can catch a feeling, express a mood, tell a story, or comment on just about anything.

Which of these things does "The Circle Game" do? Does it give you any ideas for a song of your own?

•The Circle Game•

Yesterday a child came out to wonder,
Caught a dragonfly inside a jar.
Fearful when the sky was full of thunder,
And tearful at the falling of a star.
Then the child moved ten times round the seasons,
Skated over ten clear frozen streams.
Words like "when you're older" must appease him,
And promises of someday make his dreams.
    And the seasons, they go round and round,
    And the painted ponies go up and down.
    We're captive on the carousel of time.
    We can't return, we can only look behind
    From where we came
    And go round and round and round
    In the circle game.
Sixteen springs and sixteen summers gone now,
Cartwheels turn to car wheels through the town.
And they tell him, "Take your time, it won't be long now,
Till you drag your feet to slow the circle down."
    And the seasons, they go round and round,
    And the painted ponies go up and down.

We're captive on the carousel of time.
We can't return, we can only look behind
From where we came
And go round and round and round
In the circle game.
So the years spin by and now the boy is twenty,
Though his dreams have lost some grandeur coming true.
There'll be new dreams, maybe better dreams, and plenty,
Before the last revolving year is through.
And the seasons, they go round and round,
And the painted ponies go up and down.
We're captive on the carousel of time.
We can't return, we can only look behind
From where we came
And go round and round and round
In the circle game.

—Joni Mitchell

Think & Respond

What does the child seem to want as he grows up? Why does the image of a carousel, or merry-go-round, seem appropriate? How does Joni Mitchell use verses to organize the ideas in her song?

INVITATION
TO
Write

A song can deal with very basic feelings, very ordinary experiences. Joni Mitchell uses the image of a revolving carousel to symbolize the passage of time as a child grows to adulthood.

Write the words for a song that expresses a feeling or idea, tells a story, or describes a scene.

E XPLORING   YOUR   WORLD

1. Capture a mood or a feeling.   Your own song could spring from feelings of sadness, jealousy, anger, love, confusion, or wonder. Try to remember specific occasions when you felt any of these feelings powerfully. A **cluster** may generate usable details about feelings you want to explore further.

2. Read and listen to songs.   You may get inspired by reading other song lyrics or listening to songs. Look for interesting lines, clever rhymes or rhythms, powerful images, and effective use of repetition.

3. Listen to language.   Carry around a notebook so that you can jot down interesting language you come across—from books, movies, TV shows, even everyday conversation. A popular phrase, for example, might give you a line for a song.

 Writer's Choice   You can simply write the lyrics for a song, but you may want to compose a musical accompaniment. If you put your lyrics to music, you might choose to write the words first and then find a suitable melody, or you might write words to go with an already-written melody.

DRAFTING YOUR SONG

1. Start with a line or a phrase. Look for a line, perhaps from your freewriting, that has a ring to it, that feels good to your ear. Joni Mitchell, for example, might have started with a line like "the seasons, they go round and round."

2. Develop an idea. Try to hit on one main idea for your song. This might grow out of your catchy line, or it could be a feeling, a simple statement, or a very short story. Each verse could then carry the story forward or present a different example.

3. Use figurative language. Like other poems, songs often suggest much in few words. They do this by using vivid images and imaginative comparisons. "The Circle Game," for example, compares the passage of time to the movement of a carousel. A boy who has lived ten years—ten winters—has "skated over ten clear frozen streams."

4. Consider rhyme and repetition. Remember, however, that rhyming is optional in poetry and song. Don't let a search for rhymes distract you from thinking about what you want to say. Forced rhyming can make your song sound more like a jingle. You can use inexact rhymes, like "seasons" and "appease him." You may want to repeat key lines or phrases. Many songs, like "The Circle Game," benefit from a repeated refrain, or chorus.

PROBLEM

SOLVING

"How can I use similes and metaphors?"

To learn more about figurative language, see

• Handbook 27, "Using Poetic Devices," pages 318–321

Writing
TIP

You can use a rhyming dictionary to get ideas for rhymes.

1. Read your song lyrics aloud. Listen to their rhythm. Do the lyrics sound as if they could be sung? Do you like the sound of the words? Does a tune suggest itself to you? If so, try to sing your song into a tape recorder or pick it out on a guitar, piano, or other instrument.

2. Look at your song's form. Verses of a song are like the paragraphs of a story. Your song may have just one verse; more likely it will have two or three, perhaps divided by a refrain.

3. Share your song lyrics. In a spirit of fun and good will, read or sing your song to friends, and listen to their songs. Share useful comments.

PROBLEM SOLVING

"How can I find better words to make my ideas clear?"

For help in choosing the right words, see

• Handbook 25, "Meaning and Word Choice," pages 314–315

Grammar TIP

For song lyrics, you may decide not to capitalize the first word of each line or not to punctuate normally. You might use contractions that are normal in speech, like "Hey, good lookin'."

PUBLISHING AND PRESENTING

• **Have a concert.** Perform your song for your class or for a larger group in your school.

• **Record your song.** Make an audiocassette recording of your song. If you have a video camera, you may want to produce a music video, designing specific visuals to go with your song.

• **Publish a songbook.** Collect the song lyrics your class wrote and publish them in a book, with or without musical notation.

Spring boards

Literature Write about a milestone in the life of a literary character or your favorite author. You might compose your story in the form of a journal entry written by the character, trying to capture his or her individual voice.

Science Present a news bulletin about an important scientific break-through, such as the discovery of antibiotics or of the structure of the DNA molecule. If you prefer, write a diary entry as if you were the scientist who made the discovery. You may choose to fictionalize your account, setting your news bulletin in the future.

SPEAKING AND LISTENING

Tape-record interviews with members of your family about important incidents in their lives. You could ask about their memories of historic events or scientific discoveries or about their experiences in coming to this country.

Art Make a painting, sculpture, or drawing to convey an important event in your life. Your piece may be representational or abstract, but it should express the mood and significance of the event.

History Become a historical figure and narrate an important event from your life, stressing the significance of the incident. For example, you could present the March on Washington as told by Dr. Martin Luther King, Jr. You could also choose someone who was not famous—for example, a pilgrim sailing to America.

Sentence

Imitating Sentences

Professional writers vary their sentences to add richness and interest to their writing. By imitating their sentences, you can learn new ways to compose, structure, and punctuate your own writing. Notice how the writer of the following description varies the rhythm of each sentence.

Model A   In her attic bedroom, Margaret Murry, wrapped in an old patchwork quilt, sat on the foot of her bed and watched the trees tossing in the frenzied lashing of the wind.

Model B   Behind the trees, clouds scudded frantically across the sky.

Model C   Every few moments, the moon ripped through them, creating wraithlike shadows that raced along the ground.

Madeleine L'Engle, *A Wrinkle in Time*

▶ **ON THE MARK**   Use commas to set off introductory elements, interrupters, and appositives.

A. Chunking Sentence Parts   People read and write sentences in meaningful "chunks." By dividing sentences into parts, or chunks, you can see how together the parts express a complete thought. Choose the sentence in each pair below that is divided into meaningful chunks. Explain how each chunk relates to those around it.

1. **a.** In her attic / bedroom, Margaret Murry, / wrapped in an old / patchwork quilt, / sat on the foot of her bed / and watched the trees / tossing in / the frenzied lashing of the wind.
    b. In her attic bedroom, / Margaret Murry, / wrapped in an old patchwork quilt, / sat on the foot of her bed / and watched the trees / tossing in the frenzied lashing of the wind.

2. **a.** Behind the trees, / clouds scudded frantically / across the sky.
    b. Behind / the trees, clouds / scudded frantically across the sky.

3. **a.** Every / few moments, the / moon ripped through them, creating wraithlike shadows that / raced along the ground.
    b. Every few moments, / the moon ripped through them, / creating wraithlike shadows / that raced along the ground.

B. Identifying Imitations   Find the sentence in each pair below that can be divided into chunks that match the structure of the chunks in the model.

1. Choose the sentence that imitates Model A.
   a. Prancing around the ring and led by Mrs. Jackson, the toy poodle resembled a miniature giraffe with cotton balls on its feet and a sneering look on its face that, in a person, would have seemed conceited.
   b. After his escape, the fox, tired from his race across the field, stood in the mouth of the hole and observed the dogs sniffing the ground for a scent.

2. Choose the sentence that imitates Model B.
   a. In the morning, blackbirds cackled annoyingly in the trees.
   b. An expert swimmer, Albert had no trouble getting a summer job.

3. Choose the sentence that imitates Model C.
   a. Each Thursday, Mr. Samuels went to the mall, meeting several friends who strolled there with him.
   b. Feeling somewhat anxious, Janie was practicing her hardest piece, a composition that had to be played very fast.

C. Unscrambling and Imitating Sentences   Unscramble the sentence chunks below to create sentences that match the models on page 46. Then write correctly punctuated sentences that imitate the models.

1. Write sentences that imitate Model A.
   played at the highest possible volume / and sent the chaperones scurrying for the controls of the stereo / the music / reverberated against the walls of the cafeteria / during the dance

2. Write sentences that imitate Model B.
   Joon sketched quickly / on his drawing board / with his pencil

3. Write sentences that imitate Model C.
   creating a wave / that spread around the stadium / during the baseball game / the fans raised their arms.

Grammar Refresher   See Handbook 44, "Using Prepositions, Conjunctions, and Interjections," pages 540–541, for more on prepositional phrases, and Handbook 47, "Using Verbals," pages 599–601, for more on participial phrases.

Sketch Book

- You're in your room. You hear a roar. You look out the window. Something strange is happening to the house across the street! Describe what you see.
- Describe the most amazing thing you ever saw.

THE HOUSE ON MAPLE STREET

It was a perfect lift-off.

Show, Don't Tell

You can use facts, details, even dialogue to re-create an event you've witnessed. Rewrite the *telling* sentences below to capture a reader's interest and *show* what is happening.

- Our player scored the winning point.
- The storm caused a great deal of damage.

2

Observation and Description

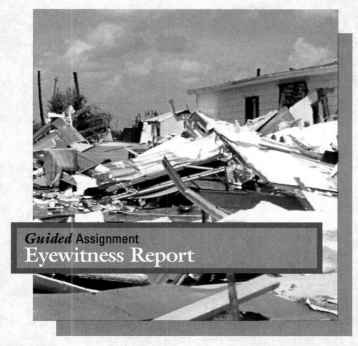

Guided Assignment
Eyewitness Report

Related Assignment
Field Notes

When you're on a vacation, you can take snapshots of sights you want to remember—a violet-orange sunset, a funny street performer, a misty coast. However, how do you capture a moment in time or a special event?

In this workshop you will use your powers of observation and description to vividly re-create an event in an eyewitness report. Then, in a related assignment, you will have a chance to use the same skills to capture observations and thoughts in the form of field notes about a subject of personal interest to you.

Eyewitness Report

Starting from
LITERATURE

Have you ever felt as if you had experienced an event in history just by reading about it? The main goal of an eyewitness report is to give you that kind of experience. Eyewitness reporters strive to bring events to life through print.

In this 1992 eyewitness report, journalist Deborah Sontag takes you to Florida's coast to show how survivors of Hurricane Andrew coped with the destruction caused by the storm. As you read her account, notice the words, phrases, and images that help you to feel as though you were there.

from *The New York Times*

AMID THE RUBBLE by Deborah Sontag

The night Hurricane Andrew hit the Florida coast, Ronald Bruscia, 46, Pamela Jones, 41, and Pamela's son, Scott, 13, had huddled around candles in the bathroom with a mattress propped against the door. Listening to the wind tear off sections of the roof above them, the three promised themselves that if they came through that night alive, they would stop leading selfish lives. Five days later, journalist Deborah Sontag spent twenty-four hours with these three survivors. The following is her report.

It was ninety-two degrees at noon Saturday, the fifth day after Hurricane Andrew. Ronald Bruscia maneuvered his van around mounds of brush and tangles of fallen power line. Shards of glass flew from his shattered windshield as he drove toward a friend's house that had collapsed during the storm.

The friend had offered fifty gallons of gasoline in exchange for help in moving, and Mr. Bruscia was eager for the trade. . . .

[He] swerved around pretzels of metal railing and bumped over downed wires that, the radio kept warning, could still be live.

Mr. Bruscia screeched to a halt as a hog waddled across the street.

"That pig just blew into the neighborhood during the storm," he said. . . .

1 P.M. [Later,] Mr. Bruscia and Ms. Jones, heading home with their gasoline, saw a Federal Express truck making a delivery to a house without walls.

"What the . . . ?" Mr. Bruscia started to say, before he realized and leapt out of the van.

"Ice!" Ms. Jones cried. "They're delivering ice, God bless them. Ice is gold." . . .

2:30 P.M. The storm clouds darkened. Mr. Bruscia and his neighbors clambered on and off their makeshift roofs, trying to secure the new plywood, the tar paper, and the plastic sheeting with extra nails.

Relatively speaking, the families on Martinique Drive were lucky. The storm only took half their roofs, most of their ceilings, all of their windows, and an entire bedroom here and there. They had no belongings, but for the most part, they still had their walls. . . .

5 P.M. The family unloaded charcoal, bottled water, cans of chili, and other goods that Mr. Bruscia's sister had driven down from Orlando.

Ms. Jones had salvaged a large bell from their boat, and she rang and rang it to let the neighbors know provisions had arrived. "I was about ready to give up this morning, but now I feel better," she said.

Thunder rumbled. "Uh oh, maybe not," she said. . . .

Gnats and mosquitoes swirled in the gusting winds as the rain started falling in sheets.

"About this moment is where you have people finally going over the edge," Mr. Bruscia said. "Not me, though. I spent enough years living on that edge to know how to cling on real tight."

Think & Respond

What was your reaction to this report? Consider the impression it made on you. Then look for sensory details and bits of dialogue that helped to create this impression.

One Student's Writing

Reading a STUDENT MODEL

Have you ever, in a letter or a conversation, tried to share something exciting or strange you witnessed? How did you go about it? Were you successful?

As you read Rene Froehmer's eyewitness account, decide whether she achieves her goal of vividly recreating a fight that she witnessed.

Fight
by Rene Froehmer

As the two teen boys began yelling, everybody in the area, including me, knew that a fight was going to occur. They were in each other's face, yelling rude remarks.

"So, do you wanna fight?" the smaller boy said. "Come on!"

The other guy wouldn't budge. He knew that if he started the fight, he wouldn't be at this school for long.

Finally, the smaller boy couldn't wait any longer. He hit his enemy on the shoulder of his white T-shirt. The second boy reacted quickly to this, as if it had happened to him many times before.

By now there was a large crowd surrounding the two, cheering for their favorite. The circle grew and grew as the larger boy punched his opponent in the face and stomach many times until he fell to the ground. Once he was on the ground, there was no hope for him. He was kicked many times before, finally, a teacher came and broke up the fight. The audience booed because the fight was over and so was the entertainment.

A strange thing happened that makes me remember this fight clearly. As the smaller boy walked off with blood all over his face, he smiled with his light red teeth showing.

I was confused about why the boy smiled. Was he relieved that it was over? Was he pleased that he'd gotten the bigger kid in trouble? Was he just trying to look as if he wasn't hurt? I don't know.

All I do know is that I definitely will not forget that fight and that boy's weird smile.

Think & Respond

Respond as a Reader
► Could you "see" the fight?
► Tell about an event you've witnessed that made as strong an impression on you as this fight made on Rene Froehmer.

Respond as a Writer
► What words and phrases does Rene use to create excitement and tension at the beginning of this account?
► What detail of this account stands out the most for you? Why do you think you remember that one best?

INVITATION
TO
Write

Eyewitness reports, like Deborah Sontag's story about the survivors of Hurricane Andrew and Rene Froehmer's account of a fight, make it possible for events to touch our lives.

Write an eyewitness account of an interesting or special event that you experienced. Try to make your readers feel as if they were there.

PREWRITE AND EXPLORE

PROBLEM
S O L V I N G

"What's the best way to write down what I observe?"

To find out more about ways to record what you observe, see

- Handbook 3, "Graphic Devices for Writing," pages 227–231

- Handbook 32, section on "Taking Notes," page 341

- Handbook 37, "Critical Listening and Observing," pages 363–366

1. Be on the lookout for interesting events. Any event observed with interest and attention can make an engaging subject. To find an event, try one or more of the following activities.

Exploring Topics

- **School scout** Situations worth reporting can be found right in your own school. Pay attention to what goes on around you as you sit in homeroom, the cafeteria, or the auditorium and while you're outside on break.

- **Roving reporter** See what's going on at places like video arcades, roller rinks, bowling alleys, shopping malls, and parks.

- **News hound** Newspapers and local magazines can tip you off to many local happenings, from concerts to political gatherings and sports events. Pick one or two to attend.

2. Observe and record details, impressions, and dialogue. Good reporters rely on more than just their memories. They take detailed notes on the scene. When you're at an event, record *all* your sense impressions—not just sight and hearing—to gather as many details as possible and get an overall impression. You might **list,** make a **sketch,** or create an **observation chart.**

Also note as precisely as possible any comments or bits of conversation that seem meaningful. A bit of dialogue can be even more memorable than a collection of sensory details. For instance, think about the power of this quotation from Deborah Sontag's report: "They're delivering ice, God bless them. Ice is gold."

3. Pick a topic.   Is there one event or some strong image that keeps coming to mind? If so, perhaps your topic has already chosen you. If not, you may want to try freewriting about events you've witnessed to see which one interests you most. You may not be able to pick a topic until after you have drafted for a while.

4. Look for a focus.   What had the biggest impact on you? This could be a sound, an image, a bit of dialogue, a key event, or even a general impression. Make this the focus of your account. In other words, when you write your account, make sure that this thing comes across to your readers just as strongly as it did to you. If you can't find a focus now, try drafting for a while. Also bear in mind that as you draft, your focus may change.

Grammar
═ TIP ═

If you use direct quotations in your report, be sure to use quotation marks correctly. For help, see Handbook 49, "Punctuation," pages 664–665.

One Student's Process

While scouting around her school for events, Rene Froehmer witnessed a fight. Since her thoughts kept returning to this fight, she chose it as her topic. Then, after reviewing her notes on the event, Rene decided to focus on the fact that the bigger kid didn't want to fight, but the smaller one did.

<u>Fight</u>

in each other's face
lots of yelling
fists clenched
big kid doesn't want to
   fight, but smaller one
   does—why?
✔ smaller kid shoves first
big kid is suddenly all
   over him
✔ Has he fought before?

✔ Was he kicked out of other
   schools for fighting?
✔ Was he afraid he'd be
   kicked out of our school?
crowd forms circle
cheering
teacher breaks it up
blood all over smaller kid's
   face, but he's smiling
big kid is hauled to office

Writer's Choice Some writers prefer to draft carefully; others take a more adventuresome approach. You can select details from your notes now to create a plan for drafting or just see which details come to mind as you put ideas on paper.

DRAFT AND DISCOVER

1. Begin writing. You can start by writing about any part of the event that interests you. For example, you might begin by writing about the moment of greatest excitement, by relating your first impressions of the scene, or by describing an image that keeps coming to mind. Then work your way backward or forward from this material to fill out the rest of your account.

2. Think about your goals. Your main goal should be to get your readers to feel as if they were in the center of the action. A second goal is to give your account a clear and vivid focus.

Rene Froehmer thought she wanted to focus on the fact that the bigger boy didn't want to fight but the smaller boy did. As she drafted, however, she realized that what kept coming to mind was the odd fact that the bloodied smaller boy had smiled. So she switched her focus to the strange smile.

3. Work with your draft. Try using different details in different drafts of your account to see which ones best help you to accomplish your goals. Notice the details Deborah Sontag selects to show how people were working together cooperatively.

> The storm clouds darkened. Mr. Bruscia and his neighbors clambered on and off their makeshift roofs, trying to secure the new plywood, the tar paper, and the plastic sheeting with extra nails.

4. Give your account a shape, and check your organization. Look at your report as a whole. Does it have a strong opening, a well-developed middle, and an ending that effectively brings your account to a close? Have you organized your details sensibly and linked them with transitions where necessary?

PROBLEM
S O L V I N G

"How do I write a strong beginning and an effective ending?"

For information on ways to begin and end compositions, see

- Handbook 16, "Introductions," pages 278–280
- Handbook 17, "Conclusions," pages 281–283

5. Take a break. Once you've finished your first draft, put it aside for a few hours or even a few days. Then use the following questions to help you and your readers review this draft.

Questions for Yourself
- What have I done to help readers feel as if they were actually at the scene themselves? What more could I do?
- Does the image or moment I focused on come across clearly?
- What did I discover about this event by writing about it?

Questions for Your Peer Readers
- What words and phrases helped you to feel that you were at the scene?
- What parts did you have trouble "seeing"?
- What was missing? What do you want to know more about?
- What images, moments, and ideas do you recall most vividly?
- Was the account easy to read and understand? What, if anything, is unclear?
- What could I do to make my report flow more smoothly and naturally?

One Student's Process

Here is part of Rene's first draft. Read it and then review the peer comments. What comments, if any, would you add?

As the two teen boys began yelling, everybody in the area knew that a fight was going to occur. I was on my way over to a friend's house, but when I heard the yelling, I stopped to watch. They were in each other's face, yelling rude remarks. But I got the impression that the smaller kid wanted to fight more than the other one did. Finally, the smaller boy couldn't wait any longer and hit his enemy.

Grammar TIP

Using the present tense helps your readers feel that the story is unfolding as they're reading about it. If you use the present tense, don't suddenly switch to the past tense or the future tense. Such switches can confuse your readers.

Peer Reader Comments

I like the way you get right into the action.

What were they yelling?

What makes you think this? Where did he hit him? I need more details to picture this clearly.

PROBLEM
S O L V I N G

"How can I 'show' rather than 'tell' a story?"

For more information on showing instead of telling, see

• Handbook 13, "Show, Don't Tell," pages 262–267

1. Review your responses and goals. Look at your peer responses as well as your own notes and goals. Then decide which changes you might want to make.

2. Show, don't tell. In the body of your composition, look for general statements or conclusions. Think about replacing them with the sensory details and quotations from which you drew these conclusions in the first place.

Deborah Sontag could have just told her readers that the hurricane victims were still struggling to survive. Instead, she uses sensory details and quotations to show these people dealing with their hardships.

> [He] swerved around pretzels of metal railing and bumped over downed wires that, the radio kept warning, could still be live.
>
> Mr. Bruscia screeched to a halt as a hog waddled across the street.
>
> "That pig just blew into the neighborhood during the storm," he said.

3. Check your opening and closing. Your beginning should interest your readers in your account. Your ending should leave them with something to think about.

If your opening and closing still need work, sensory details might help you to improve them. Sensory details can help your readers understand what something or someone looks, smells, tastes, feels, and sounds like. For example, Rene Froehmer first involves readers in the fight with descriptive statements such as, "They were in each other's face, yelling rude remarks." Likewise, she uses sensory details to create a vivid closing image of a bloodied young boy smiling with "light red teeth."

Paragraphs at Work Each paragraph in an eyewitness report should convey a single main idea or impression. When you revise your account, check the content of your paragraphs.

- Make sure that each paragraph conveys only one main idea or impression.
- Make sure that the sentences in each paragraph contain enough sensory details to develop one idea or impression adequately.
- Eliminate details that don't belong, or move them to other paragraphs where they do belong.

One Student's Process

After thinking about her peer readers' comments and questions, Rene decided to take out unnecessary information and add specific dialogue and details. Notice how her changes affected one part of her draft.

¶ The other guy wouldn't budge. He knew that if he started the fight, he wouldn't be at this school for long.

As the two teen boys began yelling, everybody
                          including me,
in the area knew that a fight was going to occur.

I was on my way over to a friend's house, but

when I heard the yelling, I stopped to watch. They
¶ "So do you wanna fight?" the smaller boy said.
were in each other's face, yelling rude remarks.
"Come on!"
But I got the impression that the smaller kid

wanted to fight more than the other one did.

¶Finally, the smaller boy couldn't wait any longer.
He
and hit his enemy, on the shoulder of his white T-shirt.

The second boy reacted quickly to this, as if it had happened to him many times before.

Writing
TIP

Think about what your audience needs to know to understand the event you've witnessed. Then provide them with that background information.

Standards for Evaluation

DESCRIPTIVE
W R I T I N G

An eyewitness report

- uses sensory details, dialogue, and action verbs to show what was observed, bringing the event to life

- has a clear focus

- provides readers with the information they need to understand the event

- presents details in a sensible order that is easy to follow

L I N K I N G
GRAMMAR AND WRITING

Action Verbs

An action verb tells that something is happening, has happened, or will happen. A linking verb, on the other hand, simply states that something exists, or it links a subject with a word that describes or renames it. To help readers feel as if they were actually at the scene of an event, look for ways to use action verbs rather than linking verbs. Notice how an action verb can improve a sentence.

The wind was on her face.
The wind cooled her face.

Now compare these two versions of a sentence from "Amid the Rubble." Which one would you say conveys a more powerful image?

Version 1
Gnats and mosquitoes appeared in the gusting winds as the rain started falling in sheets.

Version 2
Gnats and mosquitoes swirled in the gusting winds as the rain started falling in sheets.

P R O O F R E A D

1. Proofread your work. Correct any errors in grammar, usage, and mechanics.

2. Make a clean copy of your account. Is your eyewitness report ready to publish? Give it a final once-over, using the Standards for Evaluation shown in the margin. Then make a clean final copy.

- **Publish your report in a school or local newspaper.**
  Newspapers often publish community-interest stories. Submit your report for publication. Include a suggested headline and any photographs you may have of the event.

- **Arrange an oral reading.**   Read your account to a group interested in the event you witnessed. Share any photos you may have.

- **Create a "News of the Week" bulletin board display.**
  Mount your eyewitness account on a current events bulletin board. Then, as you and your classmates write new eyewitness reports, replace the "old news" with "new news."

REFLECT ON YOUR WRITING

WRITER TO WRITER

There aren't even phrases in the languages for half the things happening just on the block where I live, not yet anyhow.
**Toni Cade Bambara,
novelist, short story writer, and editor**

**FOR YOUR
PORTFOLIO**

1. Add your report to your portfolio.   While the eyewitness report is still fresh in your mind, you might want to write some notes to yourself about your writing process. Answering the following questions can help you get started. Attach your notes to your final draft before putting your draft in your portfolio.

- How did I find an event for my report?
- In what ways was the process of writing an eyewitness account different from writing other kinds of narratives?
- What writing techniques were particularly useful to me?
- Were my peer readers' responses helpful? Why or why not?
- What would I do differently next time?

2. Explore additional writing ideas.   See the suggestions for writing field notes on pages 64–65 and Springboards on page 66.

Field Notes

Starting from LITERATURE

Have you ever spotted an animal— say a deer or a strange bird—and held your breath, hoping not to frighten it away? The novelist Douglas Adams and the zoologist Mark Carwardine had many such moments during the year they spent observing unusual animals. As you read Adams's tale of one of their many encounters, try to put yourself in his place. How would you have felt? What would you have done?

from

LAST CHANCE TO SEE

by Douglas Adams and Mark Carwardine

JUST AS WE WERE ABOUT TO GIVE UP and go back, we tried one more turning, and suddenly the forest seemed to be thick with gorillas. A few feet above us, a female was lounging in a tree, idly stripping the bark off a twig with her teeth. She noticed us but was not interested. Two babies were cavorting recklessly ten feet from the ground in a very slender tree, and a young male was chugging through the undergrowth nearby on the lookout for food. We stared at the two babies in astounded fascination at the wonderful wild abandon with which they were hurling themselves around each other and the

terrible meagerness of the tree in which they had elected to do it. It was hard to believe the tree could support them, and indeed it couldn't. They suddenly came crashing down through it, having completely misunderstood the law of gravity, and slunk off sheepishly into the undergrowth.

We followed, encountering one gorilla after another until at last we came across another silverback lying on his side beneath a bush, with his long arm folded up over his head, scratching his opposite ear while he watched a couple of leaves doing not very much. It was instantly clear what he was doing. He was contemplating life. He was hanging out. It was quite obvious. Or rather, the temptation to find it quite obvious was absolutely overwhelming. . . .

I crept closer to the silverback, slowly and quietly on my hands and knees, till I was about eighteen inches away from him. He glanced around at me unconcernedly, as if I was just someone who had walked into the room, and continued his contemplations. I guessed that the animal was probably about the same height as me—over six feet tall— but I would think about twice as heavy. Mostly muscle, with soft grey-black skin hanging quite loosely on his front,

covered in coarse black hair.

As I moved again, he shifted himself away from me, just about six inches, as if I had sat slightly too close to him on a sofa and he was grumpily making a bit more room. Then he lay on his front with his chin on his fist, idly scratching his cheek with his other hand. I sat as quiet and still as I could. . . .

After a quiet interval had passed, I carefully pulled the pink writing paper out of my bag and started to make the notes that I'm writing from at the moment. This seemed to interest him a little more. I suppose he had simply never seen pink writing paper before. His eyes followed as my hand squiggled across the paper, and after

a while he reached out and touched first the paper and then the top of my ballpoint pen—not to take it away from me, or even to interrupt me, just to see what it was and what it felt like. I felt very moved by this and had a foolish impulse to want to show him my camera as well.

Think & Respond

Discuss with classmates your reactions to Douglas Adams's account. What parts were most exciting? Why? Do you think you might have reacted the way Adams did? List some of the details you think probably came straight from Adams's notes. What do you notice about these details you listed?

INVITATION
TO
Write

Field notes used to be thought of as strictly a scientist's way of recording observations made in the natural world—that is, "the field." Today, however, writers in many professions have discovered the benefits of taking field notes.

Think of something in the natural world that you find interesting or want to learn more about. Observe it and write field notes in which you record your observations, thoughts, and feelings.

F INDING A SUBJECT

1. Think of subjects of interest that can be observed. For ideas, complete each of the following sentence starters four or five times.

- I want to know more about . . .
- I'm really fascinated by animals like . . .
- Why do people . . .

2. Pick a subject. Freewrite on a few subjects, and then choose the one that interests you most.

3. Decide on a purpose. Do you want to learn more about your subject? Are you hoping to see the effects or results of something? Will you compare it with another subject?

4. Observe your subject. Plan a suitable observation period. For instance, if you've arranged to observe a snake, you may want to see how it behaves before and after a feeding.

5. Record the data you obtain from all your senses. Be alert to the sounds things make, their colors under various conditions, and any smells they give off. Also record when events occur. Take notes on any important measurements such as distance, height, or weight. Draw sketches or diagrams if they would be useful.

Writing
TIP

Try creating the kind of three-column chart many scientists use. Label the left-hand column "Time," the center column "Actions and Details Observed," and the right-hand column "Personal Reactions, Impressions, and Comments." Then fill in each column with appropriate information.

1. Notice what is important.   In your notes, look for the following:

- **Patterns of events or other details**   For instance, does your subject change color whenever it hears a loud noise?

- **Especially exciting, interesting, odd, or funny details**
Adams includes an amusing incident involving two baby gorillas playing on a slender tree.

- **Details that make a strong impression on you**

- **Strong reactions or feelings**   "I felt very moved by this," Adams writes, "and had a foolish impulse to want to show him my camera as well."

- **Conclusions you draw from your observations**   For example, "It was instantly clear what he [the silverback gorilla] was doing. He was contemplating life. He was hanging out."

- **Examples that support your conclusions**

2. Write a summary.   In your summary, you might cover the important details you observed and comment on them, discuss your impressions of the subject, or draw conclusions.

Writer's Choice   If your subject is likely to be unfamiliar to most people, you may want to compare it to something people commonly recognize. Similes, metaphors, and other poetic devices are especially good for making such comparisons.

- **Publish a report or present your findings to a group.**
Pick a focus for your report and decide what goals you want to accomplish. Include sketches, photographs, lists, and any other kinds of data you gathered "in the field."

- **Create a display.**   Use diagrams, sketches, photographs, or objects related to your subject to create a display for your classroom, school, or local library.

PROBLEM
S O L V I N G

"How do I draw conclusions or make generalizations from my notes?"

For help in drawing conclusions and making generalizations, see

- Handbook 31, "Critical Thinking and Writing," pages 337–339

Spring boards

Science

Go into the field—be it kitchen, zoo, or back yard—and write field notes on something you observe. Then use your notes to create a report in which you present your information as if it were new, groundbreaking material. In your conclusion, explain why your readers (scientists) should be excited about your discoveries.

MEDIA

Write and present an on-the-scene news report about an event you witnessed. Try to include photographs or a videotape, statements from other witnesses and people who were involved, and documents or other items that might shed light on what happened.

Art

Create a drawing, painting, collage, sculpture, or other type of artwork to show your impression of an event you observed. Title your piece and add to it a brief written explanation of what it shows.

Literature

Imagine that you're a character from literature who witnessed an important event. Write an entry for this character's diary. For example, what might Angie Lowe or Cochise from Louis L'Amour's story "The Gift of Cochise" have written after their first meeting? Include the character's comments, thoughts, and feelings.

THEATER

Collaborate with a group of classmates to script a reenactment of an event you witnessed. Feel free to include a narrator to provide background information and commentary. Then perform your reenactment.

After the Alaskan Oil Spill, Sigrid Holmwood, Age 11

on the LIGHT side

Who Flang That Ball?

A reporter is interviewing Infield Ingersoll, a former shortstop known for his colorful language.

"Well," he said, "it was the day us Wombats plew the Pink Sox . . . "

"*Plew* the Pink Sox?" I interrupted. "Don't you mean *played?*"

Infield's look changed to disappointment. "Slay, slew. Play, plew. What's the matter with that?"

"*Slay* is an irregular verb," I pointed out. . . .

He paused belligerently, and then went on. "What I'm tryin' to do is easify the languish. I make all regular verbs irregular. Once they're all irregular, then it's just the same like they're all regular.

That way I don't gotta stop and think."

He had something there. "Go on with your story," I said.

"Well, it was the top of the fifth, when this Sox batter wang out a high pop fly. I raught for it."

"*Raught?*"

"Past tense of verb to reach. Teach, taught. Reach,—"

"Sorry," I said. "Go ahead."

"Anyhow I raught for it, only the sun blound me."

"You mean blinded?"

"Look," Infield said patiently, "you wouldn't say a pitcher winded up, would you? So, there I was, blound by the sun, and the ball just nuck the tip of my glove—that's nick, nuck; same congregation as stick, stuck. But luckily I caught it just as it skam the top of my shoe."

"*Skam?* Could that be the past tense of *to skim?*"

"Yeah, yeah, same as swim, swam. . . . Well, just then the umpire cell, 'Safe!' Naturally I was surprose. Because I caught that fly, only the ump cell the runner safe."

"*Cell* is to *call* as *fell* is to *fall,* I surpose?" I inquired.

"Right. . . . so I yold at him, 'Robber! That decision smold!'"

W. F. Miksch

Sentence

Compound Subjects and Compound Verbs

You can add information to your sentences by including more than one subject or verb. You can also use compound subjects and compound verbs to add rhythm and variety to your sentences. Notice how the compound subjects and compound verbs in the sentences below make each sentence more complete.

Model A   Jewels, pins, and brooches glittered in her tangle of weedy hair. *(compound subject)*   **Lloyd Alexander, "The Foundling"**

Model B   Mrs. Jones stopped, jerked him around in front of her, put a half nelson about his neck, and continued to drag him up the street. *(compound verb)*   **Langston Hughes, "Thank You, M'am"**

Model C   Johnny and I stretched out on our backs and looked at the stars. *(compound subject and compound verb)*

S. E. Hinton, *The Outsiders*

▶ **ON THE MARK**   Place a comma after every item except the last item in a series of three or more subjects or verbs. Do not use a comma with two subjects or two verbs.

A. Combining Sentences   Make a new sentence by replacing the italicized part in the first sentence with the detailed information underlined in the second sentence. Eliminate any words in the second sentence that are not underlined. The new sentence will contain a compound subject or verb. Punctuate correctly.

1. He *did several things.* He stood up and eased his shoulders, turned his feet in their ankle sockets, rubbed the back of his neck.

Harper Lee, *To Kill a Mockingbird*

2. *We* were seated at the dining-room table having lunch. We were Daddy, Mama, Doodle, and I.   **James Hurst, "The Scarlet Ibis"**

3. He *performed several jobs.* He sorted the new crates, stacked the canned goods, and lugged the filthy garbage pails out back.

Robert Lipsyte, *The Contender*

B. Unscrambling and Imitating Sentences Unscramble each set of sentence chunks below to create a sentence that matches one of the models on page 68. Then write a correctly punctuated sentence of your own that imitates each model. Be sure each of your sentences contains a compound subject or compound verb.

1. Write sentences that imitate Model A.
on the ferry boat / traveled across the bay / cars, trucks, and vans

2. Write sentences that imitate Model B.
turned himself around in the middle of his flight / lifted the ball above his head / the star player / and proceeded to jam it through the hoop / leaped

3. Write sentences that imitate Model C.
and landed on the air mattress / the firefighter and the cat / leaped down from the roof

C. Expanding Sentences Use your imagination to expand the parts of sentences given below by adding compound subjects or compound verbs in the places indicated. Be sure to use commas to separate the items in each series.

1. Mr. Jamison picked up his briefcase, *(add two more actions that he did)*.
Mildred D. Taylor, *Roll of Thunder, Hear My Cry*

2. In her room, Jane locked the door against the sound of the playing children, *(add two more actions that Jane did)*.
Mary Elizabeth Vroman, "See How They Run"

3. The insects buzzed, *(add four more sounds that the insects made)* as the air grew warmer in the sunset. **Richard Adams, *Watership Down***

4. There was a pontoon bridge across the river, and *(add five things crossing the bridge)* were crossing it.
Ernest Hemingway, "Old Man at the Bridge"

5. Every muscle, *(add two more things)* was tired, dead tired.
Jack London, *The Call of the Wild*

Grammar Refresher To learn more about compound subjects and verbs, see Handbook 39, "The Sentence and Its Parts," pages 403–405.

Sketch Book

*The local groceries are all out of broccoli,
Loccoli.*
> Roy Blount, Jr., "SONG AGAINST BROCCOLI"

*I wish that I
Were up to my knees
In my mother's mac-
Aroni and cheese.*
> Roy Blount, Jr., "SONG TO MY MOTHER'S MACARONI AND CHEESE"

*Parsley
Is gharsley.*
> Ogden Nash, "FURTHER REFLECTION ON PARSLEY"

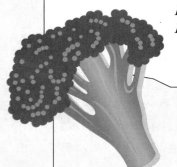

- Write a love note to your favorite food. You can use poetry or prose.

- Describe in ten or fewer words the best thing you've seen lately.

- Roy Blount, Jr., and Ogden Nash made up the words "loccoli" and "gharsley" to describe their feelings. What words can you make up to describe people, places, or things you like or dislike?

Show, Don't Tell

Poetry creates pictures or feelings for a reader with carefully chosen sensory words and images. Turn each *telling* sentence into a *showing* line of poetry by using more vivid words.

- The day was gloomy.
- The child jumped for joy.

3

Narrative and Literary Writing

Guided Assignment
Writing a Poem

Related Assignment
Developing a Script

Even without knowing it, you've probably written some kind of poetry. You may have played with the sounds of words or the pictures they create. Perhaps you've written a valentine or put some rap lyrics together. Your everyday life is full of material for poetry. This workshop will help you to turn some of your own thoughts and experiences into poems. In the related assignment you'll do a different kind of literary writing as you create a dramatic scene through dialogue—characters speaking and interacting with one another.

71

Writing a Poem

Have you ever tried to capture in a few words something you saw, remembered, felt, imagined, or wanted to do? That's what these three writers did. "The Base Stealer" creates a feeling of tense movement. "Celebration" describes a powerful experience that a writer wants to have again. "the drum" is built around a strong, clear image. As you read these poems, notice how much life each manages to pack into a few words.

CELEBRATION

I shall dance tonight.
When the dusk comes crawling,
There will be dancing
    and feasting.
I shall dance with the others
    in circles,
      in leaps,
        in stomps.
Laughter and talk
    will weave into the night,
Among the fires
    of my people.
Games will be played
And I shall be
    a part of it.

—*Alonzo Lopez*

The Base Stealer

Poised between going on and back, pulled
Both ways taut like a tightrope-walker,
Fingertips pointing the opposites,
Now bouncing tiptoe like a dropped ball
Or a kid skipping rope, come on, come on,
Running a scattering of steps sidewise,
How he teeters, skitters, tingles, teases,
Taunts them, hovers like an ecstatic bird,
He's only flirting, crowd him, crowd him,
Delicate, delicate, delicate, delicate—now!

—Robert Francis

the drum

daddy says that the world is
a drum tight and hard
and i told him
i'm gonna beat
out my own rhythm

—Nikki Giovanni

Think & Respond

What idea or feeling do you
think each writer was trying to
capture? Which of these poems
do you like the most? What
appeals to you in that poem?

One Student's Writing

Everyone's life contains both good and bad times, sudden whims or memories, moments of grief or laughter or surprise. Any of those moments could become the seed of a poem. Read these poems, all written by eighth graders. Note that Tiffany Shue builds a little story around something familiar, a teddy bear. In "A Life Is Gone," Jim McConnell uses sense images to work through some difficult emotions about the death of his brother. Trang Phan plays a "what-if" game to create "Creatures from Outer Space."

The Teddy Bear

There was a little teddy bear,
who belonged to a girl I knew,
that was loved so much,
the fur started falling off of it.
Pretty soon its right eye fell off.
That did not stop the girl
from taking the bear everywhere she went.
Now, twenty-five years later,
she still has that bear.
She also has two girls of her own.
One girl reminds me
very much of her mother.
That little girl has a teddy bear,
that also is showing much wear.
And travels too.

Tiffany Shue

Creatures from Outer Space

This unknown planet contains creatures
different from our own.

Like dogs with no fur,
Tigers that don't roar.
Cats without whiskers,
And eagles that don't soar.

Like woodpeckers that don't peck,
Lions with no mane.
Zebras without stripes,
And kittens that aren't tame.

Like hyenas that don't laugh,
Squirrels that hate nuts.
Birds with no beaks,
And lambs that give haircuts.

Like cheetahs that run slow,
Ladybugs that are men.
Flamingos that are blue,
And giraffes that live in dens.

Like roosters that don't crow,
Tortoises that beat the hare.
Owls that don't give a hoot,
And wooly mammoths that are bare.

Where is this place?
And where do we look to find?
Oh, I don't know.
Maybe in our minds!

Trang Phan

A Life Is Gone

It is cold.
The trees rustle
as the wind nips
my face.

A child's lonely cry
known only to one.
He lies motionless
and can not be seen.

A face hidden
from the world.
It is cold.
It is so cold.

Jim McConnell

Think & Respond

Respond as a Reader

▶ What favorite toy or object of yours comes to mind as you read "The Teddy Bear"?

▶ What was your first reaction to "A Life Is Gone"?

▶ Could you create any other creatures from outer space?

Respond as a Writer

▶ How did the writer link the ending of "The Teddy Bear" to the rest of the poem?

▶ How does a sense of cold contribute to the feeling of "A Life Is Gone"?

▶ What effect does rhyme have in "Creatures from Outer Space"?

INVITATION
═ TO ═
Write

Each of the six poems you have read grew out of something seen, remembered, imagined, or strongly felt. The
writers found that poetry was the best way to express
their ideas.

**Now write a poem that expresses something you
have experienced, felt, or thought about in your
own life.**

PREWRITE AND EXPLORE

1. Let ideas come from anywhere.   Anything can trigger a
poem. It might be something you see, read, laugh at, remember,
worry over, or wonder about. The starting point for your poem
might be a bit of language: a phrase, something someone said,
words that stick in your mind. A dream you had, if put into words,
might become a poem. The following activities may help you to
discover a "poetic moment."

Exploring Topics

• **Memories**   What images or experiences from your past
  often come back to you? These might be pleasant memories,
  such as a birthday party or a peaceful summer day. The images
  also could be difficult ones, such as a death, a disappointment,
  or a fright. Try writing "I remember" at the top of a sheet of
  paper. Then keep writing, listing whatever comes to mind.

• **The world around you**   Be alert to scenes and sounds,
  emotions, episodes between people in your everyday life. You
  may be in the cafeteria, in class, at a party, at a sports or religious event, or outdoors in a park. Carry a small notebook to
  sketch or **freewrite** about what you see, hear, smell, and feel.

- **Reading literature**   Read as many different kinds of poetry as you can. You could even launch your poem with a line borrowed from someone else's poem. It becomes yours as you change it to fit your needs.

2. Discover your poem.   Read over your notes. Underline words, feelings, and ideas that seem to stand out. Look for connections between some of the things you underlined. Jotting down these connections on a new piece of paper might give you the beginning of a poem. If you start two or three poems, one will gradually emerge as the one you want to work on more.

3. Explore your ideas.   The key is to write as much as you can about your subject or subjects. Keep jotting words, phrases, and ideas around the lines you have already written. Freewriting is another good way to explore your subject. Try drawing a picture of your subject and then freewriting about what you have drawn.

One Student's Process

Tiffany Shue loved her big sister but wasn't sure how to write about her in a poem. She began freewriting and then underlined what seemed to mean the most to her.

My big sister, I love her so much. She always took care of me, she was my hero, she was so grown up in high school and still had time for me, but she was really a shy person deep inside. She slept with her old teddy, she took it on overnights. I understood, I had stuffed animals too. She's married now, but I still love my big sister, and the girls too, my littlest niece especially, she looks just like my sister and even talks like her, their baby pictures are just alike. She even has a teddy too, it kind of reminds me of the other one. She brought it last time they came over. My mom and dad even noticed.

COMPUTER TIP

With a word processor you can easily try out different ways of arranging lines or stanzas. You can also copy any line or refrain that you want to repeat.

1. Begin shaping your poem. You may already have many of the words you'll use. Try rearranging them. Experiment with different line lengths. Think about ways of grouping ideas and dividing your material into smaller units, as Trang Phan did with a stanza for each group of creatures. Aim for economy: cut out words you don't need. Remember that most poetry is tightly focused, often concentrating on a single idea or feeling.

2. Play with images. An image is a mental picture that appeals to any of the senses. For example, in "The Base Stealer," several images help to give a picture of the jumpy, waiting runner: a tightrope-walker, a dropped ball, a kid skipping rope, an ecstatic bird. Take advantage of any imaginative comparisons like these that come into your mind.

3. Listen to the sounds. Most poetry is meant for the ear. Read your poem aloud as you write it. Listen to the vowels, the consonants, and the rhythms. Listen for words that sound like what they mean. In "The Base Stealer," lively verbs—"teeters, skitters, tingles, teases"—all sound like something nervous, bouncy, quivery. In "A Life Is Gone," the repeated sound of "cold" increases the feeling of loneliness and grief.

 Writer's Choice Do you want to write your poem in free verse, or do you want your poem to rhyme and have a regular beat? If you want to use rhyme, be careful not to fall into too much of a singsong pattern. Poetry thrives on playful and imaginative use of language, but it doesn't have to rhyme.

4. Think about your draft. If possible, put your poem aside for a few hours or even a day or two. Then test it on your ear by reading it aloud. Does it seem to express what you meant to say? If not, don't be too critical yet. You may decide to stop working on this poem and work on a different one. When you're satisfied with your poem, you may want to read or show what you've written to classmates and see how they respond. The questions on the next page can help you review your work.

PROBLEM SOLVING

"I can't get my poem to say what I want it to."

For tips on word choice, see

• Handbook 25, "Meaning and Word Choice," pages 314–315

Questions for Yourself
- What main feeling, idea, or experience do I want to convey in my poem?
- Do any words or lines seem unnecessary to the meaning or impact of my poem?
- What parts of the poem feel most right for me?

Questions for Your Peer Readers
- What feeling, idea, or experience does my poem create for you?
- Which words, lines, or sections of my poem interest you or stand out the most?
- Which line or part of my poem is most important to you? Why?
- Which parts of my poem puzzle you?

One Student's Process

Here is Tiffany's first draft, with her friends' comments on the side. What would some of your comments have been?

Two Girls

When I was little,
My big sister always took care of me.
She was already a teenager, but she was shy.
When she slept over with girlfriends,
she always took her old teddy bear,
that was so worn out
the fur started falling off of it.
My big sister is a mother now,
with girls of her own.
One girl reminds me
Very much of her mother.
She even has a teddy bear too,
just like her mother.

Peer Reader Comments

I wonder what the first lines have to do with the rest of the poem.

I like the teddy bear. It makes me remember when I was little.

They both had teddy bears. Maybe you could use that idea more.

PROBLEM
SOLVING

"My words don't seem as exciting as my idea does."

For new ways to express your ideas, see

• Handbook 27, "Using Poetic Devices," pages 318–321

1. Review your readers' comments. Review the comments and think about whether you want to change your poem. If your readers didn't like your favorite part, should you still keep it? That's your choice. After all, you're the poet here.

2. Think about how your poem looks on the page. Look for a natural place to begin each line. Longer lines may produce an effect like conversation. Shorter lines may create more emphasis. In "Creatures from Outer Space," the lines fall into a regular pattern and a capital letter begins each line. In "Celebration," short lines seem right: "in circles,/ in leaps,/ in stomps." Check books of poetry to see how other poems look.

LINKING
GRAMMAR AND WRITING

Effective Modifiers

Adjectives and adverbs, if carefully chosen, can add detail, affect the mood, and make your images stand out. Notice the revisions involving modifiers in the second stanza of "A Life Is Gone."

Original

A child's cry
known only to one.
He lies there
and can not be seen

Revised

A child's lonely cry
known only to one.
He lies motionless
and can not be seen.

The adjective *lonely,* in the first line, helps to set a somber mood. It also echoes with *only* in the second line. The adverb *motionless,* in the third line, stresses a feeling of desolation.

For more information on modifiers, see Handbook 43, "Using Modifiers," pages 506–507 and 511–513.

3. Check your words once more. Are your words as specific as possible? Do they call up the picture you want?

One Student's Process

After reading her classmates' comments, Tiffany decided to focus on the teddy bears that belonged to her sister and her niece. With this new focus, she added some details and crossed out others. Then she realized she needed a different title.

~~Two Girls~~ The Teddy Bear

~~When I was little,~~
There was a little teddy bear,
~~My big sister always took care of me.~~
who belonged to a girl I knew,
~~She was already a teenager,~~ but she was shy.

~~When she slept over with girlfriends,~~

~~she always took her old teddy bear,~~
loved so much
that was ~~so worn out~~

the fur started falling off of it.

~~My big sister is a mother now,~~
she also has two
with ~~two~~ girls of her own.

One girl reminds me

Very much of her mother.
That little girl
She even has a teddy bear, too,

~~just like her mother.~~

that also is showing much wear.
And travels too.

Pretty soon its right eye fell off.
That did not stop the girl
from taking the bear everywhere she went.
Now, twenty-five years later,
she still has that bear.

COMPUTER TIP

Working on a word processor, you can experiment with various line lengths and stanza breaks. Some programs will help you to make a poem into different shapes.

Paragraphs at Work   Poems don't have paragraphs, but they may have groups of lines, or stanzas. The "Creatures" poem is an example. Stanzas can work like paragraphs by introducing new ideas in a poem. You may want to start a new stanza at the following points:

- when the feeling in your poem changes
- when you describe a new image
- when you want to emphasize something

PROOFREAD

1. Proofread your poem.   Check your grammar, spelling, punctuation, and capitalization. It is often useful to punctuate poetry as if it were prose, unless you have some reason not to. The same is true of capitalization, unless you decide to start each line with a capital. Poetry does not always follow formal grammar. In "A Life Is Gone," for example, notice that "A face hidden / from the world" is a sentence fragment.

2. Make a clean copy of your poem.   Are you ready to prepare your poem for publication? If so, the Standards for Evaluation can help. After making final changes, you can write out a clean copy.

PUBLISH AND PRESENT

- **Present a poetry reading.**   Join with a group of friends and classmates to read poems aloud for other students. You might choose appropriate musical accompaniment, either live or recorded, for each poem.

- **Create an anthology.**   Arrange your poems by theme or type to form a class poetry anthology. Find a way to present them by using fine handwriting or by using a word processor.

- **Submit poems for publication.**   Your teacher can help you send your poems to your school or local newspaper or to a literary magazine.

- **Make poetry posters.**   Combine artwork and poetry in colorful posters you can hang in the school hallways.

Standards for Evaluation

LITERARY WRITING

A poem

- usually centers around a particular idea, feeling, story, or experience
- often creates specific, concrete images
- usually produces part of its effect with the sounds of its words
- uses few words, all chosen with great care

- **Find imaginative presentations.** Write poems in fancy handwriting and frame them. Put poems on greeting cards or T-shirts, or stitch them on samplers. Turn poems into illustrated children's books or into songs.

REFLECT ON YOUR WRITING

WRITER TO WRITER

Remember to be alive to everything, not just to what you're feeling, but also to your pets, to flowers, to what you are reading.

May Sarton, poet

1. Write an introduction to your poem. Before you add your poem to your portfolio, write an introduction for it, telling readers about the poem and about your experience in writing it. In this introduction, reflect on some of the following questions.

FOR YOUR
PORTFOLIO

- Where did my poem come from? How did I decide what to write about and how to get started?
- How would I compare writing a poem to doing other kinds of writing? Did my poem surprise me in any way?
- In what ways did my readers help—or not help—me in writing this poem?
- What was I trying to accomplish with this poem? How well do I think I have accomplished it?
- What parts of my poem am I now the most and the least satisfied with?
- Would I like to write more poetry?

2. Explore other writing ideas. See the suggestions in Springboards on page 89.

Developing a Script

Starting from LITERATURE

Shakespeare wrote, "All the world's a stage." He also knew that putting actors on a stage is one of the best ways to tell a story. For that reason, drama is at least as old as the ancient Greeks and as up-to-date as tonight's TV shows.

The script for the movie *Stand and Deliver* was written by Ramon Menendez and Tom Musca. The film is about Jaime Escalante, a high school math teacher who dares to believe his students can learn more than anyone expects them to. In the following scenes he asks students to commit themselves to doing extra work.

PRODUCTION

from *Stand and Deliver*

SCENE	TAKE
36	4

by RAMON MENENDEZ and TOM MUSCA

[Escalante classroom interior—day. The beginning of the second year. The classroom is . . . upbeat looking . . . colorful. Posters with success as the theme decorate the walls. Escalante stands at the door as the students march in. He hands each of them a piece of paper. . . . Javier reads the piece of paper he was handed.]

JAVIER: Oh, come on! Contracts? You mean you can't trust us by now?

ESCALANTE: For those of you making the commitment you will be preparing yourself for the Advanced Placement Test. Make sure you have one, make sure it's signed before you come to class tomorrow.

ANA: We have to come here an hour before school, take your class two periods and stay until five?

ESCALANTE: Believe it or don't.

PANCHO: Saturdays? We gotta come on Saturdays? And no vacations?

ESCALANTE: Yep. Pass the A.P. exam and you get college credit.

CLAUDIA: Big deal.

LUPE: Kimo,[1] we're seniors. This is our year to slack off. *[The students get up and begin to file out. . . .*

(Next day) Escalante stands by the door collecting signed contracts from the students as they enter.]

ESCALANTE: Thank you very much. You don't got it signed, you don't get a ticket to watch the show. Thank you, Mr. Kung Fu. Good morning, good morning. Mr. Blue Eyes, thank you very much. Elizabeth, my tailor! Sophia, my Loren. Hey, get a haircut. One more time I gotta tell you. Thank you very much. *[Pancho hands in his contract.]* Hey! You didn't. . . . *[Escalante pushes past some students to Pancho.]* Get out of the way. *[to Pancho]* Here. You didn't sign it.

PANCHO: Come on, Kimo. I gotta put school on hold.

ESCALANTE: Go back until you sign it.

PANCHO: My uncle offered me a job operating a forklift Saturdays and Sundays. I'll be making time and a half.

ESCALANTE: So what?

PANCHO: Two years in the union and I'll be making more than you.

• • •

[Pancho's car, interior—night. Escalante is at the wheel.]

PANCHO: Kimo, I don't want to let you down, but the money I'll be making will buy me a new Trans Am.

ESCALANTE: No one cruises through life, Pancho. Wouldn't you rather be designing these things than repairing them? You can't even do that if they got fuel injections. *[He downshifts roughly.]*

PANCHO: Kimo, you're gonna strip my gears, man.

[Escalante speeds up and begins to really play at the gear shift.]

ESCALANTE: What's the big problem?

PANCHO: Orale,[2] Kimo.

ESCALANTE: Don't panic, Johnny. Just watch out for the other guy. Right or left?

[Escalante speeds up. A fork in the road.]

PANCHO: Where are we going?!

ESCALANTE: Right or left?

PANCHO: Go right! Go right!

ESCALANTE: *[Escalante veers right at the last moment. He speeds up and comes to a screeching halt in front of a sign that reads "Dead End."]* All you see is the turn. You don't see the road ahead.

---

1. **Kimo** nickname.
2. **orale** (ō rä' lä) *Spanish:* come on.

Think & Respond

How would you react to this teacher? How does he seem to motivate his students? How does the dialogue help shape your impression of each character? How do the stage directions add to the story?

Developing a Script

The script you have just read presents two brief scenes that are part of a longer story. It uses stage directions as well as actors' dialogue to indicate how the scenes could be performed for an audience.

Now write a script for a dramatic scene. You may make up the events or take them from your life or from a story you have read.

THINKING ABOUT YOUR SCENE

1. Think about possible stories.   List moments in your life when you experienced or witnessed something memorable. Also think about family stories. Imagine the center of this memory or story. What happened, and where? Who said what to whom, and why? What was the result? Try freewriting to produce a dramatic scene from this material.

2. Look for a story to adapt.   You may not want to make up your own scene. In that case, choose one from a short story, novel, legend, religious story, or historical event that you are familiar with. Look for a moment in the story where the characters face some challenge or learn an important lesson. Choose a short scene with a single, clear event.

3. Choose a type of presentation.   Scenes for the stage, for film (movies or TV), or for radio all have advantages. A radio script allows you to travel widely through time and space because your listeners can use their imaginations freely. Scripts for film and stage can make use of strong visual effects like gestures and costumes. Think about what you want to accomplish in your script; then make your choice.

"I don't know how to decide what kind of scene makes a good script."

To get an idea of the kind of scene that works well as a script, skim library books containing one-act plays.

4. Plan your script.   Imagine how your scene might look if performed, or how it would sound on radio or tape. Think about the main effect you want to create for the audience. If you are adapting a story, decide whether you will need to add anything to the original. Consider how you will open and close your scene.

DRAFTING YOUR SCRIPT

1. Set the scene.   The first part of your script will include brief stage directions in order to identify the characters, set, and props or to describe these to a listening audience.

2. Get your characters talking.   In drama, good dialogue is nearly everything. It should sound natural while always carrying the story forward. The first lines your actors speak should "grab" your audience, giving an idea of the characters and setting and referring to earlier events if necessary.

3. Present a dramatic action.   After your scene begins, the dialogue should begin to reveal some central problem or conflict among the characters and show how that problem develops. Don't worry if you find yourself writing dialogue that wasn't part of the original story, or even adding a new event or character. You can do whatever seems best for your script.

4. Look for an effective ending.   Your ending might show the action building to a climax or coming to an end. It might show a problem being solved or a conflict being settled. If there is no solution to the problem, you can show how the characters react to that fact. Even if the end of your scene is not the end of the story, your audience should feel that something has happened.

Writing
TIP

A radio script can have a narrator, who introduces setting and characters. Sound effects and background music can be used to set the mood.

PROBLEM
SOLVING

"I'm not used to writing dialogue."

For tips on effective dialogue, see

- Handbook 29, "Writing Dialogue," pages 324–327

Edward James Olmos plays math teacher Jaime Escalante in the film *Stand and Deliver.*

REVIEWING YOUR SCRIPT

1. Put yourself in the place of the audience.   Now read over your script, imagining you are not familiar with the story it is based on. Ask yourself these questions:

- Does the script tell the story I want it to tell?
- Have I captured the sound of real speech?
- Would an audience find the scene interesting, even without knowing the whole story?
- Do I give the audience enough information about the background, setting, and characters so that they can follow the story?

2. Try out a performance.   Probably the best way to shape a script is to try it out on an audience. Plays are often revised during rehearsals and even during the first performances. You might have friends read your script aloud so that you can decide which parts seem most, or least, effective.

PUBLISHING AND PRESENTING

- **Perform your scene with classmates.**   You can select actors, a stage designer, a props manager, a costumer, musicians, and any other assistants you need. Remember that some skits can be performed very effectively with few props and no scenery. Your audience may be members of your class or of another class.

- **Videotape your scene.**   You might show it to your classmates, friends, or family.

- **Tape your script as a radio drama.**   Find creative ways to get the sound effects or music you need. Play your tape for classmates.

- **Present your script as a dramatic reading.**   Select some helpers and plan a Reader's Theater presentation with appropriate costumes and props. You can perform it for your class or for others.

Lou Diamond Phillips rehearses during the filming of *Stand and Deliver.*

Springboards

Music

Find a poem or script that would benefit from musical accompaniment. Write or perform this music, or choose appropriate recorded music for the performance.

MEDIA

Write a newspaper review of a TV program, a radio show, a movie, or a play that you felt strongly about—or rewrite the ending of the story.

History

Write a poem or a radio drama about a character from history or a famous historical event. The character could be the speaker in a poem or the narrator of a radio story.

Speaking and Listening

Choose a scene from a play, a scene to be performed by two or three actors. Prepare a performance of this scene for the class.

Sentence

Words in a Series

Good writers sometimes use nouns or adjectives in a series to add smoothness and detail to their sentences. Notice how the words in a series make the sentences below more vivid.

Model A   It was a day something like right now, *dry, hot, and dusty.*

> **Ernest Gaines, *The Autobiography of Miss Jane Pittman***

Model B   I would gather *wildflowers, wild violets, honeysuckle, yellow jasmine, snakeflowers, and water lilies,* and with wire grass we'd weave them into *necklaces and crowns.*

> **James Hurst, "The Scarlet Ibis"**

Model C   *Cheerful and willing,* he went about every task with eagerness and good grace.   **Lloyd Alexander, "The Foundling"**

▶ **ON THE MARK**   In a series of three or more nouns or adjectives, use a comma after every item except the last one.

A. Combining Sentences   Make a new sentence by putting the underlined parts into the first sentence as a series. Decide where the series fits best. Write the complete sentence, putting commas between items in the series.

1. The chin was now clean. It was also <u>polished, soft</u>.

> **Hernando Téllez, "Lather and Nothing Else"**

2. She finished her breakfast and then went for her coat and hood. She also got <u>her school books and her satchel</u>.   **Daphne du Maurier, *The Birds***

3. He was more than a tough boy. He was also more than a <u>long, rawboned</u> boy.   **Carl Sandburg, *Abraham Lincoln: The Prairie Years***

4. I hated the tests. I also hated <u>the raised hopes and failed expectations</u>.

> **Amy Tan, *The Joy Luck Club***

5. The light lay like gold rind over the turf. The light was <u>full and smooth</u>. It also lay over <u>the furze, yew bushes, and the few wind-stunted thorn trees</u>.

> **Richard Adams, *Watership Down***

B. Unscrambling and Imitating Sentences   Unscramble each set of sentence chunks below to create a sentence that matches the structure of one of the models on page 90. Then write a correctly punctuated sentence of your own that imitates each model. Be sure each of your sentences contains a series.

1. Write sentences that imitate Model A.
   cold, melting, and delicious / a lot like an ice-cream cone / it was a treat

2. Write sentences that imitate Model B.
   novels, short stories, plays, newspaper articles, essays, and magazines, / Becky would read / she'd remember their contents for years and years / and with her photographic memory

3. Write sentences that imitate Model C.
   the runner headed toward the finish line / tired and aching / with determination and persistence

C. Expanding Sentences   Become a partner with a professional writer. Use your imagination to expand the parts of sentences given below by adding a series of nouns or adjectives where indicated. Be sure to use commas to separate the items in each series.

1. The house was silent, *(add two more adjectives describing the house)*.
   Cynthia Voigt, *Homecoming*

2. My mother's voice was like a cool dark room in summer—*(add three adjectives describing the mother's voice)*.   **Eugenia Collier, "Marigolds"**

3. He loved his vegetable plot, *(add two more things he loved)*.
   Lloyd Alexander, "Coll and His White Pig"

4. There was a camera store, a newsstand, *(add three other kinds of stores)*, and several other shops including a shoeshine stand tended by a boy of about Slake's age.   **Felice Holman, *Slake's Limbo***

5. On the dashboard in front of him, Brian saw dials, switches, *(add three more things Brian saw)* that were wiggling and flickering. . . .   **Gary Paulsen, *Hatchet***

Grammar Refresher   For more on punctuating series of nouns and adjectives, see Handbook 49, "Punctuation," pages 644–645.

- What if pigs could fly? What if the earth were flat? What if . . . ? Ask yourself a "what if" question, and then try to answer it.

- What would you like to change about yourself? How would your life be different if you made the change?

- What lessons have you learned? Write about an experience that taught you a lesson.

Show, Don't Tell

When you show how one event influences another event, you use facts, examples, and personal experiences to prove your point. Turn one of the *telling* sentences below into a *showing* passage, using examples that illustrate your point.

- Something made her change.
- Movies can start a trend.
- Creative advertising can really sell a product.

4

Informative Writing: Explaining *How*

Guided Assignment
Cause-and-Effect Explanation

Related Assignment
Describing a Process

A song on the radio makes you think of a friend. You wonder how your life will change if your family moves to another city. You try to figure out why your muscles are sore and then remember that you cleaned the garage over the weekend. Cause-and-effect relationships are everywhere.

In this workshop, you'll learn how to explain cause-and-effect relationships. You'll also learn how to describe a process. What's more, as you write about relationships and processes, you'll probably come to understand them better than ever before.

Cause and Effect

from

KRAKATOA
THE GREATEST OF THEM ALL

by Margaret Poynter

Starting from LITERATURE

Did you realize that just the sound of a volcano exploding can shatter windows for hundreds of miles around? Did you know that a volcanic eruption can create a tidal wave?

In this article, journalist Margaret Poynter describes the chain of destructive events triggered by three volcanoes erupting at the same time. As you read her account, notice the images and similes she uses to help you vividly picture the effects of this triple blast.

Krakatoa was a small island made up of three volcanoes—Perbuwatan, Danan, and Rakata—in the Sunda Strait of Indonesia.... On August 26, 1883, Krakatoa's three volcanoes began to erupt, the noise shaking houses a hundred miles away. Steam rose to a height of seven miles, and dust fell as far as three hundred miles from the island.

By the end of the day, Krakatoa was hidden by clouds of smoke and ash. Loud explosions occurred almost every ten minutes, and stones were tossed high into the air as lightning flashed through the inky black sky. The only other light came from a shower of glowing mud that looked like thousands of fireflies. It covered the ships in the area that were trapped by the mass of floating volcanic rock.

Meanwhile, more openings appeared on the slopes of the volcanoes, and hundreds of gallons of water rushed through them. The plug in the main vent still held firm, and the internal pressures grew. At dawn the next day, the sides of the island started to burst open, and the first of four huge explosions was heard. An hour later came a second; then there was silence for over three hours.

At 10:02 that morning, a gigantic explosion occurred, making the loudest noise ever reported by human beings! The sound waves cracked windows and walls for two hundred miles around. In Burma, fifteen hundred miles away, the noise sounded

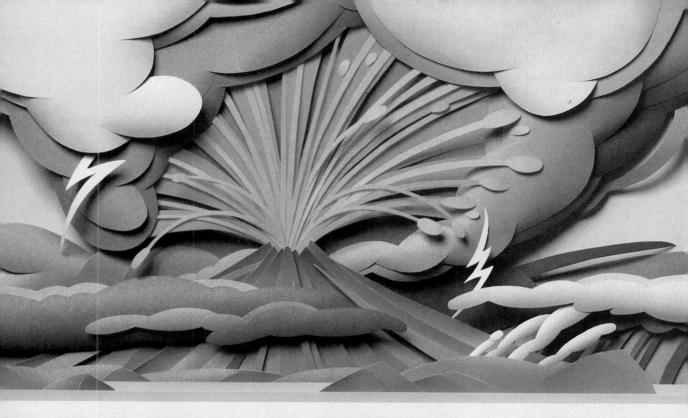

like gunfire at sea. A man on an island in the Indian Ocean east of Africa heard the noise from Krakatoa four hours later. The sound waves had traveled three thousand miles!

The eruption caused a cloud of dust to rise fifty miles into the air, and at least five cubic miles of rock and dirt were blown out of the inside of the volcano. Since there wasn't enough rock left to support it, the peak collapsed into the crater of the volcano, carrying two-thirds of the island with it. . . .

The ocean had been greatly disturbed by all the activity, and tidal waves, or *tsunamis* (tsoo-nah-mees), were formed. The largest, created by the 10:02 explosion and the island's collapse, rushed away from Krakatoa at a top speed of 350 miles per hour. As the huge wave approached land, it grew stronger and higher. A wall of water as high as a ten-story building crashed down on the coast of Java. Within minutes it destroyed three hundred villages, and parts of Sumatra were covered with eighty feet of water. . . .

For many months after the eruption, the Indonesian sea was full of floating rocks. The pillar of dust was caught up in the winds of the upper atmosphere, where it orbited the earth for several years! The dust was so thick that it formed a wall between the earth and the sun for two years. The average temperature of the earth dropped almost one degree. Strange blood-red sunsets were seen in many places. The sun appeared to be green or blue, and sometimes the moon seemed to be wearing a green halo.

Several years passed before the last of the dust fell back to earth. By that time, a bit of Krakatoa had been left in every part of the world.

Think & Respond

Which of the effects Poynter describes surprised or impressed you most? What did you learn from Poynter's article that you hadn't known before? Now look at how she organizes the effects she presents. How does this organization help you to understand what happened?

One Student's Writing

Margaret Poynter's purpose in writing the article on Krakatoa was to show the multiple effects of that island's triple eruption. The author of the following article, Steve Ginensky, an eighth-grade student, also focuses on effects—effects he fears are going unnoticed. However, Steve not only wants to share information, he wants to make a point about it. Read Steve's article to discover the point he wants to make.

Wake Up and Smell the Spray Paint
Steve Ginensky

If you're like most of the students at this school, you don't think gangs are causing us too much trouble yet. However, since gangs started trickling into our school and neighborhood last spring, they've caused us all plenty of problems. Just look at the things we've lost since gangs became a part of our town.

We've lost the freedom to dress as we please. Gang members identify each other by the way they wear their hats. Therefore, boys have been warned not to wear hats to school. "You could get jumped just for wearing a hat the wrong way," explains Peter Dubnik. The teachers won't allow anyone wearing gang colors or symbols into the school either. Also, since gang members have been known to beat people up for their jackets and gym shoes, many students now feel that they can't safely wear their expensive gym shoes and sports team jackets out of the house. "I wouldn't wear my new jacket until my name was permanently stitched on the back," said Teresa Ruiz, "and even then I was kinda scared to wear it."

We've lost peace of mind too. Instead of breezing through the halls thinking only about the friends we might meet, we have to deal with extra hall security guards and monitors as well as the police officer that patrols the grounds. These

Wrong Moves, Clothes, Colors Provoke Violent Gang Response

RIVER CITY (UPI)—The list of do's and don'ts associated with gang activity is long and intricate. People unaware that certain colors, signs, or types of clothing can be the symbols of gangs, are often ~~related violence.~~ Police say precaution is the

guards watch our every move, making us all feel uncomfortable. "I can't stand being looked at as if I were a gang member," says Josh DeStefano. Other students have told me the same thing.

We've also lost our feelings of trust in each other. Most of us don't share our locker combinations with friends anymore. As Joey Goldberg explains, "A gang member could buy it off someone and steal your things." Most kids even get worried when they see a large group gathering.

Finally, we've lost the freedom to go where we please. Gang graffiti is a warning to keep out. So we stay away from any place it appears, which includes all our old favorite hangouts. Gangs have taken over Delaney Woods, the old mill, and even our own playground (after school). The only place we seem to have left is the mall.

We've lost a lot because of gangs. We've lost the freedom to dress as we please. We've lost peace of mind. We've lost our feelings of trust in each other. We've even lost our old hangouts. So the next time you think gangs aren't causing you any problems, think again. You're as much a victim of gang violence as the kid who's gotten beaten up by a gang for his jacket. The only difference between you and that kid is that he can file a complaint with the police department. What are you going to do? Wake up and smell the spray paint—before it's too late.

Think & Respond

Respond as a Reader

▶ How do you think you would feel if you were in Steve's school?

▶ Have you or people you know had any experiences with gangs? In a small group, discuss how you might respond—or have responded—to gang violence or threats of violence.

Respond as a Writer

▶ What kinds of details does Steve use to support his ideas?

▶ Why do you think Steve uses so many quotes from students?

Cause-and-effect explanations like Margaret Poynter's article about Krakatoa and Steve Ginensky's piece about the effects of gangs make people aware of important relationships between events.

Now explain a cause-and-effect relationship that you think is important or interesting.

PREWRITE AND EXPLORE

1. Take time to wonder. Why do people crack their knuckles? How did the light bulb change people's lives? Find something that sparks your curiosity by freewriting to come up with "why" and "how" questions, or by engaging in some of the activities below.

Exploring Topics

- **Capturing your questions** What might happen if I change schools? What causes tornadoes to form? Record what you wonder about as you go through your day. Then share your notes.

- **Peeking into the past** How has the computer influenced modern life? What were the causes of the French Revolution? Browse through history books to find inventions and events that interest you.

- **What's news?** Look through newspapers and magazines to find current events and recent discoveries that concern or interest you. **List** these items. Then predict or speculate about their effects on you and your future.

- **"Ah ha!" experiences** Have you figured something out about people or events? Do you have a theory or an idea you're eager to explore? Jot down your theories, ideas, and speculations.

2. Begin exploring.   Once you have several topics, freewrite, research, or brainstorm to answer any of these questions: "What happened?" "What might happen?" and "What caused it?"

After you've explored for a while, choose the topic you'd most like to explain to others. Begin to examine it more closely.

3. Gather information.   If you need to know more about your topic, conduct library research or interviews, or do experiments.

4. Notice relationships.   As you try to see the connections among your details, keep the following points in mind.

- One cause can have more than one effect.

- One effect may have many causes.

- In a true cause-and-effect relationship, one event doesn't only happen later than another. Instead, the second event actually happens *because* the first event occurred.

5. Sort out your details.   Try drawing a cause-and-effect chart. Start with one cause and work forward, noting its effects. Or, begin with an effect and work backward, noting its causes. Add details that support your ideas and, if possible, a conclusion.

"Have I described a true cause-and-effect relationship?"

For help in checking your reasoning, see

- Handbook 31, "Critical Thinking and Writing," pages 337–339

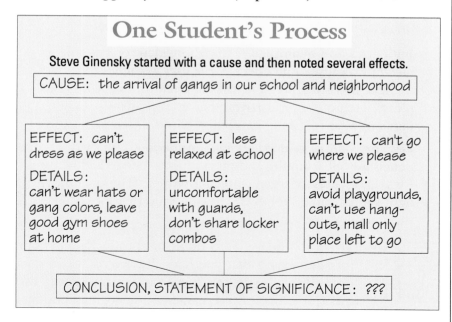

One Student's Process

Steve Ginensky started with a cause and then noted several effects.

CAUSE: the arrival of gangs in our school and neighborhood

EFFECT: can't dress as we please

DETAILS: can't wear hats or gang colors, leave good gym shoes at home

EFFECT: less relaxed at school

DETAILS: uncomfortable with guards, don't share locker combos

EFFECT: can't go where we please

DETAILS: avoid playgrounds, can't use hang-outs, mall only place left to go

CONCLUSION, STATEMENT OF SIGNIFICANCE: ???

Cause-and-Effect
Explanation   **99**

1. Start writing. Focus on whatever is clearest to you, then work backward or forward as you figure things out. Also, as you draft, feel free to explore additional causes or effects.

2. Be on the lookout for your purpose and goals. As Steve explored the effects of gangs, he realized that he and his friends had been overlooking lots of changes in their lives. He became concerned about these changes and the fact that no one was noticing them. So he decided his purpose for writing would be to point out these gang-related changes. His personal goal would be to wake his friends up "by shaking them up," as he put it.

As you write, think about your purpose and goals. Do you simply want to describe certain causes or effects? Do you want to persuade your readers to think or act in a certain way? What feelings or thoughts do you want your readers to get from your writing?

3. Elaborate on ideas. Is there more you can say? Try showing what you mean by adding some of the following details.

- **Facts and statistics** Include startling or impressive facts and statistics. For instance, "The sound waves cracked windows and walls for two hundred miles around."

- **Incidents and examples** Use an incident or example to illustrate a cause or an effect. Steve uses examples to support the idea that students have lost the freedom to dress as they please. He notes, for instance, that teachers won't allow students to wear certain color combinations to school.

- **Sensory details and figurative language** Use vivid sensory details as well as similes and metaphors to paint vivid pictures for your readers. Margaret Poynter writes, "The only other light came from a shower of glowing mud that looked like thousands of fireflies."

 Writer's Choice You don't have to include in your draft everything that you have discovered about your topic. Instead, you can focus on explaining just the causes or effects of your cause-and-effect relationship.

PROBLEM SOLVING

"How can I do a better job of showing instead of telling?"

For help in showing instead of telling, see

- Handbook 13, "Show, Don't Tell," pages 262–267

Writing
TIP

Dialogue and anecdotes can help bring to life a cause-and-effect explanation. They can also help your readers to feel personally touched by the causes or effects you are describing.

4. Organize your material. Here are three good ways to organize cause-and-effect writing:

- **Cause to effect** Start by describing the causes. Then move on to the effects. Steve, for example, first identifies a single cause and then describes several effects.

- **Effect to cause** Begin by telling what happened. Then explain or speculate on why it happened. If what happened is especially exciting or interesting, describing it first is a good way to grab your reader's attention.

- **Chronological order** If, like Margaret Poynter, you are describing a series of causes and effects in which each effect also acts as a cause, you may want to present each event in the order it occurs or might occur.

5. Examine your draft. Use the following questions to help you and your peer readers review your draft.

REVIEW YOUR WRITING

Questions for Yourself
- Are there any other possible causes or effects I might want to include?
- Have I emphasized the most important causes and effects?
- Have I shown clear connections between causes and effects?
- Have I explained my ideas with facts, incidents, and anecdotes?

Questions for Your Peer Readers
- Why do you think I wrote this essay?
- Do the connections I've made between causes and effects seem reasonable? Which connections are the strongest, or most reasonable? Which are weakest?
- Have I left out any causes or effects? If so, what are they?
- What questions do you have? What would you like to know more about?

PROBLEM SOLVING

"How do I organize my material?"

For help with cause-and-effect organization, see

- Handbook 8, "Types of Organization," pages 239–243

COMPUTER TIP

You can experiment with different ways of organizing the details in cause-and-effect writing by using the block move (cut and paste) command.

Cause-and-Effect
Explanation

Peer Reader Comments

The beginning of this paragraph doesn't seem as strong as the end.

You sound really frustrated. Why?

I like the last sentence.

One Student's Process

Here is the conclusion of Steve's first draft. Read it and then look at the peer comments. What comments, if any, would you add?

We've lost a lot because of gangs. We've lost the freedom to dress as we please, peace of mind, trust in each other, and even our old hang-outs. Why doesn't anyone else besides me see these things? Is being beaten up for your jacket or gym shoes the only kind of effect of gangs you guys can recognize? Why won't anybody wake up and smell the spray paint?

R EVISE YOUR WRITING

1. Review your responses.   Read your peer responses as well as your own notes to pinpoint the strengths and weaknesses of your writing. Then decide which changes you might want to make.

2. Have you stayed on track?   You may have discovered new causes or effects as you drafted. If so, now is the time to ask yourself if they belong in your composition.

3. Check your organization and add transitions.   If your cause-and-effect relationships are unclear, try organizing your details differently. Adding transitions can also help make relationships clearer.

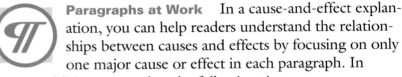

Paragraphs at Work   In a cause-and-effect explanation, you can help readers understand the relationships between causes and effects by focusing on only one major cause or effect in each paragraph. In addition, remember the following tips.

- Transitions in your topic sentence can help you clarify cause-and-effect relationships.
- All the details in your paragraph should help develop the major cause or effect that is the focus of that paragraph.

4. Think again about your purpose and goals. Did your peer readers understand your purpose for writing? One way to help your purpose come across clearly is to state it in your introduction. Also remember that your purpose and goals may change as you draft.

5. Review your conclusion. In your conclusion, you may simply want to restate or summarize your main ideas. However, you can also comment on these ideas, make a proposal, or call your readers to action.

After reviewing his peer readers' comments, Steve realized that his conclusion wasn't helping him get his message across. So he decided to rewrite the ending to get his readers to realize he wanted them to take some action.

One Student's Process

Read Steve's revised conclusion to see his changes.

We've lost a lot because of gangs. We've lost the freedom to dress as we please, peace of mind, trust in each other, and even our old hang-outs. ⊙ We've lost ⊙ We've lost our feelings of We've lost

~~Why doesn't anyone else besides me see these things? Is being beaten up for your jacket or gym shoes the only kind of effect of gangs you guys can recognize? Why won't anybody wake up and smell the spray paint?~~ —before it's too late.

So the next time you think gangs aren't causing you any problems, think again. You're as much a victim of gang violence as the kid who's gotten beaten up by a gang for his jacket. The only difference between you and that kid is that he can file a complaint with the police department. What are you going to do?

PROBLEM
S O L V I N G

"How do I know when to paragraph in a longer piece of writing?"

For more help with paragraphing in longer pieces of writing, see

- Handbook 11, "Paragraphs in Longer Writing," pages 252–254

Cause-and-Effect
Explanation **103**

1. Proofread your work. Correct any errors in grammar, capitalization, usage, and spelling.

2. Make a clean copy of your paper. Use the Standards for Evaluation in the margin to check your paper one last time. Then make a clean final copy.

Writing **TIP**

The words *effect* and *affect* are often confused. To use them correctly, remember that an **e**ffect is an **e**nd result and **a**ffect means to **a**ct on.

Standards for Evaluation

INFORMATIVE
W R I T I N G

A cause-and-effect explanation

- focuses on a true cause-and-effect relationship
- offers reasonable explanations of cause-and-effect relationships
- shows clear connections between causes and effects
- presents causes and effects in a sensible order
- uses facts, examples, and other details to illustrate each cause and effect

LINKING
MECHANICS AND WRITING

Punctuating Transition Words and Phrases
Transition words and phrases can help you to make the connections between causes and effects clear. When you begin a sentence with a transition word or phrase, set off that word or phrase with a comma.

Original
Gang members identify each other by the way they wear their hats. Boys have been warned not to wear hats to school.

Revised
Gang members identify each other by the way they wear their hats. <u>Therefore</u>, boys have been warned not to wear hats to school.

For more information on punctuating sentences with introductory elements, see Handbook 49, "Punctuation," page 646.

- **Arrange an oral presentation.** Share your explanation with a group that might be interested in understanding the cause-and-effect relationship you have described. If possible, consider demonstrating the cause-and-effect relationship to this group as part of your presentation.

- **Create a book-on-tape.**   Record your explanation along with those of your classmates to form a book-on-tape. Make this "book" available at the learning center in your school.

- **Make a cause-and-effect chart.**   Use your prewriting chart and notes as well as your final paper to prepare a poster-sized cause-and-effect chart that explains your cause-and-effect relationship. Then display your poster alongside others on a bulletin board.

REFLECT ON YOUR WRITING

WRITER TO WRITER

Have something to say, and say it as clearly as you can.
Matthew Arnold, poet and critic

FOR YOUR
PORTFOLIO

1. Add your explanation to your portfolio.   Now that you have written about a cause-and-effect relationship, what are your thoughts about this type of informative writing? Write down your reactions and attach your notes to your final draft. Answering the following questions may help you to focus your thoughts.

- What did I learn about finding ideas for cause-and-effect writing?

- What did I discover as I started writing about my cause-and-effect relationship? Did it seem simpler or more complicated once I began exploring it?

- How did I organize my details? Why? Did I make any changes in my organization during revision? If so, why?

- What was the most difficult part about writing this explanation? What techniques helped me with this part?

- Were my peers' responses helpful? Why or why not?

- If I were to rewrite my paper again, what would I change?

2. Explore additional writing ideas.   See the suggestions for describing a process on pages 108–109 and Springboards on page 110.

Describing a Process

Would you like to learn how to sky-dive? charm a snake? create a mummy? Some things you can learn by doing. Other things require some instruction. Of course, even with an instruction manual in hand, you probably wouldn't actually want to create a mummy. However, you may be curious enough about the mummification process to want to find out more about it.

In this article, Aliki unravels the mysteries of mummification. As you read her article, notice what else you learn about mummification besides the steps in the process.

FROM
MUMMIES

BY ALIKI Egyptians believed everyone had a *ba*, or soul, and a *ka*, an invisible twin of the person. They believed that when a person died, the ba and ka were released from the body and lived on in the tomb. The ba would keep contact with the living family and friends of the dead. The ka traveled back and forth from the body to the other world.

In order for a person to live forever, the ba and ka had to be able to recognize the body so they could return to it. That is why the body had to be preserved, or mummified.

A mummy is a corpse that has been dried out so it will not decay. The earliest Egyptians were mummified naturally. The corpse was buried in the ground and the hot dry sand of Egypt dried out the body. . . .

As time went on, burials took many more steps. The dead were wrapped in shrouds of cloth. . . . They were buried in caves or in pits lined with wood or stone.

Bodies not buried directly in the sand were exposed to dampness, air, and bacteria, and they decayed. People therefore learned how to embalm, or mummify, their dead. It took centuries of practice to perfect the art. Embalmers became so good that the mummies they made remained preserved for thousands of years. Mummification was a long, involved, and costly process. . . .

MADE IN EGYPT

The embalmers first took out the inner organs. They removed the brain through the nose with metal hooks. Then they made a slit in the left side of the body. They took out the liver, lungs, stomach, and intestines through this slit. Each of the organs was embalmed in a chemical called natron. It was put in its own container called a canopic jar. The heart was left in place. The embalmers later used stuffing to shape the thorax and stomach cavity.

In some cases, small bundles of natron wrapped in linen were stuffed inside the body. The outside was covered with natron too. The chemical dried out the body the same way the sand had done.

Then the body was carefully bound with long, narrow strips of linen. Fingers, toes, arms, and legs were wrapped separately. Sometimes, linen shrouds were placed between the layers of binding. Every few layers were glued together with resin.

[Small figurines of gods] were tucked in between the mummy's wrappings. Jewelry items such as rings, bracelets and necklaces were also placed between the layers of wrappings.

In some cases, the bound head was covered with a portrait mask. If anything happened to the mummy, the ba and ka would still be able to recognize it. The mask, too, was bound. Then the body was wrapped in a shroud and given a last coat of resin. The mummy was finished. . . .

Think & Respond

What surprised or impressed you about this process? Discuss your thoughts and reactions with your classmates. Then look back over the article to see how Aliki interests her audience in the mummification process. Notice, also, how Aliki helps her audience to understand unfamiliar terms.

INVITATION
▬ TO ▬
Write

Aliki makes the complicated process of embalming easy to follow by explaining it in a step-by-step way. By breaking a process down into its steps, you, too, can help others to understand it. In fact, you'll probably come to understand it better yourself.

Now write a description of a process in which you tell how to do something, how something works, or how something happens.

PLANNING YOUR EXPLANATION

1. Ask "I wonder how" questions. Have you ever wondered how to develop a photograph, how Velcro works, or how a caterpillar changes into a butterfly? List several "I wonder how" questions. As you list, think about processes that explain the workings of everyday items around your house, events in nature, and recent inventions or technology. Then choose a process that interests you.

2. Investigate the process. If the process is something you can do yourself, give it a try, or watch someone else do it. Take notes on what happens so you can describe the process carefully step by step. If the process is something you can't do or watch, try finding information in the library or interviewing an expert.

3. Map out the steps. Once you understand how the process works, arrange the steps in chronological order—the order in which they happen. To do this, you may want to create a timeline, flow chart, or even some sort of diagram such as the one in the margin showing the basic steps in the mummification process. You may want to include such a chart or a diagram with your final written explanation.

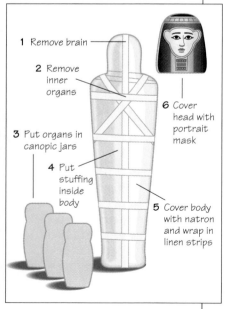

1 Remove brain
2 Remove inner organs
3 Put organs in canopic jars
4 Put stuffing inside body
5 Cover body with natron and wrap in linen strips
6 Cover head with portrait mask

DRAFTING YOUR EXPLANATION

1. Start your draft. Describe the process in the order that it is done or takes place. You may want to begin by writing about whatever you know best and then fill in the rest of the steps.

2. Think about your reasons for explaining this process. Why did you choose to write about this process? Point out what is unusual or interesting about the process or how it might be useful.

3. Consider the needs of your audience. Provide background information, definitions of terms, and lists of needed materials. Also use sensory details and examples to make your process clear.

REVIEWING YOUR WRITING

1. Ask a classmate to read your work. Have a peer reader identify any terms you need to define or any spots in your draft where steps seem to be missing or unclear. If you have explained how to do something, you may want to see if your reader can actually perform the process from your written instructions.

2. Check your organization. For help in checking your organization, ask yourself the following questions:

- Do I identify my process in my introduction?
- Does each paragraph cover only one main step in the process?
- Are the steps in their proper order?
- Would adding transitions make the order of my steps clearer?

PUBLISHING AND PRESENTING

- **Present an oral report in person or on videotape.** Consider using illustrations, photographs, or other props. If possible, you might even demonstrate the process.

- **Create a class booklet.** Group the explanations by their subject matter. Add a table of contents, title page, and cover. Then lend the booklet to the school or local library.

PROBLEM SOLVING

"How do I present the steps in my process?"

For help in presenting the steps in your process, see

- Handbook 9, "Effective Paragraphs," pages 244–247

Grammar **TIP**

As much as possible, use precise nouns. For example, don't say *container* if you mean *thermos*.

Spring boards

Science Think up an invention that the world needs. It could be something practical or something fanciful. Describe your invention, tell how it works, and explain how it will affect the world.

Literature Throughout history, people have thought up myths to explain strange natural events or remarkable human behavior. Write a myth of your own to explain an event or a behavior.

History What if the South had won the Civil War? Imagine a different outcome to a well-known historical event. Then describe what your life would be like today as a result of that outcome.

Speaking and Listening

At what are you an expert? Explain one of your hobbies or skills in an oral presentation.

Geography How has your community changed over the years? Why? Explain the effect one physical change has had on your community.

110

Send Out for a Sniglet

What do you call those little squares in a waffle? How about *squaffles?* This word is an example of a "sniglet"—a word that doesn't appear in the dictionary, but perhaps should. Here are some other familiar things with new names. You might try making up sniglets of your own.

bobble gesture (bah′bol jes′cher) n. The classroom activity of not knowing an answer but raising one's hand after determining a sufficient number of other people have also raised their hands, thus reducing the likelihood of actually being called on.

erdu (uhr′dew) n. The left-over accumulation of rubber particles after erasing a mistake on a test paper.

gazinta (gah zin′tah) n. Mathematical symbol for division; also the sound uttered when dividing out loud. (Example: "Four *gazinta* eight twice.")

grackles (grak′elz) n. The wrinkles that appear on the body after staying in water too long.

gyroped (jy′roh ped) n. a kid who cannot resist spinning around on a diner stool.

hangle n. A cluster of coat hangers.

laminites (lam′in itz) n. Those strange people who show up in the photo sections of brand-new wallets.

mittsquinter n. A ballplayer who looks into his glove after missing the ball, as if, somehow, the cause of the error lies there.

Rich Hall and Friends

Hmmm, a HanGLe

Sentence

Series of Sentence Parts

A series of similar sentence parts can add detail and power to writing. The repetition of similar sentence parts and similar words (*-ness* words in Model A, the word *cursing* in Model B, and the word *because* in Model C) adds emphasis and rhythm to the sentences below. This device is called **parallelism.**

Model A	She grieved over the <u>shabbiness of her apartment, the dinginess of the walls, the worn-out appearance of the chairs, the ugliness of the draperies.</u> **Guy de Maupassant, "The Necklace"**
Model B	His teeth chattered, and he began to gibber to himself, <u>cursing the day, cursing himself, cursing everybody.</u> **Liam O'Flaherty, "The Sniper"**
Model C	As I continued my delivery, I began to chuckle small bits of contentment to myself <u>because Mr. Brewer had invited me to his shop for haircuts, because the gringo customer had smiled at me, and because now all the gringos of the town would know me and maybe accept me.</u> **Daniel Garza, "Everybody Knows Tobie"**

▶ **ON THE MARK**   Use commas to separate sentence parts used in a series.

A. Combining Sentences   Make a new sentence by putting the underlined series of the second sentence into the first sentence at the caret (∧). Write the complete sentence, putting commas between the sentence parts in the series.

1. He galloped with the herd that day, ∧ . He galloped <u>across the plain, down to the river, up into the hills</u>.   **Julius Lester, "The Man Who Was a Horse"**

2. He went everywhere the slightest hope drove him, ∧ . He went <u>to the police station, to the newspapers to post a reward, to the cab companies</u>.   **Guy de Maupassant, "The Necklace"**

3. ∧ The roses came alive day by day, hour by hour. They were <u>rising out of the grass, wreathing the tree trunks and hanging from their branches, climbing up the walls and spreading over them with long garlands that fell in cascades</u>.   **Frances Hodgson Burnett, *The Secret Garden***

B. Unscrambling and Imitating Sentences   Unscramble each set of sentence chunks below to create a sentence that matches the structure of the model on page 112. Then write a correctly punctuated sentence of your own that imitates each model. Be sure each of your sentences contains a series.

1. Write sentences that imitate model A.
   the coziness of the campsite / we marveled at / the stillness of the evening / the fragrant smell of the pine needles / the brightness of the stars

2. Write sentences that imitate model B.
   praising the entire school / praising the students / and he began to speak to the assembly / praising the teachers / the principal stood

3. Write sentences that imitate model C.
   as I did my chores / and after all the clothes in the hamper were washed and dried / after I had put the dishes from the dishwasher into the cabinet / I began to make my plans for what I would do / after I had shopped for dinner

C. Expanding Sentences   Follow the directions in parentheses to add sentence parts that are parallel in structure to the underlined portion of each sentence. Be sure to use commas to separate the items in each series.

1. It was a guy's room with all his stuff, <u>a hockey stick,</u> *(add two other sentence parts that begin with* a *and tell what he had in his room).*
   Richard Peck, *Voices After Midnight*

2. I'd be chugging along through the fall and the winter, <u>enjoying school during the week,</u> *(add three other sentence parts that begin with* enjoying *and tell other things this person liked to do).*   **Robert Lipsyte, *One Fat Summer***

3. The day had been one of the unbearable ones, <u>when every sound had set her teeth on edge like chalk creaking on a chalkboard,</u> *(add one more sentence part that begins with* when *and gives a reason the day had been unbearable).*
   Dorothy Canfield Fisher, "The Apprentice"

Grammar Refresher   Verbal phrases are often used in series. To learn more about verbals and verbal phrases, see Handbook 47, "Using Verbals," pages 596–605.

> *It all started when Gilbert's older cousin Raymundo brought over* The Karate Kid *on video. Never before had a message been so clear, never had Gilbert seen his life on TV. As he sat in the dark with a box of Cracker Jacks in his lap, he knew that he, Gilbert Sanchez, a fifth-grader at John Burroughs Elementary, was the Karate Kid. Like the kid on the screen, he was pushed around by bullies. He too was a polite kid who did his homework and kept to himself. And, like the kid in the movie, Gilbert wanted to be strong enough to handle anyone who tried to mess with him.*
>
> Gary Soto, "THE KARATE KID"

- Have you ever compared yourself to someone in a movie or to someone famous? Write about the similarities you discovered.

- In what ways are you like your best friend? How are you different?

Show, Don't Tell

When you compare and contrast two subjects, you show how the subjects are alike and different. Turn one of the following *telling* sentences into a *showing* paragraph.

- Our parents' generation is different than our generation.

- The present can be like the past.

5

Informative Writing: Explaining *What*

Guided Assignment
Comparison and Contrast

Related Assignment
Consumer Report

Have you ever told a friend that some unusual food "tastes just like chicken, only . . . you know . . . different"? Have you ever known twins who looked very much alike but had quite different personalities? The world is filled with such interesting similarities and differences.

In this workshop you will have the opportunity to explain or describe something or someone through comparison and contrast. In a related assignment, you will create a consumer report.

Guided
ASSIGNMENT

Comparison and Contrast

Starting from
LITERATURE

Our solar system has nine planets, each with its own unique characteristics. What would life be like on another planet— Mars, for example? Brad Darrach and Steve Petranek wondered too, and decided the simplest way to explain the red planet would be to show how it was similar to and different from the earth. As you read their informative essay, from *Life* magazine, notice how they compare and contrast these two planets in our solar system.

Oh, what a fascinating walk you could take near the Martian equator next December, in the middle of a summer day. The weather would be perfect—high 60s and a bright orange Creamsicle-colored sky—but shirtsleeves would be out. You'd be wearing a light space suit to keep your blood from boiling because the "air" on Mars is so thin, about the same density as Earth's at 20 miles above sea level. The space suit would help with two other problems—the deadly ultraviolet light from the Sun, and the unbreathable Martian atmosphere, which is 95 percent carbon dioxide, with traces of nitrogen and argon.

The physical act of walking would seem effortless; you could endlessly hop, skip or jump along because gravity is only about a third of what it is on Earth. A 100-pound woman would feel as if she weighed 38 pounds, and a world-class athlete could run 100 meters in less than five seconds. The vista would remind you of the Arizona and California deserts—fine sand littered with rocks and boulders. But the sand would be pink and reddish-brown, because Martian soil is about 13 percent iron, much of which has turned to rust. Of course, there wouldn't be any cacti or scrub plants like tumbleweed, any darting lizards or rabbits. The terrain would be much drier than any desert on Earth, so dry that an ice cube placed on the ground would quickly disappear, evaporating before it could melt, going straight from solid to vapor.

You could walk just about anywhere you wanted on

A LAND OF STAGGERING PROPORTIONS

by
Brad Darrach
and
Steve Petranek

Mars, because the entire surface is land; there are no lakes, rivers or oceans. All the water is underground or frozen at the north and south poles. There's as much land on Mars as there is on Earth, even though Mars is only half as big as Earth and weighs only a tenth as much. Because of its weaker gravity, Mars is not as dense as Earth; it's puffed up. A thousand feet below the surface of Earth you would probably hit solid rock, but a thousand feet below the crust of Mars you would find porous material, perhaps even a gravelly slurry of rock and ice.

A day's walk on Mars would offer about as much Sun time as on Earth; Mars rotates once every 24 hours, 37 minutes. But the summer would last twice as long because Mars takes 687 days to orbit the Sun.

A trek to any of Earth's natural wonders would pale by comparison to what can be seen on Mars. Mount Everest, at just over 29,000 feet, would seem a foothill compared to the Tharsis bulge, a broad raised equatorial plain the size of the United States. On Tharsis sit extraordinary volcanoes, among them Olympus Mons, at 90,000 feet the highest known elevation in the solar system. The mighty Colorado River's cut through the Grand Canyon would seem a drainage ditch next to Valles Marineris, a gorge that would stretch from Seattle to Miami. . . .

You could spend a lifetime on the surface of Mars and never run out of new formations to see . . . . Just one thing, though. You would want to get back to base before dark. Most nights, even in summer, the temperature drops to about -125° F.

Think & Respond

What aspects of the Martian environment do you find most intriguing? Why? Give some examples from the essay that show how the authors help you to understand the environment of Mars.

One Student's Writing

Thor!
The Wonder Dog?

Have you ever dreamed about something for a long time and then had your dream come true? How did what you finally got compare to your fantasy? Rick Shen's dream came true when his mom announced the family was getting a dog. As you read Rick's essay, notice how his family's new pet compared to what he had in mind.

By Rick Shen

When my mom announced at dinner one night that our family was finally getting a dog, I couldn't have been happier. I'd been listening to my friend Laura brag about her dog, Sam, forever. Sam's parents were national champions. Sam was faster than a Corvette. Sam could leap 10 feet in the air to catch a Frisbee. Sam brought the newspaper in every night. Listening to Laura, you'd think Sam did her math homework too. I decided my dog would do anything Sam could do, only better.

The next day, Mom brought Thor home from the animal shelter. I named him Thor even before I saw him because I remembered from English class that Thor is the Norse god of thunder, and I wanted my dog to be powerful and fast. Mom told us that Thor had been abandoned by his owners and had fallen off a bridge into the river. I guess I should have realized right then that he wasn't going to be the most coordinated

dog in the world. But I didn't— at least not until Mom brought him in the front door. I looked at Thor and my heart sank. This was going to be my wonder dog? How was I ever going to face Laura and Sam?

You see, Sam is a golden retriever. Golden retrievers are sporting dogs. You can take them hunting, for companionship and to bring back any game birds you've brought down. Like all golden retrievers, Sam has long, silky, reddish-golden hair, a long tail, and a happy face. Sam always looks like she's smiling. Golden retrievers are great with little kids and make terrific pets.

Thor, on the other hand, is a dachshund, a hound. About all he has in common with Sam is that both dachshunds and golden retrievers are used for hunting. Instead of long, silky, golden hair, Thor has short, wiry, blackish-brown hair. His legs are about two inches long, and his stomach practically sits on the ground. Even with his head

In This Issue
How to Choose the
Right Veterinarian

THE DOG-OWNERS MAGAZINE

Bow Wow

Septe
Vol. 12

raised up, he can't be more than 12 inches tall. Thor looks sort of like a sausage with legs. Dachshunds are also good with little kids, although when Thor howls I think a little kid would get scared. Thor howls because dachshunds don't bark exactly like other dogs do.

When I told Laura I had gotten a dog, she suggested we take our dogs to the park to play one Saturday morning. That's when I realized how else Thor was different from Sam.

Laura threw the Frisbee and Sam ran after it. At the last second Sam jumped up high and grabbed it out of the air. Now it was our turn. I threw the Frisbee and Thor ran underneath it. At the last second, it hit Thor in the head. He had tried to jump up, but dachshunds just weren't made for jumping.

Then Laura asked Sam to sit and shake her hand. Sam did both things easily. I told Thor to sit. Dachshunds don't sit like other dogs. Thor sort of leans over until the back part of his body flops on the ground. Then he tries to keep his front half steady. Shaking hands in this position isn't easy. We finally gave up. By the end of the afternoon, I think Thor was better friends with Sam than I was with Laura.

That was last year. By now I've grown to love Thor a lot. He'll never chase sports cars or catch Frisbees like Sam, although he has learned to shake hands. I guess people will always ask about his funny shape. And I don't let him get anywhere near the river. Thor will never be a wonder dog, but we've become really great buddies, and that's good enough for me.

Think & Respond

Respond as a Reader

▶ Do you think Rick's first impressions of Thor are understandable? Why?

▶ Did you ever dream big dreams for one of your own pets? Did your dreams come true?

Respond as a Writer

▶ How does Rick lead up to his comparison of golden retrievers and dachshunds?

▶ How does Rick organize his comparison and contrast?

INVITATION
═ TO ═
Write

Like Brad Darrach and Steve Petranek, Rick Shen used comparison and contrast techniques as part of an informative essay. In both pieces of writing, the authors explained and described by showing how things are alike and different.

Write an informative essay that uses comparison and contrast to explain or describe something or someone.

P REWRITE AND EXPLORE

1. Look for comparisons and contrasts.   When you compare and contrast persons or things, you try to find similarities and differences. What types of comparisons interest you? To find out, try some of the following activities.

Exploring Topics

- **One on one**   Which team is better, the Chicago Bulls or the Los Angeles Lakers? What are the differences between laser discs and videocassettes? Which exercise gives you the best workout—cross-country skiing or tennis? Get together with some classmates and **brainstorm** to create a list of people, objects, and ideas you could compare and contrast, one on one. Make a list of the ideas you come up with.

- **Decisions, decisions**   Personal decisions often involve comparison and contrast. Which summer camp will you attend? What clubs will you join at school? Which jeans will you buy? Recall decisions you have made in the past, or think about decisions you're facing now. **Freewrite** about one that involved comparing or contrasting two choices.

PROBLEM
S O L V I N G

"How can I find a topic I care about?"

For additional suggestions for finding a writing topic, see

- Handbook 1, "Discovering Writing Ideas," pages 218–223

- **Time machine**   If you could travel forward into the future or back to the past, what would be different? What would be the same? Choose a new lifetime and make a **chart** that shows what things are different and what things are the same.

- **Reading literature**   Have any of your favorite stories or novels been made into movies? How are the two versions alike? How are they different? **Freewrite** about one such example.

What types of ideas have you gathered? Which one strikes you as the most interesting, unusual, or challenging? Choose one you'd like to explore in a comparison and contrast essay.

2. Investigate similarities and differences.   To explore your topic, you need to find a way to sort out similarities and differences. One way is to figure out what features you want to compare and contrast. For example, if you were comparing compact discs and tapes, you might consider such features as sound quality, durability, and cost. Then you could make a chart to show how your two subjects measure up.

Another way is to make a Venn diagram. In the outer part of each circle, list what is different about each subject you are comparing. In the space where the circles overlap, list the similarities.

One Student's Process

Rick Shen used a Venn diagram to help him clearly see how Sam and Thor were alike and different.

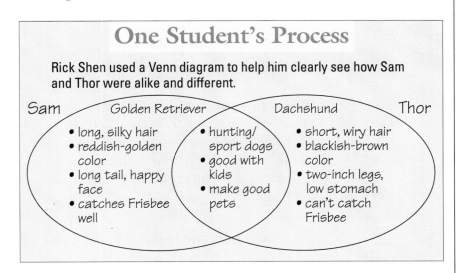

Sam   Golden Retriever   Dachshund   Thor

- long, silky hair
- reddish-golden color
- long tail, happy face
- catches Frisbee well

- hunting/ sport dogs
- good with kids
- make good pets

- short, wiry hair
- blackish-brown color
- two-inch legs, low stomach
- can't catch Frisbee

3. Think about your purpose. As you begin gathering details and ideas for your comparison, ask yourself, "What am I trying to accomplish with this comparison?" Do some freewriting about your purpose.

DRAFT AND DISCOVER

1. Begin writing. Start writing whatever part of your essay you feel most comfortable with. If you've thought of a great beginning, start there. If one similarity or difference stands out, write about it first. Don't worry about organization at this point.

 Writer's Choice You don't have to limit your draft to the information in your charts, diagrams, or other prewriting notes. If new ideas occur to you as you write, include them in your draft.

2. Organize information clearly. At some point in your drafting process, you will want to begin organizing the information you're presenting. Here are two techniques you can try.

- **Feature by feature** Present a feature and explain how each subject is similar or different with regard to that feature. Darrach and Petranek organized their essay in this way.

Feature I	Feature II
subject A	subject A
subject B	subject B

- **Subject by subject** Present all the information about one subject first and then move on to the next subject, showing how it is similar or different. Rick Shen used this type of organization in the third and fourth paragraphs of his essay.

  Subject A
     feature I, feature II, feature III, feature IV
  Subject B
     feature I, feature II, feature III, feature IV

3. Write an intriguing introduction.   Start your essay with an introduction that makes the reader want to read on. Darrach and Petranek start by telling you that a midday walk on Mars would be fascinating. You read on to find out why and how. Rick Shen starts out with a story, telling you that his new dog will be better in every way than Laura's. You read on to find out if his prediction turns out to be true.

Paragraphs at Work   When you write a comparison, you want to draw attention to the similarities and differences between the subjects. Your writing will be clear and easy to follow if you present only one subject or feature in each paragraph. Remember these tips.

- Begin a new paragraph for each subject or feature.
- Support the main idea of each paragraph with details or examples that illustrate specific similarities and differences.
- Delete any details that are not directly related to the main idea of the paragraph.

4. Think about your draft.   Do you want to share your writing with a peer reader now, or should you make some changes first? The following questions can help you review your draft and get the help you need from your peers.

REVIEW YOUR WRITING

Questions for Yourself
- Have I accomplished what I set out to do with this comparison?
- Would my point be clearer if I organized my information differently?
- Have I forgotten to mention any important similarities or differences?

Questions for Your Peer Readers
- Why do you think I chose to compare these subjects?
- Which points of comparison helped you the most?
- Is there anything else you'd like to know about these subjects?

One Student's Process

Notice the comments Rick's peer readers made about this part of his first draft. What comments would you have made?

Sam is a golden retriever. Golden retrievers are sporting dogs. You can take them hunting, for companionship and to bring back any game birds you've brought down. Like all golden retrievers, Sam has golden hair, a long tail, and a happy face. Golden retrievers are real good with little kids and make great pets. Thor is a dachshund. Dachshunds are hounds who hunt by running along with their noses to the ground. Thor has blackish-brown hair.

I didn't know any of this about golden retrievers.

What makes a dog's face happy?

You didn't tell me enough about Thor.

Writer's Choice Would including a chart, drawing, or diagram help your readers understand your comparison more clearly?

REVISE YOUR WRITING

1. Review your responses. Your own reactions and the reactions of your peers can help you see how effectively your draft uses the techniques of comparison and contrast. Did you discover any places in your writing where you need to supply additional details or examples to explain a comparison or contrast more completely? Were your peer readers able to follow your explanation easily, or do you need to strengthen your organization? Would transitional words and phrases make your ideas flow more smoothly? At this point you can choose to make minor changes or completely rethink your essay.

2. Use transitions to point out similarities and differences.
Transitions can help you draw attention to points of comparison and contrast. Use such words and phrases as *both, also,* and *similarly* to draw attention to similarities. Use *but, instead,* and *on the other hand* to signal differences.

3. Decide what changes you want to make. You may want to make only minor changes, or you may want to strike out in an entirely new direction. Always keep in mind that the purpose of revision is to rethink what you have written. Making changes doesn't mean you've made mistakes—you've just found clearer, more interesting, more informative ways to express your ideas.

One Student's Process

After thinking about the peer responses he got and his own concerns, Rick made the following changes in his draft.

Sam is a golden retriever. Golden retrievers are sporting dogs. You can take them hunting, for companionship and to bring back any game birds you've brought down. Like all golden retrievers, Sam has ^long, silky, reddish- golden hair, a long tail, and a happy face. ^Sam always looks like she's smiling. Golden retrievers are real good with little kids and make great pets. Thor is a dachshund. Dachshunds are hounds who hunt by running along with their noses to the ground. Thor has ^short, wiry blackish-brown hair.^

His legs are about two inches long, and his stomach practically sits on the ground.

GRAMMAR **AND** WRITING

Comparative and Superlative Forms

Whenever you use comparison and contrast, you will be comparing at least two subjects. Sometimes you may be working with more than two subjects. Depending on how many subjects you're comparing and contrasting, you will need to use different forms of adjectives and adverbs.

Use the **comparative** forms of adjectives and adverbs when you are comparing or contrasting two subjects.

> Diamonds are <u>harder</u> than rubies.

Use the **superlative** forms of adjectives and adverbs when you are comparing or contrasting three or more subjects.

> Diamonds are the <u>hardest</u> of all precious stones.

Rick Shen used the comparative form to compare Sam with a sports car.

> Sam is <u>faster</u> than a Corvette.

Had Rick wanted to compare Sam with more than one other subject, he would have used the superlative form.

> Of all the dogs in the park that day, Sam was <u>fastest</u>.

Standards for Evaluation

INFORMATIVE
W R I T I N G

Comparison and contrast writing

- introduces the subjects being compared in an interesting, intriguing manner
- discusses how the subjects being compared are similar and different
- organizes ideas logically, using feature-by-feature or subject-by-subject organization
- includes transitional words and phrases to make similarities and differences clear
- ends with a satisfying conclusion

PROOFREAD

1. Proofread your work. Check your informative essay for errors in grammar, spelling, punctuation, and capitalization.

2. Make a clean copy of your paper. Use the Standards for Evaluation in the margin to make one final check of your writing. Then prepare a final copy of your informative essay.

- **Add graphics to your essay.**   Photographs, drawings, and other visual aids can add interest to your informative essay.

- **Participate in a paper exchange.**   Exchange essays with students in another class at your school or even at a different school. Attach a letter to the essay you've been asked to respond to, telling the writer what you liked about his or her work.

- **Make a bulletin board display.**   Include a comparison and contrast chart about your subjects.

REFLECT ON YOUR WRITING

1. Add your writing to your portfolio.   You have now written your own informative essay based on comparison and contrast. How did your writing experience go? Did you find this type of writing enjoyable? What was the most interesting or frustrating part of your writing experience? Write a brief note to yourself or your teacher that talks about your writing process. These questions may help you focus your thoughts.

> FOR YOUR
> **PORTFOLIO**

- What did I learn about these subjects by comparing and contrasting them? Did anything surprise me?

- Was I surprised by any of the responses I got from my peer readers? Did I make any of the changes my peer readers suggested?

- Did I enjoy exploring comparisons and contrasts? Did this assignment give me any ideas for other comparisons I would like to investigate?

- Other than in an informative essay like Brad Darrach's and Steve Petranek's, in what types of writing could I use comparison and contrast techniques?

2. Explore additional writing ideas.   See the suggestions for writing a consumer report on pages 130–132 and Springboards on page 133.

Roller Rover (1987), William Wegman.

Consumer Report

Reading a
CONSUMER REPORT

How do you decide what basketball shoe or blue jeans to buy? With so many brands to choose from, you have to be a smart consumer to get the most for your money. One way to spend your cash intelligently is to check out similar products in a consumer magazine. As you read this consumer report about frozen yogurt, think about the features of this warm-weather treat that the author focuses on. What other features would you have compared?

from ZILLIONS

WHY IS EVERYBODY EATING FROZEN YOGURT?

Why is frozen yogurt the fastest growing new food of the 1990's?

It's cold and sweet. Smooth and creamy. A lot like ice cream—but with a difference. Frozen yogurt has less fat and fewer calories. In these nutrition-conscious 90's, a healthier choice that tastes terrific is sure to find new fans.

Did we say *tastes terrific?* Whipping air and sugar into icy yogurt may not sound tempting to your taste buds. Isn't yogurt just sour milk? Doesn't it have a certain tang? It can't really compare to ice cream, can it? To find out, we asked 26 *Zillions* readers around the country to visit local frozen yogurt stores and check out some low-fat flavors.

What They Thought

Each member of the Yogurt Team tasted chocolate and one other flavor at three different stores. In all, they visited 80 stores and tried 160 samples. . . . Everyone found a favorite, and (surprise! surprise!) no one complained about this assignment. "Frozen yogurt doesn't taste as sour as I thought it would," said Adam. Cammie agreed: "I was really amazed at the similarity to ice cream."

The kids found the best samples were smooth (not icy), fairly sweet, with a gentle yogurt tang and good flavor.

Even the richest frozen yogurts don't pack the flavor punch of fine ice cream, but the worst ones "tasted like cardboard," said Sarah. . . .

Why Switch?

Okay, it tastes good. So does ice cream. Why would you want to trade your old favorite for a swirl of yogurt? Because of two things you don't want lots of: calories and fat. . . .

Premium ice creams . . . are made with more cream and have less air whipped into them than regular ice creams. . . . That makes them *much* higher in fat and calories than frozen yogurt. Doctors say Americans should cut down on fat. Eating too much can lead to health problems, like heart disease.

Our testers found that switching to frozen yogurt is a delicious way to drop some fat, even for kids who don't choose snacks for nutrition reasons.

ICE CREAM VS. FROZEN YOGURT

Premium Ice Cream	330 calories	20 grams of fat
Regular Ice Cream	180 calories	9 grams of fat
Frozen Yogurt	150 calories	3 grams of fat

If you drown your treat in M&Ms, coconut, sprinkles, nuts, syrup, and such, the calories (fifty for a tablespoon of nuts) will climb. So will the cost of your order. Most stores dish up a hefty swirl of yogurt, but "it's not cheap," complained Michael. Our testers paid between $1 and $1.50 for a plain "small" portion. An 80-cent cone was the only real bargain. Most other stores offer an inexpensive kiddie cup that might satisfy many kids.

Frozen Assets

So the heat has hit and you're willing to give frozen yogurt a try. What should you order? Some kids liked the chocolate, but Esther recommends "sticking to unusual flavors. Classic flavors aren't quite as rich." Most testers especially enjoyed flavors like peach, raspberry, lime cooler, and peanut butter fudge.

No matter what flavor you pick, you may find you agree with Brian: "I never thought of going into a frozen-yogurt store before. But now that I've tried it, I'll definitely go back!"

Think & Respond

What else do you want to know about frozen yogurt that this report doesn't tell you? Why do you think the author presented the information about fat and calories as a chart? Do you think the quotations from the taste-testers are convincing? Why or why not?

INVITATION
TO
Write

As a consumer you are faced with a wide variety of products—so many, in fact, that making an intelligent choice can be difficult. Comparing products in an organized way, such as by creating a consumer report, can help you—and your readers—make wise decisions.

Write a consumer report to help people decide which brand, model, or type of product they should buy.

PLANNING YOUR
CONSUMER REPORT

1. Choose a product. Have you purchased something lately that you were dissatisfied with? Are you thinking of buying something in the near future, but you're not sure which brand or model really suits your needs? How could you have made a better choice last time and make the right choice this time? Discuss these questions with classmates, and brainstorm a list of products you'd like to investigate. Which product would you like to report on?

2. Set your standards. Before you can evaluate a product, you have to decide what you expect from it. For example, if you were evaluating different brands of frozen yogurt, you might look for such features as delicious taste, good nutritional value, low fat and calories, and a reasonable price.

Make a list of the features you think your product should have. Then arrange those features in a chart you can use to present your evaluation of each individual brand.

3. Gather information. Now it's time to find out how the individual brands of the product you've chosen to evaluate measure up. On the next page are some evaluation techniques you can try.

PROBLEM
SOLVING

"How can I present information visually?"

For more information on using charts and graphs, see

• Handbook 34, "Creating Graphic Aids," pages 349–351

- **Read product labels.**   Labels often include useful information that can help you better understand the product's features.

- **Try out the product.**   The best way to check out a product is to wear it, taste it, use it, ride it—in other words, try it out.

- **Take a survey.**   Talk to people who use the product you're investigating. Why do they like or dislike it? What are its best or worst features?

Record your findings on your chart. In addition, write down what people have to say about the product. You may want to include their quotations in your final report.

Studying advertisements for your product can help you identify important features.

WRITING YOUR

CONSUMER REPORT

1. Start writing.   Your chart and notes tell you what you discovered about your subject. What, however, will you *say* about your findings? Do some freewriting about your product evaluation. Did your findings surprise you in any way? Do you have any recommendations you want to make?

2. Shape your report.   There are many ways to present a consumer report. However, you will want to include these elements:

- **Introduction**   Tell your readers what product you are evaluating and the purpose of your evaluation. Are you rating individual brands? Are you judging how useful the product is?

- **Explanation of your method**   Tell your readers about the standards you used and how you went about your evaluation.

- **Your findings**   Present your evaluations, plus any reactions or personal opinions you think are useful. You might choose to write about each brand in turn, telling how it measured up to your standards. Another option is to present each of your standards in turn, explaining how the individual brands rate.

- **Conclusion**   You might want to summarize the information, recommend one brand, or even recommend that people not buy this product at all.

Writer's Choice Do you want to develop a rating system for judging individual brands? For example, you could give each brand a certain number of stars or a letter grade depending on how well it measures up to your standards.

REVIEWING YOUR REPORT

1. Size up your audience. Your goal is to help consumers like yourself make intelligent product decisions, so think about what your readers need to know. Have you given them enough background information about the product? Are there any special terms or concepts you should define?

2. Check your accuracy. In order to be useful, your information must be reliable. Check to make sure you spelled brand names correctly and listed prices, ingredients, and other details accurately.

SHARING YOUR REPORT

- **Create a consumer magazine.** Make copies of the magazine available to the rest of the school.

- **Submit your report to your school or community newspaper.** You might suggest that the newspaper consider running a regular column of consumer reports.

- **Give a demonstration.** Bring samples of the products you evaluated to class and show how they measure up to each other.

- **Hold a consumer conference.** Present and discuss the consumer reports as a group.

Spring**boards**

MEDIA   Imagine you work for the advertising agency that just won the account for your favorite product. Create an advertisement or commercial that compares and contrasts the product with its main competitor.

Colored Campbell's Soup Can (1965), Andy Warhol

Music

Many songs have been recorded by more than one artist. Choose such a song, and compare and contrast the versions by different musicians or musical groups.

Speaking and Listening   What if you could have helped elect Abraham Lincoln or Thomas Jefferson or any other President? Choose a presidential candidate (from the present or the past) and write a campaign speech comparing your candidate with his opponent.

Science   We take for granted many inventions that have made our lives easier. What if the telephone, the automobile, or the computer had never been invented? Choose an invention, and then compare and contrast what life would be like if it didn't exist.

Sentence

Adding Sentence Parts

You can make your sentences more informative by adding sentence parts at the beginning of sentences (sentence openers), between the subject and the verb (S-V splits), or at the end of a sentence (sentence closers). Read the sentences below without the underlined sentence parts. Then notice how the underlined parts make each sentence more interesting and complete.

Model A, Sentence Opener	<u>When we were about a hundred yards from the foot of the mountain,</u> we stopped and sat on a bench.
	William Pene du Bois, *The Twenty-One Balloons*
Model B, S-V Split	John, <u>the oldest of the children left at the home place,</u> sat at the end of the table facing his mother.
	Irene Hunt, *Across Five Aprils*
Model C, Sentence Closer	Rachel is sitting in the library during seventh period, <u>writing in her notebook</u>.
	Norma Fox Mazer, *After the Rain*

▶ **ON THE MARK** Use commas to set off sentence openers, closers, and S-V splits from the rest of the sentence.

A. Combining Sentences Make a new sentence by putting the underlined part of the second sentence into the first sentence in the position indicated *(sentence opener, closer, or S-V split)*. Write the complete sentence, using commas to set off the addition from the rest of the sentence.

1. Benno can see that the sun has moved way over to the river, and it is beginning to get cold. He sees this as he lies <u>curled up near the chimney of a building two houses away from his</u>. *(sentence opener)*

   Felice Holman, *Secret City, U.S.A.*

2. I didn't own a suit, but I had a sport coat, and I got a pair of leather penny loafers for the occasion. The new shoes led to <u>unsneakering my feet</u>.
   (sentence closer)   **Richard Peck, *Remembering the Good Times***

3. Charlie Bond sat facing them. He was <u>a pleasant-faced youth of twenty</u>. *(S-V split)*

Oliver La Farge, "The Little Stone Man"

B. Unscrambling and Imitating Sentences   Unscramble each set of sentence chunks below to create a sentence that matches the structure of one of the models on page 134. Then write a correctly punctuated sentence of your own that imitates each model. Be sure each of your sentences contains a sentence opener, S-V split, or sentence closer.

1. Write sentences that imitate Model A.
we lay on our blankets / when we were only little kids / and napped / in the first grade of elementary school

2. Write sentences that imitate Model B.
nominated for most unusual behavior / playing his imaginary harmonica / Weird Walter / the looniest of the kids / stood on the bleachers

3. Write sentences that imitate Model C.
dreaming of supper / was dozing in his doghouse during the storm / Snoopy

C. Expanding Sentences   Use your imagination to add sentence openers, S-V splits, and sentence closers to the sentences below. Follow the directions in parentheses.

1. The heat hit my face like a steamy towel, and I gasped for air. *(Add a sentence opener that begins with* when *and tells why it was so hot.)*

Robert Lipsyte, One Fat Summer

2. The black stallion raised his head and whistled when he saw him. *(Add a S-V split that begins with an* -ing *word and describes the stallion.)*

Walter Farley, The Black Stallion

3. The stray dogs had a pen out back. *(Add a sentence closer that begins with* a *and describes the pen for the dogs.)*   Gary Paulsen, <i>The Monument</i>

Grammar Refresher   Sentence openers, S-V splits, or sentence closers are often subordinate clauses. To learn more about subordinate clauses, see Handbook 45, "Using Compound and Complex Sentences," pages 560–570.

Sketch Book

- Who gets your vote? Give some convincing reasons to support the candidate you choose. Be original; be daring; have fun!

- What's your pet peeve? Jot down some of your thoughts.

- Tell the story of an argument you had recently. Who was right? Who won?

Show, Don't Tell

When you present both sides of an issue, show your readers all the important arguments, both pro and con. Use the following *telling* sentence to write two *showing* paragraphs, one paragraph for each side of the argument.

- All students should wear uniforms to school.

6

Persuasion

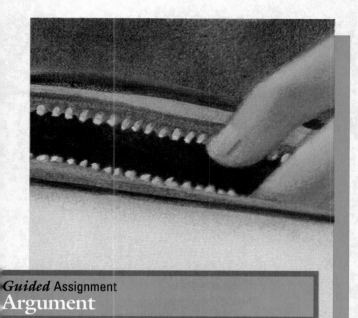

Guided Assignment
Argument

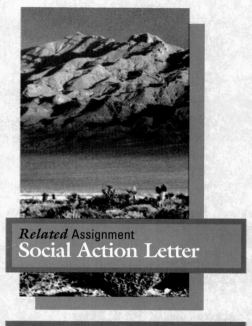

Related Assignment
Social Action Letter

Related Assignment
Writing for Assessment

Persuasive writing allows you to use the power of language to educate and influence people and to help others understand how *you* see the world. In this workshop you will have the chance to argue both sides of an issue of your choice. In one related assignment you will be able to present your views in a social action letter to an official who can help make those ideas a reality. In another assignment, you will learn how to present your ideas effectively and persuasively in a writing assessment situation.

Have you ever felt strongly about an issue but changed your mind when someone made a good case for the other side? Most important issues have more than one side. The one you agree with often depends on how convincing the speaker's or writer's arguments are. As you read this article notice the arguments that Lauren Tarshis gives to support each position.

by Lauren Tarshis

PRIVACY
AND TEENS

from Scholastic Update

IT WAS LUNCHTIME at Miami Southridge High School, and Tara McClary and a group of her friends were relaxing before afternoon classes . . . when a school security guard rounded them up and ushered them to the school office. "We didn't know what was going on," she says.

What was going on, she soon learned, was a drug search. Since Tara wasn't into drugs and had never been in trouble at school, the idea of a drug search didn't particularly concern her.

Paul Cooper, the assistant principal who led the search, didn't find any drugs that afternoon. But while sifting through the contents of Tara's purse, he discovered another type of contraband: six unsigned and unauthorized hall passes. Tara insisted that she had found the passes crumpled up on a classroom floor. But Cooper slapped her with a five-day suspension.

[Tara's father] was angry at Cooper and the school administration for what he claims is a serious violation of his daughter's Fourth Amendment rights, which protect Americans from unreasonable searches and seizures.

The Fourth Amendment is key to Americans' right to privacy. It states that government officials (like the police) cannot conduct a search without "probable cause"—good reason to suspect they'll find something illegal.

[On the other hand,] law enforcement officials and many school administrators say that the Fourth Amendment can interfere with their ability to preserve order and student safety.

They point to increased violence in schools, particularly in cities. Tara's school, for instance, is located in a particularly rough section of Miami. The school doesn't have a crime problem. But the surroundings are infamous for drug traffic. And there have been a number of shootings on or close to school property. Cooper and other Southridge administrators insist that student searches are vital to keeping the peace at Southridge. "Would you want your kids in a school where there might be weapons?" he asks.

[Others], like former Supreme Court Justice William Brennan, insist that young people deserve full Fourth Amendment coverage, particularly in school. "Schools cannot expect their students to learn the lessons of good citizenship when the school authorities themselves disregard the fundamental principles underpinning our constitutional freedoms," Brennan once wrote.

Legal experts on both sides of the student-rights issue agree that the courts need to set down more specific guidelines about student searches. They say that many rights violations occur because administrators don't know when a search crosses constitutional boundaries.

Tara and her father are hoping that her case will help clarify the constitutional rights of students.

Think & Respond

Which do you think is more important—students' privacy or their safety? Which of Lauren Tarshis's arguments influenced your thinking?

One Student's Writing

You probably don't always agree with your parents. Has listening to each other's point of view ever helped you come to an agreement? A junior high school student, Utica Norr, tried to present both the parents' and young people's points of view on an issue that was important to her.

As you read her writing, notice if her arguments change your own feelings on the issue.

War of the Words
by Utica Norr

Picture this. It's a summer afternoon in a small town. A boy comes home with a cassette of "Death Watch" by Eye C and his father throws it away because it has "disgusting lyrics." You may be thinking that this argument is between a father and son and doesn't concern you. But this incident is just one example of a controversial issue that affects us all.

The argument about songs with explicit lyrics has two sides. One side is that these songs often have an important message and that young people should be able to make their own decisions about what to listen to. Most kids probably would support this side. The other side is that the swearing, racism, and violence toward authority and especially toward women in the songs is a bad influence on children. Most parents would support this side. Many even want these recordings banned from the stores.

Most kids, and the musicians themselves, don't believe that the explicit language is harmful. They believe that young people are being exposed to this type of language all the time, even in their own homes. They also believe that the message of the song should be more important than the language.

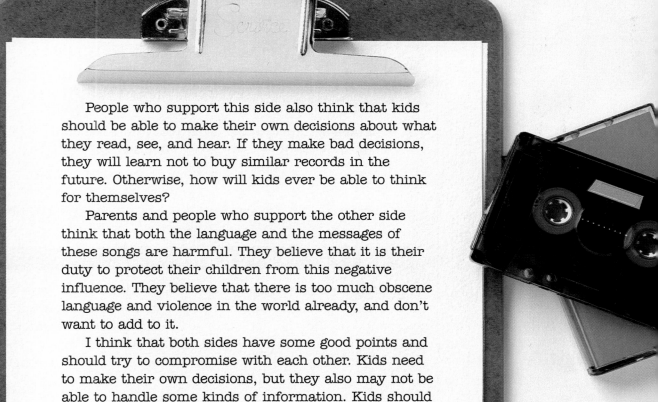

People who support this side also think that kids should be able to make their own decisions about what they read, see, and hear. If they make bad decisions, they will learn not to buy similar records in the future. Otherwise, how will kids ever be able to think for themselves?

Parents and people who support the other side think that both the language and the messages of these songs are harmful. They believe that it is their duty to protect their children from this negative influence. They believe that there is too much obscene language and violence in the world already, and don't want to add to it.

I think that both sides have some good points and should try to compromise with each other. Kids need to make their own decisions, but they also may not be able to handle some kinds of information. Kids should try to understand their parents' concern and should act responsibly and make the best decisions they can. Parents should trust their children and talk freely with them. If they don't someone else will.

Think ▼ *Respond*

Respond as a Reader

▶ What is your point of view on this issue?

▶ How practical do you think Utica's compromise position is?

Respond as a Writer

▶ Did Utica's introduction draw you into her writing? Why or why not?

▶ Why do you think she presents young people's side of this issue first?

INVITATION
== TO ==
Write

Lauren Tarshis and Utica Norr each explored an issue that was important to her. Both writers persuasively present two sides of a controversial issue. As a result, readers are able to draw their own conclusions.

Examine a controversial issue that interests, concerns, or angers you and write an argument that presents both sides of the issue.

P REWRITE AND EXPLORE

1. Identify a controversial issue. What subject in the news or in your personal life do you and your friends or parents disagree on? Should people who don't recycle be fined? Should community service be a requirement for graduation from high school? The following activities can help you discover an issue you feel strongly about.

Exploring Topics

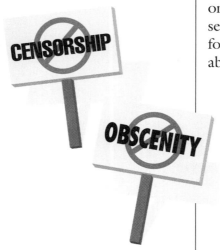

- **Power play** What if you had the power to change anything you wanted? How would you change your life, your school, the world? **Freewrite** about how people might argue against your ideas and how you would help them see your point of view.

- **Media march** Tune in on important current issues by watching or listening to news or talk shows. Read the editorials and the letters to the editor in your local newspapers. What issues make you want to voice your opinion? **Brainstorm** various sides of these issues with friends.

- **Reading literature** Stories and plays often explore controversial issues. Make a **list** of some issues dealt with in your favorite literary works.

2. Look at your issue from both sides.   Once you identify an issue that you want to explore, examine it from all sides. It's important to understand your issue thoroughly. The following activities can help you investigate your issue.

- **Research your issue**   Learn what other people think about your subject. You can locate recent magazine articles by using the *Readers' Guide to Periodical Literature* or your library's computerized index. Conducting interviews or taking opinion polls is another way to gather information.

- **Debate your issue**   Hold an informal debate or discussion about your subject with a few friends. Have each person take a different position and present arguments to support it. Challenge or offer additional support for each other's statements to make the strongest possible case for each side.

3. Sort your information.   Listing the ideas you have gathered about your issue in a chart may help you organize them. Divide a piece of paper in half. In one column list the arguments that support one side of the issue; in the other column list the arguments for the opposing side.

PROBLEM
S O L V I N G

"How can I find support for both sides of my issue?"

To help you find sources of information, see

- Handbook 35, "Making Use of the Library," pages 352–361
- Handbook 36, "Interviewing Skills," page 362

One Student's Process

Utica Norr had been arguing with her parents about the lyrics of a song that she liked. She decided that writing about the issue might help her clarify her own position and understand her parents' point of view better. She made the following chart to organize her ideas.

What I believe
Songs often have serious
   messages.
Language is not as impor-
   tant as the message.
Kids hear bad language
   all the time anyway.
Kids should make their
   own decisions about
   what they hear.

What my parents believe
These songs are a bad
   influence on kids.
Kids need to be protected.
There's enough violence
   in the world already.
Offensive songs should
   be banned from the
   stores.

Writer's Choice   You don't have to continue with a subject just because it's the one you started exploring. If you lose interest in your topic, find another one that interests you more.

DRAFT AND DISCOVER

1. Start writing.   You can begin writing any part of your argument that you are comfortable with and have ideas about. At some point you will need to clearly state your issue and its two sides. Some writers find that setting down that statement when they begin writing helps them to focus as they draft.

2. Support both sides of the issue.   The statements you make about each side of your issue must be backed up by solid evidence. Try to present each side fairly and support it as well as you can. Here are some kinds of evidence you can use.

Types of Support for Arguments

	Definition	Example
Facts	Statements that can be proved	"Death Watch" by Eye C was the best-selling single in 1992.
Statistics	Facts that involve numbers	Over two million copies of the single have been sold.
Incidents and examples	Events or specific cases that illustrate a point	Tim's dad threw away Tim's copy of "Death Watch."
Opinions	Personal feelings or beliefs	Tim's dad thinks the song has disgusting lyrics, but I don't agree.

3. Organize your arguments.   You can organize your writing in two basic ways—point by point or side by side.

- **Point by point**   Discuss one point from each side of the issue, then the next point from each side, then the next, until you have covered all the points you want to make.

- **Side by side**   Discuss all the points on one side of the issue first, then all the points on the other side.

PROBLEM

S O L V I N G

"What kinds of information can I use to support my arguments?"

For help in developing your writing ideas, see

- Handbook 12, "Methods of Elaboration," pages 255–261

For example, notice that Utica used the side-by-side organization. First she presented all the arguments on the young people's side and then all those on the parents' side.

4. Think about your draft.   Are you ready for some feedback, or do you want to continue to work independently? If you want, get the reactions of some friends. Try answering these questions.

REVIEW YOUR WRITING

Questions for Yourself
- What is most important to me about this issue?
- How can I state the argument more clearly?
- What reasons matter most to me?
- Have I presented both sides fairly?

Questions for Your Peer Readers
- What part of my argument seems strongest to you?
- What do you want to know more about?
- What don't you understand about the issue or about my arguments?

One Student's Process

Utica understood the young people's point of view on song lyrics very well, so that's where she began her draft. She wasn't sure how others would react, though, so she decided to ask some classmates for their comments.

> Most kids don't believe that the explicit language is harmful. My friend had to ask her older brother what some of the words meant. They also believe that the message of the song should be more important than the language. Also, young people should be able to make their own decisions about what they read, see, and hear. If they make bad decisions, they can learn from their mistakes. Otherwise, how will kids ever be able to think for themselves?

COMPUTER TIP

As you draft your writing, keep your prewriting notes visible on a split screen.

Peer Reader Comments

I think this is your strongest argument.

Don't forget people who think the message is just as bad as the language.

I don't get it. What do they learn from buying offensive music?

1. Review your responses.   Reread your writing and think about your own reactions and your peer readers' responses. How can you strengthen your arguments and the way you present them?

2. Put yourself in your reader's place.   Who will be reading your writing? Think about your audience's interests and experience and make sure you have given them enough background information to understand the issue. Remember to define any words that may be unfamiliar to readers.

3. Check your reasoning.   Review your writing to see if your explanation of the issue is logical. Have you drawn conclusions based on evidence you've provided? If you state your own opinions, make sure you support them with sufficient facts and examples.

4. Make sure your introduction and conclusion are strong. The beginning and ending of your writing are often the things that stick in readers' minds. Your introduction should make people want to keep reading. A question, surprising fact, or anecdote is a good way to create interest. Your conclusion might summarize the two sides of the issue, restate your position on the issue, invite readers to make up their own minds, or call for some action.

Notice how Utica draws readers into her writing by relating an interesting anecdote. She ends by offering her solution, one that both young people and their parents might support.

Paragraphs at Work   In presenting an argument, it is usually a good idea to start a new paragraph for each side or point you present. Also, stating in a topic sentence what each paragraph is about can help readers follow your argument easily. Remember these points.

• You could present each side or point of the argument in a separate paragraph.
• You may want to begin each paragraph with a topic sentence that states the subject of the paragraph.

5. Decide which changes you want to make.   Remember that this is *your* work, and you alone decide how to revise it.

PROBLEM SOLVING

"How can I improve my introduction and conclusion?"

For help beginning and ending your writing, see

• Handbook 16, "Introductions," pages 278–280
• Handbook 17, "Conclusions," pages 281–283

Writing
TIP

Use transitional words and phrases—for example, *however, nevertheless, on the other hand,* and *in contrast*—to show when you are shifting to another part of your argument.

One Student's Process

After thinking about her peer readers' comments and her own reactions to her draft, Utica made the following changes to her draft.

Most kids don't believe that the explicit language is harmful. ~~My friend had to ask her older brother what some of the words meant.~~ They also believe that the message of the song should be more important than the language. ~~Also, young people~~ should be able to make their own decisions about what they read, see, and hear. If they make bad decisions, they ~~can~~ learn ~~from their mistakes.~~ Otherwise, how will kids ever be able to think for themselves?

, and the musicians themselves,

People who support this side think that kids

will

not to buy similar records in the future

They believe that young people are being exposed to this type of language all the time, even in their own homes.

1. Proofread your work. Errors in grammar, capitalization, punctuation, and spelling can confuse readers and weaken the impact of your argument. Double-check your writing for accuracy.

LINKING
GRAMMAR AND WRITING

Avoiding Loaded Adjectives

Adjectives are powerful words, and they can sway readers to one side or the other of an argument. For example, saying someone is "brave" would be a compliment, while calling the same person "foolhardy," "rash," or "reckless" would be an insult. When choosing adjectives, pay attention to their **connotations,** the emotional associations people make with words.

Notice how Utica replaced a loaded adjective with a more neutral one when she revised her writing.

Original
One side is that these songs often have an incredible message and that young people should be able to make their own decisions.

Revised
One side is that these songs often have an important message and that young people should be able to make their own decisions.

For more information on the connotations of words and using adjectives correctly, see Handbook 25, "Meaning and Word Choice," pages 314–315 and Handbook 43, "Using Modifiers," pages 505–533.

---

2. Make a clean copy of your work. Are you satisfied with your writing now? If so, do a final check of the content using the Standards for Evaluation shown in the margin and decide if you want to make any additional changes. Then make a final copy.

Standards for Evaluation

PERSUASIVE
WRITING

An argument
- describes the issue clearly
- supports the writer's position with good evidence
- treats both sides fairly
- has a logical organization
- uses appropriate language for the audience
- concludes strongly with a summary of the issue, the writer's position, or a call for action

PUBLISH AND PRESENT

- **Submit your argument as a letter to the editor.** Share your ideas with a general audience by submitting your writing to your local or school newspaper for publication.

- **Present your argument as a pamphlet.** Design and produce a pamphlet based on your writing. Distribute it to an organization that is interested in your issue.

- **Stage a debate.** Working with a friend, choose a controversial issue you both care about and stage a debate for your class. Then hold a class discussion in which students vote for one side of the argument, explaining the reasons for their choices.

REFLECT ON YOUR WRITING

FOR YOUR
PORTFOLIO

1. Add your writing to your portfolio. Now that you have read two arguments and written one of your own, think about what you have learned. Write a paragraph or two that focuses on your writing process and attach it to your final piece. The following questions may help you focus your thinking.

- How did I decide on which issue to write about?

- What did I learn about myself or about my beliefs as I explored this issue?

- What was hardest for me about doing this kind of writing? What was easiest?

- Did I fairly present the side of the issue I don't agree with?

- What comments from my peers were most helpful? What kinds of help would I ask for next time?

- What did I learn about writing that I could use in completing other writing assignments?

2. Explore additional writing ideas. See the suggestions for writing a social action letter on pages 152–154 and Springboards on page 159.

Social Action Letter

Reading a
SOCIAL ACTION LETTER

You alone may not be able to change the world, but by letting the people in power know how you feel about important issues, you can have a real impact. For example, one junior high school student, Jennica Thuet, wrote her congressperson, urging him to vote against a plan to bury radioactive waste near her home. Do the arguments in her social action letter convince you?

Mr. Peter Hoagland
Congress of the United States
House of Representatives
Washington, D.C. 20515-1309

Dear Mr. Hoagland:

Why take the chance? This question is being asked all over Nevada.

Yucca Mountain in northwest Nevada has been chosen as the first geologic repository for spent fuel and high-level radioactive waste.

I am against this project because even though these pellets will be carefully buried in Yucca Mountain, how do we know that in the future the radiation won't seep into the groundwater, or that a volcanic eruption won't cause radiation to spill out?

I don't want any transport trucks in my neighborhood. If there's an accident, the canisters could be shattered, therefore releasing radiation.

Please consider a less populated state for this project and leave Nevada alone.

In fact, why not put this issue on the ballot? If I were old enough to vote, I think you know what my decision would be.

"No."

Sincerely,

Jennica Thuet

Jennica Thuet

Think & Respond

Which of Jennica's arguments was most convincing to you? Do you think that the language and tone of her letter are appropriate? Why or why not?

INVITATION
═ TO ═
Write

Jennica Thuet wrote a letter to her congressional representative to try to prevent the mountains near her home from becoming a dumping ground for radioactive waste. Writing gives you power. With well-chosen words directed to the right people, you, too, can help bring about changes in your world.

Choose an issue that is important to you. Write a social action letter to a public official stating your concern and calling for action.

DISCOVERING AND EXPLORING
YOUR ISSUE

1. Find an issue that matters to you. What social issues do you care deeply about? You might start by thinking of events that have touched your own life.

2. Stop, look, and listen. The advice that helped you cross the street safely as a child can also help you discover an issue that demands social action.

- **Stop** and think about social action organizations you have heard about—Greenpeace or Students Against Drunk Driving, for example. You might brainstorm as a class to come up with a list of these groups. Then check the library or write to each group for more information.

- **Look** in the newspaper for articles about issues that concern you. Write your reactions to them in your journal.

- **Listen** to your friends and family talk about events that had a major impact on their lives. Share your own experiences, too. Did someone's child get lead poisoning from eating peeling paint? Was someone's life saved by using a seat belt? Try freewriting about one of these issues.

3. Explore your issue. Try these techniques.

- **Loop it.** Freewrite for five minutes about your issue. Pick out the most important thought or feeling in that writing. Use that idea as the basis for another freewriting loop, and so on. Keep looping until you have enough ideas to work with.
- **Talk it over.** Discuss your issue in a small group. Take notes during the discussion and, later, freewrite about your ideas.

PLANNING AND DRAFTING
YOUR LETTER

1. Think about your audience. A social action letter expresses your personal feelings and calls for action. To be effective, however, it must be addressed to the person or group with authority to act on the issue. The following chart should help you direct your letter to the appropriate people.

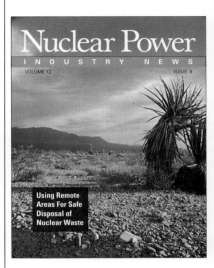

Social Action Letter

Audience	Type of Issue	Form of Letter
Government or corporate officials	Laws or business policies (a factory dumps harmful wastes into a river)	Business letter to an individual
Citizens of your community	Community activities (a neighborhood watch program may prevent crime)	Open letter or petition
Family and friends	Family or neighborhood concerns (an empty lot can become a playground)	Personal letter or flyer

 Writer's Choice Do you want to get together with other students and write a letter collaboratively? You could also write the letter on your own and ask others to join you in signing it. The choice is yours.

2. Start writing. Once you have some ideas about your issue, begin putting them down on paper. You may already have some freewriting or prewriting notes that can help get you started. Don't worry if you still have questions about your issue—your opinions may still be valid.

3. Support your statements. Be sure to support your position on the issue with convincing evidence. Presenting facts, statistics, and the opinions of experts can help persuade people to take the action you recommend.

REVIEWING YOUR LETTER

1. Reread your draft. Look over your writing to be sure you have included all the important points you want to make. Your letter should clearly state the issue and your position on it. You might want to ask several classmates to respond to your work and to offer additional arguments you could use to support your case.

2. Focus on the action. Your letter should tell the addressee exactly what action you want him or her to take on your issue. Notice how Jennica ended her letter with a call to action—and a very personal reason why her congressperson might want to comply.

3. Proofread your letter. Factual or grammatical errors in your letter can prevent people from taking it seriously. Before making a clean copy, be sure that your facts, grammar, capitalization, punctuation, and spelling are correct. Also check to be sure you have addressed the appropriate person or organization and that you have the correct mailing address.

PROBLEM
SOLVING

"How do I set up my letter?"

For correct letter format, see

• Appendix, page 684

PUBLISHING AND PRESENTING YOUR LETTER

- **Mail it.** If you've written to a government or corporate official, just drop your letter in the mail. Be sure to include your return address and to keep a copy for yourself.

- **Display it.** If you've written an open letter to your school or community, display it on a poster. Create an eye-catching layout and headings for your letter. Use colors and illustrations or photographs to enhance the content.

- **Read it aloud.** If you've written an open letter to friends or people in the community, read it aloud at an informal gathering.

Writing for Assessment

Tests. Nobody likes them, but everybody has to take them. Knowing what to expect on a test, however, can help you do your best. There are basically two types of tests. In one type, you are asked to write an essay to show your knowledge of a school subject, like history or science. In the other type of test, a *writing assessment,* you must write to express your own thoughts or feelings.

Look at the two essay-test questions and two prompts for a writing assessment on this page. What key words tell you what you are expected to do?

• ***Health***   In a short composition, explain the health risks of smoking. Include facts and examples that show the risks to both smokers and the people around them.

• ***English***   Choose a character from *The Red Pony* who changes in some important way during the story. Write at least three paragraphs describing the causes of the change and its effects on the character.

• ***Writing Assessment***   Imagine that the magazine *Awesome Audio* has asked readers to submit statements endorsing their favorite piece of audio equipment. Write a letter to the editor describing your favorite piece of equipment and tell why it is important to you.

• ***Writing Assessment***   Imagine that your city has a new law that all bicycle riders must wear helmets. Supporters say that the law will reduce injuries. Others say that helmets are costly and confining. Write an editorial for your local newspaper expressing your opinion on this issue.

INVITATION
═ TO ═
Write

Test taking can make you panic—or it can be your chance to shine. Knowing how to analyze test questions and learning how to respond to them can help you relax and do your best on any type of test.

Following the directions in the fourth prompt on page 155, express your views in an editorial.

Aₙₐₗᵧzᵢₙg tₕₑ ₚᵣₒₘₚₜ

1. Identify the important information. Writing prompts tell you what you are being asked to do on the test. As you read a prompt, look especially for these three pieces of information:

- what you'll write about—topic
- whom you'll write for—audience
- the form your writing will take—format

2. Look for key words. Prompts also include key words that suggest the best writing strategies to use. Some of these words and strategies are shown below.

Key Words	Strategy
Describe, define	Identify main qualities; give specific facts or sensory details about each.
Narrate, tell how, trace the steps, describe the process	Tell sequence of events or steps in a process in chronological order.
Explain, analyze, compare, contrast, show causes and effects	Present the main points of a topic. Develop each point with facts, examples, or other specific details.
Persuade, convince, give reasons, express your opinion	State your point of view and support it with facts, examples or anecdotes.

1. Budget your time. For example, on a thirty-minute writing test, you might prewrite for ten minutes, draft for fifteen minutes, and revise and proofread during the last five minutes.

2. Do some prewriting. A list, cluster, or quick freewriting can help you gather your thoughts. Keep in mind the strategy suggested by the prompt. For example, if you need to write a description, list the subject's characteristics and note sensory details.

3. Organize your thoughts. Make an informal outline or numbered list of your main ideas.

One Student's Process

Clifford Merrill decided to respond to the third writing prompt. He analyzed the prompt, then planned his response.

<u>Topic</u>: Favorite audio equipment; <u>Audience</u>: Audio magazine readers; <u>Form</u>: Letter to editor; <u>Strategy</u>: Describe equipment, tell what it means to me and why.
1. General statement—My tape player's the best.
2. Descriptive details
3. Uses—a) relaxing after school   b) listening with friends, sharing new music.

PROBLEM

S O L V I N G

"What is the most logical order in which to present my ideas?"

For help in organizing your response logically, see

• Handbook 15, "Coherence," pages 273–277

DRAFTING YOUR RESPONSE

1. Jump right in. Get to the point immediately. You might begin with a one- or two-sentence summary of your answer. Then cover the points in your prewriting list or outline. Be sure to include specific details, facts, or examples about each point.

2. Stick to the point. Cover each of your main ideas in a separate paragraph and make sure that every sentence in the paragraph relates to that idea. Use transitional words between paragraphs to link your ideas.

3. Write a strong conclusion. You might summarize the points you have made or restate your main idea in a different way.

REVIEWING YOUR RESPONSE

1. Reread the prompt. Have you answered the questions fully? Make any changes between the lines or in the margins.

2. Proofread your work. Check your grammar, capitalization, punctuation, and spelling and correct any errors.

One Student's Process

Here's how Clifford's test paper looked when he had finished.

To the Editor, <u>Awesome Audio</u> magazine:

You can stop looking right now. No piece of audio equipment can beat my tape player.

It's not really much to look at. It has the basics—a handle, a row of buttons, an earphone jack, a microphone, and a cassette holder. It also has powerful speakers, despite their compact size.

Looks mean very little to me, however. It's the music it plays that's more important. I listen to tapes every day after school and on the week-ends with my freinds, we trade tapes and record new ones, telling jokes or stories. The player is portable, so it goes where I go. That's why my tape player means so much to me.

Sincerely,
Clifford Merrill

Springboards

Literature

Think of a character in a short story, poem, or novel who chooses between two different courses of action. Explain why you agree or disagree with the character's choice.

SCIENCE

Some scientists now believe that we cannot save all endangered plant and animal species because we don't have the money or the technology. Write an editorial that either sides with the scientists or proposes a different approach.

A r t

Some people think that artists should be free to express their feelings in any way they want, including forms that others might find offensive or immoral. Write a letter to a local art museum, asking the director to either include such artwork in or exclude it from the museum's collection.

M E D I A

Think about a controversial movie you have heard about. Write a letter to a friend that explains both sides of the controversy.

Sentence

Adding Lists

Good writers sometimes add information or an explanation to sentences in the form of lists. Notice how the repetition of similar words or sentence parts in the underlined lists adds clarity, detail, and rhythm to the sentence.

Model A	I advocate the establishment of shrines in recognition of baseball greats: <u>Ty Cobb, Tris Speaker, Shoeless Joe Jackson, Ruth, Gehrig, Mantle, Mays, DiMaggio, and a few dozen others</u>. **W. P. Kinsella, *Shoeless Joe***
Model B	They began to ransack the floor: <u>pulled suitcases and boxes off shelves, tore clothes off hooks in the closets, pulled beds away from walls</u>. **James Thurber, "The Night the Ghost Got In"**
Model C	He showed him the different methods of propagation: <u>from seed, from cuttings, or from layering</u>. **John Christopher, *The Guardians***

▶ **ON THE MARK**   Use a colon to separate a list from the rest of the sentence. Use commas to separate the items in the list.

A. Combining Sentences   Make a new sentence by putting the underlined list of the second sentence into the first sentence. Write the complete sentence, putting a colon before the list.

1. Animals took shape. The shapes were of <u>yellow giraffes, blue lions, pink antelopes, lilac panthers cavorting in crystal substance</u>.
   Ray Bradbury, "There Will Come Soft Rains"

2. The mountains were miles away from the house of the family, and sometimes they were altogether hidden by weather. The weather consisted of <u>clouds, rain, or wind alive with dust</u>.
   Paul Horgan, "To the Mountains"

3. When I went inside, there was the new milliner, seated at a table littered with things. The things were <u>feathers, bird wings, satin bows, stiff tape, bolts of velvet, linen, silk, and so on, and several life-sized dummy heads</u>.
   Olive Ann Burns, *Cold Sassy Tree*

B. Unscrambling and Imitating Sentences Unscramble each set of sentence chunks below to create a sentence that matches the structure of one of the models on page 160. Then write a correctly punctuated sentence of your own that imitates each model. Be sure each of your sentences contains a list separated from the rest of the sentence by a colon.

1. Unscramble the chunks to match the structure of model A.
   recommends the enjoyment / our music appreciation teacher / rock, classical, reggae, new age, opera, jazz, blues, rap, and a couple of others / of many forms of music

2. Unscramble the chunks to match the structure of model B.
   wrapped dishes and glasses in paper / placed refrigerated foods safely in a picnic chest / they started to pack their belongings / stacked books in piles on the floor

3. Unscramble the chunks to match the structure of model C.
   by adding / the writing teacher / by changing / and by deleting / taught the class practical ways to revise

C. Expanding Sentences Use your imagination to add a list to the end of each sentence below. Be sure to answer the question in parentheses and to use commas to separate the items in each series.

1. I was faced with two choices: *(What were they?)* **Mark Mathabane,** *Kaffir Boy*

2. When I stepped out into the bright sunlight from the darkness of the movie house, I had only two things on my mind: *(What were the two things?)*
   S. E. Hinton, *The Outsiders*

3. The men in the seat were tired and angry and sad for they had got eighteen dollars for every movable thing from the farm: *(What things from the farm did they sell?)* **John Steinbeck,** *The Grapes of Wrath*

4. She had come to San Francisco in 1949 after losing everything in China: *(What things had she lost?)* **Amy Tan,** *The Joy Luck Club*

Grammar Refresher For more on using colons to introduce lists, see Handbook 49, "Punctuation," pages 657–658.

- Write down the first two thoughts that come to mind after seeing this piece of sculpture. Freewrite about one of your thoughts.

- Does anything puzzle you or confuse you about this sculpture? Explore your reactions to it.

- Create a work of art—drawing, collage, or sculpture—and share it with a friend. Write about your friend's reaction.

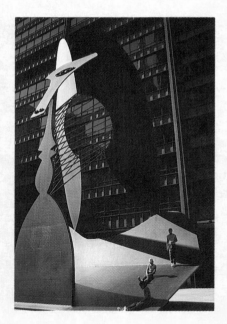

Show, Don't Tell

When you respond to a piece of writing, try to show the connections the selection has to you and to things in your own life. Turn one of the *telling* sentences below into a *showing* paragraph, using examples to support your feelings.

- The story impressed me.
- What that person did made me mad.

Responding to Literature

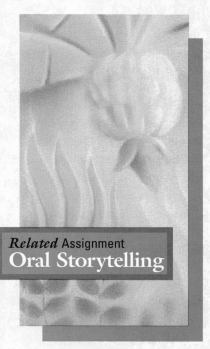

Guided Assignment
Analyzing a Story

Related Assignment
Oral Storytelling

P art of the fun of reading a good book or watching a movie comes afterwards when you can talk it over with friends. You might compare notes, argue about a character, or complain about the ending.

What you've really been doing is analyzing the work—figuring out what you think about it. Analysis is a good way to understand and enjoy something more. This workshop will help you learn how to analyze a literary work. In the related assignment you can bring the meaning of a story to life by retelling it orally.

Analyzing a Story

A short story can affect readers in many different ways. As you read a story, you might be fascinated by how the events unfold. Your friend, on the other hand, might notice one character in particular. A third person might wonder about the story's message. All of you might find parts you don't totally understand. As you read this excerpt from the short story "Dancing for Poppa," be aware of your reactions —what you are thinking, feeling, wondering, or noticing about the story.

"Dancing for Poppa" explores a young person's reaction to the death of a family member. After her grandfather's funeral, Connie remembers his love for her and his desire for her to become a ballerina. It was Poppa who bought Connie's first pair of pink ballet slippers, drove her to dance class, and proudly applauded her first recital solo. Connie is struggling with some difficult decisions about what she wants and what others expect of her.

from
Dancing for Poppa

by
Pat MacEnulty

◆

Poppa always thought I would be a ballerina. And I guess I did, too, until I was about fourteen and realized that even though I was quite good, I wasn't good enough to be a star for a major ballet company, and I didn't want to be in a company if I was just going to be a member of the corps. I had been a star in Miss Bell's senior class, and that had spoiled me for anything but the spotlight.

For the first five years, I had been a mainstay of the back row, but I started coming to the school and practicing by myself early in the mornings, and one day Miss Bell asked me to

lead the class. In our eighth-grade recital I had my first solo. Poppa embarrassed me by standing up and clapping at the end of my performance, and he kept clapping long after it was time for the next girl to come on. He cried afterward, saying, "I am young again when I watch you up there dancing like a fairy princess. It makes me young."

A week before his death I visited him in the hospital. He wanted to know what my plans were, whether I was going to New York to try out for the American Ballet Theatre.

"No, Poppa," I told him. "I'm going to Florida State with Cathy and my other friends from school."

"But I thought you liked performing," he said, crossing his hands. An IV tube was stuck in his arm, and he had lost at least thirty pounds, but his eyes had the same dark intensity as ever.

"I love it, but it's not enough for me. I want to do more with my life, maybe help people somehow." I couldn't explain, but I knew there was more to life for me than the stage, even if I had been good enough to be a star. He didn't say he was disappointed, but his smile seemed weak. Maybe that was just the illness. . . .

"Come with us to your grandmother's, Connie," my mother said after [the funeral, as] I collected the plates from around the living room and took them into the kitchen.

"Would you mind if I didn't?" I leaned against the sink. I had not been able to cry for Poppa the way everyone else had. If I could have just cried, maybe my knees wouldn't have felt as though they would sink like sandbags to the floor.

"Yes, Connie, I would mind very much." But my father overheard us from the dining room and came into the kitchen.

"Let her stay here, honey. She's been so strong for everyone else," he said and he gave my mother a long look. "They were very close," he added in a voice so soft he must have thought I couldn't hear him. . . .

Soon the house was quiet except for the running water as I rinsed off the dishes before loading them into the dishwasher. . . . The house was back to normal, as if Poppa had never died, as if he would come in any moment and say, "How's my princess?"

I sat in the living room on the couch where earlier Aunt Lynn and Aunt Maryjane had been discussing Poppa's will. He had left enough to take care of Grandma and a few tokens for members of the family. He had left me a framed photograph of the Degas statue the *Little Ballerina*, which sat on the coffee table next to the catalog from the college where I had been accepted.

I opened the catalog. . . . When I came to the page of dance classes, I stopped a moment to daydream. I imagined being on stage, felt the warmth of the lights and the tightness of the costume with its sequins and straps. I looked back at the catalog and noticed something I hadn't seen before. Just below the list of dance courses was a section of dance-therapy classes. I had never even heard of dance therapy, but it made sense. I turned to the course descriptions and found that there was even a major for dance therapy.

"Dance makes people happy," Poppa had said one Christmas after a family dinner. "Even a little baby knows how to dance. Before she can walk or talk, she'll start bouncing when she hears music.". . .

He was right. Dancing had always made me happy. And watching me dance had always made Poppa happy. It occurred to me that perhaps Poppa didn't want me to cry for him. Maybe he just wanted me to be happy. . . .

I walked to my bedroom and found my toe shoes hanging by their laces in the closet. I stuffed some fresh lamb's wool in the toes,

pulled on my tights and leotard, and went back into the living room. We had a recording of *Swan Lake*, and I lowered it onto the turntable. The music started, soft and sad. Instead of dancing the traditional version, I made up my own steps. My arm swung above my head and I rose up on my toe and stretched my leg out in an arabesque. My leg rose higher and straighter than it ever had before. Then I brought my foot to my knee. My body had a life of its own as I twirled. It seemed that I twirled in slow motion and that sitting on the couch, Poppa was shouting and clapping, "Bravo!" My torso stretched taller than ever and I could pirouette three times in one continuous spiral. Every movement was perfect. I played side one and then side two and then I started over again. I danced until, with bleeding toes, I landed in a lake of dreams.

The next morning my mother woke me up and said, "Hey, you slept in your ballet clothes. Might as well get up. You've only got a couple of weeks left until summer vacation is over. Better enjoy every minute of it."

She opened the window before she left. I rolled over in my bed and inhaled the last notes of my childhood. Outside a breeze danced through the leaves of a chinaberry tree, and it sounded like distant applause.

Think & Respond

How did the story make you feel? How do you feel about the way Connie resolves her problem? Does anything about the story puzzle or confuse you? How would you describe this story to someone else? Share your ideas with other readers of the story.

One Student's Writing

Applause for Connie
By Annie Maxwell

Many young people are faced with a dilemma when it comes to choosing a career. This, I think, is the main message of Pat MacEnulty's "Dancing for Poppa." In this touching short story the main character, Connie, is faced with the problem of deciding her future. She must consider her goals, but she also wants to be sensitive to the desires of her family. Connie is mainly concerned about the wishes of "Poppa," who is her grandfather, her friend, and "the one who knows her dreams."

Throughout the story, Connie does not know what to do with her life. Her family wants her to attend college, but her beloved Poppa wants her to become a ballerina. She realizes the importance of Poppa's hopes for her even more when he dies; she feels that she desperately needs to express her gratitude to her deceased grandfather. After all, she didn't even know she liked dancing until Poppa gave her her first ballet shoes.

Toward the end of the story, Connie discovers a possible compromise. She can major in dance therapy. That way she can go to college and still dance. At this point I thought Connie's struggle had been resolved and drawn to a logical conclusion. Then I read the ending for the first time, and I was confused. It seemed to hold out the possibility of Connie following another path. In particular, I had problems with two statements.

I was puzzled by the sentence "I inhaled the last notes of my childhood," but I quickly decided that it refers to Connie leaving childhood and its hobbies. She's going on to study dance therapy in college—going on to becoming an adult. I had more trouble though with the final sentence: "Outside a breeze danced through the leaves of a chinaberry tree and it sounded like distant applause." Does the breeze represent Poppa and show that now his spirit is free because Connie has made her decision, or does it represent Connie's final dance for Poppa? Does the distant applause stand for more applause to come for Connie because she will become a ballerina, or is it a sign of approval for her decision to go into dance therapy?

After studying these lines, I decided they are meant to show that through Connie's decision to pursue a career that includes ballet, she has resolved her conflict. The ending proves that not only is Connie satisfied with her choice, but also that Poppa's wishes are fulfilled. What convinced me most of all was the description near the end of the story of Connie's final performance for Poppa. She dances the best ever, and she imagines Poppa sitting on the couch clapping for her, congratulating her on her decision and her dancing. (Earlier, Connie had not been able to cry for her grandfather. This dance is her way of crying.)

I feel satisfied that Connie was happy and was going to continue with dance through dance therapy. The breeze in the end represents this last dance and the distant applause is the reassurance of Connie's first happiness as an adult.

Think & Respond

Respond as a Reader

► What do you think you would do if you were faced with a decision similar to Connie's?

► Can you think of a time when you were torn between what you wanted to do and what your family wanted you to do?

Respond as a Writer

► How does Annie help the reader to understand the background of the problem she will discuss?

► How does Annie support her interpretation of the ending?

Analyzing a Story

INVITATION
TO
Write

Annie Maxwell chose to write about the ending of "Dancing for Poppa" in order to sort out—to analyze—her reactions to the story. By doing so she found a deeper meaning to the story. Writing an analysis is a good way to appreciate a literary work and come to understand it better.

Choose a short story and write an essay in which you analyze some part of it.

PREWRITE AND EXPLORE

1. Find a story. Think about a story—or even a novel or play—that you found challenging, liked or disliked strongly, or were unable to forget. For short stories, you might consider "Dancing for Poppa," "The Dinner Party" by Mona Gardner, or "A Cap for Steve" by Morley Callaghan. To help you make your choice, try one or more of the following activities.

Exploring Topics

- **First impressions**   You can **freewrite** about your initial reactions—the kinds of things you might tell a friend who had just asked you about the story.

- **Text rendering**   A good way to dig into a story is to meet with classmates who also have read it. Each person reads aloud whatever lines or phrases seem particularly important, interesting, or troubling. Some passages might get called out more than once. This process often gives you unexpected ideas about the story.

After you've explored your choices, choose the story you are most interested in. Think about ideas that you'd like to follow up.

2. Reread and record.   Read the story again. This time, jot down what you notice, think, feel, or wonder about. For example:

- Questions you have about characters, actions, or setting

- Lines that interest, puzzle, amuse, or anger you

- Ideas you agree with, want to argue about, or remember

- Memories, thoughts, or feelings triggered by your reading

A double entry journal is a good tool for recording and exploring reactions to important or confusing lines or passages. Write the lines from the story in one column and your reactions in a second column.

One Student's Process

Annie found certain passages troubling. She created this double-entry journal to explore the meaning of those key passages. The notes from her first reading are shown in blue. As she reread the story, she added new thoughts.

Quotes from story	Ideas
"I rolled over in my bed and inhaled the last notes of my childhood."	• What does this have to do with anything? • Is she leaving the hobbies of childhood behind? • Is she becoming an adult, going into dance therapy?
"Outside a breeze danced through the leaves of a chinaberry tree and it sounded like distant applause."	• Does this mean she's going into ballet after all? • Does the breeze represent Poppa—his spirit free now and her mind at rest? • Or does it represent her last dance for Poppa? • The applause could be a sign of approval for her decision to study dance therapy.

Writer's Choice   You might want to make notes on a photocopy of the work you are analyzing. You can also highlight or underline important passages.

3. Explore your reactions.   Read the story one more time, and keep taking notes. See if your understanding changes as you read the story again.

4. Find a focus.   An analysis is more than a summary. It often means looking at a work from a certain angle—examining a particular feature, noticing how one element of a story helps make the story more effective or interesting. Look through your journal and mark any entries that seem especially interesting or thought provoking. You could focus on any of the following:

- **Plot**   Are the events believable, predictable, surprising?
- **Theme**   Does the story teach an idea you agree with? Why do you agree or disagree?
- **Character**   Do the characters act in ways that fit their personalities? Are the characters presented as stereotypes?
- **Confusing elements**   Where does the story confuse you? You could explore parts that puzzle you and look for solutions.

Detail of *The Ballerina* (1875–1877), Edgar Degas.

PROBLEM SOLVING

"How can I tell my readers about the story as briefly as possible?"

For help writing a summary, see

- Handbook 33, "Writing Paraphrases and Summaries," pages 346–348

DRAFT AND DISCOVER

1. State your focus in a sentence.   Then freewrite to discover more about what you think. Consider what details you could use to explain your ideas. Don't worry if your thoughts seem disorganized, or even contradictory. You can sort out your ideas—or even change your mind—once you get something on paper.

2. Begin organizing your draft.   Most literary analyses follow this general pattern:

Introduction   Give the title, the author of your story, and enough background for readers to understand the story. Explain the focus of your analysis. Show why you found the subject interesting.

Body Present your analysis. Show—don't just tell—what you think about your subject. Explain the steps in your reasoning. Refer specifically to the story, and use quotations to support your argument. Summarize where necessary. Like Annie, you may want to explore a topic or problem that puzzles you. Notice some of the various ways to organize analyses.

Organizing the Body

Analyzing a Problem Passage
- Show where the problem part fits into the whole story.
- Explain any problems you had understanding the passage.
- Explore some possible meanings or interpretations, possibly picking the best and explaining why it is the best.

Analyzing a Character
- Show what the character is like at the beginning.
- Show how the character changes.
- Show how the character is different at the end.

Analyzing Themes or Ideas
- Summarize the story.
- State what you think the theme is and what you think it means.
- Agree or disagree with the theme or idea and give your reasons.

Closing Summarize important points, and state your feelings about the story or conclusions you have reached.

3. Think about your draft. After you've put your analysis aside for a while, read it again with fresh eyes. The following questions can help you and your peers respond to your draft.

R E V I E W   Y O U R   W R I T I N G

Questions for Yourself
- What is the focus of my essay?
- How do my details support this focus?
- How have I shown that this topic interested me?
- What additional information do my readers need?

Questions for Your Peer Readers
- What title would you give my essay? Tell me in your own words what you think it is about.
- What part of my essay is most important or interesting?
- How does my essay give you a better or different understanding of the story?

One Student's Process

In this part of Annie's first draft, she thought about possible meanings of the breeze mentioned at the end of the story. Afterwards, she asked her peers to react to her interpretation.

> So does the breeze represent Poppa and show that his spirit is free because Connie has made her decision, or does it represent Connie's final dance for Poppa. Does the distant applause of the wind stand for more applause to come because she will become a ballerina, or is it a sign of approval for her decision to go into dance therapy. After reading and studying these lines, I decided they are meant to show that she has resolved her conflict. The ending proves that not only is Connie satisfied with her choice, but also that Poppa's wishes are fulfilled.

Peer Reader Comments

These are interesting ideas. I hadn't thought of them.

I still don't understand how the ending proves this.

REVISE YOUR WRITING

1. Review your responses. Think about how you answered your own questions. How did the responses from your peer readers help you see your writing differently?

2. Look over your argument. Have you supported your analysis with enough well-chosen details, such as reasons, examples, and quotations from the story?

 Paragraphs at Work In a literary analysis, paragraphs need to flow logically. For example, look on page 173 at the suggested method of organization for analyzing a problem passage. This list could serve as an outline for a brief analysis of a passage. Each of the points could be covered in a paragraph. So remember these tips.

- Consider an outline like one of those on page 173.
- Write a paragraph for each point in the outline.
- Support each main idea with specific details.

PROBLEM SOLVING

"Have I given enough reasons to explain my interpretation?"

For help with elaborating on ideas, see

- Handbook 12, "Methods of Elaboration," pages 255–261

3. Decide what changes you want to make. While it's helpful to consider the responses of your readers, you need to trust yourself most of all.

Writing
TIP

Remember to include details from the story that will help you show, not tell, how you reached your conclusion.

One Student's Process

After reviewing her peers' comments, Annie decided she needed to present more evidence to back up her interpretation of the ending.

> through Connie's decision to pursue a career that includes ballet,

So does the breeze represent Poppa and show that his spirit is free because Connie has made her decision, or does it represent Connie's final dance for Poppa? Does the distant applause ~~of the wind~~ stand for more applause to come because she will become a ballerina, or is it a sign of approval for her decision to go into dance therapy? After reading and studying these lines, I decided they are meant to show that she has resolved her conflict. The ending proves that not only is Connie satisfied with her choice, but also that Poppa's wishes are fulfilled.

> What convinced me most of all was the description near the end of the story of Connie's final performance for Poppa. She dances the best ever, and she imagines Poppa sitting on the couch clapping for her, congratulating her on her decision and her dancing. (Earlier, Connie had not been able to cry for her grandfather. This dance is her way of crying.)

Grammar
TIP

To show the relationship between two contrasting ideas you are explaining, try combining the two ideas with the conjunction *or* or *but*. Remember to use a comma.

Analyzing a Story   **175**

1. Proofread your writing. Look for errors in grammar and spelling. Be sure you have used quotation marks correctly. Also, since you will be referring to a novel, short story, or play, be especially careful in the handling of punctuation and capitalization of titles.

Grammar
═ TIP ═

Remember to use quotation marks when you quote lines exactly. When you put a passage in your own words, do not use quotation marks.

Standards for Evaluation

INTERPRETIVE
W R I T I N G

A story analysis

- identifies the author and title and briefly summarizes the work
- shows why the writer found the subject interesting
- clearly focuses on one feature of the work
- presents an interpretation of that feature
- supports the interpretation with reasons, examples, quotations, or other evidence

---

L I N K I N G
MECHANICS AND WRITING

Writing Titles

When you write titles, the first and last words and all other important words should be capitalized. The titles of poems, short stories, and songs should be enclosed in quotation marks. The titles of books, plays, magazines, very long poems, and motion pictures are normally set in italics. You can indicate italics by underlining.

Example

Pat MacEnulty, the author of "Dancing for Poppa," is also the fiction editor for Sun Dog magazine.

For more information on correct punctuation of titles, see Handbook 49, "Punctuation," pages 666–667.

2. Make a clean copy of your analysis. Did you accomplish what you wanted to with your analysis? Read it over one more time as you think about the Standards for Evaluation shown in the margin. If you are ready for publication, make a final copy.

P U B L I S H   A N D   P R E S E N T

- **Hold a reading.** Read your essay aloud to a small group of classmates who have read the same work. You might want to discuss similarities and differences in your analyses. Then share at least one essay from each group with the whole class.

- **Post your analysis.**   Make a bulletin board display that groups together analyses written about the same work.
- **Publish a class collection.**   Share the collection with other classes.

REFLECT ON YOUR WRITING

WRITER TO WRITER

If one cannot enjoy reading a book over and over again, there is no use in reading it at all.

Oscar Wilde, playwright and poet

1. Add your analysis to your portfolio.   Now that you've read Annie's analysis and written one of your own, summarize what you learned in a brief introductory note for your paper. Consider how you put together this essay, how peer responses may have helped, and what you think of your analysis now that you've written it. Some of these questions may help you focus your thinking.

- What was the hardest part of writing my analysis? Is there any way to make it easier next time?

- What did I enjoy most or find easiest to do?

- What part of my essay do I like best, and what would I like a reader to appreciate most?

- If I were to write it again, how would I change this essay?

2. Explore additional literary ideas.   See the suggestions for oral storytelling on pages 180–181 and Springboards on page 182.

FOR YOUR
PORTFOLIO

At age 100, arthritis sufferer Clare Willi stays limber thanks to dance therapy.

Oral Storytelling

Starting from LITERATURE

When you were younger, you probably listened to many stories that started "Once upon a time." People have always loved hearing stories—and telling them too. As a storyteller you can use your voice to bring out the drama, the suspense, and the humor in your story. As you read this folk tale, think about how you might tell it yourself.

from

Why Monkeys Live In Trees

by Jessie Alford Nunn

IN KIKUYULAND. . . there lived a mother tortoise and a monkey who were very close friends. One day the tortoise borrowed some money from the monkey, promising to pay it back in six months' time. The months passed, and the tortoise had not come to pay her debt, so the monkey went to her house to ask for the money, but found only the tortoise's young daughter at home.

"Where is your mother, my child?" asked the monkey.

"Alas, I do not know," the little one replied sadly. "Indeed, it has been six months since I last saw her."

Every day the monkey went to the tortoise's house, but every day the answer was the same. . . .

Now the wily tortoise was at home all the time, but she lay very still behind the house, and being the very color of *murram* (earth), escaped detection by the monkey.

At last, however, she became tired of hiding. . . .

"The next time he comes," she told her child, "simply turn me upside-down, and he will think I am a grinding stone."

So the following day, when the monkey appeared, the daughter quickly turned her mother upside-down and began to grind millet on the bottom of her shell. Exasperated at the thought of yet another fruitless visit, the monkey became furious. Enraged, he picked up the grinding stone and hurled it as far as possible into the thick bush. . . .

Not at all hurt by this treatment because of the protection provided by her hard shell, the mother tortoise calmly picked herself up and strolled nonchalantly back into her house.

"Good afternoon, friend," she said pleasantly to the monkey. "I am sorry to have been away so long. Have you come to collect the money I borrowed from you?"

"Yes, I have," growled the monkey. "Oblige me by giving it to me right away."

"Why certainly, my dear friend," replied the tortoise in a sweet voice. "It is stored right here in the grinding stone."

"In the grinding stone?" screeched the monkey.

"Yes, indeed. . . . But I don't see my favorite grinding stone. Where can it be?"

With much chagrin, the monkey had to confess that he had just thrown the stone into the thick bush.

"Ah, well," returned the tortoise blithely, "don't worry; just go out and search for the grinding stone, and when you find it, you'll have your money."

So the monkey went into the bush but he could see nothing. Up the branches into the trees he scampered, looking and worrying. . . . All the other monkeys came around to ask what he was doing, and he persuaded them to help him search. Soon the trees were alive with monkeys hunting, running up and down in the swinging branches from first dawn to lantern dark.

At this very moment, if you go into the forest and look into the trees, you will find the entire monkey family swinging from branch to branch and tree to tree, still hunting and searching for the grinding stone that holds the money.

Oral Storytelling

INVITATION
— TO —
Write

Oral storytelling is a way you can entertain listeners with your own interpretation of a story. You can make any story come alive by using your voice in different ways when you tell the story.

Choose a story you would like to tell and tell it in a way that will entertain your listeners.

Writing
— TIP —

It's a good idea to put marks and notes to yourself on a photocopy of the story. These will remind you which words to emphasize or how to read certain passages.

CHOOSING A STORY

1. Find a story to tell. You may wish to retell "Why Monkeys Live in Trees." You could also look through collections of folk tales, myths, and legends. Here are some other possibilities:

- scary stories
- stories from camp
- urban folklore
- holiday stories
- family tales or legends
- stories you make up

2. Reread the story. Think about what makes the story a good one to tell. Is it the suspense, the interesting characters, or the humor? If the story is long, you might choose one key part to tell.

PRACTICING YOUR STORY

1. Use your voice for different effects. You want your listeners to experience the story through your voice as well as through the author's words. Try using a tape recorder to practice your presentation. By playing back the tape you can evaluate your performance. Think about ways you can vary your presentation and bring out the special features of the story when you read it aloud. Look at the suggestions on the following page.

- **Pitch**   Help your listeners identify characters by using high pitch for some characters, low for others.

- **Volume**   Consider where a loud or forceful tone will be best and where speaking more softly is more effective. Volume can be used to create mood or for emphasis.

- **Pace**   Speed up your speaking when the action heats up; slow down to increase suspense. Pause for dramatic effect.

- **Dialect**   Let your characters speak in dialect where appropriate—if you think you can do this convincingly.

- **Gestures**   Facial expressions and effective gestures can help you put your story across.

2. Try out different approaches.   A good way to practice is to work with someone else. Try using different approaches and commenting on each other's presentations. See which effects work best.

3. Prepare an introduction.   Think about what your listeners need to know about the story. Do you need to give any background about the story or its author? Are there any words or ideas you should explain beforehand? You also might want to explain why you chose to tell this story. For example, does it have some special meaning for you, or is there a particular message you want to convey?

 Writer's Choice   You could make your reading a multimedia presentation by adding music, props, costumes, or other special effects.

PUBLISHING AND PRESENTING

- **Hold a round robin.**   Get together with other class members and take turns telling your stories.

- **Be a storyteller.**   Make arrangements to tell your story to a group that would be interested in it. You might choose another class, a group of younger children, or a family gathering.

- **Make a recording.**   Use a tape recorder to record your tale. You might want to add music or other special effects.

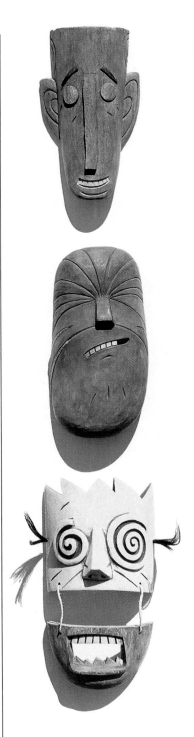

Oral Storytelling   **181**

Spring**boards**

Media
You and one of your classmates have been chosen as the Roger Ebert and Gene Siskel of your school. Choose a classmate and then choose a movie to review. In front of the class, share your reviews and then comment on the similarities and differences in your analyses.

CURRENT EVENTS
Time magazine has chosen you to analyze an important issue facing teenagers today. Choose an issue and then write your analysis of it.

History
What if you had been on hand when President Abraham Lincoln gave the Gettysburg Address? How would you have responded to it? Choose an important historical speech and write an analysis of it.

Art
What do you see when you look at a painting or a sculpture? Choose a work of art and write an analysis of it.

SPEAKING & LISTENING
Choose a scene from a story or play you like. Then, with some of your classmates, act out the scene for the rest of the class.

Cucaracha (1948), Alexander Calder.

Private? No!

So you don't think punctuation makes a difference?
Which of these signs is more inviting?

> **Private
> No Swimming
> Allowed**

> **Private?
> No. Swimming
> Allowed.**

Willard Espy, who writes interesting books about language, came
up with this demonstration of what a small change in punctuation will do.
Here are some of his other examples:

The butler stood by the door and called the guests' names as they arrived.
The butler stood by the door and called the guests names as they arrived.

The murderer protested his innocence. An hour after, he was put to death.
The murderer protested his innocence an hour after he was put to death.

I'm sorry you can't come with us.
I'm sorry. You can't come with us.

The escaping convict
dropped, a bullet in his leg.
The escaping convict
dropped a bullet in his leg.

Go slow—children.
Go slow, children.

A clever dog knows its
master.
A clever dog knows it's
master.

Do not break your bread or roll in your soup.
Do not break your bread, or roll in your soup.

Sentence

Adding Extensions

Effective writers occasionally use a dash to signal an extension or afterthought at the end of a sentence—like a P.S. at the end of a letter. Using a dash allows you to add information that is related to the idea in a sentence but is not essential.

Model A   It was just the most beautiful thing to have a really and truly best friend—<u>a friend that you could enjoy.</u>

Rosa Guy, *The Friends*

Model B   There, on the farther side of the clearing, dark, heavy forms were making a silent advance—<u>a sea of thick, powerful black bodies with short bristles, small black snouts, and long yellowish tusks.</u>   **Tom Gill, "Jungle Wars"**

Model C   My mother had trouble persuading me to carry one because I was a lady, but I now realized that a handkerchief was an invaluable tool for a counter-spy—<u>to erase fingerprints, and so forth.</u>   **Katherine Paterson, *Jacob Have I Loved***

▶ **ON THE MARK**   Use a dash to separate nonessential material from the rest of the sentence. Place a period at the end of the extension or afterthought.

A. Combining Sentences   Make a new sentence by putting the underlined part of the second sentence into the first sentence as an extension or afterthought. Write the complete sentence, putting a dash before the extension or afterthought.

1. At the time I thought the blame for my unhappiness had to be fixed. The blame had to be fixed <u>on Caroline, on my grandmother, on my mother, even on myself</u>.   **Katherine Paterson, *Jacob Have I Loved***

2. With rattlesnake speed, Maniac snatched the book back. He snatched it back <u>except for one page, which stayed, ripped, in Mars Bar's hand</u>.

Jerry Spinelli, *Maniac Magee*

3. Each morning she would get up at six, and walk all the way from Thirteenth Avenue to First Avenue. The walk was <u>a distance of about two miles to and fro</u>.

Mark Mathabane, *Kaffir Boy*

B. Unscrambling and Imitating Sentences   Unscramble each set of sentence chunks below to create a sentence that matches the structure of one of the models on page 184. Write a correctly punctuated sentence of your own that imitates each model and contains an extension or afterthought.

1. Write sentences that imitate Model A.
   a toothache that Jeremy couldn't stand / to get a really nasty and throbbing toothache / it certainly was a terrible time

2. Write sentences that imitate Model B.
   now, toward the goal line of the visitors / a fullback with strong, punishing long strides / fast, powerful Klemsky was running the ball / in black jersey, battered silver helmet, and grass-stained silver pants

3. Write sentences that imitate Model C.
   but Sally finally agreed that a big dog would be the best pet for her / the pet store owner had difficulty convincing Sally to buy a big dog / to watch the house and everything else / since Sally was so tiny

C. Expanding Sentences   Use your imagination to add an extension to the end of each sentence. Be sure each extension answers the question in parentheses.

1. There Trufflehunter called at the mouth of a little hole in a green bank, and out popped the last thing Caspian expected—*(What popped out?)*
   C. S. Lewis, *Prince Caspian*

2. All was well until one day they met a thunderstorm—*(What was the thunderstorm like?)*   **J.R.R. Tolkien, *The Hobbit***

3. When Slake sat down to dine in the evening, his dinner awaited him in his shirt pocket—*(What was his dinner?)*   **Felice Holman, *Slake's Limbo***

4. I was halfway across the dump area when I saw something I didn't like— *(What did you see?)*   **Stephen King, "The Body"**

Grammar Refresher   Extensions and afterthoughts are often sentence fragments that do not by themselves express a complete thought. To learn more about sentences and fragments, see Handbook 39, "The Sentence and Its Parts," pages 382–383.

Sketch Book

Desert Metropolis, Robert McCall.

- Where do you think people will live in the future? Write down some of your thoughts.

- What have you wondered about recently? What puzzles you? Make a list of things that you would like to know more about.

- If you could meet any person in history, who would it be? Explain why you would like to meet the person you picked.

Show, Don't Tell

When you write a report, you can show your knowledge by using concrete details. Your sources of information—such as books, eyewitness accounts, and interviews—can help you find the facts and examples you need. Add examples to one of the *telling* sentences below, turning the statement into a *showing* paragraph.

- Technology changes quickly.
- News programs today provide more entertainment than information.

8

Informative Writing: Reports

Guided Assignment
Research Report

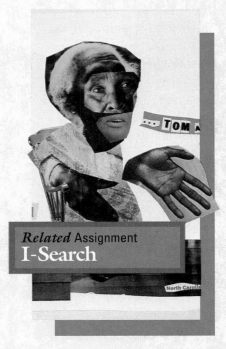

Related Assignment
I-Search

What is a research report? It is more than library books and magazine articles, more than note cards and outlines and getting all your facts right. Writing a research report is about questions and answers, about *your* questions and *your* answers. It's about discovery—finding a subject you're curious about, uncovering information in a variety of places, and then sharing what you've discovered with others.

In this workshop, you'll have the opportunity to research subjects you're curious about and to report on what you learn.

Research Report

Reading a
STUDENT MODEL

Do you ever hear reports on TV or radio that leave you with unanswered questions? Do you ever wish you could find answers to those questions yourself—if you only had the time? When you write a research report, you take the time. You ask questions, look for answers, and write up your findings to share with others.

Tom Witosky's social studies report reflects his interest in his Native American ancestry. As you read, think about how Tom combines what he learns about history with an issue that is important today.

CAHOKIA MOUNDS

city of the sun

state historic and world heritage

Tom Witosky
Mr. Swanson
Social Studies
9 February 1994

Respecting the Heritage of the Mound Builders

Hundreds or even thousands of years from now, what will happen to our remains? Will our graves become tourist attractions for future generations?

That may seem impossible, but it is not. In fact, it has happened to ancient cultures of American Indians called mound builders. In many places around the country, the mounds have been excavated. Some of the mounds were burial sites, and people's remains have been displayed on the site of the mound or are stored and studied in museums around the country. As a result of protests by modern American Indian groups, the displays have been closed and museums have returned some of the remains to the Indian groups that claim them. The controversy over respect for the dead and for Native American heritage versus the historical importance of the mounds continues today.

To understand the controversy, we need to first understand the mounds themselves and the people who built them. The term "mound builders" is used to describe several different groups of early North American Indians. Between about 1000 B.C. and A.D. 1500, they built mounds of earth as burial places and sites for temples. Tens of thousands of mounds were built in river valleys in the Midwest, the South, and parts of the East.

There were three main groups of mound builders. One major

About a thousand year
Mississippian people b
the mounds in Illinois
died out — but Indi
pr   t the display
and artif

Monk's Mound—Cahokia

group was the Adena culture. They began building mounds as burial places in about 700 B.C. They piled dirt, stones, and other materials over the dead, who were buried with personal belongings such as stone pipes and trinkets of copper, shell, and mica (Franklin 32). One of the largest mounds, Grave Creek Mound in Moundsville, West Virginia, is 70 feet high. The Adena also made some mounds shaped like animals. The most famous is the Great Serpent Mound near Hillsboro, Ohio. It is shaped like a huge snake and is about one quarter of a mile long (Snow).

Another major group of mound builders was the Hopewell culture. Between 100 B.C. and A.D. 500, they built mounds that were more elaborate than the Adena's. Some were circular or octagonal. Hopewell mounds were often surrounded by miles of earthen walls. Pearl necklaces, obsidian blades, and birds and fish made of beaten copper were buried inside the mounds. Paula Franklin says that "the objects found inside with the burials are of great beauty and superb workmanship. . . . The Hopewell people were the finest Indian metal workers in North America" (33).

The third major group was the Mississippian culture. It lasted from about A.D. 700 to the 1700s. The Mississippians made some of the most complicated mounds. Some were burial places, but others were bases for temples. These were large, flat-topped mounds similar to pyramids. One of them, called Monk's Mound in Cahokia, Illinois, is 100 feet high, 1,000 feet long, and 700 feet wide. It is considered the largest man-made earthen structure in the world (Franklin 33).

Eventually, the native peoples stopped building mounds, and their cultures died out. No one is sure why. Possible reasons are revolts, wars, floods, famines, or diseases (Baldwin 175-176). We do know that the age of the mound builders ended around the time the first European explorers came to America.

When the Europeans first saw the mounds, they thought they must have been built by some unknown race that had vanished from the earth (Silverberg 3). One of the first colonists to explore the mounds was Thomas Jefferson. This is his description of what he found in a mound in Virginia:

> At the bottom I found bones; above these a few stones,
> then a large interval of earth, then a layer of bones, and
> so on. The bones nearest the surface were least decayed.
> I guessed that this barrow [mound] might have a thousand
> skeletons. (Franklin 30)

Since Jefferson's time, many archaeologists have dug into mounds to learn about the mound builders. In the process, they have discovered valuable information about the history of early Indian cultures. However, their actions and the actions of other people who have dug up the mounds to take artifacts or to put bones on display have upset some Indian groups. These people believe the mounds are sacred resting places that should not be disturbed.

One controversy happened near Lewistown, Illinois, at a place called Dickson Mounds. A museum on the site of one mound displayed artifacts and 234 skeletons of Mississippian men, women, and children. Everything had been kept exactly as it was found. People looked at the graves from a raised platform (Ina).

For years, Indian groups criticized this exhibit, saying it was sacrilegious, racist, and demeaning. Most Indian groups think that

**Illinois to [...]
an Exhibit [...]
Indian Skele[...]**

SPRINGFIELD, Ill., Nov.28 (A[...]
Jim Edgar of Illinois has ann[...]
that he plans to close a state ex[...]
of 234 Indian skeletons at Dick[...]
Mounds Museum next spring,[...]
say that American Indian groups[...]
move that American Indian groups[...]
bridging the gulf [...] ween Indians
and the state. [...]
Indian gro[...]
criticized th[...]
saying the [...]
racist and [...]
tribes b[...]

**Indian Burial
Site Focus of
Controversy**

WATERFORD TOWNSHIP, Ill.—The last
major battle in the bitter controversy over rights to Native American
remains and funerary objects is
underway here at Dickson Mounds,
a small, inauspicious rural muse[...]
surrounded by cornfields.
Located about 40 miles
west of Peoria in the arch[...]
cally rich Illinois River [...]
museum is built aroun[...]
nation's foremost N[...]
burial sites and is [...]
exhibits Native A[...]

someone's soul cannot rest if his or her bones are uncovered and shown in a public display ("Illinois"). James Yellowbank of the Indian Treaty Rights Committee said, "These people are American Indians and entitled to rest in peace regardless of whether they died 10 years ago or 10,000 years ago" (Culloton). He also said, "We want them reburied properly and left alone" ("Illinois").

On the other hand, museum displays teach people about the past. Archaeologists study the artifacts they uncover and use them to understand history. Willard Boyd, president of Chicago's Field Museum of Natural History, said, "We clearly believe it is appropriate to have remains in the collections for purposes of continuing research. We can learn more and more from them as techniques of research [improve]" (Wilson).

Complaints have caused museums and the U.S. government to change the way they handle bones and artifacts. Museums such as the Smithsonian Institution and the Field Museum have agreed to remove remains from display and return them to groups that can prove that they are descendants. Congress passed the Indian Graves Protection and Repatriation Act in 1990, which gives Indian groups a say in the handling of remains (Ina). The Dickson Mounds Museum is still open, but the exhibit of the burial excavation has been sealed off and closed to the public.

Today, the controversy continues. Modern Indian groups are still fighting for recognition and due respect for their sacred sites. Even so, our understanding of other cultures and of our own history has been enhanced by the research that has been done on the historic mound sites.

Illinois to Shut an Exhibit of Indian Skeletons

SPRINGFIELD, Ill., Nov.28 (AP)—Gov. Jim Edgar of Illinois has announced that he plans to close a state exhibit 234 Indian skeletons at Dickson unds Museum next spring, a that American Indian groups g the gulf between Indians state.

and others have um for years, acrilegious, t Indian can-

al of sy

p, Ill.–The last bitter controver- Native American nerary objects is at Dickson Mounds, picious rural museum y cornfields. about 40 miles south- eoria in the archaeologi- Illinois River valley, the n is built around one of the 's foremost Native American al sites and is the only one that ibits Native American skeletons

Works Cited

Baldwin, Gordon C. <u>America's Buried Past</u>. New York: Putnam's, 1962.

Culloton, Dan. "House Panel Foils Burial Site Closing." <u>Chicago Tribune</u> 21 Mar. 1991, sec. 2: 2.

Franklin, Paula Angle. <u>Indians of North America</u>. New York: McKay, 1979.

"Illinois to Shut an Exhibit of Indian Skeletons." <u>New York Times</u> 29 Nov. 1991: A30.

Ina, Lauren. "Indian Burial Site Focus of Controversy." <u>Washington Post</u> 10 Nov. 1991: A24.

Silverberg, Robert. <u>Mound Builders of Ancient America</u>. Greenwich: New York Graphic Society, 1968.

Snow, Dean. "Mound Builders." <u>The World Book Encyclopedia</u>. 1990 ed.

Wilson, Terry. "Protesters Assail Dickson Mounds." <u>Chicago Tribune</u> 4 Jan. 1991, sec. 1: 3.

③

Great Serpent Mound (near ___ Ohio — built ___

A ___

Think & Respond

Respond as a Reader

► What did you learn about the mound builders that you didn't know before?

► What do you think about the Dickson Mounds controversy? Should museum displays like this one stay open?

Respond as a Writer

► What does Tom do to get you interested in his report?

► Find three different kinds of details Tom uses to support his ideas.

INVITATION
— **TO** —
Write

As Tom Witosky investigated the burial mounds of his Native American ancestors, he found a way to connect what he had learned about the past to a recent controversy. Writing a report means learning about an interesting subject and sharing what you learn with others.

Choose a subject that interests you and research it in several sources. Then write a short research report that tells what you have learned.

P REWRITE AND EXPLORE

1. Find a subject you'd like to investigate. Consider your interests—both in and out of school—and think about subjects you've been wanting to learn more about. Has something been in the news lately that intrigues you? Do you have a special hobby? Has a concept in one of your classes caught your interest? Try one or more of these activities to help you find a subject.

Exploring Topics

This falcon-shaped copper cutout from the Hopewell culture dates back to the Middle Woodland period (200 B.C.–A.D. 1). Likenesses of birds such as this one often played an important part in Hopewell funeral ceremonies.

• **From A to Z** At your library, browse through books and magazines, flip through some volumes of an encyclopedia, or scan a computer index. What catches your eye? Make a **list** of subjects you would like to know more about.

• **From the familiar to the strange** What's familiar to you may be unfamiliar to someone else. What—or whom—do you know that others don't? Make a **chart** listing names of people, places, or things you know a bit about. For example, you might include figures in history, cultural traditions and customs, or places you've lived or visited. Then make some notes about one or two items in your chart. What do you already know? What do you want to find out?

- **From the mystery files**   The world is full of mysteries, puzzles that have yet to be solved. Is there a Loch Ness monster? Does Bigfoot exist? What is a black hole? Who—or what—made England's crop circles? What is the purpose of Stonehenge? Make a list of unanswered questions and **freewrite** about the ones that interest you most.

2. Suit yourself.   Teachers in different subject areas may ask you to write research reports. Try to find ways you can tailor your writing to your own interests. For example, if you are assigned a science report on outer space, and if astronomy is your hobby, you could focus on theories about distant galaxies. If you have an interest in science fiction, you could write about futuristic space stations or about the prospect of life on other planets.

3. Check out your ideas.   You may wish to talk to classmates about your topic possibilities. A friend may help you find a fresh angle on an idea, suggest other topics, or mention possible resources.

 Writer's Choice   Do you want to share your expertise with others by choosing a topic you already know quite a bit about? Would you rather increase your own knowledge by tackling something that is totally new to you? The choice is yours.

4. Find a focus.   The hardest part of choosing a report topic is finding a focus. If your topic is too broad, there will be too much information to cover in a short report. If your topic is too narrow, you won't be able to find enough information. Doing some reading on your general topic can help you find a focus that's right for you.

For example, you might have trouble writing a short research report on the topic of computers. The subject is too broad. If you read a few articles about new applications for computers, however, you might come across the subtopic "computers in architecture." This idea might be just the right size for your purposes.

Ceremonial deer mask made from carved cedar and shells, found at the Spiro Mound site near Spiro, Oklahoma.

PROBLEM SOLVING

"How can I find a focus for my report?"

To learn how to make your topic the right size, see

- Handbook 2, "Focusing a Topic," pages 224–226

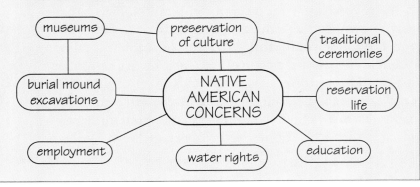

One Student's Process

Tom Witosky's social studies class was asked to write a report on some aspect of Native American culture. After talking to an uncle who works for the Native American Rights Fund in Colorado, Tom decided to write a report on a contemporary Native American concern. He explored possible topics in this cluster and decided to write about burial mound excavations.

5. Examine your purpose and goals. Is there a point you want to make about your subject? Is there something specific you want to learn? Even if you are completing an assignment for your teacher, think about what *you* want to get out of the project. Finding a goal—a reason to care—early in your writing process will help you research and write your report. Keep in mind, though, that your reasons for writing may change as you work.

6. What do you want to find out? Before you begin your research, jot down a list of questions about your topic. These questions can guide your search for information. Cross out questions as you find answers to them and add new questions as you learn more about your topic.

Writing
TIP

Many of your sources will mention other books or articles on the same topic that could be key to your research. Check the book or article's bibliography, and watch for in-text references to other sources.

RESEARCH YOUR TOPIC

1. Look for sources. Begin investigating your topic by looking for sources in your school or local public library. Handbook 35, "Making Use of the Library," pages 352–361, can help you make the most of your library's resources. You might also try exploring unconventional sources of information, so think creatively. Can government agencies or your local chamber of commerce help? Are there experts you could interview?

2. Make a written record of the sources you might use. It's too early to tell which sources you'll actually use when you write your report. However, you should still create a source card for each book or article you think might be useful. Write down the publication information from your sources, using a separate index card for each source. Here are a few of the source cards Tom made as he conducted his research.

Be sure to give each source card a number, as shown on these samples. Numbered source cards can help you in two ways. First, when you take notes, you can refer to the source of the information by number instead of writing down the title or author over and over again. Second, your source cards will help you assemble your Works Cited list, an alphabetized list of the sources you actually used in writing the report.

3. Preview your sources. Before you begin taking notes from a source, check to see if it answers any of your questions. Look over the book's table of contents and the index to find the sections that apply to your specific topic. If you're skimming an article, read the title and any headings that are in bold type. Handbook 32, "Study and Research Skills," pages 340–345, can help you make the most of the time you spend with your sources.

Source Card for Book

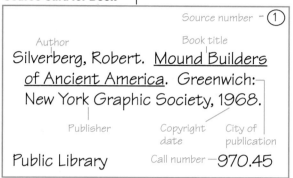

Source Card for Newspaper or Magazine Article

Source Card for Encyclopedia Entry

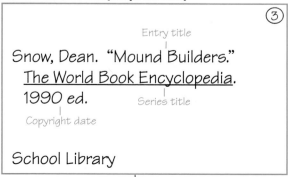

"How can I take notes and use source material in my writing?"

For information on how to use sources, see

• Handbook 33, "Paraphrases and Summaries," pages 346–348

4. Take notes from your sources. Take notes on another set of index cards. Include the facts, anecdotes, or statistics that you think will later be useful in your writing. Use a new card for each piece of information. That way, you can move the cards around, organizing and reorganizing your ideas and information when you're ready to write a draft.

5. Use your own words. To help you understand what you read, record important information in your own words. Rewriting information can help you uncover what you don't understand or what else you need to find out about. However, if you come across statements you think are particularly interesting or well said, copy them word for word and enclose them in quotation marks.

Tom Witosky found several newspaper articles that discussed a controversial exhibit of a burial excavation at the Dickson Mounds Museum in Illinois. He recorded information from each article on several note cards. Here are two of them.

Source card number — ②

About a thousand years ago, the Mississippian people built some of the mounds in Illinois. Their culture died out—but Indian groups today protest the display of Mississippian skeletons and artifacts. p. A24 — Page number from source

Note written in Tom's own words

⑥

Beliefs: Souls can't rest if their bones are uncovered and shown in a public display. James Yellowbank of the Indian Treaty Rights Committee said, "We want them reburied properly and left alone." p. A30

Quotation copied word for word

Writing
TIP

If you later discover that a source doesn't contain the information you need, throw away the source card and return the book or magazine to the library. Make new source cards as you conduct more research.

6. Begin to focus your research. As you gather information and take notes, your report should begin to take shape in your mind. Try making a list of the main points you think you'll want to cover, then sort your note cards into groups under each of those points. Do you think you have enough information on each point? If not, do some more research to uncover what you need.

One Student's Process

Tom's list of main points turned into a preliminary outline for his report. He knew he'd probably make some changes in the organization of the parts of his report once he started drafting. This is what his early outline looked like.

1. Introduction
2. Excavating mounds
   —Dickson Mounds example
3. Different points of view
4. Conclusion

DRAFT AND DISCOVER

1. Start writing.   Use your rough, preliminary outline and your notes to help get you started. Do you have a lot of note cards for one particular section of your report? You might begin there, drafting the part of your report you've learned the most about. As you write, keep yourself open to new ideas and insights. Does your explanation of the topic raise new questions in your mind? Does it suggest another focus that might be more interesting to you? You may want to do additional research and rework your outline as you strike out in new directions.

2. Think about organization.   What's the best way to organize your ideas? There's no one right way to organize a research report; many possibilities are open to you. For example, you might want to use chronological order for any historical material or biographical information in your report. You might use order of importance or order of familiarity for other sections. Once you start drafting and see how your ideas fit together, you'll be able to judge which organizational techniques will work best for your topic and for the information you want to present.

COMPUTER TIP

If you write your paper on a word processor, set your file to double space the entire paper. Set your tabs at five spaces and ten spaces from a one-inch left margin. Each new paragraph should be indented five spaces, and long quotations set off separately should be indented ten spaces.

PROBLEM SOLVING

"How can I organize my draft?"

For more information on organizing ideas, see

- Handbook 8, "Types of Organization," pages 239–243

One Student's Process

Tom started drafting the part of his report he knew the most about: the controversial Dickson Mounds Museum exhibit. He realized, though, that he would need to provide background information on the history of the mounds and the people who built them. Tom did more research, then revised his outline. Notice the chronological order in the outline's first section.

The Mound Builders

Introduction
I. Mound builders—three cultures
   A. Adena (700 B.C.)
   B. Hopewell (100 B.C.)
   C. Mississippian (A.D. 700–1700)
II. Discovery of the mounds
   A. Thomas Jefferson
   B. Archaeologists
III. Controversial displays
   A. Dickson Mounds
      1. Indians' ideas
      2. Archaeologists' ideas
   B. Museums
   C. Result of conflict
Conclusion

PROBLEM

S O L V I N G

"I need to make a formal outline, but I'm not sure how."

For help creating a formal outline for your writing, see

• Appendix, page 683

Writer's Choice   Some writers like to create formal outlines that include headings and subheadings for every section of their writing. Others prefer to make a rough outline, listing only key words for the report's main sections. Use the approach that works for you or that meets your class requirements.

3. Write an introduction and a conclusion.   Your opening paragraph should draw readers into your report and clearly state your topic. For example, you might begin with a thought-provoking question, as Tom Witosky did. You could also open with an interesting fact about your topic or tell a brief anecdote. Your introduction should also include a **thesis statement** that tells the main idea or overall purpose of your report.

Your closing paragraph might summarize your main points, make a prediction, propose an action, or draw a conclusion.

4. Give credit where credit is due. You don't need to credit either your own ideas or information that is considered common knowledge and can be found in several sources. (It is considered common knowledge, for example, that many mound-building groups lived near rivers.) However, you do need to give credit when you use someone else's ideas, facts, or information—even when you put that information in your own words. You must also give credit to the source of direct quotations.

There are several ways to credit your sources, so check with your teacher to see which method he or she prefers. You can use these Modern Language Association guidelines—as Tom did—to help you credit sources correctly.

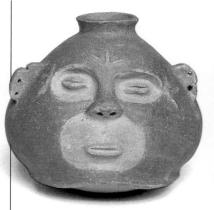

Mississippian mound builders made this head-shaped pottery bottle. The vessel, which stands six inches high and is equally as wide, is painted with ochre, an earth-tone pigment. The bottle could be hung or carried by stringing leather straps through the holes in the ears.

Guidelines for Crediting Sources in Text

- **Work by one author** Put the author's last name and the page number in parentheses: (Silverberg 3). If the author's name is mentioned in the sentence, put only the page number in parentheses: (3).

- **Work by more than one author** Put the authors' last names and the page number in parentheses: (Erdoes and Ortiz 87). If a source has more than three authors, give the first author's last name followed by *et al.*, and the page number: (Milner et al. 21).

- **Work with no author listed** Give the title or a shortened version and the page number: ("Ancient" 30).

- **One of two or more works by the same author** Give the author's last name, the title or a shortened version, and the page number: (Silverberg, The Old Ones 145).

---

5. Think about your draft. Look back over your work and decide if you want to make changes now or first see what people think of your draft. The questions on the following page can help you and your readers review your draft.

Questions for Yourself
- Have I answered all my questions about my topic? Did I find good sources, or should I look for more information?
- Is my report clearly organized? Does it flow smoothly from beginning to end, or are there parts I should rearrange?

Questions for Your Peer Readers
- What would you say is the main point of my report?
- Do you now know more than you did about my topic?
- Which parts seemed confusing or out of place?

One Student's Process

Tom showed his draft to a friend whose comments appear in the margin. How would you have responded?

Another major group of mound builders was the Hopewell culture. They built mounds that were more elaborate than the Adena's. Some were circular or octagonal. Hopewell mounds were often surrounded by miles of earthen walls. All kinds of artifacts were buried inside the mounds. The objects found inside with the burials are of great beauty and workmanship. The Hopewell people were the finest Indian metalworkers in North America.

Peer Reader Comments

I didn't know anything about the history of the mounds—it's really interesting. When did the Hopewell people build their mounds?

What was buried there? Can you give some details?

This doesn't sound like you. Did you forget to cite your source?

REVISE YOUR WRITING

1. Review your responses. Your reactions and those of your peers should help you see if your writing is on target. You may find it helpful to revise your outline before you write another draft. Check to see if you've **plagiarized,** or used the words or ideas of others without giving credit. Check your notes and either add a citation or use an exact quotation from one of your sources instead.

Paragraphs at Work Each heading in your outline should be discussed in one or more separate paragraphs.
- Discuss one aspect of your topic in each new paragraph.
- Write a topic sentence for each paragraph.
- Include in each paragraph only those details and examples that support the paragraph's main idea.

2. Confirm the facts. Accuracy is essential in a report. Make sure the dates, statistics, names, and other facts are correct and that you have properly credited your sources.

3. Create a Works Cited list and attach it to your report. A Works Cited list is an alphabetized list of only those sources you cited in the text of your report. Here are models to help you write and punctuate the entries in your list.

Book—One author
Silverberg, Robert. <u>Mound Builders of Ancient America</u>. Greenwich: New York Graphic Society, 1968.

Book—Two or more authors
Erdoes, Richard, and Alfonso Ortiz, eds. <u>American Indian Myths and Legends</u>. New York: Pantheon, 1984.

Book—No author given
<u>The Times Atlas of the World</u>. Rev. ed. London: Times, 1984.

Newspaper or Magazine Article—Author given
Ina, Lauren. "Indian Burial Site Focus of Controversy." <u>Washington Post</u> 10 Nov. 1991: A24.

Newspaper or Magazine Article—No author given
"Illinois to Shut an Exhibit of Indian Skeletons." <u>New York Times</u> 29 Nov. 1991: A30.

Article from Encyclopedia or Other Reference Work
Snow, Dean. "Mound Builders." <u>The World Book Encyclopedia</u>. 1990 ed.

Interview
Boyd, Willard. Telephone interview. 15 Nov. 1992.

Writing
═══ **TIP** ═══

When you make your Works Cited list, use the source cards you made as you conducted research. They should contain all the publication information you need.

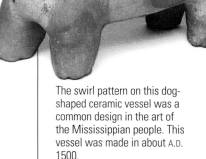

The swirl pattern on this dog-shaped ceramic vessel was a common design in the art of the Mississippian people. This vessel was made in about A.D. 1500.

Research Report **203**

This two-thousand-year-old Adena figurine stands eight inches high. The Adena inhabited areas of what is now Ohio.

PROOFREAD

1. Proofread your work. Carefully reread your report, looking for mistakes in grammar, spelling, usage, and mechanics.

LINKING
MECHANICS AND WRITING

Using Quotations and In-text Citations

- Copy quoted passages word for word.
- Use ellipses (. . .) in your quotation to show where you've left out material.
- Follow the guidelines on page 201 for crediting sources.

2. Make a final copy.   Review the Standards for Evaluation in the margin. Have you met the requirements of the assignment? Make any necessary changes and neatly write or print out a clean copy.

PUBLISH AND PRESENT

- **Present your report to another class.**   If your report deals with a topic in another subject area, such as science or social studies, give an oral presentation in that class.
- **Create a class encyclopedia.**   Gather reports and arrange them alphabetically or by subject.
- **Turn your written report into a multimedia presentation.** Bring in photographs, illustrations, or maps related to your topic. You could also play an audiotape of a piece of music or a recording of an interview you conducted during your research.

REFLECT ON YOUR WRITING

WRITER TO WRITER

The element of discovery takes place, in nonfiction, not during the writing but during the research.

Joan Didion, novelist and essayist

Add your writing to your portfolio.   First, write the story of your research and attach it to your finished piece. These questions may help you focus your thoughts.

- How did you find your topic? Did you change your topic once you began your research? Why or why not?
- Were you surprised by what you learned about your topic?
- How did you find your information? Did you wish you had more information as you drafted your report? Did you have too much?
- In what other writing situations could you use research skills?

INFORMATIVE WRITING

A research report

- has an interesting introduction that clearly states the topic and the purpose
- contains facts and details to support main ideas
- presents information in a logical order
- uses information from multiple sources
- gives credit for the ideas and facts of others
- ends with a strong conclusion
- includes a Works Cited list

FOR YOUR **PORTFOLIO**

Related ASSIGNMENT
I-Search

she said

North Carolina

Starting from LITERATURE

I-Search reports, like research reports, present information gathered from a variety of sources. An I-Search, however, has a personal focus. Why do you want to know more about your topic? How are you finding out what you need to know? What are you discovering about yourself along the way?

Read author Alex Haley's story of his search for information about his family history. He later incorporated what he learned into his autobiographical book *Roots*. How do you think he would answer the questions above?

from THE NEW YORK TIMES

My Furthest-Back Person

by ALEX HALEY

One Saturday in 1965 I happened to be walking past the National Archives building in Washington. Across the interim years I had thought of Grandma's old stories—otherwise I can't think what diverted me up the Archives' steps. And when a main reading-room desk attendant asked if he could help me, I wouldn't have dreamed of admitting to him some curiosity hanging on from boyhood about my slave forebears. I kind of bumbled that I was interested in census records of Alamance County, North Carolina, just after the Civil War.

The microfilm rolls were delivered, and I turned them through the machine with a building sense of intrigue, viewing in different census takers' penmanship an endless parade of names. After about a dozen microfilmed rolls, I was beginning to tire, when in utter

206   Workshop 8

astonishment I looked upon the names of Grandma's parents: Tom Murray, Irene Murray . . . older sisters of Grandma's as well—every one of them a name that I'd heard countless times on her front porch.

It wasn't that I hadn't believed Grandma. You just *didn't* not believe my Grandma. It was simply so uncanny actually seeing those names in print and in official U.S. government records.

During the next several months I was back in Washington whenever possible, in the Archives, the Library of Congress, the Daughters of the American Revolution Library. . . . In one source or another during 1966 I was able to document at least the highlights of the cherished family story. I would have given anything to have told Grandma, but, sadly, in 1949 she had gone. So I went and told the only survivor of those Henning front-porch storytellers: Cousin Georgia Anderson, now in her eighties in Kansas City, Kansas. Wrinkled, bent, not well herself, she was so overjoyed, repeating to me the old stories and sounds; they were like Henning echoes: "Yeah, boy, that African say his name was *'Kin-tay'*; he say the banjo was *'ko,'* an' the river *'Kamby Bolong,'* an' he was off choppin' some wood to make his drum when they grabbed 'im!" Cousin Georgia grew so excited we had to stop her, calm her down, "You go

'head, boy! Your grandma an' all of 'em—they up there watching what you do!" . . .

I was on a jet returning to New York when a thought hit me. Those strange, unknown-tongue sounds, always part of our family's old story . . . they were obviously bits of our original African *"Kin-tay's"* native tongue. What specific tongue? Could I somehow find out?

Back in New York, I began making visits to the United Nations Headquarters lobby; it wasn't hard to spot Africans. I'd stop any I could, asking if my bits of phonetic sounds held any meaning for them. A couple of dozen Africans quickly looked at me, listened, and took off—understandably dubious about some Tennesseean's accent alleging "African" sounds.

Think & Respond

Discuss Alex Haley's essay with your classmates. How did Haley present the details of his re-search process along with infor-mation about his family history? What do you know of your own family history? How could you find additional information?

PROBLEM
S O L V I N G

"How can I find a topic I care about?"

For more information about finding ideas to suit your purpose, see

• Handbook 1, "Discovering Writing Ideas," pages 218–223

• Handbook 4, "General Purpose and Personal Goals," pages 232–233

INVITATION
═ TO ═
Write

The stories Alex Haley grew up hearing on his grandmother's front porch inspired him to research his family history. An I-Search records the research process from a very personal point of view. Writing an I-Search is a chance to explore a subject you care about and to share your research with others.

Research a topic that is personally important to you. Then write an I-Search report that tells about the topic and your experiences finding out about it.

R ESEARCHING YOUR
I-SEARCH REPORT

1. Find a topic.   Since an I-Search paper is a personal research report, you'll want to choose a topic you feel strongly about. If you're not sure what you want to research, try listing your personal goals or interests, or just start asking yourself "I wonder why" questions. You might also check your journal to see what's been on your mind lately. Then choose the topic you care about most.

2. Think about your purpose.   Make some notes in your journal about why this topic is important to you. For example, are you interested in flying because you'd like to become a pilot? Do you want to learn more about dyslexia because you or someone you know is affected by it? Getting a clear idea of why you want to write about your topic can help you focus your research.

3. Research your topic.   You should go about your research in the same way that you would for any other research paper. Gather information from a variety of sources and keep track of your own reactions to what you learn. For example, if you discover that some of your first ideas about your topic weren't true, make some notes about how your new understanding affects you.

Keep track of your research process. Are you solving a mystery, where each clue leads you on a search for additional clues? Are you discouraged because you cannot find information easily or because you discover there are no clear answers to some of your questions? Write down your thoughts and reactions as you conduct your research.

Writing
TIP
You might try charting your progress and discoveries on a time line or story line as you research.

WRITING YOUR REPORT

1. Set the stage.   You might begin with an explanation of why it's important for you to learn more about your topic. A brief anecdote or story that explains why you care about the topic is one way to start. You might also show what you already know or think is true about your topic and what else you need to find out.

2. Tell your story.   If you'd like, write your paper as a personal narrative. Show the steps of your research, reporting the information you gather and your reactions to the experience. Since an I-Search paper is a personal research report, your reactions are just as important as the facts you gathered. Remember that an I-Search paper can have a more personal and informal tone than other research reports.

Writing
TIP
You don't need to recount every single step of your research. Focus on the key steps, the ones where you learned important information or had significant personal reactions.

3. Wrap it up.   The conclusion to your I-Search should sum up what this personal research experience meant to you. Did your investigation back up your original ideas? Did you come to a new understanding or appreciation of your topic? How did your attitudes or ideas about the topic change? What advice do you have for other people who might be interested in researching this topic further? Remember that your personal reaction to the experience is what counts.

1. Reread your draft. You chose this topic because it had a special meaning to you. Does that meaning come through in your report? Check to see if you need to do more to explain why you care about this topic. Also check to make sure you have covered the topic thoroughly, explaining what you have learned.

2. Share your report. An I-Search report has two goals—to provide information and to explain the experiences you had while gathering that information. Ask your classmates whether your paper meets both goals. Is there anything else your readers want to know?

3. Check for accuracy. Like any other research report, an I-Search report should contain facts that are accurate. Double-check statistics, dates, and other details. Also be sure you have given proper credit to your sources. Then revise your report using your own reactions and any thoughts from your peers you want to respond to. Proofread your final draft carefully.

Publishing and presenting

- **Hold an "I-Search Day."** Classmates can share their reports orally.

- **Submit your paper to a school or community newspaper.** Your paper could make an interesting feature story.

- **Share your findings.** If a person or group of people would benefit from hearing about your experience, distribute copies of your report or share it orally.

Spring boards

Speaking and Listening

Imagine you are a television reporter on the scene for a major event in world history. You can choose an event from the past several years, such as the Persian Gulf War, or an event much earlier, such as the signing of the Declaration of Independence. Work with others to prepare an in-depth report for the evening news.

Sports

Trace the history of your favorite sport. How and where did it begin? How have the rules and equipment changed over time? What other cultures have similar games?

MUSIC

What kind of music do you enjoy most? Check into the origins of your favorite music and explore how it has developed.

Geography

Choose a place you would like to visit—an exotic, distant land or a historic site in your state—and find out all you can about it. Then write a travel brochure for the place, describing its main attractions. Illustrate your brochure with maps, photos, or drawings of your own.

Sentence

Reviewing Sentence Composing Skills

In the preceding Sentence Composing exercises, you studied several ways professional writers add detail, emphasis, and variety to their writing. These methods include using compound subjects and verbs, series of words, series of sentence parts, sentence openers, sentence closers, lists, and extensions.

A. Identifying Sentence Composing Skills   The sentences below are from *Across Five Aprils,* a novel about the Civil War by Irene Hunt. Each sentence illustrates one of the sentence composing skills you have studied. For each sentence, write the letter identifying the skill illustrated in the underlined part.

> **a.** compound subject   **f.** S-V split
>
> **b.** compound verb   **g.** sentence closer
>
> **c.** series of words   **h.** sentence with a list (colon)
>
> **d.** series of sentence parts   **i.** sentence with extension (dash)
>
> **e.** sentence opener

1. She had borne twelve children, four of whom were dead—<u>perhaps five, for the oldest son had not been heard from since he left for the gold fields of California twelve years before</u>.

2. A cupboard of heavy walnut put together with wooden pegs stood near the fireplace and held <u>dishes, food, and cooking utensils</u>.

3. <u>When the barn was burned to a pile of glowing coals,</u> the men asked Jethro to draw water from the stock well to throw around the edges of the coals.

4. McClellan, <u>the most promising young officer in his class at West Point,</u> was the general who either didn't move at all or moved ineffectually.

5. He looked at the faces around him, and they spun in a strange mist of color: <u>black eyes and blue eyes, gray hair and gold and black, pink cheeks and pale ones and weather-beaten brown ones</u>.

6. <u>Ellen, the two young women, and Jethro</u> stood in the yard and watched silently.

7. The sun was getting low by the time he reached the ruins of what had been the county's first schoolhouse, <u>a landmark known as the eight-mile point north of Newton</u>.

8. The restaurant was warm and clean, full of the fragrance of <u>roasting meat, freshly baked wheat-flour bread, and strong, rich coffee</u>.

9. He lay with his face close to the earth, <u>clutching the fresh spring grass with both hands</u>.

10. He <u>picked up Tom's letter, read it again, smoothed it carefully, and returned it to the envelope</u>.

11. Jethro, <u>understanding the situation more fully now that he was older,</u> wondered at his father's intervention that afternoon.

12. They say, too, that hundreds of people climbed up on rooftops to watch the flight—<u>as if it were a circus of some kind</u>.

B. Matching and Imitating Sentences   Each sentence below can be divided into chunks that resemble the chunks in one of the sentences in Exercise A. Write the number of the sentence in Exercise A that each sentence imitates. Then write your own imitation.

1. Janine sat with her feet up to the fire, stretching her damp, chilled toes with growing contentment.

2. Michele had invited ten friends, nine of whom were coming—perhaps ten, since one friend had not called back before Michele went to the store for refreshments fifteen minutes ago.

3. Thom, the unpredictable new member of the cross-country team at Jefferson School, was the runner who either led from the start or lagged behind.

4. When the beach was deserted after sunny afternoons in the summer, the beachcomber used his metal detector to find items beneath the sand to sell at the recycling center in town.

5. The cellar was humid and dank, full of the smell of rotting wood, long-neglected furniture, and damp, mildewed cloth.

The Wedding: Lover's Quilt #1 (1986), Faith Ringgold. This African-American folk artist pieced together images and text in three quilts that tell the story of a couple's life. In this quilt, the couple is shown at their wedding.

Writing Handbook

MINI-LESSONS

Calvin and Hobbes
by Bill Watterson

- What important thoughts do *you* have? Jot down some ideas that are on your mind.
- Draw a picture that shows what you are feeling or thinking about right now.
- How do you figure things out? Describe how you made a recent decision.

Writing Process

Where do you think the idea for this movie came from? It could have started with a writer doodling on a piece of paper—perhaps drawing Martians invading Indianapolis.

Writing isn't just a matter of putting words down on paper. It's a process of figuring out what you're thinking and how you want to express your thoughts. The handbooks that follow can help you explore, write, and polish your ideas.

How Do I Find a Topic?

Discovering Writing Ideas

Where do writing ideas come from? They can come from just about anywhere—observations, experiences, memories, conversations, dreams, or imaginings. The writer Alice Walker got the idea for her book *The Color Purple* from a remark her sister made. Maya Angelou's book *I Know Why the Caged Bird Sings* is based on her memories of growing up in the South during the 1930s. The idea for Roald Dahl's book *Charlie and the Chocolate Factory* came from a note in a journal: "What about a chocolate factory that makes fantastic and marvelous things—with a crazy man running it?"

Like Walker, Angelou, and Dahl, you are constantly surrounded by good writing ideas. All you have to do is start looking. The techniques presented in this handbook can help you find a topic you really care about. Try them out and use the ones that work for you.

PERSONAL TECHNIQUES

One of the best places to look for writing ideas is inside yourself. You can begin by exploring your own memories, interests, and imagination.

Do you remember learning to ride a bicycle? a trip to visit your grandmother? your twelfth birthday? Your life is full of experiences that can yield good writing ideas. To help jog your memory, try any of the following techniques:

- **Look** through your journal, family photo albums, and scrapbooks. List people, places, and things that have been important to you.

- **Recall** significant events. A time line might help you remember events from different periods of your life.

- **Talk** to a friend or family member about incidents from your childhood or experiences you've shared.

Taking Stock of Your Interests What do you most like to do? Watch horror movies? Study the sky through a telescope? Play soccer? Your own interests can be a good source of writing ideas. Questions like the ones below can help you identify your interests:

- What books and magazines do I like to read?
- What is my favorite sport?
- What kinds of television programs do I like?
- What do I do in my free time?
- What would I like to learn more about?
- Who are my heroes?

WRITER TO WRITER

You'd be surprised to know how many everyday things will trigger a great idea. I always keep a piece of paper handy—you never know when that great idea will come!
Jennifer Wilson, student, Mount Clemens, Michigan

Responding to Triggers Sometimes just a word or a picture can set your thoughts in motion. Simply focus on a word or image—the first one that comes to mind or one that you find in your journal. Then jot down ideas and questions that occur to you as you think about it.

Answering Reporters' Questions When reporters gather information for a news story, they ask basic questions beginning with *who, what, where, when, why,* and *how.* These questions can help you find ideas for writing, too. Suppose your social studies teacher has assigned a paper on the Civil War. You might ask questions like the ones on the next page to help you identify a topic:

Nighthawks (1942), Edward Hopper.

- Who were the leaders of the Union and of the Confederacy?
- What were some of the consequences of the war?
- Where were the major battles fought?
- When did the war begin?
- Why was the war fought?
- How did average soldiers feel about the war?

Asking Creative Questions   In the movie *Big,* the actor Tom Hanks plays a young boy who, incredibly, grows up overnight. The idea for that movie probably came from asking the question "What if?" Asking that question can help you come up with writing ideas that are just as original. Even questions that seem ridiculous can lead to promising writing ideas. Here are some examples:

- What if I changed a familiar object in some way? (What if a mattress were filled with water?)
- What if I used a familiar object in a new way? (What if a surfboard were used as a water ski?)
- What if I put two things together in a new way? (What if a television and a telephone were combined?)
- What if a person had never existed or an event had never happened? (What if television had not been invented?)
- What if relationships between people or things were changed? (What if your cat kept you as a pet?)
- What if things happened differently? (What if people got younger instead of older? What if people lived underwater?)

What if . . . ?

Gleaning   Just as some people collect baseball cards, you can collect ideas by gleaning, or gathering, ideas from the world around you. Whenever you come across something that intrigues you—something you see, hear, read, or experience—jot down your thoughts, feelings, and observations in your journal. When you need a writing idea, just look through your collection.

Sharing Techniques

When you're searching for ideas, you might also try getting a little help from your friends. Working with other people is often more effective than working alone.

Brainstorming   One way to come up with a lot of ideas quickly is to brainstorm. Get together with a few friends or classmates. Choose someone to record the group's ideas on the chalkboard or on a large sheet of paper. Pick a topic and then try to come up with ideas as fast as you can. Don't stop to comment on any of the ideas. One person's ideas may spark other ideas, like a chain reaction. After about five or ten minutes, review your list for potential writing ideas.

Here are the results of a brief brainstorming session in which students began with the topic *oceans:*

oceans	Pacific	dolphins	submarines
waves	Atlantic	shipwrecks	*Alvin* submersible
tides	salt water	coral reefs	Jacques Cousteau
sharks	tidal waves	whales	scuba diving

Discussion   Although brainstorming can help you generate ideas quickly, a discussion can help you explore a topic in more depth. Here are some guidelines for holding a discussion:

- Agree on a general topic for discussion.
- Give each person a chance to speak and to ask questions about or to react to what others have said.
- Listen carefully and respectfully to what others have to say.

Afterwards, jot down notes about the discussion and ideas you would like to develop in a piece of writing.

Your pen or pencil can also lead you to new ideas. Just putting your thoughts on paper can help get them flowing.

Freewriting   The only rule in freewriting is "Keep writing." To begin, set a time limit, say five minutes. Pick a topic or start by writing down the first words that come into your head. If you get stuck, keep writing the same words over and over until a new thought occurs to you. Don't worry about grammar, spelling, punctuation, or logic, and don't stop to read what you've written. Just keep writing. When the time is up, read through your freewriting. Circle any ideas you'd like to explore further. You can even do more freewriting to develop one of those ideas.

Here's how one student used freewriting to come up with a topic for a social studies report on Alaska:

Student
MODEL

> Alaska. What do I know about it? Lots of snow and ice. Ice and snow, snow and ice. Cold. Gold. Forty-niners. It's the forty-ninth state. The Gold Rush. Somewhere I read about a new gold rush for liquid gold—oil. There's some kind of battle between Eskimos who hunt caribou for food and the oil companies. They want to drill wells where the caribou herds migrate. I wonder what's going to happen. Maybe I could write about that.

Listing   Like brainstorming, listing is a good way to generate writing ideas quickly. First pick a topic. Then start listing all the related ideas that occur to you. Don't stop to judge your ideas— just get thoughts down as fast as you can.

Using a Journal   Sometimes the best ideas occur to you when you're not even looking for them. That's why many writers regularly record their observations, thoughts, and feelings in a journal. You can do the same. Your journal is just for you. You can use it to explore your ideas, sort out your feelings, record your experiences, and dream about the future. You can also use it to keep clippings of newspaper and magazine articles, quotes, cartoons, photographs, and anything else that interests you.

When you need a writing idea, thumb through your journal and see what catches your eye. Then use one of the techniques presented in this handbook to explore the idea further.

Graphic Techniques

Sometimes "seeing" your ideas in graphic form can help you clarify them. For help with using graphic devices, see Handbook 3, "Graphic Devices for Writing," pages 227–231.

Practice Your Skills

A. Choose one of the topics below or study the photograph on this page. Then use two of the following techniques to generate writing ideas: recalling, answering reporters' questions, asking creative questions, or gleaning. Compare the results of the two techniques. Which technique worked better for you?

Little Sparrows (1969), Jill Freedman.

rain	winning	sports
mountains	spiders	careers
honesty	change	
music videos	high school	

B. In a small group, choose one of the topics below and use brainstorming or discussion to develop writing ideas.

adventure	travel	freedom
frustration	Mars	amusement parks
grandparents	animals	
winter	discovery	

C. Look through your journal, or use freewriting, listing, or a graphic device, to come up with writing ideas on one of the following topics.

making decisions	friendship	racism
sharing	disappointments	popularity
writing	volunteering	
telephones	disease	

How Do I Make My Topic the Right Size?

Focusing a Topic

As any photographer will tell you, there is more than one way to focus on a scene. Sometimes a sweeping, overall view works

best. At other times a close-up is more effective. The same is true of writing. Part of choosing a writing topic is bringing the ideas into focus by giving them sharpness and clarity. Many of the techniques for finding a topic discussed in Handbook 1 can also help you focus a topic.

Loon Lake, Maine, (1990), William Wegman.

QUESTIONING

Asking questions about a topic is a good way to find a focus. Suppose that your social studies teacher has assigned a two-page paper on Mexico. That topic is too broad to cover in two pages, so you might begin to narrow it by asking questions that begin with *who, what, where, when, why,* and *how.*

- Who are some famous Mexican artists?
- What are some major events in Mexican history?
- When did Mexico gain its independence from Spain?
- Why did the United States and Mexico fight a war?
- How has the geography of Mexico affected its history?

If your topic is too narrow, you can also use questioning to expand it. For example, suppose that you are writing a four-page report on space exploration. After watching a science program on television, you become interested in pictures of the United States taken from the Landsat satellites. There is not enough nontechnical information on this topic for a four-page report. However, you can ask questions such as these to find a broader topic:

- Who invented the Landsat satellites?
- What are some other kinds of artificial satellites?
- Where are satellites like Landsat built and launched?
- When was the first artificial satellite put into orbit?
- Why are artificial satellites useful?
- How have Landsat images been used?

LOOPING

Another way to limit or expand a topic is to use looping. This is a special kind of freewriting. (See Handbook 1, "Discovering Writing Ideas," pages 218–223.) First, choose a writing topic. Then freewrite about it for five minutes without stopping. When the time is up, read through what you have written and look for a possible focus for your writing. State that focus in a sentence and use it as a starting point for more freewriting.

You may need to repeat this looping process several times before finding a topic that's just the right size. For example, after freewriting three loops on the topics "sleep," "napping," and "relaxation," one student discovered her writing topic—"hypnosis."

USING GRAPHIC DEVICES

Graphic devices such as clusters and idea trees can also help you focus a topic. (See Handbook 3, "Graphic Devices for Writing," pages 227–231, for examples of these graphics.) As you use a cluster or an idea tree to limit a broad topic, try to think of specific parts of the larger topic. Then think of even narrower ideas associated with each of those parts. That way, the ideas will get more focused as you move farther from the center.

For example, one student made the cluster on the next page to narrow the topic "new technology" so that it could be covered in a five-page report.

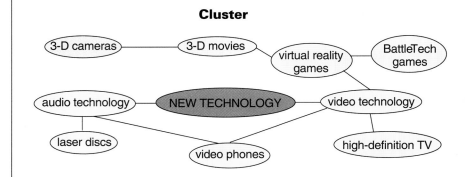

Cluster

3-D cameras — 3-D movies — virtual reality games — BattleTech games

audio technology — NEW TECHNOLOGY — video technology

laser discs

video phones

high-definition TV

B RAINSTORMING

Brainstorming can not only help you find writing topics but
also help you take the next step and focus your topic. You can
brainstorm alone, with a partner, or in a small group. First pick a
topic. Then jot down all the related ideas that you or other people
suggest. Don't stop to discuss or criticize the ideas. Just keep writing them down. At the end of the session, you will probably have
found a topic that is just the right size for your writing project.

In addition to brainstorming, techniques such as listing and
questioning can help you expand your topic if its focus is too
narrow. (See Handbook 1, "Discovering Writing Ideas," pages
218–223.)

Practice Your Skills

For each topic listed below, use one of the strategies presented in
this handbook to find one topic that is narrower and one that is
broader in focus. Tell which strategy you used to find each topic.

Dr. Martin Luther King, Jr.   science fiction
the moon   sports played on ice

Graphic Devices for Writing

When people want to make sure that they've gotten their message across, they often say, "Do you see what I mean?" Seeing is an important part of understanding. Sometimes putting your thoughts in visual form—in a graph or a chart—can help you both develop and organize your writing ideas.

GRAPHICS TO DEVELOP IDEAS

Some graphic devices that are especially helpful in exploring and developing ideas are clusters, idea trees, observation charts, and pro-and-con charts.

Clusters   A cluster can help you explore a general idea to see how its parts are related. To make a cluster, write the general topic in the center of your paper and circle it. Write down related ideas as you think of them. Circle each of these ideas and draw lines connecting them to the main topic or to related ideas. (Look on the opposite page for an example of a cluster.)

Idea Trees   An idea tree is especially useful for breaking down a general topic into its parts. Start by writing the general topic at the bottom or top of your paper. Then think about subtopics that are related to that topic. List these on "branches" growing out of the main topic. Keep dividing each new topic into subtopics until you have generated enough ideas or have found a topic to write about. One student used the idea tree on the next page to find an aspect of bats that she wanted to write about—how they navigate in the dark by echolocation.

40

A. Shachot

Graphic Devices
for Writing   **227**

Idea Tree

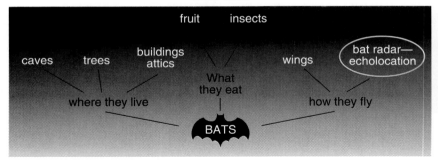

Observation Charts   A good way to come up with details for descriptive writing is to use an observation chart. First, think of a person, place, thing, or experience you want to write about. Then list the five senses as column headings. Try to recall or imagine details about your topic, focusing on each sense in turn.

After you've finished, look over your list for vivid images and unexpected observations. These may be good starting points for writing. For example, after making the following observation chart, one student decided to write a story about a camping trip from the point of view of his feet.

Observation Chart

Camping Trip				
Sight	**Sound**	**Touch**	**Taste**	**Smell**
moose grazing brother's footprints in mud light filtering through trees brilliant stars	crunch of dry leaves and twigs underfoot crackle of campfire	rough fir tree bark icy water of stream on feet warm mud between toes painful blisters	sweet and salty trail mix bitter berries	wood smoke pine needles wildflowers dirty socks

Pro-and-Con Charts   When you're trying to develop material for persuasive writing, you need to evaluate the advantages and disadvantages of an idea. A pro-and-con chart can help you. First, divide a sheet of paper into two columns. Then list the advantages, or pros, of your idea in one column and the disadvantages, or cons, in the other.

For example, one student who wanted to start a paper-recycling program at her school decided to write a letter to the student council. She used the following pro-and-con chart to explore the advantages and disadvantages of her idea.

Pro-and-Con Chart

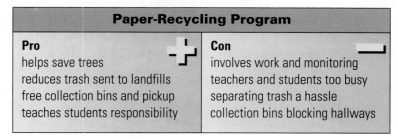

Paper-Recycling Program	
Pro	**Con**
helps save trees	involves work and monitoring
reduces trash sent to landfills	teachers and students too busy
free collection bins and pickup	separating trash a hassle
teaches students responsibility	collection bins blocking hallways

GRAPHICS TO ORGANIZE IDEAS

Once you have generated and developed your ideas, you can also use graphics to help you organize your writing and visualize its structure. Devices that are particularly helpful include idea-and-details charts, classification frames, compare-and-contrast charts, and Venn diagrams.

Idea-and-Details Charts   If you have trouble separating main ideas and supporting details, try using an idea-and-details chart. You can rank the details by numbering them in order of their importance. Some writers use this graphic instead of an outline.

Idea Chart—"Smart" TVs

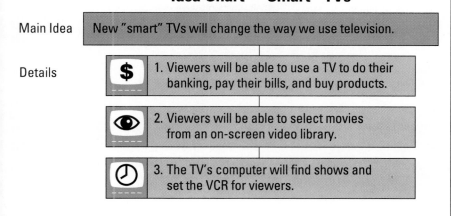

Main Idea — New "smart" TVs will change the way we use television.

Details

$ 1. Viewers will be able to use a TV to do their banking, pay their bills, and buy products.

2. Viewers will be able to select movies from an on-screen video library.

3. The TV's computer will find shows and set the VCR for viewers.

Classification Frames When you write, you may need to break an idea down into its parts or group several ideas in categories and consider how they are related. A classification frame can help you picture these relationships.

For example, one student was having trouble organizing a report on the martial arts. He knew that all of the styles could be used for exercise and for self-defense, but he didn't know how to group them. While making a classification frame, he found that the styles fell into two groups, depending on body contact.

Classification Frame

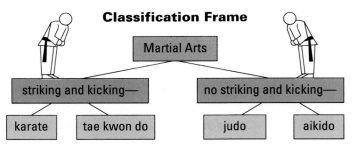

Martial Arts

striking and kicking—

no striking and kicking—

karate   tae kwon do   judo   aikido

Compare-and-Contrast Charts A compare-and-contrast chart can help you clearly see the similarities and differences between two or more subjects. You can then use the chart to help you organize your writing by either subject or characteristic. Here is a compare-and-contrast chart that a student used in preparing a science report on forests.

Compare-and-Contrast Chart

Characteristics	Subjects Being Compared	
	Tropical rain forest	Temperate forest
Location	near the equator	eastern North America, western Europe, eastern Asia
Climate	warm and wet all year	warm summers and cold winters
Types of trees	mostly broad-leaved evergreens	mostly broad-leaved deciduous
Shrubs	thin layers	possibly dense layers

Venn Diagrams   A Venn diagram is another graphic way of comparing and contrasting two subjects. A Venn diagram consists of two overlapping circles. Shared characteristics go in the overlapping area. Outside areas contain the characteristics unique to each subject. A Venn diagram comparing types of forests is shown here.

Venn Diagram—Tropical Rain Forest vs. Temperate Forest

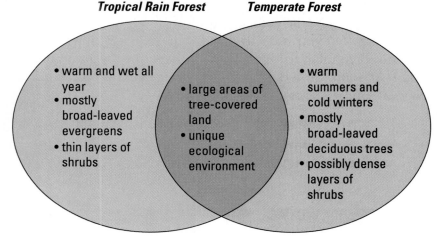

Tropical Rain Forest

Temperate Forest

- warm and wet all year
- mostly broad-leaved evergreens
- thin layers of shrubs

- large areas of tree-covered land
- unique ecological environment

- warm summers and cold winters
- mostly broad-leaved deciduous trees
- possibly dense layers of shrubs

Practice Your Skills

A. Choose one of the following topics and use a cluster map, an idea tree, or an observation chart to explore it further. Compare your results with those of a classmate who chose the same topic.

caves   cities   California   football   whales   deserts

B. Choose an issue about which you care and people disagree. With a partner, create a pro-and-con chart to explore different sides of the issue.

C. List the graphic device that would be most helpful for organizing information on each of the following topics.

1. Going to the movies versus watching movies on TV
2. Walking through the woods in mid-October
3. Types of Latin American music

What Is My Purpose for Writing?

General Purpose and Personal Goals

Imagine that you are directing a skit for a class performance. As you work with the actors, you must decide what you want to accomplish. Do you want to make your audience laugh? Do you want to force them to think? Do you hope they will do a little of both? At some time during your writing process, you must ask yourself similar questions:

- What is my **purpose,** or general reason for writing?
- What are my **personal goals,** or things I want my writing to accomplish for myself and my readers?

PURPOSE

There are hundreds of reasons for writing. These purposes generally fall into four categories: **to express yourself, to entertain, to inform,** and **to persuade.** For example, after arguing with your best friend, you may write in your journal the apology you couldn't say to her face. You might write a card to someone who needs cheering up. Sometimes you may have two or even more purposes for writing. For example, you might write to inform your classmates about your favorite rock group and to persuade them to listen to the group's music.

Sometimes you know your purpose before you begin writing or can state it after doing some freewriting or brainstorming. Often, though, you discover your purpose as you write. You may even find your purpose changing as you continue to draft and revise. To help clarify your purpose for writing, ask yourself questions like the ones below:

- Why did I choose to write about this topic?
- What effect do I want my writing to have on my readers?

PERSONAL GOALS

Your personal goals are the specific things you want to achieve with this piece of writing. These goals might involve ways the writing can help you understand an idea, or they might simply focus on the impression you want to make. Asking yourself questions such as the following can help you identify your personal goals:

- What aspects of this topic mean the most to me?
- What specific feelings or thoughts do I want my readers to get from this piece of writing?

For example, imagine you are writing a story for your school newspaper about a recent basketball game. Your purpose might be to inform your classmates about the game. However, one of your several personal goals might be to point out the contributions of a player you think the coaches and fans don't really appreciate. In another piece of writing, your purpose might be to persuade readers to visit Mammoth Cave in Kentucky. A personal goal, however, could be to re-create the sense of wonder you felt inside the cave.

Practice Your Skills

A. Choose a piece of writing from your portfolio, or think of a topic you want to explore in a future piece of writing. Then state your purpose and your personal goals for that writing.

B. The purpose of the following paragraph is to provide information. Rewrite the paragraph to persuade readers that some television programs are more worthwhile than others. As you think about this topic, list your personal goals for writing. Include specific examples of television programs in your new paragraph.

> What is the first thing many students do when they get home from school? After raiding the refrigerator, they turn on the TV. They have a variety of television programs to choose from. These programs include sitcoms, soap operas, talk shows, sports programs, travelogues, newscasts, variety shows, cartoons, educational shows, science and nature programs, and full-length movies.

General Purpose and
Personal Goals   **233**

Who Is My Audience?

Audience

If a tree falls when there's no one around to hear it, does it make any sound? People have argued about that question for centuries and still don't know the answer. One thing we *do* know, though, is that wherever people are, there's almost always someone else around to hear them. We live, work, play, and talk with other people. When we write, we write to other people.

IDENTIFYING YOUR AUDIENCE

WRITER TO WRITER

My favorite audience is teenagers. Because I am one, I can relate to them.

Mousumi Behari, student, Aurora, Colorado

Sometimes your audience is chosen for you. For example, the audience for the writing you do at school is usually your teacher and classmates. At other times, however, you decide who your readers will be. If you want to write a short story about a baby sitter, you might choose to write for parents and other adults or for people your age. Even if you choose not to share your writing with anyone else, you still have an audience—yourself.

Knowing who will read your writing can help you decide on your purpose and personal goals. It can also help you choose what kinds of details, language, sentences, and tone to use. As you think about your readers, ask yourself the following questions:

- How much do they already know about my topic?
- What will they be most interested in?
- What will they agree with? disagree with?
- What kind of language can I use to help them understand what I am saying?

Writing
— TIP —

You can make even the most difficult ideas understandable in your writing. Just be sure to use language and examples that are familiar to your readers.

One student wrote a report on humpback whales for her science class. When her younger brother started asking questions about it, she decided to rewrite the report for children her brother's age. Notice how each piece of writing is appropriate for its audience.

Middle-School Audience

The most unusual thing about a humpback whale is the way it behaves. One of its playful behaviors is called tail slapping. A humpback stands on its head and slaps the water with its flukes. The most spectacular humpback behavior is called breaching. A whale jumps out of the water, arches over, and lands on its side or back.

Third-Grade Audience

Like you and your friends, a humpback whale loves to play. One of its favorite games is tail slapping. The whale stands on its head and slaps the water with the side of its tail. The water splashes and crashes. Breaching is the most exciting game to watch. The whale shoots out of the water and straight up into the air. Then it turns over and lands on its side or back with a huge splash.

Practice Your Skills

Rewrite the following paragraph, adjusting tone, sentence length, and word choice so that it appeals to third graders.

About 63 million years ago, coinciding very closely with the disappearance of the dinosaurs, the world went through a great change of climate. It got colder. This may very well have killed the dinosaurs. While it is true that a big body keeps its heat for a long time, it is also true that it takes a very long time to regain it once it is lost. . . . A series of bitterly cold nights could have drained a big dinosaur of its heat beyond all recovery. With its body badly chilled, it might not be able to summon sufficient energy to move its huge bulk and browse. So a steady cooling of the climate . . . may well have led to the death of the large herbivores.

David Attenborough, *The Living Planet*

How Do I Draft My Writing?

Drafting to Learn

Like Regina, many writers have learned that drafting, or trying out their ideas on paper, can help them discover what they think and feel.

HOW TO APPROACH DRAFTING

The most important thing to remember about drafting is that there is no right way to do it. Sometimes you might want to be adventuresome and just dive right into your writing. At other times, you might want to proceed more carefully, planning what you want to say beforehand. Feel free to try different methods and use the one that works best for you and your writing project.

Adventuresome Drafting

When you draft in an adventuresome way, you just begin writing. You can start with the beginning, the middle, or the end—any part you have ideas about. You don't even need to know what your writing will eventually be about. Just write freely, letting one idea spark the next and following wherever your ideas lead. Adventuresome drafting works particularly well for writing that does not require much research or planning. For example, this kind of drafting can help you discover your opinions for a movie review, the ending of a short story, or the lyrics for a song.

Careful Drafting

Like some writers, you may prefer a more careful approach. Think through a writing plan or make an outline before you begin drafting. Then follow your plan as you write, developing your ideas and filling in details as you go. Because you will already have thought through your ideas, you will be able to concentrate on **bridge building**—exploring and showing the connections between ideas. Careful drafting is a good way to develop reports, business letters, and other kinds of formal writing.

WHEN TO STOP DRAFTING

Since drafting is the process of trying out ideas on paper, keep writing until you are satisfied with your ideas. You may need to make many drafts—changing direction or even starting over—before you're ready to revise and polish your writing.

Once you have produced a draft you feel good about, take a break and reread what you have written. Note your own and your peer readers' reactions and write in the margins any specific ideas you have for improving your draft. Then set the draft aside for a few hours or a day. This break will help you see your writing more objectively and revise it more effectively.

Practice Your Skills

Choose from your portfolio a piece of writing that you especially like, and think about the writing process you went through. Then write a letter to yourself or your teacher, answering questions such as the following. Attach the letter to your writing and return it to your portfolio.

- Did I use an adventuresome or a careful approach in drafting this writing?

- What discoveries did I make during drafting?

- How many drafts did I write before I was satisfied that my ideas were clear and complete?

- What would I do differently in drafting a similar piece of writing?

Writing
TIP

If you're not sure which kind of drafting to use, try mixing both approaches. Begin with a general plan, but explore new ideas and directions as they occur to you.

What Writing Forms Can I Choose?

Forms of Writing

One very creative man asked his girlfriend to marry him by painting his proposal on a large billboard near her office. She said yes! She might have married him anyway, but the unusual form of his proposal certainly helped get his message across.

Unlike this marriage proposal, most writing takes a form more typically suited to its topic and audience. For example, you probably wouldn't write instructions on how to pop popcorn in the form of a poem. This doesn't mean, however, that you shouldn't experiment with surprising and creative forms. That's part of what makes writing fun.

FORMS OF WRITING

A **form** of writing is a shape or structure that the writing takes. Which of the forms listed below have you used? The next time you do a piece of writing, try using a different form.

Forms of Writing

announcement	journal entry	poem
autobiography	letter to the editor	postcard
book review	limerick	poster
family history	movie review	report
friendly letter	news report	short story
instructions	play	speech

Practice Your Skills

Suggest a suitable form for writing about each of these topics.

- what to do during an earthquake
- an important event in your life
- your thoughts and feelings about your family
- the need to expand school-bus service

Types of Organization

Do you ever feel lost as you make your way through a piece of writing? Like Snoopy, do you long for a landmark or a compass to help you find your way?

If a piece of writing presents ideas in an organized way, readers won't have to worry about where they are and where they are going. They can relax and follow the various guideposts the writer provides.

How should you organize your writing so it is easy for your readers to follow? There is no single right way. The answer depends on the type of writing you are doing. There also is no single right time in the writing process to think about organization. Some writers like to work out a structure before they write the first word. Others prefer to just start writing. These writers organize their material as they work on their revision. Use the method and type of organization that work for you and your particular piece of writing. This handbook describes several types of organization you can try.

WRITER TO WRITER

There are no right or wrong answers in writing.
Nina Ramundo, student, Hamilton, Ohio

PEANUTS reprinted by permission of UFS, Inc.

MAIN IDEA AND
SUPPORTING DETAILS

Many types of writing can be organized into main ideas and details that support those ideas. For example, in the paragraph on the next page, notice that in the first sentence Anne Frank states her main idea—she feels alone even though she is surrounded by family and many friends. She then provides details and examples that support her feeling of isolation.

Let me put it more clearly, since no one will believe that a girl of thirteen feels herself quite alone in the world, nor is it so. I have darling parents and a sister of sixteen. I know about thirty people whom one might call friends . . . . I have relations, aunts and uncles, who are darlings too, a good home, no—I don't seem to lack anything. But it's the same with all my friends, just fun and joking, nothing more. . . . We don't seem to be able to get any closer, that is the root of the trouble.

Anne Frank, *Anne Frank: The Diary of a Young Girl*

ORDER OF IMPORTANCE OR DEGREE

You might want to organize your ideas by order of importance or degree. You can use any quality that suits your subject, such as most to least useful or older to younger, for example. In the following introduction to a report about health, the writer starts with the most familiar disease and ends with the least familiar.

It's a battleground out there, and the worst part is that you can't even see the enemy. Every time you breathe or eat, thousands of invisible organisms—bacteria, viruses, and fungi—threaten your health. You have all probably lost the battle to the viruses that cause the common cold, mumps, or chicken pox. You may even know someone who had polio or scarlet fever. Hopefully, however, you'll never experience diseases like meningitis, elephantiasis, or breakbone fever.

CHRONOLOGICAL ORDER

In your writing, you often tell about events that happened over a period of time. Biographies, histories, and stories are usually told in chronological order—the order in which events took place. You can also use chronological order to explain a process, give directions, or support an argument. Using transitional words and exact dates or other time references can help make the order of events clear.

> **At six-thirty** the sky was still dark, the rain falling steadily. **An hour later:** rain. **Two hours later:** no change. I got up, washed, ate some fruit and cheese. I draped across the bunk and read, occasionally looking into the gray obscuring rain, listening to thunder (puts the sugar in the cane), watching Spanish moss (a relative of the pineapple) hang still in the trees like shredded, dingy bedsheets. **At ten-thirty** the rain dropped straight down as if from a faucet; I was able to leave the front windows half open. I didn't know then, but in April in coastal Louisiana you don't wait for the rain to stop unless you have all day and night. Which I did.
>
> **William Least Heat Moon, *Blue Highways***

Literary
M O D E L

Writing
— **TIP** —

Transitional words that indicate chronological order include *first, immediately, last, later, meanwhile, next, soon,* and *then.*

CAUSE-AND-EFFECT ORDER

In various types of writing, you explain why something happened. For example, in a science paper, you might tell why the sky is blue. In a research report, you could show why the Soviet Union broke apart. In a story, you might want to suggest why a character acted in a certain way. An effective way to organize this type of writing is by using cause-and-effect order. In the following paragraph about football, notice how the writer uses the transitional words *because* and *so* to point out the cause and its effect.

> Why are there fewer barefoot punters than place kickers? [The answer is] **because** punts are executed on the outside rather than the inside of the foot. If you kick a punt on the same spot as a place kick, the ball won't spiral properly. The outside of the foot is a little more susceptible to pain and injury than the inside of the foot, **so** there are fewer barefoot punters.
>
> **David Feldman, *Why Do Dogs Have Wet Noses? and Other Imponderables of Everyday Life***

Professional
M O D E L

Cause

Effect

SPATIAL ORDER

To help your readers understand what something looks like, you might present the details in the way you see them. This is called **spatial order.** You can organize the details from near to far, top to bottom, or left to right, for example.

The writer of the following paragraph uses spatial order to describe the inside of a government office. Notice how she uses transitional words to make the description clear for readers.

> **Inside,** the place was gray. There were rows of long benches like church pews facing each other across a middle aisle that led to a central desk. **Beyond** the benches and the desk, four hallways led off to a maze of partitioned offices. **In opposite corners,** huge fans hung from the ceiling, humming from side to side, blowing the heavy air for a breeze.
>
> **Paulette Childress White, "Getting the Facts of Life"**

CLASSIFICATION

When you are writing about a number of ideas, consider classifying them into groups or categories. For example, in the following passage about the *Titanic,* a passenger ship that sank in 1912, the writer classifies people on the ship by social status.

> In fact, the *Titanic* was a kind of floating layer cake, composed of a cross-section of the society of the day. **The bottom layer** was made up of the most lowly manual laborers toiling away in the heat and grime of the boiler rooms and engine rooms located just above the keel. **The next layer** consisted of steerage or third-class passengers— a polyglot mixture hoping to make a fresh start in the New World. **After that** came the middle classes—teachers, merchants, professionals of moderate means—in second class. **Then finally,** the icing on the cake: the rich and the titled.
>
> **Robert D. Ballard, *The Discovery of the* Titanic**

COMPARISON-AND-CONTRAST ORDER

An important part of classifying subjects is noting how they are the same and how they are different. You can compare and contrast two subjects by discussing the characteristics of one subject first and then those of the other subject. You can also discuss the characteristics one by one, first in one subject and then in the other. The following comparison is organized by characteristic.

Professional
MODEL

Comparison

Contrast

The washer-dryer [designed for a space station] uses 1.1 gallons of water to clean each pound of clothes—**compared with** a typical seven gallons per pound for Earth's current models—and uses 20 percent less energy than other machines. It holds seven pounds of clothes—about half the amount of a conventional machine—though it could be sized for larger loads. **Rather than** agitating clothing for cleaning, it extracts soil with a detergent solution.

Mariette DiChristina, "Appliances from Space"

Practice Your Skills

Write the type of organization you would use to make each group of ideas into a paragraph. Then write a paragraph.

1. • ping-pong table in center of basement
   • gas furnace in far left corner
   • inside basement door—washer and dryer on left, rug and weights on right
   • stacks of boxes in far right corner and along back wall

2. • senses of humans: sight is most highly developed sense; senses of hearing and smell not as keen as in dogs
   • senses of dogs: smell is most highly developed sense; better sense of hearing than people; poorer sight than people

3. • Lee became angry with the coach.
   • Lee was late for soccer practice.
   • The coach made him sit out the next game.
   • Lee quit the soccer team.

Types of Organization   **243**

What Is a Good Paragraph?

Effective Paragraphs

You are listening to some musicians as they tune up and practice their riffs and scales. It's a strange jumble of noise—guitar, keyboard, bass, and percussion, each doing something different. Then a conductor brings the group together, and music begins. The separate players are now a group with a common goal.

Like the group of musicians, a **paragraph** is made up of individual parts that work together toward a common goal. Each sentence in a paragraph helps to develop an idea or accomplish a purpose. Paragraphs can be any size and can be used in many different ways. Usually, they are part of a longer piece of writing, such as a lab report or a story. Some writing, however, such as an essay-test response, may be only one paragraph long.

WHAT IS A GOOD PARAGRAPH?

No matter what their size and purpose, all good paragraphs have two things in common—unity and coherence. For a paragraph to have **unity,** each of its sentences must relate to the main idea of the paragraph. For a paragraph to have **coherence,** the sentences must be presented in an order that makes sense. (For more information on unity and coherence, see Handbooks 14 and 15, pages 268–277.)

Is the following passage a good paragraph?

Literary
MODEL

I was assigned to Bunk 7, the Senior Girls. The inside of our bunk was like a long bedroom, with ten cots, five on each side, lined up against the walls. There were windows, but they had no glass, only screens and canvas shades that rolled down on the outside. The floors were raw planks that looked like they'd give you splinters regularly, and the walls were unfinished pine with exposed beams between the windows. A jail, I thought, must look a lot like this.

Ellen Conford, *Hail, Hail Camp Timberwood*

This is a good paragraph because all the sentences help describe the bunk room at a summer camp. They are also logically connected to one another—the paragraph moves from a general description of the room to the specific details.

Read the next paragraph. Does it have unity and coherence?

> I gripped the bat and clenched my teeth. Now it was up to me. Sweat dripped down my face as I stared at my enemy—the pitcher on the mound. He just transferred to our school. I hadn't had a hit in five games and I had already struck out twice in this game. What had happened to my magic touch?

Are any sentences unrelated to the main idea?

The purpose of the paragraph above is to describe the batter's nervousness. The sentence about the pitcher transferring to the school does not help develop that idea. Therefore, the paragraph is not unified. Now read another paragraph.

> The land began to shudder and then just split open. The sidewalk was twisted like a rubber band and our thirty-foot-tall pine tree was tossed across the street the way someone would toss a matchstick. Suddenly, without warning, the earthquake struck. Miraculously, nobody was hurt. We sure were scared, though. We were having a picnic in the back yard on a beautiful summer afternoon.

Are any events out of order?

The paragraph is unified because all the sentences describe the experience of an earthquake. However, the events are not presented in an order that makes sense. Therefore, the paragraph is not coherent. The revised paragraph follows.

Student MODEL

Notice how repositioning two sentences improves coherence.

> We were having a picnic in the back yard on a beautiful summer afternoon. Suddenly, without warning, the earthquake struck. The land began to shudder and then just split open. The sidewalk was twisted like a rubber band and our thirty-foot-tall pine tree was tossed across the street the way someone would toss a matchstick. Miraculously, nobody was hurt. We sure were scared, though.

Uses of Paragraphs

Paragraphs can serve many purposes. Some common purposes are listed below.

Purposes of Paragraphs

Introduce a piece of writing	Define
Tell a story	Show cause and effect
Describe	Connect two ideas
Compare and contrast	Persuade
Explain	Conclude a piece of writing

The main purpose of the following paragraph is to explain how submersibles—boats that can operate underwater—work.

Professional MODEL

> Submersibles are designed for use at great depths. They need to be able to sink, to rise, and also to float underwater. They do this by altering their weight with a system of ballast tanks which can hold either air or water. If a craft's ballast tanks are flooded with water, the craft's weight increases. If the water is then expelled by compressed air, the weight decreases. By adjusting the amount of water in the tanks, the craft's weight and buoyancy can be precisely regulated.
>
> **David Macaulay, *The Way Things Work***

The following paragraph compares two kinds of relationships—relationships with parents and friendships with peers.

Literary MODEL

> Sam stopped, bent down to tie his sneaker, and looked up at his oldest friend. He couldn't remember when he didn't know Benjy. It was a good thing, Sam was thinking, to be able to go back that far with somebody who wasn't a parent. You had no choice with parents, and they had no choice with you. You're stuck with each other. But if he and Benjy didn't choose, and didn't keep choosing, to like each other, there'd be no reason for them to keep going home from school together and hanging out with each other on the weekends.
>
> **Nat Hentoff, *This School Is Driving Me Crazy***

Practice Your Skills

A. Indicate whether each of the following paragraphs displays unity and coherence. If necessary, rewrite the paragraph to correct the problem.

1. First Officer Thims took a deep breath and punched in the coordinates for the next destination on the ship's computer. This was his third, uneventful year as navigator for the *Fantasy,* an interstellar cruise ship. Each year the ship carried vacationers to all the popular galactic ports of call—the red sand beaches of Io, the underground pyramids of Mars, and the golf courses on Pluto. He had once gotten a hole in one on the thirteenth hole because the force of gravity was only a fraction of Earth's.

2. As a young man, Ernest Hemingway worked in Europe as a newspaper correspondent. He also wrote short stories. Unfortunately, the suitcase was stolen from a train platform. All but two of the many stories Hemingway had started were lost. One year he and his wife were getting ready to vacation in Switzerland. His wife carefully packed in a suitcase most of the stories he was working on. Hemingway wanted to work on the stories while he and his wife were away. Hemingway was crushed by the loss, but he kept writing.

B. Identify the purpose or purposes of each of the following paragraphs.

1. The members of the photography club need a darkroom, and we are asking for your support. Students need to learn more than reading, writing, and arithmetic at school. For example, student photographers can learn real-world skills if we can work in a darkroom. The photography club is willing to hold fund-raising events to raise the money needed for basic equipment and supplies. If the school will give us a room, we'll take care of the rest.

2. Dodging boulders the size of small cars, she steered the kayak down the river. The water roared, and the spray sparkled in the late afternoon sun as the kayak shot through the rapids. She felt as if she could touch the red canyon walls rising steeply on either side of her. The thin slice of dark blue sky was so far above her head that it made her dizzy to look at it.

This computer-enhanced image shows Io, one of Jupiter's moons.

How Do I Create a Paragraph?

Developing Paragraphs

Mosaics, such as this one below by Lupus, are made up of hundreds of pieces put together in precise patterns. To create a mosaic, the artist may first develop an overall design and then develop the details with the individual pieces.

Like a mosaic, a piece of writing is made up of smaller parts, or paragraphs. The process that writers go through in creating a piece of writing may be similar to the way an artist works. Often writers first think about the overall purpose of their writing and then work on individual paragraphs. Not all writers work this way, however. Some writers like to begin writing just to get their ideas on paper. Then they organize their material into paragraphs as they revise.

WRITING A TOPIC SENTENCE

A **topic sentence** makes the main idea of a paragraph clear and tells readers what to expect from the paragraph. In addition, a good topic sentence can serve as a lead to catch the readers' attention and make them want to keep reading. However, as you will see later, not all paragraphs have a topic sentence.

Which of the following topic sentences would make you want to read the rest of a paragraph?

1. I am going to tell you how to fix a flat bicycle tire.
2. Imagine a computer that responds to the sound of your voice or reads even the most illegible handwriting.
3. The giant octopus has been called the "devilfish"—with good reason.
4. This paragraph is about windsurfing.

The second and third sentences probably caught your interest. What would you do to improve the first and fourth sentences?

Every paragraph is different, so no single kind of topic sentence—no matter how good it is—will work all the time.

Untitled classical head (1991), Lupus.

Fortunately, however, there are several techniques you can choose from to write an effective topic sentence for any paragraph.

- **State an unusual fact or intriguing detail.**

  Mozart had an older sister who may have been just as talented as the famous composer, but she never got a chance to fully develop her genius—just because she was a girl.

- **Ask a question.**

  How can you make a healthy meal choice at a fast-food restaurant?

- **Give a command.**

  Try to remember what it was like to be four years old.

DEVELOPING YOUR MAIN IDEA

To write an effective paragraph, you need more than just a main idea. You need to support that idea with additional details, or **elaboration.**

The type of supporting details you use will depend on the main idea or purpose of your paragraph. Here are several types of details you can choose from.

Types of Supporting Details

Facts and statistics statements that can be proved

Sensory details words that appeal to the five senses

Incidents events that illustrate your main idea

Examples specific cases or instances that illustrate your main idea

Quotations the words of an expert or an authority

Grammar
TIP

When using direct quotations, be sure to enclose the person's words in quotation marks.

If the purpose of your paragraph is to describe a setting in a short story, you might use sensory details. On the other hand, if your purpose is to support an opinion, you might use facts and statistics. (For more information about elaboration, see Handbook 12, "Methods of Elaboration," pages 255–261.)

Notice the many sensory details the writer used in elaborating the following paragraph.

> I sit on my air mattress and wait to stop sweating. Fifty miles of caverns plunge and snake and twist away from me in every direction, passages of impenetrable darkness, like damp black velvet pressing against my face. The disk of light from my helmet lamp sweeps across the walls of the tunnel as I turn my head. The surface is white, glittering with gypsum crystals, and crystals loosened by my body heat snow gently onto my hands. The air smells clean and wet, like fresh laundry, and the silence is absolute. It must be like this in outer space, I think, but I am a thousand feet underground.
>
> **Tim Cahill, "The Splendors of Lechuguilla Cave"**

Logical Flow of Details   Notice that the paragraph above does not have a topic sentence. In many paragraphs—especially in paragraphs that relate events or that tell a story—the main idea is not stated directly; it is only implied. This type of paragraph will have unity and coherence if the sentences all relate to the purpose of the paragraph and if the supporting details flow in a sensible way from one to another.

Like the paragraph above, the following paragraph does not have a topic sentence. However, the paragraph is unified because all the sentences relate to its purpose—describing the setting and action in a story. The paragraph is coherent because the details are presented in a way the reader can follow—the order in which they happened.

> They were silent the rest of the way back to their grandmother's dock. The two children climbed out there. Dicey took the line and tied it around one post. Then she sat on the edge of the dock and held the boat steady with her feet while her grandmother lifted the motor up and rocked it into a resting position inside the boat. The metal propeller blades dripped water into the bay like sullen raindrops.
>
> **Cynthia Voigt, *Homecoming***

ORGANIZING YOUR PARAGRAPH

Whether or not a paragraph has a topic sentence, details must be presented in a sensible order. The type of order you choose will depend upon the purpose of your paragraph. For more information on ways of organizing the details in a paragraph, see Handbook 8, "Types of Organization," pages 239–243.

Practice Your Skills

A. Decide which of the following topic sentences are weak. Then revise them to make them stronger.

1. This is a story about a cat.
2. Whom do you see when you look in the mirror
3. Prairie-dog towns are so well organized that they even have their own security systems.
4. One kind of summer job you can try is starting your own business.
5. My topic is the Australian outback.

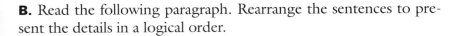

Prairie dogs on "sentry duty" watch for danger.

B. Read the following paragraph. Rearrange the sentences to present the details in a logical order.

"What is your destination?" Instead of finding the rough draft of her English composition, Anna found herself staring at a message blinking insistently on the screen. OK, thought Anna, I'll play along. It had seemed like any other afternoon, until Anna turned on her computer to do her homework. She thought for a moment and then typed in the words "the moon." As she watched the screen, something very strange happened. Maybe this was some new computer game of her brother's.

C. Write a paragraph about each of the following topics. Vary the types of topic sentences and elaboration you use. Remember that not every paragraph needs a topic sentence.

- a place you like to visit
- how something works
- an important incident in your life

Developing
Paragraphs   **251**

How Do I Use Paragraphs?

Paragraphs in Longer Writing

Imagine that you're driving in an unfamiliar place at night. It's so dark that you can barely see the side of the road. There are no landmarks, no signs to tell you where you are, and no place to rest. You realize with a sinking feeling that you're lost!

That's what it might feel like to read a book without paragraphs. In writing, paragraphs are like the signs along a road. They signal the reader: Pay attention! New idea here! Paragraph indents also break up the page, giving readers' eyes a rest and helping them keep track of where they are on the page.

WHEN SHOULD I PARAGRAPH?

Few writers know exactly how many and what kinds of paragraphs they will write when they begin drafting. Some writers try out different idea groupings and create paragraphs as they draft. Other writers just get everything on paper during drafting and wait to group ideas into paragraphs when they revise their writing. Here are some suggestions to help you paragraph your writing.

Guidelines for Paragraphing

Begin a new paragraph when
- a new idea is introduced or the topic changes
- there is a major change in setting or action
- the speaker in a dialogue changes

Make sure your paragraphs include
- only one main idea
- adequate elaboration
- no unrelated details
- a logical order of presentation

In the following passage, notice how Helen Keller begins a new paragraph to introduce a new idea—that people who can see don't really use that gift.

> I have often thought it would be a blessing if each human being were stricken blind and deaf for a few days at some time during his or her early adult life. Darkness would make people more appreciative of sight; silence would teach them the joys of sound.
>
> Now and then I have tested my seeing friends to discover what they see. Recently I was visited by a very good friend who had just returned from a long walk in the woods, and I asked her what she had observed. "Nothing in particular," she replied. I might have been incredulous had I not been accustomed to such responses, for long ago I became convinced that the seeing see little.
>
> **Helen Keller, "The Seeing See Little"**

Toshio Mori begins a new paragraph each time the speaker changes in the following dialogue between the owner of a flower shop and a sales clerk.

> Mr. Sasaki ran excitedly to the front. "Teruo! She forgot to pay!"
>
> Teruo stopped the boss on the way out. "Wait, Mr. Sasaki," he said. "I gave it to her."
>
> "What!" the boss cried indignantly.
>
> "She came in just to look around and see the flowers. She likes pretty roses. Don't you think she's wonderful?"
>
> "What's the matter with you?" the boss said. "Are you crazy? What did she buy?"
>
> "Nothing, I tell you," Teruo said. "I gave it to her because she admired it, and she's pretty enough to deserve beautiful things, and I liked her."
>
> "You're fired! Get out!" Mr. Sasaki spluttered. "Don't come back to the store again."
>
> **Toshio Mori, "Say It with Flowers"**

Room in Brooklyn (1932), Edward Hopper.

Practice Your Skills

Act as peer editor for the following piece of writing, paying special attention to paragraph breaks, unity, and coherence. Write instructions for revising the passage. (For example, "Begin a new paragraph with sentence __." or "Delete sentence __.") Note that one paragraph should be repositioned.

Equipment such as this hydraulic lift helped to create remarkably realistic special effects in the film *Jaws*.

1In the movie *Jaws,* a giant shark gobbles up a fisherman. **2**In the movie *Who Framed Roger Rabbit?* an actor and a cartoon character race through the streets in a cartoon car. **3**Have you ever watched a movie with great special effects and wondered, "How did they do that?" **4**Surprisingly, special effects rely on just a few basic filmmaking techniques. **5**One of the secrets behind many special effects is a technique called stop-motion photography. **6**A filmmaker shoots the frames of a film one at a time and then combines them to make the action look continuous. **7**For example, stop-motion photography helped turn actor Lon Chaney, Jr., into a monster in the movie *The Wolf Man.* **8**Chaney was the son of a famous silent film star. **9**First the filmmaker shot a few frames of the actor. **10**Then the makeup crew added pieces of hair to Chaney's face and hands. **11**A few more frames were shot, and the process was repeated until Chaney had become a full-fledged werewolf. **12**Other special effects rely on the use of models and miniatures which can be photographed to look like live action. **13**The shark in *Jaws,* for example, was really three different mechanical models, each designed to be used in different scenes. **14**In the 1976 movie *King Kong,* the giant ape was actually a Styrofoam model just forty feet high. **15**The original King Kong movie was made in 1933. **16**Combining live action with animation like this can produce astonishing illusions. **17**The next time you watch a movie, you won't have to ask, "How did they do that?" **18**You'll know how. **19**Some of the most complex special effects involve a process called composite photography. **20**For instance, in the film *Who Framed Roger Rabbit?* the cartoon characters' actions were drawn and photographed on one piece of film—the live actors' movements on another. **21**The two pieces of film were then combined so that it looked as if the "Toons" and the humans were on screen together.

How Can I Develop My Ideas?

Methods of Elaboration

How many times have you said to someone you were talking to, "You know what I mean?" When you write, however, you don't have a chance to ask that question. Your writing should give readers enough specific details, or **elaboration,** so that they understand your ideas completely and aren't left with any unanswered questions.

TYPES OF ELABORATION

You can use many types of details to elaborate on your ideas. These details include facts, statistics, sensory details, incidents, examples, quotations, and graphic aids. The details you choose should fit your purpose, audience, and topic.

Facts and Statistics A statement that can be proved is a **fact.** An example of a fact is "Greg LeMond of the United States won the Tour de France bicycle race in 1986, 1989, and 1990." A **statistic** is a fact stated in numbers. "Cyclists in the Tour de France usually cover between 2,500 and 3,000 miles" is a statistic. You can find such statements in a sports encyclopedia.

Facts and statistics are especially useful in supporting opinions. For example, Mariolle and Shermer used facts and figures to show that U.S. women have dominated cycling for years.

In 1984, many TV viewers saw Americans Connie Carpenter Phinney and Rebecca Twigg win the gold and silver medals in the first cycling event ever held for women in the Olympics. It was no accident. American women have been prominent in international cycling competition since 1969, when Audrey McElmury won the road race at the World Championships in Brno, Czechoslovakia. She was the first American champion, male or female, in 57 years. Since 1945, Americans have won a total of 35 medals at the Worlds and 27 of them were won by women.

Elaine Mariolle and Michael Shermer, *The Woman Cyclist*

Professional
MODEL

Fact

Fact

Statistic
Statistic

Methods of
Elaboration   **255**

Sensory Details   You can help readers experience what you are writing about by showing how something looks, sounds, smells, tastes, or feels. These sensory details can help you bring a description or narration to life. To find sensory details, try recalling, observing, or imagining. Then look for specific nouns and active verbs to describe these details.

In the following paragraph, notice how the writer uses sensory details of smell, sound, and sight to make readers feel as if they're standing right beside him as he tracks the gorilla.

Smell ——

Sound ——

Sight ——

> The musty, somewhat sweet odor of gorilla hung in the air. Somewhere ahead and out of sight, a gorilla roared and roared again, *uuua-uuua!* an explosive, half-screaming sound that shattered the stillness of the forest and made the hairs on my neck rise. I took a few steps and stopped, listened, and moved again. The only sound was the buzzing of insects. Far below me white clouds crept up the slopes and fingered into the canyons. Then another roar, but farther away. I continued over a ridge, down and up again. Finally I saw them, on the opposite slope about two hundred feet away, some sitting on the ground, others in trees.
>
> **George B. Schaller, *The Year of the Gorilla***

Incidents   Sometimes, describing a brief event, or **incident,** can help you explain an idea. In the following passage the writer uses an incident to show the importance of following the proper procedure.

> *Seek help.* Just as police are trained to call for backup during emergencies, so the rest of us should guard against going it alone if help is available.
>
> When fire was reported in an office building in Hartford, firefighters were startled to see how far the blaze had progressed by the time they arrived. Construction workers on the scene had tried to put the fire out themselves. "By the time they called the fire department," says [fire captain] Fred Crocker, "smoke was up to the third floor. It was amazing nobody died." Crocker points out that the proper sequence is to call for help first, and *then* try to handle the problem.
>
> **Reynolds Dodson, "Control Your Crisis"**

When relating an incident, be sure to include enough details to support your idea and to leave out ones that might be confusing. Notice how Dodson described the fire by using sensory details and by quoting the firefighter's own words.

WRITER TO WRITER

"In your writing you want to have all of the what, when, where, how, *and* why.*"*

Jamie Lentz, student, Hamilton, Ohio

Examples   Sometimes a "for instance," or **example,** can also help you elaborate on an idea. A well-chosen example often can be more effective than a whole page of explanation.

In the following paragraph, notice how the writer uses examples to show how Olympic track-and-field coach Bob Kersee gives his athletes the winning edge.

Professional **MODEL**

> Kersee is a keen student, staying abreast of all the latest training developments and scientific research. He knows all about weight training, diet, muscles, massage, and techniques for throwing, running, and jumping. He sees himself as a "detail" person. He carefully studies videotapes of his athletes' performances and watches for the smallest change in form or the tiniest adjustment. What he notices may add only an inch to a long jump or shave just hundredths of a second off a sprint, but at the highest levels of track and field, those differences can decide who wins and who finishes last.
>
> **Jay Jennings, "Jackie Joyner-Kersee and Bob Kersee: Track's Wedded Winners"**

Example of new training developments

Example of Kersee's techniques

Quotations   Quoting people directly can be a powerful way to elaborate on and support your ideas. In choosing quotations to include in your writing, however, just as in choosing incidents, be sure that they make your point clearly. Also be sure to copy the words exactly and to credit the writer or speaker.

For example, the writer of the passage on the next page uses a quotation from an expert to support his statements about space junk.

Methods of
Elaboration   **257**

> There's all sorts of junk whizzing around in Earth orbit, bits and pieces of spacecraft that nobody ever cleaned up. The military's early warning radar can spot the big pieces—those four inches long and up. . . . Researchers even know a lot about the tiny pieces, less than two-hundredths of an inch across. . . .
>
> But between four inches and two-hundredths of an inch lies a lot of garbage about which little is known. "These things have a closing speed of ten miles per second," says Richard Goldstein, a radar specialist with the Jet Propulsion Laboratory in Pasadena. "That means that if you're ten miles away from a piece of debris, you have one second to duck."
>
> **"Looking for Trash,"** *Discover*

Graphic Aids   You've probably heard the expression, "A picture is worth a thousand words." That certainly can be true. So, if you have to present a large amount of information in a small space in your writing, consider using **graphic aids** such as maps, tables, and diagrams. For example, the following diagram shows a figure skater doing the complicated triple axel jump. Describing this movement in words would be very difficult and would take a great deal of space.

Counting the turns   A triple axel in figure skating is hard to follow because the motion is so rapid. The skater makes three and one-half turns in less than one second.

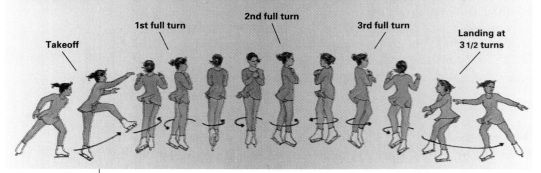

Takeoff   1st full turn   2nd full turn   3rd full turn   Landing at 3 1/2 turns

Presenting information graphically can also make the relationships between ideas clear. Notice that the bar graph on the next page shows at a glance how the distribution of Peace Corps volunteers changed from 1967 to 1992.

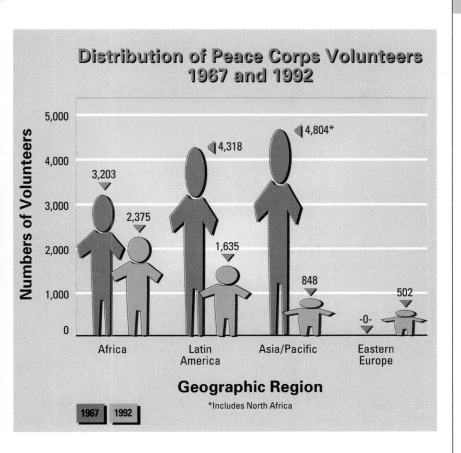

Distribution of Peace Corps Volunteers 1967 and 1992

Numbers of Volunteers

5,000
4,000
3,000
2,000
1,000
0

Africa: 3,203 / 2,375
Latin America: 4,318 / 1,635
Asia/Pacific: 4,804* / 848
Eastern Europe: -0- / 502

Geographic Region

*Includes North Africa

1967 1992

SOURCES OF ELABORATION

Even if you know what type of elaboration you need to develop your writing ideas, you still have to gather specific details. What sources or methods will best help you gather the information you need?

Questioning What do you know about your topic? Asking questions can help you find out. The answers to the questions are the details you can use to elaborate on your writing. The questions you can't answer can help direct your research. A student made the chart on the next page as she was working on a report about the guitarist Les Paul. Notice that she included reminders to herself in the chart.

Details About Les Paul

Who?   guitarist Les Paul
What?   helped develop modern electric guitar
When?   early 1950s? (FIND THE EXACT DATE!)
Where?   (DOESN'T MATTER)
Why?   wanted a different sound
How?   attached pickups below strings of an acoustic guitar

Exploring   The same methods that are useful for exploring writing ideas can also be used to generate details that elaborate on those ideas. These methods, which are presented in Handbook 1, "Discovering Writing Ideas," pages 218–223, include recalling, brainstorming, freewriting, listing, and using a journal.

Research   The library is a storehouse of many types of resource materials you can use to help you elaborate on your ideas. For more information about finding and evaluating library sources, see Handbook 35, "Making Use of the Library," pages 352–361.

People who have special knowledge about your topic can also be good sources of information. Before contacting an expert, make a list of questions you want to ask. Then arrange an interview and take good notes. Finally, double-check any answers that sound wrong. Even experts can make mistakes.

Graphic Devices   Another good way to find details is to use graphic devices such as clustering, charting, and analysis frames. These devices can help you learn what you know and what you need to find out about a topic. (See Handbook 3, "Graphic Devices for Writing," pages 227–231.)

Practice Your Skills

A. Choose two of the following main ideas. Then elaborate each idea in a brief paragraph by following the suggestions in parentheses.

1. Airports are interesting places.
   (*Suggestion:* Give examples. Include sensory details that describe what you see, hear, smell, taste, and touch.)

2. There is nothing spookier than a deserted street at night. (*Suggestion:* Give sensory details or tell about an incident. The incident can be real or made up.)

3. Changing a tire on a bicycle is easy if you know how. (*Suggestion:* Research the topic by watching someone change a tire or by doing it yourself. Draw a diagram or use another graphic aid to make your explanation clear.)

4. A pet's antics are amusing to watch. (*Suggestion:* Give examples or tell about an incident.)

5. _____ is the best team in the league. (*Suggestion:* Choose a team. Give facts or statistics from a recent newspaper or magazine article. Consider including a graphic aid.)

6. Our town has changed in the past thirty years. (*Suggestion:* Research the topic by interviewing older relatives or family friends. Include examples and a quotation from one of them.)

7. _____ was the most important day of my life. (*Suggestion:* Tell about an incident.)

8. The best video game is _____. (*Suggestion:* Use specific examples from the game.)

B. Imagine that you have to write about each main idea listed below. Name the method of generating details that will help you produce the most interesting and informative piece of writing. Then list the types of details you might use.

1. Different kinds of music fit different moods.
2. Certain species of whale are in danger of becoming extinct.
3. Soccer is the world's most popular sport.
4. Riding a bicycle in a large city can be dangerous.
5. Off in the distance, I heard a waterfall and a person shouting.
6. Athletic shoes are now made for every possible purpose.

How Can I Use Elaboration Techniques?

Show, Don't Tell

Eduardo sent Ana this postcard from summer camp.

> Dear Ana,
>   Camp is great! I can't believe all the people I'm meeting and the things I'm learning to do!
>   Ciao,
>   Eduardo

After reading Eduardo's postcard, Ana had lots of questions. She wondered what the people he was meeting were like. She was curious about all the activities and what he was learning to do. She wanted details to *show* her about the camp, so she wrote back asking her questions. Here is Eduardo's reply.

> Dear Ana,
>   You have to meet Aaron. He's a crack-up. He's always telling jokes. Another guy is giving me guitar lessons. Today we hiked to Lake Navajo. We even learned how to water ski. Tonight is the cookout. We'll all sit around the campfire and tell ghost stories.
>
>   Miss you,
>   Eduardo

Eduardo's first postcard *tells* about camp in a general way. The second one, however, *shows* what happens at camp. The details about friends, water-skiing, and ghost stories show Eduardo's active day.

In Handbook 12, "Methods of Elaboration" (pages 255–261), you learned about a variety of supporting details that you can use to develop your ideas. Asking yourself questions like the ones Ana asked Eduardo can help you think of supporting details.

Show-Don't-Tell Strategies

Showing a Feeling When you write about your important experiences, you may focus on showing your feelings. Notice how Gary Soto uses striking comparisons and vivid description to show his disappointment over his new jacket.

Telling

I couldn't believe my mother gave me such an ugly jacket!

Showing

When I needed a new jacket and my mother asked what kind I wanted, I described something like bikers wear: black leather and silver studs with enough belts to hold down a small town. . . . The next day when I got home from school, I discovered draped on my bedpost a jacket the color of day-old guacamole. I threw my books on the bed and approached the jacket slowly, as if it were a stranger whose hand I had to shake. . . . I stared at the jacket, like an enemy, thinking bad things . . .

Gary Soto, "The Jacket"

Showing an Event When you're reporting an event, don't try to include every detail. Instead, focus on the most important and vivid details. You might also include dialogue.

Telling

The raft began to capsize.

Showing

"Hang on!" a crewman shouted over the crash of waves. Suddenly, the whoops of excitement turned to cries of alarm. In the fast and furious chute of Crystal Rapids, the three-ton, 38-foot long raft had pitched onto a rock and stopped dead. A crewman bellowed orders to stay put. But when the raft heeled to an angle of 70 degrees, John yelled into Tyler's ear, "Jump."

Peter Michelmore, "Capsize at Crystal Rapids"

What had he expected? What did he receive? How did he feel?

Literary **MODEL**

What did the characters see and hear? What were the passengers doing?

Professional **MODEL**

Showing Cause and Effect   When you write about a situation and its results, use specific details to make each point clear. You might include first-hand observations, facts, examples, and expert opinions, for example. The telling sentence below states a connection between rope jumping and tennis. The showing paragraph, however, provides specific details and the experience of an expert to explain the cause-and-effect relationship.

How does rope jumping affect your skill? What does rope jumping do that helps you play a better game?

Professional
MODEL

Telling
Rope jumping can improve your tennis game.

Showing
   The big appeal for tennis players is that rope jumping mimics many movements you execute on the court. Tennis is played on the balls of the feet. You're constantly moving in short, controlled steps, much the way you move while jumping rope. Improve your jumping ability and you'll get to the ball quicker.
   "One of the biggest problems tennis players have is being out of position," says Greg Moran, the head pro at the Four Seasons Racquet Club in Wilton, Conn., who has been jumping rope for ten years. "You need short steps to adjust to the ball. if I stop jumping rope for a while, I feel heavy-footed and slow on the court."

Susan Festa Fiske, "Jump To It"

Showing Comparisons and Contrasts   When you compare or contrast two subjects, use the same set of details to show their similarities or differences. Notice how the following writer contrasts Saturday and Sunday. Each paragraph focuses on the same kinds of details in the same order, but each paints a sharply different picture. The concluding sentence neatly summarizes the contrasts of the two days.

What's the difference in the way each day feels? What do you do differently on each day?

Telling
Saturday feels different from Sunday.

Showing

Without the help of an alarm clock, at 8:30 sharp Saturday morning, I wake up brimmed with energy and ready to take on any activity that floats my way. The sun is pouring bars of golden liquid in my window and the blue jays are singing merrily at the top of their musical voices. Anticipating a whole day to do whatever I want, I eagerly throw on my clothes and spring down the stairs. In a flash, I'm out the door and running.

On Sunday, though, my mother is shaking me and saying, "It's past 11:00. Get up, there's work to do." With a deep groan I open my eyes and am immediately blinded by the terrible glare of the sun beaming hot and stuffy directly on me. Very slowly I claw my way out of bed, and in a drained, limp state of semi-consciousness, stumble sheepishly down the stairs. Saturday was freedom; Sunday means mowing the lawn.

Showing an Opinion When writers argue for something they believe in, they use facts and examples to support their point of view. Using evidence based on research strengthens your argument. Notice how the writer in the model below supports one side of a controversial issue.

Telling

Animal research is good because it has produced major advances in medicine.

Showing

Anyone who has looked into the matter can scarcely deny that major advances in medicine have been achieved through basic research with animals. Among these are the development of virtually all modern vaccines against infectious diseases, the invention of surgical approaches to bone and joint injuries and eye disorders, the discovery of insulin and other hormones, and the testing of new drugs and antibiotics.

Frederick A. King, "Animals in Research: The Case for Experimentation"

What medical advances have been made? What are different examples?

Professional
MODEL

Other Show-Don't-Tell Strategies

Showing a Cliché A cliché is an overused expression, such as *She was as quiet as a mouse* or *I could hardly believe my eyes,* that has become meaningless and dull because it has been repeated over and over again. To avoid using a cliché, try to find fresh words or descriptive details that will show the meaning and add interest. Here is an example.

What made him such a model of health? Why did he seem so fit?

Student
MODEL

> ### *Telling*
> He was the picture of health.

> ### *Showing*
> He was off once more to play basketball, running full-speed, leaving the exercise room far behind. Dodging through the crowded corridors, leaping over benches, and sliding down banisters, in no time he found himself at the entrance to the basketball court.

Showing an Idea in a Single Sentence When writers strengthen their writing by showing instead of telling, they don't always develop whole paragraphs to add specific details and descriptions. Sometimes one or two sentences can be just as effective as an entire paragraph. In the excerpt below, Alice Walker uses only a single sentence to *show* instead of *tell* what the baby is doing in her mother's lap.

What gestures was the baby making? Why did she seem happy?

Literary
MODEL

> ### *Telling*
> The baby was happy in her mother's lap.

> ### *Showing*
> Once in her mother's lap she rested content all the way home, sucking her thumb, stroking her nose with the forefinger of the same hand, and kneading a corner of her blanket with the three fingers that were left.
>
> **Alice Walker, *The Color Purple***

Practice Your Skills

A. Rewrite the following telling sentences to turn them into showing paragraphs. Use the writing strategies in parentheses.

1. It felt great to be alive. (Show your feelings through sensory details.)
2. The mood was somber. (Show the mood through a comparison.)
3. The game was a close one. (Show the suspense by focusing on a single moment.)
4. Students should (should not) be allowed to watch television as much as they want. (Show reasons to support your opinion.)
5. He was a new person after a week's vacation. (Show the different ways his vacation affected his outlook.)
6. The words *skinny* and *trim* suggest different meanings. (Show the contrast in meanings by giving specific examples.)
7. Athletic shoes can vary in price, depending on where you buy them. (Show facts and statistics to support this statement by researching local stores.)
8. Video games are too violent. (Support your opinion with descriptive details and specific examples.)
9. My two friends are as different as night and day. (Show this cliché.)
10. Cable television has changed viewing habits. (Show the effects of cable television by using facts and examples.)

B. Write a showing paragraph for each sentence.

1. We took a risk.
2. The sea is full of mystery.
3. The streets were crowded.
4. I could tell the book was going to be good.
5. Mothers can be different from fathers.
6. American diets are changing.
7. Homework is (is not) necessary to improve learning.
8. The grass is always greener on the other side of the fence.

C. Write a showing sentence (or two) for each telling sentence.

1. I was annoyed.
2. The speaker captured our attention.
3. Dogs are different from cats.
4. Exercise can improve health.

How Do I Make My Writing Unified?

Achieving Unity

You go to the mall to buy a new pair of jeans and come home with new shoes, a magazine, and two shirts. What happened? You got distracted by the shoe store, the bookstore, and the rack of shirts you had to pass on your way.

As you write, you can become just as distracted by fond memories, vivid details, and interesting ideas. However, if you include everything that interests you, your main idea may not come across very clearly. For example, read the following paragraph.

> What do the scent of seaweed and the aroma of an apple-spice mixture have in common? Both can relax you. Odors can also jog memories. The scent of seaweed makes me think of the beach. Researchers have found that people who sniffed the essence of seaweed became as much as 17 percent calmer than they had been beforehand. People who smelled an apple-spice fragrance were soothed in the same way. Sometimes people scent their homes with apple-spice fragrance.

That paragraph contains many interesting details. Yet the paragraph's main idea isn't very easy to follow. Notice how much more clearly the main idea comes across when the details unrelated to it are removed.

Student
MODEL

> What do the scent of seaweed and the aroma of an apple-spice mixture have in common? Both can relax you. Researchers have found that people who sniffed the essence of seaweed became as much as 17 percent calmer than they had been beforehand. People who smelled an apple-spice fragrance were soothed in the same way.

A paragraph has **unity** if all of its sentences support the same main idea or purpose. A composition has unity if all of its paragraphs work together to achieve the same goal. It is usually much easier to grasp the main idea of a unified paragraph, such as the one you just read, than to grasp the main idea of a paragraph lacking in unity. Therefore, as a writer you should always try to give your paragraphs and compositions unity.

WAYS TO ACHIEVE UNITY

To achieve unity in a paragraph, do the following:

- Make sure that your paragraph focuses on one main idea.
- Check to be sure that all of the sentences in the paragraph relate to its main idea.
- Use a topic sentence if necessary.

Follow this advice to achieve unity in a composition:

- Start a new paragraph each time you begin a new idea.
- Make sure that all of the paragraphs in the composition help to achieve its goal.

Performers from the Cirque du Soleil use lights, costumes, movements, and music to create a unified aerial ballet.

Unity with Topic Sentences

A **topic sentence** states the main idea or purpose of a paragraph. Stating your main idea in a topic sentence can help you to stay focused on this main idea as you write and revise. In the following paragraph, the main idea is stated in a topic sentence, and the rest of the sentences help to develop this idea.

> Manuel was middle-aged, patient, and fatherly. He bent down on his haunches to talk to kids. He spoke softly and showed interest in what we had to say. He cooed "good" when we made catches, even routine ones.
>
> **Gary Soto, "Baseball in April"**

Literary
MODEL

Writing
TIP

To create unity in a longer narrative, think of the main event as a series of separate incidents. Then develop each incident in a separate paragraph.

Literary
MODEL

Literary
MODEL

Unity Without Topic Sentences

You do not always have to use a topic sentence to create unity in a paragraph. Instead, you can try the following method:

- Decide on an overall goal for the paragraph.
- Make sure that each sentence supports that goal.

You can use this approach in all kinds of writing. Some examples are given below.

Narrating an Event   If your overall goal in writing a paragraph is to capture an event, then make sure that each of your sentences helps to develop this event. For example, each sentence in the following paragraph helps the reader feel a young woman's terror.

> The canoe was thrown violently into the air, and I felt myself free-falling. The boat was gone. I had lost hold of my lifeline. The impact [of the mammoth wave] was so savage it forced the breath from my lungs. I felt myself spiraling down into a current of suffocating foam, buried in a turmoil of furious water. A powerful sucking force was swallowing me. All I could think was, *This is it, Michelle.*
>
> **Michelle Hamilton with Rachelle Hamilton, "Swept to Sea"**

Describing a Character   If your overall goal in writing a paragraph is to describe a character, then make sure that all of your sentences tell something about that character. For example, each sentence in the following paragraph describes Grandpa.

> When we got to my house, Grandpa was sitting on the patio. He had on his red shirt, but today he also wore a fringed leather vest that was decorated with beads. Instead of his usual cowboy boots, he had solidly beaded moccasins on his feet that stuck out of his black trousers. Of course, he had his old black hat on—he was seldom without it. But it had been brushed, and the feather in the beaded headband was proudly erect, its tip a brighter white. His hair lay in silver strands over the red shirt collar.
>
> **Virginia Driving Hawk Sneve, "The Medicine Bag"**

Practice Your Skills

A. Revise the following paragraph by eliminating those sentences that are unrelated to the main idea stated in its topic sentence.

What do fireflies and vampire bats have in common? They are both nocturnal, or active only at night. By day, fireflies hide. At night, however, they flash a greenish yellow light to find one another. My science teacher says that this blinking is like a mating call. He also says that female fireflies don't have any wings. On the other hand, all vampire bats have big blue-black wings. Vampire bats sleep all day. Then, on dark nights, they fly out in search of other mammals to prey upon. Vampire bats can puncture your skin and drink your blood.

B. Determine the overall goal of the following paragraph. Then revise the paragraph to give it unity by eliminating those sentences that fail to support this goal.

We began hiking into the canyon at high noon without water. There are supposed to be snakes and scorpions at the bottom of the canyon. At the top, mules were the only creatures we saw. Down we marched, the hot sun feeling good on our backs. Two hours later, the sun didn't feel so good. We were sweaty, sunburned, and thirsty. Aloe is supposed to be really good for treating sunburn. On my next hike, I intend to take along plenty of aloe and water. Soon our throats were as dry as the orange canyon dust, so we decided to turn around. That's when we panicked.

C. Create a unified paragraph about one of the following topics. You may use a topic sentence or just make sure that each sentence in your paragraph helps to achieve the same goal.

1. a scary event (getting lost, being chased by a dog)
2. a person who is special to you (friend, relative, teacher)
3. a fun or interesting place (carnival, museum, vacation spot)

Headline Howlers

Food is Basic to Student Diet
Bridgeport (CT) Post 1/18/78

COLD WAVE LINKED TO TEMPERATURES
Daily Sun/Post (San Clemente, CA) 1/17/77

Fish and Game to Hold Annual Elections
Berkshire Courier (Great Barrington, MA)

THE FUTURE IS GETTING CLOSER
Post-Crescent (Appleton, WI)

Lead-lined Coffins Termed Health Risk
The Washington Post

Police Can't Stop Gambling
Detroit Free Press 7/1/75

JUVENILE COURT TO TRY SHOOTING DEFENDANT
Deseret News (Salt Lake City, UT)

Town OK's Animal Rule
The Asheville (SC) Citizen 3/2/77

Shut-Ins Can Grow Indoors With Lights
The Miami Herald 7/21/78

Robber Holds Up Albert's Hosiery
Buffalo Evening News 9/19/75

CHICAGO DAILY NEWS

WOMAN BETTER AFTER BEING THROWN FROM HIGH-RISE

School Board Agrees to Discuss Education
Philadelphia Evening Bulletin 10/8/74

MILK DRINKERS TURN TO POWDER
Detroit Free Press

Man Eating Piranha Mistakenly Sold as Pet Fish
The Milwaukee Journal 7/16/76

How Can I Make My Ideas Easy to Follow?

Coherence

Imagine reading a recipe that first tells you to frost a cake and then tells you to bake it. The recipe would be pretty difficult to follow, and the resulting cake would be a mess. To make details easy to follow, you need to present them in a clear, sensible order. Keep these points in mind as you read the following paragraph.

> Since they were three years old, Judit, Zsuzsa, and Zsofia Polgar have been playing chess with amazing results. At fifteen, Judit became the youngest chess grandmaster ever. The sisters earn enough money from tournaments and appearances to support themselves and their parents. She is now sixteen and the top-ranked female chess player in the world. Judit was beating her father at the game by the age of five. She and her sisters dominated the women's Chess Olympiad when Judit was twelve.

Do you think the information in that paragraph is clear? To decide, compare the paragraph with this revision.

Student
MODEL

> Since they were three years old, Judit, Zsuzsa, and Zsofia Polgar have been playing chess with amazing results. **By the age of five,** Judit was beating her father at the game. **When Judit was twelve,** she and her sisters dominated the women's Chess Olympiad. **At fifteen,** Judit became the youngest chess grandmaster ever. **Today, at the age of sixteen,** Judit is the top-ranked female chess player in the world. **In addition,** the sisters **now** earn enough money from tournaments and appearances to support themselves and their parents.

The revised version of the paragraph is **coherent**—that is, all of its details flow logically from one to another. To ensure that your paragraphs are coherent, make sure your details are arranged in a sensible order. Then link your details with connecting words that help make their relationship clear.

The connecting words that show how details are related are called **transitions.** You can use transitions to point out relationships in time and space, to show order of importance, and to show cause-and-effect relationships. You can also use transitions to clarify whether details are similar or different. Look at the following list to become familiar with some of the many words and phrases that can serve as transitions.

Transition Words and Phrases

Chronological Order	first second always then next	later soon before finally earlier	afterwards meanwhile eventually next week tomorrow
Spatial Order	in front behind next to nearest	lowest above below outside	underneath on the left on the right in the middle
Degree	mainly strongest weakest first	second third most important less important	equally important most significant least significant best
Comparison	similarly likewise in addition	like than as	neither . . . nor either . . . or by comparison
Contrast	however by contrast yet	but unlike instead	nevertheless as opposed to on the other hand
Cause and Effect	since because thus therefore	so due to as a consequence accordingly	for this reason if . . . then as a result owing to

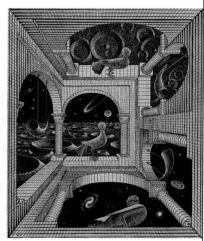

Other World (1947), M. C. Escher. © 1947 M. C. Escher/ Cordon Art–Baarn–Holland.

Chronological Order   Transitions that show relationships in time help make clear the order in which events occurred, as in the following paragraph.

> **Then** we sat on the big snowbank at the edge of the rink and just watched. It was cold **at first** even with my skating pants on, sitting on that hard heap of snow, but **pretty soon** I got warm all over. He threw a handful of snow at me and it fell in a little white shower on my hair and he leaned over to brush it off. I held my breath. The night stood still.
>
> **Maureen Daly, "Sixteen"**

Spatial Order   Transitions such as those in the following paragraph help to point out where details are located in space.

> Tall trees grew **down in the canyon** and **leaned out over** a deep hole of clear water. **In the trees** nested hundreds of long-shanked herons, blue ones and white ones with black wing tips. . . . And **beneath them, down in the clear water,** yard-long catfish lay on the sandy bottom, waiting to gobble up any young birds that happened to fall out of the nests.
>
> **Fred Gipson, *Old Yeller***

Degree   Transitions can help you to clarify relationships of degree of importance or any other quality. In the following paragraph, transitions rank clues by their degrees of reliability.

> Some people appear older than they actually are. The Carnival age-and-weight guesser Willy "the Jester" Stewart is seldom fooled, however. **Some of the best clues to people's ages,** according to Willy, come from their hands. If a girl is wearing a wedding ring, she's old enough to be married. **A less reliable clue** is braces. Nowadays people may get braces later in life. **The least certain sign of age** may be gray hair. "Gray hair is a fooler," says Willy.

Comparison and Contrast   Transitions that introduce points of comparison help readers know when to look for similarities.

Fluent language is very important to keep a reader's interest.

Chakkarin Burudpakdee, student, Clementon, New Jersey

Transitions that introduce contrasts signal readers to look for differences. Notice the use of transitions in the next paragraph.

Student
MODEL

> **Like** mountain bikes, specially designed off-road wheelchairs have enabled thrill-seeking riders to blaze new trails over rocks and down steep mountainsides. **Both** types of all-terrain vehicles let riders whip around sharp corners and fly off jumps. **Unlike** its two-wheeled counterpart, **however,** an off-road wheelchair has four wheels, a low-slung seat, and disc brakes.

Cause and Effect   To show that details are linked in a cause-and-effect relationship, use transitions such as *because* and *therefore.* Look at how transitions in the following passage connect weightlessness with some of its effects on appearance.

Professional
MODEL

> [When I'm weightless] I *look* a little different, though—all astronauts do. **Since** the fluid in our bodies is not pulled toward our feet as it is on Earth, more of this fluid stays in our faces and upper bodies. This makes our faces a little fatter and gives us puffy-looking cheeks. We are also about an inch taller while in orbit **because** in weightlessness our spines are not compressed.
>
> **Sally Ride with Susan Okie,** *To Space and Back*

Using Synonyms

Sometimes writers weave sentences together with **synonyms**—different words with similar meanings. By linking your sentences with synonyms, you can avoid repetition and add variety as well as information to your writing. For instance, notice how synonyms of *message* both strengthen the coherence of the following paragraph and add variety to its sentences.

> The principal got the **message** first. He passed the **news** to the teachers. However, a student must have overheard the teachers talking about the **announcement,** for by the afternoon everyone seemed to have the **information.** Of course, by then the **story** had become exaggerated. Still, there must be some truth to the **tale** I heard—and what I heard is that we're all going to be in a movie!

Practice Your Skills

Revise the following paragraphs to improve their coherence. Feel free to rearrange and combine sentences in addition to adding transitions.

1. If you don't want to get struck by lightning during a thunderstorm, this advice is for you. If you're stuck outside, sit or crouch down. Do this away from tall trees. Stay away from water and metal, because they are both good conductors of electricity. Head indoors when it starts raining. That's the best thing you can do.

2. Throughout the day, everybody's body changes in predictable ways. If you're like most people, your mind is most alert during a certain few hours. These are the late morning hours. On the other hand, sometime between 8:00 and 11:00 P.M., you begin to feel sleepy. Between 3:00 and 4:00 P.M., you regain your energy. In those late afternoon hours, athletic activities seem easier than at any other time of day. By comparison, early in the afternoon, your energy level tends to drop. Just before supper time, your senses of taste and smell become quite sharp. However, at the same time, so may your tongue. Five o'clock is prime time for arguments. Your eyesight is at its sharpest at a particular time of day too. That time of day is noon.

How Do I Introduce My Writing?

Introductions

W R I T E R   T O   W R I T E R

The hardest part [of writing] is deciding where to begin.
Amity Baca, student, Denver, Colorado

Amity Baca is not the only writer who has trouble getting started. Most people face that problem at one time or another. One way to get beyond the hurdle of putting down that first word is not to worry about beginning with an introduction. Just start writing any part of your piece that you have ideas about. As you write, your purpose or focus will become clearer. Then you will better know how to begin.

VARIETIES OF INTRODUCTIONS

An introduction has two purposes—to capture your audience's attention and to present the main idea of your writing. There are as many varieties of introductions as there are ways of saying hello. For example, you may say "Hi," "How ya doin'," "What's new?" or just "Hello," depending on the situation. Choosing an introduction is similar. Here are some approaches to try.

Sharing an Unusual Fact

Beginning your writing with a startling or interesting fact can make your audience want to keep reading. Why does the following introduction make you want to learn more about what trees have to say?

Professional
MODEL

> Some gardeners talk to their plants. Scientists have learned that plants can "talk," too. During long periods without rain, trees make high-pitched sounds. The message: They're weak from thirst.
>
> *National Geographic World,* **"The Trees Are Talking"**

Presenting a Lively Description

A vivid description can capture your readers' imagination and welcome them into a whole new world. Notice how the following description almost makes you want to put your hands into your pockets to warm them.

> Winter came upon us like the sudden opening of a tomb. Almost overnight it seemed that the last multicolored banners of autumn leaves had been wrenched from the trees by the wind and built up in great moldering piles that smelled like plum cake when you kicked them. Then came the early-morning frost that turned the long grass white and crisp as biscuit, made your breath hang in pale cobwebs in front of you and nipped at your fingertips with the viciousness of a slamming door.
>
> **Gerald Durrell, *A Bevy of Beasts***

Asking a Question

Asking a question in your introduction can get your readers thinking about the answer your writing will provide. The following opening is an intriguing example.

> Do you eat like a bird and still gain weight? Believe it or not, you may be eating in your sleep.
>
> Sleepeating is an unusual but far-from-rare phenomenon, according to Neil Kavey, director of the Sleep Disorders Center at New York's Columbia Presbyterian Medical Center. Kavey recently wired up three people thought to be sleepeaters in a scientific attempt to show that they would try to eat in their sleep. Sure enough, they did.
>
> **Paul McCarthy, "Snacking in Your Sleep"**

Relating an Incident

An interesting or humorous story can draw readers into your writing by making them part of the action. The anecdote on the next page invites readers to share the real-life adventure of four children in a Costa Rican rain forest.

The roar of a howler monkey boomed through the treetops. Down below, four kids stopped walking and looked up. But the jungle was too dark and thick with leaves for them to see anything. Henri tried to copy the monkey's call. But his yell sounded more like a small hoot than a howl.

"No question who's king of *this* jungle," Cynthia said with a little chuckle.   **Chris Wille, "Kids Saved It!"**

Using Dialogue

Quoting people's own words can add interest to an introduction. The following dialogue introduces an article about a driving instructor in New York City.

Professional
MODEL

"O.K., start the engine, put your foot on the brake, and put it in D for dumb," Bob Kousoulos said.

Ely Quezada, terror etched on her face, did as instructed.

"Now, remember, I don't know anything," Ms. Quezada said.   **N. R. Kleinfield,
"It's a Harrowing Drive on the Learning Curve"**

Practice Your Skills

A. Rewrite one of the following weak introductions, using a technique you learned in this handbook.

1. I'm going to tell you how to remember names better.
2. There's no more enjoyable activity than playing basketball. (or building model cars, or walking the dog, etc.)
3. My summer vacation was fun.

B. Choose a writing topic from the following list. Then write *two* different introductions for a piece of writing about that topic.

physical fitness	being different	training a pet
learning to cook	a favorite team's	allowances
skin care	latest victory	boys' sports and
making friends	chocolate	girls' sports
household chores	clothing styles	

How Do I Conclude My Writing?

Conclusions

Think of how good it feels to fit the final piece into a jigsaw puzzle. The picture is complete and everything finally makes sense. In your writing, you can give readers that feeling of satisfaction by ending with a strong conclusion.

WRITING CONCLUSIONS

There are many ways to end a piece of writing. However, every conclusion should give readers a feeling of completeness. It should leave them with a strong final impression that supports your purpose for writing. It should not introduce new information or unrelated ideas. Here are some types of conclusions that you might try.

Restating the Main Idea

One way to complete your writing is to remind readers of the main points you've made. The following paragraph concludes an essay that presented guidelines for preparing vegetarian meals. Notice how the first sentence of the conclusion links it with what has gone before.

Professional
MODEL

> Using these basic guidelines, it's relatively easy to plan well-balanced vegetarian meals that are low in fat, calories, and cholesterol, as well as high in carbohydrates and fiber. A vegetarian diet can be just as healthy, nutritious, and delicious as any other diet around.
>
> **Carol Bialkowski, "The Veg Edge"**

Asking a Question

Another good way to end your writing is to ask readers a question that sums up what you have told them and leaves them with something to think about. The conclusion shown on the next page does just that.

With devotees such as [former Lakers basketball star Kareem] Abdul-Jabbar, it's no wonder hatha yoga has become a new fitness craze—it's even been dubbed "yogarobics." So even if you're not quite ready for chanting and not the least bit interested in perfecting the double lotus, you can still enjoy yoga. After all, what other exercise routine builds the mind as much as the body?

Emerald, "Yoga Yo' Body"

Making a Recommendation

When you are writing to persuade, you can use your conclusion to tell readers what you want them to do. The following paragraph concludes an article persuading people that they can get the jobs they want. It tells readers the simple steps for success.

From my standpoint, that's what it's all about. Prepare to win. Never stop learning. Believe in yourself, even when no one else does. Find a way to make a difference. Then go out and make your own tracks in the snow.

Harvey B. Mackay, "Get the Job You Want"

Ending with the Last Event

If you're telling a story—either real or imaginary—you can just end with the last thing that happens. The book *The Pig-Out Blues* tells the story of a young girl's struggle to get along with her mother and to accept herself. It ends with an important moment of understanding.

"I love the spread. It will be perfect for my room. Thank you." She squeezed my hand and started the motor.

"Now, if I were you," Mother said, "I'd do the whole bedroom in vivid colors."

"But I'm not you," I said quietly.

She nodded. Out of the wall that was between us came one brick at a time.

Jan Greenberg, *The Pig-Out Blues*

Generalizing About Your Information

A good way to conclude many types of writing is to make a general statement that shows the overall importance of what you've said. The following paragraph concludes an article about the many roles a father can play in his children's lives. Notice that it clearly explains what all these roles have in common.

> Despite all that mothers provide, children feel safe and protected with their fathers. Read into it whatever you want. Nothing can change the need for a dad.
>
> **Ralph Kinney Bennett, "What Kids Need Most in a Dad"**

Practice Your Skills

A. Decide which of the following conclusions are well written and which are not. Rewrite any weak ones.

1. Together again after twenty years, mother and child walked down the dim corridor into the sunlight of a June morning. Their search for each other was over.
2. Well, that's all I have to tell you about why you should be concerned about the messy conditions in the town park. Please be neater and don't throw stuff in the bushes.
3. No matter which of the after-school clubs you decide to join, you will make new friends, take pride in your new skills, and have an enjoyable time. Club presidents will sign up new members next Tuesday afternoon. Join a club and be an active member of our school.
4. So that's why bike riders should wear safety helmets. I think wearing them is a good idea. Don't you? Furthermore, it would be a good idea for skateboarders to wear helmets too. I should have mentioned that before. Skateboarders can have just as many accidents as bike riders.

B. Choose from your portfolio a piece of writing that you want to revise. Use one of the techniques presented in this handbook to make your conclusion stronger.

How Can Others Help Me Improve My Writing?

Peer Response

When you were a young child, you picked up crayons, pencils, or pens and scribbled on every scrap of paper you could find. Long before you knew how to form letters or draw objects, you were experimenting with putting ideas and feelings down on paper. Remember how good it felt when people responded to your early work, praising it and displaying it on the refrigerator door?

Sharing your work with others and hearing their responses can be as satisfying now as it ever was. It still feels good when people read your writing and tell you how much they like it. Praise, however, is just one aspect of **peer response**—the comments friends or classmates make about your writing. Working with others on your writing can help you discover new ideas, decide what else you want to say, and see how well you've communicated your ideas.

USING PEER RESPONSE

You can ask peer readers for help at any point in your writing process—from prewriting to final revision. For example, before you begin writing, you might ask your readers how much they know about your topic. Later, you might ask readers to listen to a first draft and tell you where they think you might be headed with your writing. As you revise, you can ask your readers if your organization makes sense or if there's anything else they would like to know. You can also read your draft to a friend without asking for any response at all. This gives you the opportunity to hear what you've written.

You can help your peer readers provide you with the most useful kinds of feedback by following these guidelines:

- Tell your readers where you are in your writing process. Are you still trying out ideas, or have you completed a draft?
- Ask questions that will help you get specific information about your writing—ones that require more than "yes" or "no" answers.

- Encourage your readers to be open and honest when they respond to your work. It's OK if you don't agree with them—you always get to decide which changes to make.

Just as you may ask others to read and respond to your writing, they may ask the same of you. Follow these guidelines when you act as a peer reader for someone else:

- Be respectful and considerate of the writer's feelings.
- Make sure you understand what kind of feedback the writer is looking for before you respond. If you are asked for help with organization, don't comment on word choice.
- Always use "I" statements. Saying "*I* like your ending" or "It would help *me* understand your point if you would . . ." reminds the writer that your impressions and advice may not be the same as someone else's.

TRYING RESPONSE TECHNIQUES

Four of the most useful peer-response techniques you can use are **pointing, summarizing, replying,** and **identifying problems.** Here is part of a piece of student writing. The writer's questions and the reader's answers on the next page show how these peer response techniques work.

Student
MODEL

It was a perfect day for a bike ride, and Kim had borrowed her brother's new bike—a shiny red twelve-speed—to ride to a friend's house. Kim rode along Eleventh Avenue, where a new building was going up. She stopped to watch the construction and looked through a hole cut in the wooden fence surrounding the site. Huge bulldozers scooped up mounds of earth. Cranes, like giant mechanical birds, pecked at a pile of lumber.

Kim turned around to get the bike, but it was gone! She could hardly believe it. In the short time that she had stopped to watch the construction, someone had taken the bike. Her brother's bike. The one he had saved his money all year to buy.

Pointing   "What parts of my draft do you particularly like or dislike? Which words or phrases stick out in your mind—for better or worse?"

"I like your description of the construction site. I could really see the crane! I like the words *scooped* and *pecked.*"

Summarizing   "What do you think I'm trying to say? What's my main idea?"

"A girl borrows her brother's bike and someone steals it. Now she has to tell her brother about the loss. Is that your story's main idea?"

Replying   "What do you know about my topic? Has anything like this ever happened to you? What else do you want to know?"

"I once borrowed my sister's backpack and then lost it, so I know how Kim feels. I'd like to hear more about what's going on in Kim's mind. What's she going to tell her brother?"

Identifying Problems   "Did you have any trouble with my writing? Where did you get lost or confused?"

"Where was the bike when Kim looked through the fence? Wasn't she on it?"

Practice Your Skills

A. Choose a piece of writing from your portfolio and share it with others. Be sure to ask for the kind of feedback you want.

B. Imagine that the paragraph below is from the first draft of a friend's science report. Your friend is ready for peer response and asks you to point, summarize, reply, and identify problems in the writing. Write your responses to the questions on this page for each of these response techniques.

Living things have found ways to survive in very unusual places. For example, colonies of giant mussels and clams live in total darkness along volcanic vents in the ocean floor. Ghostly white crabs scramble over the rocks. Enormous tube worms, some measuring ten feet, sway in the ocean's current. How can this underwater world survive without sunlight?

How Do I Evaluate and Improve My Draft?

Revising

Have you ever made a project out of clay? As you worked, you probably pinched and pulled the clay many ways before the form pleased you.

When you write, you also pinch and pull and reshape. When you revise, you may even end up starting over. Because you are rethinking your ideas, revision involves much more than simply copying your piece and adding a comma or two.

TYPES OF REVISION

The changes you make in your writing usually fall into two categories: revising for ideas and revising for form. When you add new ideas, develop old ones, or delete unrelated ideas, you are **revising for ideas.** When you change the organization and presentation of your ideas, you are **revising for form.** Use the following charts to identify and solve problems in your writing.

Revising for Ideas

Problem	Solution
• My opening isn't catchy enough to make the reader continue reading.	• Begin with an interesting fact, story, or quotation.
• I didn't present my most important idea early enough.	• State the main idea in a sentence near the beginning.
• The reader might need more information or details.	• Add more details in places that left you asking *who, what, where, when, how,* or *why.*
• Some ideas or details are unnecessary. Others distract from the main idea.	• Delete or move any idea that does not relate to the main idea.
• My conclusion doesn't tie my ideas together.	• Summarize the main idea and the supporting details.

Revising for Form and Language

Problem	Solution
• My readers can't tell where ideas begin and end.	• Start a new paragraph for each idea and for each change of speaker or setting.
• My ideas don't seem to be ordered logically.	• Check the order by jotting down each idea in a time line, a flow-chart, or an outline.
• My ideas don't flow smoothly from one sentence to another.	• Link the sentences, using transition words such as *now, later, then, next, finally, therefore,* and *however.*
• This idea or detail doesn't work well here.	• Move or delete details that aren't related to main idea.
• Another word might get my meaning across better.	• Use a dictionary or thesaurus to find alternative words that state more precisely what you want to say.

The passage below is from a writer's first draft. Notice the various revision strategies used to revise the draft.

Student
MODEL

Detail added

More accurate word

Moved sentence up to keep
related details together
Begin a new paragraph for
each new idea
Not related to the topic

Detail added

Loggerheads are the most common kind of sea turtle. They have thick, reddish brown shells and huge heads. *The shape of their head gives them their name.* They are ~~powerful~~ *good* swimmers and can travel more than forty miles a day. They live in tropical waters around the globe. Adults *can* weigh as much as 450 pounds. These ancient creatures are now in danger. ~~Green turtles are, too.~~ Each year many thousand*s of* loggerheads drown in shrimp nets. Others choke on plastic trash *floating in the sea.* Their nesting sites on beaches have been destroyed by homes and hotels. Loggerheads are now a threatened species.

Practice Your Skills

A. Revise the passage below, making any changes in ideas or form you think are needed. Delete unrelated ideas or details.

Dolphins use sound in special ways. Bats do too. Dolphins have a special organ, called the melon, on their forehead. The fatty tissue in the melon lets dolphins focus sound waves into narrow beams. These sound waves are powerful enough to stun fish. The sound waves are also used to communicate. Dolphins are very intelligent in captivity. People are only now discovering how complex and varied dolphin "speech" is. Dolphins use squeaks and whistling noises to talk to one another. Some whistles are "names." Other whistles warn of danger and identify sources of food. The whistles let one dolphin tell other dolphins who it is and where it is. Many experiments are underway to learn more about it.

B. Select a piece of your writing you wish to review again or a piece of writing you are currently developing. Revise it for ideas and for form, using the charts to help you. Then discuss your revisions with one or more classmates. Explain why you made each change.

C. Revise the passage below. Make any changes in ideas or form you think are needed. Delete unrelated ideas or details.

Even today we have much to fear from the great power of natural forces. We don't have the knowledge yet to predict with total accuracy when volcanoes will go off. We have no control at all over the shifting of the giant plates of rock forming the crust of the earth. We also can't predict when earthquakes will occur. Our knowledge of weather is just as limited. On radar we can see a hurricane forming. We can't tell accurately if or where it will hit land until just before it does. Have you ever seen a hurricane? It's really something. We cannot prevent droughts or control the causes of major floods. We can make artificial snow, though. Scientists are hard at work trying to understand all these forces. Maybe within our lifetime they will find the answers.

A satellite view of Hurricane Andrew as it passed over the Bahamas on its way to Florida on August 23, 1992.

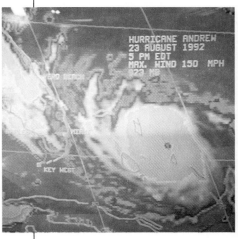

How Can I Polish My Writing?

Proofreading

Before a space shuttle takes off from its launch pad at Cape Canaveral, technicians at mission control always perform a last-minute check of the shuttle's vital systems. The ship's computers must be operating correctly, fuel pressure must be at the right level, electrical systems must check out. The shuttle doesn't fly until all the status lights at mission control are green.

Before you present your writing to a public audience, you, too, should perform a last-minute check. You'll want to look for and correct run-on sentences, incorrect verb tenses, and errors in capitalization, punctuation, spelling, and pronoun usage. Don't let your writing "fly" until everything checks out properly.

STRATEGIES FOR PROOFREADING

The following proofreading strategies will help you to search for and correct errors in your writing:

Proofread more than once.   Don't try to catch every possible error in just one proofreading session. Proofread your writing several times, perhaps looking for different kinds of mistakes each time. Put aside your writing between proofreadings. When you go back to it, you may see errors you didn't notice before.

Proofread for complete sentences and end punctuation. Look over your sentences. Is each one actually a sentence? Does it have a subject and a verb? Does it express just one complete thought? When you're satisfied that you've eliminated any fragments or run-ons, check your end punctuation. First decide whether each sentence makes a statement, asks a question, or expresses a strong feeling. Then be sure you've used the correct end punctuation for each type of sentence.

Proofread for initial capitals.   Remember that every sentence should begin with a capital letter. Also, read carefully to identify proper names and be sure that they begin with capital letters.

Proofread for commas within sentences.   Notice where you pause naturally as you read your writing aloud. Such a pause may mean that a comma is needed.

Proofread for other punctuation.   Be sure that you correctly used punctuation marks in abbreviations, dates, and addresses. For quotation marks, parentheses, and other punctuation marks used in pairs, be sure that you used both opening and closing marks.

Proofread for confusing words.   Watch for such words as *your* and *you're, peace* and *piece,* and *accept* and *except* that are often misused and misspelled.

Proofread for spelling.   Check the spelling of each word by reading your writing backwards, one word at a time. When you think a word may be misspelled, circle it. Then use a dictionary to check the spelling of all the circled words.

Proofreading Checklist

Step 1: Check the forms of words.
- Did I use correct verb tenses?
- Did I use any adjectives where I should have used adverbs?
- Did I use *-er/-est* and *more/most* correctly in comparisons?
- Did I use all forms of *be* and other irregular verbs correctly?
- Did I use the correct forms of pronouns?

Step 2: Check sentence structure and agreement.
- Are there any run-on sentences or sentence fragments?
- Do all verbs agree with their subjects?
- Do all pronouns agree with their antecedents?
- Did I keep all verb tenses consistent?

Step 3: Check capitalization, punctuation, and spelling.
- Did I use the correct form for every plural noun?
- Did I capitalize the first word of each sentence?
- Did I capitalize all proper nouns and proper adjectives?
- Is any punctuation mark missing or not needed?
- Did I spell all words, including possessive forms, correctly?

Use these proofreading symbols to mark the changes you want to make in your draft.

Proofreading Symbols

∧ Add letters or words.
⊙ Add a period.
≡ Capitalize a letter.
‿ Close up space.
⌄ Add a comma.

╱ Make a capital letter lowercase.
⌱ Begin a new paragraph.
∿ Switch the positions of letters or words.
— or ℘ Take out letters or words.

Notice how the symbols are used in the following passage.

> Beetles were eating Australia's cane sugar. So
> australians imported cane toads to eat the
> Beetles⊙ since the beeteles fly and the toad
> don't, the plan has worked not well. Now the
> people do'nt know how to get rid of the toads.

Possibly the world's largest cane toad, weighing in at almost four pounds, this specimen was found by Myrt and John Deambrogio in northeastern Australia.

Practice Your Skills

Proofread the passage below for mistakes in grammar, capitalization, punctuation, and spelling. Rewrite the passage correctly.

The Call of the Wild is more than a book about a dog it's a book about survival. The hero is a dog name Buck. Buck is stole from his home in california and taken to the Arctic. The land is hostile. In the winter, the temperture can reach sixty-six degrees below zero. The dogs that pull the dog sled are hostile. They fight like wolfs. Any dog that falls in a fight is kill by the pack. The dog trainers is hostile. They use clubs to make the dogs' obey. the dogs that dont are killed. Buck survives cuz he is smart. He can adapt, and other dogs can't. Bucks primitive instincts take over.

How Can I Publish My Writing?

Sharing and Publishing

When you perform in a talent show, run in a race, or compete in a band contest, you are sharing your achievements by letting others see your accomplishments. But how do you share a poem or a story that you have written? You announce its completion. You publish it!

WAYS TO SHARE AND PUBLISH YOUR WRITING

When possible, share and publish your writing in a creative way. Here are a few suggestions.

Creative Publishing Ideas

- Present writing that is related to a special day or event over the school's public address system or at a school assembly.

- Include the finished product in a collection of your other writings. Add a cover, an acknowledgment page, and a table of contents. Then display the book in your classroom or elsewhere in the school.

- Work with friends and classmates to dramatize one of your scripts or to perform a song for other classes, for parents, or for interested community groups.

- Submit your writing to the school or community newspaper, to magazines that publish student writing, or to organizations that sponsor writing contests.

- Tape-record your writing, and illustrate the writing with transparencies. Then use an overhead projector to show the illustrations to the class as you play the tape.

- Read one of your short stories aloud to a class of younger students. Ask the students to illustrate parts of the story on a roll of paper. Display the finished product on a wall.

Sketch Book

- What style of music is your favorite? Tell why you like it.
- If the singer on this page met the singer on the next page, what would they talk about? Write the dialogue of their conversation. Try to use words that show the personalities of both musicians.
- What can you tell about people by the way they dress?

Style

WRITING
HANDBOOKS

When a classical singer like Kathleen Battle learns a new piece, she starts with the written notes. She soon adds her own interpretation, however. Her personal style comes through.

You, too, have your own personal style. The way you talk, the way you dress, the way you act, and the way you think are all your own. So is the way you write. In these handbooks you will learn ways you can make your unique qualities come through in your writing.

How Can I Create Strong Sentences?

Correcting Sentence Errors

What an experience! There were auditions. For a whole week. The best part was performing. Because we all wore costumes.

Talking with a friend about drama club, you would probably have no trouble understanding these words. Reading these words, however, might leave you confused about where thoughts begin and end. This handbook will help you identify and revise problem sentences so that you can communicate clearly and concisely.

REVISING SENTENCE FRAGMENTS AND RUN-ONS

Sentence fragments and run-ons interfere with a reader's understanding. A fragment leaves out a major part of a sentence. A run-on contains two or more sentences that should be separate.

Correcting Sentence Fragments

Do some of your sentences leave a reader asking *whom* or *what* the sentence is about or *what happened?* A **sentence fragment** does not express a complete thought. The subject, the verb, or sometimes both are missing. Often you can change a fragment into a complete thought by supplying the missing part.

Fragment	For almost a week *(What happened?)*
Sentence	For almost a week we rehearsed.

Other times you can join the fragment to an existing sentence.

Sentence	The best part was performing.
Fragment	Because we all wore costumes
Revised	The best part was performing because we all wore costumes.

Rewriting Run-on Sentences

Watch for sentences that do not clearly show where one idea ends and the next one begins. A **run-on sentence** consists of two or more sentences written incorrectly as one. Run-ons may occur because the writer either used no end mark or used a comma instead of a period to end the first complete thought. One way to revise a run-on is to use the proper end mark after the first sentence and to capitalize the first letter of the next sentence.

Run-on	Scottie raced up the court his defender closed in.
Revised	Scottie raced up the court. His defender closed in.

Run-on	The referee watched closely, Scottie took his time.
Revised	The referee watched closely. Scottie took his time.

If the ideas are closely related, you may revise the run-on by joining the ideas with a semicolon.

Run-on	Scottie faked a shot, his defender wasn't fooled.
Revised	Scottie faked a shot; his defender wasn't fooled.

Grammar
TIP

Remember that a comma is not strong enough to join two complete thoughts.

Practice Your Skills

A. Correct each sentence fragment in the following passage.

What's your hobby? Some people enjoy doing ceramics. Because it relaxes them. They enjoy watching the clay take shape. As their hands and fingers move. Other people are collectors. They collect things such as stamps. Baseball cards. Or comic books. Some people race remote-control cars. And airplanes. Whatever your hobby is. Invite a friend to join you.

B. Improve the following paragraphs. Revise each run-on sentence.

Why not visit a county fair this summer? County fairs are exciting city people in particular enjoy these festivals.

Teenagers show their farm animals in the livestock contest, everyone is nervous. Judges inspect each animal they award blue ribbons to the best.

Other activities are entertaining too. You're assured of some fun at the pig race, you can cheer your favorite logger in the lumberjack contest, don't miss out on the fun!

REVISING STRINGY SENTENCES

Do your sentences go on and on? A **stringy sentence** loosely connects two or more ideas with the word *and*.

Stringy   The temperature fell below zero, and a water main under the street burst, and soon we had our own skating rink, and then a work crew turned the water off.

A reader may have difficulty sorting out the ideas and seeing the relationship between them. To revise the sentence begin by separating each of the ideas.

Separate ideas   The temperature fell below zero.
A water main under the street burst.
Soon we had our own skating rink.
Then a work crew turned the water off.

Think about how ideas are related and combine them with words such as *because, when, after, before, if, then, next, later, soon, although, as,* and *until.* To clearly show the relationships, you can also rearrange and reword the other ideas or leave them separate.

Revised   A water main under the street burst when the temperature fell below zero. Soon we had our own skating rink. Then a work crew turned the water off.

Practice Your Skills

Separate the ideas in each stringy sentence. Then recombine the closely related ideas and rearrange and reword as necessary.

1. Greg's front tire has hit a bump, and he has lost control, and the bike is swerving into the railing, and Greg's chance to win the Tour de France is gone now.
2. The woman searched nervously for the ticket, and the conductor looked angry, and she dumped out the entire contents of her purse, and she found the crumpled stub.
3. Ada began to make the batter, and she went to get the eggs, and she found she was one short, and she would have to go to the store.

4. The wind was blowing, and many garbage cans toppled over, and soon the whole block became covered with debris.

5. The doorbell rang, and I answered it, and a person in a delivery service uniform handed me a mysterious package.

REVISING EMPTY SENTENCES

Check that each of your sentences really contributes to the ideas you are expressing. An **empty sentence** either repeats an idea or makes a claim without giving enough supporting details.

Eliminating Repeated Ideas

If the words in different parts of a sentence or in several sentences have the same meaning, delete the repeated idea.

Repetitive   Are you a procrastinator, and do you put things off until tomorrow? (A procrastinator is a person who puts things off. Delete the second clause.)

Revised   Are you a procrastinator?

Sometimes you can combine sentences so that an idea is not repeated.

Repetitive   The canoe trip began at the river's source and ended at the mouth. The canoeists paddled the whole river. Then they continued into Lake Erie. (You can delete the second sentence and combine the first and third sentences.)

Revised   The canoe trip began at the river's source and continued to the river's mouth and into Lake Erie.

Adding Supporting Details

Watch for sentences that leave a reader asking *why?* Always support a claim with reasons, facts, or examples.

Unsupported   Musicals are the best shows to see. (The sentence does not explain why they are the best.)

Revised   Musicals are the best shows to see because the lyrics tell a story and the dances are fun to watch.

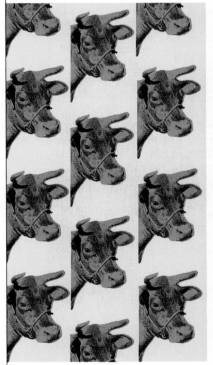

Cow Wallpaper (1966), Andy Warhol.

Correcting
Sentence Errors   **299**

Practice Your Skills

Revise the empty sentences below. Add details or delete repeated ideas as necessary. Write *Correct* if no revision is needed.

1. Many athletes have quick reflexes and they react fast.
2. Swimming is good for you.
3. Ten thousand people went to last night's concert in the park. The open-air concert was outdoors. Everyone had to leave when the downpour started.
4. I like baseball because you play it outdoors, you learn teamwork, you develop a number of athletic skills, and besides, you can pretend you're Hank Aaron.
5. The drama club is presenting the popular musical *The Wiz* in the school auditorium on Friday and Saturday evenings at eight o'clock.
6. Richard shared a secret with me. He told me something that he had never told anyone else before.

REVISING PADDED SENTENCES

Are all the words in your sentence important to the meaning of the sentence? A **padded sentence** contains unnecessary words that make it difficult for a reader to follow the ideas. You can strengthen your writing by taking out the padding. Sometimes you can remove the padding by deleting the extra words that merely repeat an idea. Other times you can take out the padding by simplifying or reducing groups of words to shorten phrases.

Deleting Extra Words

Some expressions contain extra words that you can remove.

Padded   Hank Aaron is famous on account of the fact that he hit 755 home runs during his career in major-league baseball. (The expression *on account of the fact that* contains words that don't add to the meaning of the sentence.)

Revised   Hank Aaron is famous because he hit 755 home runs during his career in major-league baseball.

Henry "Hank" Aaron at bat in 1963, as a player with the Milwaukee Braves (later the Atlanta Braves). Hank Aaron left his mark on baseball by breaking Babe Ruth's home-run record in 1974.

Ways to Remove Padding

Padded: because of the fact that   **Better:** because, since
in spite of the fact that   although
call your attention to the   remind you
      fact that
what I want is   I want
what I want to say is   (Just say it!)
what I mean is   (Just say it!)

To make your sentences clearer and less wordy, avoid the following padded expressions:

Expressions to Avoid

the point is	the reason is	being that
the thing is	it happens that	it would seem that

Reducing Groups of Words

Sentences that contain word groups beginning with *who is, which is,* or *that is* can be simplified by taking out those words.

Wordy   I left my hat on the bench, which is near the snack bar.
Revised   I left my hat on the bench near the snack bar.

Wordy   The person who is behind the counter is my dad.
Revised   The person behind the counter is my dad.

Practice Your Skills

Revise this passage by shortening the padded sentences.

> Because of the fact that there was little snow that winter, the water levels in the reservoirs were low. What the town faced was a hot and waterless summer. The reason that young people were upset was because the town pool, which was a source of odd jobs for teenagers, had to be closed. Furthermore, people who were in town could not water lawns or wash cars. Let me point out that no one wanted a summer like that one again.

How Can I Vary My Sentences?

Sentence Variety

A composer uses a variety of tones, rhythms, melodies, and harmonies to create a pleasing arrangement of sounds. Similarly, you can vary sentence type and length as well as the way you begin and end sentences to add interest and impact to your writing.

UNDERSTANDING KINDS OF SENTENCES

Sentences are the basic structures you use to express your thoughts. Here are some types of sentences you can use to add variety to your writing.

A **simple sentence** has only one subject and one predicate.

> The lead guitarist ran onstage.

A **compound sentence** contains two or more simple sentences combined with a conjunction or a semicolon.

> The lights flicked on, and the lead guitarist ran onstage.
> The lights flicked on; the lead guitarist ran onstage.

A **complex sentence** has one main clause and one or more subordinate clauses.

> Fans cheered when they saw their favorite guitarist.

(For more about compound and complex sentences, see Grammar Handbook 45, pages 556–561.)

Varying Length and Structure

Change the rhythm of your writing by occasionally varying the types of sentences as well as the length of sentences you use.

> Then it happened. The stage lights went out. The excited fans cheered continuously because they wanted an encore. The stage remained dark, however. The concert was over.

Carlos Santana, musician and songwriter.

Varying Sentence Beginnings

Make your writing more interesting by beginning each sentence differently. Try using some of these sentence openers.

Opener	Sentence
Adverb	*Suddenly,* the amplifier went dead.
Prepositional phrase	*Within minutes,* a stagehand found a blown fuse.
Verb form (*-ing*)	*Hurrying,* the stagehand searched for a new fuse.
	Replacing the fuse solved the problem.
Verb form (*to*)	*To start* the concert, the group played its best-known hit.
Adverb clause	*When the music started,* the audience cheered loudly.

Practice Your Skills

A. Revise the paragraph below to improve sentence variety:

1. Join sentences 2 and 3 to form a compound sentence using *but.*
2. Join sentences 4 and 5 to form a complex sentence beginning with *when.*
3. Vary the beginnings of sentences 1, 6, 7, 8, and 9 by moving the underlined parts. Use commas as necessary.

> [1]The microprocessor was developed <u>in 1971</u>. [2]The microprocessor is a tiny computer chip. [3]It has had a big effect on the computer industry. [4]Inventions such as video games appeared. [5]This happened when smaller computers became possible. [6]Video games became popular <u>quickly</u>.
> [7]Video games are fun <u>because they have realistic graphics and interesting sound effects</u>. [8]A player must have good coordination and good reflexes <u>to win</u>. [9]A player's greatest challenge, <u>however,</u> is concentrating.

B. Choose a piece of writing from your writing portfolio. Use some of the strategies you learned in this handbook to improve sentence variety and to clarify your ideas.

How Can I Craft Better Sentences?

Sentence Combining

A stained-glass window may consist of thousands of pieces of glass of varying sizes, shapes, and colors. An artist arranges the pieces of glass to form interesting designs and pictures.

Likewise, the sentences you write may contain a variety of different details. You can arrange the words and phrases in a sentence to show how ideas are related and to make your writing more interesting.

COMBINING SENTENCES AND SENTENCE PARTS

Short sentences can work well for expressing single ideas. Sometimes, however, you may want to show that there is a connection between two or more ideas. You can use a conjunction to join words, groups of words, or sentences that are related.

Combining Related Sentences

There are a variety of possible relationships between ideas. You can use either a coordinating conjunction or a subordinating conjunction to join ideas, depending on the kind of relationship you wish to show.

Using Coordinating Conjunctions   Two sentences of equal importance may contain similar ideas, contrasting ideas, or a choice between ideas. You may show the relationship between these complete thoughts by combining the sentences with a **coordinating conjunction,** such as *and, but,* or *or.*

Join sentences that are equally important and contain similar ideas with a comma and the word *and.*

Separate	The cover of this book is torn.
	Some of the pages are missing.
Combined	The cover of this book is torn, **and** some of the pages are missing.

Use a comma and *but* to join sentences that present differing but equally important thoughts on the same topic.

Separate   Few readers know the name Theodor S. Geisel.
             Many recognize this writer's pen name Dr. Seuss.

Combined   Few readers know the name Theodor S. Geisel, **but** many recognize this writer's pen name Dr. Seuss.

When sentences offer a choice between equally important thoughts, combine the sentences with a comma and the word *or*.

Separate   Is the library still open? Has it already closed?

Combined   Is the library still open, **or** has it already closed?

Using Subordinating Conjunctions   If the ideas in two sentences express relationships of time or cause, you can combine the sentences with a **subordinating conjunction,** such as *because, when, after, before, until, unless,* or *if.* A subordinating conjunction shows that the idea in the main sentence is more important than the idea that has been added. For more information on subordinating conjunctions, see Handbook 45, "Using Compound and Complex Sentences," pages 560–561.

Separate   Kim will enjoy this book.
             She likes mysteries.

Combined   Kim will enjoy this book **because** she likes mysteries.

When you begin a sentence with a subordinating conjunction, place a comma between the ideas.

Separate   Ian mended the book.
             He put it on the shelf.

Combined   **After** Ian mended the book, he put it on the shelf.

Combining Sentence Parts

Just as you can use *and, but,* or *or* to join complete sentences, you can use one of these conjunctions to join parts of two sentences that contain related ideas. However, do *not* place a comma before a coordinating conjunction that joins sentence parts. Delete repeated words or ideas. Study the examples shown on the next page.

Look for opportunities to combine sentences with subordinating conjunctions when you write about relationships such as cause and effect.

Separate	Photographers consider lighting.
	They plan composition.
Combined	Photographers consider lighting **and** composition.
Separate	The photo is very small. *It is* remarkably clear.
Combined	The photo is very small **but** remarkably clear.
Separate	Is this lens for all kinds of pictures?
	Is this lens for only close-ups?
Combined	Is this lens for all kinds of pictures **or** only close-ups?

Practice Your Skills

A. Use the word in parentheses to combine each pair of sentences. Drop repeated words and ideas. Add commas where necessary.

1. In the past people could eat produce only in season. Now many fruits and vegetables are available year-round. (*but*)
2. Airplanes deliver ripe raspberries in winter. They deliver fresh bananas every month of the year. (*and*)
3. It's winter in the United States. It's summer in Australia. (*when*)
4. The United States imports produce during the winter. The United States exports produce during the summer. (*and*)
5. Out-of-season produce is expensive. Delivery costs are so high. (*because*)
6. Do you prefer the way it was in the past? Do you prefer the way it is now? (*or*)

B. Combine each pair of sentences with *and, but, or, because,* or *after.* Delete repeated words and add commas where necessary.

[1]The steam whistle sounds. The paddle wheel stops. [2]Passengers quickly step off the steamboat. It is tied to the pier. [3]They can't wait to see Mark Twain's boyhood home in Hannibal, Missouri. They can't wait to see the surrounding countryside. [4]Will the visitors join the fence-whitewashing contest? Will they tour the dark passages of the cave? [5]The tomboy contest would be interesting. The frog-jumping contest might be more fun to watch. [6]Most visitors find these attractions especially interesting. They have read *Huckleberry Finn* or *Tom Sawyer.*

ADDING WORDS AND
WORD GROUPS

Using conjunctions is one way to join related ideas. You can also combine sentences by moving details from one sentence to another. The newly formed sentence is often a tighter, more effective way of expressing the ideas.

Adding Single Words

Sometimes details in one sentence can contribute important information to another sentence. When the idea you want to add to the main sentence is only a single word from another sentence, move that key word to the main sentence and delete the remainder of the related sentence.

Separate This aquarium contains many colorful fish.
The fish are tropical.

Combined This aquarium contains many colorful **tropical** fish.

Separate Special filters and a heater are necessary to maintain the correct environment.
These special filters are charcoal. *The heater is* electric.

Combined Special **charcoal** filters and an **electric** heater are necessary to maintain the correct environment.

Sometimes you must add either a comma or the word *and* when you move an important detail into the main sentence.

Separate The Smithsonian has a zoo. *It is a* small *zoo.*
It is an unusual *zoo. It is an* insect *zoo.*

Combined The Smithsonian has a **small, unusual insect** zoo.

Separate One cockroach sits in a display. *The display was* carefully prepared. *The display is* elaborate.

Combined One cockroach sits in a **carefully prepared and elaborate** display.

Wood sculptor Patrick Bremer relaxes with one of his creations, a six-foot-tall praying mantis. More insect sculptures greet visitors at the Smithsonian Institution's Insect Zoo, part of the Museum of Natural History.

Sentence Combining **307**

Adding Words That Change Form

Sometimes you must change the form of an important word before you add it to a main sentence.

Adding -y or -ly   What word change was made in this example?

Separate	Our guide led us along the trail.
	The trail had rocks.
Combined	Our guide led us along the **rocky** trail.

Words that end in *-ly* often fit in more than one place in the main sentence.

Separate	We followed the guide. *We were* cautious.
Combined	**Cautiously,** we followed the guide.
	We **cautiously** followed the guide.
	We followed the guide **cautiously.**

Separate	We trudged up the mountain.
	We were slow. *We were* quiet.
Combined	**Slowly and quietly,** we trudged up the mountain.
	We **slowly and quietly** trudged up the mountain.
	We trudged up the mountain **slowly and quietly.**

Adding -ed or -ing   Notice the changes in these examples.

Separate	Our guide showed us a trail on the map.
	The map had many details.
Combined	Our guide showed us a trail on the **detailed** map.

Separate	We inched closer to the mountaintop.
	The mountaintop glistened.
Combined	We inched closer to the **glistening** mountaintop.

Adding Groups of Words

You can also combine sentences by moving groups of words.

Separate	Many people enjoy hot-air ballooning.
	The people fly balloons over the countryside.
Combined	Many people enjoy hot-air ballooning **over the countryside.**

Separate	Balloonists meet at huge rallies. *They hold the rallies* to compete with one another.
Combined	Balloonists meet at huge rallies **to compete with one another.**

Before adding a group of words to a main sentence, you may need to change the ending of one word in the group.

Separate	A propane burner heats the air in the bag. *The burner* rests inside the basket of the balloon.
Combined	A propane burner **resting inside the basket of the balloon** heats the air in the bag.

Practice Your Skills

A. Combine the following sentences, deleting unnecessary words. You may need to change the forms of some words.

1. The teen club sponsored a trip to a local park. The trip was by bus. The trip was to an amusement park.
2. The club had rented a school bus. The bus was ancient. It was rickety.
3. We got off the bus. We were glad. The bus was uncomfortable.
4. We waited in a line at the Ferris wheel. We were patient. The line was long.
5. We watched the people riding the roller coaster. The people screamed. We were fearful.

B. Combine each group of sentences.

[1]The National Weather Service issued a warning. The warning was about a storm. [2]Rains had struck the towns. The rains were torrential. The towns were along the coast. [3]Now the storm was turning. Its turn was sudden. It was turning inland. [4]Winds and hail accompanied the rains. The winds raged. The hail pelted. [5]Many travelers were stranded. This happened when the airport closed. The closing was temporary. [6]The National Weather Service urged people to take precautions. The people live near the path of the storm. The service also urged people to evacuate the area.

You become a good writer just as you become a good joiner [carpenter]—by planing down your sentences.

Anatole France, novelist and critic

COMBINING WITH *WHO, THAT,* OR *WHICH*

Perhaps you have written two sentences that provide details about the same person, place, or thing. You can avoid repetition by combining such related sentences with *who, that,* or *which* or by using an appositive.

Using *Who*

When two sentences give details about a person, you can combine the sentences by using the word *who* to replace *he, she, they,* or another word that names the person.

Separate	Runners seldom get muscle injuries. *They* stretch regularly.
Combined	Runners **who stretch regularly** seldom get muscle injuries.

Notice in the combined sentence above that the added detail "who stretch regularly" is necessary for you to understand which runners are seldom injured. When an added detail is essential to the meaning of the sentence, do not set off the added words with commas.

Separate	Laurence Yep has published many books. Laurence Yep wrote *Dragonwings.*
Combined	Laurence Yep, **who wrote *Dragonwings,*** has published many books.

In the combined sentence above, the added detail "who wrote *Dragonwings*" is not needed in order to understand the main idea of the sentence. The added words provide extra information about Laurence Yep, so they are set off with commas.

Using *That* or *Which*

If the common element in related sentences is a place or a thing, use *that* or *which* to combine the sentences. The word *that* or *which* replaces the words that name the place or thing.

Use *that* when the added detail is an essential element that identifies or explains an idea in a main sentence. Do not set off such essential elements with commas.

Separate   Workers in a field uncovered a steamboat. *The steamboat* had sunk in the Missouri River in 1856.

Combined   Workers in a field uncovered a steamboat **that had sunk in the Missouri River in 1856.**

Use *which* when the added detail is a nonessential element that merely provides extra information about an idea in a main sentence. Use commas to set off nonessential elements.

Separate   Poodles were once used as hunters and retrievers. *Poodles* now make smart and friendly house dogs.

Combined   Poodles**, which now make smart and friendly house dogs,** were once used as hunters and retrievers.

Using Appositives

Sometimes you can combine closely related sentences by using an appositive instead of the word *who, that,* or *which*. An **appositive** is a noun or phrase that explains one or more words in a sentence. Do not set off an appositive with commas if it adds an essential detail to the main idea of the sentence. Do use commas if the appositive adds extra information to the main idea.

Separate   Spike Lee has made many films about social issues. *He* is an African-American director.

Appositive without Commas   The African-American director **Spike Lee** has made many films about social issues.

Appositive with Commas   Spike Lee**, an African-American director,** has made many films about social issues.

In the first combined sentence on the previous page, the director's name is essential for understanding which director has made films about social issues, so the name is not set off with commas. In the second combined sentence, the added detail is extra information about Spike Lee. It is set off with commas.

Practice Your Skills

A. Use *who, which,* or *that* to combine each pair of sentences. Add commas if needed. Delete any unnecessary words.

1. The pier on Main Street draws a variety of visitors. The pier extends nearly a block into the ocean.
2. Some people fish mostly for enjoyment. These people spend a relaxing afternoon dangling a hook and line in the water.
3. Other hardy men and women work long hours for low pay at the pier. These people fish for a living.
4. Tourists wave to the departing fishing boats. These tourists stroll to the waterfront before dawn.
5. Anglers catch many kinds of fish. The fish swim close to shore.
6. The local waters provide plenty of food for fish. These waters are full of plankton.
7. Small fish often consume plankton. Plankton is microscopic plant and animal life.
8. These small fish become food for the larger fish. The larger fish lurk nearby.

B. Use appositives to combine the following pairs of sentences. Add commas where they are needed.

1. A popular form of recreation involves going underwater while breathing with the aid of air tanks. The form of recreation is scuba diving.
2. Navy divers are called frogmen because of one distinctive piece of equipment. That piece of equipment is their swim fins.
3. One of the devices used by novice divers allows them to breathe underwater. The device is a snorkel.
4. An important part of the aqualung lets scuba divers control the flow of air from their air tanks. It is the regulator.

5. A potentially fatal condition faced by divers is caused by rising too quickly to the surface. The condition is the bends.

C. Combine the following sentences. Delete the words in italics and follow the directions that are given in parentheses.

1. Behind the library is a pond. *It* is great for skating during the winter. (Use *that.*)
2. Sometimes skaters must watch for thin ice. *These skaters* go out on the pond early in the season. (Use *who.*)
3. The sheriff's office sends a patrol car past the pond. *The office* is several blocks away. (Use commas and *which.*)
4. One watchful deputy has rescued several skaters. *His name is* Jefferson Douglass. (Use an appositive.)
5. In midwinter the pond is covered by a layer of ice. *The ice* is often eight or more inches thick. (Use *that.*)
6. Several teenagers shovel snow from the ice. *These teenagers* also work as lifeguards in the summer. (Use commas and *who.*)
7. Ye Old Woodworks donated two wooden sleds to the town. *Ye Old Woodworks is* a well-known local carpentry shop. (Use an appositive.)

D. Revise the following passage, using what you know about combining sentences. Some sentences can remain the same.

¹People often need patience. ²These people are learning a new sport. ³Not everyone has the physical strength of a natural athlete. ⁴Not everyone has the ability of a natural athlete. ⁵A natural athlete masters any sport. ⁶A natural athlete does it easily. ⁷Soccer may take years to master. ⁸Soccer requires precise footwork. ⁹Tennis is another difficult sport to learn. ¹⁰Tennis requires speed and stamina. ¹¹Bowlers must have good eye-hand coordination. ¹²These athletes try to knock over ten wooden pins. ¹³The pins are at the end of a wooden lane. ¹⁴In all sports, practice and persistence are important factors. ¹⁵These factors lead to improved skills and winning scores.

HANDBOOK

25

What's the Best Word for Me to Use?

Meaning and Word Choice

Does a character in your story like to *talk,* or is *gossip* a better word? What about *chat* or *blab?* How can you decide which word to use? How you choose words depends on your purpose for writing and on your audience.

DENOTATION AND CONNOTATION

Words have two types of meanings. A **denotation** is a dictionary definition of a word. A **connotation** is a feeling or thought that a word suggests.

Two words may have similar denotations but very different connotations. Here are some examples.

| **Positive Connotation** | slender | curious | thrifty |
| **Negative Connotation** | skinny | nosy | stingy |

AUDIENCE

When you choose words, consider your **audience**—your readers or listeners. Ask yourself questions like the following:

- Who is my audience?
- What are their ages and backgrounds?
- What do they already know about the subject?
- What do they need to know?

These questions help you focus on your audience. For example, to a friend you might describe a computer game as *awesome.* However, you might describe the same game to your grandmother as *exciting.* (For more information about audience, see Writing Handbooks 4 and 5.)

Fat or *plump?*

314   Writing Handbook

FORMAL AND INFORMAL ENGLISH

Choose words that are suited to the occasion, or situation. If you were writing a letter to a friend about litter around your school, you would use words from everyday speech and possibly some slang to express your feelings. However, if you were writing to the school board about the same problem, you would choose words that made your letter sound more dignified.

Standard English includes both formal and informal English. Business letters, legal documents, and technical articles are written in formal English. **Formal English** has a serious tone, longer sentences, and sometimes includes technical vocabulary. Friendly letters, advertisements, and magazine and newspaper articles are written in informal English. **Informal English** has a casual tone, shorter sentences, and simpler vocabulary than formal English. Slang is sometimes a part of informal English. **Slang** consists of popular, faddish words and phrases spoken by members of a particular group. Note these examples of different language styles.

Formal	Exposure to rock music at high decibel levels can cause auditory damage.
Informal	Listening to loud rock music can hurt your hearing.
Slang	Blasting hip-hop from a boom box can kill your ears.

Practice Your Skills

A. Rewrite this formal invitation to make it informal.

The graduating class of Kennedy Middle School cordially invites you to attend commencement exercises on the evening of June 14, 19— at seven o'clock. The Honorable Jorge Ruiz, mayor of Springfield, will deliver a congratulatory address to the students. Principal Cynthia Davis will distribute the diplomas. In celebration of the graduates, a reception will be held in the school's gymnasium immediately following the ceremony.

B. Find an advertisement in a magazine. List the words that are used to make the product seem appealing. For each word, list another with a similar denotation but a different connotation.

Writing
TIP

A thesaurus can help you find the right word to say exactly what you mean. Be sure to choose words carefully, however. Remember that the synonyms listed in a thesaurus can have very different connotations.

COMPUTER
TIP

Some word processing programs have built-in thesauruses that you can use to find the right word for your purpose, audience, and occasion.

WRITING
H A N D B O O K
26

How Can I Make My Writing Sound Like Me?

Developing a Personal Voice

Your writing has a distinctive sound, or voice. Of course, an entry you write in your journal will read very differently than a geography report on tropical rain forests. However, if you are expressing what you really think or know in words that come naturally to you, your personal voice will come through.

KEEP IT NATURAL

Young writers often don't trust their natural voices. They think they have to use complex words and long, complicated sentences to make their writing seem impressive. One student began the first draft of an article for the school newspaper this way.

> I'd like to raise a strenuous objection to the presentation of commercials before feature films. This obnoxious trend is an affront to the movie viewer who has paid to see a film, not to be subjected to a barrage of advertising.

In reading her draft aloud, she realized that the vocabulary was probably too difficult for most of her audience to understand. More importantly, it didn't sound like her at all. She decided to revise her draft to make it more informal.

Student
MODEL

> When I went to see *Star Trek VI* recently, I got more than I bargained for. As the lights dimmed, instead of the *Starship Enterprise,* a commercial for a candy bar appeared on the screen. I felt used. I go to the movies to see a feature film, not commercials. Yet I'm part of a captive audience and can't fast-forward through these ads. I believe that theater operators are taking unfair advantage of moviegoers by showing commercials before films.

BE TRUE TO YOURSELF

Another way to develop a personal voice is to write about the things you feel, think, and believe—not what you think others want to hear. Does this letter really sound like a student's opinion?

> A recent study showed that U.S. students spend too much time watching television and not enough time reading and doing homework. As a result, their scores on reading tests continue to decline. Parents must put strict limits on the amount of time their children spend watching television.

When the student revised this draft to express her real feelings, her writing became more authentic and thus more powerful.

Student
MODEL

> Many people blame television for students' low reading test scores. Kids may spend more time watching television than they do reading or doing their homework. However, there are other problems—schools are often overcrowded and funds for education have been cut back. If kids today are having trouble reading, it's not just television's fault.

How to Develop Your Writing Voice

- WRITE in your journal regularly.
- FREEWRITE before you begin drafting.
- TALK out your ideas before writing them down.
- READ your work aloud.

Practice Your Skills

Rewrite the following paragraph using your personal voice.

> It is absolutely essential for each individual person to develop his or her unique potential. A person must never allow himself or herself to be limited by other people's expectations of what he or she is capable of achieving in his or her life. An individual's future is in his or her own hands.

How Can I Make My Language Richer?

Using Poetic Devices

> My first bike got me nowhere, though the shadow I cast as I pedaled raced along my side. The leaves of bird-filled trees stirred a warm breeze and litter scuttled out of the way. Our orange cats looked on from the fence, their tails up like antennas. I opened my mouth, and wind tickled the back of my throat. When I squinted, I could see past the end of the block. My hair flicked like black fire, and I thought I was pretty cool riding up and down the block, age five, in my brother's hand-me-down shirt.
>
> **Gary Soto, *A Summer Life***

What images came to mind as you read Gary Soto's paragraph? Did you see the cats' tails sticking up like antennas? Could you feel the wind tickling the back of your throat? Perhaps you imagined the boy's black hair flicking like flames in the wind.

Figurative language enables you to show one thing by comparing it to something else. When you use figurative language, you present your readers with vivid pictures they can see and with sensations they can feel. You make your poems, song lyrics, short stories, and other pieces of writing come to life.

TYPES OF FIGURATIVE LANGUAGE

Some types of figurative language help your readers to compare persons or things that are basically different. Three common figurative devices are **similes, metaphors,** and **personification.**

Simile

What might a baseball mitt and a mousetrap have in common? A **simile** uses the word *like* or *as* to compare two different persons or things. Notice how Annie Dillard's simile on the next page compares the feeling of catching a baseball in a mitt to snaring a mouse in a trap.

> On the catch—the grounder, the fly, the line drive—you could snag a baseball in your mitt, where it stayed, snap, like a mouse locked in its trap.
>
> **Annie Dillard, *An American Childhood***

When Dillard wrote this simile, she first identified what she wanted to describe: catching a baseball. Then she zeroed in on a specific feeling she wanted to highlight: the sensation of catching a baseball in a mitt. She thought of something else to compare that sensation to: the snapping of a trap as it snares a mouse. Dillard used *like* to compare the first thing to the second. Follow the same pattern to write your own similes.

Metaphor

When you compare one thing to another without using the word *like* or *as,* you are writing a **metaphor.** What is the airplane compared to in the metaphor that follows?

> The plane is your planet and you are its sole inhabitant.
>
> **Beryl Markham, *West with the Night***

Markham needed a metaphor that described the lonely feeling she experienced when she flew solo. Then she thought of something that might create that same feeling: being the only person on a planet. Finally, she compared the plane to a planet and the passenger in the plane to the only person on a planet. The reader must think about how it might feel to be the only person on a planet in order to understand the loneliness Markham felt when she flew.

Personification

When you give human qualities to nonhuman things, such as plants, animals, places, and objects, you are using **personification.** Gary Soto used personification when he wrote that "wind tickled the back of my throat." In the example on the next page, what human qualities does F. Scott Fitzgerald give to the moon?

> [Dexter] . . . watched the even overlap of the waters in the little wind. . . . Then the moon held a finger to her lips and the lake became a clear pool, pale and quiet.
>
> **F. Scott Fitzgerald, *Winter Dreams***

To use personification, identify which human quality you want to give to a nonhuman subject. Then let your subject take on that quality, as Fitzgerald did when he wrote that "the moon held a finger to her lips."

Avoiding Clichés

When you write, try to create original expressions instead of using clichés. **Clichés** are expressions, such as *time is money* and *sly as a fox,* that are not effective because they have been overused.

cliché	spread like wildfire
alternative	spread quicker than a rumor in a small town

Cool as a cucumber

SOUND DEVICES

In addition to figurative language, you can use sound devices to create images. Devices such as **onomatopoeia, alliteration,** and **assonance** create pleasing patterns of sound in your writing.

Onomatopoeia

Do you think of the actual sounds when you hear the words *screech, fizz, clang,* and *murmur?* Words such as these are examples of **onomatopoeia.**

Literary
MODEL

> The sounds were coming from just across the river, to the north, and they were a weird medley of *whines, whimpers,* and small *howls.*
>
> **Farley Mowat, *Never Cry Wolf***

Alliteration

In **alliteration** the words you use repeat a beginning consonant sound to create a mood in your writing.

> *D*rum on your *d*rums, *b*atter on your *b*anjoes,
> *s*ob on the long cool winding *s*axophones.
> **Carl Sandburg, "Jazz Fantasia"**

Assonance

Another sound device, **assonance,** uses the repetition of vowel sounds to give special emphasis to words.

> Asl*ee*p h*e* wh*ee*zes at his *e*ase.
> H*e* only wakes to scratch his fl*ea*s.
> **Ted Hughes, "Roger the Dog"**

Practice Your Skills

A. Rewrite the sentences below, following the directions given.

1. His hair stood up straight and stiff. (Use a simile.)
2. The house had been recently painted. (Use personification.)
3. Her hands moved quickly across the piano keys. (Use a metaphor.)
4. The basketball dropped through the net. (Use onomatopoeia.)
5. The noisy river flowed through the canyon. (Use alliteration or assonance.)

B. Replace the underlined clichés in the paragraph below with more original language.

> ¹The howling of the wind was <u>clear as a bell</u>. ²My room grew <u>dark as night</u>. ³No one had to <u>hit me over the head</u> to make me understand. ⁴I ran <u>quick as a wink</u> to shut my window. ⁵Outside I saw my bike being <u>bounced around like a basketball</u>.

Who Will Narrate My Story?

Point of View

Is the human a zoo visitor or the lion's next meal? That depends on the point of view.

THREE POINTS OF VIEW

In narrative writing, **point of view** refers to who is telling the story. There are three basic points of view: first person, third person, and second person. The point of view you choose depends on whom you want to tell your story.

A story narrated by someone who takes part in the action is written from the **first-person point of view.** This point of view reveals the feelings and thoughts of the narrator and uses such first-person pronouns as *I, me, my, we,* and *our.* Letters, journals, opinion essays, and autobiographies are written from the first-person point of view.

Literary
MODEL

> I could feel the game. I could feel everything that was going on. It was as if every player had a string on him and the strings were all tied to me. Anytime anybody moved, I could feel it. I saw everything and knew what everybody was doing. We started coming back. The ball felt good in my hands.
> **Walter Dean Myers, *Hoops***

A story told by someone who observes and describes the action, but doesn't take part in it, is told from the **third-person point of view.** A third-person narrator will use such third-person pronouns as *he, she, him, her, they,* and *them.* This point of view is used in many types of writing, but it is especially helpful when the writer wants the narrator to be an objective observer of the action.

> The stars were coming out behind him in a pale sky barred with black when the hobbit crept through the enchanted door and stole into the Mountain. It was far easier going than he expected. This was no goblin entrance, or rough Wood-elves' cave.   **J.R.R. Tolkien, *The Hobbit***

Literary
MODEL

The **second-person point of view,** indicated by the pronoun *you,* is used when the writer wants to address the reader directly. This point of view is most often found in instructions, explanations, advice, or directions.

Practice Your Skills

A. The paragraph below is written from the first-person point of view. Rewrite it as a third-person narrative.

> I went on lathering his face. My hands began to tremble again. The man could not be aware of this, which was lucky for me. But I wished he had not come in. Probably many of our men had seen him enter the shop. And with the enemy in my house I felt a certain responsibility.
>
> I would have to shave his beard just like any other, carefully, neatly, just as though he were a good customer, taking heed that not a single pore should emit a drop of blood. Seeing to it that the blade did not slip in the small whorls. Taking care that the skin was left clean, soft, shining, so that when I passed the back of my hand over it not a single hair should be felt.   **Hernando Téllez, *Lather and Nothing Else***

B. Write a paragraph based on one of the topics below, using the first-person point of view. Then write a second paragraph on a different topic using the third-person point of view. In what ways are the paragraphs different?

a childhood memory   an embarrassing moment
an argument   a frightening experience

How Do I Create Dialogue?

Writing Dialogue

"What is the use of a book," thought Alice, *"without pictures or conversations?"*

Lewis Carroll, *Alice in Wonderland*

Of course, Alice is exaggerating. Not every piece of writing has—or needs—pictures and conversations. However, these elements *can* make your writing interesting and exciting to read. In fact, you can use conversation, or **dialogue,** in any kind of writing. Letting people speak for themselves can launch your writing right off the page and into readers' memories.

FICTION AND NONFICTION

In fiction and nonfiction, dialogue can provide important information about the characters, the action, and the setting—the who, what, and where—of your topic.

Characters

In your writing, you can let people reveal who they are by what they say and how they say it. For example, in the following passage from an autobiographical essay, Richard Wright lets readers discover his characters by quoting their own words.

> My mother met me at the door.
> "They b-beat m-me," I gasped. "They t-took the m-money."
> I started up the steps, seeking the shelter of the house.
> "Don't you come in here," my mother warned me.
> I froze in my tracks and stared at her.
> "But they're coming after me," I said.
> "You just stay right where you are," she said in a deadly tone. "I'm going to teach you this night to stand up and fight for yourself."
>
> **Richard Wright, "The Right to the Streets of Memphis"**

Action

Dialogue can also give readers details about events. The following passage is from a nonfiction account of a near tragedy in an abandoned mine. Notice how readers learn that something has happened to the boy Josh through the comments of the people who were with him.

> [Scout leader Terry] Dennis settled by the mine entrance to wait for the others. When [Scoutmaster Kevin] Weaver's group emerged almost an hour later, Josh was not with them.
>
> "Where's Josh?" Dennis shouted, suddenly apprehensive.
>
> "I thought he went with you," Weaver said.
>
> "Have we lost him?" Dennis screamed.
>
> "Maybe Josh came out by himself," Weaver replied. The group fanned out through the underbrush, calling Josh's name. Dennis checked the sleeping bags. *I should have kept him with me. What if he's fallen down a shaft?*
>
> **Per Ola and Emily d'Aulaire,**
> **"Lost Beneath the Mountain"**

Setting

Rather than just describing where events take place, let dialogue do the work for you. In the following passage, the characters are lost in a snowstorm. Their conversation describes the setting.

> "I think I know where we are! That old split post just back there's where we made a takedown running coyotes with Dad's hounds this fall. If I'm right, this is Miller's north meadow, and there's a strip of willows down ahead there, off to the right—" . . .
>
> "How far to a house?" she finally asked, her lips frozen.
>
> "There's no house along this fence if it's the Miller's," Chuck had to admit. "It just goes around the meadow, three, four miles long."
>
> "You're sure—" the teacher asked slowly, "—sure there's no cross fence to the ranch? You might get through, find help in time—"
>
> **Mari Sandoz, "Winter Thunder"**

PLAYS AND SKITS

In plays and skits, dialogue must tell almost everything the audience needs to know about the characters' thoughts and feelings and about events that happen offstage. **Stage directions** provide details about the setting and about characters' appearance and behavior.

In the following passage, notice how A. A. Milne uses the stage directions in parentheses. They describe what the characters look like, how they speak, and what they are doing. The dialogue reveals the characters' personalities and sets the humorous tone of the play. As in many plays, the dialogue is not enclosed in quotation marks.

Literary
MODEL

> **A Voice** (*Announcing*). His Excellency the Chancellor! [The Chancellor, *an elderly man in horn-rimmed spectacles, enters, bowing.* The King *wakes up with a start and removes the handkerchief from his face.*]
>
> **King** (*With simple dignity*). I was thinking.
>
> **Chancellor** (*Bowing*). Never, Your Majesty, was greater need for thought than now.
>
> **King.** That's what I was thinking. (*He struggles into a more dignified position.*) Well, what is it? More trouble?
>
> **Chancellor.** What we might call the old trouble, Your Majesty.
>
> **King.** It's what I was saying last night to the Queen. "Uneasy lies the head that wears a crown" was how I put it.
>
> **A. A. Milne, *The Ugly Duckling***

WRITING DIALOGUE

No matter how you use dialogue in your writing, the following guidelines can help you make it effective and easy for your audience to follow. Reading your dialogue aloud is a good way to see if it sounds like a conversation real people would have. It can also help you find ways to give each person his or her own special way of speaking.

Guidelines for Writing Dialogue

- Make the dialogue sound like real speech. You can include slang and sentence fragments.

    "Hey, whatcha doin', Silas?" Lucy asked.

- Identify the speaker and tell how the person is speaking by using a speaker's tag.

    "Can I come too?" Lucy begged. "Please, please."

- Set off the speaker's exact words with quotation marks.

    "There's almost nothing I'd rather do than scuba dive," Silas said.

"I've even seen sharks and stingrays," Silas continued.

- Begin a new paragraph each time the speaker changes.

    "I'm not afraid," boasted Lucy. "I'm not. I'm not."
    "Well, I can't wait all day," Silas said over his shoulder. "Step on it if you're comin'."

- The first words of quotations are capitalized.

- End marks are usually placed inside quotation marks as you see in these examples.

Practice Your Skills

The following passage is from an autobiographical essay. Using dialogue, rewrite it as part of a short story.

> The day of the first game some of us met early at Hobo Park to talk about how we were going to whip them and send them home whining to their mothers. Soon others showed up to practice fielding grounders while waiting for the coach to pull up in his pickup. When we spotted him coming down the street, we ran to him, and before the pickup had come to a stop, we were already climbing the sides. The coach stuck his head from the cab to warn us to be careful. He idled the pickup for a few minutes to wait for the others, and when two did come running, he waved for them to get in the front with him. As he drove slowly to the West Side, our hair flicked about in the wind, and we thought we looked neat.   **Gary Soto, "Baseball in April"**

Sketch Book

- What do you want to grow up to be? Write about your hopes and your goals.

- How do you find out things you want to know? Tell about some of your strategies.

- Have you ever gotten words mixed up and used the wrong one in a conversation? Tell about the experience.

Academic Skills

The Librarian (1556), Giuseppe Arcimboldo.

You won't find any thesaurus bones in the natural history museum. You won't find any synonyms in a tyrannosaurus.

You *can* find ways to think more clearly, study more effectively, and use the information in books more skillfully. In these handbooks you will learn skills that can keep you from becoming extinct as a student.

Academic Skills **329**

How Do I Strengthen My Vocabulary?

Developing Vocabulary

Consider for a moment how your vocabulary has grown over the years. By the age of eighteen months, you could probably say about fifty words and understand around two hundred. You learned words easily by listening to people around you. As you grew, you stored thousands of words in your memory.

Unfortunately, developing your vocabulary by listening to others becomes less effective as you get older. You must now develop new techniques for learning words.

Guidelines for Learning New Words

1. **Read.** One of the best ways of developing a large vocabulary is reading. If you read about a variety of subjects, you will encounter many new and useful words.

2. **Ask about the meanings of unfamiliar words.** When someone uses a word you don't understand, ask what the word means. Besides increasing your vocabulary, inquiring about the meaning shows that you are truly interested in understanding the person's ideas.

3. **Keep vocabulary lists.** Reserve a part of your notebook or learning log to be used as a "vocabulary bank." When you encounter a new word, write it down. Later on, look up the word in a dictionary and jot down its meaning. You might also include a sentence that shows how the word is used. Then make a point of working the word into your writing and conversation. These techniques will help to make the word stick in your mind.

4. **Use context clues.** When you read or listen, be alert for clues to the meanings of unfamiliar words. Later in this handbook, you will read about four types of clues you can use.

5. **Use word parts.** Often you can dissect an unfamiliar word into a base word and other parts to help you determine the meaning of the word. This handbook will explain how. See pages 333–335 for details.

Study the picture on this page. Can you guess the meaning of the word *baguette?* If you guessed "a long, thin loaf of bread," you're right. Chances are, the **context**—the pictures and words that surround the word—helped you infer its meaning. When you **infer,** you draw a conclusion based on the facts that are given and on what you know from experience.

Several types of context clues are used by writers. The next few pages describe these clues.

Definition or Restatement Clues

A new or unfamiliar word may be defined directly, or its meaning may be restated in other words. Often a comma, a dash, or parentheses are used to set off the meaning clue. In the example below, notice how the commas help you know that *salutation* means "greeting."

> The *salutation,* or greeting, appears at the beginning of a letter.

Some words that signal definitions or restatements are *in other words, that is, or, this means,* and *to put it another way.*

Example Clues

A writer might choose to use one or more examples to clarify the meaning of a new or unusual word.

> *Primates,* including squirrel monkeys, baboons, chimpanzees, and gorillas, take very good care of their young.

Although the meaning of *primates* is not given, the word *including* signals that the animals named are all types of primates. From these examples, you might infer that primates are such mammals as monkeys and the apes. Example clues commonly use the following words and phrases: *like, especially, for example, for instance, including, such as, to illustrate, this, these,* and *other.*

Developing
Vocabulary

331

Comparison or Contrast Clues

Sometimes the meaning of a new or unusual word is compared or contrasted with something the reader will understand. Read the sentence below. Notice how the word *like* sets up a comparison that helps you infer that arid land is dry like a desert.

> The new land was *arid,* like the dry, barren desert through which the settlers had come.

In the example that follows, the word *while* is used to introduce a contrast. It helps you infer that an aloof attitude is the opposite of one that is friendly and outgoing.

> Jamal acted *aloof,* while Ed was friendly and outgoing.

Comparisons and contrasts are often signaled by words and phrases such as *but, although, in comparison, in contrast, on the other hand, similarly, like,* and *as.*

Clues from General Context

In some instances, no direct clue to the meaning of a word is given. Instead, the meaning is hinted at in the sentences surrounding the word, as in this example.

> The house was *dilapidated.* Its windows were broken. Its doors were off their hinges. Its paint was peeling. Wind whistled through cracks in the attic walls, and the floorboards creaked.

Although the word *dilapidated* is not directly defined, the broken windows and doors, the peeling paint, and the cracks in the walls help you know that *dilapidated* means "run-down and neglected."

Practice Your Skills

A. Using the context clues given in the sentences, write the meanings of the italicized words and phrases.

1. *Poaching,* the unlawful hunting of protected animals, has put several species on the endangered list.

Writing TIP

Use context clues in your own writing to define words that your readers might not understand.

2. *Fossil fuels,* such as petroleum, coal, and natural gas, are formed from plants that lived long ago and are used as sources of energy.
3. Most of us agreed, but Hector *dissented.*
4. *Stalactites* hung like icicles from the roof of the cave.
5. The Wild Cats are a *formidable* basketball team. Taller than most teams and quick on their feet, the Wild Cats can out-play most opponents. They haven't lost a game all season.

B. Rewrite each of these sentences, adding a context clue to help readers understand the meaning of the italicized word. Use a dictionary if necessary. Be sure to use each type of context clue at least once.

> EXAMPLE   Martina tried to *rectify* her mistake.
> Martina tried to *rectify*, **or correct,** her mistake.

1. The *venue* for the trial has yet to be decided.
2. Please be *frank* in your comments about my report.
3. Pat was not surprised to learn that she had developed *myopia.*
4. Archaeologists uncovered many *artifacts.*
5. Chris *deliberated* for hours about how to begin his speech.

ANALYZING WORD PARTS

Another good way to determine the meaning of an unfamiliar word is to analyze its parts. A complete word to which word parts are added is called a **base word.** If you take word parts that cannot stand alone and add them to a base word, new words are formed. The word *illiterate,* for example, is made by adding the word part *il-,* which means "not," to the base word *literate,* meaning "able to read and write." *Illiterate* means "not able to read and write."

Prefixes

A word part that is added to the beginning of a word is called a **prefix.** The chart on the next page lists some common prefixes.

Calvin and Hobbes
by Bill Watterson

Prefix	Meaning	Examples
bi-	two	bicycle, biplane
de-, dis-	lower, opposite	devalue, disagree
fore-, pre-	before, ahead of time	forewarn, precook
il-, im-, in-, ir-, non-, un-	not	illegible, improper, incapable, irregular, nonsense, unknown
mid-	middle	midway, midyear
mis-	wrong, badly	misspell, misbehave
re-	back, again	renew, recall
sub-	under, less than	subzero, subdivision
super-	above, more than	superstar, supermarket
trans-	across, to the other side of	transcontinental, transfusion, transplant
tri-	three	tricycle, triangle

Suffixes

A word part added to the end of a word is called a **suffix.** A suffix can change the part of speech of the base word to which it is added. The spelling of the base word may also change. For example, the final letter may be dropped or doubled.

Adding a **noun suffix** to a base word forms a noun.

Noun Suffix	Meaning	Examples
-an, -ant, -eer, -er, -ian, -ier, -ist, -or -ship, -ment, -ness, -hood	one who does or makes something the state or condition of, act or process of	auctioneer, baker, physician, actor kinship, motherhood

Adding a **verb suffix** to a base word forms a verb.

Verb Suffix	Meaning	Examples
-ate	to form, produce	orchestrate
-en	to make, cause	deepen
-ify, -fy, -ise, -ize	to become, cause, make	solidify, legalize

Adding an **adjective suffix** to a base word forms an adjective.

Suffix	Meaning	Examples
-able, -ible	able to be	manageable, sensible
-al	relating to	natural
-ful, -ous, -ive	full of, having the characteristics of	harmful, poisonous, sportive
-ish	like, similar to, of or belonging to	foolish, yellowish, Spanish
-less	without, not able or likely to	seamless, tireless
-like	relating to	childlike, lifelike

Practice Your Skills

A. Make four columns on your paper. Label them *Base Word, Prefix, Suffix,* and *Meaning.* For each word, write the base word and the prefix or suffix (or both) in the appropriate columns. In the last column, write a definition of the word, based on its parts.

1. brotherhood   **3.** irresistible   **5.** finalize

2. disrespectful   **4.** subtotal   **6.** awaken

B. Write the new word you form by adding the appropriate prefix or suffix (or both) from the charts to the base word in parentheses in each sentence.

1. Maurice Sendak, a (write) and (illustrate) of children's books, has also been a set designer for operas.
2. If you are tired, a snack or a short nap may (vital) you.
3. Few toys are really (break).
4. The first solo (Atlantic) airplane flight was made by Charles Lindbergh in 1927.
5. The trial lawyer asked for a (play) of the taped conversation.
6. The criminal gave his captors a (murder) look.
7. When you (view) an article, be sure to read the titles, the subtitles, the illustrations, and the captions.
8. Recycling your cans, bottles, and newspapers is an easy way to demonstrate your (commit) to a cleaner environment.

How Words Earn Their Keep

If you are having trouble with your vocabulary, maybe you aren't paying your words enough. Humpty Dumpty gave this advice about how to treat words to Alice when she went *Through the Looking Glass.*

"When *I* use a word," Humpty Dumpty said in rather a scornful tone, "it means just what I choose it to mean—neither more nor less."

"The question is," said Alice, "whether you *can* make words mean so many different things."

"The question is," said Humpty Dumpty, "which is to be master— that's all."

Alice was too much puzzled to say anything, so, after a minute, Humpty Dumpty began again. "They've a temper, some of them— particularly verbs, they're the proudest: adjectives you can do anything with, but not verbs. However, *I* can manage the whole lot of them! Impenetrability! That's

what *I* say!"

"Would you tell me, please," said Alice, "what that means?"

"Now you talk like a reasonable child," said Humpty Dumpty, look- ing very much pleased. "I meant by 'impenetrability' that we've had enough of that subject, and it would be just as well if you'd men- tion what you mean to do next, as I suppose you don't mean to stop here all the rest of your life."

"That's a great deal to make one word mean," Alice said in a thoughtful tone.

"When I make a word do a lot of work like that," said Humpty Dumpty, "I always pay it extra."

Lewis Carroll

How Can I Tell If I'm Thinking Clearly?

Critical Thinking and Writing

> Our principal and the school board are considering renaming the gymnasium in honor of Coach Harvey. Let our school be the first in this area to honor our town's most famous citizen. Coach Harvey was the finest high school and college coach of this century. Everybody in Norristown admires him.

Suppose that you read this letter to the editor in your school newspaper. Do any of the statements sound exaggerated or misleading? For example, does it seem likely that in one hundred years there hasn't been a better coach than Coach Harvey?

You read and hear statements like these every day—in radio and television commercials, in magazine and newspaper ads, and in casual conversations. How do you know which ones to believe? The ability to think critically will help you judge the truth of statements like these.

Critical thinking is an important skill to bring to your writing too. Carefully examining your ideas and the words you use to express them will help you make your case strongly and clearly.

ERRORS IN REASONING

Detecting errors in thinking can help you avoid problems in your writing. Here are some common errors in reasoning.

Overgeneralization   A statement so broad that it cannot be true is an overgeneralization. Words such as *everyone, no one, always, never, best,* and *worst* often signal overgeneralizations.

> Everybody in Norristown admires Coach Harvey.
>
> (There must be at least one person in town who doesn't admire the coach—or who hasn't even heard of him.)

Circular Reasoning   Repeating a statement in other words rather than supporting it with good reasons is called circular reasoning.

> Baseball is exciting because it is thrilling to the fans.
>
> (We don't know why it's exciting.)

Either/Or Argument   Stating that there are only two choices in a situation when other alternatives actually exist is an either/or argument.

> Either my parents will have to increase my allowance, or I won't have any social life at all.
>
> (There are other ways to earn money for social activities.)

False Cause-and-Effect Statement   A statement wrongly implying that one event caused another is a false cause-and-effect statement.

> The neighbor's dog barked all night. The next day I failed a test. I'd get better grades if the dog were quiet.
>
> (Failing a test has more to do with lack of preparation than with lost sleep caused by a barking dog.)

IMPROPER APPEALS TO EMOTION

Be alert for statements that appeal to your emotions—your feelings of pride, insecurity, affection—rather than to your intelligence. Weed these kinds of statements out of your own writing. They weaken your arguments and leave them open to attack.

Bandwagon Appeal   A statement that suggests a person should think or act like everyone else is a bandwagon appeal.

> Really fashionable teens wear Hiker boots. Get a pair today.
>
> (We don't know anything about the boots themselves.)

Exaggeration   A statement that makes something seem larger or better than it actually is involves exaggeration.

It was the most fantastic concert ever shown on TV.

(There is no way to decide which concert is the "most fantastic . . . ever shown.")

Loaded Language   Certain words arouse people's emotions. This kind of loaded language takes advantage of the connotations or emotional associations of words.

The movie *Star People* is action-filled and thrilling.
The movie *Star People* is scary and violent.

(Which sentence makes the movie more appealing?)

Name-calling   Criticizing someone's personal qualities is a type of loaded language known as name-calling.

Sue's locker is a mess. Don't elect her class president.

(Sue could still be a good class president.)

Weak Testimonial   A testimonial is a statement of support for a product or idea by a famous person. A testimonial is weak if the person has no special knowledge about that product or idea.

Actor Marvin Bosner wears a Rock Mountain jacket.

(Simply wearing it says nothing about the jacket's quality.)

Insufficient Support   In your reading, listening, and writing, be alert for strong statements that are not supported by facts.

The candidate's plan to reform health care is worthless.

(We aren't told what the plan is or why it is worthless.)

Practice Your Skills

Identify the errors in reasoning and the emotional appeals in the following ad. Then rewrite it to correct the errors.

Come to Fun 'n Sun theme park to experience the most incredible ride of a lifetime. There's nothing like it on earth; everyone who's in the know realizes that this ride has no equal. The singer Chelsea Nelson says there is nothing more enjoyable. You can't help but enjoy yourself because everything is so much fun.

How Can I Become a Better Student?

Study and Research Skills

Have you ever imagined a magic spell for doing homework? Even though no such spell exists, there are study skills you can use that will have a powerful effect on your school work. By using proven study methods and learning specific reading skills, you will marvel at your success in school.

UNDERSTANDING YOUR ASSIGNMENTS

One of your most important jobs as a student is keeping track of your assignments. The guidelines below can help.

Organizing Your Assignments

1. **Log your assignments.**   List all assignments in a notebook or folder. Your notes should answer these questions: What needs to be done and when? What form will the final product take? What supplies or other materials will you need?

2. **Keep a weekly schedule.**   Record your assignments and your study times on a weekly calendar. The calendar allows you to see at a glance what needs to be done every day.

3. **Divide long assignments into parts.**   If you're writing a speech, for example, divide your assignment into small tasks. Go to the library one day. Create an outline the next day, and begin your draft on yet another day.

COMPUTER
TIP

Weekly schedules and calendars are available for many personal computers. Check with your computer software dealer.

TAKING NOTES

Do you ever look at your notes and find that you don't understand them? You need time and practice to learn how to take notes well. The strategies on the next page will help you become a first-class note taker.

- **Keep a notebook.**   Keep all your notes in one place. You might use small notebooks, one for each class or subject area.

- **Identify each set of notes.**   Write the subject and date in the upper right-hand corner of the page.

- **Use a modified outline form.**   Use phrases to record main ideas in your notes. Then, below the main ideas, indent and write down related ideas.

- **Write key facts and ideas.**   Be critical. Don't try to record everything. Look for phrases such as *most important, for these reasons, for example, to review,* and *to summarize.*

- **Use symbols and abbreviations.**   Here are some symbols and abbreviations often used in notes. If you wish, you can make up your own symbols and abbreviations.

&	and	w/o	without	=	equals
Amer	American	def	definition	re	regarding
~	approximately	y	why	s/b	should be

- **Review your notes regularly.**   Set aside time each day to review your notes.

Notice how one student uses a modified outline form and other guidelines to structure her notes about dinosaurs.

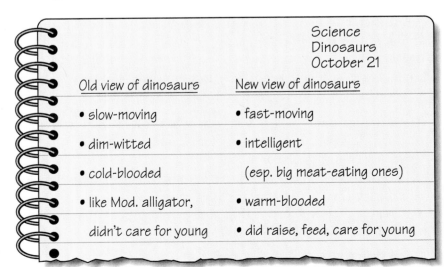

Science
Dinosaurs
October 21

Old view of dinosaurs	New view of dinosaurs
• slow-moving	• fast-moving
• dim-witted	• intelligent
• cold-blooded	(esp. big meat-eating ones)
• like Mod. alligator,	• warm-blooded
didn't care for young	• did raise, feed, care for young

Study and
Research Skills   **341**

USING THE KWL STUDY METHOD

One way to study is to use the KWL study method. When you use this method, ask yourself three key questions:

> **K:** What do I already **know?**
> **W:** What do I **want** to know?
> **L:** What did I **learn?**

Answer the first question by listing what you already know about the subject. Then create a list of questions about the subject, ones that show what you want or need to learn. These questions can begin with the question words *who, what, where, when, why,* or *how.* Look for answers to your questions as you study. Finally, answer the third question and make a list of what you have learned.

You can use the KWL method for any kind of studying. Use it to study chapters from a book or notes from a class. Apply the KWL study questions when doing a report or a project. This method will help you whether you are studying alone or with a group.

KEEPING A LEARNING LOG

Another excellent approach to studying involves keeping a learning log. A **learning log** is a notebook or folder in which you write about what you want to learn, are learning, and have learned. Some students keep their notes in their learning logs. Use the following activities to generate material to include in your log:

1. Start a learning journal and write what you learned from projects, class presentations, problems, and successes.
2. Make a list of goals for all your classes.
3. Keep rough drafts, outlines, or summaries of writing ideas for future essays.
4. Create a "Topics for Writing" list by jotting down ideas while reading, talking with friends, or watching TV.

5. Freewrite about subjects that interest you.
6. Keep in your log the lists that you make when using the KWL study method.
7. Record questions or comments about homework assignments or class lectures.
8. Formulate a "What I Learned Today" (WILT) list to chart how much you've grown and progressed.
9. On the left side of a two-column page, record notes from books, discussions, or lectures. Reserve the right side for ideas and reactions to your notes.
10. Establish a place in your log to jot down memorable quotes that you read or hear.
11. Set aside a "Reader Response" section for feelings and reactions to your reading.
12. Brainstorm about your dreams and the role that learning plays in fulfilling those dreams.

UNDERSTANDING WHAT YOU READ

One way to improve your understanding of what you read is to **preview** the material first. When previewing a reading selection, follow these steps:

1. Read the title.
2. Read any headings or words printed in special type.
3. Examine any illustrations, maps, diagrams, charts, or other graphics. Read all captions, labels, and headings on the graphics.
4. Read the first and last paragraph closely. Then skim the selection's paragraphs to find the main ideas.
5. Read the summary or conclusion, if the selection has one.
6. List questions that you predict the author will answer about the subject.

Once you have previewed the selection, read it actively. **Reading actively** means responding as you read. Respond aloud or in writing to what the author is saying. Some of the types of responses that you might make are listed on the next page.

- **Write answers to your preview questions.** Jot down these answers as you read the selection.
- **Ask questions.** Record any additional questions that you think of or that the author raises.
- **Record main ideas and key terms.** Look for main ideas as you read. Note the topic sentences of paragraphs. Write down all key terms and definitions that appear in the selection.
- **Respond critically to the selection.** Record your own ideas and opinions about the author's subject. Do not simply accept everything that the author says. Ask yourself why you agree or disagree.

Once you have finished reading, **review** your notes. Recopy them or organize them if necessary. Then make a list of what the selection has taught you. Write down all questions that remain unanswered.

Practice Your Skills

A. Take notes on the following passage. Use a modified outline form and abbreviations.

> The pyramid of Khufu, called the *Great Pyramid,* contains more than 2 million stone blocks that average 2.5 short tons (2.3 metric tons) each. It was originally 481 feet (147 meters) tall, but some of its upper stones are gone now and it stands about 450 feet (140 meters) high. Its base covers about 13 acres (5 hectares). . . .
>
> The burial chamber is inside the Great Pyramid. A corridor leads from an entrance on the north side to several rooms within the pyramid. One of the rooms is called the *Queen's Chamber,* although the queen is not buried there. The room was planned as the king's burial chamber. But Khufu changed the plan and built another burial chamber, called the *King's Chamber.* The *Grand Gallery,* a corridor 153 feet (47 meters) long and 28 feet (8.5 meters) high, leads to Khufu's chamber. It is considered a marvel of ancient architecture.
>
> ***The World Book Encyclopedia,* 1992**

B. Preview the selection by reading the title, heading, and words in special print. Write down three questions that you predict the author will answer. Then read the passage closely and record its main ideas. Jot down answers to your questions, and write your critical response to the selection.

Hinamatsuri: A Japanese Doll Festival

Japanese children are especially lucky, because there is a holiday just for them! . . . This festival is called *Hinamatsuri,* the Girls' Doll Festival. *Hina,* pronounced hee-na, is the Japanese word for doll, and *matsuri* means festival. . . . Every year this festival is held on March 3. . . .

HISTORY OF THE FESTIVAL

This festival began so long ago that people are not really sure why or how it first started. It may have begun over two thousand years ago, when the third day of the third month was called "the day of the snake" in Japan and China. This was a day of cleansing. Little dolls were used as symbols for human beings—people would "give" all their impurities and bad thoughts to these dolls, which were cast off into streams. . . .

The *Hinamatsuri* dolls are very special. They are ceremonial dolls, often handed down from mother to daughter through the generations. . . . But the dolls are not played with like ordinary dolls—they are for display only.

DESCRIPTION OF THE DOLLS

The *Hinamatsuri* dolls represent the emperor, the empress, and all the figures of the royal court. In Japan there is a long tradition of respect and loyalty for the emperor. . . .

The most important dolls, of course, are the emperor and empress, called the *Dairisama.* They sit on the top shelf of the *hinadan.* . . . The other members of the court sit on the shelves below the emperor and empress. In a full set of dolls, there may be seven ladies-in-waiting, five musicians, two pages, and three guards. . . .

For most of the year the dolls are carefully wrapped up and put away in boxes, so it is always a special treat when March 3 comes and the dolls are displayed.

from *Cricket,* August 1992

An empress doll from a Japanese *Hinamatsuri* doll set. Such dolls reflect the ancient Japanese tradition of honoring royalty.

How Do I Put Things in My Own Words?

Writing Paraphrases and Summaries

When you put an orange through a juicer, what do you get? You get the juice and the pulp—in other words, the best parts of the orange. The unimportant part, the rind, is left behind.

When you write a paraphrase or a summary of a piece of writing, you also want to get at the best parts of the writer's work. You restate the writer's most important ideas in your own words, leaving out the unimportant details.

PARAPHRASING

When you **paraphrase** a passage from a book or a magazine, you restate the writer's ideas in your own words. Do not simply use synonyms to replace the writer's original language. Instead, think about the passage and then rewrite it in your own words, using your own voice. Here are some guidelines:

Guidelines for Paraphrasing

1. **Identify the main idea.** Find the main idea and write it in your own words.

2. **List supporting details.** List all the supporting details in the original passage. Include sensory details, examples, facts, and opinions. Write these details in your own words and keep them in their original order.

3. **Simplify the language.** Use familiar words to simplify the way you present the main idea and supporting details. Try not to change the tone of the passage.

4. **Revise your work.** When you've finished paraphrasing, revise your work. Make sure that the final product is in your own words, uses simple vocabulary, has the same content as the original, and is about the same length.

COMPUTER
—TIP—

When writing a paraphrase on a computer, save the different drafts in separate files. This makes it easy to try out changes or keep original material when revising your work.

Suppose you are writing a report about the Native American mound builders you learned about in Workshop 8. You read the following passage that discusses a specific type of mound structure:

> Some Indians built still another kind of mound. This was the effigy mound in the shape of a living creature, almost always an animal. Most effigy mounds are in southern Wisconsin and in nearby areas of Illinois and Iowa, although Ohio has some, too. All kinds of animals are represented. There are bears, deer, panthers, wolves, turtles, and birds.
>
> **Paula Angle Franklin,** *Indians of North America*

Here is one way you could paraphrase Paula Franklin's paragraph:

> According to Paula Angle Franklin, some Native Americans created mounds that were in the shape of living animals. These mounds can be found within southern Wisconsin, Illinois, Iowa, and Ohio. The animals depicted in these mounds vary: bears, deer, panthers, wolves, turtles, and birds (33).

Main idea

Supporting Ideas

SUMMARIZING

A summary is usually one-third the length of the original. To **summarize** a passage, rephrase the original material in fewer words. Try to capture the original's key ideas. Follow these steps:

Guidelines for Summarizing

1. **List the main idea.** Read the original material closely. Rewrite the main idea in as few words as possible.

2. **Select details.** Select the most important points to support the main idea.

3. **Rewrite ideas.** Rewrite key ideas, using simpler language and combining ideas.

4. **Revise your summary.** Reread your draft and make sure it is in your own words. Remember that the tone of your summary should match the original.

You can use summarizing to help you write a report, take notes, or study.

Here is a summary of the passage on Native American mounds:

> Native Americans built effigy mounds in the Midwest. These mounds resembled different animals.

Student
MODEL

PROBLEM
S O L V I N G

"How can I cite a source correctly?"

To find out the correct form for citing a source, see

• Writer's Workshop 8, page 201

PLAGIARISM

When you paraphrase or summarize an original idea, or quote a passage directly, always give credit to the original source to avoid plagiarism. **Plagiarism** is the dishonest practice of presenting another person's ideas or language as your own.

You can avoid plagiarism by citing your sources as you write. These steps will help you avoid plagiarism:

• **Credit all direct quotations.** Use quotation marks when quoting directly from a source. Do not use quotation marks when you are paraphrasing or summarizing another person's ideas.

• **Credit all ideas that are not your own.** However, you do not need to credit a source if the material you paraphrase or summarize is general knowledge.

Practice Your Skills

Read the following selection carefully. Jot down its topic sentence and supporting ideas. Then paraphrase the paragraph. Finally, use your paraphrase to write a summary.

> The rain forests are vanishing. By some estimates, nearly half of the rain forests that existed a century ago have already been cut down, and more are being destroyed, at a rate of 43,000 square miles (111,000 sq km) per year, an area roughly half the size of Pennsylvania. Within half a century, there may be no rain forests left at all. And for every square mile of rain forest that is removed, untold thousands of plants are killed, and an important animal habitat is lost.
>
> **Christopher Lampton, *Endangered Species***

How Can I Use Charts and Graphs in My Writing?

Creating Graphic Aids

Calvin knows that a visual aid will help make his report interesting and memorable. You too can use visuals, or **graphic aids,** in your writing to help your readers understand and remember information, especially information involving numbers. Some common graphic aids are line graphs, bar graphs, and circle graphs.

Line Graphs

If you were writing a report on world hunger, you might want to show how population increases affect world hunger. A line graph is a good way to show how the world population is growing. Here are the steps for creating the line graph shown below:

- **Research the topic.** Look through an encyclopedia or a reference book to find statistics on world population.
- **Create a grid.** Label your grid. The vertical scale goes up the left side of the grid. It shows population size. The horizontal scale goes across the bottom of the grid. It shows time.
- **Plot the information.** Plot the points on your grid, pairing each year with its matching population number. Use a ruler to draw lines connecting the points.

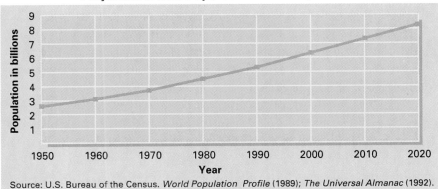

Projected World Population Growth, 1950–2020

Source: U.S. Bureau of the Census. *World Population Profile* (1989); *The Universal Almanac* (1992).

Calvin and **Hobbes**
by Bill Watterson

Creating
Graphic Aids   **349**

Bar Graphs

Suppose you are writing a report on the problem of homelessness. You want to compare the problem in six cities. A good way to compare numerical information is to create a bar graph.

To make a bar graph, first gather information and create a grid. Write the "name variables," in this case the names of the cities, along one side of the graph. Arrange the "number variables," or the sizes of the homeless populations, along the other. Use these variables to mark the length of each bar on the graph. In this case, the bars are drawn from the left side of the graph and end at the points marked on the grid.

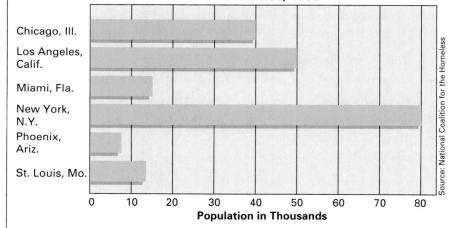

Estimated Numbers of Homeless People in Six Cities, 1989

Source: National Coalition for the Homeless

Circle Graphs

If you were writing about teenagers' attitudes toward TV, you might conduct a poll and show the results in a circle graph like the one on the next page. In this example, the circle represents the total number of people polled.

To make a circle graph, list the information you want to represent. Draw a circle and divide it into "pie slices." Label each slice. To determine the size of each slice, you must figure out what percentage, or part of the whole, it represents. For example, if 200 students are polled and 20 of them answer that television has too many reruns, these 20 are represented by 10 percent of the circle.

What Bothers You Most About TV?

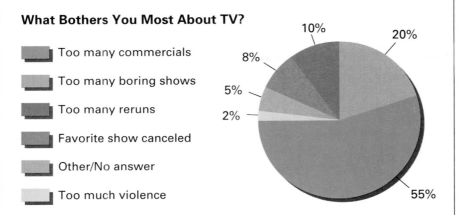

- Too many commercials
- Too many boring shows
- Too many reruns
- Favorite show canceled
- Other/No answer
- Too much violence

10%   20%
8%
5%
2%
55%

Practice Your Skills

A. Use the graphs in this handbook to answer these questions.

1. Between 1970 and 1990, by approximately how many people did the world population grow?
2. In 1989, what was the difference between the homeless population in New York and in St. Louis?
3. According to the circle graph, what are the two aspects of television that bother students the most? What aspect bothers them the least?

B. Use the information in the table below to draw a line graph. Be sure to include a title and headings in the appropriate places.

Average Attendance at Chicago Bulls Professional Basketball Games, 1966–1990

Year	Attendance in Thousands
1966	4.5
1970	10.0
1974	10.5
1978	9.0
1982	7.0
1986	16.0
1990	18.5

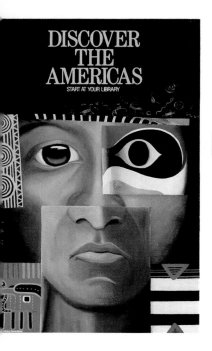

How Can I Locate Information?

Making Use of the Library

A typical modern library is very different from a library of twenty years ago. In the past, libraries did not offer videotapes, artwork, CDs, photographs, laser discs, or computers. Public readings, children's story time, movies, and workshops were among the other services not available. The library of today has become an important community resource center.

HOW LIBRARIES ARE ORGANIZED

With so much to offer, libraries can be confusing places. It's important to learn how libraries organize their materials.

The Sections of the Library

Most libraries are organized into the following sections:

Section	Contents
The Stacks	shelves of fiction and nonfiction books
Catalog and Index	card catalogs, computer catalogs, and indexes
Reference	atlases, encyclopedias, and other fact-filled works
Periodicals	magazines, newspapers, and journals
Audiovisual	audiotapes, tape recorders, CDs, films, filmstrips, projectors, laser discs, and records
Children and Young Adult	materials for toddlers, children, and teenagers
Special Services	rooms for story readings, lectures, computer users, job searches, and community services

How the Books Are Arranged

Library books are usually grouped into the following main types: **fiction, nonfiction, biography and autobiography,** and **reference.**

Fiction   Novels, short story collections, and mysteries are classified as fiction. You will find these books shelved in alphabetical order according to the author's last name.

Nonfiction   Books that contain only factual information are nonfiction. Libraries use one of two systems for classifying these books: the Dewey Decimal System or the Library of Congress System. The **Dewey Decimal System** divides nonfiction books into ten subject categories and into subcategories as shown below.

Dewey Decimal System

000–099	General Works (encyclopedias, bibliographies)
100–199	Philosophy (self-help, psychology)
200–299	Religion (the Bible, mythology, theology)
300–399	Social Science (law, education, economics)
400–499	Language (books on grammar, dictionaries, foreign languages)
500–599	Science (mathematics, biology, chemistry)
600–699	Technology (medicine, inventions, cooking)
700–799	Fine Arts (painting, music, theater, sports)
800–899	Literature (poetry, plays, essays)
900–999	History (biography, geography, travel)

Very large libraries use the **Library of Congress System** to classify nonfiction books into twenty-one subject categories. Each category is assigned a letter of the alphabet. A librarian can provide you with a guide to this system.

Biography and Autobiography   A **biography** is a nonfiction book about a person's life. An **autobiography** tells the author's own life story. Biographies may be kept in the 900's section or they may be shelved in a special section. In either case, biographies are shelved alphabetically according to the name of the person the book is about.

Reference Books These sources include almanacs, encyclopedias, dictionaries, and other fact-filled works. Reference books are shelved in the reference section and are labeled with an *R* or *REF.* Usually you cannot check out reference books.

Catalog Systems

One of the first steps in using a library or doing research is finding out what materials are available. A **catalog system** lists all the materials a library has to offer.

No matter what catalog system a library uses, you can find a listing for a book by looking it up in one of three ways: by the author's last name, by the first word of the title, or by the subject the book is about. Two common types of library catalog systems are card catalogs and on-line computer catalogs.

Card Catalogs

A card catalog is a file of cards for all the materials in the library. The cards are filed alphabetically and are usually kept in drawers in a cabinet.

Guide Cards These cards are labeled with letters or general headings and extend above the other cards in the catalog. They help you quickly locate the specific entry card you need. To find entry cards on the California gold rush, for example, you would look in the G drawer between the guide cards *Gold Coins* and *Goldberg, Isaac.*

Entry Cards There are usually three file cards for each book: an author card, a title card, and a subject card. To find a book about the California gold rush, you could look for a subject card labeled *GOLD RUSH* or for a title card labeled *The Great American Gold Rush.* An author card would be filed under *B* for Rhoda Blumberg. Each type of entry card provides the same information about a source. Study the subject entry card that follows.

Conditions were primitive in the California gold fields of the 1850s. Here a woman brings lunch to three miners.

Subject Card

Call number

```
            CALIFORNIA—GOLD DISCOVERIES ———— Subject
   x979.4
   Blumb.R   Blumberg, Rhoda 1926- ———————— Author
             The great American gold rush/Rhoda  Title
             Blumberg.
               --New York: Bradbury Press, c1989. — Copyright
             135 p.: ill.; 29 cm. Bibliography:     date
             p. 130-131. Includes index.          Size

             Summary: Describes the emigration
             of people from the East Coast of
             the United States and from foreign
             countries to California to pursue
             the dream of discovering gold.

             1. Voyages to the Pacific coast ———— Other ways
             I. Title         II. Author           the book
                                                   is listed
```

Publisher
Length
Illustrated

Cross-reference Cards Some of the cards between the guide cards may begin with the words *See* or *See also.* These cross-reference cards suggest other related subject, title, or author entries. When researching a topic, you may find cross-reference cards useful for finding additional sources.

Computerized Catalogs

Many libraries list all their materials on a computer. To find a specific source, you use a computer terminal to search for listings. Computerized systems vary, so ask your librarian for help.

Computer Searching Generally, you use a terminal keyboard, and begin a search by typing the subject, the author's last name, or the title. A screen appears with choices for related listings. For example, if you type the words *California gold rush,* the choices *California—Gold discoveries, California—Gold discoveries— Fiction,* and *California—Gold discoveries—Songs and music* may appear. Select a choice and the screen displays a list of book titles on that subject. Choose a title, and the computer provides an entry with information similar to that found on an entry card in the card catalog. Compare the computer entry on the next page with the subject card you studied earlier.

Computer Catalog Author Entry

```
   AUTHOR:   Blumberg, Rhoda
    TITLE:   The great American gold rush
PUBLISHER:   Bradbury Press [1989]
 SUBJECTS:   Voyages to the Pacific coast. Overland journeys
to the Pacific.


## ----Call number ------Volume  Material   Location   Status
1       x979.4/Blumb.R            Juv. Book  CHILDRNS   Available


Enter: F          to see Full title record.
>>                          Enter ? for HELP.
```

Special Features   Most computerized catalogs show whether a source is available or checked out. In addition, some systems can provide a printout of all the sources available on a subject, including sources in neighboring libraries.

LOCATING AND USING MATERIALS

Once you know what sources are available, your next step is to find the materials you need. Libraries use **call numbers,** codes of letters and numbers, that tell you where a book is shelved.

Understanding Call Numbers

To find a book in the stacks, you match the call number on the catalog entry with the call number printed on the spine of the book. Some libraries use a letter code before the Dewey number to tell you the section of the library where the book is kept. A list of commonly used letter codes is shown below.

R, REF = Reference	B, BIO = Biography
C, CHILD = Children's	X, J, JUV = Juvenile
X, Y, YA = Young Adult	AV = Audiovisual
P, PER = Periodicals	SC = Short Story Collection
SF = Science Fiction	MYS = Mystery

Other parts of the call number also help you locate a book. Look at the call number below for *The Great American Gold Rush* by Rhoda Blumberg.

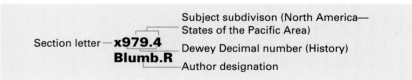

Section letter — **x979.4** — Subject subdivison (North America—States of the Pacific Area)
Blumb.R — Dewey Decimal number (History)
— Author designation

In this call number, the letter *x* tells you that this book is in the young adult section. The 979.4 is the Dewey number. The Dewey number tells you to go to the 900 section of the shelves. In the 900s, look for books with the same subcategory number. Then, since books are arranged alphabetically by the author's last name, look for the author designation, *Blumb.R.*

Research Resources

Imagine being able to find the answer to every question you ever had. In the reference section, you are surrounded by the most up-to-date information sources. Such a variety of materials not only allows you to answer questions but also to learn a variety of viewpoints on a topic. The chart below lists some of the most useful resources.

Library References

Reference	Contents	Examples
Encyclopedias	articles on various topics	*Encyclopaedia Britannica*
Almanacs and Yearbooks	current facts and unusual information	*Facts on File, The Information Please Almanac*
Atlases	detailed maps and geographical information	*The National Geographic Atlas of the World*
Vertical File	pamphlets, booklets, and clippings of topics	
Periodicals	newspapers, magazines, and journals	*Chicago Tribune, Time, The Reading Teacher*

Writing
TIP

If there is a bibliography in a reference source you use, examine it for possible additional research sources.

Making Use of the Library

Using Periodical Indexes

A reference work that lists articles from magazines and newspapers is called a **periodical index.** The two types of periodical indexes—printed and computerized—are valuable tools.

Printed Indexes   The *Readers' Guide to Periodical Literature* is a printed index published monthly. Articles are listed by subject and author. At the end of the year, the issues are bound into one volume. Study this excerpt from the *Readers' Guide:*

Excerpt from the *Readers' Guide*

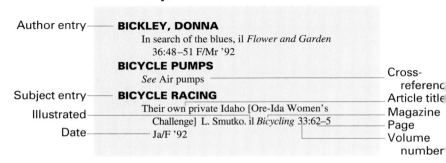

Author entry — **BICKLEY, DONNA**
In search of the blues, il *Flower and Garden*
36:48–51 F/Mr '92
BICYCLE PUMPS
See Air pumps —————————————— Cross-reference
Subject entry — **BICYCLE RACING** ———————— Article title
Illustrated ————— Their own private Idaho [Ore-Ida Women's
Challenge] L. Smutko. il *Bicycling* 33:62–5 ——— Magazine
Page
Date ————————— Ja/F '92 ———————————— Volume number

Computerized Indexes   Computerized indexes such as *InfoTrac, ProQuest,* and *Uncover* list periodicals by subject and sometimes by author for the period of years covered by the index. A librarian can help you use the index. Look at this entry from *ProQuest:*

Computerized Periodical Index Entry

```
TITLE:        Bernard Hinault On: Bike Fit
AUTHORS:      Drake, Geoff
JOURNAL:      Bicycling  Vol: 33  Iss: 2  Date: March 1992
              pp: 86-87
Jrnl Code:    GBIK  ISSN: 0006-2073  Jrnl Group: Lifestyles
ABSTRACT:     Five-time Tour de France winner Bernard
              Hinault offers guidelines for proper bike fit,
              including information on saddle setback, frame
              height and saddle/handlebar distance.
              Photograph; Table
SUBJECTS:     Bicycles; Bicycle racing
NAMES:        Hinault, Bernard
TYPE:         Feature
LENGTH:       Medium (10-30 col inches)
```

Microforms   Usually, recent periodicals are shelved in the periodical section. However, many libraries save space by using **microforms,** pieces of film that show pages from certain recent and all older periodicals. When the microforms are rolled-up strips of film, they are called **microfilm.** When the microforms are film cards, they are called **microfiche.** Check with a librarian to learn which issues of periodicals are stored on microforms. The library has special machines that you must use to read microforms. A librarian will gladly instruct you on how to use the machines.

Experts

Experts aren't just "talking heads" on TV. Your friends, relatives, teachers, librarians, and school administrators may be experts you can interview. Often you can find experts at local organizations such as businesses, museums, and clubs. A good interview can provide interesting material for a report. For more information about interviewing, see Handbook 36, "Interviewing Skills," page 362.

Government Agencies

Many libraries have special sections that contain government publications. In addition, the government agencies listed in a telephone book can provide information about federal issues. The General Services Administration publishes a catalog that lists free or inexpensive government pamphlets on many subjects. You can receive this free catalog by writing to: Consumer Information Catalog, P.O. Box 100, Pueblo, CO 81002.

For information about local issues, you can contact your town hall or mayor's office. For information on state issues, you might try the office of your state legislator.

Computer Services

Computer information services offer on-line encyclopedias and dictionaries, as well as news, weather, and sports reports. If you have the use of a computer, a modem, and a telephone line, you can access an information service. A librarian may be able to provide you with a listing of available computer services.

COMPUTER
TIP

Some libraries also provide on-line computer bulletin boards that display community information and notices of upcoming events.

The Media

"The media" refers to all of the communication methods used by people. There are two main kinds of media: audiovisual and print.

Audiovisual Media Audiotapes, CDs, computer programs, films, filmstrips, laser discs, photos and slides, transparencies, and videotapes are examples of audiovisual media. Two types of audio-

visual media are broadcast and narrowcast. **Broadcast media** send messages from one point to many points through network TV or radio programs. You can sometimes purchase transcripts of these broadcasts for a slight fee. **Narrowcast media** send messages from one point to one point through cable or telephone wires. You can receive narrowcast messages through computer networks, pay-per-view television, and facsimile machines.

Print Media Any media printed on paper—books, letters, fliers, posters, magazines, newspapers—are considered print media.

Whenever you use media sources, it is important to think critically about the sources and to use the information responsibly. Ask yourself these questions as you evaluate the media sources:

Evaluating Media Sources

- Have my sources presented different views of the topic?
- Are my sources reliable?
- Is the information from each source accurate?
- Are my sources as current as possible?
- Have my sources provided unbiased information or are they trying to persuade me?
- Have I discussed my interpretation of the information with a peer?

Practice Your Skills

A. Find and list the call number of one book in each of the following general categories:

1. mythology
2. foreign languages
3. biology
4. plays

B. Follow the directions for each item. Use your library's card catalog or computer catalog to find the information requested.

1. Find a book about Mexico. List the title, the author, and the call number.
2. Find the title of a book by Virginia Hamilton.
3. Find the title of a biography about any sports hero.
4. Find a collection of short stories or poems. List the title of the collection and its editor or editors.

C. Use reference works in your library to answer the following questions. Write the answer to the question and the name and type of the reference work that you used. (encyclopedia, almanac, atlas, etc.)

1. How many people now live in Brazil?
2. In what part of California is the town of Santa Rosa located? Whom is the town named after?
3. Who founded Howard University, and when was it founded?
4. What were the high and low temperatures in your town last Monday?

D. Use the *Readers' Guide* or a computerized periodical index to find two magazine articles, one that is on the shelves and one that is on microfiche, for each of the following subjects:

1. Texas
2. solar energy

E. List all the sources you would use for the following topics. Explain why you would use each source.

1. space shuttle astronauts and scientists
2. early settlers in your town

How Can I Become a Good Interviewer?

Interviewing Skills

Have you ever noticed how quotes from interesting people or experts on a subject can make a newspaper or magazine article come alive? For this reason, reporters value interviews as an important way of gathering information. You can use interviewing to add firsthand information and interest to many kinds of writing, such as eyewitness reports, research papers and I-Search papers. These guidelines will help you conduct a successful interview.

Guidelines for Interviewers

Planning the Interview

1. Contact the person you want to interview. Arrange to meet.
2. Learn about the subject and the person before the interview.
3. Make a list of questions that require more than yes-or-no answers. For example "What was it like . . ." or "How do you . . ."

Conducting the Interview

1. Listen carefully and take accurate notes. If necessary, ask the person to slow down or to repeat or explain statements.
2. Ask permission if you want to tape-record or quote the person.
3. Be flexible. Follow your plan, but be willing to ask follow-up questions during the interview.
4. Thank the person, and then review and rewrite your notes while the interview is fresh in your mind.

Practice Your Skills

Rewrite the following questions so that they require more than a yes-or-no answer.

1. Do you like being a jet pilot?
2. Are you trained to fly other types of aircraft?
3. Do you have any hobbies?
4. Were you scared on your first solo flight?
5. Are you glad you chose this career?

How Can I Become a Good Listener?

Critical Listening and Observing

Stop! Close your eyes. Notice what you hear for the next twenty seconds.

You may have heard two classmates whispering or a videotape from another classroom. You have just used your sense of hearing. But were you really listening? When you **listen,** you also try to understand and make use of what you hear.

When and why do you listen? You listen to the news to become informed, to TV or radio to be entertained, to commercials to learn about products, and to conversations to gather the ideas of friends. To make the best use of what you hear, however, you must become a critical listener. As a **critical listener,** you not only hear but also think about and evaluate the messages.

IMPROVING LISTENING SKILLS

Before you can become a critical listener, you need to sharpen your basic listening skills.

Strategies for Effective Listening

Do
- think about why the topic might be important to you
- keep an open mind
- listen for the speaker's purpose and main ideas
- try to anticipate the speaker's next point
- summarize as you listen
- take notes if appropriate

Don't
- tune out the speaker
- become distracted
- let your own thoughts and feelings interfere
- try to remember too many details
- jump to conclusions
- let note taking get in the way of your listening

EVALUATING WHAT YOU HEAR AND SEE

Today we rely on a variety of sources for information, especially TV. In order to understand what you hear, you must be able to evaluate, or judge the value of, the speaker's ideas. Don't assume that the speaker's ideas are valid or truthful just because he or she is a so-called expert, a newscaster on TV, or even a relative. Be skeptical!

Weigh the Evidence

Often speakers use a mix of facts and opinions to support main ideas. Even a newscaster, whose job is to present only facts, may mix opinions with the facts of a story. As a critical listener, you must be able to tell the difference between fact and opinion and judge the soundness of both. Then you can decide if a speaker has presented his or her conclusions fairly. Ask yourself these questions.

Facts	*Opinions*
• Can I prove the facts by asking an expert or checking resource materials?	• Are the opinions reasonable and based on the facts?
• Are there enough facts to support the main ideas?	• Is the speaker qualified to give knowledgeable opinions?
• Have I heard all the facts? Have I heard facts that support the other side of the issue?	• How does the opinion compare with my own experience? with that of people familiar with the subject?

Some speakers use faulty reasoning when discussing issues. In advertisements, political statements, and other types of persuasive speeches, these errors in reasoning may be deliberate attempts to mislead listeners. Learn to recognize faulty reasoning so that you can judge the value of messages. (See also "Critical Thinking and Writing," pages 337–339.)

Look Beyond the Words

Sometimes the words of a message may be right, but something still doesn't ring true. Don't be afraid to trust your own judgment. You may not be an expert, but you probably know enough about a topic to do some questioning. In addition to the words, consider the speaker's motive and point of view and any nonverbal messages that accompany the speaker's words. Also notice visual images and symbols that may affect your opinion.

Motive and Point of View   A citizen presents an editorial on the "sound off" segment of a local news program to complain that skateboarders and Rollerbladers on public sidewalks are safety hazards. How would your evaluation of the complaint be affected if you knew that the citizen was preparing to run for a position on the village board? Is the citizen really concerned about the welfare of villagers, or could the speech be a preview of campaign issues? Always ask yourself what reason a speaker has for taking a certain position.

Nonverbal Messages   A political candidate broadcasts a campaign message from his living room. He wears a shirt with the sleeves rolled up, sits casually in a relaxed position, and smiles a great deal. Does his appearance make his ideas seem more believable? Facial expression, posture, gestures, and dress are all ways good speakers get a message across. However, it is important to think about whether these elements have been purposely crafted to create a certain impression.

Visual Images and Symbols   One network reports a criminal's parole hearing and shows a police photo of the criminal, while another network reports the same story but shows a family photo of the criminal hugging his elderly mother. How does each photo affect your opinion about the parole issue?

Now imagine a TV commercial for automobile tires that shows toddlers happily sitting in and around tires. Do you associate the safety and happiness of children with that brand of tires? As a critical listener, think about how your judgment is affected by the associations you make. Notice the symbols and pictures that accompany what you hear.

Critical Listening
and Observing   **365**

Practice Your Skills

A. Look at the picture below. List any nonverbal messages and visual images you see. Explain what effect they might have on a listener. Then read the excerpt from General Schwarzkopf's speech to Congress after the 1990–91 Persian Gulf War. Write a brief analysis of it. Identify the purpose and any special phrasing used to accomplish the purpose.

. . . We also want to thank our families. It is you who endure the hardships and separations simply because you choose to love a soldier, a sailor, an airman, a marine, or a coast guardsman. But it is your love that gave us strength in our darkest hours. You are truly the wind beneath our wings. Finally, and most importantly, [thanks] to the great American people. The prophets of doom, the naysayers, the protesters, and the flag burners . . . said you would never stick by us. But we knew better. We knew you would never let us down. By golly, you didn't. Since the first hour of Desert Shield until the last minute of Desert Storm, every day in every way all across America, you shouted that you were with us. Millions of . . . students, millions and millions of families, untold numbers of civic organizations, . . . factories, companies and workplaces, millions of senior citizens, and just plain Americans—never let us forget that we were in your hearts and you were in our corner. Because of you, when that terrible first day of the war came, we knew we would not fail; we knew we had the strength of the American people behind us, and with that strength we were able to get the job done, kick the Iraqis out of Kuwait, and get back home. From all of us who proudly served in the Middle East in your armed forces, thank you to the great people of the United States of America.

B. Watch a newscast on television. Write a short evaluation, noting both the positive and the negative qualities of the broadcast.

on the LIGHT side

Howta Reckanize American Slurvian

In his book *Anguished English,* Richard Lederer describes a familiar style of pronunciation called Slurvian.

Everywhere we turn we are assaulted by a slew of slurrings. We meet people who *hafta, oughta,* or are *gonna* do something or who *shoulda, woulda,* or *coulda* done it. . . . Here's a typically American exchange:

"Jeet jet?"

"No, jew?"

"Sgo."

Translation: "Did you eat yet?" "No, did you?" "Let's go." . . .

To help you translate Slurvian into English . . . I offer [this] glossary.

Bar. To take temporarily. "May I bar your eraser?"

Dense. A tooth expert. "Yuck! I have a dense appointment today."

Forced. A large cluster of trees. "Only you can prevent forced fires."

Less. Contraction of "let us." "Less learn more about Slurvian."

Lining. Electrical flash of light. "We abandoned our picnic when we heard the thunder and saw the lining."

Mere. A reflecting glass. "Mere, mere on the wall, who's the fairest one of all?"

Mill. Between the beginning and the end. "A table stood in the mill of the room."

Mince. Units lasting 60 seconds. "I'll be back in a few mince."

Neck store. Adjacent. "I'm in love with the girl neck store."

Nigh. Opposite of day. "She woke up screaming in the mill of the nigh."

Win. Movement of air. "He was awakened in the mill of the nigh by flashes of lining and gusts of win."

How Can I Perform Better on Tests?

Test-Taking Strategies

"Is this going to be on the test?" That's a question you've probably heard or asked many times. One that is just as important is this: "What type of test will it be?" If you know the kind of test, you can decide how to prepare for it. In this lesson you will learn some helpful strategies for taking classroom and standardized tests.

TAKING CLASSROOM TESTS

Classroom tests cover topics studied in class. In a social studies class, for example, you might be given a test on Spain's conquest of the Inca empire. Here are some ways to prepare for taking a classroom test:

1. **Learn what the test will cover.** Ask your teacher what ideas will be covered and what types of questions will appear on the test.

2. **Plan your study time.** Don't cram for the test at the last minute. Instead, spread out your study times.

3. **Review all written materials and list the key facts.** Quickly reread any notes, textbook chapters, or handouts. Then make a list of key facts and concepts such as names, vocabulary words, dates, events, and math formulas.

4. **Memorize the key facts.** Here are some tips:
   - Read your list of facts aloud.
   - Make and use flash cards.
   - Make up silly sentences to remember groups of facts ("**M**any **v**ery **e**ager **M**artians **j**uggled **s**oft, **un**ripe **p**ears" = **M**ercury, **V**enus, **E**arth, **M**ars, **J**upiter, **S**aturn, **U**ranus, **N**eptune, **P**luto).

5. **Rest and relax.** Go to bed early the night before a test.

In the following sections you will learn how to answer the different types of questions that can appear on classroom tests.

Answering Objective Questions

In answering an **objective question,** look for one brief, correct answer. The following information describes four types of objective questions and gives some strategies for answering them.

A **true-false question** is really a statement. Your job is to tell whether the statement is true or false. Use these strategies:

- If even one small part of a statement is false, the whole statement is false.
- Words like *all, always, every, never,* and *only* often but not always appear in false statements.
- Words like *generally, most, often, probably, some, sometimes,* and *usually* often appear in true statements.

> (T) F   Colorblindness is generally more common among males than among females.

Matching questions ask you to match items in one group with items in a second group. Try these strategies:

- Check to see if you are allowed to match some items more than once or if some items will not be used at all.
- Read all of the items. Then match the ones that you know.
- Cross out items as you match them, unless they can be used more than once.

> Write the letter of each poem title next to the correct author's name.
>
> **a.** "Casey at the Bat"   _c_ **1.** Lilian Moore
>
> **b.** "The Raven"   _b_ **2.** Edgar Allan Poe
>
> **c.** "The First"   _e_ **3.** Eloise Greenfield
>
> **d.** "The Dream Keeper"   _d_ **4.** Langston Hughes
>
> **e.** "Way Down in the   _a_ **5.** Ernest Lawrence
> Music"   Thayer

PEANUTS reprinted by permission of UFS, Inc.

A **multiple-choice question** asks you to choose the best answer from a group of answers provided. These strategies may help you:

- Read all choices. Ignore the ones that are obviously wrong.
- Choose the best answer from the ones that are left.

> **1.** Which is the most abundant mineral in your body?
>   **A.** iron   **B.** magnesium   **C.** sodium   **D.** calcium

A **fill-in-the-blank** or **completion question** asks you to write a brief answer on a blank line. Use these strategies:

- First fill in the answers you are sure of.
- Then go back and reread the questions you left blank.
- If several words are needed, write all of them.

> **1.** The battle that ended the American Revolution happened in 1781 at _Yorktown, Virginia._

Answering Short-Answer Questions

Classroom tests also often contain short-answer questions. These questions are especially good for testing both specific knowledge and understanding of a subject area.

A **short-answer question** asks you to give a short, written answer. Give these strategies a try:

- Read the directions completely.
- Answer in complete sentences if asked to do so.
- Make sure that your grammar, spelling, punctuation, and capitalization are correct.

> Answer the question below in a complete sentence.
>
> **1.** Of all the living creatures on earth, which has the largest population?
> _The beetle has the largest population on earth._

Grammar
TIP

The answer to a fill-in-the-blank or completion question should fit grammatically into the sentence.

Answering Essay Questions and Writing Prompts

Like a short-answer question, an **essay question** asks for a written answer, but the answer to an essay question is longer and more complex. In science class, for example, you may be asked to explain the process of photosynthesis.

A **writing prompt** asks you to write a short composition. It may tell you the form your composition should take and the audience for whom you should write. Here is an example of a writing prompt:

> **1.** In a letter to your principal, state your opinion about the recent decision to shorten your school's lunch period.

Understanding the Question   Try the following strategies:

- **Locate** the topic about which you are to write.
- **Find** key words that tell you what to do, such as *compare, explain, identify,* or *describe.*
- **Identify** the form, such as a letter or an essay.
- **Determine** the audience, such as sports fans.

Writing the Response   Be sure to follow these guidelines:

1. **Read** all parts of an essay question. Pay careful attention to the form and audience stated in a writing prompt.
2. **Organize** your ideas on scratch paper before you write.
3. **Proofread** your response. If you left out an important idea, insert it. Correct any mechanical errors.

Practice Your Skills

Write a response to one of the following writing prompts.

1. Write a brief essay for your classmates called "How Not to Take a Test." In your essay, explain four things that a student definitely should not do when he or she takes a test.
2. Choose a music video, television program, or movie and write a review for your school newspaper. Tell students whether or not they should see the production and why.

PROBLEM

S O L V I N G

How can I find out more about essay tests?

For more information about assessment, see Writer's Workshop 6, pages 155–158.

COMPUTER TIP

Some on-line services contain special help and question-and-answer departments for students who will be taking standardized tests.

An *oshiya*, or "pusher-in," helps a man into a crowded subway during rush hour in Japan.

A **standardized test** covers several areas of knowledge. One type of standardized test, an **achievement test,** is designed to find out what you have learned over several years. Subjects covered on an achievement test include math, vocabulary, reading, grammar, usage, science, and social studies. You can't really study for a standardized test. However, you can learn strategies for answering the test questions.

Answering Reading Comprehension Questions

Reading comprehension tests are used to find out how well you understand what you have read. You are asked to read passages that are followed by questions that may ask you to do such things as state the main idea, recall details, or draw a conclusion. In some tests the questions may have more than one correct answer. Read the test directions carefully. Then follow these steps:

- Read the questions before you read the passage.
- Look for answers to the questions as you read.
- Read all of the answer choices. Then choose the best answer. If several answers are allowed, choose all correct answers.

Read the following passage. Then answer the question below. The question may have more than one correct answer.

The United States imports many Japanese products, including cars, televisions, and VCRs. At the same time, Japan imports many things from the United States, including English words. Recent Japanese borrowings from the English language include *ice cream*, *taxi*, and *rush hour*. Many teachers in Japan dislike the imported English words, which they think of as slang. Nevertheless, Western popular culture and English words continue to be popular among Japanese teens.

1. Which English words have been borrowed by the Japanese?
   A. boyfriend   **B.** taxi   **C.** airplane   **D.** ice cream

Answering Grammar, Usage, and Mechanics Questions

A **grammar, usage, and mechanics question** tests your language skills. You are given a sentence with several parts underlined. Your job is to decide which of the underlined parts contains an error. If no part contains an error, the answer is "No error."

The error occurs in part C. The word *are* should be *is.*

> The <u>principal,</u> <u>in addition to</u> the teachers, <u>are</u> here. <u>No error.</u>
>   **A**   **B**   **C**   **D**

Use these strategies for answering similar questions:

- Read the entire sentence, not just the underlined parts.
- Check word choice, punctuation, capitalization, sentence structure, agreement, and other grammatical issues.

Answering Vocabulary Questions

Standardized tests often contain two types of vocabulary questions. These are synonym questions and antonym questions.

A **synonym question** asks you to find words that are similar in meaning. An **antonym question** asks you to find words that are opposite in meaning. Try these strategies:

- Read all the answers and then choose the best one.
- Choose similar words for synonym questions and opposite words for antonym questions.

> Choose the word most similar in meaning to the underlined word.
> **1.** <u>affluence</u>
>   **A.** poverty   **B.** wealth   **C.** happiness   **D.** freedom
>
> Choose the word most opposite in meaning to the underlined word.
> **2.** <u>affluence</u>
>   **A.** poverty   **B.** wealth   **C.** happiness   **D.** freedom

Answering Analogy Questions

In an **analogy question,** you must determine how two given words are related. Then you must choose a word that makes the second pair of words relate to each other in the same way as the first pair. Some analogies have fill-in-the-blank lines.

> **1.** <u>Lion</u> is to <u>pride</u> as <u>wolf</u> is to _____.
>   **A.** den   **B.** cub   **C.** pack   **D.** kin

In the analogy above, you must decide how *lion* and *pride* are related. Follow these steps:

- Make a sentence using the first pair of words that shows their relationship: A group of *lions* is called a *pride.*
- In the sentence, replace the first pair of words with the second pair: A group of <u>wolves</u> is called a _____.
- Complete the sentence: A group of *wolves* is called a *pack.*

Some analogies use symbols instead of the words *is to* and *as.* Follow the same steps as above to help you complete this type of analogy.

> **1.** earthquake ⟶ destruction : humor ⟶ _____
>   **A.** joke   **B.** comedy   **C.** comedian   **D.** laughter

In the analogy above, the correct answer is "D. laughter." An earthquake causes destruction, and humor causes laughter.

TAKING TESTS

When taking a test, follow these steps:

1. When you first receive your test, skim over it. Note the types of questions and which sections will require more time to complete, such as a section with essay questions. Plan your time accordingly.

2. Carefully read the questions and all possible answers.

3. Answer all the questions you know. Make a mark next to the questions you can't answer, and go back to them later.

4. On answer sheets, fill in each answer circle darkly and completely. Be sure that you mark each answer in the correct place. If you make a mistake, erase and re-mark neatly.

5. Review your answers, proofreading where appropriate. Correct any confusing answers or illegible handwriting.

Practice Your Skills

A. Reread the passage on page 372. Then answer these questions. There may be more than one correct answer to each question.

1. What conclusions can you draw from the passage?
   A. People in the United States buy Japanese products.
   B. Western culture influences people throughout the world.
   C. The United States has imported many words from Japan.
   D. Japan imports ice cream from the United States.

2. According to the passage, what group in Japan opposes the importing of English words from America?
   A. business leaders **B.** politicians **C.** teenagers **D.** teachers

B. Choose the word closest in meaning to the underlined word.

1. extravagant
   A. new **B.** outdated **C.** excessive **D.** wild

2. distinguished
   A. smothered **B.** famous **C.** friendly **D.** right

C. Complete these analogies:

1. slice ⟶ pie: foot ⟶ _____
   A. sock **B.** yard **C.** shoe **D.** inch

2. chick ⟶ hen: child ⟶ _____
   A. baby **B.** adult **C.** person **D.** youngster

3. mathematics ⟶ numbers: music ⟶ _____
   A. orchestra **B.** notes **C.** piano **D.** conductor

4. meat ⟶ beef: fruit ⟶ _____
   A. bean **B.** peanut **C.** peach **D.** cabbage

Day of the Dead candelabrum (1992), Oscar Soteno. On November 2, All Souls Day in the Catholic Church, Mexicans and Mexican Americans celebrate *El Dia de los Muertos* (the Day of the Dead). Families honor the dead by visiting cemeteries, where they light candles and decorate graves with flowers. Day of the Dead folk art often features humorous skeletal figures that engage in the customary activities of the living.

Grammar and Usage Handbook

MINI-LESSONS

Skills

Directions   One or more of the underlined sections in the following sentences may contain an error in grammar, usage, punctuation, spelling, or capitalization. Write the letter of each incorrect section. Then rewrite the section correctly. If there is no error in an item, write *E*.

> **Example** The <u>North American</u> <u>continent</u> does not end at the
>   **A**   **B**
> <u>Pacific Ocean</u>. It continues under the <u>Ocean</u> for about forty-five miles.
>   **C**   **D**
> <u>No error</u>
> **E**
>
> **Answer** D—ocean

1. <u>Wow Some</u> of those geysers in <u>Yellowstone National Park</u> <u>spouts</u> water one
    A   **B**   **C**
   hundred <u>feet</u> into the air. <u>No error</u>
       D   **E**

2. On <u>february</u> 5, 1976, Maude Tull had her <u>driver's</u> <u>license</u> <u>renewed. She</u> was 104
       A   **B**   **C**   **D**
   years old at the time. <u>No error</u>
                  E

3. The famous <u>pony express system</u>, which carried mail from <u>Missouri</u> to California,
             A   **B**
   <u>was</u> in operation for only eighteen <u>monthes</u>. <u>No error</u>
   C   **D**   **E**

4. <u>King Richard I</u> of <u>England, also</u> known as Richard the <u>Lion-Hearted, spent</u> only
      A   **B**   **C**
   about half a year in his own <u>country. During</u> his entire rule. <u>No error</u>
                 D   **E**

5. <u>Cockroachs</u> are hard to get rid <u>of, and</u> they have been around for a long
     A   **B**
   <u>time. They</u> have <u>existed</u> on the earth for 250 million years. <u>No error</u>
     C   **D**   **E**

6. Have you ever <u>laid</u> in the <u>ocean, if</u> you have, you <u>know</u> that salt water holds a
           A   **B**   **C**
   person up <u>better</u> than fresh water does. <u>No error</u>
         D   **E**

7. A <u>Siberian</u> husky has a <u>thick, oily</u> <u>undercoat. Which</u> keeps water away from the
     A   **B**   **C**

<u>dogs'</u> skin. <u>No error</u>
 D   **E**

8. My cousin and <u>me</u> <u>were</u> amazed that frozen yogurt is so <u>healthful and tastes</u> so
          A **B**   **C**

<u>well</u>. <u>No error</u>
 D   **E**

9. The <u>lungs</u> and hearts of the natives of the <u>Andean</u> region <u>is</u> larger than those of
    A   **B**   **C**

people who live at <u>Sea</u> level. <u>No error</u>
           D   **E**

10. <u>Yellowstone National Park</u> has long been famous for <u>it's</u> many active geysers.
    A   **B**

There <u>is</u> also hot springs, mud volcanoes, fossil <u>forests, and</u> a glass mountain.
     C   **D**

<u>No error</u>
 E

11. The <u>Great Sandy</u> and the Simpson <u>are</u> two of the <u>desserts</u> of Australia. Of the
     A   **B**   **C**

two, the Great Sandy is <u>biggest</u>, covering about 150,000 square miles. <u>No error</u>
           D   **E**

12. The United States <u>produces</u> more cheese than <u>any country</u>, but the <u>French</u> <u>eat</u>
               A   **B**   **C** **D**

more cheese per person than people in the United States eat. <u>No error</u>
                                      E

13. That letter <u>has set</u> on your desk for several <u>days</u>. <u>To</u> <u>whom</u> is it <u>addressed</u>?
          A   **B**   **C**   **D**

<u>No error</u>
 E

14. Robin Hood was a <u>legendary</u> hero. <u>Him</u> and his men <u>robbed</u> from the rich and
             A   **B**   **C**

<u>gived</u> to the poor. <u>No error</u>
 D   **E**

15. <u>"An</u> old Irish <u>superstition"</u>, explained Tim, "says <u>your</u> going to have bad luck if
   A   **B**   **C**

you meet a weasel on the <u>road."</u> <u>No error</u>
                   D   **E**

Sketch Book

Animals talk to each other, of course. There can be no question about that; but I suppose there are very few people who can understand them. I never knew but one man who could. I knew he could, however, because he told me so himself. . . . According to Jim Baker, some animals have only a limited education, and use only very simple words, and scarcely ever a comparison or a flowery figure; whereas, certain other animals have a large vocabulary, a fine command of language, and a ready and fluent delivery; consequently these latter talk a great deal; they like it; they are conscious of their talent, and they enjoy "showing off."

MARK TWAIN
"BAKER'S BLUE-JAY YARN"

- What animal would you like to talk to? How would that animal speak? Write the dialogue of your conversation.

- Which animals have limited educations, and which ones like to show off? Write down your speculations.

- Have you ever been misunderstood? How did it happen? Why did it happen? Tell about the experience.

The Sentence and Its Parts

No matter whom you talk to, you want to be understood. The way you put your words together—the sentences that you make—can determine how well you succeed.

In this handbook you will learn what makes up sentences and how you can structure sentences to get your message across—to any audience.

SENTENCES AND SENTENCE FRAGMENTS

A **sentence** is a group of words that expresses a complete thought; a **sentence fragment** does not express a complete thought.

A complete thought is clear. Which of the following groups of words expresses a complete thought?

1. Close by the whale
2. The whale jumped clear of the water
3. Suddenly, a great splash

The second group of words expresses a complete thought. It is a complete sentence.

Sentence fragments do not express complete thoughts. The reader cannot be sure of what is missing or of the author's meaning.

A sentence fragment may be missing a subject, a verb, or both. You may wonder *What is this about?* or *What happened?*

Fragment	The huge whale (*What happened?*)
Sentence	The huge whale jumped high into the air.
Fragment	Eagerly watched for whales (*Who watched for whales?*)
Sentence	On the boat, tourists eagerly watched for whales.

You can correct a sentence fragment by supplying the missing information. Sometimes a fragment can be corrected by joining it to a complete sentence.

Practice Your Skills

A. CONCEPT CHECK

Sentences and Sentence Fragments   Write *S* for each complete sentence and *F* for each sentence fragment.

1. I saw a TV show yesterday
2. The show was about dolphins
3. Actually a kind of small whale

Writing
TIP

Always express yourself in complete thoughts to avoid confusing your reader.

Writing Theme
Whales

4. Dolphins are quite intelligent
5. Playful animals that seem to enjoy games
6. Under the water in the big tank
7. The dolphins can be very entertaining
8. Just for the fun of swimming in front of an audience
9. Dolphins have a well-developed sense of hearing
10. They communicate complex messages
11. A variety of chirps, whistles, and squeaks
12. Can be heard for great distances under water
13. Dolphins live in groups, or pods
14. Swim in oceans around the world and even in some rivers
15. Because dolphins breathe air and are warm-blooded

B. REVISION SKILL

Correcting Sentence Fragments   Rewrite the following letter. Make the ten fragments into sentences.

> Dear Elena,
>   Yesterday I had a thrilling adventure. My parents and I sailed far out to sea. On a large boat. The passengers boarded the boat. Early in the morning on Cape Cod in Massachusetts. We were at sea for several hours, looking for whales. Almost gave up. Finally, one of the passengers sighted whales. At least twenty or thirty of them. Our boat got very close. A few of the whales leaped into the air. Splashed everyone. When they landed. No one complained! The whales seemed playful. They even seemed to enjoy our company. Got especially close. It pushed its head out of the water right next to the boat. Almost touched it! Time passed so quickly. Soon we had to leave. And return to port. Was sad. I hated leaving the whales. I'll always remember that trip.
>   Christine

C. APPLICATION IN WRITING

Writing Complete Sentences   Write a letter to a friend describing your vacation experience with dolphins in a small cove. Change the five sentence fragments from the following list into complete sentences, and use the sentences in your letter.

the large rubber raft
swimming nearby all afternoon
wanted me to play too

rubbed against the raft
played tag with each other

FOR MORE PRACTICE
See page 408.

The Sentence
and Its Parts   **383**

The **subject** of a sentence tells *whom* or *what* the sentence is about. The **predicate** tells what the subject *does* or *is*.

Every sentence has two basic parts: the subject and the predicate. The **subject** tells *whom* or *what* the sentence is about. The **predicate** tells something about the subject.

Subject	Predicate
(Who or what)	(What is said about the subject)
Playful puppies	chew on everything.
Lion cubs	sleep about twenty hours a day.

Each sentence expresses a complete thought. Think of the sentence as telling who did something or what happened. The subject tells *who* or *what*. The predicate tells what was *done* or what *happened*.

Who or What	Did or Happened
The deer	leaped over the high fence.
The opossum	curled into a ball.
The horse	galloped gracefully across the field.

Practice Your Skills

A. CONCEPT CHECK

Subjects and Predicates   Make two columns on your paper. Label them *Subject* and *Predicate*. Write the proper words from each sentence in the columns.

1. Monarch butterflies are beautiful and interesting animals.
2. We saw several in our yard.
3. Monarchs have black bodies and orange wings with black borders.

Writing Theme
Animal Behavior

4. These butterflies spend the summer in the United States.
5. Fall weather sends them south.
6. They fly about eleven miles per hour.
7. Thousands of these insects may gather together in huge flocks.
8. Some of them will travel as many as three thousand miles.
9. The flocks spend the winter in a remote valley in Mexico.
10. The butterflies head back north in the spring.

B. DRAFTING SKILL

Sentence Completion   Use each group of words below to form complete sentences. You may wish to add a subject or predicate, or both where necessary. Tell which part you added.

11. wolves
12. are feared unnecessarily
13. have been the subject of many folk tales
14. their piercing eyes and sharp teeth
15. a German shepherd
16. have a bushy tail
17. the pups, or young wolves
18. live in a den dug into the ground
19. are related to the jackal and the dog
20. the color of their fur
21. the gray wolf, the red wolf, and the prairie wolf
22. sometimes called timber wolf and coyote
23. because wolves roam prairies and pasture land
24. can be dangerous to livestock
25. now an endangered species as a result of overhunting

C. APPLICATION IN WRITING

Describing an Animal   Brainstorm a list of experiences you have had with animals. Think about household pets, animals you have seen at the zoo, or animals that live in the wild. Choose one experience and write a description of that experience. When you have finished, underline the subject once and the predicate twice in each sentence.

FOR MORE PRACTICE
See page 408.

The Sentence
and Its Parts

SIMPLE SUBJECTS AND PREDICATES

A **verb** is a word that tells about action or that tells what someone or something is. The **subject of the verb** is the most important part of the complete subject.

In every sentence, a few words are more important than the rest. These key words make the basic framework of the sentence.

The young **musician** **played** skillfully.
His **hands** **moved** rapidly across the strings.

The subject of the first sentence is *The young musician.* The key word in this subject is *musician.* The predicate in the sentence is *played skillfully.* The key word is *played.* Without this word you would not have a sentence.

The key word in the subject of a sentence is called the **simple subject.** It is the subject of the verb.

The key word in the predicate is called the **simple predicate.** The simple predicate is also called the **verb.**

Finding the Verb and Its Subject

The verb and its simple subject are the basic framework of every sentence. The rest of the sentence is built around them. To find this framework, first find the verb. Then ask *who* or *what* before the verb. The answer identifies the subject.

That musician plays the zither. *Verb:* plays
Who or what plays? musician
Simple subject: musician

You can tell a fragment from a sentence easily by carefully identifying the subject and verb. A fragment will be missing a subject or verb or both.

Fragment   Lively music (*What about it? What happened?*)
Sentence   Lively music *poured from the unusual instrument.*
Fragment   From the unusual instrument.

Looking at the Sentence as a Whole

You have learned how to identify a simple subject, or key word in the subject. The **complete subject** is the simple subject plus any words that modify or describe it.

> EXAMPLE   The young musician played skillfully.

The young musician is the complete subject. It is made up of the simple subject plus the modifiers *the* and *young*.

Similarly, the **complete predicate** is the verb plus any words that modify or complete the verb's meaning. What is the complete predicate in the example sentence above? What is the simple predicate, or verb?

Sentence Diagraming   For information on diagraming subjects and predicates, see page 692.

Practice Your Skills

A. CONCEPT CHECK

Simple Subjects and Predicates   Label two columns *Verb* and *Simple Subject*. In the correct column, write the verb and its simple subject for each of the following sentences.

Writing Theme
Unusual Musical
Instruments

1. The kazoo is a musical instrument about six inches in length.
2. It resembles a tube in appearance.
3. In the early 1900s, people called the kazoo a Sonophone.
4. Alabama Vest invented this popular musical instrument.
5. Even nonmusical people play the kazoo.
6. Perhaps this fact explains the instrument's popularity.
7. Stores sell more than one million kazoos every year.
8. Some musicians view this instrument as more than a toy.
9. Those kazooists play metal kazoos.
10. Recently, four professional kazooists formed a very unusual quartet.
11. They call this quartet Kazoophony.
12. During concerts they wear tuxedos and no shoes.
13. Kazoophony performs silly songs such as "The 1813 Overture" and "Swine Lake."
14. On a more serious side, the University of Chicago formed an informal kazoo marching band.
15. Leonard Bernstein even wrote a part for kazoo in *Mass*.

B. REVISION SKILL

Precise Word Choice   Act as a peer reader for the author of the passage below. First, write and label the subject and verb from each sentence. Then suggest words that are more precise as replacements for the underlined subjects or verbs.

[16]Besides all his other accomplishments, Benjamin Franklin <u>made</u> a most unusual musical instrument. [17]Franklin <u>called</u> his invention the armonica. [18]The <u>thing</u> consisted of thirty-seven glass bowls on a long rod. [19]A mechanism <u>moved</u> the bowls rapidly. [20]The <u>person</u> placed a finger on a spinning bowl. [21]The bowl vibrated from the pressure of the finger. [22]Each glass bowl <u>made</u> a different tone.

[23]<u>People</u> throughout Europe and the United States loved the armonica. [24]Unfortunately, the vibrations of the bowls damaged the nerves of the player's fingers. [25]Soon, no one <u>used</u> the armonica anymore.

CHECK ✔ POINT
MIXED REVIEW · PAGES 382–388

Write *S* for each complete sentence, *F* for each sentence fragment. Then identify and label the missing element needed to form a complete sentence: *Subject, Verb,* or *Subject and Verb.*

1. Orson Welles was one of Hollywood's most creative actors and directors.
2. First great success as a radio broadcaster.
3. In the radio broadcast *The War of the Worlds,* Welles.
4. Many listeners believed Martians had landed on Earth.
5. Began a long and distinguished career.
6. The remarkable movie *Citizen Kane.*
7. The character of Kane was based on William Randolph Hearst.
8. This colorful ruler of a newspaper publishing empire.
9. Portrayed a publishing tycoon's ambition and ruthlessness.
10. The brilliant director, Orson Welles, also played the lead.
11. First appeared in movie theaters in 1941.
12. Hearst tried to stop its release.
13. Because of inventive filmmaking techniques.
14. Still consider it one of the greatest American films of all time.
15. Viewers for years to come.

Writing Theme
Orson Welles

FOR MORE PRACTICE
See page 408.

THE VERB PHRASE

A **verb** may consist of one word or of several words.

Sometimes the **main verb** in a sentence is used with one or more **helping verbs.** A main verb and one or more helping verbs make up a **verb phrase.**

Helping Verbs	+	Main Verb	=	Verb Phrase
might have		gone		might have gone
will		see		will see
are		driving		are driving
could		go		could go
could be		riding		could be riding

Sometimes the parts of a verb are separated from each other by words that are not verbs. In each of the following sentences, the parts of the verb phrase are printed in bold type. The word in between is not part of the verb phrase.

> The old cowpoke **could** always **tell** a good story.
> He **is** finally **buying** a new horse.
> The trail boss **has** often **made** camp here.
> Longhorn cattle **would** sometimes **stampede** unexpectedly.
> Cowhands **must** occasionally **ride** great distances.

Some verbs are joined with other words to make contractions. When naming verbs that appear in contractions, name only the verb. The word *not* and the contraction *n't* are adverbs. They are never part of a verb or a verb phrase.

Contraction	Verb
hasn't *(has not)*	*has*
couldn't *(could not)*	*could*
we're *(we are)*	*are*
I've *(I have)*	*have*
we'd *(we had or would)*	*had* or *would*

Two young rough-and-ready cowboys scrape off the trail dust and don clean duds for the camera.

Practice Your Skills

A. CONCEPT CHECK

Verb Phrases Write the verb or verb phrase in each sentence.

1. In the late 1800s, vast herds of cattle were raised in Texas.
2. The cattle owners couldn't easily get their beef to market.
3. This problem may have contributed to the growth of the West.
4. Before long, in response to the need for a transportation system, railroads slowly advanced westward.
5. Cowhands would drive the cattle to the railheads, or end of the existing rail lines.
6. Railheads would eventually grow into cow towns.
7. Cow towns moved west with the railroads.
8. Cattle arrived in Sedalia, Missouri, for the first time in 1866.
9. By 1867, Abilene, Kansas, had become a main railhead.
10. A few years later, railroads reached Dodge City, Kansas.
11. Cow towns did not always have good reputations.
12. After cattle drives, cowhands were often seeking some fun.
13. The celebrations should have been happy.
14. However, fights and shootings would often occur.
15. Dodge City is still remembered as the roughest cow town of all.

B. APPLICATION IN LITERATURE

Verbs and Verb Phrases Write and label each *Main Verb* and *Helping Verb* in the numbered sentences below.

[16]During a trail drive, cowboys would move thousands of cattle across the range to railroad stations. [17]From there the cattle were shipped to markets for sale in the East.

[18]A cowboy's work could be difficult and dangerous. [19]There were hardships involved in tending cattle. . . .

[20]Commonly, cowboys didn't call one another by their real names. [21]Within his first week at the bunkhouse, a new man was generally given a nickname. [22]Often the name described something about him. [23]For example, a redhead might be called "Red" or "Sunset," and a sorrowful-looking man "Gloomy." . . .

[24]After sunset at a roundup, the cowhands would spend some time together. [25]A cowboy might bring an accordion, a fiddle, or a banjo to a roundup. [26]As in the early West, a cowhand today will often enjoy a song after work.

Elaine Landau, *Cowboys*

FOR MORE PRACTICE
See page 409.

SENTENCES BEGINNING WITH *HERE* AND *THERE*

When *here* or *there* is the first word in a sentence, the word can be an adverb or merely an introductory word.

Sentences Beginning with *There*

Many sentences begin with the word *there*. Sometimes *there* is used as an adverb modifying the verb to tell where something is or happens.

> There is the cave entrance. (The cave entrance is *there*.)
> There stands the guide. (The guide stands *there*.)
> There are some unusual cave fish. (Some unusual cave fish are *there*.)

In other sentences, *there* is only an introductory word that helps get the sentence started. It is not necessary to the meaning of a sentence.

> There are many large caves in the United States.
> (Many large caves are in the United States.)

In most sentences beginning with *there,* the subject follows the verb. To find the subject, first find the verb. Then ask *who* or *what.*

> There is a deep pool in this cave.
> *Verb:* is
> *Who or what is?* pool.

Sentences Beginning with *Here*

In sentences beginning with *here,* the word *here* is always an adverb telling where about the verb.

> Here is another cave opening. (Another cave opening is *here*.)
> Here are some very long stalactites. (Some very long stalactites are *here*.)

Writing **TIP**

Sentences that begin with *here* and *there* can be helpful when you are explaining a process, or how to do something.

Practice Your Skills

A. CONCEPT CHECK

Sentences Beginning with *Here* and *There*   Write the simple subject and the verb in each sentence.

1. There are three experienced cavers in your group.
2. Here at this point you can go down into the cave.
3. There is only one way down.
4. Here the path becomes very steep and slippery.
5. There are no lights of course.
6. Here you will need a flashlight.
7. There, just a little beyond the opening, the cave ceiling gets extremely low.
8. There you must crawl on your hands and knees.
9. There goes a bat!
10. Here are hundreds of bats hanging from the ceiling.

B. REVISION SKILL

Sentence Variety   The overuse of *here* or *there* at the beginning of sentences can create dull, repetitive writing. Rewrite the following paragraph. Revise sentences **12, 13, 15, 16, 19,** and **20** so that they do not begin with *here* or *there.* You may want to drop *here* or *there,* or you may want to reposition the words. Underline the subject once and the verb twice in the sentences of your revised paragraph.

> EXAMPLE   There are unusual animals in caves.
> Unusual <u>animals</u> <u>live</u> in caves.

[11]There can be many animals in caves. [12]Here, near the cave entrance, certain animals live part of the time. [13]There may be bears, rats, porcupines, and various birds and insects in this part of the cave. [14]Here the animals leave the cave for part of the day. [15]There are other animals somewhat farther back in caves. [16]There are bats, crickets, spiders, cockroaches, certain kinds of owls, and other animals in this sort of twilight zone area. [17]Many animals in the deepest reaches of the cave never leave the darkness. [18]There are blind animals, such as fish and salamanders, as well as many insects. [19]Here you will also find animals with no skin color at all. [20]There, in total darkness, skin color would not be visible.

FOR MORE PRACTICE
See page 409.

OTHER SENTENCES WITH UNUSUAL WORD ORDER

> The subject does not always come at the beginning of the sentence.

The usual order of words in a sentence is *subject-verb*. Writers and speakers often vary the order to make more interesting sentences. You have seen examples of a varied pattern in sentences beginning with *here* and *there*. In questions, too, sentence order is often *verb-subject*:

> Is that the space shuttle? (That is the space shuttle?)
> Would you travel in space? (You would travel in space?)

Other sentences begin with phrases or adverbs:

> Finally the countdown began. (The countdown finally began.)
> Into the darkness zoomed the space shuttle. (The space shuttle zoomed into the darkness.)
> At the beginning the flight was rough. (The flight was rough at the beginning.)

To find the subject in a sentence that has an unusual word order, first find the verb. Then ask *who* or *what*.

> Did the space colonists worry? *Verb:* did worry
> *Who* or *what did worry?* colonists
> *Subject:* colonists

In **imperative sentences,** which state commands or requests, the subject is usually not given. Since commands and requests are always directed to the person spoken to, the subject is *you*. Because the *you* is not given, we say that it is understood.

> *(You)* Check all the gauges and instruments carefully.
> *(You)* Watch out for that asteroid!

Sentence Diagraming　For information on diagraming imperative sentences, see page 692.

Practice Your Skills

A. CONCEPT CHECK

Unusual Word Order   Label two columns *Subject* and *Verb*. Write the subject and verb for each sentence below.

1. Picture yourself as a crew member of the European Space Agency's Spacelab.
2. In November 1983 you and three other scientists journeyed into space.
3. Within the roomy lab, you monitor many instruments.
4. Past the window in the ceiling streaks a meteoroid.
5. Frequently, such events interrupt the team's work.
6. From this mission may come answers to many questions.
7. In zero gravity, do roots grow down?
8. Will trees grow horizontally rather than vertically?
9. Apparently, gravity limits a plant's growth on earth.
10. Can a plant grow forever in space?

B. REVISION SKILL

Sentence Variety   Revise the following passage to improve the sentence variety. Follow the directions in parentheses.

> **11**Humans might be living in colonies on Mars *in the future.* (Move the italicized phrase.) **12**You can imagine what that might be like. (Use an imperative.) **13**People's homes lie underground. (Use verb-subject order.) **14**You can guess why. (Use a question.) **15**Colonists enjoy 50 degree weather on hot days *near the equator.* (Move the italicized phrase.) **16**Frigid temperatures of about 100 degrees below zero Fahrenheit exist *elsewhere.* (Move the italicized adverb.) **17**Residents are quite comfortable inside their underground homes, *however.* (Move the italicized adverb.) **18**Advanced equipment *constantly* controls temperature and humidity. (Move the italicized adverb.) **19**A spacesuit is a necessity at all times *on the surface.* (Move the italicized phrase.) **20**The danger of harmful radiation lurks throughout the atmosphere. (Use verb-subject order.)
>
> **21**One drawback of each colony is *clearly* size. (Move italicized adverb.) **22**You can wander through the entire area very quickly. (Use an imperative.) **23**You will do what to amuse yourself? (Use verb-subject order.) **24**You will *perhaps* get bored. (Move italicized adverb.)

C. APPLICATION IN WRITING

Writing a Letter   Imagine that a year ago you participated in settling the first space colony on Mars. Now you are writing a letter home to a friend. In your letter, describe the space settlement or your experiences there. Use your imagination. Write at least five sentences with the verb coming before the subject.

FOR MORE PRACTICE
See pages 409–410.

CHECK ✔ POINT
MIXED REVIEW • PAGES 389–395

Writing Theme
Dreams

Write each of the following sentences on your paper. Underline the subject once and the verb or verb phrase twice.

1. Watch out!
2. That flying monster is getting much too close!
3. Suddenly, behind you appears another one.
4. Out of the darkness comes yet a third.
5. Whew! You're only dreaming.
6. Every night your mind will spin new dreams—possibly five or six times.
7. What is the reason for dreams?
8. There is no certain answer.
9. Scientists have learned a little about dreams, though.
10. Your dream may have been triggered by an anchovy pizza at dinner or a scary movie later in the evening.
11. Was your day very busy?
12. During the night your brain may reshape the day's happenings.
13. There is often little similarity between real events and the dream version of those events.
14. However, out of the dreams may come important solutions to problems or questions.
15. Here in your dreams may also lie the idea for a new invention or a great artistic creation.

The Sentence
and Its Parts

OBJECTS OF VERBS

> **Objects of verbs** are words that complete the meaning of a sentence.

Some verbs complete the meaning of spoken or written sentences without the help of other words. The action that they describe is complete.

> The waves *rose.*   Yoko *is swimming.*

Some verbs do not express a complete meaning by themselves. They need to be combined with other words to complete the meaning of a sentence.

> Chris saw _____. (Saw who or what? Chris saw *Mike.*)
> Rosa wears _____. (Wears what? Rosa wears *goggles*.)

Direct Objects

The word that receives the action of a verb is called the **direct object** of the verb. In the sentences above, *Mike* receives the action of *saw. Goggles* receives the action of *wears.*

Sometimes the direct object tells the *result* of an action.

> Sara won the *race.*   She received a *trophy.*

To find the direct object, first find the verb. Then ask *whom* or *what* after the verb.

> We cheered the winner.   The swimmers left the water.
> *Verb:* cheered   *Verb:* left
> *Cheered whom?* winner   *Left what?* water
> *Direct object:* winner   *Direct object:* water

A verb that has a direct object is called a **transitive verb.** A verb that does not have an object is an **intransitive verb.** A verb may be intransitive in one sentence and transitive in another.

Intransitive   They were swimming.
Transitive   They were swimming the English Channel.

Direct Object or Adverb?

Many verbs used without objects are followed by adverbs that tell *how, where, when,* or *to what extent.* These words are adverbs that go with or modify the verb. Do not confuse them with direct objects. The direct object tells *what* or *whom.*

To decide whether a word is a direct object or a modifier of the verb, decide first what it tells about the verb. If it tells *how, where, when,* or *to what extent,* it is an adverb. If it tells *what* or *whom,* it is a direct object.

> Brian swam *slowly.* (*Slowly* is an adverb telling *how.*)
> Kathy swam a tough *race.* (*Race* is a direct object telling *what.*)

Verbs can also be followed by a phrase that tells *how, when,* or *where.* A direct object is never found in such a phrase.

> Cara swam *across the pool.* (*Across the pool* tells *where* Cara swam.)

Practice Your Skills

A. CONCEPT CHECK

Direct Objects   Write the verb or verb phrase from each of the following sentences. Then write the direct object. If a sentence does not have a direct object, write *None.*

1. Some competitive swimmers will attempt almost any long-distance course.
2. The English Channel has challenged the best of them.
3. These remarkable athletes must swim tirelessly for at least twenty-one miles.
4. Cold water, rough seas, and strong currents persist.
5. The first crossing of the Channel occurred in 1875.
6. Captain Matthew Webb achieved this milestone.
7. He swam doggedly for almost twenty-two hours.
8. No one else successfully swam the Channel for the next thirty-six years.
9. Now people swim it almost every year.
10. The best swimmers now cross the English Channel in less than ten hours.

B. APPLICATION IN LITERATURE

Direct Objects   Identify the italicized verbs in the following selection as *Transitive* or *Intransitive.* If the verb is transitive, write the direct object.

    11Diana Nyad *sat* back on her heels. . . **12**For three weeks Diana's living room floor *had been covered* with maps. **13**They *showed* every major body of water in the world. **14**The champion swimmer *was searching* for a route. . . .

    15For days on end, Diana *bent* over the maps and charts in her New York apartment. **16**She *made* list after list of water temperatures, wind speeds, and currents. **17**Each day she *crossed* out certain places and added new ones. **18**Finally, in April 1977 her goal *came* into view.

    19She *would swim* nonstop from Cuba to Florida—130 miles through shark-filled waters. **20**The crossing *would take* . . . sixty hours, maybe sixty-five.

Valjean McLenighan, *Diana: Alone Against the Sea*

Indirect Objects

Some words tell *to whom* or *for whom* something is done. Other words tell *to what* or *for what* something is done. These words are called the **indirect objects** of the verb.

> King Kong showed **Fay Wray** deep *affection.* (showed *for* Fay Wray)
> He gave **her** a *gift.* (gave *to* her)

In the sentences above, the words in bold type are indirect objects. The words in italics are direct objects.

The words *to* and *for* are never used with indirect objects. The words *to* and *for* are prepositions. Any noun or pronoun following *to* or *for* is actually the object of the preposition.

> The mad scientist gave the *monster* a brain. (*Monster* is the indirect object of *gave.*)
> The mad scientist gave a brain to the *monster.* (*Monster* is the object of the preposition *to.*)

Sentence Diagraming   For information on diagraming direct objects and indirect objects, see page 692.

Writing
━━ **TIP** ━━

Objects of verbs help you express complete thoughts in your writing. Notice the difference:
  Joe cooked.
  Joe cooked me dinner.

Practice Your Skills

A. CONCEPT CHECK

Indirect Objects   Label three columns *Verb, Indirect Object,* and *Direct Object.* In the columns, list whichever of these parts of speech you find in each sentence.

1. Many moviegoers love monster movies.
2. Fans will gladly tell you their favorites.
3. However, monster movies often do not receive good reviews.
4. Critics assign them poor marks for production and writing.
5. Sometimes these movies depend on low-budget special effects.
6. Dull writing can give monster movies predictable endings.
7. In spite of such flaws, fans show these movies great loyalty.
8. The 1931 Academy Award for best picture went to *Cimarron.*
9. Few people in recent generations have even heard of that movie.
10. However, another 1931 movie, *Frankenstein,* would still fill a theater.

B. REVISION SKILL

Sentence Expansion   Identify the verb in each sentence as either *T,* transitive, or *I,* intransitive. Then rewrite each sentence that contains an intransitive verb. Use one of the choices from the word bank as a direct object in your revised sentence.

| EXAMPLE | Monsters chase through dark streets. *I* |
| | Monsters chase their prey through dark streets. *T* |

WORD BANK	his terrified victims spellbinding scripts
	audiences a variety of roles
	the world

11. Monster movies can entertain by using special effects.
12. Screenwriters have written for countless horror films.
13. You have no doubt seen Count Dracula.
14. This favorite has been stalking through movies since silent films.
15. King Kong, Wolf Man, and Mr. Hyde awakened us to other horrors.
16. A weird collection of monsters performs in the *Star Wars* movies.
17. However, these odd creatures generate smiles instead of fear.
18. Other movies have brought viewers dangers of a different sort.
19. Germs from outer space attack Earth in *The Andromeda Strain.*
20. In *The Invasion of the Body Snatchers,* plant monsters take over.

Writing Theme
Monster Movies

FOR MORE PRACTICE
See page 410.

The Sentence
and Its Parts   **399**

PREDICATE WORDS AND LINKING VERBS

> **Linking verbs** connect the subject with a word or group of words in the predicate.

Not all verbs express action. A verb may simply say that the subject exists. Such a verb may also link the subject of a sentence with a word or group of words in the predicate. A verb that links the subject with words in the predicate is called a **linking verb.**

Mustangs *are* wild horses.
Mustangs *were* once a common sight in the Southwest.
Bronco *is* another name for a wild horse.

The most common linking verb is the verb *be.* This verb has many forms. Study these forms of *be* to make sure that you can easily recognize them:

be   been   is   was
being   am   are   were

The verbs *be, being,* and *been* can also be used with helping verbs. Here are some examples:

might be   is being   have been
could be   are being   might have been
will be   was being   would have been

The words linked to the subject by a linking verb like *be* are called **predicate words.** There are **predicate nouns, predicate pronouns,** and **predicate adjectives.**

The mare is a *thoroughbred.* (predicate noun)
That pony is *mine.* (predicate pronoun)
The colt was *frisky.* (predicate adjective)

Notice how the subjects and the predicate words in the above sentences are linked by *is* or *was.*

Here are some other common linking verbs:

seem   feel   become   look   remain
appear   taste   grow   sound

Like *be,* these verbs can have various forms (*seems, appears, felt*), or they can be used with helping verbs (*will appear, could feel, might have become*).

The *story* seems *believable.* (predicate adjective)
You sound *excited.* (predicate adjective)
My *brother* has become an *expert.* (predicate noun)

Sentence Diagraming   For information on diagraming predicate words following linking verbs, see page 692.

Practice Your Skills

A. CONCEPT CHECK
Predicate Words   Write the predicate words in the following sentences.

1. Horses are central figures in many stories of fact and fiction.
2. Pegasus is a winged horse in Greek mythology.
3. Bellerophon was the owner of this special creature.
4. With the help of Pegasus, Bellerophon became the slayer of a fire-breathing monster.
5. The hero grew famous after this deed.
6. He felt very proud of his accomplishment.
7. According to the myth, Pegasus eventually became a constellation.
8. Sleipnir was the horse of Odin, a god in Norse mythology.
9. This animal must have looked very odd indeed.
10. His eight legs were no doubt his strangest feature.
11. Another of Sleipnir's characteristics, the capability of running on both land and water, seems quite unusual too.
12. Comanche, a cavalry horse, became a part of United States history.
13. He was the only survivor of Lieutenant Colonel George Custer's "last stand."
14. A horse from Roman history, Incitatus, must have appeared quite grand in his ivory manger.
15. Did his oats taste especially good in such elegant surroundings?

Writing
━━ TIP ━━

Using linking verbs with predicate adjectives is one way to create vivid sensory description.
   The lemonade tasted *cool* and *tart.*

Writing Theme
Horses

B. APPLICATION IN LITERATURE

Predicate Words Draw four columns on your paper. Label them *Subject, Verb, Direct Object,* and *Predicate Word.* Write in the columns the parts you find in each sentence in the passage below. Notice how the writer has used these structures to include vivid details.

> [16]She was a cream-colored mare with a black forelock, mane, and tail and a black stripe along the middle of her back. [17]Tall, slender, and high-spirited, . . . she was the most beautiful of horses. [18]Colonel Carter had bred and reared her with me and my uses in mind. [19]She was a careful cross of a mustang mare and a thoroughbred stallion. . . . [20]And she had a sense of fun. . . . [21]She . . . flung her head high in the air . . . [22][She] tucked her nose affectionately under his [Carter's] arm.
>
> [23]"I have handled her a lot," he said. [24]"She is as kind as a kitten. . . . [25]You can spoil her by one mistake. . . . [26]And she is unbroken."

Lincoln Steffens, *Boy on Horseback*

C. APPLICATION IN WRITING

Writing a Letter Imagine that you have just been given the pet horse you have always longed for. Write a letter to a friend, describing the experience and your horse. After completing your letter, review it yourself or ask a classmate to read it. Look for predicate words and direct objects that could be changed to make your letter more specific. Here are some examples.

My colt is nice. (*affectionate*)
I gave him some food. (*oats*)

FOR MORE PRACTICE
See page 410.

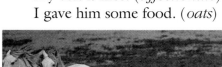

COMPOUND SENTENCE PARTS

> A **compound subject** has two or more parts. A
> **compound predicate** has two or more parts. Many
> parts of a sentence may be compound.

Every part of the sentence you have studied in this handbook
can be compound—subjects, verbs, direct objects, indirect
objects, and predicate words.

If the compound form has only two parts, there is usually a
conjunction (*and, or, but*) between them. If there are three or
more parts, the conjunction usually comes between the last two of
these parts. Use a comma after every part but the last.

Using compound sentence
parts is a way to streamline
your writing. Compound sentence parts also show a
close relationship between
ideas.

Compound Subjects

> *Anne* and *Marc* are building a time machine.
> The *future* and the *past* will be within their reach.

Compound Verbs

> The time machine *thundered, crackled,* and *spewed* smoke.
> People *laughed* and *jeered.*

Compound Objects of Verbs

Direct Objects:
> They tried new *theories* and *strategies* for time travel.
> They will visit tenth-century *London* and third-century *Egypt.*

Indirect Objects:
> We wish *Anne* and *Marc* luck.
> They will bring *Cathy* and *me* a souvenir from the future.

Compound Predicate Words

> The time machine was *small* and *round.*
> It looks *fragile* and *unsafe.*

Sentence Diagraming   For information on diagraming compound sentence parts, see page 693.

Practice Your Skills

A. CONCEPT CHECK

Compound Sentence Parts   Write the compound parts in each of the following sentences. Then write whether each is a *Compound Subject, Verb, Object,* or *Predicate Word.*

1. Many people talk and dream about time travel.
2. Movie scripts and books have been written about it.
3. Yet, time travel remains a mystery and a scientific puzzle.
4. To some people, time travel seems impossible and ridiculous.
5. No one has ever seen objects or travelers from the future.
6. Therefore, people don't travel and will never travel in time.
7. On the other hand, physicists and other scientists agree on the possibility of time travel.
8. Time travelers and time machines must go faster than light.
9. Traveling at light's speed may sound fantastic and absurd.
10. Nevertheless, a hundred years ago you couldn't have convinced critics and disbelievers of the future existence of jet planes.

B. REVISION SKILL

Sentence Combining   Make the following paragraphs more precise and interesting by combining each numbered pair of sentences into a single sentence with a compound part.

 11Time travel is popular. It is also exciting. **12**Several good books have been written about it. Movie scripts have also been written about time travel. **13**"The Time Machine," a short story by H. G. Wells, takes us on a trip through time. The movie *Back to the Future* takes us on a trip through time too. **14**In Wells's short story, we meet the Morlocks in the year 802,701. Wells also introduces the Eloi at this same time. **15**The Morlocks are technologically more advanced than the Eloi. They are more cruel and inhumane as well. **16**Wells's story shows you a possible future for humans. It shows me a possible future too.

 17People may laugh about the consequences of time travel in *Back to the Future*. They also may worry about its consequences. **18**The hero, Marty McFly, travels back in time to 1955. He meets his parents then. **19**Marty almost gives his parents a different future. He almost gives himself a different future too. **20**The audience sees the complications of time travel. They see its dangers too.

C. APPLICATION IN WRITING

Writing a Travel Journal   Imagine that you have been given the opportunity to take a trip through time. Choose a time and place to visit. Think about what you might see and experience. Then write a brief journal entry describing your first day. Use compound parts in at least half of your sentences.

FOR MORE PRACTICE
See page 411.

C H E C K ✔ P O I N T
MIXED REVIEW · PAGES 396–405

Writing Theme
Hannibal's Elephants

Write each of the sentences below on your paper. Underline any compound parts. Then write *D.O.* over all direct objects, *I.O.* over all indirect objects, and *P.W.* over all predicate words.

> EXAMPLE   Hannibal's army threatened
>   D.O.   D.O.
>   <u>Rome</u> and its <u>cities</u>.

1. Rome and Carthage both had mighty empires 2,200 years ago.
2. For several centuries, these cities fought bloody battles and very long wars.
3. A general by the name of Hannibal led the army of Carthage in one of the most famous wars.
4. Hannibal was a great soldier and leader.
5. Hannibal often used elephants in battle.
6. They frightened and pushed aside enemy soldiers.
7. Hannibal brought thirty-eight elephants and fifty thousand troops to Italy.
8. The elephants were a problem for Hannibal.
9. With great difficulty he brought them to Italy from Spain across high mountains.
10. Deep snow and narrow mountain trails were dangerous for the elephants.
11. Food and water were not always available in large enough quantities.
12. The elephants weren't really effective or successful in Italy.
13. Their appearance in Italy must have given soldiers and peasants a surprise, though.
14. For about fifteen years, Hannibal's army gave the city of Rome considerable trouble.
15. Hannibal fought well but never conquered Rome.

AVOIDING RUN-ON SENTENCES

> A **run-on sentence** is two or more sentences written incorrectly as one.

When two sentences are incorrectly written as one, the result is a **run-on sentence.** Sometimes no punctuation mark is used between run-on sentences. At other times, a comma is incorrectly used.

Incorrect   Folk tales are old their origin is unknown.
Incorrect   Folk tales are old, their origin is unknown.
Correct   Folk tales are old. Their origin is unknown.

As you can see, a run-on sentence confuses readers. You can avoid run-on sentences by using a period or other end mark to show the reader where each complete thought ends. For other ways to correct run-on sentences, see Handbook 22, page 297 and Handbook 45, pages 556–559.

Practice Your Skills

A. CONCEPT CHECK

Run-on Sentences   Identify and label each of the following sentences as *Run-on* or *Correct.*

1. Almost everyone has heard of Mother Goose the tales and rhymes have been told for generations.
2. Most Mother Goose tales are older than the first Mother Goose books the tales were told orally before they were published.
3. These entertaining tales have been told in many languages.
4. For example, the stories and rhymes were popular in France in the 1600s.
5. Many of the Mother Goose tales come from England they were written for adults as a form of political criticism.
6. In the United States, Mother Goose tales first appeared in 1786.
7. People argue about whether there really was a Mother Goose no one is sure.
8. Some people think she was real others insist she was fictional.
9. Mother Goose may have been Elizabeth Goose, she was a grandmother living in Boston during the colonial period.
10. Others think the real Mother Goose lived in an earlier time.

B. REVISION SKILL

Correcting Run-On Sentences   Rewrite the run-on sentences, correcting the mistakes. Write *Correct* if the item does not contain a run-on.

11. Jakob and Wilhelm Grimm collected folk tales.
12. "Little Red Riding Hood" is one of their most famous tales, "Snow White" is another.
13. The brothers worried about the loss of the oral German folk tales, the young men preserved them on paper.
14. The tales recorded by the Grimms had been told for centuries, they were passed on from one generation to the next.
15. The Grimms collected tales between 1807 and 1814, they collected them from farmers in villages.
16. Nineteen of the tales were told by an elderly woman.
17. All tales were recorded faithfully and exactly.
18. The first printed volume of the brothers' tales appeared in 1812, it held eighty-six tales.
19. The second contained seventy tales, it appeared in 1815.
20. The Grimms were influenced by German history, they also wrote about German myths.

FOR MORE PRACTICE
See page 411.

C H E C K ✔ P O I N T
MIXED REVIEW · PAGES 406–407

Writing Theme
Toothpaste

Write each of the sentences, correcting all run-on sentences. If a sentence contains no run-ons, write *Correct*.

1. A tube of toothpaste looks innocent inside are some weird ingredients, though.
2. White toothpaste is made partly of chalk.
3. Chalk comes from shellfish it scrubs your teeth clean.
4. Gel toothpastes use silica for scrubbing silica is found in sand.
5. There are other ingredients, too, such as mouthwash and fluoride.
6. These ingredients are held together by a substance this special substance comes from seaweed.
7. Today our toothpaste seems plain, the first toothpastes were made from coral, fish bone, burnt eggshells, and porcelain.
8. Those early toothpastes may also have included insect bodies.
9. The insects were used for coloring the toothpaste.
10. What is used for color today, could it still be insect bodies?

The Sentence
and Its Parts   **407**

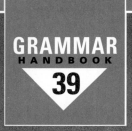

GRAMMAR
HANDBOOK
39

Writing Theme
Adventures

A. Identifying Sentences and Sentence Fragments   Write *S* for each sentence and *F* for each sentence fragment.

1. All schools and classrooms are not alike
2. Outward Bound is one of the oldest wilderness schools
3. Held on sheer cliff walls or violent rivers
4. Teaches self-confidence and cooperation with others
5. You may feel a rush of fear
6. Leaping from the side of a cliff
7. Your companions' strong arms and legs help support you
8. Sometimes the fear and uncertainty
9. At the end of the course
10. You'll have new courage and greater self-confidence

B. Complete Subjects and Predicates   Write each sentence. Draw a line between the complete subject and complete predicate.

11. The study of ancient people can often lead to real adventure.
12. Thor Heyerdahl wrote a book, *The Ra Expedition,* about his experiences in 1970 as an explorer.
13. Heyerdahl sailed a boat, the *Ra,* from Africa to the West Indies.
14. The boat was made of papyrus reed, a kind of plant.
15. Some of the earliest boats were made from papyrus.
16. Ancient Egyptians also made paper from papyrus.
17. Heyerdahl and his crew sailed this paper boat across the entire width of the Atlantic.
18. They provided support for a theory about the ancient Egyptians, a people of North Africa.
19. These people may have reached America long before the Vikings.
20. Heyerdahl's voyage on the *Ra* took about two months.

C. Finding Verbs and Simple Subjects   Draw two columns and label them *Simple Subject* and *Verb.* Write the verb and its simple subject for each of the following sentences.

21. Some people find great excitement and adventure in wild places.
22. Sometimes they turn their interest into a profession.
23. Jane Goodall chose her profession as a zoologist that way.
24. Her research on chimpanzees made her famous.
25. She devoted her efforts to wild animals in their native habitat.
26. She stalked wild animals as part of her job.

27. Goodall's work took her to the wildest forests and jungles.
28. Dangerous and unpredictable animals were a constant threat.
29. She patiently observed her subjects for days and even years.
30. Precise field notes described all of the animals' activities.

D. Finding Main Verbs and Helping Verbs Label two columns *Main Verb* and *Helping Verb*. Write the appropriate words from each sentence in the columns.

31. The fifteen-year-old commander is speaking to Mission Control.
32. Something has suddenly gone wrong with the main fuel tank.
33. It couldn't have happened at a worse time in the mission.
34. The astronauts can't find a solution.
35. Tension is quickly building in the shuttle.
36. The crew members aren't worried, though.
37. The shuttle crew is only working in a simulator, or model.
38. They'll get another chance at the mission.
39. They're attending the U.S. Space Camp in Huntsville, Alabama.
40. Since 1982, thousands of boys and girls have gone to this camp.

E. Sentences with *Here* and *There* Write the simple subject and the verb in each sentence. Tell whether *there* or *here* is used as an adverb or as an introductory word.

41. There are many kinds of adventure available to you.
42. Here in Antarctica many people seek adventure.
43. There were mainly scientific expeditions in the past.
44. There are now many recreational adventurers as well.
45. There may be many reasons for the increased interest.
46. Here is a frozen wonderland of almost untouched wilderness.
47. Here are giant glaciers, huge icebergs, and active volcanoes.
48. There are penguins, whales, seals, and many birds in Antarctica.
49. Here you will find many places for skiing, hiking, and exploring.
50. There are tours traveling regularly to Antarctica.

F. Sentences with Unusual Word Order Write the following sentences. Underline each subject once and each verb twice.

51. Do archaeologists live quiet, uneventful lives?
52. "Not always," might have responded Louis Leakey.
53. Remarkable were the adventures of this famous scientist in Africa.

54. Can you picture Leakey in an open truck on a sunny African veldt?
55. Calmly lounging on the road are twelve lions.
56. Suddenly after him charge all of them!
57. Watch out!
58. Barely does he escape in time.
59. Quite an adventure, don't you think?
60. Around every corner may be wild adventure for an archaeologist.

G. Recognizing Transitive and Intransitive Verbs   Write the verb in each numbered sentence. Label the verb *Transitive* or *Intransitive*. If the verb is transitive, write the objects of the verb and identify each as *D.O.*, direct object, or *I.O.*, indirect object.

[61]A little imagination and planning can give you an adventure anytime. [62]Load your bike with a tent, sleeping bag, water bottles, extra clothes, and a little food. [63]Now, take off! [64]A bicycle trip promises you great challenges. [65]It offers riders almost unlimited freedom. [66]The route, destination, and schedule are entirely up to you. [67]A train or plane can even take you to unusual starting points. [68]Europeans have enjoyed bicycle trips for decades. [69]In the United States, some people go on long trips every year. [70]Bicycle travel has never been as popular here as in some other places, though.

H. Objects and Predicate Words   Label four columns on your paper *Verb, Direct Object, Indirect Object,* and *Predicate Word.* Write these parts from each sentence in the columns.

71. Everyone is occasionally restless for a new experience.
72. Dan Jelsema was an average teenager living in Michigan.
73. Dan had a dream; he wanted adventure.
74. His dream seemed fantastic: a sea voyage around the world.
75. However this young man had experience.
76. His father had taught him much about sailing.
77. This training gave Dan confidence.
78. The eager sailor felt ready for the test.
79. With a boat full of provisions, Dan began his journey.
80. The dream became a reality.

I. Finding Compound Parts of a Sentence Write the compound parts in the following sentences. Tell whether they are *Compound Subjects, Verbs, Objects,* or *Predicate Words.*

81. French astronomer Serge Brunier and seven other amateur astronomers wanted to establish the world's highest observatory.
82. They researched and chose as a site Ojos del Salado, a mountain in South America.
83. Ojos del Salado is 22,572 feet high and icy.
84. It also has a dry atmosphere and low pollution.
85. In this clear, thin air the stars appear clearer and brighter.
86. On maps, Ojos del Salado looked accessible and climbable.
87. The determined astronomers drove as far as possible and then began their hike.
88. They took observations at 19,000 feet but never climbed to the mountain's top.
89. The effects of the altitude gave Brunier and his friends great problems.
90. Thin air and waist-deep snow forced them to stop 1,000 feet short of the summit.

J. Avoiding Run-on Sentences Rewrite correctly the run-on sentences in the paragraph. If a sentence does not need to be rewritten, write *Correct.*

[91]Jacques Cousteau was one of the first ocean explorers, he made many contributions to the field of oceanography. [92]He made one especially important contribution it was the development of oxygen tanks for diving. [93]Previously, divers could not go far under water they wore heavy diving suits. [94]These had metal helmets air was pumped down a tube from a boat. [95]These diving suits were dangerous and clumsy Cousteau's invention was a big step forward. [96]It made possible the exploration of the world's oceans. [97]Cousteau studied all kinds of ocean life people had almost no knowledge of these plants and animals before. [98]He explored shipwrecks he searched for the lost civilization of Atlantis. [99]Cousteau also studied pollution in the ocean, plants and animals were being killed. [100]Cousteau made people aware of the ocean now people think more about keeping it healthy.

Writing Theme
Australia

A. Identifying Subjects and Verbs   Write the simple subject and the verb or verb phrase from each sentence. Identify each *Main Verb* and *Helping Verb.*

1. The continent of Australia is halfway around the world.
2. Even by plane, a trip there is a long journey.
3. In your imagination, you can easily go there in a second.
4. At first, you may notice very little difference between Australia and your home in the United States.
5. The cities, especially, may look similar to those here.
6. The cities lie mainly along the east coast of Australia.
7. The people speak English.
8. Their stores have many of the same items as ours.
9. You'll even recognize the name of their currency—dollars.
10. Before long, though, you may see a great many differences.

B. Identifying Verbs, Objects, and Predicate Words   Write the verbs, direct objects, and predicate words in the following sentences. Label each *Verb, Direct Object,* or *Predicate Word.*

11. The great interior of Australia seems unpopulated.
12. This vast area is the outback.
13. Most Australians of the outback raise livestock.
14. Their ranches are called "stations."
15. These stations are usually huge.
16. One of medium size might cover two hundred square miles.
17. You could build three cities the size of Washington, D.C., on such a station.
18. Most of the outback is extremely dry.
19. In some sparsely vegetated places, fourteen acres of pasture land will feed only one sheep.
20. Despite the harsh land and the isolation, the lonely outback has been the home of a few hardy Australian families for generations.

C. Identifying Compound Sentence Parts   Write the compound parts in each of the following sentences. Then write whether each is a *Compound Subject, Verb, Object,* or *Predicate Word.*

21. Two interesting Australian animals are the wombat and platypus.
22. The grass-eating wombat is large and powerful.

23. It weighs up to eighty-eight pounds and lives in burrows deep in the ground.
24. The platypus has the tail and fur of a beaver.
25. However, the snout and feet are like those of a duck.

D. Identifying Fragments and Run-ons   Identify each of the following sentences as *Fragment, Run-on,* or *Correct.*

26. For tens of thousands of years
27. Australia was rich in plants and animals no people lived there
28. About 40,000 years ago, the first people arrived
29. These people, the Aborigines, probably came to Australia on rafts they came from Southeast Asia
30. Great forests and many rivers, swamps, and lakes
31. People must have had easy lives they spread across the continent
32. Then the land began to dry out
33. Many of the large animals became extinct life got difficult
34. Adapted to the changes in their land
35. Life again became good for the Aborigines

E. Correcting Fragments and Run-ons   Rewrite the following sentences to correct fragments and run-ons.

36. Great Britain once shipped convicts to the American colonies the practice ended during the American Revolution
37. Overcrowded prisons in Britain
38. Looked for another place for its convicts
39. In 1788, eleven British ships landed in Australia they brought settlers and about seven hundred convicts
40. The settlers and convicts suffered greatly the first year food shortages, cold weather, and lack of shelter made life difficult
41. Worked together to build the new Australian colonies
42. Improved after two or three years
43. Spent only a little time behind bars
44. The convicts worked as laborers many were soon pardoned
45. In the first 80 years, more than 160,000 convicts were sent to Australia the settlements grew rapidly

Observation and Description

An eyewitness report lets readers experience an event as if they were actually there. (See Workshop 2.) When you revise an eyewitness report, make your descriptions as vivid as possible. Use compound sentence parts to help your readers understand relationships more clearly. Also look for ways to add interest to your writing by varying sentence openers.

Revise and proofread the following draft of an eyewitness account. Begin by following the directions at the bottom of the page. Then proofread the passage, paying particular attention to correcting sentence fragments and run-ons. Also look for other errors in grammar, capitalization, punctuation, and spelling.

[1]Supporters of Lisa Vogel gathered in the ballroom of the Grant Hotel. [2]People jammed every corner of the vast room, they seemed ready for a big celebration. [3]They carried Campaign Posters. [4]They also had ballons and noise-makers. [5]They waited anxiously for the votes to be counted. [6]The result's were finally announced. [7]After what seemed like hours. [8]The people roared. [9]They threw confetti. [10]They released thier balloons. [11]They chanted the candidates name. [12]Then Vogel walked onto the stage of the ballroom, looking happy. [13]She stepped to the microphone and thanked all the people for there support. [14]She promised to be the best sentor the People had ever elected. [15]As she left the stage. [16]The crowd responded with thunderous applause.

1. In sentence 1, explain who Lisa Vogel is by adding the phrase "the candidate for state senator." Set off the phrase with commas.

2. Combine sentences 3 and 4 to make a sentence with compound objects of the verb.

3. Improve sentence variety by changing sentence 5. Begin with the word "anxiously."

4. Add this detail in an appropriate place: "The results showed that Vogel was the winner."

5. Combine sentences 8, 9, 10, and 11 to form a sentence with a compound verb.

6. Make sentence 12 more descriptive by replacing the phrase "looking happy" with the phrase "with a broad grin on her face."

Poetic License

License plates can say a lot with just a few letters or numbers. C if U can figure out these license pl8s.

HIS XLNC

YRU MAD

XQUS ME

N E 14 10S

IM A QT

CUL8R

BOY 1DER

B GRRR8

H2O SKR

W84ME2

2TH FERY

2 KWIK4U

SOR 2TH

1 DR FUL

GR8DA2U

(Answer: His excellency; Why are you mad?; Excuse me; Anyone for tennis?; I'm a cutie; See you later; Boy wonder; Be great; Water skier; Wait for me too; Tooth fairy; Too quick for you; Sore tooth; Wonderful!; Great day to you.)

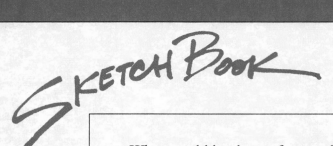

- What would be the perfect meal? Describe it in detail.

Kids' Favorite Foods

Hot dogs
45%

Chicken nuggets
52%

Cheeseburgers
42%

Macaroni and cheese
41%

Pizza
82%

Source: Gallup Poll of 1,034 parents of 3 to 11-year-olds. Respondents could choose more than one.

- What would be a good name for a rock band? a football team? a town in the desert? a newly discovered planet? Think up as many creative names as you can.

- What's on your top-ten list? Choose a category, such as food, athletes, or video games, and make out your top-ten list.

Using Nouns

- **What Is a Noun?**
- **Singular and Plural Nouns**
- **Possessive Nouns**

Cheese, sausage, tomatoes, mushrooms, green peppers, olives. . . . You need nouns to order a pizza with everything on it. Nouns name what you want—pizza and toppings of your choice.

Without nouns, writers couldn't name the people, places, things, and ideas they write about. By choosing precise nouns, you can make your writing clear and expressive.

A **noun** names a person, a place, a thing, or an idea.

All words may be classified into groups called **parts of speech**. A **noun** is the part of speech that names a person, place, thing, or an idea. You use nouns every day when you speak and write. Notice the nouns naming persons, places, and things that are printed on the game cards below.

Many nouns name things you can see.

Person	Place	Thing
stranger	orbit	short story
Edgar Allan Poe	Mars	half-moon
Agatha Christie	outer space	spyglass
water-skier	New Orleans	shadow

Some nouns name things you cannot see, such as ideas, feelings, and characteristics.

Idea	Feeling	Characteristic
justice	surprise	curiosity
fantasy	fear	courage
evil	suspense	imagination
faith	happiness	self-confidence

As you can see in the charts on the previous page, some nouns are compound (more than one word), and some of these compound nouns are hyphenated. In this handbook you will learn to recognize different kinds of nouns and to use specific nouns to make your writing more precise.

Common Nouns and Proper Nouns

All nouns can be described as either common or proper. A **common noun** is the general name of a person, a place, a thing, or an idea. A **proper noun** is the name of a particular person, place, thing, or idea. Proper nouns always begin with capital letters.

Common Nouns	Proper Nouns
author	Sir Arthur Conan Doyle
detective	Sherlock Holmes
assistant	Dr. Watson
villain	Professor Moriarty
country	England
city	London
street	Baker Street

Proper nouns are important to good writing. They make your writing more specific, and therefore clearer.

Practice Your Skills

A. APPLICATION IN LITERATURE

Common Nouns and Proper Nouns   Write the italicized nouns in the following sentences. Identify each one as a Common Noun or a Proper Noun. Be sure to capitalize the proper nouns.

[1]"Many noble *russians* lost everything. [2]I, luckily, had invested heavily in [foreign] *securities*, so I shall never have to open a *tearoom* in *monte carlo* or drive a *taxi* in *paris*. [3]Naturally, I continued to hunt—*grizzlies* in your *rockies, crocodiles* in the *ganges, rhinoceroses* in *east africa*. . . . [4]Hunting was beginning to bore me! [5]And hunting, remember, had been my *life*. [6]I have heard that in *america, businessmen* often go to pieces when they give up the *business* that has been their *life*."

[7]"Yes, that's so," said *rainsford*.

Richard Connell, "The Most Dangerous Game"

Writing
TIP

Using specific common nouns and proper nouns makes your writing more vivid and colorful. For example, the common noun *giant* creates a clearer picture than the common noun *creature*. The proper noun *Cyclops* names a more specific being than the common noun *giant*.

Writing Theme
Science Fiction and Suspense

B. PROOFREADING SKILL

Capitalizing Proper Nouns Rewrite the following paragraphs, correcting errors in grammar, capitalization, punctuation, and spelling. Pay special attention to the capitalization of proper nouns. (15 errors)

Ray bradbury is an author of science fiction and suspense stories. Whether set on mars or in the midwestern united states, his stories are full of excitement and suspense. Bradbury has followed in the tradition of such well-known writers as jules verne and Edgar Allan Poe Jules Verne, a native of france, was the first writer to specialize in science fiction stories. In some of his adventure tales, the characters take unusual trips. For example, Phileas fogg travels around the world, and captain nemo journeys under the sea. The details and explanations in the stories make Verne's science fiction beleivable.

Edgar Allan Poe, on the other hand, wrote frightening suspense stories. They take place in such locations as spain, paris, and the United States. One of his tales is a chilling murder mystery. Set on a street called the Rue Morgue. Poe is considered the creater of the modern detective story. In three stories a private detective named C Auguste dupin investigates a crime. All three authors—Bradbury, Verne, and Poe—capture the reader's attention through well-told tales.

C. APPLICATION IN WRITING

Using Common and Proper Nouns Ray Bradbury, Jules Verne, and Edgar Allan Poe have all written stories filled with suspense. Write a paragraph about one of your own favorite suspense stories.

Before you begin writing, study the following list of common nouns. Choose five that relate to your topic. Then substitute proper nouns for the common nouns. Include the proper nouns in your paragraph.

detective	villain	organization
city	country	crime
heroine	hero	planet
book	movie	robot
author	actor	alien

FOR MORE PRACTICE
See page 428.

CHECK ✔ POINT

Writing Theme
Newsmakers

A. Write the italicized nouns in the following sentences. Identify each one as a Common Noun or a Proper Noun. Capitalize the proper nouns.

1. Have you read about *mary hays* in a *class?*
2. She worked as a *nurse* during the *american revolution.*
3. During the war her *husband, john,* joined the *continental army.*
4. Like many *wives* of colonial *soldiers,* Mary traveled with her husband.
5. One bitter *winter* they camped at *valley forge, pennsylvania.*
6. Despite the weather, they did not give up the *cause* for *freedom.*
7. During the *summer* of 1778, Mary earned her *nickname, molly pitcher.*
8. At the *battle of monmouth, men* were dropping from fatigue.
9. Mary heard the soldiers' *cries.*
10. She grabbed a *pitcher* and brought them *water.*
11. After the *battle george washington* made her an army *sergeant.*
12. Molly Pitcher became a *symbol* of colonial women's *devotion* to the *united states of america.*

B. Make three columns on your paper. Label the columns *Person, Place,* and *Thing or Idea.* Write each of the nouns in the following sentences in the correct column.

13. One afternoon, headlines stunned people throughout the world.
14. The *Challenger,* a space shuttle, had exploded above Cape Canaveral.
15. Viewers watched in horror as television showed the explosion.
16. Newscasters with teary eyes reported the tragedy.
17. It was the worst accident in the history of NASA.
18. All the astronauts aboard the shuttle lost their lives.
19. One of those astronauts, Christa McAuliffe, taught at a high school in New Hampshire.
20. She was the first teacher selected by the government of the United States to travel into space.
21. Her goal was to educate students all over the world.
22. She had planned to broadcast lessons from the *Challenger.*

SINGULAR AND PLURAL NOUNS

> A **singular noun** names one person, place, thing, or idea.
> A **plural noun** names more than one person, place, thing, or idea.

A noun may be either singular or plural. The singular noun *teacher* refers to only one teacher. The plural noun *teachers* refers to more than one teacher. Here are guidelines for forming plurals.

Forming Plurals

1. To form the plural of most singular nouns, add -s.

painters   museums   shelters   events   attitudes

2. When a singular noun ends in s, sh, ch, x, or z, add -es.

dresses   brushes   coaches   boxes   waltzes

3. When a singular noun ends in o, add -s to make it plural.

concertos   cameos   pianos   solos   patios

For some nouns ending in an o preceded by a consonant, add -es.

heroes   potatoes   echoes   tomatoes   vetoes

4. When a singular noun ends in a y preceded by a consonant, change the y to i and add -es.

story—stories   activity—activities   library—libraries

When the y is preceded by a vowel (a, e, i, o, u), just add -s.

alley—alleys   essay—essays   survey—surveys

5. To form the plural of many nouns ending in f or fe, change the f to v and add -es or -s.

leaf—leaves   self—selves   scarf—scarves
half—halves   life—lives   shelf—shelves
loaf—loaves   wife—wives   thief—thieves

For some nouns ending in *f,* add *-s* to form the plural.

motif—motifs   proof—proofs   belief—beliefs

6. Some nouns have the same spelling in both the singular and the plural.

series   species   trout   sheep   moose

7. The plurals of some nouns are formed in special ways.

child—children   tooth—teeth   ox—oxen
woman—women   mouse—mice   man—men

If you can't figure out the correct spelling of a plural noun, a dictionary can help. Look at the dictionary entry for the word *elf,* below. Notice that the entry includes the plural form, *elves.* Most dictionaries show the plural of a noun if the plural is formed in an irregular way.

elf (elf) ***n.**, *pl.* **elves** (elvz) ⟦ ME < OE *ælf,* akin to OHG *alb* (Ger, nightmare), prob. < IE base **albho-,* white > L *albus,* white: prob. basic sense "whitish figure" (in the mist) ⟧ **1** *Folklore* a tiny, often prankish imaginary being in human form, supposedly exercising magic powers and haunting woods and hills; sprite **2** a small child or being, esp. a mischievous one — **elf'like'** *adj.*

Practice Your Skills

A. CONCEPT CHECK

Plural Nouns   Write the plurals of the italicized nouns.

1. Many *child* and *adult* think that they cannot write *poem.*
2. The poet Kenneth Koch tried to change *opinion* about poetry by teaching poetry *class* to young *student* in New York City.
3. Koch published their work in his book about *wish, lie,* and *dream.*
4. He encouraged his *student* to make unusual *comparison* about *thing* in their *life.*
5. One young poet compared bumpy *mattress* to the *back* of *camel.*

Use a thesaurus to help improve your writing. A thesaurus lists synonyms for words. For example, the noun *writer* has many noun synonyms, such as *author, novelist, poet, journalist, playwright,* and *screenwriter.* A thesaurus can help you choose the most precise noun to say exactly what you mean.

Writing Theme
Inspirations

6. Some described the sounds of *piano, radio, mouse,* and crying *baby.*
7. *Youngster* described the colors of *sky, volcano, sheep,* and *goldfish.*
8. Others wrote about *beach, waterfall,* and *leaf.*
9. Writing as a group, one class created a poem about comic-book *hero.*
10. Koch's *pupil* learned to explore their *fantasy* and *belief.*
11. They wrote about what they saw during their *holiday,* read in *book,* or heard on their *stereo.*
12. Koch used creative *activity* to help young *author* sharpen their *sense.*
13. To inspire them, he played records of *concerto, symphony,* and jazz *composition.*
14. With their *eye* closed, *student* listened to the music.
15. The music helped them imagine strange *story* and *scene.*

B. PROOFREADING SKILL

Plural Nouns   Write the following paragraph, correcting errors in grammar, capitalization, punctuation, and spelling. Pay special attention to the plural spellings of plural nouns. (15 errors)

In the winter of 1983, eleven-year-old Trevor Ferrell saw individuals and families. Living on the streets. They warmed there hands over ashs and huddled in doorwayes. Trevor decided to help these people by offering them blankets. Soon his family, and friends were giving away coats, scarfs, and sweaters. They bought loafs of bread and made sandwichs to give away. Then they decided to open a home for some people from the streets, they called it trevor's Place. Volunteers—childrens, men, and women—from nearby communitys and churchs donated time and money. Trevor inspired many people, including the president of the united states, by showing that kindness can turn ordinary individuals into heros.

C. APPLICATION IN WRITING

Using Plural Nouns   People, places, things, and ideas can be sources of inspiration. Write a paragraph about something or someone you find inspiring. Include the plural forms of nouns. Check a dictionary if you are unsure of the correct plural spellings.

As part of his campaign to help the homeless, eleven-year-old Trevor Ferrell offers a hot beverage to a homeless woman.

FOR MORE PRACTICE
See page 428.

A **possessive noun** shows who or what owns something.

The noun following a **possessive noun** may name a thing or a quality.

Thing   Yoki's raincoat   Bianca's umbrella
Quality   storm's fury   Bob's courage

Forming Possessives of Nouns

Type of Noun	Rule	Examples
Singular noun	Add an apostrophe and *s*.	Mr. Ross's plight tornado's path
Plural noun ending in *s*	Add an apostrophe.	the Rosses' home victims' losses
Plural noun not ending in *s*	Add an apostrophe and *s*.	children's fears women's boots

Practice Your Skills

A. CONCEPT CHECK

Possessive Nouns   In each sentence find the noun that should be possessive. Write the correct possessive form of that noun.

1. For years scientists gave hurricanes women names.
2. In 1978, however, scientists began giving hurricanes men names as well.
3. For example, the hurricane that slammed into South Carolina coast in 1989 was called Hugo.
4. The Caribbean islands were the first to feel Hugo fury.
5. This storm winds, waves, and rains caused widespread destruction.
6. The hurricane damaged homes, businesses, and merchants stores.
7. The destruction affected the islands tourist industry.
8. Worst of all, though, people lives were lost.
9. The Red Cross began relief efforts after the hurricane end.
10. Victims of the decade most costly storm also received aid from the government.

Writing
TIP

Use the possessive forms to make phrases more concise.
Hurricane Andrew destroyed *homes of people.*
Hurricane Andrew destroyed *people's homes.*

Writing Theme
Storms

B. DRAFTING SKILL

Sentence Completion   You are a newspaper reporter writing about one family's experience during a tornado. Write each sentence, using the correct possessive form of the word in parentheses.

11. Kris _____ two children were playing outside. (Jacobs)
12. Suddenly, the _____ siren warned citizens of a nearby tornado. (city)
13. Kris took her children and the _____ dog to the basement. (family)
14. The _____ loud noise sounded like a speeding train. (twister)
15. The _____ tearful eyes grew wide with fear. (children)
16. Their _____ soothing voice seemed to calm them. (mother)
17. After the siren blew the all-clear notice, the Jacobses and other families inspected their _____ condition. (homes)
18. Fortunately, the tornado did not severely damage many _____ homes. (families)
19. However, some _____ houses were destroyed. (neighbors)
20. Men, women, and children were frightened, but everyone in the community survived the _____ worst tornado. (season)

C. PROOFREADING SKILL

Possessive Nouns   Write the following paragraph, correcting errors in grammar, capitalization, punctuation, and spelling. Pay special attention to the possessive forms of words. (15 errors)

Midwesterners fear the sight of a tornadoes' funnel cloud. They know that a twisters powerfull force can level a town in minutes. One illinois mans' memory of a tornado. That struck his town in 1965 has never faded. John Boden vividly recalls the storms devastation. The tornado tore families homes from their foundations. Turned a plane upside down, and uprooted trees. One families pool table sat undisturbed in the basement, but the rest of the house was blown away. The twister damaged the towns businesses and totaly destroyed one building. Boden still remembers the residents fear and shock after the tornado. Yet the communitys' citizens and businesspeople began at once to rebuild there town.

FOR MORE PRACTICE
See pages 428–429.

CHECK ✓ POINT
MIXED REVIEW • PAGES 422–426

A. Write the sentences, changing each singular noun in parentheses to either its plural or its possessive form. Some nouns need to be both plural and possessive.

1. (Fairy), ghosts, and (witch) appear in many legends.
2. Some legends are about strange (species) such as sea serpents.
3. Other legends praise (hero) remarkable achievements.
4. For example, John (Henry) life is celebrated in ballads, stories, and songs.
5. Like many folk (hero), John Henry was probably a real person.
6. He was an African American who worked for railroad (company) during the 1870s.
7. One day, John Henry met his (foreman) challenge.
8. Which could dig a tunnel faster, John Henry's hammer or his (boss) powerful steam drill?
9. John Henry hammered faster than the (company) drill.
10. This contest symbolizes (worker) struggles against being replaced by (machine).
11. (Artist) have also featured John Henry in their paintings.
12. Palmer C. (Hayden) painting *His Hammer in His Hand* shows John Henry walking proudly down a railroad track.

B. Correct each incorrect plural or possessive italicized noun in the following sentences. If a word is correct, write *Correct.*

13. *Sailors* tall tales are amazing *storys.*
14. They portray folk *heroes lifes* and incredible adventures.
15. New England *sailors* invented fantastic *seamen,* such as Alfred Bulltop Stormalong, or Stormy.
16. Few could match this *superheros* enormous size or *abilitys.*
17. *Stormys* height was measured in fathoms, not *foots* and *inchs.*
18. *Ships* cooks were always busy preparing special *dishs* for Stormy.
19. He once helped a cook steam *salmons* in pots full of the *seas* fog.
20. Stormy drank *whales* milk through a fire hose and enjoyed eating *ostriches* eggs.
21. After his *feasts* Stormy picked his huge *tooths* with a marlinespike, a pointed iron tool.
22. These tall tales still capture the *readers* attention.

GRAMMAR
HANDBOOK
40

Writing Theme
Sports Standouts

A. Identifying Common and Proper Nouns   Write the italicized nouns in the following paragraph. Identify each one as *Common Noun* or *Proper Noun.* Capitalize the proper nouns.

1*gertrude ederle* was an excellent *swimmer.* **2**In 1922, she broke seven amateur swimming *records* in one *afternoon* at *brighton beach,* New York. **3**In the 1924 *olympic games,* she helped the U.S. relay *team* win a gold *medal.* **4**However, many believe her greatest *achievement* occurred in 1926. **5**In that *year* she swam the *english channel.* **6**She was the first *woman* to swim across this body of water. **7**She swam from *calais, france,* to *dover, england,* and finished the *swim* in record *time.* **8***ederle* returned home a *heroine.* **9**A *parade* in *new york city* welcomed her. **10**The citizens of the *united states* were proud of their amazing *champion.*

B. Forming Plurals of Nouns   Write the correct plural form of each italicized noun in the following sentences.

11. Nancy Lopez started playing golf when she was eight *year* old.
12. She competed in *match* with other *child.*
13. Lopez's *coach* quickly recognized her talent.
14. She was the first girl to play with *boy* on a high school golf team.
15. In 1977, she competed in professional *tournament* for *woman.*
16. Soon afterward, she became one of the greatest *rookie* in the history of the *Lady* Professional Golf Association (LPGA).
17. *Photo* of Lopez appeared in many sports *magazine.*
18. Over the years Lopez has received many *trophy* for her *victory.*
19. Many people admire Lopez's *series* of *success.*
20. Lopez has strong *belief* about the role of hard work in the *life* of successful *athlete.*

C. Forming the Possessives of Nouns   Find the nouns that should be possessive. Write the correct possessive form.

21. Tennis history is filled with athletes amazing achievements.
22. In the 1970s and 1980s, Sweden Bjorn Borg was one of the sport finest players.
23. During his successful career, he earned his opponents admiration.
24. Reporters stories also praised Borg for his accomplishments.
25. Borg helped win his country first Davis Cup.

26. The tennis star triumphs included becoming a Wimbledon champion five times in a row.
27. Another triumph was winning the men championship six times at the French Open.
28. In 1978, Borg won three nations major tournaments.
29. However, Borg never won tennis grand slam.
30. He also failed to win two other countries national championships.

D. Forming the Plurals and Possessives of Nouns

Write the correct plural or possessive form of each italicized noun in these sentences.

31. *Jackie Robinson* professional baseball career began in 1945.
32. Robinson played for the *Monarch,* an all-African-American team.
33. At that time no African *American* were playing in the *nation* major leagues.
34. In the late 1940s, the Brooklyn *Dodgers* president, Branch Rickey, hired Robinson to play on his team.
35. *Rickeys* decision was a bold step and helped to end prejudice in professional baseball.
36. At first Robinson faced *bias* against African Americans.
37. He had to contend with *players* cruel remarks and *fans* insults.
38. Eventually, they showed their respect for his outstanding *abilityes*.
39. For many years he was his *team* most valuable player.
40. In 1962, Robinson was elected to *baseballs* hall of fame.

E. Using Plural and Possessive Forms Correctly

Write the following sentences, correcting the errors in plural and possessive forms.

41. Jim Thorpes great-grandfather was Black Hawk, one of the famous Native American chieves of the 1800s.
42. As a young man, Thorpe attended class at the Carlisle Indian Industrial School, where he played on the schools football team.
43. From 1915 to 1930, Thorpe achieved fame as one of professional footballs' heros.
44. He could kick the football eighty yard and outrun his opponentes.
45. Such displayes of strength and speed earned him peoples' praise.
46. Many authoritys consider Thorpe to be the most talented football player who ever lived.
47. In 1950, a journalists association selected Thorpe as the centuries greatest male athlete.

GRAMMAR
HANDBOOK
40

Writing Theme
Miniature Worlds

A. Identifying Nouns   Write the italicized nouns in the following sentences. Label each one *Common Noun* or *Proper Noun*. Capitalize the proper nouns.

1. *Bacteria* are tiny one-celled *organisms.*
2. They are able to thrive in almost any *environment* on *earth.*
3. Scientists have discovered bacteria in icy regions of *antarctica* and in the hot *springs* of *yellowstone national park.*
4. Using a simple *microscope, anton* van Leeuwenhoek first observed bacteria around 1675.
5. He was an amateur *scientist* in *holland.*
6. During the late 1800s, a French *chemist* and a German *physician* made important contributions to the study of bacteria.
7. In *france, louis pasteur* showed that bacteria cause milk to sour and change wine to vinegar.
8. He identified the kinds of bacteria that cause different chemical *changes.*
9. In *germany, robert koch* discovered that specific bacteria cause certain *diseases.*
10. Koch also developed *techniques* for isolating and growing bacteria.

B. Forming Plurals   Write the plural of each of the following nouns.

11. doll house	16. eyelash	21. shadow box	26. inch
12. woman	17. roof	22. miniature	27. hobby
13. couch	18. drapery	23. piano	28. foot
14. curio	19. glass	24. scarf	29. elk
15. model	20. knife	25. display	30. goose

C. Forming Possessives   Write the possessive form of each italicized noun. If the italicized noun is plural, be sure to use the plural possessive form.

31. The Thorne Miniature Rooms, displayed at the Art Institute of Chicago, are one of the *city* popular attractions.
32. The lifelike settings have fascinated the *museum* visitors since the exhibit opened in 1954.
33. Narcissa Niblack Thorne, the *rooms* creator, began collecting miniatures during her childhood.
34. Later, with several *people* help, Thorne began making shadow-box displays of her miniatures.

35. She used *architects* drawings to design some of the rooms.

36. Thorne decorated the rooms with *weavers* colorful rugs and tapestries.

37. This *designer* attention to detail made her rooms seem magical.

38. The *shadow boxes* charm enchanted viewers of all ages.

39. In 1932, Thorne's first set of rooms was displayed at a benefit for the Architectural *Students* League.

40. The same rooms were then shown at *Chicago* Century of Progress Exposition in 1933.

41. Other rooms were on exhibit at a *World* Fair in 1939.

42. Some of *Thorne* shadow boxes were donated to charities for sale.

43. Thorne also created two rooms for a *children* hospital.

D. Using Plural and Possessive Forms   Write the following sentences, correcting errors in plural and possessive forms.

44. Did you know that some full-grown horses are shorter than ponys?

45. Miniature horses stand less than three foot tall.

46. Miniatures, however, are not natures smallest horses.

47. Horses earliest ancestor's lived millions of years ago.

48. They stood between ten and twenty inches' tall.

49. In contrast, todays miniature horses are much larger.

50. The first modern miniatures were probably the pets of Europes' royal familys.

51. Later, in the 1700s, some miniatures performed tricks in circus.

52. Monkies often rode on small horses to entertain the audience.

53. Sometimes miniatures played comic roles in clowns acts.

54. Other miniatures spent their lifes hauling coal in underground mines.

55. They obeyed their masters commands and became coal miners reliable companions.

56. Today some miniatures are raised as childrens' pets.

57. Others are bred to perform at rodeoes.

58. The miniatures compete in different class of events.

59. Some shows feature the miniatures jumping abilities.

60. Before the shows the miniatures are groomed, and sometimes their hoofs are painted.

61. The best horses earn winners prizes.

62. Whether or not they win blue ribbons, miniature horses always receive an audiences' applause.

WRITING CONNECTIONS
Elaboration, Revision, and Proofreading

Informative Writing: Explaining *What*

Writing a consumer report is an effective way to analyze information about a product or service. (See Workshop 5.) When you revise a consumer report you have written, make sure you present accurate information in a logical order. Use precise nouns to make details and examples more specific.

On your paper revise the draft of a consumer report below. Follow the directions at the bottom of the page. Proofread your revision, paying special attention to errors in the use of nouns. Also look for other errors in grammar, capitalization, punctuation, and spelling.

¹In the late 1970s, akio morita convinced his company to design a tiny portable tape player with lightwieght headphones. ²The idea of Morita became a commercial success. ³Today, several companys in our country and japan market little portable stereos. ⁴Many corporations also make large stereo systems and big-screen televisions. ⁵Many different models are now available to consumers' who enjoy music. ⁶Some models have radios, cassette players or combinations of both ⁷Some even play compact discs. ⁸What kind of portable stereo to buy depends on you're needs. ⁹Consider the cost, the size, the quality, and the features. ¹⁰Portable stereoes with only radios are the smallest, lightest, and least expensive. ¹¹Models with only tape players are ideal. ¹²If you listen just to cassette recordings. ¹³Portable Compact disc players are the largest and most expensive, but they are a worthwhile investment for true music lovers. ¹⁴A recording of a piece of music on a compact disc most closely resembles a live performance. ¹⁵More expensive tape players have Dolby, a noise-reduction system.

1. Delete the sentence that does not support the main idea of the report.
2. Make sentence 2 more concise by changing the phrase "the idea of Morita" to a phrase containing a possessive form.
3. Make the phrase "our country" in sentence 3 more precise by changing it to a proper noun.
4. Move sentence 15 to a more logical position.
5. Divide the passage into two paragraphs.

A Collection of Nouns

Speakers of English have had a great deal of fun making up words for groups of things. You're already familiar with some of these—a *school* of fish, a *herd* of cattle, a *flock* of sheep or birds. If you hear of a *swarm,* you probably think of bees. But do you know what a *clutch* is? It's a bunch of eggs—a *clutch* of eggs in a nest. Then there's the word *brood,* which is related to *breed* and means a family of young animals—such as newly-hatched birds.

Some of these words have an interesting connection to the animals they name. For example, a *pride* of lions seems quite fitting for the king of beasts. Was it the quality of wisdom that led to a *parliament* of owls? How about a *leap* of leopards, a *plague* of locusts, a *gaggle* of geese, and a *shrewdness* of apes?

What does an *exaltation* of larks make you picture?

Most of these words have been around for almost six hundred years. However, some are newcomers. In a book titled *An Exaltation of Larks,* James Lipton put together a collection of these group terms and even added some new ones. Playfully making a connection to the thing named, he suggested a *piddle* of puppies. How about a *wince* of dentists, an *intrusion* of cockroaches, or a *shush* of librarians? Lipton also suggests a *stand* of flamingoes, a *dash* of commuters, and a *wobble* of bicycles.

If this all seems confusing, why not send your questions to a *wrangle* of philosophers, or better yet, add some collective nouns of your own. Can you think of any?

a Leap of Leopards

433

Sketch Book

- Imagine that you and your family were at Niagara Falls. Write a postcard to a friend telling about your experiences.

- Tell the story of an adventure you and your friends had.

- What is your most prized possession? Describe something that is special to you, and tell why it is special.

Using Pronouns

NIAGARA
DAREDEVIL

Can you imagine telling what you did on your summer vacation without using such words as *I, we, he, she,* and *they?* If a person tries to write without using pronouns, a person quickly discovers that a person's writing sounds very awkward and wordy.

The sentence you just read certainly shows that problem! Pronouns take the place of nouns. By using pronouns effectively, you can make your writing flow smoothly.

A **personal pronoun** is a word that is used in place of a noun or another pronoun.

Personal pronouns are used to refer to nouns that name persons or things. Study the following examples.

Awkward   Jane put on Jane's boots. Then Jane went hiking.
Improved   Jane put on her boots. Then she went hiking.

Note how the personal pronoun *her* helps the writer avoid repeating the same noun. Also notice how the pronoun *she* acts as a bridge to connect the two sentences.

To use personal pronouns to make your writing concise, you should understand how they are classified. First, pronouns are classified by **person:**

1. Pronouns in the **first person**—*I, my, me, we, our,* and *us*—refer to the person(s) speaking.
2. Pronouns in the **second person**—*you, your, yours*—refer to the person(s) spoken to.
3. Pronouns in the **third person**—*he, his, him, she, hers, her, it, its, they, their, them*—refer to some other person(s) or thing(s) that is being spoken of.

The personal pronoun *it* usually replaces a noun that stands for a thing or an animal. *It* is never used in place of a person.

Second, personal pronouns are classified by **gender.** Pronouns in the **masculine gender** refer to male people. Pronouns in the **feminine gender** refer to female people. Pronouns in the **neuter gender** refer to animals or things.

Lewis studied *his* map. (*His* is in the third person, masculine gender.)
Ilsa said the compass was *hers.* (*Hers* is in the third person, feminine gender.)
The parrot flapped *its* wings. (*Its* is in the third person, neuter gender.)

Writing
TIP

Pronouns can help you express your ideas smoothly when you are writing about literature. Notice how Annie Maxwell uses pronouns in her analysis of "Dancing for Poppa" on pages 168–169.

Practice Your Skills

A. APPLICATION IN LITERATURE

Personal Pronouns   Write the personal pronoun(s) in each sentence. Then identify each as *First Person, Second Person,* or *Third Person.*

1During my stay in the Kelabit highlands, I looked across the wide, green valley to study the mountains that marked the border of Kalimantan. **2**They were only a few miles away, and I knew that this time I would reach them. **3**A few nights before I left, Pedera Ulan gave me some travel advice for the land beyond the mountains. **4**"You must obtain a *surat jalan* (walking letter). . . . **5**It is your letter of introduction. **6**For your safety always travel from one headman to another. **7**Each headman will write you a new letter. . . ."

8I was warned to take only guides who had been arranged by the headman. **9**This was because a guide who is answerable to the head of his village will take care of you. **10**He is responsible for your safety and well-being. . . . **11**Any local who violates the code of village hospitality can expect his family and their descendants to bear the guilt of his actions.

Eric Hansen, *Stranger in the Forest*

Eric Hansen rides an express cargo boat up the Baram River, Sarawak, Borneo.

B. REVISION SKILL

Using Pronouns to Avoid Repetition   Revise the following draft by writing pronouns to replace the words in italics.

12Borneo is very densely forested in *Borneo's* interior. **13**Eric Hansen managed to penetrate *Borneo.* **14***Eric Hansen* walked through *Borneo's* dense jungles to find the Penan people. **15**The Penans spend *the Penans'* lives as nomads. **16**Hansen's Penan guides taught *Hansen* survival skills in the rain forest. **17**Most important to *Hansen* was *Hansen's* sense of humor. **18**At night the guides told *Hansen* stories of *the guides'* people. **19**Hansen adapted "Cinderella" for *the guides.* **20**Cinderella worked for *Cinderella's* ugly sisters, and *Cinderella* fell in love with the son of a headman of a Penan village. **21**The guides enjoyed *Hansen's* story, and *the guides* asked *Hansen* to tell *the story* often.

A personal pronoun has three forms: the **subject form,** the **object form,** and the **possessive form.**

In English, personal pronouns have three special forms. Like nouns, they have a **possessive form.** In addition, they have a **subject form** and an **object form.**

> *She* is a writer. (subject form)
> A lyric poet is *she.* (subject form as predicate pronoun)
> This poem was written by *her.* (object form)
> It is *her* best one. (possessive form modifying a noun)
> The idea was *hers.* (possessive form as a predicate pronoun)

Notice that the subject form of a pronoun may be used as the subject of the sentence or as a predicate pronoun. You may recall that predicate pronouns follow linking verbs and rename the subject of the sentence. The object form may be used as the direct or indirect object or as the object of a preposition. The possessive form is used to show ownership.

The Subject Form of Pronouns

A personal pronoun is used in the subject form (1) when it is the subject of a sentence or (2) when it follows a linking verb as a predicate pronoun. Here are the subject forms of personal pronouns:

The Subject Form of Pronouns			
Singular	I	you	he, she, it
Plural	we	you	they

> *I* love to write. (subject of a sentence)
> *He* is also a writer. (subject of a sentence)
> The illustrator is *she.* (predicate pronoun)
> The playwrights were *they.* (predicate pronoun)

The Object Form of Pronouns

A personal pronoun is used in the object form (1) when it is the direct or indirect object of a verb or (2) when it is the object of a preposition. A preposition is a connecting word such as *of, for, to, with,* or *by.*

The Object Form of Pronouns

Singular	me	you	him, her, it
Plural	us	you	them

The critics praised *her.* (direct object)
The screenwriter thanked *us.* (direct object)
The audience asked *him* many questions. (indirect object)
The autograph is for *me.* (object of a preposition)

The Possessive Form of Pronouns

The possessive form of a pronoun is used to show ownership. There are two groups of personal pronouns in the possessive form: (1) those used like adjectives to modify nouns and (2) those used like nouns as subjects, predicate words, objects of verbs, or objects of prepositions.

Pronouns Used to Modify Nouns

Singular	my	your	his, her, its
Plural	our	your	their

Pronouns Used Alone

Singular	mine	yours	his, hers, its
Plural	ours	yours	theirs

Your story is in the folder. (modifying a noun)
This editorial on sports eligibility in the school newspaper is *mine.* (used alone)
Our deadline is today. (modifying a noun)
Are these notes *yours?* (used alone)

Writing
TIP

You may often hear sentences such as the following: "Yes, this is her." "Hi! It's me."

The object forms are sometimes used in casual conversation. Writing is more formal; be sure to use the subject form as the predicate pronoun.

Practice Your Skills

A. CONCEPT CHECK

Pronoun Forms Write the correct pronouns from those given in parentheses. Then label each as *Subject Form, Object Form,* or *Possessive Form.*

1. Because of (me, my, mine) strong curiosity, (I, me, my) often wonder how people get started in their careers.
2. How certain writers got their start has fascinated (I, me, my).
3. (They, Them, Their) often had surprising beginnings.
4. Many of (they, them, their) wrote, but they worked at other jobs too.
5. Much to (I, me, my) surprise, Robert Frost worked as a chicken farmer, but (he, him, his) wasn't very successful.
6. In later years, Frost explained (he, him, his) failure.
7. (He, Him, His) was just too lazy for farming!
8. Doris Lessing also had to work at other jobs; (she, her, hers) was a rocky beginning.
9. (She, Her, Hers) left school at the age of fifteen.
10. Jobs such as nursemaid, typist, and telephone operator gave (she, her, hers) a steady income.
11. Eventually, recognition as a writer was (she, her, hers).
12. Anton Chekhov, Arthur Conan Doyle, and William Carlos Williams earned (they, them, their) living as physicians.
13. Sometimes (they, them, their) medical experiences provided (they, them, their) with material for (they, them, their) writing.
14. (We, Us, Our) have to admire a writer like Kenneth Grahame who worked full time at a bank and wrote in (he, him, his) spare time.
15. It was (he, him, his) who created Toad, Rat, Mole, and all the other lovable characters in *The Wind in the Willows.*
16. Perhaps the dreary bank work gave (he, him, his) the urge to create an imaginary world.
17. However, it was never (he, his, him) intention to have the tales published; (he, him, his) wrote (they, them, their) as entertainment for (he, him, his) son.
18. Because these writers survived (they, their, theirs) hardships, adventure and entertainment can be (we, us, ours).
19. In (we, us, our) world today, it's still very hard to start as a beginning author and work (you, your, yours) way up.
20. However, a writer's life can be (you, your, yours) if (you, your, yours) are willing to work at something else too.

B. PROOFREADING SKILL

Using Pronoun Forms Correctly   The writer of the following paragraph has made some errors. Rewrite the passage, correcting all errors, especially those of pronoun forms. (10 errors)

> For you and I, fans of westrens and Pioneer novels, it's a good thing that Louis L'Amour wrote so many stories. However, for he, just as for many other writers, a number of unusual jobs were a necesity. He worked as a caretaker of a mine a boxer, and a lumberjack. Was even a hobo and a merchant sailor. Truly, the life of a wanderer was him. Many of L'Amour's experiences are described in his book *Education of a Wandering Man.* Its pages are filled with fascinating storys. In later years he wrote, "A wanderer I had been through most of mine early years, and now that I had my own home, my wandering continued, but among books."

C. APPLICATION IN WRITING

Describing a Process   Carefully study the picture below. Write a brief explanation of the process that is shown. Be sure to use subject, object, and possessive pronouns correctly.

FOR MORE PRACTICE
See page 463.

Write the italicized pronouns in the following sentences. Label each pronoun *Subject, Object,* or *Possessive.*

1. *My* friend Mike belongs to a superstitious family.
2. Strange practices come naturally to *them.*
3. *His* grandfather always carries a rabbit's foot.
4. *It* is the left hind foot of a rabbit that was caught in a graveyard.
5. *Its* power is supposed to be great.
6. Mike's grandmother was an actress in *her* youth.
7. Once *she* accidentally whistled in a dressing room.
8. The other actors made *her* leave the room, turn around three times, and spit to remove the bad luck.
9. Those actors—a very superstitious group were *they.*
10. A list of *their* practices would fill several pages!

A tourist surveys hex sign artist Johnny Ott's collection of signs decorated with a sunburst motif, an ancient symbol meaning "welcome."

11. Mike's father, on the other hand, collects horseshoes; *he* says that even the Romans thought *they* were lucky.
12. *His* always hang over the back door.
13. Long ago, people carried *them* to ward off the "evil eye."
14. The belief is that the iron gives *them* special powers.
15. Mike's mom, however, does not believe in *it.*
16. Instead, *she* collects Pennsylvania Dutch hex symbols.
17. *They* do not have a farm; therefore, *it* is impossible to follow the custom of putting *them* on a barn.
18. A brightly colored hex symbol hangs above *her* desk.
19. Anyone can quickly tell which desk is *hers.*
20. Mike's aunt Matilda is different; *hers* are really outdated superstitions.
21. Matilda once scolded *him* for sweeping dirt out the door.
22. "*You* just swept away the luck of this house.
23. *Yours* is a thoughtless generation!" *she* shouted.
24. Apparently, *he* was supposed to sweep the dirt into the fireplace.
25. However, *he* explained to *her* that *their* modern home is not equipped with an open hearth!

PRONOUNS IN COMPOUND
SUBJECTS AND OBJECTS

In a compound subject or a compound object, use the same pronoun that you would use if the pronoun stood alone.

Speakers and writers seldom make mistakes when they use one personal pronoun in a sentence. However, they may have to pause to think when two pronouns, or a pronoun and a noun, are used together in compound sentence parts. For example, would you say *between you and I* or *between you and me?* Study the following examples and read the pointers below.

> *Mario and she* went to the theater. (compound subject)
> I joined *Sue and them.* (compound direct object)
> Mario gave *Sue and me* a program. (compound indirect object)
> It was very helpful to *Sue and me.* (compound object of a preposition)

Read the sentences above a second time. This time, drop out the noun in each compound part. For example, read "*She* went to the theater." Each sentence should sound complete and sensible when the pronoun is used alone.

Whenever you are in doubt about which form of the pronoun to use in a compound sentence part, drop out the noun or the other pronoun and read the sentence with just one pronoun.

> The conductor smiled at (he, him) and (I, me).
> The conductor smiled at *him.*
> The conductor smiled at *me.*

Remember to use only *I, we, he, she,* or *they* as predicate pronouns after forms of the verb *be.*

> The narrator is *she.*   The stage manager will be *I.*

Practice Your Skills

A. CONCEPT CHECK

Pronouns in Compound Subjects and Objects   Write the correct pronouns from those given in parentheses.

1. Between you and (I, me), I used to not like opera at all!
2. However, Ryan and (I, me) went to see *Carmen*.
3. It was the first opera for both (he, him) and (I, me).
4. The playbill gave other members of the audience and (we, us) a summary of the story.
5. Carmen and a band of gypsies are in Seville, Spain; (she, her) and (they, them) are camped outside the city.
6. A young soldier, Don José, sees the gypsies and (she, her).
7. José must choose between (she, her) and Micaela, his sweetheart from home.
8. Carmen was two-timing (he, him) and Escamillo the toreador.
9. Escamillo and (he, him) fight for Carmen's love.
10. José feels he must stop Escamillo and Carmen; he must prevent (he, him) and (she, her) from being together.
11. His solution, stabbing the fickle Carmen, surprised my friend and (I, me).
12. After the show, the audience and (we, us) clapped loudly.

B. REVISION SKILL

Using Pronouns in Compound Subjects and Objects   Rewrite the following paragraph, correcting errors in pronoun use.

[13]My brother and me had heard of an opera called *The Barber of Seville*. [14]The story, though, was a new one for him and I. [15]It has a lot of romance and intrigue, which are important for I and for many people. [16]The composer, Gioacchino Rossini, put humor into this opera too. Him and his music have lasted for almost 180 years; perhaps humor is the reason. [17]The two lovers in the story are Count Almaviva and Rosina, but him and her are kept apart by her guardian. [18]Figaro, the barber, likes Almaviva and she, so he figures out how to bring the count and she together. [19]Figaro and the count provide a variety of clever plans and disguises that keep all of we in the audience happy. [20]One night, for example, Rosina and Almaviva plan to elope, but them and their plans run into trouble. [21]In the end, him and her really do get married. [22]So love always triumphs, as you and me know.

FOR MORE PRACTICE
See page 463.

POSSESSIVE PRONOUNS

AND CONTRACTIONS

A **possessive pronoun** never has an apostrophe; a **contraction** always has an apostrophe.

A **contraction** of a pronoun and a verb is formed by omitting one or more letters from the verb and inserting an apostrophe in place of the letters that have been left out. Note that *who* is a pronoun that is used to ask a question. As an interrogative pronoun, it is in the subject form. You will learn more about interrogative pronouns later in this handbook.

Writing
━ TIP ━

Avoid contractions in certain types of writing, such as reports and business letters. Contractions are more appropriate for written dialogue and informal writing.

| it + is *or* has = it's | they + are = they're |
| you + are = you're | who + is *or* has = who's |

Some **possessive pronouns** sound like contractions. Because the words sound alike, they are sometimes confused. Note that *whose* is the possessive form of the pronoun *who*. It is used to ask a question and to modify nouns.

Possessive Pronouns	*Contractions*
its	it's
your	you're
their	they're
whose	who's

| *Incorrect* | The school celebrated it's victory. |
| *Correct* | The school celebrated its victory. |

| *Correct* | You're (You are) late for the test. |
| *Correct* | Who's (Who is) the debater whose notes you have? |

Follow these two simple rules for using possessive pronouns and contractions correctly:

1. If the word you want to use stands for two words, it is a contraction and needs an apostrophe.
2. Never use an apostrophe in a possessive pronoun.

Practice Your Skills

A. CONCEPT CHECK

Possessive Pronouns and Contractions   Write the correct word given in parentheses in the following sentences. If the word is a contraction, also write the words the contraction represents.

1. The South Koreans have worked hard to improve (their, they're) educational system.
2. (Their, They're) now rightfully proud of the schools.
3. No doubt, (your, you're) probably used to beginning school in the fall.
4. The South Korean school year begins (its, it's) term in March.
5. (Your, You're) school year usually has 180 days.
6. In South Korea (their, they're) used to 210 days in a school year.
7. (Whose, Who's) eligible to go to college in South Korea?
8. Only students (whose, who's) scores are excellent on the entrance examination may go.
9. (Its, It's) a very competitive test.
10. Only half of the high-school graduates may continue (their, they're) education in colleges or universities.

B. REVISION SKILL

Using Possessive Pronouns and Contractions Correctly
Revise the following dialogue, correcting errors in the use of pronouns and contractions. If a sentence is correct, write *Correct.*

11. LUIS: Your face looks familiar. Your one of the new exchange students, right?
12. RITA: Yes, I am the one whose from South America.
13. LUIS: Do the other exchange students like they're classes here?
14. RITA: Oh, yes, they're so much more relaxed here.
15. LUIS: Relaxed! Your not saying that it's easier here!
16. RITA: Your always complaining about tests and quizzes.
17. In my school, you're grade depends on one final examination.
18. LUIS: Whose in your classes there? Are they coed?
19. RITA: Oh no! Most schools aren't mixed. Their separate.
20. Its strange for me to be in a class with boys.

FOR MORE PRACTICE
See page 464.

CHECK ✓ POINT

Writing Theme
A World Language

Write the correct pronoun or contraction given in parentheses.

1. (Its, It's) said that English is the world's lingua franca.
2. (Your, You're) probably wondering what a lingua franca is.
3. Recently a Japanese girl, a Brazilian boy, and (I, me) represented our schools at a conference in Saudi Arabia.
4. English was quite useful to (she, her) and (he, him).
5. No one else could speak (their, they're) languages.
6. So the other people and (we, us) spoke English.
7. When a language is used between groups that have no other language in common, (its, it's) called a lingua franca.
8. We learned that the Chinese, (whose, who's) language is difficult for Westerners, are also learning English.
9. "(Their, They're) all learning English," one visitor said.
10. We learned that the British Broadcasting Corporation produced a television series; (its, it's) title was *Follow Me.*
11. It was shown to the Chinese; (their, they're) response was good.
12. English gives the British and (they, them) a lingua franca.
13. Communication exists between the British and (we, us).
14. Yet (they, them) and (we, us) speak our own kinds of English.
15. So if the Chinese learn British English, (we, us) and (they, them) should be able to communicate too.
16. One problem occurred to other students and (I, me).
17. (Whose, Who's) going to decide which variety of English will be the lingua franca?
18. Native speakers of English include, among others, the British, the Australians, the New Zealanders, and (we, us).
19. If you are from Britain, American English is different from (your, you're) English.
20. For example, (your, you're) probably not familiar with the word *flashlight,* but you know *torch.*
21. (Whose, Who's) English will be used?
22. Dictionaries and phrase books can help you and (I, me).
23. (Its, It's) been estimated that about 130 million students are learning English as a second language.
24. Perhaps you and (I, me) should feel a little embarrassed.
25. (Their, They're) learning another language, but not many of us have learned anything except English!

THE FAR SIDE By GARY LARSON

The Far Side cartoon by Gary Larson is reprinted by permission of Chronicle Features, San Francisco, CA.

Using Pronouns   **447**

INDEFINITE PRONOUNS

> An **indefinite pronoun** is a pronoun that does not refer to a specific person or a specific thing.

Pronouns like *everyone* and *somebody* do not refer to any definite person or thing. They are called **indefinite pronouns.**

Singular Indefinite Pronouns

another	anything	everybody	neither	one
anybody	each	everyone	nobody	somebody
anyone	either	everything	no one	someone

Possessive pronouns that refer to indefinite pronouns should agree in number with the indefinite pronoun.

> Neither believed *his* eyes. (Not *their* eyes)
> Each strained *his or her* neck to see. (Use *his or her* if the person being referred to can be either male or female.)

An indefinite pronoun used as a subject must agree in number with its verb. Do not be confused by phrases that come between a singular indefinite pronoun and the verb.

> Each of these men has a boat. (The subject is *each*, not *men.*)

Plural Indefinite Pronouns

both	many	few	several

Several reported *their* findings. Many *are* verifiable.

The pronouns *all, some, any,* and *none* may be singular or plural, depending on their meaning in the sentence.

> All of my story is true.   All of the reporters are here.
> None of the lake is foggy.   None of the photos are sharp.

Practice Your Skills

A. CONCEPT CHECK

Indefinite Pronouns   Write the indefinite pronoun from each sentence. Then write whether it is *Singular* or *Plural*.

Writing Theme
Lake Monsters

1. Anything is possible if you keep an open mind.
2. Everyone has heard about the lake monster in Scotland.
3. However, few know about other lake monsters.
4. Some of the supposed monsters are said to live in North America.
5. No one has photographed the Ogopogo monster in Canada.
6. Many suggest that these monsters are plesiosaurs.
7. None of the evidence confirms the existence of prehistoric large water reptiles.
8. Anyone can tell you that even thirty years ago, such creatures were spotted in Canada.
9. One of the observers claimed to have seen a "creature resembling a large snake."
10. Another reported a "reptile-like beast."
11. Neither had solid proof of the creature.
12. Both, though, stood by what they described.
13. None of their claims have been verified.
14. Perhaps somebody has evidence but is afraid to show it.
15. Everything about the monster remains a mystery.

B. CONCEPT CHECK

Verbs and Indefinite Pronouns   For each sentence, write the indefinite pronoun and then write the correct form of the verb.

16. Nobody (know, knows) much about the Loch Ness monster.
17. Some of the Loch Ness visitors (have, has) photographed it.
18. All of the photographs of the monster (is, are) unclear.
19. (Does, Do) everybody know that Loch Ness is in Scotland?
20. Many of the observers (has, have) given their descriptions of the monster.
21. (Has, Have) anybody here seen the famous film of the monster?
22. Many (believes, believe) some animal does live in the lake.
23. Some (call, calls) it "Nessie, the Loch Ness Monster."
24. All of the evidence (indicates, indicate) a creature with a small head and a long neck.
25. Each of the photographs (make, makes) people want more.

FOR MORE PRACTICE
See page 464.

A **demonstrative pronoun** is used to single out one or more persons or things referred to in the sentence. An **interrogative pronoun** is used to ask a question.

Demonstrative pronouns help you point out certain persons and things. Interrogative pronouns help you ask questions.

The **demonstrative pronouns** are *this, that, these,* and *those. This* and *these* point to persons or things that are near. *That* and *those* point to persons or things that are farther away.

This is a gazebo.   *These* are the local stores.
That is the town square.   *Those* are the restaurants.

The **interrogative pronouns** are *who, whose, whom, which,* and *what.* You use them to ask questions.

Who is the mayor?   *Which* is her house?
Whose is the blue house?   *What* did you ask me?
Whom should I see to learn about the local history?

Practice Your Skills

A. CONCEPT CHECK

Demonstrative and Interrogative Pronouns   Write the correct demonstrative or interrogative pronouns given in parentheses.

1. (This, That) is the general store we are entering now.
2. (Who, Whom) owns the store?
3. Let me see! (Who, Whom) can we ask?
4. I remember! (This, That) is the Kellers' store.
5. (This, That) is their diner across the street too.
6. (Whose, Whom) are the other stores?
7. (Which, What) is the one you want to know about?
8. Well, to (who, whom) does the clothing store belong?
9. I'm sorry! (Which, What) did you ask me?
10. Never mind! (These, Those) are beautiful quilts on the counter over there.

Writing
TIP

You can use demonstrative pronouns to connect your ideas in a paragraph. Demonstrative pronouns used in this way are called **transitions.**

The puppy in the middle had white paws. I chose the puppy in the middle.

The puppy in the middle had white paws. *That's* the one I chose.

Writing Theme
Small Towns

---

11. (These, Those) right in front of you were made by Grandma Keller's quilting group.
12. Look! Are (these, those) old-fashioned candies on the far counter?
13. (This, That) in my hand used to be called penny candy.
14. (Which, What) are the ones on the strips of paper called?
15. I think (these, those) are called buttons.

B. DRAFTING SKILL

Using Demonstrative and Interrogative Pronouns   Write the following sentences, adding the correct demonstrative and interrogative pronouns.

16. _____ could resist a town called Nameless?
17. _____ is one of the places mentioned in the book *Blue Highways.*
18. By _____ was the book written?
19. William Least Heat Moon was the author. _____ is one of the places he visited, right here on the map.
20. _____ are some of the other places he visited?
21. Dime Box, Hungry Horse, and Salt Wells— _____ are all places in his book.
22. _____ did he like better, Nameless or Wolf Point?
23. I don't know. _____ can I ask to find out?
24. May I use those travel books? _____ are they?
25. _____ on this shelf are all mine, but _____ over there are my mother's.

Portrait of Orleans (1950), Edward Hopper.

C. APPLICATION IN WRITING

Dialogue   Imagine that you are giving someone a tour of your favorite small town. Write a brief dialogue between you and your friend in which you point out attractions of the town and your friend asks you questions. Be sure to include at least four demonstrative and interrogative pronouns in your dialogue.

FOR MORE PRACTICE
See page 465.

Using Pronouns   **451**

USING _WHO_, _WHOM_, AND _WHOSE_

The words _who, whom,_ and _whose_ may be used as **interrogative pronouns** to ask questions.

Who, whom, and _whose_ are often used to ask questions. When that is their function, they are called **interrogative pronouns.** _Who_ is the subject form. It is used as the subject of a verb. _Whom_ is the object form. It is used as the direct object of a verb or as the object of a preposition.

> _Who_ taught you how to do origami? (_Who_ is the subject of _taught._)
> _Whom_ did you ask? (_Whom_ is the object of _did ask._)
> For _whom_ is this gift? (_Whom_ is the object of _for._)

Whose is the possessive form. It can modify a noun: _Whose work_ is this? Alone, it can be the subject or object of a verb.

> _Whose_ paper sculptures did you see? (_Whose_ modifies _sculptures._)
> _Whose_ did you like? (_Whose_ is the object of _did like._)
> _Whose_ are those paper dragons? (_Whose_ is the subject of _are._)

Practice Your Skills

CONCEPT CHECK

Who, Whom, and _Whose_   Complete these sentences with _who, whom,_ or _whose._

1. _____ knows the origin of origami?
2. _____ did you ask about it?
3. Well, _____ is the expert here?
4. Let me see. To _____ should I direct you?
5. _____ skill in paper folding is best?
6. That is, _____ is the most delicate work?
7. _____ is likely to receive the blue ribbon?
8. _____ are those wonderful origami figures that move?
9. I don't know. _____ are you looking at?
10. For _____ did you buy this paper rose?

CHECK ✔ POINT
MIXED REVIEW · PAGES 448–452

A. Write the correct verb from those in parentheses.

1. Believe it or not, everything about tugboats (is, are) interesting.
2. Each (has, have) its own history of adventure and work.
3. Any of the stories (is, are) worth telling.
4. People are aware of some jobs tugs do, and many (knows, know) that tugs help huge ships into harbor.
5. Few, however, (is, are) aware of their rescue work.
6. (Has, Have) anybody read *Tugboat: The Moran Story?*
7. Some of the book (describes, describe) daring rescues.
8. One of the saddest (was, were) the story of the *Saale* and the *Main.*
9. Both (was, were) destroyed by fire, despite the valiant efforts of fireboats and tugboats.
10. All of Hoboken (was, were) seen from a great distance; the blaze was so enormous.
11. Some of the crew members (was, were) saved.
12. (Does, Do) anything compare with such a frightening fire?

B. Complete the following sentences by adding the correct demonstrative and interrogative pronouns.

13. Welcome aboard! _____ is a tugboat, the *Seaworthy.*
14. Careful! Pieces of equipment are everywhere, and _____ at your feet are hawsers.
15. _____ is a hawser? Well, it is a heavy rope used for mooring the boat or for pulling cargo.
16. For _____ of the crew do you have questions?
17. _____ is the question about the posts? Is it yours?
18. _____ over there are called bitts. Deckhands connect the hawsers to the bitts on the tug.
19. _____ connects them to the barge? We deckhands do!
20. _____ is the most interesting job of all the crew members?
21. _____ is the captain in the distance. His is the best job.
22. _____ seems harder, the deckhand's job or the captain's? The deckhand's job is harder physically, but the captain's is more difficult.

REFLEXIVE AND INTENSIVE PRONOUNS

Pronouns that end in *-self* or *-selves* are called either **intensive** or **reflexive pronouns.**

The reflexive and intensive pronouns are *myself, yourself, herself, himself, itself, ourselves,* and *themselves.*

A **reflexive pronoun** refers to an action performed by the subject of the sentence. The meaning of the sentence is incomplete without the reflexive pronoun.

> We pride *ourselves* on our creativity. (If you remove *ourselves,* the meaning of the sentence is incomplete.)
> Erika bought *herself* a needlepoint kit.

An **intensive pronoun** is used to emphasize a noun or a pronoun. It does not add information to a sentence, and it may be removed without changing the meaning of the sentence.

> I *myself* have an unusual hobby. (If you remove *myself,* the meaning of the sentence does not change.)
> Zeke made this paper *himself.*

Practice Your Skills

A. CONCEPT CHECK

Reflexive and Intensive Pronouns   Write the reflexive and intensive pronouns in the sentences. Then label them *Reflexive* or *Intensive.*

1. I myself have never tried mud walking.
2. Willem, a Dutch visitor, has done it many times himself.
3. "If you want to give yourself a treat," he says, "you should try it!"
4. The Dutch themselves call the activity *Wadlopen.*
5. Each year about 30,000 people revitalize themselves by walking through the mud off the coast of the Netherlands.
6. The Netherlands itself is not particularly muddy, but the West Frisian Islands are, especially at low tide.

Writing
—— **TIP** ——

When you use a reflexive pronoun, recall that it must refer to a noun or a pronoun that comes before it.
Incorrect: Bob and myself attended the meeting.
Correct: Bob and I attended the meeting.

Writing Theme
Unusual Pastimes

7. "I have to buy myself a new pair of tennis shoes after a trip from the mainland to a nearby island," says Willem.
8. The monks in the Middle Ages made the trip themselves.
9. However, such a monk was not enjoying himself.
10. He himself was taking cattle to pasture on an island.
11. You may ask yourself about the sanity of mud walking.
12. People on the islands wonder about it themselves.
13. My sister Celia said she would be willing to try it herself.
14. She often challenges herself by doing strenuous activities.
15. Willem invited us to find out for ourselves that walking knee-deep in mud is, indeed, strenuous.

FOR MORE PRACTICE
See page 465.

B. DRAFTING SKILL

Using Reflexive and Intensive Pronouns   Write the correct reflexive or intensive pronoun to complete each sentence.

16. Have you ever prepared _____ for a competition?
17. The Jamaicans _____ were in a quandary.
18. They wanted to train _____ for bobsled competitions.
19. However, even one snowflake by _____ is unheard of on their island, not to mention a snow storm.
20. Preparation _____ presents some challenges.
21. "We _____ practice sledding on the beach!" said one aspiring bobsledder.
22. "I made _____ a dummy sled with wheels."
23. He also times _____ on how fast he can push the sled.
24. Enthusiasts on Jamaica and other islands in the Caribbean have formed _____ into a group.
25. "We pride _____ on being goodwill ambassadors first, and bobsledders second," added another sand sledder.

The Jamaican bobsled team trained on sleds with wheels to prepare for the 1992 Winter Olympics in Albertville, France.

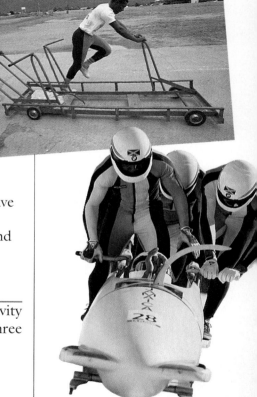

C. APPLICATION IN WRITING

Personal Narrative   Write a paragraph about an unusual activity you have done with your friends or classmates. Use at least three of the following reflexive and intensive pronouns.

myself	yourselves	herself
ourselves	himself	themselves

PRONOUNS AND THEIR ANTECEDENTS

> The **antecedent** of a pronoun is a noun or another pronoun for which the pronoun stands.

A personal pronoun, you remember, is used in place of a noun. This noun is the word to which the pronoun refers and is called its **antecedent.** The noun usually comes first, either in the same sentence or in the sentence before it.

We talked to *Greg. He* is the computer expert.
　　(*He* stands for *Greg. Greg* is the antecedent.)
The *students* had turned on *their* personal computers.
　　(*Their* stands for *students. Students* is the antecedent.)

Pronouns may be the antecedents of other pronouns.

Does *everybody* have *her* manual? (*Everybody,* which is singular, is the antecedent of *her.*)
All of the students have brought *theirs.* (*All* is plural here and is the antecedent of *theirs.*)

Pronoun and Antecedent Agreement

A pronoun must agree with its antecedent in number. Here, the word *agree* means that the pronoun must be the same in number as its antecedent. The word *number* means *singular* or *plural.* The pronoun must be singular if the word it stands for is singular, and it must be plural if the word it stands for is plural.

The programmers tested *their* new software.
　　(*Programmers* is plural; *their* is plural.)
Mr. Johnson turned on *his* terminal.
　　(*Mr. Johnson* is singular; *his* is singular.)
Nobody left *his* or *her* workstation.
　　(*Nobody* is singular; *his* and *her* are singular.)

When the antecedent refers to both males and females, many people prefer to use the phrase *his or her.*

Writing
TIP

To avoid *his or her* phrases, try using plural subjects.
　Each student turned on his or her computer.
Better:
　All the students turned on their computers.

Practice Your Skills

A. CONCEPT CHECK

Pronoun-Antecedent Agreement Write the pronouns and their antecedents from the following sentences. Note how the pronouns can link sentences together and avoid awkward repetition.

Writing Theme
Computers

1. Engineers can now fit computer circuitry into a tiny square. They call the square a chip.
2. Mr. Saez held up a chip. It was quite small.
3. Ms. Estes held up a quartz rock. She explained that silicon comes from quartz.
4. Silicon is important because it is used to make chips.
5. Because of this technology, many people now own their own personal computers.
6. Anyone can buy his or her own PC at a relatively low price.
7. Computer chips are used in many things. They can be found in watches, cars, games, and telephones.
8. Have you ever seen a computer chip with your own eyes?
9. Daryll says that he saw a chip under a microscope. He thought it looked like the view of a city from an airplane.
10. Tricia said she once saw an interesting picture. It showed an ant carrying a computer chip.
11. When the chip was first developed, scientists called it the integrated circuit.
12. The first completely electronic digital computer was built in 1946. It was huge compared to the computers of today.
13. Less than fifty years ago, only top-level scientists used computers. They were an elite group.
14. Now, even children use computers in their classrooms for both games and lessons.
15. We have come to rely on the tiny chip in almost every part of our lives. It helps us do everything from telling time to balancing our budgets.

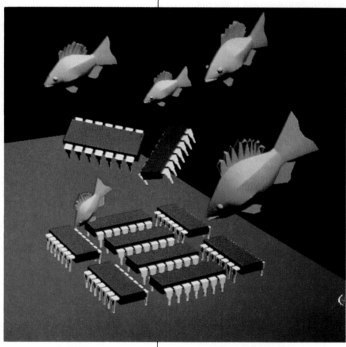

Fish and Chips © 1985 Vibeke Sorensen. Produced at the Caltech CSCGG.

B. DRAFTING SKILL

Using Pronoun-Antecedent Agreement   Write the following sentences, adding pronouns that agree with the antecedents.

16. Juanita Lewis says computers changed _____ life.

17. Blind since birth, Lewis runs _____ own company.

18. Ira Gold, a paraplegic, agrees. _____ uses a computer to write a weekly advice column.

19. People with disabilities have discovered that computers can open many doors for _____.

20. Not everybody must use _____ fingers and type on a keyboard to input information.

21. Because of voice-activation technology, Juanita and Ira can now dictate _____ letters and reports to the computer.

22. Thanks to some very clever software programs, anybody can add voice activation to _____ computer.

23. One of the software packages has 30,000 words in _____ program.

24. Interestingly, Shakespeare used about 30,000 words in _____ writing.

25. The creators of the software designed _____ program to recognize this large number of words.

C. PROOFREADING SKILL

Correcting Errors in Agreement   Rewrite the following passage, correcting all errors, especially errors in pronoun-antecedent agreement. (15 errors)

"Someone may spend their life joining groups, but that's not for me," said Millie. "Then I bought myself a computer and didn't know what to do next! Millie and others have found ansers to his or her questions by joining computer user groups one of the oldest groups got their start in 1977. Today the group has 32,000 people on it's membership list. Anyone who owns a computer can increase their knowlege by sharing information in a group. "We talk about programs, PCs, and problems in their group. A software company even asked us to test a brand-new computer game. The Company actually used one of their suggestions to improve the game." All of the members' enjoyed. Giving his or her opinions of the game.

A computerized voice synthesizer allows a disabled person to communicate without speaking.

FOR MORE PRACTICE
See page 466.

C H E C K ✔ P O I N T

Write the correct pronoun to complete each sentence. Be sure that each pronoun agrees with its antecedent.

1. Some people must be born with adventure in _____ heart.
2. Why else would they subject _____ to all kinds of danger?
3. Anyone with an ounce of common sense would not leave the safety of _____ home.
4. I _____ can't understand what makes them do it.
5. Sir Francis Chichester often challenged _____.
6. When Sir Francis was sixty-five, _____ sailed alone around the world.
7. More recently, a woman proved _____ equal to the same challenge.
8. Naomi James undertook this adventure in 1977. _____ sailing companion was a kitten named Boris.
9. The voyage lasted about 272 days, and _____ was filled with beautiful sights, dangerous storms, and countless problems.
10. Would you be able to spend that much time all by _____?
11. The ship's rudder gave Naomi problems. _____ tried to repair _____ herself.
12. Five days before Christmas, a powerful storm pounded the ship. _____ howling winds created massive waves.
13. Fortunately, Naomi kept a log of _____ journey.
14. We can read parts of her journal _____ in *Alone Around the World.*
15. By reading Naomi's book, we can take _____ on a thrilling adventure without leaving _____ chairs!
16. Neither Sir Francis nor Naomi can be blamed if _____ was frightened. Both _____ and _____ faced fierce dangers alone.
17. Naomi wrote: "I know that the . . . hours and days of this voyage have enriched _____ life immeasurably."
18. Sir Francis was knighted after _____ voyage.
19. After _____ voyage, Naomi was named Dame Commander of the Order of the British Empire.
20. Sadly, Boris the kitten received no honors. _____ trip ended when a wave swept _____ overboard.

> When using phrases like *we girls* and *us boys,* choose the correct pronoun by dropping the noun and saying the sentence with only the pronoun.

You may need to decide which of two similar pronouns is the correct choice. The following are some useful suggestions.

We and *Us* Used with Nouns

When you use phrases such as *we students* and *us workers,* be sure that you use the correct pronoun. To tell which pronoun to use, drop the noun and say the sentence without it:

Problem	(We, Us) boys study hard.
Solution	We study hard. = We boys study hard.
Problem	The mayor thanked (we, us) girls.
Solution	The mayor thanked us. = The mayor thanked us girls.

Using the Pronoun *Them*

The word *them* is always a pronoun. It is always used as the object of a verb or a preposition.

> The speaker greeted *them.* (direct object of a verb)
> She gave *them* a booklet. (indirect object of a verb)
> The data was useful to *them.* (object of the preposition *to*)

Using *Those*

You have already learned that *those* can be used as a demonstrative pronoun (page 450). Sometimes, however, *those* is used as an adjective. An adjective is a word that modifies a noun or a pronoun. If a noun appears immediately after it, *those* is probably an adjective. Used without a noun, *those* is a pronoun.

> *Those* are the new career posters I ordered. (pronoun: subject of a verb)
> *Those* posters are outdated. (adjective modifying *posters*)

Writing
TIP

Remember that careful writers never use *them* as an adjective. For example, "them pictures" is incorrect. "Those pictures" is correct.

Practice Your Skills

A. CONCEPT CHECK

Problem Pronouns   Write the correct pronoun in parentheses from each sentence.

1. (We, Us) students started a newsletter about careers.
2. Finding unusual jobs was important to (we, us) writers.
3. Many careers sound dull. (Them, Those) are ones to avoid.
4. An employment agency invited (we, us) reporters to a career fair.
5. "(Them, Those) are interesting exhibits," I said.
6. One of (them, those) career speakers was especially interesting.
7. A bill collector told (we, us) students about his work.
8. "(We, Us) collectors perform an important service," he said.
9. "Some people truly want to pay their bills. (Them, Those) are the ones I try to help."
10. "I help (them, those) find ways to pay their debts."
11. "In fact, (we, us) callers need to be understanding."
12. "However, when people lie, it is hard to make (them, those) tell us the truth."

B. REVISION SKILL

Correcting Pronoun Errors   Write the paragraph below, correcting errors in the use of *we, us, them,* and *those.* If a sentence is correct, write *Correct.*

> [13]Many of we inventors have long lists of inventions that failed. [14]We try to forget them inventions. [15]Often it is not enough for us inventors to create a successful product. [16]Often us creators also have to design and make the machines that produce the products. [17]Those are usually the hardest to invent. [18]When people have problems, I simply try to solve those. [19]Most of we inventors are just creative problem solvers. [20]Them problems spark ideas in our minds, and we search for solutions. [21]The solutions sometimes present us inventors with other problems. [22]Them answers lead us to other questions until we creators find the final solution.

Writing Theme
Unusual Careers

FOR MORE PRACTICE
See page 466.

The prone bicycle shown here was demonstrated at the Human Powered Vehicle Festival in England. It puts the rider in a more powerful, if less comfortable, position than does a conventional bike.

Write the correct pronoun or adjective given in parentheses for each sentence. Some items covered earlier in this handbook are included.

1. Folk dances can be a mystery to (we, us) uninformed people.
2. (Them, Those) dances are often used for storytelling.
3. For example, Hawaiians use (them, their) hula dances to tell stories or describe places.
4. We can picture the places as dancers portray (them, those) with graceful movements.
5. The meaning of the dances is sometimes not clear because most of (them, those) have ancient origins.
6. (We, Us) dance fans enjoy watching dance dramas from India.
7. (Them, Those) are especially intricate dances.
8. All parts of the body are used in (them, those) to tell a story—even the eyes.
9. One of the dance styles, *Kathakali,* tells a complete story in (its, their) movements.
10. In some ways it seems like ballet to (we, us) observers.
11. *Manipuri* is one of (them, those) styles of dance that mimic nature.
12. A dancer portrays animals or weather in (his or her, their) movements.
13. Some dances from Balkan countries give (we, us) students of the dance some insight into history.
14. (Them, Those) dances reenact historic battles.
15. Male dancers usually portray Christians, Moors, or Turks in (them, those).
16. I could almost picture (me, myself) as a participant in a folk dance I saw while on vacation in Mexico.
17. The dancers wore traditional costumes, and (they, them) performed a battle between winter and summer.
18. During the dance, devils and death figures move in and out among (them, those) brightly clothed dancers.
19. Of course, it did not surprise (we, us) spectators that summer was victorious.
20. We thoroughly enjoyed (us, ourselves) even if we did not understand all the details of the dance.

GRAMMAR
HANDBOOK
41

Writing Theme
Traveling
Entertainment

A. Using Personal Pronouns Write the correct pronoun from those given in parentheses. Then write whether the pronoun is in *Subject, Object,* or *Possessive* form.

1. Frontier settlers who lived along rivers had almost no entertainment in (they, them, their) lives.
2. William Chapman changed that. (He, Him, His) built the first showboat in 1831 in Pittsburgh with the intention of taking her south.
3. (She, Her, Hers) was named the *Floating Theatre*.
4. Chapman and (he, him, his) family headed for New Orleans.
5. (They, Them, Their) gave shows from landing to landing.
6. Talented people were (they, them, their).
7. At first the program was limited, but he expanded (it, its) by adding plays, songs, and dances.
8. Edna Ferber described showboats in (she, her, hers) novel.
9. (She, Her, Hers) was a lively and accurate account.
10. Lucky are (we, us, our) that Ferber wrote *Show Boat*.
11. Showboats are no longer available to (we, us, our).
12. (We, Us, Our) could have had such great fun!
13. The entertainment provided by motion pictures and the transportation cars offered finished (they, them, their) off.
14. In 1943, the showboat *Golden Rod* made (she, her, hers) last trip.
15. (She, Her, Hers) was the last of the great showboats.

B. Using Pronouns in Compound Subjects and Objects Write the correct pronoun from those given in parentheses.

16. You and (I, me) have heard of the Ringling brothers.
17. John Ringling is the most familiar to (we, us) and others.
18. (He, Him) and his brothers began in a small way.
19. The arts were important to (they, them) and their mother.
20. Their father and (she, her) often disagreed.
21. Performing seemed a waste of time to (he, him) and others of his age.
22. Thus, he never gave (she, her) or his sons any encouragement.
23. A stubborn group were (they, them) and John.
24. Their first show took John and (they, them) far from home.
25. Throughout the Midwest, (he, him) and (they, them) performed plays, music, acrobatics, juggling, and clowning.

C. Using Possessive Pronouns and Contractions Write the correct word from those given in parentheses.

26. LIZ: (Whose, Who's) books are on the table?
27. TOM: (Their, They're) mine.
28. LIZ: (Your, You're) reading about equestrian shows?
29. TOM: (Its, It's) sad that (their, they're) not more popular.
30. LIZ: (Whose, Who's) this book about?
31. TOM: George Washington. The shows owe (their, they're) popularity partly to him.
32. He attended John Bill Ricketts's show of daring horsemanship and was (its, it's) greatest fan.
33. LIZ: (Your, You're) example surprises me. I didn't know horse shows went back that far.
34. TOM: Well, Liz, (your, you're) lack of knowledge is not unusual.
35. Unfortunately, (their, they're) part in our history is unknown to many.

D. Finding Indefinite Pronouns Write the indefinite pronoun from each sentence. Then choose the correct verb for the pronoun from those given in parentheses.

36. Probably all of us (has, have) seen puppet shows.
37. Many (thinks, think) of puppets as children's entertainment.
38. However, none of the early shows (was, were) just for children.
39. Each (was, were) entertainment for adults as well.
40. Someone may still (remembers, remember) *Uncle Tom's Cabin* being presented by a traveling marionette company.
41. No one in the audience (was, were) ever disappointed.
42. Some of this kind of entertainment (has, have) changed in recent years.
43. Today, some of the puppeteers (performs, perform) in malls.
44. Everything (is, are) uncertain about the future of puppetry.
45. Few (wants, want) to see puppets disappear, but no one (is, are) able to revive interest in traveling puppet theaters.
46. Another of the problems (is, are) television.
47. With puppets on the screen, nobody (goes, go) to real shows.
48. In China everyone still (enjoys, enjoy) puppet shows.
49. All of the expenses (is, are) paid by the government.
50. Otherwise, none of the shows (makes, make) enough money.

E. Finding Demonstrative and Interrogative Pronouns   Write and label each *Demonstrative* and *Interrogative* pronoun.

51. Which of the exhibits do you want to see?
52. What can I tell you?
53. This is the greatest traveling menagerie in the world.
54. These before you are exotic South American talking birds.
55. Whom are you addressing, sir?
56. Of course, those are purebred macaws and cockatoos.
57. Who thinks my animals are not authentic?
58. That, over there, is Madame Zazu, a trained cockatoo.
59. Whose is the brand new straw hat with the blue band?
60. Well, this is the rest of it. Madame Zazu was hungry!

F. Using Interrogative Pronouns   Write the following sentences, adding the correct interrogative pronouns, *who, whom,* or *whose.*

61. _____ name is linked with the great circus managers?
62. To _____ are you referring?
63. _____ called himself the "Prince of Humbugs"?
64. _____ is the man known for labeling the exit the "exhibit of the egress" and tricking spectators into thinking they were seeing another exhibit like the tigress or the lioness?
65. _____ is this nickname? It's P. T. Barnum's, of course.

G. Using Reflexive and Intensive Pronouns   Write the correct reflexive or intensive pronoun to complete each sentence.

66. At the circus we laugh (pronoun) silly over the antics of clowns.
67. Shakespeare (pronoun) wrote about clowns.
68. I found out for (pronoun) how clowns learn their craft.
69. Circus clowns do not train (pronoun); they go to college.
70. Irvin Feld (pronoun) started Clown College in 1968.
71. The college has distinguished (pronoun) as the only professional clown school.
72. Students throw (pronoun) into their studies and into the ring.
73. Peggy Williams is proud of (pronoun) as one of the first women to graduate from the college.
74. The art of clowning is (pronoun) kept a secret.
75. Three of the greatest clowns—Lou Jacobs, Otto Griebling, and Bobby Kay—taught the first classes (pronoun).

H. Finding the Antecedents of Pronouns   Write the antecedents of the pronouns in italics in the following sentences.

76. After World War II, the circus in the United States seemed on *its* way out.
77. Circus acts and circus stars were losing *their* appeal.
78. At the time, Irvin Feld, the owner of Ringling Bros. and Barnum & Bailey Circus, was in Italy, and *he* saw "an act so spectacular that you get shivers up *your* spine."
79. The act was Gunther Gebel-Williams and *his* family.
80. Gunther married a lovely model, and *she* entered the circus.
81. Sigrid started in 1969. Everything scared *her* at first.
82. Gunther's son made *his* debut by riding a giraffe.
83. Stepdaughter Tina developed *her* own act with horses.
84. No one in *his or her* act outshone the great Gebel-Williams.
85. Many have showered *their* praises on this unique trainer.
86. "Gunther was the greatest all-around circus performer of his time," wrote John Culhane in *his* book *The American Circus.*
87. Gunther trained horses first. *They* are the most difficult.
88. Then Gunther advanced to elephants. *He* considers *them* to be highly intelligent animals.
89. We have held *our* breath as Gunther trains *his* tigers.
90. "I thank the animals who have done well . . . . All of *my* animals have come to expect *me* after the show."

I. Using Pronouns   Write the correct words given in parentheses in the following sentences.

91. Traveling comes naturally to (we, us) balloonists.
92. Balloons are exciting, and people love to see (those, them).
93. (Those, Them) are the comments of fans of commercial ballooning.
94. (We, Us) pilots take our special balloons on the road.
95. (Those, Them) are the ones with faces or special shapes.
96. Flying at shows is dangerous for (we, us) performers.
97. I often refuse to perform at (those, them).
98. Mid-afternoons are the worst; (those, them) are the windiest times of day.
99. (We, Us) commercial balloonists try hard to please our clients.
100. However, if the weather is bad, we must sometimes disappoint (those, them).

GRAMMAR
H A N D B O O K
41

Writing Theme
Music

A. Personal Pronouns Write the correct pronoun from those given in parentheses for each sentence.

1. Music is the bond between Ivan and (I, me).
2. (Our, Ours) is a special relationship.
3. (He, him) and (I, me) are interested in electronic music.
4. A dedicated pair are (we, us).
5. Electronic music got (it, its) start around 1950.
6. Musicians in Paris developed (them, their) own style.
7. (They, Them) and (them, their) followers called (it, its) *musique concrete,* or concrete music.
8. Musical, natural, and electronic sounds were mixed by (they, them) and altered electronically to suit the music.
9. Ivan writes (him, his) own music and gives it to (I, me).
10. It is (I, me) who can be called the electronic whiz.

B. Pronouns and Contractions Label each italicized word as *Possessive, Demonstrative, Interrogative,* or *Contraction.*

11. *Who* started jazz in the United States?
12. *It's* largely attributed to former slaves from West Africa.
13. Later, gospel singers added *their* influence.
14. For *whom* did early jazz musicians play?
15. *They're* known to have played at weddings, funerals, and other community events in New Orleans.
16. *Those* were the times when people first heard jazz.
17. *What* are the songs they sang?
18. *That* is a good question. Much of *their* music was improvised.
19. Composer W. C. Handy helped jazz in *its* development.
20. *Whose* is the song "Memphis Blues"?
21. *This* is one of his.
22. *You're* sure it's Handy's song?
23. *Who's* known as "Satchmo"?
24. Louis Armstrong, the trumpeter, is, to answer *your* question.
25. *These* are some of his recordings; you may borrow them.

C. Indefinite, Reflexive, and Intensive Pronouns Identify each italicized pronoun as *Indefinite, Reflexive,* or *Intensive.* For indefinite pronouns, identify each as *Singular* or *Plural.*

26. I consider *myself* a purist about music.
27. *All* of today's computer music is not bad, I will admit.

Using Pronouns   **467**

28. Personally, I find that *everything* about computerized music makes me shudder!
29. How can *anyone* enjoy mathematical music?
30. Imagine, *someone* must convert sounds into numbers to produce music.
31. *Some* of my best friends think I am crazy.
32. They *themselves* listen only to those awful sounds.
33. However, how can you call *yourself* an expert if you do not also listen to music made from instruments?
34. It is true that *many* of the great musicians were spontaneous.
35. Musicians must train *themselves* how to interpret music and how to be creative.
36. *No one* can interpret emotions with fake, computer instruments!
37. With artificial sounds are we depriving *ourselves* of the clear notes produced by real instruments?
38. *Few* think computers are more exciting than musicians that perform live.
39. I *myself* have seen many great, exciting performers.
40. I still think *anything,* including piano lessons, is more exciting than music from a computer!

D. Agreement and Other Problems   Some sentences below contain errors in pronoun use or pronoun-antecedent agreement. Write the sentences correctly. If a sentence does not contain an error, write *Correct.*

41. Us kids are forming our own band and will play homemade instruments.
42. None of us has played a light-bulb rattle before.
43. We are willing to try our hand at it, though.
44. Joe's mother would not let we creators use her good crystal glasses as instruments.
45. Of course everyone know that crystal makes the best sound.
46. Them glasses, filled with water, make a singing tone.
47. Leon's father let him use a saw to make rasps.
48. Them are the bumps you have to rub with a stick in order to make sound.
49. All of we budding musicians has also made panpipes out of plastic tubing.
50. Those are the instruments we are most proud of!

WRITING CONNECTIONS

Elaboration, Revision, and Proofreading

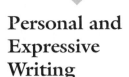

Revise the following autobiographical incident by using the directions at the bottom of the page. Then proofread the passage, looking especially for errors in the use of pronouns. Also check for other grammatical errors and errors in capitalization, punctuation, and spelling.

¹I'll never forget the first time I saw a rattlesnake. ²People have many mistaken ideas about snakes. ³Jim and Willie and me was camping in the mountains, and Jim and Willie and me decided to go for a hike. ⁴Each of my friends had their own idea about where we should go, but we finally settled on a trail. ⁵Jim and myself lead the way, and Willie followed. ⁶I started to step over a rock and noticed something in the way. ⁷Its funny now as I think about all the things that went through my mind so quickly. ⁸I realized that the thing in the way was a snake. ⁹I noticed that it was a big snake. ¹⁰I heard the hiss and the awful Rattles. ¹¹All at once I yelped. ¹²I leapt into the air. ¹³I jumped backward. ¹⁴Jim and Willie looked frozen; neither could move their legs. ¹⁵The snake slithered into the bushes, and us hikers watched more carefuly where we stepped after that.

1. Delete the sentence that doesn't belong.

2. Use a pronoun to avoid repeating the names in sentence 3.

3. After sentence 4, add these details to set the scene: "We headed up the rocky side of a hill, winding back and forth between the boulders."

4. Make the order of events clear by adding introductory words ("first," "then," and "finally") to sentences 8, 9, and 10.

5. Combine sentences 11, 12, and 13 to make one sentence.

Personal and Expressive Writing

Writing about autobiographical incidents is a good way to record your experiences and to share them with others. (See Workshop 1.) When you write about personal experiences, you can use pronouns to avoid repeating names and to make your writing flow smoothly. Make sure, however, that you use the proper forms of pronouns and that each pronoun agrees with its antecedent in number.

Skills

Directions   One or more of the underlined sections in the following sentences may contain an error in grammar, usage, punctuation, spelling, or capitalization. Write the letter of each incorrect section. Then rewrite the section correctly. If there is no error in an item, write *E*.

Example   As they get older, <u>humans</u> get taller; mountains get
                                    A
<u>shorter. Old</u> mountains such as the <u>Appalachians</u> have been
     B   **C**
gradually wearing down for <u>centurys</u>. <u>No error</u>
                                 D   **E**

Answer   D—centuries

---

1. My <u>Cousin</u> Juan is visiting <u>Grandpa</u> in Milwaukee. They will meet Grandma and
        A   **B**
   <u>myself</u> at the <u>zoo</u>. <u>No error</u>
     C   **D**   **E**

2. The woolly <u>monkies</u> of the <u>Amazon River</u> basin <u>have</u> fingerprints—or
                A   **B**   **C**
   fingerprint-like ridges—on <u>their</u> tails. <u>No error</u>
                                 D   **E**

3. Although <u>Columbus's</u> ships landed in <u>America. They</u> did not land in what is now
              A   **B**
   the United States. His crews' first contact with the New World <u>was</u> in the <u>Bahamas</u>.
                                                                    C   **D**
   <u>No error</u>
     E

4. The nine <u>planet's</u> orbits take them varying <u>distances</u> from the <u>sun, Jupiter</u>, for
              A   **B**   **C**
   example, is 507 million <u>miles</u> away at one point and 460 million miles away at
                             D
   another. <u>No error</u>
              E

5. The wife of John Adams, one of the signers of the <u>Declaration of Independence</u>,
                                                       A
   was named Abigail. <u>Her</u> and her husband argued because <u>women's</u> rights <u>were</u>
                        B   **C**   **D**
   not mentioned. <u>No error</u>
                    E

6. Both <u>trouts</u> and <u>salmon</u> <u>migrate</u> to fresh water to <u>spawn</u>. <u>No error</u>
          A   **B**   **C**   **D**   **E**

---

7. Ocean oases are created when warm water spurts up from inside the <u>earth's</u> crust

A
to warm the cold ocean <u>floor. Each</u> of these oases <u>support</u> hundreds of

B **C**
underwater <u>creatures</u>. <u>No error</u>

D` **E**

8. "I think; therefore, <u>i am,"</u> <u>said</u> the <u>French</u> philosopher <u>René Descartes</u>. <u>No error</u>

A **B** **C** **D** **E**

9. <u>It's</u> not true that a camel survives without water by storing moisture in its

A
<u>hump, it</u> is the <u>camel's</u> efficient <u>kidneys</u> that help it conserve water. <u>No error</u>

B **C** **D** **E**

10. The circle of huge pillars called Stonehenge puzzles many of <u>us</u> astronomers. <u>It</u>

A **B**
may have been used as a <u>reference</u> point in the study of stars and <u>planets</u>.

C **D**
<u>No error</u>

E

11. Somebody <u>has</u> left <u>their</u> <u>keys</u> on the table, but neither of the keys <u>fit</u> the lock.

A **B** **C** **D**
<u>No error</u>

E

12. <u>Us</u> Americans often <u>hear</u> the 1930s <u>referred</u> to as "the golden age of radio," but

A **B** **C**
the number of <u>radioes</u> sold in 1971 was more than twice the number sold in

D
1937. <u>No error</u>

E

13. Before <u>signing</u> up for craft <u>activities. Each</u> of the campers should make

A **B**
<u>themselves</u> a <u>sandwich</u> and tidy up the cabin. <u>No error</u>

C **D** **E**

14. A neutron <u>star</u> can be <u>smaller</u> than an average-sized <u>island</u>. <u>It's</u> diameter may be

A **B** **C** **D**
no more than ten miles. <u>No error</u>

E

15. You may not be familiar with the name <u>Dr. G. W. A.</u> <u>Bonwill, but</u> you no doubt

A **B**
know his <u>invention. It</u> was <u>he</u> who gave us the safety pin. <u>No error</u>

C **D** **E**

Sketch Book

- Write a description of what a place such as a beach or an amusement park is like when it is filled with people. Then write a description of what this same place is like when no one is around.

- What is the funniest or scariest thing that has happened to you lately? Tell the story of what happened.

- You're the coach, and you've just called timeout. Give a pep talk to your team. Tell them what you want them to do.

Using Verbs

GRAMMAR
H A N D B O O K
42

Untitled painting (1987), Keith Haring.

- **What Is a Verb?**
- **Verb Phrases**
- **Principal Parts of the Verb**
- **Verb Tenses**
- **Progressive Verb Forms**
- **Active and Passive Verb Forms**
- **Troublesome Pairs of Verbs**

There is a verb to describe everything you do. There are even verbs to describe doing nothing at all. No sentence is complete without a verb. Verbs tell what action is going on, state that something exists, or link ideas.

In this handbook, you will learn ways you can use verbs to make your writing more precise, interesting, and vivid.

WHAT IS A VERB?

> A **verb** expresses an action, states that something exists, or links the subject with a word that describes or renames it.

When you speak or write, you use two kinds of verbs. These are **action verbs** and **linking verbs.**

Action Verbs

Some verbs express actions: They *crowned* their new queen. The action may be one that you cannot see: She *wanted* power.

Whether you can see the action or not, an action verb says that something is happening, has happened, or will happen.

Linking Verbs

A few verbs do not tell about an action. They may express a state of being, or they may link the subject with a word or words that describe or rename the subject.

> She *is* here. (expresses state of being)
> The country *seems* prosperous. (links subject with description)

These verbs are called **linking verbs** because they can be used to connect, or link, the subject with some other word or words that describe it.

Linking Verbs			
be (am, are, is, was, were, been, being)	look	smell	appear
	seem	taste	sound
became	feel	grow	remain

Some linking verbs can also be used as action verbs.

Linking Verbs	**Action Verbs**
The feast looked delicious.	The king looked at his meal.
The food smelled wonderful.	The king smelled the food.

Writing
═ TIP ═

Lively action verbs can add energy and interest to your writing. Notice the verbs Robert Francis uses in "The Base Stealer" on page 73 to show the ball player's teasing actions.

Practice Your Skills

A. CONCEPT CHECK

Linking Verbs and Action Verbs   Write each verb from the following sentences. Then label each verb *Action* or *Linking.*

Writing Theme
Royalty

1. Queen Christina of Sweden seems an interesting historical figure.
2. She became a queen-elect in 1632, at the age of only six.
3. As a girl she appeared wild and tomboyish, with a great love for her studies.
4. She usually studied for about twelve hours a day.
5. As an adult, she often wore men's wigs, coats, and shoes.
6. Her masculine clothes and manners shocked people.
7. However, she was an able queen.
8. She brought an end to the costly Thirty Years' War.
9. She also supported foreign study, school reforms, and the arts.
10. Yet, Christina remained queen only until 1654.

B. APPLICATION IN LITERATURE

Recognizing Verbs   Write the italicized verbs from the following selection. Label each verb *Action* or *Linking.*

> [11]Guinevere *became* Arthur's queen. [12]The splendor of Arthur's kingdom *overwhelmed* her. [13]She quickly *established* herself in his court, and King Arthur's knights *were* devoted to her. [14]She *seemed* happy and confident as queen.
> [15]In the meantime, Merlin, the magician, also *fell* in love. [16]The lake where Arthur *received* his famous sword also *had* a great rock. [17]Underneath the great rock *was* a palace. [18]The Lady of the Lake *lived* there. [19]One day she *cast* a spell on Merlin. [20]Under the influence of her spell, Merlin *joined* her. [21]No one ever *saw* Merlin again.
>
> **Thomas Malory, *The Legend of King Arthur*,**
> **based on a retelling of *Le Morte Darthur***

C. APPLICATION IN WRITING

Description   Imagine that you have just been named king or queen. Write a paragraph describing the day of your coronation. Include each of the following verbs. Use one of these verbs twice, once as an action verb and once as a linking verb.

tasted   smelled   felt   looked

FOR MORE PRACTICE
See page 496.

VERB PHRASES

A **verb phrase** consists of a main verb and one or more helping verbs.

A **verb phrase** consists of more than one verb. It is made up of a **main verb** and one or more **helping verbs.**

Helping Verbs	Main Verb	Verb Phrases
had	taken	had taken
might have	taken	might have taken
must have been	taken	must have been taken

Some verbs, such as *do, have,* and *be,* can be used either as main verbs or as helping verbs. Here are their forms:

do	have	be	is	were
does	has	am	was	been
did	had	are		

The examples below show how they can be used.

Used as Main Verbs	Used as Helping Verbs
Will you *do* the job?	I *do ride* the bus every day.
Who *has* bus fare?	He *has seen* the monorail.
Where *were* they?	The girls *were bicycling.*

Helping Verbs

can	shall	will
could	should	would
may	might	must

Sometimes helping verbs and main verbs are separated by words that are not verbs.

I *did* not *ride* the subway today.
You *must*n't *waste* gasoline.
Can we *solve* the air pollution problem?
We *should* certainly *improve* public transportation.

Practice Your Skills

A. CONCEPT CHECK

Verb Phrases   Make two columns on your paper. Label them *Helping Verbs* and *Main Verbs.* Write the parts of the verb phrases from the following sentences in the correct column.

1. Automobile companies have stopped development of steam-powered cars.
2. These cars just can't travel very fast.
3. Other types of zero-emission cars will soon be on the roads, however.
4. Zero-emission cars do not produce any pollutants.
5. Your first car could be powered by electricity from batteries.
6. Electric coils in the roads themselves also may provide the power for tomorrow's cars.
7. Future automobiles will probably have small engines.
8. So these cars should look much more streamlined than today's models.
9. Of course, at first these cars will cost more money.
10. However, wouldn't you spend a little more for the sake of our environment?

B. DRAFTING SKILL

Using Helping Verbs   Complete the following sentences by adding one or more helping verbs that fit the meaning. (For some sentences, suggestions are given in parentheses.)

EXAMPLE   Transportation problems _____ _____ addressed. (Show necessity.)
Transportation problems must be addressed.

11Transportation_____ become a major problem for our country. **12**Gasoline use and automobile exhaust fumes _____ _____ reduced greatly. (Show necessity.) **13**As a result, planners _____ looking into new forms of transportation. **14**Some cities _____ already created special ways to help workers. **15**Thanks to these services, public car pools and special buses _____ carrying thousands of people to and from work each day. **16**Some manufacturers _____ developed electric people-mover systems. **17**Someday, these electric "trains" _____ carry workers, shoppers, and other travelers from place to place.

18 _____ you know about these systems from amusement parks or airports? **19**Better rail systems _____ also help. (Show possibility.) **20**In France and Japan, trains already _____ reach two hundred miles per hour. **21**Future travelers _____ also ride on magnetic levitation vehicles or maglevs. (Show possibility.) **22**Powerful electric motors _____ move these vehicles along, several inches above the ground, at speeds up to three hundred miles per hour.

C. APPLICATION IN WRITING

Writing for a Newspaper   Imagine that you have invented a time machine that allows you to visit your community in the year 2013. Write a description of your experiences for your local newspaper, comparing how people travel today with how they might get from place to place in 2013. As you write, remember that verb phrases can make your descriptions more interesting and more specific.

FOR MORE PRACTICE
See pages 496–497.

Writing Theme
J.R.R. Tolkien

C H E C K   P O I N T
MIXED REVIEW • PAGES 474–478

Write the verbs and verb phrases from the following sentences. Label each *Action* or *Linking.*

1. What reader doesn't enjoy the works of J.R.R. Tolkien?
2. Tolkien spent most of his years at England's Oxford University.
3. Tolkien was a professor of medieval languages.
4. He didn't seem like a person with strange worlds in his head.
5. Tolkien probably would have remained an unknown Oxford professor for the rest of his life.
6. However, during the 1930s he became a novelist.
7. He wrote strange and wonderful fantasies.
8. Tolkien created a new race of fictional beings—the hobbits.
9. Hobbits looked like small people with furry feet.
10. They lived in comfortable holes in the sides of hills.
11. Tolkien's first fantasy novel, *The Hobbit,* appeared in 1937.
12. Later, he published *The Lord of the Rings,* a trilogy.
13. The three novels in the series tell the heroic tale of the hobbits.
14. The trilogy begins with the discovery, by the hobbit Bilbo Baggins, of an evil, magic ring.
15. This is truly a classic story of adventure and excitement.

PRINCIPAL PARTS OF THE VERB

The many forms of the verb are based on its three **principal parts:** the **present,** the **past,** and the **past participle.**

Verb forms change to show when an action occurred. These forms, called *tenses,* are based on the three **principal parts** of the verb: the *present,* the *past,* and the *past participle.*

Regular Verbs

For all **regular verbs,** the past and the past participle are spelled alike. They are made by adding *-d* or *-ed* to the present form. The past participle is used with a helping verb.

Present	Past	Past Participle
help	helped	(has) helped
rescue	rescued	(has) rescued
rush	rushed	(have) rushed
support	supported	(have) supported

The spelling of many regular verbs changes when *-d* or *-ed* is added. (See page 686 for a review of spelling rules.)

knit + -ed = knitted   pay + -d = paid
carry + -ed = carried   lay + -d = laid
cry + -ed = cried   say + -d = said

Practice Your Skills

CONCEPT CHECK

Regular Verbs   Make three columns on your paper labeled *Present, Past,* and *Past Participle.* Write the principal parts of the following regular verbs in the correct column.

1. save	**6.** assist	**11.** prevent	**16.** donate
2. provide	**7.** relieve	**12.** carry	**17.** hurry
3. sob	**8.** aid	**13.** train	**18.** travel
4. share	**9.** worry	**14.** try	**19.** tug
5. use	**10.** pay	**15.** nap	**20.** enroll

Irregular Verbs

Hundreds of verbs follow the regular pattern of adding -*d* or -*ed* to form the past and the past participle. Verbs that do not follow this pattern are called **irregular verbs.** There are only about sixty frequently used irregular verbs. For many of these, the past and the past participle are spelled the same. The past participle is used with a helping verb.

fight	fought	(have) fought
make	made	(has) made

For a few irregular verbs, like *hit* and *cut,* the three principal parts are spelled the same. They offer no problems. Most verb problems come from irregular verbs with three different forms. For example, the irregular verbs *throw* and *ring* have three different forms:

throw	threw	(had) thrown
ring	rang	(have) rung

If you are not sure about a verb form, look it up in the dictionary. If the verb is regular, only one form will be listed. If the verb is irregular, the irregular form or forms will be listed.

Common Irregular Verbs

Present	Past	Past Participle	Present	Past	Past Participle
begin	began	(have) begun	know	knew	(have) known
break	broke	(have) broken	lie	lay	(have) lain
bring	brought	(have) brought	ride	rode	(have) ridden
choose	chose	(have) chosen	ring	rang	(have) rung
come	came	(have) come	run	ran	(have) run
do	did	(have) done	see	saw	(have) seen
drink	drank	(have) drunk	sing	sang	(have) sung
eat	ate	(have) eaten	speak	spoke	(have) spoken
fall	fell	(have) fallen	steal	stole	(have) stolen
freeze	froze	(have) frozen	swim	swam	(have) swum
give	gave	(have) given	take	took	(have) taken
go	went	(have) gone	throw	threw	(have) thrown
grow	grew	(have) grown	write	wrote	(have) written

Practice Your Skills

A. CONCEPT CHECK

Irregular Verbs   Write the correct form of the irregular verb given in parentheses.

Writing Theme
Humanitarians

1. The idea for the Red Cross (arose, arisen) in the 1860s.
2. War had (broke, broken) out in Italy in 1859.
3. During a tour of the country, Jean Henry Dunant had (rode, ridden) across a battlefield at Solferino.
4. He (saw, seen) great misery all around him.
5. More than forty thousand soldiers (lay, lain) dead or wounded.
6. By the end of his tour, he had (brought, brung) together volunteers to help the wounded.
7. After three years, Dunant's ideas had (grew, grown).
8. In 1862 he (wrote, written) "Recollections of Solferino."
9. In this pamphlet, Dunant (spoke, spoken) passionately about assistance for the victims of war and natural disasters.
10. Many people soon (knew, known) of Dunant's plans.
11. People from sixteen nations (go, went) to a series of meetings in Geneva, Switzerland.
12. By 1863, a new organization had (laid, lay) out its basic plan.
13. It had also (chose, chosen) its symbol, a red cross on a white background, and its name, the Red Cross.
14. Twelve nations (came, come) to sign the charter in 1864.
15. Eighteen years later, the United States still had not (make, made) the decision to sign this charter.
16. The American Red Cross finally (began, begun) in 1882.
17. Some branches have (took, taken) other symbols, such as a red crescent in Muslim countries, and a red Star of David in Israel.
18. The Red Cross has (wrote, written) rules for the treatment of wartime prisoners.
19. We (known, know) these rules as the Geneva Convention.
20. The Red Cross has always (done, did) much for people in need.
21. For example, if you have ever (fell, fallen), you may have used first-aid skills that you learned from the Red Cross.
22. The Red Cross also (takes, taken) in blood during blood drives.
23. It (freezes, frozen) the blood and uses it in an emergency.
24. Victims of earthquakes and other natural disasters have (sang, sung) the praises of the Red Cross for years.
25. Volunteers from all over the world have (given, gave) their time and money to this worthy cause.

After Hurricane Andrew struck southern Florida in August 1992, residents had great difficulty getting safe drinking water.

Clara Barton (1937), Mathilde M. Leisenring. The founder of the American Red Cross, Clara Barton, was called "the angel of the battlefield" for her tireless efforts helping wounded soldiers during the Civil War.

B. DRAFTING SKILL

Using Correct Verb Forms   Write the past or past participle form of each verb in parentheses.

26. In 1861, tensions (grow) between the North and South in the United States.

27. Soon the Civil War (break) out.

28. Clara Barton, a clerk in the U.S. Patent Office, had (go) to the battlefields as a nurse.

29. Thousands of soldiers had (fall) in battle.

30. They (lie) in makeshift hospitals.

31. Barton (bring) valuable supplies of food, drink, and medicine.

32. Wounded men gratefully (eat) and (drink) Barton's provisions.

33. By 1864 her humanitarian activities had (begin) to be famous.

34. She had (do) wonders for the sick and wounded.

35. People had (speak) of her as the "Angel of the Battlefield."

36. At first, the government (give) her no encouragement.

37. Later, it (choose) a different path, one of support for her work.

38. In 1865, church bells (ring) and people (sing) in celebration of the end of the war.

39. Then Barton (run) a bureau that tried to locate men missing in action.

40. She had (come) up with another form of help for those in need.

C. PROOFREADING SKILL

Checking Verb Forms   Write the following paragraph, correcting all the errors in grammar, capitalization, punctuation, and spelling. Pay particular attention to the verb forms. (15 errors)

By the end of the Civil War, Clara Barton had grew very tired in 1869 she went to switzerland for a long-overdue rest. The international Red Cross had already begun to operate their. Barton soon known all about it. She spoke to it's organizers and quickly seen how she could help them. Once again she choose to be in a dangerous situation. This time she went to the front lines of the Franco-Prussian War and give aid to the soldiers. By 1873, she had returned to america, where she begun the American branch of the Red Cross she also wrote several books about her ideas. Clara Barton run the United States Red Cross from 1882 to 1904. Under her direction, the Red Cross helped the victims of natural disastors as well as victims of warfare.

FOR MORE PRACTICE
See page 497.

VERB TENSES

> Different forms of the verb are used to show the time of an action or the time of a state of being. These forms are called the **tenses** of the verb.

A verb has different forms, called **tenses,** to indicate whether an action takes place or a condition exists in the present, past, or future. Verbs change in the ways shown below to indicate time differences.

Verb Forms To Indicate Time Differences

The spelling of the present form of the verb may change:		A helping verb may be used:		
invent	invented	will grow	has grown	had grown
see	saw	will protect	has protected	had protected

A verb has three simple tenses and three perfect tenses.

The Simple Tenses

The most common tenses of the verb are the **simple tenses:** present, past, and future. You use these tenses most often in your speaking and writing. Correctly using the tenses helps you convey clearly what you mean.

The **present tense** places the action or condition in the present time. The present form of the verb is used for the present tense: *find, make, play.*

The **past tense** places the action or condition in the past. The past tense of a regular verb is formed by adding *-d* or *-ed* to the present form: *replaced, looked.* The past tense of an irregular verb is shown by changing the spelling within the word: *grow, grew; begin, began.*

The **future tense** places the action or condition in the future. The future tense is formed by using the word *shall* or *will* before the present form: *shall need, will eat.*

Writing TIP

A story that is told or written in many different tenses can confuse the listener or reader. The sequence of events is hard to understand if the tenses change too often.

The Perfect Tenses

Sometimes you want to show that an action was completed or that a condition existed before a given time. In that case, use one of the perfect tenses.

The **perfect tenses** are formed by using *has, have,* or *had* before the past participle. They are formed as follows:

Present Perfect	have gone, has gone, has been gone
Past Perfect	had gone, had been gone
Future Perfect	shall have gone, will have gone

Practice Your Skills

A. CONCEPT CHECK

Verb Tenses   Write the verbs from the following sentences. Beside each verb, write its tense.

1. Most ivory comes from the tusks of elephants.
2. Until the late 1800s, people had made jewelry, piano keys, and billiard balls from ivory.
3. By the 1860s, however, the supply of ivory had dwindled.
4. A New England maker of billiard balls offered $10,000 for a good substitute for ivory.
5. John Wesley Hyatt won the prize with celluloid, a form of plastic.
6. He had acquired the patent for celluloid from a British professor.
7. Celluloid has now been replaced by newer plastics.
8. Because of the invention of plastic, the demand for ivory has dropped.
9. With any luck, the elephant population will not perish.
10. Inventors will have contributed to the elephant's survival.

B. DRAFTING SKILL

Using Different Tenses   Complete each of the following sentences with the form of the verb given in parentheses.

11. An elephant (present of *have*) the largest ears of any animal.
12. It also (present of *possess*) the keenest sense of smell.
13. If given an unlimited supply of food, an elephant (future of *consume*) as much as five hundred pounds.

14. In some parts of Africa, elephants (present perfect of *eat*) all the available foliage.
15. By the time it is an adult, a typical elephant (future perfect of *grow*) to a weight of ten thousand pounds.
16. One of the largest known elephants (past of *weigh*) over two hundred pounds at birth.
17. By the time they die, most elephants (future perfect of *live*) only fifty or sixty years.
18. At one point, elephants (past perfect of *become*) an endangered species.
19. People (past perfect of *hunt*) them for years.
20. Hunters (past of *be*) eager to sell the elephants' ivory.

C. APPLICATION IN WRITING

Problem and Solution   Write two brief paragraphs. In the first paragraph, describe one of the endangered species in our world. In the second paragraph, explain the history of the species. Be sure your verb tenses show a logical sequence of events.

FOR MORE PRACTICE
See pages 497–498.

CHECK ✔ POINT
MIXED REVIEW • PAGES 479–485

Writing Theme
Ballet

A. Write the correct form of the verbs given in parentheses.

1. As of this year, the ballet will have (exist, existed) for more than three hundred years.
2. Over the years, audiences have (went, gone) to performances in formal halls as well as in school auditoriums.
3. This year alone, millions of people will (see, seen) a ballet.
4. The dancers especially will (entertain, entertained) them.
5. Ballet (develop, developed) from the parties of Italian nobles.
6. For years the nobles had (gave, given) fancy entertainments.
7. In the 1500s, they had (begin, begun) dance contests among themselves.
8. In 1547 an Italian noblewoman, Catherine de Medici, (came, come) to Paris as France's new queen.
9. She (introduce, introduced) Italy's dance entertainments to France.
10. She also (bring, brought) a gifted musician, Balthazar de Beaujoyeulx.

11. In honor of Catherine's wedding, he (organize, organized) a magnificent spectacle of dancers.
12. Beaujoyeulx had (wrote, written) music and dance compositions that took over five hours to perform.
13. Actors (recited, recite) poems and (sing, sang) songs for the show.
14. By the 1600s, French ballet had (became, become) very important to the French people.
15. Finally, in 1661, King Louis XIV (established, establish) the Royal Academy as a school for professional dancers.

B. Write the verbs from the following sentences. Beside each, label its tense.

16. Probably no other painter has ever captured scenes from the ballet as well as Edgar Degas.
17. From 1854 to 1859, Degas painted scenes from history such as battles and portraits of famous people.
18. However, he eventually focused on scenes from his life in Paris, such as scenes from ballet classes.
19. These paintings show ballerinas' movements in casual or even awkward positions.
20. Such moments had never been the subject of paintings before.
21. Degas also created daring new compositions.
22. For instance, in some of his pictures, parts of his subjects are not visible; the figures extend beyond the edge of the painting.
23. These pictures seem like snapshots of fleeting moments.
24. No wonder they have captivated viewers for years.
25. Surely they will be popular for many more years.

Ballet Rehearsal (1885), Edgar Degas.

PROGRESSIVE VERB FORMS

> The **progressive form** of the verb shows continuing action.

Sometimes we tell the time of an action like this:

I *am* playing.   (instead of I *play*)
I *was* playing.   (instead of I *played*)

In situations like these, we use a form of the verb *be* plus the **present participle,** a verb form that ends in *-ing.* A verb phrase made up of one of the forms of *be* and a present participle is called a **progressive form.**

The progressive form of a verb shows continuing action. For instance, "I am playing" shows that my playing is going on right now, whereas "I play" shows that I can or do play. Here are the progressive forms of *play* that are used with *I:*

I am playing.	I have been playing.
I was playing.	I had been playing.
I will (shall) be playing.	I will (shall) have been playing.

Sports announcers often use the present progressive to convey the excitement of the action as it occurs:

"The ball is *heading* deep into center field.
It's *going.* It's *going.* It's gone!"

Practice Your Skills

A. CONCEPT CHECK

Progressive Verb Forms   Write each verb phrase from the following sentences.

Writing Theme
Sports Action

1. In another minute we will have been broadcasting this tense tennis match for four hours.
2. We will be continuing, though, until the very end of the match.
3. The crowd has been standing on its feet for much of the action.
4. Our current champion has been serving well all day.
5. Earlier in the tournament, he had been faulting often.

6. This afternoon, though, he is concentrating on his serves.

7. From now on he should be delivering each serve flawlessly.

8. His opponent, however, is returning those serves consistently.

9. Earlier, his opponent was hitting a lot of ground strokes.

10. Now he is smashing one overhead shot after another.

B. REVISION SKILL

Using Progressive Forms Rewrite each of the following sentences. Change the verbs to the progressive form.

11. Today I broadcast from the site of the U.S. Open.

12. For several days the greatest names in tennis have gathered here.

13. They have practiced for hours each day.

14. Now, however, they face the real test.

15. This morning the first matches of the tournament will get underway.

16. Already, spectators file into the stands.

17. Players arrive for their first matches.

18. Some will stay for only the first rounds.

19. Others, though, hope for a longer run in the tournament.

20. In the end, of all the players who will have prepared for the thrill of victory, only two—one man and one woman—will come home singles champions.

C. APPLICATION IN WRITING

Writing a Script Imagine that you are auditioning for a job as a sports announcer. Write the script you would use for your tryout. Select an appropriate sports event and describe the quickly changing action. Mix present tense and progressive forms to make your description as exciting as possible.

FOR MORE PRACTICE
See page 498.

ACTIVE AND PASSIVE VERB FORMS

When the subject of the sentence performs the action, the verb is **active.** When the subject of the sentence receives the action or expresses the result of the action, the verb is **passive.**

In addition to showing the time of an action, you can use verbs in still another way to express exactly what you mean.

Suppose oil has been leaked into the harbor. If you know who or what did it, you can say something like this:

Our motorboat leaked oil into the harbor.

Suppose that you do not know who or what leaked the oil or that you do not want to say who or what did it. You can say this:

Oil was leaked into the harbor.

In the first sentence, the subject says who or what performed the action. The verb of this sentence is **active.** In the second sentence, the subject says who or what received the action. The verb of this sentence is **passive.** The word *passive* means "acted upon."

The passive form of a verb consists of some form of *be* plus the past participle. Only transitive verbs, those that take objects, can be changed from active to passive:

Active	**Passive**
Beebe explored the sea.	The sea was explored by Beebe.
The bathysphere helped him.	He was helped by the bathy-sphere.

Practice Your Skills

A. CONCEPT CHECK

Active and Passive Verb Forms   Write the verbs from the following sentences. Label each one *Active* or *Passive.*

1. The sea's depths were first explored by an American naturalist.
2. His name was Dr. William Beebe.
3. Beebe built the first bathysphere during the 1920s.
4. This small chamber carried two scientists down into the sea.

5. In 1930 the bathysphere was lowered for the very first time.
6. Beebe traveled three thousand feet into the inky deep.
7. At two thousand feet below the surface, Beebe was overwhelmed by the unexpected sight of bright lights and colors.
8. The sea was illuminated by bioluminescent fish.
9. Chemicals within the fish gave them a glow, like fireworks.
10. Sights like these had never been seen before by human eyes.

B. REVISION SKILL

Avoiding the Use of *You* In formal writing, the pronoun *you* should be used only to mean "you, the reader." In some cases, changing a verb from the active to the passive will eliminate awkward *you* constructions. Rewrite the following paragraph, using passive verbs in sentences 11, 13, and 14. In sentences 12, 15, and 16, supply a new subject.

The bathysphere with the two scientists descends slowly into the depths of the sea. **11**You feel a gentle tug. The cable has neared its end, and the bathysphere floats in an undersea world. **12**At first, you can see only blackness. **13**You might describe this darkness as "perpetual night." However, the black world is not completely without light. **14**You can observe hundreds of fish. Each glows with its own colored lights. **15**For instance, nearby you notice a bright liquid discharge from a deep-sea shrimp. **16**Soon you can enjoy a spectacular display of living fireworks.

C. REVISION SKILL

Using Active Verbs In the following paragraph, identify each of the italicized verbs as *Active* or *Passive*. Also make the writing stronger and more straightforward by changing passive verbs to active verbs.

17Undersea exploration *has come* a long way. **18**Years ago, people *could dive* only about two hundred feet underwater. **19**Diving suits with air hoses *were used* by them. **20**Then William Beebe *went* half a mile down in his bathysphere. **21**However, cables always *connected* it to the surface. **22**Cables *are* not *needed* by a newer invention, the bathyscaph. **23**Instead, when the craft must return to the surface, ballast *is released* by the craft to make it lighter. **24**The bathyscaph *has reached* depths of over six miles. **25**Still, it only *can go* down or up.

FOR MORE PRACTICE
See pages 498–499.

CHECK POINT

Writing Theme
Transportation
of the Future

A. Write each verb from the following sentences and identify the tense. Also state if the verb is in the progressive form.

1. Early automobiles used steam, gas, and electricity for power.
2. By 1924, however, gasoline had become the major power source.
3. Unfortunately, gasoline adds to air pollution problems.
4. So, for decades U.S. inventors have had an important goal.
5. They have been developing an inexpensive, pollution-free car.
6. Electric cars returned for a short while in the 1960s.
7. Recently, General Motors has been working on a new car.
8. The inside of this car will eventually contain a complex system of batteries and motors.
9. General Motors engineers are still working on the design for the electrical storage systems.
10. New car owners will be facing different issues in the future.
11. By the year 2000, inventors will have been working on electric vehicles for more than a century.
12. Their hard work will have paved the way for future designers.

B. APPLICATION IN LITERATURE

Write the italicized verbs from the following passage. Label each verb as *Active* or *Passive.*

[13]As we approach the Cape, we *see* again the rocket and its launching tower from far off over the lagoon. [14]It *is illumined* with searchlights, the newest and most perfected creation of a scientific age—hard, weighty metal.

[15]We *watch* the launching with some of the astronauts and their families, from a site near the Vehicle Assembly Building. [16]Our cars *are parked* on a slight rise of ground. . . . [17]A jet of steam *shoots* from the pad below the rocket. [18]"Ahhhh!" The crowd *gasps,* almost in unison. [19]Now great flames *spurt, leap, belch* out across the horizon. [20]Clouds of smoke *billow* up on either side of the rocket, completely hiding its base. [21]From the midst of this holocaust, the rocket *begins* to rise. . . . [22]as if the giant weight *is pulled* by an invisible hand out of the atmosphere.

Anne Morrow Lindbergh,
"Morning—The Bird Perched for Flight"

Many writers find several pairs of verbs confusing. These verbs include *sit* and *set, lie* and *lay, rise* and *raise, let* and *leave*, and *learn* and *teach*.

These pairs of verbs cause trouble because they are similar in meaning and often similar in appearance.

Using *Sit* and *Set*

Sit means "to be in a seated position." The principal parts of the verb *sit* are *sit, sat*, and *sat.* Example: *Sit* on the chair.

Set means "to put or place." The principal parts of the verb *set* are *set, set*, and *set.* Example: *Set* the cage down.

Using *Lie* and *Lay*

Lie means "to rest in a flat position." The principal parts of the verb *lie* are *lie, lay*, and *lain.* Example: It *lies* on the table.

Lay means "to put or place." The principal parts of the verb *lay* are *lay, laid*, and *laid.* Example: *Lay* the slides on the counter.

Using *Rise* and *Raise*

Rise means "to move upward." The principal parts of the verb rise are *rise, rose*, and *risen.* Example: The moths *rise* quickly in the air.

Raise means "to move something upward" or "to lift." The principal parts of the verb *raise* are *raise, raised*, and *raised.* Example: *Raise* the window.

Using *Let* and *Leave*

Let means "to allow or permit." The principal parts of the verb *let* are *let, let,* and *let.* Example: *Let* the spider go free.

Leave means "to depart" or "to allow something to remain where it is." The principal parts of the verb *leave* are *leave, left,* and *left.* Example: *Leave* the window closed.

Using *Learn* and *Teach*

Learn means "to gain knowledge or skill." The principal parts of the verb *learn* are *learn, learned,* and *learned.* Example: I *learned* a lot about those insects.

Teach means "to help someone learn" or "to show how or explain." The principal parts of the verb *teach* are *teach, taught,* and *taught.* Example: That book *taught* me a lot about insects.

Practice Your Skills

A. CONCEPT CHECK

Verb Pairs   Write the correct verb from the ones given in parentheses.

Writing Theme
Attack and Defense
in Nature

1. Studying insects closely can (learn, teach) us much about how they protect themselves.
2. An insect that (lays, lies) motionless on a leaf can become food for some other animal.
3. If other species (leave, let) this creature alone, however, it can be a predator, or hunter.
4. It will (lay, lie) there waiting for its prey.
5. Many species will not (let, leave) the slightest chance for a meal go by.
6. For example, a spider (lies, lays) a trap with its web.
7. Then the spider (sits, sets) patiently near its web.
8. It will (lay, lie) there motionless for hours.
9. Experience seems to have (learned, taught) moths how to escape from sticky spider webs.
10. Detachable scales on the moth's wings (leave, let) the moth get away from a hungry spider.
11. When the moth (sits, sets) on the spider's web, its wings don't stick.

12. Soon it (rises, raises) its body and flies to safety.
13. The moth (leaves, lets) some of its wing scales behind, stuck to the web.
14. This (raises, rises) another question.
15. What other insects can (set, sit) on a spider web and then escape?

B. REVISION SKILL

Using the Right Verbs　Revise the sentences that contain errors in verb choice. Write *Correct* if a sentence contains no errors.

16. Nature's moths usually leave scales on spiders' webs.
17. However, nature has learned spiders new tricks as well.
18. The orb weaver, for example, is a spider that has learned the difference between moths and other types of prey.
19. The spider instantly raises up to attack any moth.
20. Other clever spiders sit traps for male moths.
21. An odor exactly like that of a female moth raises from the body of the spider.
22. Some spiders also have lain special traps for moths.
23. These spiders raise vertical "skyscraper webs" more than two hundred times their own size.
24. A smaller web might leave a moth escape.
25. In a skyscraper web, however, a moth leaves so many scales on the web that the moth cannot fly.

C. PROOFREADING SKILL

Using Verbs Correctly　Write the following paragraphs, correcting any errors in grammar, capitalization, punctuation, and spelling. Watch especially for errors in verb choice. (10 errors)

Learning about self-defense in the animal world might learn us something about our own defenses. Animals' defense systems include shells and spines some creatures, like armadillos, have hard, protective shells. Others, like porcupine's and hedgehogs, have sharp spines. Under attack, these animals lie safely inside their "armer."

Some insects and mammals roll themselves up into a ball. this protects soft body parts. When attacked, a hedgehog quickly rolls up in this way. Then it sets on the ground, without rising its head and with only it's needle-sharp spines exposed. Enemys often will let a hedgehog alone rather than risk an injury to themselves.

FOR MORE PRACTICE
See page 499.

CHECK ✔ POINT

The following sentences are part of an imaginary interview between a reporter and Donald McKay, builder of the renowned clipper ships of the 1800s. Write the correct verb from the pair in parentheses.

1. REPORTER: We are (setting, sitting) here today with shipbuilder Donald McKay. How fast were your sailing ships?
2. McKAY: Well, *The Champion of the Seas* (taught, learned) the steamboats a lesson. Her record was unbeaten for twenty-five years.
3. REPORTER: How did you (set, sit) such a record?
4. McKAY: We simply (raised, rose) as much canvas as possible.
5. Sometimes, five rows of sails were (raised, risen) on each mast.
6. REPORTER: Who (learned, taught) you to sail this way?
7. McKAY: Experience has (learned, taught) me everything.
8. REPORTER: What cargo did the ships carry to (raise, rise) money?
9. McKAY: In the early days, we (laid, lay) bags of tea in most holds. Later, ships carried gold, silver, or passengers.
10. Passengers would (set, sit) on deck as often as possible.
11. They didn't like to (lay, lie) below deck.
12. REPORTER: (Teach, Learn) me about a typical voyage. Tell me, please, what was a day aboard ship like?
13. McKAY: Well, we often sailed before the sun (raised, rose).
14. We hoped the weather would (leave, let) us alone to sail freely.
15. My ship has often (laid, lain) still in the water on windless days and my hopes would (raise, rise) at any hint of breeze.
16. REPORTER: Did you (leave, let) the crew relax at any time?
17. McKAY: No skipper has ever (left, let) a crew become too relaxed. The sea is too dangerous for that.
18. REPORTER: As you (set, sit) here today, which would you say is your favorite among your ships?
19. McKAY: If you (let, leave) me choose a favorite, it would be the *Great Republic,* the biggest wooden ship ever built.
20. REPORTER: Thank you, Donald McKay. We'll (let, leave) you to your work.

Clipper Ship "Dreadnought" off Tuskar Light, (1856), Nathaniel Currier. Lithograph.

GRAMMAR
H A N D B O O K
42

Writing Theme
Toys

A. Identifying Verbs Make two columns on your paper. Label them *Action Verbs* and *Linking Verbs.* Write the verbs from the following sentences in the correct columns.

1. Toys often have interesting histories.
2. Yo-yos, for example, first became popular in the United States during the 1930s.
3. However, they were not a new invention at the time.
4. People in the Philippines used yo-yos for many years.
5. Their yo-yos worked as weapons as well as toys.
6. In Europe, people made toys like yo-yos almost three thousand years ago.
7. Some toys, though, are even older than the yo-yo.
8. In ancient Egypt, children pulled and rolled toys from place to place.
9. Egyptian children played ball too.
10. They also enjoyed toy animals of various kinds.
11. In ancient Greece and Rome, children often pushed hoops.
12. They floated toy boats in local lakes and ponds.
13. Greek and Roman children also rode hobbyhorses.
14. Toys like these remain popular today.
15. Some good ideas last forever.

B. Identifying Verb Phrases Write the verb phrases from the following sentences. Underline the helping verbs once and the main verbs twice.

16. Did you ever spin a toy top?
17. You can find these wonderful toys almost all over the world.
18. In China and Japan, children have played with tops and spinners for thousands of years.
19. Historians have uncovered evidence of tops in ancient Egypt.
20. Some tops might have appeared more than five thousand years ago.
21. Can you picture ancient-Egyptian children and their tops with the great pyramids in the background?
22. Archaeologists have discovered wonderful tops at the sites of ancient Native American communities.
23. People must have made them by hand from hollow nuts and gourds.
24. Further north, Inuit children have always used ivory tops.

25. Their tops might have been carved from walrus tusks.
26. In Europe, children have had tops and spinners since Roman times.
27. Over the years, tops have come in all shapes and sizes.
28. A twist of the wrist will start some tops.
29. Others are spun with the help of a string.
30. Once a top has been started, it will turn for a long time.

C. Using Irregular Verbs   For each sentence write the correct form of the verb given in parentheses.

31. Do you ever (took, take) a kite out on a breezy day?
32. Not much has been (written, wrote) about the very first kites.
33. Kites probably (begin, began) in China about three thousand years ago.
34. By 200 B.C. kites had even (went, gone) into battle.
35. Bamboo pipes (rode, ridden) up into the air on the kites.
36. The sound of these whistles usually (frozen, froze) the enemy in its tracks.
37. Over the years kites have (did, done) other useful things.
38. During the construction of a bridge in the 1840s, kites (bring, brought) equipment across the Niagara River.
39. Airplane designers have also (chose, chosen) kites as models.
40. For example, the Wright brothers had (saw, seen) kites in action before they built their first airplane.

D. Recognizing Verb Tenses   Make two columns: *Verbs* and *Verb Tenses*. In the first column, write the verbs from the following sentences; in the second, write the tenses of those verbs.

41. Dolls are among the world's most popular toys.
42. They will probably remain popular for years to come.
43. People have not always used dolls as toys, however.
44. In ancient Egypt, people buried special dolls with the dead.
45. According to Egyptian religious beliefs, these dolls became servants in the afterlife.
46. In ancient Greece, young girls gave their dolls away shortly before marriage.
47. For centuries this had been a sign of the girls' adulthood.
48. In most parts of Europe, dolls became popular children's toys in the 1700s.

49. Dolls from that era do not have the sophisticated appearance of dolls today.
50. Back then, woodcarvers had become doll makers.
51. Many of their dolls have survived to this day as puppets.
52. By the 1800s, many dolls had been made from papier-mâché.
53. Today, doll collectors still have china dolls, with china faces and heads.
54. In the future, doll makers will probably use high-tech materials for dolls.
55. By then, dolls will have become more lifelike than ever.

E. Using Progressive Forms Rewrite the following sentences, using the progressive forms of the verbs.

56. Surfers will always ride the big waves.
57. However, during the 1950s, surfers had searched for alternatives to waves.
58. These surfers looked for a new approach to the sport.
59. For years they had noticed youngsters on roller skates.
60. This everyday sight gave some surfers an idea.
61. Soon surfers attached roller skates to their surfboards.
62. Thanks to these inventive surfers, people have enjoyed skateboards for years.
63. Since the 1950s, fun-seekers have ridden skateboards.
64. Today, people skateboard more than ever before.
65. They still find excitement in the speed of the ride.
66. In the past, skateboarders practiced on local streets.
67. Now they use elaborate ramps too.
68. Some cities have built parks with skateboard ramps.
69. Without a doubt, skateboarders will develop new ways of practicing their skills.
70. Maybe even more people will take up the sport in the future.

F. Identifying Active and Passive Forms Write each verb from the following sentences. Label each *Active* or *Passive*.

71. Puppets have been around for thousands of years.
72. Today the simplest puppets are finger puppets.
73. The puppeteer's own hands and fingers form the puppets.
74. The puppet's face is usually drawn on the person's hands or fingers.

75. Hand puppets are used by both professional and amateur puppeteers.
76. Hand, or glove, puppets usually are topped by a hollow head.
77. Puppeteers place their hands inside this hollow head.
78. A glove or piece of cloth forms the puppet's body.
79. The puppet's arm movements are controlled by the puppeteer's fingers.
80. During the 1950s and 1960s, hand puppets were revolutionized.
81. Jim Henson, for example, developed the Muppets, highly flexible puppets.
82. Rods and strings were used for the control of arms and legs.
83. Recently, computers have been added to the puppeteer's bag of tricks.
84. Puppets' movements and voices are created by complicated hardware and computer programs.
85. Computers make these electronic puppets incredibly lifelike.

G. Choosing the Correct Verb   Write the correct verb given in parentheses.

86. People who enjoy model trains love to (learn, teach) the hobby to others.
87. First the experts (let, leave) the person run the train.
88. Then they (learn, teach) the person to build a setting.
89. Other experts (leave, let) newcomers learn on their own.
90. No matter what their age, though, model railroaders (lay, lie) out tracks in intricate patterns.
91. They (set, sit) houses, barns, and crossings all around the landscape.
92. Model mountains (rise, raise) dramatically into the air.
93. Valleys and rivers (lie, lay) between the mountains.
94. Typical hobbyists (set, sit) for hours with their rigs.
95. Some people never (let, leave) their work alone.
96. These people are always (sitting, setting) new equipment in place.
97. Their excitement (raises, rises) with each new addition.
98. Many young people (learn, teach) about another kind of model building from kits.
99. They (set, sit) patiently with tiny pieces of plastic or wood and a small tube of glue.
100. These hobbyists (raise, rise) entire model cities.

GRAMMAR
H A N D B O O K
42

Writing Theme
Amusement Parks

A. Identifying Verbs   List the verbs and verb phrases in the following sentences. Identify each main verb as an *Action Verb* or *Linking Verb.* Underline all helping verbs.

1. For over seventy-five years, Coney Island had meant thrills, excitement, and fun.
2. However, people had been enjoying Coney Island long before the arrival of its amusement parks.
3. Sun and sand were the main attractions in the early days.
4. In the 1850s, hotels sprang up along the beach.
5. Hundreds of visitors would come for a weekend by the sea.
6. By 1860, Coney Island had become a major resort area.
7. Then, in 1875, New York City built a new railroad line.
8. It connected Coney Island with central Brooklyn.
9. Soon people would be coming to Coney Island just for the afternoon or evening instead of for a weekend or summer.
10. The brand-new amusement parks were exciting for the tens of thousands of visitors.

B. Verb Tenses and Progressive Forms   Complete the following sentences with the verb forms in parentheses.

11. In 1897, Steeplechase Park (past tense of *open*).
12. That park (present of *be*) probably the greatest symbol of Coney Island in its prime.
13. As a child, George Tilyou, the founder of Steeplechase, (past of *live*) in his parents' Coney Island hotel.
14. In the 1890s, he (past of *watch*) the construction of Coney Island's first real amusement park, Sea Lion Park.
15. He quickly (past perfect of *realize*) the appeal of the parks.
16. In fact, few people ever (present perfect of *understand*) fun, thrills, and entertainment as well as Tilyou.
17. People (future of *pay*) good money for a thrill.
18. The thrills and rides (present of *chase*) away their worries.
19. From the beginning, Tilyou (past progressive of *call*) Steeplechase "the Funny Place."
20. Soon visitors even (past progressive of *travel*) on a fantasy trip to the moon.
21. By 1980, though, everything (past perfect of *change*).
22. Steeplechase Park and Coney Island itself (past perfect progressive of *decline*) rapidly since the 1960s.
23. Today few traditional amusement parks (present of *remain*).

24. Yet people (future progressive of *look*) for relief from tension for years to come.

25. The legends of the old amusement parks, too, probably (future of *live*) forever.

C. Using Irregular Verbs Write the verb in parentheses that correctly completes each of the following sentences.

26. Most people (have ridden, rode) a carousel.

27. Surprisingly, the word carousel (begin, began) as a name for a serious war game.

28. In the original version of the game, Arab soldiers on horseback had (threw, thrown) clay balls at one another.

29. The game (gave, given) the riders practice in the arts of war.

30. This activity (grown, grew) into a sport for Europe's nobles.

31. For training, young men on human-powered carousels (take, took) stabs at targets with swords and lances.

32. By 1900, mechanical carousels had (come, came) along.

33. The horses, camels, elephants, and other fanciful creatures on these new carousels (run, ran) smoothly for hour after hour.

34. Over the years, these carousels have (bring, brought) endless enjoyment to amusement park visitors.

35. People still can (see, seen) horses and other figures from these antique carousels in parks and museums.

D. Choosing the Right Verb Write the correct verb given in parentheses.

36. In this article I will (teach, learn) you a little about Clarkson's Carnival.

37. This is the headline for my article: Mayor (Leaves, Lets) Carnival Come to Town.

38. Right now I am (setting, sitting) at the site of the carnival.

39. Off in the distance, a group of workers (lies, lays) railroad ties around the perimeter of the park.

40. The owners (leave, let) the crews alone so they can work.

41. Close by, several crews are (setting, sitting) rides in place.

42. Yesterday's crews (rose, raised) tents in the park.

43. Inside those tents, lions and tigers (lie, lay) quietly now.

44. Nearby a worker (leaves, lets) visitors feed the elephants.

45. Tomorrow, the elephant trainer will (teach, learn) the animals a new trick.

E. Using Active Verb Forms   Rewrite the following sentences, changing the verbs from the passive to the active form.

46. Most people are surprised by unusual world records.
47. For example, the heaviest load for horses—ninety-six thousand pounds—was pulled by two Clydesdales in Michigan.
48. The number of nematode sea worms, the commonest animal on earth, has been estimated by scientists at 4×10^{25} (four followed by twenty-five zeros).
49. A whale measuring 110 feet, 2½ inches was caught by sailors in the South Atlantic Ocean.
50. A speed of 739 mph was attained by a rocket-propelled car driven by Stan Barrett in 1979.
51. A ninety-six-hour surgical operation was endured by a Chicago woman.
52. A fingernail 34½ inches long was grown by Shridhar Chillal of India.
53. The world's oldest song, the shadoof chant, has been sung since the beginning of recorded time by generations of irrigation workers in Egypt.
54. Seventy-two letters are contained in the Cambodian alphabet.
55. The tallest structure in the world, a radio tower more than four-tenths of a mile high, was built by engineers in Konstantynow, Poland.

F. Using Passive Verb Forms   Rewrite the following sentences, changing the verbs from the active to the passive form.

56. You can find many surprising records in the history of sports and games.
57. A total of 8,238 people attended the largest game of musical chairs on record.
58. Enrico Rastelli of Italy juggled ten balls at one time.
59. An Australian fisherman once caught a 2,664-pound white shark.
60. Two university students in England played the longest recorded chess game—165 hours and nine minutes.
61. Skateboarder Richard K. Brown reached a record speed of 71.79 miles per hour in a prone position on a course at Mt. Baldy, California.
62. Louis Scripa, Jr., did more than sixty thousand sit-ups in twenty-four hours in Sacramento, California.

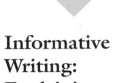

Revise the following draft of a cause-and-effect paper by using the directions at the bottom of the page. Then proofread the passage, paying close attention to correcting errors in the use of verbs. Also look for other errors in grammar, capitalization, punctuation, and spelling.

[1]A new way of cooking food was discovered accidently in 1946 by Dr. Percy Spencer, an Engineer for Raytheon Corporation. [2]Spencer was testing a magnetron tube. [3]A magnetron tube is an electronic tube that produces microwave energy. [4]Spencer reaches into his pocket for a candy bar he had brung along for a snack. [5]And found the candy bar had melted. [6]It was determined by Spencer that microwaves had heated the candy. [7]In a microwave oven, radio waves from a magnetron penetrates the food and make the water molecules in the food vibrate. [8]The vibration caused friction, which heats the food from the inside out. [9]Conventional ovens cook food in the oposite way. [10]They heated the outside of the food first and then the heat had went to the inside. [11]If you have ate food cooked by microwaves, you know it doesn't taste no diffrent from food cooked in other ways.

1. Add the information in sentence 3 to sentence 2 as an appositive.

2. Change sentence 6 to the active voice.

3. After sentence 6, add this information: His discovery led to the development of the microwave oven.

4. In sentence 10 replace the verb phrase "had went" with the precise verb "penetrates."

5. Divide the passage into two paragraphs.

Informative Writing: Explaining *How*

Cause-and-effect writing answers the questions "What happened?" and "Why did it happen?" (See Workshop 4.) When you revise this type of writing, check to see if you have used precise verbs and consistent verb tenses to explain the relationship between causes and effects.

- "Fantastic!" "Hilarious!" "Suspenseful!" "Outrageously Funny!" You've seen movie advertisements with glowing quotes from the critics. Create an ad for your favorite movie. Be sure to include some made-up quotes.

- Think of a book and a television program you've seen that you especially liked or disliked. Write a list of five terms that describe the book or program.

- Write a brief description of a scene you remember vividly. It could be something you saw yourself or something from a movie or television program.

Using Modifiers

When was the last time you saw a movie? How good was the movie? How does it compare to others you've seen? To answer questions like these, you need to use modifiers—adjectives and adverbs. Modifiers help you clarify, describe, and qualify your thoughts.

This handbook can help you choose *precise* (adjective) modifiers that you can use to express yourself *clearly* (adverb).

Writing TIP

Writers can use modifiers to bring a reader into a scene. Notice how modifiers add accuracy and detail to *Last Chance to See*, pages 62–63.

Modifiers are words that make other words more precise.

Nouns and pronouns help us name and identify things and people in the world around us. Verbs help us express action. **Modifiers** provide additional information about nouns, pronouns, and verbs. Modifiers help us describe what we have seen and heard.

Vincent van Gogh loved *bright* colors.
He painted *quickly* and *forcefully.*
He sold *only one* painting during his life.

Modifiers can also help describe feelings about things and people.

Van Gogh was *happiest* when he painted outdoors.
Bright, yellow sunflowers were a *favorite* subject.
He felt e*specially content* when painting *ordinary* people.

Remember, to change something slightly is to *modify* it. An artist can modify a painting by adding details that make the picture more interesting. Writers and speakers modify an idea or image by choosing certain describing words—modifiers.

Notice how modifiers both describe and point out the differences in the two paintings below. Behind the *yellow* sunflowers in the *copper* vase is a *roughly textured blue* background. The *blue* irises in the *gold* vase sit in front of a *bright yellow* wall.

Left, *Crown Imperial Fritillaria in a Copper Vase* (1887), Vincent van Gogh. Right, *Vase with Irises* (1890), Vincent van Gogh.

ADJECTIVES

An **adjective** is a word that modifies a noun or pronoun.

What is the difference between these sentences?

Van Gogh painted scenes of life.
Van Gogh painted simple scenes of rural life.

The difference is in the descriptive words that tell what kind of scenes and what kind of life. These words are called **adjectives.** They modify nouns or pronouns.

Some adjectives tell *how many* or *what kind* about the words they modify.

There were *many* painters.   He tried *new* techniques.
He had *few* friends.   The *older* painters disapproved.

Some adjectives tell *which one* or *which ones.*

This painting is famous.   *Those* peasants are in the field.
His paintings did not sell. *These* fields are colorful.

Self-portrait with Felt Hat
(1887), Vincent van Gogh.

Proper Adjectives

Proper adjectives are adjectives formed from proper nouns. They are always capitalized.

a Flemish painter   a French artist
a Renaissance painting a Belgian village
the Dutch countryside the Japanese watercolor

Predicate Adjectives

Sometimes a **linking verb** separates an adjective from the word it modifies. An adjective that follows a linking verb and that modifies the subject is called a **predicate adjective.** (See page 474 for information about linking verbs.)

Van Gogh seemed *lonely.*   He became *enthusiastic.*
His brother was *upset.*   The painting is *priceless.*

Pronouns Used as Adjectives

As you learned on page 450, the words *this, that, these,* and *those* can be used as demonstrative pronouns. When used alone, they are pronouns. When followed by a noun, they are adjectives telling *which one* or *which ones.*

> *Those* drawings are very old. (adjective modifying *drawings*)
> *These* are by van Gogh. (pronoun)
> *That* one was painted in Paris. (adjective modifying *one*)

The words *my, her, his, its, our,* and *their* are possessive pronouns, but they can also be classified as adjectives. These modifiers tell *which one* or *which ones.*

> *My* mother likes van Gogh's work; *her* sister does not.
> Of *his* works, *Sunflowers* is *her* favorite.
> *Our* museum collects watercolors; *its* collection is large.

Practice Your Skills

A. CONCEPT CHECK

Adjectives   Write the adjectives from the following sentences. After each adjective, write the word it modifies.

1. The Dutch painter Vincent van Gogh was extraordinary.
2. In his lifetime, this artist completed numerous paintings.
3. He was a financial failure however.
4. Many fine galleries in major cities exhibit his colorful works.
5. His early pictures were often quiet and serious.
6. At that time he favored dark colors and heavy brushstrokes.
7. Later paintings feature intense color and unusual energy.
8. Those later works often contain various shades of a special blue paint—a favorite of French painters of the time.
9. One work with that remarkable paint is very famous.
10. In that painting, *The Starry Night,* the dark sky is filled with brilliant stars.
11. The night sky moves like a stormy sea.
12. The dark city below the sky seems calm and peaceful.
13. Van Gogh studied Asian painting.
14. Japanese art influenced his painting of some peasant women washing clothes in a river.
15. He showed the simple tasks of everyday life in that picture.

The Starry Night (1889),
Vincent van Gogh.

B. APPLICATION IN LITERATURE

Recognizing Adjectives   Notice how the writer of the passage below uses adjectives to add detail and to set the tone of the passage. Read the passage, and list the adjectives.

> [16]Well over a hundred years ago a small boy ran through the moist fields and woods of Brabant in the southern Netherlands. [17]He loved the fresh, clean wind on his face; he loved to watch . . . the hidden joys of nature, the peasants at work and at rest— all the wonders of the natural world were, to him, remarkable beyond words. [18][His] name was Vincent van Gogh. He was born March 30, 1853. . . .
>
> [19]He was a quiet child but a stubborn and willful one. [20]He suffered long, dark moods that suddenly gave way to bright moments of great happiness.
>
>

Arnold Dobrin, *I Am a Stranger on the Earth: The Story of Vincent van Gogh*

C. APPLICATION IN WRITING

Description   Look carefully at the painting above. Then write a brief paragraph that describes your reactions to the painting. Use at least five adjectives in your description. Include one predicate adjective.

Writing
TIP

Think carefully about the image you want to convey. Then choose specific adjectives that describe that particular image.

FOR MORE PRACTICE
See page 529.

Using Modifiers   **509**

ARTICLES

A, an, and *the* are special adjectives called **articles.**

The is a special kind of adjective known as the **definite article.** It is used to refer to a particular thing.

> *The* climber was stranded. (a particular climber)

A and *an* are also special adjectives called **indefinite articles.** They are used when the noun does not refer to any particular thing.

> *A* guide explained the danger. (no specific guide)
> *An* avalanche may threaten climbers. (no particular avalanche)

Use *a* before a word that begins with a consonant sound (*a* hiker). Use *an* before a vowel sound (*an* accident). The first sound of a word, not the spelling, makes the difference. This means that a speaker would say *an hour* but *a hallway.*

All articles are adjectives. Use *the* with both singular and plural nouns, but use *a* and *an* only with singular nouns.

the skier	the skiers	a skier
the adventure	the adventures	an adventure

Practice Your Skills

CONCEPT CHECK

Choosing Articles   Write the correct article from those given in parentheses.

1. (A, An) hiker slipped on a sheet of ice.
2. She slid down a cliff and was stranded on (a, an) rock ledge.
3. No one knew (a, the) route she had taken.
4. (The, An) hiker's friend called the local mountain rescue team.
5. The team began the search within (a, an) hour.
6. A specially trained dog followed (a, the) hiker's scent.
7. A helicopter began (a, an) air search of the mountains.
8. The dog followed the trail to (a, the) edge of the cliff.
9. A climber from (a, the) same rescue team descended to the ledge.
10. (A, An) rope was attached and the hiker was pulled to safety.

ADVERBS

An **adverb** modifies a verb, an adjective, or another adverb.

Adverbs help make meaning clear by telling *how, when, where,* or *to what extent* something is true.

Adverbs Used with Verbs

Adverbs that modify verbs tell *how, when, where,* or *to what extent* an action happened. Study the following list of adverbs.

How?	When?	Where?	To What Extent?
carefully	sometimes	inside	fully
quickly	once	underground	very
sorrowfully	now	here	quite
hurriedly	finally	there	extremely

Notice how adverbs make the following sentence clearer:

The door of the tomb opened.
Finally, the door of the tomb *slowly* opened.

Adverbs make the meaning of the verb *opened* clearer.

Adverbs Used with Adjectives or Other Adverbs

Adverbs that tell *to what extent* can also modify adjectives and other adverbs.

Frequently Used Adverbs			
very	not	somewhat	more
just	nearly	so	most

Notice how the adverbs in the following sentences make the adjective and adverb more understandable and more precise.

The tomb was dark.   The guide spoke softly.
The tomb was *nearly* dark.   The guide spoke *very* softly.

Writing
TIP

Adverbs are useful in persuasive writing. By using qualifiers such as *quite, nearly,* and *somewhat,* you can avoid overgeneralization.

Forming Adverbs

Many adverbs are made by adding *-ly* to an adjective.

careful + *-ly* = carefully   slow + *-ly* = slowly

Sometimes the addition of *-ly* involves a spelling change in the adjective.

easy + -ly = easily (*y* changed to *i*)
full + -ly = fully (*ll* changed to *l*)

Some modifiers, like *soon* and *quite,* can be used only as adverbs.

The coffin was *soon* open. The mummy was *quite* well preserved.

Some other modifiers, like *late* or *first,* can be used either as adverbs or as adjectives.

The archaeologist arrived *late*. (adverb)
The *late* arrival delayed the discovery. (adjective)
Grave robbers had gotten there *first*. (adverb)
The *first* tomb was already open. (adjective)

Practice Your Skills

A. CONCEPT CHECK

Adverbs   Write the adverbs from the following sentences. Beside each adverb write the word it modifies.

1. Egyptians were highly successful with mummification.
2. The bodies, or mummies, were very carefully preserved.
3. First, Egyptian embalmers painstakingly removed the brain.
4. The intestines were often stored in jars.
5. The heart and kidneys generally remained in the body.
6. The dead person still needed these organs in the afterlife.
7. Workers covered the body with a special substance, and then they dried the body very gradually.
8. Finally, the embalmers rubbed the body with oils and spices and intricately wrapped it in fine linen.
9. The extremely dry climate aided the process of preservation.
10. This very elaborate process sometimes took seventy days.

B. REVISION SKILL

Using Adverbs   There are many adverbs available for writers to use. Write the following paragraph, replacing the italicized adverbs with other adverbs that convey a similar meaning.

> **11**When you think of mummies, do you think of the *very* old mummies of the ancient Egyptian Pharaohs? **12**It was *once* thought that the Egyptian embalmers used mysterious methods and secret formulas to preserve the bodies *totally.* **13***Today* scientists know that it was the climate, which is *extremely* dry, that prevented the bodies from decaying *horribly.* **14**Archaeologists have found bodies of poor Egyptians *also.* **15**These bodies are as ancient as those of the Pharaohs and *likewise* well preserved. **16**Yet, *surprisingly,* archaeologists have learned that these bodies were *never* embalmed.

FOR MORE PRACTICE
See page 529.

C H E C K ✔ P O I N T
MIXED REVIEW · PAGES 506–513

Write the italicized modifiers and identify them as *Adjectives* or *Adverbs*. Then write the word that each adjective or adverb modifies.

Writing Theme
Discovering New Planets

1. You *probably* know about *the* nine planets of our *solar* system.
2. Do you know that *some* scientists think there may *actually* be *more* planets?
3. *Several* astronomers *now* think there are hundreds or even thousands more in *our* solar system.
4. Scientists suspect that these planets may be *completely* covered with ice.
5. The *great* majority of these *undiscovered* planets could be a thousand times *farther* away than Pluto.
6. A few, however, may be *somewhat* closer.
7. Scientists have not *yet* found any of *these* planets.
8. The planets are probably *very* small, and so of course they are *quite* difficult to see.
9. However, a few may be *barely* visible through our *most* sensitive telescopes.
10. Astronomers are *systematically* searching for these *distant* neighbors.

A Hopi storyteller

An **adjective** modifies a noun or pronoun. An **adverb** modifies a verb, an adjective, or another adverb.

Study the following sentences. Which sentence sounds right?

The Hopi storyteller spoke *quiet.*
The Hopi storyteller spoke *quietly.*

The second sentence is the correct one. An adverb (*quietly*) should be used, not an adjective (*quiet*).

When you are not sure whether an adjective or an adverb should be used, ask yourself these questions:

1. *Which word does the modifier go with?* If it goes with an action verb (like *spoke* in the sentences above), it is an adverb. It is also an adverb if it goes with an adjective or another adverb. If it goes with a noun or pronoun, it is an adjective.

2. *What does the modifier tell about the word it goes with?* If the modifier tells *when, where, how,* or *to what extent,* it is an adverb. If it tells *which one, what kind,* or *how many,* it is an adjective. In the sentences above, the modifier tells *how* the storyteller spoke; it must therefore be an adverb.

Practice Your Skills

A. APPLICATION IN LITERATURE

Adjectives and Adverbs   Write each italicized word. Identify it as an *Adjective* or an *Adverb.* Then write the word it modifies.

¹It was a *hot* day. ²Anpao had ridden his *marvelous* Horse *very far,* hoping he might find a *friendly* village where he could make camp and get something to eat. ³He traveled *on* and on but he saw no sign of *his* people. ⁴*Finally* at midday he came upon a cluster of lodges. ⁵The people sat *listlessly* in the shade sleeping. ⁶All the lodge skins were raised to let the air in, and all the cooking fires had gone *out.* ⁷No one heard Anpao ride into camp until a chief *suddenly* awakened and shouted in surprise to see such an *elegant* warrior astride a *magic* animal.

8Anpao greeted the people *warmly,* but they were *selfish* and *unfriendly.* **9**They stared *enviously* at Anpao's possessions, and they peered at his horse. . . . **10**All they could think about were *devious* ways of getting his belongings and *his magic* animal.

Jamake Highwater, *Anpao: An American Indian Odyssey*

B. CONCEPT CHECK

Adjectives and Adverbs   Make four columns. In the first column, write each adjective and adverb. In the second column, identify its part of speech. In the third, write the word modified. In the fourth, write what the modifier tells, such as *which one, what kind, how,* or *when* and so on. List no articles.

11. Native American cultures have a very old and remarkably rich literature.
12. Their songs and tales are quite colorful.
13. Originally, these stories were not written down.
14. They were passed along orally to each new generation.
15. Usually men were the storytellers. Women were not.
16. Myths and legends strongly reinforced important values and beliefs of the community.
17. Often, stories reflected the close relationship of a people to other creatures, land, sky, and water.
18. In fact some cultures viewed the natural elements as their ancestors.
19. Sometimes the literature served a dual purpose.
20. It might provide a historical record of an important event and honor the deeds of past heroes.

This Hopi pottery tile depicts a kachina, a Hopi deity. These deities may be drawn as human, plant, or animal forms.

Adverbs and Predicate Adjectives

Recall that a predicate adjective appears after a linking verb and modifies the subject. Notice the predicate adjectives below.

The music sounds delightful. (*delightful* modifies *music*)
The people are friendly. (*friendly* modifies *people*)
The crawfish taste delicious. (*delicious* modifies *crawfish*)

You should also remember that in addition to the forms of *be,* the following words can be used as linking verbs: *become, seem, appear, look, sound, feel, taste, grow,* and *smell.*

Sometimes these verbs are used as action verbs. When they are used as action verbs, they are followed by adverbs, not adjectives. The adverbs modify the verbs and tell *how, when, where,* or *to what extent.* The problem of choosing an adjective or an adverb form is often difficult when these verbs are used.

Look at the following sentences to see when adjectives are used and when adverbs are used.

Linking Verb with Adjectives	**Action Verbs with Adverbs**
The *performer* looked *happy.*	The performer *looked up.*
The *pie* tasted *good.*	We *tasted* the pie *eagerly.*
The *audience* appears *pleased.*	A soloist *appears suddenly.*

If you are uncertain whether to use an adverb or adjective after verbs such as *sound, smell,* or *look,* ask yourself these questions:

1. Can you substitute *is* or *was* for the verb? If you can, the verb is probably a linking verb, and the modifier is probably an adjective.
2. Does the modifier tell *how, when, where* or *to what extent?* If it does, the modifier is probably an adverb.

Good and *Well*

Good and *well* have similar meanings, but they differ in their use in a sentence. Study the following sentences.

Incorrect   He tells the story *good.*
Correct   He tells the story *well.*

Good is always an adjective and modifies nouns or pronouns. Never use *good* to modify a verb; use *well.*

Well can be used as either an adjective or an adverb, depending on the situation. When used as an adjective, *well* usually refers to a person's health. For example, "I feel *well*" means "I feel healthy." Remember that "feeling good" refers to being happy or pleased.

Practice Your Skills

A. CONCEPT CHECK

Correct Forms of Modifiers   Write the correct form of the modifiers given in parentheses.

Writing Theme
Cajuns

1. Cajuns tell you (quick, quickly) that their heritage is French.
2. Over the years the French *Acadian* (gradual, gradually) became *Cadien* and (final, finally) *Cajun.*
3. These Louisiana residents will also say that their rice tastes especially (good, well) with boudin, a local sausage.
4. The popularity of spicy Cajun dishes has grown (rapid, rapidly).
5. The name of one favorite food, mudbugs, may sound (strange, strangely) to some.
6. Also known as crawfish, these shrimplike creatures look a little (odd, oddly) too.
7. The idea of popping their heads off before eating them doesn't sound too (reasonable, reasonably) either.
8. Yet natives and visitors alike will put away steaming platters of these tasty crustaceans very (rapid, rapidly).
9. If crawfish have been prepared (good, well), they taste even better than shrimp.
10. Since they are high in protein and low in fat, they are bound to keep you (good, well).

B. PROOFREADING SKILL

Correcting Adjectives and Adverbs   Write the following paragraph, correcting all errors. Pay special attention to errors in the use of modifiers. (15 errors)

   Early in the seventeenth century, settlers from Western France migrated to Nova scotia. The change did not go smooth, however. Very quick, they were caught up in the French and english rivalry for control of north America. England demanded loyalty the Acadian's declared themselves neutral. The english felt certainly that the Acadians were comiting treason. And ordered them deported. For thirty years the Acadians lived in exile, a few in Louisiana, many back in France. In 1762 spanish control of Louisiana made it possible for Acadians to be reunited with thier family members in Louisiana. Today many Cajuns point proud to their family tree and tell of this long, hard journey.

FOR MORE PRACTICE
See page 529.

Use the **comparative form** of an adjective to compare two things. Use the **superlative form** of an adjective to compare more than two.

Comparing people and things is one way of learning about the world. Someone could say, "The dinosaurs were like modern-day lizards. Many were *larger* and *more common* than modern lizards."

The Comparative

Use the **comparative form** of the adjective to compare one thing or person with another thing or group. The comparative is formed in two ways:

1. For short adjectives, such as *great* or *fierce,* add *-er.*

   great + er = greater   fierce + er = fiercer

2. For longer adjectives, such as *unusual* or *remarkable,* use *more.*

   more unusual   more remarkable

Most adjectives ending in *-ful* and *-ous* also form the comparative with *more.*

   more successful   more curious   more ferocious

The Superlative

To compare a thing or a person with more than one other of its kind, use the **superlative form** of the adjective.

   Dinosaurs were the *largest* land animals ever to live.
   However, they are not the *most ancient* animals.

The superlative of an adjective is formed by adding *-est* or by using *most.* The ending *-er* in the comparative becomes *-est* in the superlative, and *more* becomes *most.*

Notice how the adjectives in the chart on the next page change forms according to these rules.

Adjective	Comparative	Superlative
strong	stronger	strongest
fast	faster	fastest
mysterious	more mysterious	most mysterious
awkward	more awkward	most awkward

Remember these four things when using adjectives for comparison:

1. Use the comparative to compare two persons or things or two groups of things. Also use the comparative to compare a person or a thing to a group.

Comparative   A brontosaurus was *larger* than a mammoth.
Comparative   Lizards are *smaller* than their prehistoric ancestors.
Comparative   A mammoth probably was *faster* than most dinosaurs.

2. Use the superlative to compare a thing or person to more than one other of its kind.

Superlative   Sauropods were the *largest* of all dinosaurs.
Superlative   Brachiosaurus, brontosaurus, and diplodocus were giants; brachiosaurus was the *largest*.

3. Do not leave out the word *other* when you are comparing something with everything else of its kind.

Incorrect   Tyrannosaurus rex was more ferocious than any dinosaur. (This sentence says that tyrannosaurus rex was not a dinosaur.)
Correct   Tyrannosaurus rex was more ferocious than any *other* dinosaur.

4. Do not use both *-er* and *more* or *-est* and *most*.

Incorrect   The plant-eaters began to die out more sooner than the meat-eaters did.
Correct   The plant-eaters began to die out *sooner* than the meat-eaters did.
Incorrect   Dinosaurs are not the most oldest of all reptiles.
Correct   Dinosaurs are not the *oldest* of all reptiles.

Irregular Comparisons

We form the comparative and superlative of some adjectives by changing the words, as shown in the chart below.

Adjective	Comparative	Superlative
good	better	best
well	better	best
bad	worse	worst
ill	worse	worst
little	less *or* lesser	least
much	more	most
many	more	most
far	farther	farthest

Practice Your Skills

A. CONCEPT CHECK

Comparative Forms of Adjectives   Write the correct form of each adjective given in parentheses.

1. Dinosaurs are perhaps the (fascinating) of all animals.
2. We have (little) information about them than we would like.
3. It is (difficult) to learn about dinosaurs than about some other animals, because dinosaurs are extinct.
4. However, we have (much) knowledge now than ever before.
5. Dinosaurs dominated the earth for 150 million years, a (long) period than humans have inhabited earth.
6. The period of 3 million or 4 million years of human influence is indeed (brief) than the dinosaur period.
7. These mammoth reptiles were among the (successful) survivors of all creatures.
8. There were (many) plant eaters than meat eaters among the dinosaurs.
9. The brontosaurus, which was (massive) than six of today's elephants grouped together, was a plant-eater.
10. One of the (fearful) of the dinosaurs was tyrannosaurus rex.
11. It had huge teeth for tearing flesh and massive rear legs that probably made it (swift) than most other dinosaurs.
12. We have (good) methods of gathering scientific information than ever before, but the (important) question remains unanswered: Why did they disappear?

B. PROOFREADING SKILL

Errors in Comparisons   Write the following paragraph, correcting errors in grammar, capitalization, punctuation, and spelling. Pay special attention to the use of comparisons. (10 errors)

No one knows what happened to the dinosaurs. During their reign, dinosaurs were more dominant than any creature, yet they suddenly died out. One of the popularist and better supported explanations suggests that a meteor crashed into the earth the crash raised a huge cloud of dust that blocked out the sun. Without sunlight, plants died and tempratures got more colder. The suporting evidence for this theory is more concrete than the evidence for any theory. Scientists have found a likely meteor crater in mexico. About 180 kilometers in diameter.

FOR MORE PRACTICE
See page 530.

C H E C K  P O I N T
MIXED REVIEW · PAGES 514–521

Write the correct form of the modifiers in parentheses. Then identify each as an *Adjective* or *Adverb*. If an adjective is used for comparison, identify it as *Comparative* or *Superlative*.

Writing Theme
Wilma Rudolph

1. Wilma Rudolph was one of the (most great, greatest) runners in field and track history.
2. In the 1960 Olympics, she was (faster, more fast) than every other woman runner and won both the 100- and 200-meter dashes.
3. Her 400-meter relay team ran extremely (good, well) and won a gold medal.
4. Rudolph's achievements are even (incredibler, more incredible) because she had serious health problems as a child.
5. She was born (premature, prematurely) and almost didn't live.
6. Due to a bout with polio, she walked (awkward, awkwardly).
7. Doctors said her left leg would never grow (strong, strongly).
8. Few polio victims have been (more determined, most determined) to recover.
9. Slowly the leg grew (better, more good).
10. Finally, when she was twelve, she was (well, good) again.
11. At sixteen, she ran so (well, good) that she qualified for the 1956 Olympic team.
12. She made the team again in 1960, when she had the (better, best) results of all her Olympic performances.

ADVERBS IN COMPARISONS

> Use the **comparative form** of an adverb to compare two actions. Use the **superlative form** of an adverb to compare more than two actions.

Adverbs are used to compare one action with another. We say, "This clown dresses oddly, but that one dresses *more oddly*." We also say, "That trapeze artist swings *more daringly* than any other trapeze artist I've seen." Adverbs have special forms or spellings for use in making comparisons, just as adjectives do.

The Comparative

Use the **comparative** form of the adverb to compare one action with another. The comparative is formed in two ways:

1. For short adverbs, such as *soon* or *high,* add *-er.*

   The parade entered the big top *sooner* than we expected.
   The lion leaped *higher* than the tiger.

2. For most adverbs ending in *-ly,* use *more* to make the comparative.

   Sara laughed *more frequently* than Andrew.
   The horse ran *more rapidly* around the ring this time than it had earlier.

The Superlative

Use the **superlative** form of the adverb to compare one action with two or more others of the same kind.

   Of the three horses, that one runs *fastest.*
   The lion roared the *most ferociously* of all the big cats.

The superlative of adverbs is formed by adding *-est* or by using *most.* Adverbs that form the comparative with *-er* form the superlative with *-est.* Those that use *more* for the comparative use *most* for the superlative.

Notice how the following adverbs change forms.

Adverb	Comparative	Superlative
long	longer	longest
daringly	more daringly	most daringly
carefully	more carefully	most carefully

Keep these three things in mind:

1. Use the comparative to compare two actions and the superlative to compare more than two.

Comparative The acrobat jumped *higher* today than yesterday.

Superlative Of all the acrobats, that one jumped *highest*.

2. Do not leave out the word *other* when you are comparing one action with every other action of the same kind.

Incorrect Jumbo trumpeted louder than any elephant.
Correct Jumbo trumpeted louder than any *other* elephant.

3. Do not use both *-er* and *more* or *-est* and *most*.

Incorrect The performer juggled more faster than before.
Correct The performer juggled *faster* than before.

Practice Your Skills

A. CONCEPT CHECK
Comparisons Write the correct form of each adverb.

1. The Romans celebrated holidays (frequently) than we do.
2. They invented the circus as a form of celebration, and they clapped (loud) of all for the most spectacular performances.
3. Chariot races were (bitterly) contested than any modern auto race.
4. The best driver was not the one who raced (fast).
5. He was the one who (quickly) forced other drivers to crash.
6. Gladiators trained (hard) than any of today's performers.
7. Those who fought (fiercely) of all lived.
8. Each circus event was staged (elaborately) than the last.
9. Crowds cheered (long) for land battles than for races.
10. The (heavily) attended of all was Circus Maximus.

B. DRAFTING SKILL

Using Adverbs Correctly   Write the following sentences, completing each with the correct form of the adverb given in parentheses.

> EXAMPLE   Considering their size, fleas perform (dramatic—comparative) than other circus performers.
> Considering their size, fleas perform more dramatically than other circus performers.

11. No other circus entertainers capture audience attention (complete—comparative) than these tiny creatures.

12. Fleas are (natural—comparative) talented than people know.

13. Fleas can jump the (far—superlative) of all circus performers.

14. If a flea were the size of a human, it could leap over Grant's Tomb (easy—comparative) than a human can leap a five-foot wall.

15. In the flea circuses of eighteenth-century France and Italy, fleas wore the (clever—superlative) made collars imaginable.

16. Fleas performed under a magnifying glass so they could be seen (good—comparative).

17. They learned tricks (quick—comparative) than horses did.

18. Fleas pulled loads the (effortless—superlative) of all circus animals.

19. One of the (exceptional—superlative) trained fleas pulled a miniature cannon many times its own weight.

20. Records show that fleas were once the (rich—superlative) rewarded of circus performers.

C. PROOFREADING SKILL

Correct Comparisons of Adverbs   Write the following paragraph, correcting all errors. Pay special attention to comparisons of adverbs. (15 errors)

> Do you make people laugh more harder than they have ever laughed? Among your friends are you the more daring. Do you jump your bike the higher? Perhaps you should consider a circus career? The National Center for Circus Arts in france offers college training for the Circus. Students specialise in the skill they do better of all. One group, clearly the bravest, tries the trapeze. The other group, who's hearts are pounding more louder than a drum, stays on the ground. Dont think that they are necessarilly least adventuresome, however. They may end up learning how to train lions!

FOR MORE PRACTICE
See page 530.

> Use **modifiers** according to rules for their use, not according to the way you hear them used in everyday conversation.

People sometimes write things the way they hear them. Doing so may cause mistakes in writing because spoken English is sometimes less precise than written English. Here are some common adjective and adverb problems to watch for.

Them and *Those*

Them is always a pronoun. It is used only as the object of a verb or as the object of a preposition. *Them* is never used as an adjective.

Those is an adjective if it is followed by a noun. It is a pronoun if it is used alone.

> We heard *them robots* whirring down the hall. (incorrect)
> We followed *them.* (object of a verb)

> *Those* robots can talk! (adjective modifying *robots*)
> *Those* are the new robots. (pronoun)

The Extra *Here* and *There*

How often have you heard someone say "this here job" or "that there movie"? The word *this* includes the meaning of *here*. The word *that* includes the meaning of *there*.

Saying *this here* is like repeating your name every time you say *I* or *me:* "Please show me, Pat Smith, your robot."

Kind and *Sort*

Kind and *sort* are singular. Use *this* or *that* with *kind* and *sort*. *Kinds* and *sorts* are plural. Use *these* or *those* with *kinds* and *sorts*.

> I like *this kind* of story.   *Those sorts* of movies scare me.

The Double Negative

Negative words are such words as *no, none, not, nothing,* and *never.* A **double negative** is the use of two negative words together when only one is needed. Good speakers and writers take care to avoid the double negative.

Incorrect	We do*n't* need *no* more problems.
Correct	We do*n't* need *any* more problems.

Incorrect	That robot ca*n't* do *nothing* right.
Correct	That robot ca*n't* do *anything* right.

In the sentences above, the first negative is a contraction for *not.* When you use contractions like *don't* and *can't,* do not use negative words after them. Instead, use words such as *any, anything,* and *ever.*

> It *won't ever* respond to a command.
> We *haven't any* idea what is wrong.
> We *couldn't* see *anything* to reconnect.

Hardly, barely, and *scarcely* are most often used as negative words. Do not use them after contractions like *haven't* and *didn't.*

Incorrect	We could*n't hardly* continue working.
Correct	We *could hardly* continue working.

Incorrect	The robot ca*n't barely* operate.
Correct	The robot *can barely* operate.

Practice Your Skills

A. CONCEPT CHECK

Using Modifiers   Write the correct modifier given in parentheses.

1. You know that a robot is one of (those, them) machines that looks and acts human.
2. (These, This) sorts of machines are popular in movies and on TV.
3. You probably don't have (any, no) idea where the word *robot* comes from.
4. (This, This here) name was coined in 1921 by Karel Čapek, a Czechoslovakian who wrote a play called *R.U.R.* about mechanical people.

5. (Them, Those) machines were produced to serve people tirelessly.
6. Čapek needed a name for (them, those) machines; since *robot* means "work" in Czech, he chose this name for (them, those).
7. Eventually, people in the story couldn't control the robots (any, no) longer.
8. (Them, Those) robots took over the world.
9. (That, That there) play was so popular, the name *robot* stuck.
10. People now call (these, this) kinds of machines robots.

B. REVISION SKILL

Modifiers   Write the following sentences, correcting all errors in the use of modifiers. If a sentence is correct, write *Correct*.

11. Robots can't hardly be described as newcomers to entertainment.
12. In 1893, Ambrose Bierce wrote about them in a short story.
13. This here story is called "Moxon's Master."
14. A robot plays chess, but the robot isn't never a good loser.
15. After a human defeats that there robot, the robot strangles the human.
16. Ever since Bierce's chess-playing robot, books, movies, and TV haven't hardly ever missed a chance to include robots as characters.
17. Maybe you saw these sort of machines in the *Star Wars* movies.
18. Artoo Detoo and See Threepio were robot stars in them films.
19. *Star Trek* also had many of them humanlike machines.
20. Humans have a fascination with those kind of machine.

C. PROOFREADING SKILL

Correct Use of Modifiers   Write the following paragraph, correcting all errors. Pay special attention to modifiers. (15 errors)

Wouldn't you love to have a robot? That there idea isn't so far-fetched. Allready there are robots that can cut the grass vacuum the carpet and patroll for burglars. Even more advanced ones in industry and science. They do those kinds of jobs that people wouldn't hardly want to do, such as handeling explosives and cleaning up Radiation leaks. As yet, however, there aren't none quite like them you see in the movies. Experts say them advances are not far off. In fact, many Scientists feel it won't be scarcely any time at all before many homes have a robot

FOR MORE PRACTICE
See page 530.

Nellie Bly, January 25, 1890, the day she completed her record-breaking 72-day trip around the world.

A. Write each sentence, correcting the error in the use of modifiers. If a sentence is correct, write *Correct.*

1. Of all the reporters in her day, Nellie Bly tracked stories more fiercely.
2. She didn't never give up on a story.
3. Her reports took a more personal slant than most news stories of her time.
4. These sort of stories were unusual in the nineteenth century.
5. Bly got them stories by becoming part of the event she was covering.
6. Her first story for the New York *World* was one of these kind.
7. Bly pretended to be insane, trying the most strangely behavior she could imagine.
8. She was put in a hospital for the insane that provided the worse care imaginable.
9. Some of her best stories came out of those hospital experiences.
10. Thanks to Bly's courage, this here hospital improved its care.
11. Of her many accomplishments, Bly is probably better known for her trip around the world.
12. She modeled that there trip on the journey in Jules Verne's novel *Around the World in Eighty Days.*
13. It wasn't hardly a trip for a woman to take alone in those days.
14. Others had circled the earth, but she did it the more fast.
15. She traveled even most rapidly than did the hero of the novel.

B. Write the word or phrase that correctly completes each sentence.

16. Charlayne Hunter-Gault (isn't, is) hardly an ordinary journalist.
17. As an African-American teen, she (couldn't, could) barely get into the university of her choice.
18. There weren't (no, any) African-American students there then.
19. Hunter-Gault became the first African-American woman to attend (that, that there) university.
20. (Them, Those) were difficult times for her.
21. There were riots; she heard (them, those) outside her dormitory.
22. She stayed in school, despite (this kinds, these kinds) of problems.
23. It didn't (ever, never) occur to her to leave.
24. When (them, those) days were past, she became a reporter.
25. (That, That there) beginning set the stage for an amazing career.

GRAMMAR
HANDBOOK
43

Writing Theme
Alaska

A. Finding Adjectives   Write the adjectives. After each adjective, write the word it modifies. Do not write the articles.

1. Alaska was the forty-ninth state to join the Union.
2. It is our largest state, and everything about it is big.
3. It has 5,000 glaciers, 3,000 rivers, and 3 million lakes.
4. One Alaskan glacier, Malaspina, is larger than Rhode Island.
5. Mt. McKinley, in Alaska, is the tallest mountain on the continent.
6. Because Alaska is huge, many of its areas are remote and isolated.
7. Its tiny population numbers about one-half million.
8. That is less than the population of Memphis, Tennessee.
9. Most of those people live in a few cities along the coast.
10. The rest of Alaska is empty except for small, scattered towns.
11. You cannot even visit these towns by car.
12. There are no roads through vast sections of the Alaskan interior.
13. To visit many places, you must fly, walk, or take a boat.
14. Your trip will take you across vast wilderness.
15. There are huge forests and treeless prairies called tundra.

B. Finding Adverbs   Write and label the *Adverbs* and *Predicate Adjectives* from the following sentences. Then write the word each adverb or predicate adjective modifies.

16. Alaskan travelers always tell stories about the mosquitoes.
17. In some tales the mosquitoes seem much larger than life.
18. One Alaskan mosquito could never carry away a person.
19. Can two drag off a small animal?
20. Of course, such feats are not possible.
21. However, the great number of mosquitoes has not been exaggerated.
22. Water can be found everywhere, and the forty species of mosquitoes are plentiful.
23. The ground grows hard in the winter, trapping the water.
24. In spring the ground melts slowly and becomes a mosquito nursery.
25. Mosquitoes are worst in the months of May through July.

C. Choosing Modifiers   Write the correct form of the modifier.

26. In Alaska, the aurora borealis looks (fantastic, fantastically).
27. The northern lights, as this phenomenon is also called, may seem (real, really) close.

28. The borealis is (actual, actually) about 100 miles above ground.
29. The curtain of light can (easy, easily) be 150 miles high.
30. The lights may dance (crazy, crazily) over hundreds of miles.
31. They move (erratic, erratically) in amazing patterns.
32. The pale green and pinkish rose lights shine (bright, brightly).
33. People tell many (good, well) stories about the lights.
34. They say that if you whistle (good, well), the lights approach.
35. Listen (careful, carefully), and you may hear the lights sing.

D. Using Modifiers in Comparisons Write the following sentences, correcting all errors in the use of comparative forms.

36. Imagine a day more tiring than any day of your entire life.
37. You're on Kodiak Island, home of the larger bear in the world.
38. You hiked hardest than you ever have before to get back to camp by sundown.
39. You fell asleep more quick than at any other time on this trip.
40. Suddenly you awaken—your heart is pounding rapider than it did when you were hiking.
41. You hear something growling more louder than a jet taking off.
42. You peer outside and see the monstrousest bear imaginable.
43. You've always wanted to see a Kodiak bear in the worse way.
44. You couldn't have a gooder view, but you'd rather be anywhere but here.
45. The Kodiak stares directly at you and then turns and ambles into the night more slow than ice melts during an Alaskan winter.

E. Avoiding Problems with Modifiers Write the following sentences, correcting the errors in the use of modifiers. If a sentence is correct, write *Correct.*

46. Can you imagine living where there isn't no sunlight for months?
47. You'll find that kind of situations in one-third of Alaska.
48. That there part of Alaska is north of the Arctic Circle.
49. Them places can be dark and dreary.
50. Each fall, the sun in them areas sets farther south every day.
51. By November, in some places the sun doesn't hardly rise at all.
52. Soon, those places don't have no sunlight.
53. The darkness lasts longest in those places that are farthest north.
54. This here darkness lasts two months in northernmost Alaska.
55. What would your life be like in these sort of place?

Writing Theme
Walls

A. Choosing the Correct Modifier Write the correct form of the modifiers given in parentheses. Identify the correct form as an *Adjective* or *Adverb* and tell what word it modifies.

1. Thousands of years ago, everyday life must have been (hazardous, hazardously).
2. Survival depended on thinking and acting (quick, quickly).
3. Every day, people faced some (dreadful, dreadfully) new threat.
4. Hunting wild animals was a (real, really) important part of survival.
5. Wild animals in turn (continual, continually) stalked people.
6. At any moment, a saber-toothed tiger might decide that a wandering hunter would taste (wonderful, wonderfully).
7. At times, warlike neighbors may have pounded drums quite (loud, loudly).
8. No doubt, that pounding sounded (dangerous, dangerously).
9. Mere survival must often have seemed (uncertain, uncertainly).
10. The construction of walls seemed (logical, logically).
11. Some of the first walls were (actual, actually) made of bones from such prehistoric animals as the elephantlike mammoth.
12. That may have been because large trees were (rare, rarely).
13. Mammoth tusks and bones worked (good, well).
14. The tusks grew (gigantic, gigantically)—up to ten feet long.
15. Would those bone walls have made you feel (safe, safely)?

B. Modifiers in Comparisons Some of the following sentences contain errors in comparisons. Write each sentence correctly. If a sentence contains no errors, write *Correct*.

16. The Middle Ages were perhaps more warlike than any period.
17. People thought they would be most safest behind strong walls.
18. The walls were most thickest at the bottom.
19. People prepared the best they could for the worse siege.
20. Even the most strong armies failed to capture well-defended cities.
21. Cities with the greater advantages over invaders were those with walls.
22. Defenders could shoot arrows more accurate from on top of the walls than from below.
23. Defenders up above poured the most hottest oil on attackers.
24. Sometimes, however, the invaders were better equipped than the defenders within the walls.
25. They had the greatest number of soldiers between the two groups.

26. The *mangonel,* one of an attacking army's powerfullest weapons, hurled huge rocks into the city.
27. Frequently the attackers used battering rams that they hoped would break through the most fortifiedest walls or gates.
28. Sometimes the invaders were most secretive in their attack than at other times.
29. The more clever tactic of all was to dig a tunnel under the wall, hoping to surprise the defenders or to cause the wall to collapse.
30. Some of the famousest walled cities stood for hundreds of years and withstood many assaults.

C. Special Problems   Write the correct modifier.

31. Of all (them, those) walls that have been built in many parts of the world, perhaps the most incredible is the Great Wall of China.
32. Like (them, those) other walls, it was built for protection.
33. The Chinese (were, weren't) scarcely ever safe from invaders.
34. (Those, Them) enemies swept down from the north and attacked.
35. The builders of the Great Wall (were, weren't) hardly slowed down by anything.
36. (These, This) kind of wall was built from stones and earth.
37. (This, This here) wall was more than 3,600 miles long.
38. It was built over deserts, rivers, mountains, and other natural land features of (this, these) kind.
39. (That, That there) wall was first built in small sections.
40. Most of (them, those) sections were built from 224 to 214 B.C.
41. (Them, Those) first sections averaged twenty-five to thirty feet high and twenty-five feet wide.
42. A million people worked on the wall during (them, those) years.
43. About 400,000 of (them, those) laborers died.
44. Those laborers (were, weren't) hardly there from choice.
45. (That, Those) sort of laborer was actually a political prisoner.
46. China's first great emperor ordered that the individual sections of (this here, this) wall be linked together.
47. From the sixth century to the fourteenth century, the Great Wall wasn't (no, an) effective barrier against invaders.
48. The Ming emperors in the fourteenth century reinforced the wall with cement and other material of (this, these) sort.
49. Of the world's structures, there isn't (none, any) as large.
50. It is said that the Great Wall is the only one of (them, those) structures that can be seen with the naked eye from space.

WRITING CONNECTIONS

Elaboration, Revision, and Proofreading

Revise the following draft of a report for a computer club. Follow the directions at the bottom of the page, and then proofread the draft, looking for errors in grammar, capitalization, punctuation, and spelling. Pay special attention to the use of adjectives and adverbs.

[1]To stay up-to-date on whats happening in the world of computers, you need to know about laptop computers and how they compare with desktop models. [2]Both types offer a lot, but each have their own strengths and weaknesses. [3]For years the desktop type have been the most popular of the two. [4]Desktops generally have screens that are larger and clearer than those on laptops. [5]They also have the largest keyboards. [6]Some desktops have more memory capcity and can do jobs more quicker. [7]On the other hand, they are more bulkier. [8]Some laptops way as little as five pounds and are no bigger than a notebook. [9]Desktops can't be moved easy from one place to another. [10]Portibility is the main attracation of laptop models. [11]As their name implies, they are small enough to be used on a persons lap. [12]However, because of their smaller size, their screens are often more fuzzier and their keyboards more cramped.

1. Replace the vague expression "a lot" in sentence 2 with the more precise phrase "a variety of features."

2. Move sentence 8 to a more appropriate position.

3. Add the following information about laptops in an appropriate position: "Laptops generally can run on batteries and come with adapters for household current, so you can take them anywhere."

4. Add a concluding sentence that sums up the pros and cons of desktop and laptop computers.

5. Divide the passage into three paragraphs.

Informative Writing: Explaining *What*

When you compare and contrast items, you examine their similarities and differences. (See Workshop 5.) As you revise writing about comparisions and contrasts, make sure you have given specific examples to show how the items are similar and how they differ. Also look to see if you have used adjectives and adverbs effectively to draw attention to the points of comparison and contrast.

- Miniature golf is sometimes called goofy golf because the holes can be, well, goofy. What if you could design a hole for a miniature-golf course? Describe what it would be like. Make it as outrageous as you please.

- Imagine you are a golf ball being putted around a miniature-golf course. Describe your journey.

- Imagine you are a tour guide taking visitors to some of your favorite spots. Point out to your visitors where things are and what is interesting about them.

Using Prepositions, Conjunctions, and Interjections

- **Prepositions**
- **Prepositional Phrases as Modifiers**
- **Conjunctions and Interjections**

To describe miniature golf, you would probably need to use some miniature words—words like *in, on, over, under, and,* *or,* and *but.* If you play miniature golf, you might find yourself using some words like *wow, oh,* and *oops.*

These words—prepositions, conjunctions, and interjections— may be small, but they play a big role in showing relationships and linking ideas. In this workshop you will learn how to use them to explain connections and add details in your writing.

> A **preposition** is a word that links another word or word group to the rest of a sentence. The noun or pronoun after the preposition is called the **object of the preposition.**

When you write or speak, you use certain kinds of words to show ideas and you use other kinds of words to show the relationships between those ideas. **Connectives** are words that show the relationships between ideas. They join together two or more words or groups of words. **Prepositions** are one kind of connective. Notice the italicized prepositions in the sentences below.

The plane flew *through* the cloud.
The plane flew *over* the cloud.

The pilot hung *from* the plane.

The prepositions *through* and *over* join parts of each sentence. In the first sentence, *through* connects the verb *flew* with *cloud. Cloud* is the noun following the preposition and is the **object of the preposition.** *Through* points out the relationship between *flew* and *cloud.*

In the second sentence, the preposition *over* connects its object, *cloud,* with the verb *flew.* It points out a different relationship between *flew* and *cloud.*

Now look at the prepositions in the following sentences:

The pilot stood *on* the wing.
The pilot stood *under* the wing.

You can see that *on* and *under* join sentence parts. These words show the relationship between *pilot* and *wing* in each sentence. Changing the preposition from *on* to *under* changes the meaning of the sentence. Someone standing *on* a wing is above the ground. Someone standing *under* a wing is on the ground.

Below is a list of words often used as prepositions. Some of these prepositions tell *where*. Others indicate *time*. Still others show such special relationships as *reference* or *separation*. Study the prepositions in this chart and see if you can figure out the relationship that each of them shows.

Words Often Used as Prepositions

aboard	before	during	off	to
about	behind	except	on	toward
above	below	for	onto	under
across	beneath	from	out	underneath
after	beside	in	outside	until
against	between	inside	over	up
along	beyond	into	past	upon
among	by	like	since	with
around	concerning	near	through	within
at	down	of	throughout	without

Practice Your Skills

A. APPLICATION IN LITERATURE

Prepositions   Write the prepositions in the following passage. A sentence may contain more than one preposition. Write *None* if a sentence does not contain a preposition. Notice how the writer uses prepositions to clearly show the relationship between words and ideas in each sentence.

1Robin took her place before the left propeller with her hands resting on the blade. **2**I took my place beside the right propeller. **3**Father himself lay . . . on the bottom wing. **4**With his left hand he grabbed hold of the frame. **5**With his right, he took the front rudder controls. **6**He pulled back on the controls and the front rudders tilted upward. **7**He pushed forward and they tilted downward. **8**Then Father shifted his hips to the left. The rear vertical rudders twisted to the left and the wings curled slightly, as if they were alive. . . . **9**The wind drummed at the canvas over the wings. **10**The sky seemed alive and waiting.

Laurence Yep, *Dragonwings*

B. DRAFTING SKILL

Using Precise Prepositions   Write prepositions to complete the sentences below. Choose the prepositions that make clear the relationships between the words in the sentences.

11. Flying has been a dream _____ centuries.
12. _____ 1783, no one had successfully flown _____ the air.
13. _____ that year the first hot-air balloon flight was made.
14. Two Frenchmen floated _____ the ground _____ more than five miles, and they waved _____ the people standing _____ the ground _____ them.
15. _____ the 1800s, gliders were flown _____ short distances.
16. Inventors soon added engines _____ their gliders.
17. A few of these early planes could lift _____ the ground, but they could not fly very far.
18. None of these planes could be controlled _____ their flights.
19. The great dream _____ controlled, engine-powered flight was not achieved _____ 1903.
20. In that year, the *Flyer,* built _____ Wilbur and Orville Wright, made four short but successful flights _____ a single day.

Preposition or Adverb?

A word can be used as a preposition in one sentence and as an adverb in another. How can you tell the difference between a preposition and an adverb? A preposition never stands alone. It is always followed by its object, a noun or a pronoun. If the word is not followed by a noun or pronoun, it is probably an adverb.

The plane flew *past* the watchtower. (preposition)
The plane flew *past.* (adverb)

The aircraft is parked *inside* the hangar. (preposition)
The aircraft is parked *inside.* (adverb)

Practice Your Skills
A. CONCEPT CHECK

Preposition or Adverb   Write the preposition or adverb in the following sentences. Label each *Preposition* or *Adverb.*

1. Orville and Wilbur Wright were fascinated by aviation.
2. They used gliders in their first experiments.

Writing
═══ TIP ═══

Your sentences may be clearer and more specific if you use a preposition and its objects instead of adverbs. Notice the difference between "There's a bird *outside*" and "There's a bird *outside my window.*"

3. The brothers attached a gasoline engine to their first plane.
4. This two-winged airplane, the *Flyer,* could carry one person along.
5. The pilot lay between the top and bottom wings.
6. He could look over and see the engine.
7. Behind the wings, two wooden propellers whirled around.
8. In place of wheels, there were thin, wooden runners attached below.
9. One chilly December morning, Orville Wright climbed on.
10. Moments later, the plane flew through the air.

B. REVISION SKILL

Using Prepositions for Clarity   Complete each of the following sentences with a group of words from the list below.

of the wings	of the plane	to that question
for flight	above it	off the ground
of lift and thrust	on earth	in a forward direction

11. How does an airplane stay _____ during a flight?
12. The answer _____ is lift.
13. Before takeoff, planes, like all objects, are held _____ by gravity.
14. However, lift pushes a plane upward and gets it _____.
15. Lift is created by the wings _____.
16. The curved shape _____ lowers the air pressure above them.
17. With less air pressure _____, the plane can take off.
18. Another force, called thrust, is necessary _____.
19. Thrust from the plane's engines keeps a plane moving _____.
20. As long as the forces _____ are strong enough, a plane can remain in flight.

C. APPLICATION IN WRITING

Description of an Activity   Write a paragraph or two, describing one of your favorite activities. You might describe a ride on a roller coaster, a game you play with friends, or something else that you really enjoy. Try to include prepositions as you write. When you have finished, revise your description. To make your writing clearer or more specific, check to see if you should use a preposition and an object instead of an adverb.

FOR MORE PRACTICE
See page 547.

> A **prepositional phrase** consists of a preposition, its object, and any words that modify the object. A prepositional phrase can modify a noun, a pronoun, or a verb.

A **phrase** is a group of related words that lacks a subject and a verb. A **prepositional phrase** consists of a preposition, its object, and any modifiers, or words that describe the object. Look at the italicized prepositional phrase in the first example below. The preposition is *for,* its object is *light,* and the modifier, or adjective, is *green.* The entire prepositional phrase modifies the verb *watched.* Find the preposition, object, and modifier in the second example. What noun does the prepositional phrase modify?

The gentle guide dog watched *for the green light.*
The man *with the gentle guide dog* crossed the busy
    intersection.

Sometimes two or more nouns or pronouns are used as objects in a prepositional phrase.

He needs a dog *with intelligence and a good disposition.*

Prepositional phrases can be **adjective phrases** or **adverb phrases.** Adjective prepositional phrases modify nouns and pronouns. Adverb prepositional phrases modify verbs, adjectives, or other adverbs.

A guide dog wears a harness *with a stiff handle.* (adjective
    phrase modifying the noun *harness*)
Guide dogs train *for many months.* (adverb phrase modify-
    ing the verb *train*)

Sometimes one prepositional phrase immediately follows another. Read the example at the top of the next page. The first prepositional phrase is an adverb phrase. The second phrase is an adjective phrase, modifying the object of the first phrase.

A visually impaired woman practices with her guide dog in a training maze at the International Guiding Eyes Center in Sylmar, California.

The dog led him *through the door on the left.* (*Through the door* modifies *led* and tells *where. On the left* modifies *door* and tells *which one.*)

Sentence Diagraming   For information on diagraming sentences with prepositional phrases, see page 693.

Practice Your Skills

A. CONCEPT CHECK

Prepositional Phrases   Write the prepositional phrase from each sentence. Underline the preposition once and its object or objects twice.

1. Dogs throughout the world help people in many ways.
2. Guide dogs assist people without sight.
3. On farms and ranches, dogs herd livestock into corrals.
4. Watchdogs protect people from crime and danger.
5. Dogs also work with the police.
6. They help police search for missing people.
7. In large cities, police dogs help with crowd control.
8. Dogs can even find illegal drugs in packages at airports.
9. Although some people are allergic to dogs, they keep them for companionship anyway.
10. Dogs bring happiness to the people around them.

B. APPLICATION IN LITERATURE

Adjective and Adverb Phrases   Write each italicized phrase from this passage. Label each *Adjective Phrase* or *Adverb Phrase.* Then write the word or words modified by each phrase.

> **11**As a rule, Perrault traveled ahead of the team, packing the snow *with webbed shoes* to make it easier for [the dogs].
> **12**François, guiding the sled at the gee pole, sometimes exchanged places *with him* but not often. **13**Perrault was *in a hurry.* . . . **14**Always, they broke camp *in the dark,* and the first gray *of dawn* found them hitting the trail with fresh miles reeled off *behind them.* **15**And always they pitched camp *after dark,* eating their bit *of fish,* and crawling to sleep *into the snow.* **16**The pound and a half *of sun-dried salmon,* which was [Buck's] ration *for each day,* seemed to go nowhere. **17**He never had enough, and suffered *from perpetual hunger pangs.*
>
> **Jack London, *The Call of the Wild***

FOR MORE PRACTICE
See pages 547–548.

CHECK ✔ POINT

A. Write the italicized words in the sentences below. Then label each word *Preposition, Object of Preposition,* or *Adverb.*

1. Dogs were trained *by* nomadic *people over* 12,000 *years* ago.
2. These people traveled *around in search of food.*
3. Dogs helped these hunter-gatherers in many *ways.*
4. The barking *of* people's dogs warned them *about strangers* or dangerous *animals.*
5. The leftovers *from* people's *meals* were eaten *by* the *dogs.*
6. There was no waste *at* the nomads' camps.
7. The dogs' keen sense *of* smell also helped hunters.
8. The dogs followed their noses and knew when game was *near.*
9. Small animals were brought *down* by hunters' spears and arrows.
10. Dogs retrieved this game *for* their *masters.*
11. The nomads' dogs carried goods *from camp to camp.*
12. Goods were put *on* dogs' backs or pulled *along* in small *carts.*
13. Eventually, people began breeding dogs *with* specific traits.
14. Some of these dogs were bred *for* hard work.
15. Today, many *of* these *breeds* are popular house pets.

B. Write the prepositional phrases in the following sentences. Underline the preposition once and its object twice. Label each phrase *Adjective Phrase* or *Adverb Phrase.* Then write the word or words each phrase modifies.

16. Some breeds of dogs still do important work in our society.
17. Dalmatians, for example, can often be found in fire stations.
18. Originally, these spotted dogs stood guard over horse stables.
19. In 1870, a Dalmatian was given to a New York City fire company.
20. Soon, fire companies around the country had similar pets.
21. The dogs guard the equipment in the fire station and help protect firefighters from danger.
22. A Dalmatian from New York is the hero of one urban legend.
23. One day a small boy supposedly dashed in front of a fire engine.
24. The Dalmatian leaped to the rescue and pulled the child to safety—or so the story goes.
25. It sounds preposterous, but if it's true, perhaps someone gave an award to the dog.

CONJUNCTIONS AND INTERJECTIONS

A **conjunction** is a word that connects words or groups of words. An **interjection** is a word or short group of words that expresses a strong feeling.

A **conjunction** is another type of connecting word you can use to link words and ideas. Like prepositions, conjunctions show a relationship between the words they connect. Unlike prepositions, however, conjunctions do not have objects.

Coordinating Conjunctions

Coordinating conjunctions connect related words, groups of words, or sentences. The most common coordinating conjunctions are *and, but,* and *or.*

Wagons *and* livestock moved slowly in a wagon train. (connects subjects)

The wagons carried pioneers *and* their belongings. (connects direct objects)

The journey west was hard *and* dangerous. (connects predicate adjectives)

Each night, wagons gathered in a circle *or* near some natural barricade. (connects prepositional phrases)

Some wagons were lost during a trip, *but* most completed their journeys successfully. (connects sentences)

Correlative Conjunctions

A few conjunctions are used in pairs to connect sentence parts. Such pairs are called **correlative conjunctions.**

Correlative Conjunctions

either . . . or	not only . . . but also	both . . . and
neither . . . nor	whether . . . or	

Grammar
TIP

When you use a coordinating conjunction to combine two complete sentences, remember to use a comma before the conjunction. See Handbook 24, "Sentence Combining," pages 304–313, for more information on using conjunctions to combine sentences.

Notice how correlative conjunctions are used in the following examples:

> *Both* men *and* women moved west on wagon trains.
> People brought *not only* household belongings *but also* their pets and livestock.
> People rode *either* on horseback *or* in wagons.
> When times were tough, people had to decide *whether* to push on *or* head back.
> *Neither* storms *nor* other natural disasters stopped people from moving west.

Interjections

An **interjection** is a single word or short group of words that is used to express a feeling or emotion. Interjections can express such feelings as urgency, surprise, relief, joy, or pain.

An interjection that expresses strong emotion is often followed by an exclamation point. An interjection that expresses mild emotion is usually followed by a comma.

> *Let's go!* We can't rest until we reach the river.
> *Whew!* I was afraid we'd never make it.
> *Oh,* look at that beautiful valley.
> *Well,* I've never seen so many wildflowers.

Practice Your Skills

A. CONCEPT CHECK

Conjunctions and Interjections   Write the interjections and conjunctions in these sentences. Label them *Interjection, Coordinating Conjunction,* or *Correlative Conjunction.*

1. Pioneers traveled west via both water and land routes.
2. Whether they went by boat or by wagon, the pioneers had a long, difficult journey.
3. Sometimes the terrain was flat and sometimes it was mountainous.
4. More than a hundred families at a time might move their belongings and livestock in a wagon train.
5. Wagon trains often had not only an experienced scout but also a leader chosen by the pioneers.

6. Say, have you heard about Jim Bridger and Kit Carson—the famous pioneer scouts who led many wagon trains?

7. Trains went not only northwest along the famous Oregon Trail but also southwest along the Santa Fe and Old Spanish trails.

8. The pioneers took the southern route into areas that are now New Mexico and Arizona and southern California.

9. Neither the northern nor southern route was easy for the pioneers.

10. Yes, many people and animals perished along the way.

B. REVISION SKILL

Using Conjunctions   Use the coordinating or correlative conjunctions in parentheses to combine the following sentences.

EXAMPLE   Men wanted to settle in the West. Women also wanted to settle in the West. (both . . . and)
Both men and women wanted to settle in the West.

11. The pioneers traveled across the plains. Their livestock also traveled across the plains. (and)

12. Wagon trains stopped for repairs. Wagon trains stopped for supplies. (either . . . or)

13. This constant movement was hard on people and animals. It saved many lives. (but)

14. The pioneers knew they had to travel more than fifteen miles each day. If they did not travel more than fifteen miles, they would have to endure harsh winter storms. (either . . . or)

15. Those who reached their destination felt triumphant. They still faced many hardships. (but)

16. Pioneer families built their own homes. Pioneer families grew their own food. (not only . . . but also)

17. Individual families worked alone to set up their homesteads. Families worked with the help of their neighbors to set up their homesteads. (or)

18. Work was done by hand. Some work was done with the help of mules or oxen. (or)

Using Prepositions, Conjunctions, and Interjections

545

FOR MORE PRACTICE
See page 550.

19. Corn was an important part of the pioneers' diet. Meat was important too. (both . . . and)
20. Corn was easy to grow. Corn was easy to store for long periods of time. (both . . . and)

CHECK  POINT
MIXED REVIEW • PAGES 543–546

Write the interjections and conjunctions in these sentences. Label them *Interjection, Coordinating Conjunction,* or *Correlative Conjunction.*

1.	MARTHA:	Look! The Johnsons' wagon is ready to go.
2.	JOSH:	Help me get the pots and pans back into our wagon.
3.	MARTHA:	Hey! Sam and Megan are riding up front with their father and mother. Neither you nor I ever get a chance to do that.
4.	JOSH:	I don't care whether we do or we don't. I'd rather ride either inside the wagon or on horseback.
5.	MARTHA:	I suppose neither you nor I would survive if we had to walk.
6.	JOSH:	Do you really think Oregon will be perfect and wonderful?
7.	MARTHA:	Oh, I've heard both Ma and Pa say so about a hundred times.
8.	JOSH:	I've heard people say the rivers are made of milk, and they say the mountains are made of flapjacks.
9.	MARTHA:	Who told you that? Was it Sam Johnson or his sister Megan?
10.	JOSH:	Both Sam and Megan said it, but I don't believe it.
11.	MARTHA:	Wow! Wouldn't it be great if it were true?
12.	JOSH:	Pa said our cabin will be in a valley or near a river, and I believe it whether you do or not.
13.	MARTHA:	Ma says it will have not only real windows but also a wooden floor some day.
14.	JOSH:	Let's finish packing, and then we can go. Ouch! You dropped that pan on my toe!
15.	MARTHA:	Sorry! I didn't mean to drop it. Well, everything's in the wagon and fastened down.

Writing Theme
Money

A. Identifying Prepositions   Write the prepositions in the following sentences.

1. In the past, people sometimes did business without money.
2. They simply exchanged goods with each other.
3. A farmer might trade some wheat for cloth or a new plow.
4. *Barter* is the name of this trading system.
5. The barter system is still used in many places today, but trading one thing for another can be inconvenient.
6. Many historians believe that money was developed thousands of years ago by the people of ancient China and India.
7. Over three thousand years ago, these people traded knives and other metal tools for the things they needed.
8. By 1100 B.C., they had begun trading with miniature bronze tools in place of real tools.
9. These small tools eventually developed into coins, and people bought and sold things among themselves.
10. Coins were used elsewhere around the ancient world as well.
11. In the 600s B.C., Lydia, a region that is now part of Turkey, had a money system based on small, bean-shaped coins.
12. The coins were made under the king's supervision and had a special design stamped on them.
13. The Chinese developed paper money during the A.D. 600s, but it was not used in Europe for another one thousand years.
14. The use of money spread through Europe when banks issued paper bills called bank notes to their depositors and borrowers.
15. Today, people buy things with coins, paper money, checks, and credit cards, and they can even buy things electronically through computer programs.

B. Using Prepositional Phrases   Write the prepositional phrase in each of the following sentences. Label each phrase *Adjective Phrase* or *Adverb Phrase*. Then write the word each phrase modifies.

16. Over the years, the people of North America have used many kinds of money.
17. The native peoples of the continent bartered among themselves.
18. Playing cards were used as paper money during the 1600s and 1700s when Canada was a French colony.
19. Initially, coins and paper money were scarce in the American colonies.

Using Prepositions,
Conjunctions, and

20. The English government hoped that their colonies would trade only with England, so they limited the supply of money.
21. Without money, colonists could not trade with countries that wanted payment in cash.
22. As a result, coins from many nations circulated in the colonies.
23. The most common coins of all were Spanish silver dollars called pieces of eight.
24. These coins were accepted everywhere, and people often broke them into smaller pie-shaped pieces for change.
25. Making money was illegal in the colonies until 1652.
26. The Massachusetts Bay Colony first minted coins in that year.
27. The coins were silver shillings stamped with tree designs.
28. England later declared the coins illegal, but colonists used the oak tree shillings for many years anyway.
29. In 1783, independence led to a new system of money for the young nation.
30. Since that time, citizens of the United States have used both coins and paper money for their financial transactions.

C. Recognizing Interjections and Conjunctions   Write the interjections and conjunctions in these sentences. Label them *Interjection, Correlative Conjunction,* or *Coordinating Conjunction.*

31. Our class visited Washington, D.C., last week and saw many historic monuments and museums.
32. My favorite place was the Bureau of Engraving and Printing.
33. Wow! Seeing money being made was exciting!
34. I found both the giant machines and the printing process fascinating.
35. "All right!" I yelled to my friends. "This is what I call a cash machine!"
36. We examined not only the paper but also the plates that print the designs on the money.
37. Different plates print the fronts and backs of the bills.
38. Inspectors check each bill for both mistakes and imperfections.
39. Did you know that bills with mistakes are destroyed, and new bills with the same serial number are marked with a star and used in their place?
40. No, the bureau gives out neither free samples nor any of the imperfect "seconds" from its work.

A. Identifying Prepositional Phrases   Write the prepositional phrases in the following sentences. Underline the prepositions once and the objects of those prepositions twice.

1. Whales travel more than any other mammal on earth.
2. Whales migrate across vast distances to and from their breeding grounds.
3. They swim effortlessly in seawater.
4. Finback whales may make winter journeys of five thousand miles.
5. Their voyage begins deep within the Bering Sea and the Arctic Ocean and ends at their breeding grounds in the Indian Ocean.
6. It may take a month or more for the entire trip.
7. Interestingly, whales do not swim across the zone near the equator.
8. So, nearly all species of whales are divided into two groups, the northern and the southern.
9. The streamlined shape of whales helps them survive.
10. A whale's nostril, or blowhole, lies on top of its head.
11. When the whale needs a breath of air, it comes to the surface of the water.
12. The top of the whale's head breaks the sea's surface so the whale can breathe, while the rest of its body lies underwater.
13. As whales have evolved, their bones have become lighter in weight.
14. Their skeletons are now too weak for the survival of these creatures on land.
15. The weight of whales' bodies on land is too much for their light bone structures.

B. Prepositional Phrases as Modifiers   Write the prepositional phrases in these sentences. Label each one *Adjective Phrase* or *Adverb Phrase*. Then write the word each phrase modifies.

16. For centuries, European whalers traveled to the Arctic.
17. The narwhal is among the sea creatures in that region.
18. Narwhals are members of the whale family.
19. These creatures once roamed throughout the northern seas.
20. One of the whalers' favorite trophies was a narwhal's tusk.
21. This tusk grows from the narwhal's jaw, like a giant tooth.
22. Tusks are found only on adult male narwhals.
23. Many narwhals reach about fifteen feet in length.
24. Their tusks, however, may reach a length of eight feet.

Writing Theme
Whales

Using Prepositions,
Conjunctions, and
Interjections   **549**

25. The function of the narwhal's tusk remains a mystery.
26. Narwhals might use their tusks in the search for food.
27. Tusks uncover shrimps and crabs on the ocean floor.
28. Tusks also might be used in combat between narwhals.
29. Perhaps adult males fight over females at mating time.
30. During such fights, a tusk could be an effective weapon.
31. The tusks might also help narwhals in another way.
32. Tusks like these can break through ice.
33. Narwhals could make holes for breathing.
34. To this day, people do not know much about these creatures.
35. Scientists have one interesting theory about them, though.
36. Through the years, people often told tales about unicorns.
37. Supposedly, each of these gentle, horselike creatures had, in the middle of its forehead, a single horn.
38. Many legends tell about the magical powers of these horns.
39. The stories possibly originated with sailors' tales of narwhals.
40. Perhaps the strange narwhal is really the unicorn of the sea.

C. Recognizing Interjections and Conjunctions Write the interjections and conjunctions in the following sentences. Label them *Interjection, Correlative Conjunction,* or *Coordinating Conjunction.*

41. Three friends and I went on a whale watch last weekend.
42. None of us had been on a boat before, and we were excited.
43. Wow! Was it something!
44. It was not only fun but also educational.
45. We started very early, but it was worth the loss of sleep.
46. I arrived at the boat about five in the morning and met my friends, ten other whale watchers, and our crew.
47. Within moments, we cast off and headed into the ocean.
48. Whether tired or energetic, you caught the excitement in the air.
49. Boy! Some people felt wonderful being out on the open water, but I just felt queasy.
50. Both the wind and the ocean smelled great, but the water was incredibly rough!
51. Oh, did that boat rock back and forth for a while.
52. I kept crying, "Either we stop moving or I die!"
53. Thank goodness, the water calmed, and I felt better.
54. Whale ho! Suddenly a humpback whale surfaced and spouted!
55. Neither my friends nor I will forget our first view of a whale.

WRITING CONNECTIONS

Elaboration, Revision, and Proofreading

Revise and proofread this scene adapted from the short story "The Lady, or the Tiger?" Begin by using the directions at the bottom of the page. Then look for errors in grammar, capitalization, punctuation, and spelling. Pay special attention to the use of prepositions, conjunctions, and interjections.

[Scene: ¹The PRINCESS, a beautiful young woman, is alone. ²She is pacing back and forth talking to herself.]

PRINCESS: ³What can I do. ⁴Either I must send my lover to the Lady. ⁵Or to the tiger. ⁶I cant bear either idea. ⁷how could I stand to watch him open the door? ⁸How could I stand to watch him face the cruel fangs of the tiger? ⁹No, I cant think of that.

[¹⁰The PRINCESS lies down on her bed.]

¹¹Yet how will I feel if I send him to the lady. ¹²The thought of my love in the arms of the lady makes me crazy with jeolosy. ¹³At least he would still be alive. ¹⁴Oh, I wish someone could tell me what to do.

[¹⁵Sitting up in her bed and starting to cry again, the PRINCESS faces the audience.]

1. Add to sentence 1 these prepositional phrases describing the princess: "in her room" and "with a look of distress on her face."

2. Add more feeling to sentence 3 by beginning with an interjection.

3. Combine sentences 7 and 8 to form one sentence by using a compound verb. Choose a conjunction that correctly reflects the relationship of ideas. Delete words as necessary.

4. Combine this sentence with the stage directions in line 10: "She covers her face and cries for a moment."

5. Combine sentences 12 and 13 by using the conjunction *but*.

Narrative and Literary Writing

A script tells a story by presenting both the description needed to set the scene and the words the actors speak. (See Workshop 3.) When you revise a script, look for ways you can use prepositional phrases, conjunctions, and interjections to make your stage directions clear and your dialogue believable.

Using Prepositions, Conjunctions, and Interjections **551**

Skills

Directions   One or more of the underlined sections in the following sentences may contain an error in grammar, usage, punctuation, spelling, or capitalization. Write the letter of each incorrect section. Then rewrite the section correctly. If there is no error in an item, write *E*.

> **Example**   Not many <u>writer's</u> <u>have</u> mastered both poetry and
>   **A**   **B**
> <u>fiction. Alice</u> Walker is a striking <u>exception</u>. <u>No error</u>
>   **C**   **D**   **E**
>
> **Answer**   A—writers

1. People <u>growed</u> soybeans in eastern <u>asia</u> at least five thousand years ago, and the
       A   **B**
   ancient <u>Chinese</u> considered soybeans <u>their</u> most important crop. <u>No error</u>
         C   **D**   **E**

2. In colonial <u>Connecticut</u>, it was against the law for a <u>Mother</u> to kiss her child on
             A   **B**
   <u>Sunday</u>. Both of them probably felt <u>badly</u> about that. <u>No error</u>
     C   **D**   **E**

3. Yeast is a living substance that <u>sets</u> <u>quietly</u> on the shelf until warm water is added.
                            A   **B**
   Without it bread dough would just <u>lie</u> there and would not <u>rise</u>. <u>No error</u>
                         C   **D**   **E**

4. Swallowtail <u>butterflies</u> beat <u>their</u> wings more <u>slowly</u> than <u>any insect</u>, only about
            A   **B**   **C**   **D**
   five times per second. <u>No error</u>
                E

5. Some van Gogh <u>paintings</u> have been sold for more money than any painting by
               A
   <u>Rembrandt. That</u> does not mean, however, that <u>they're</u> <u>best</u>. <u>No error</u>
     B   **C**   **D**   **E**

6. Warren Spahn <u>winned</u> more games during his <u>career</u> than any other left-handed
            A   **B**
   <u>pitcher. In fact</u>, few right-handed pitchers have pitched as <u>good</u>. <u>No error</u>
     C   **D**   **E**

7. Medieval <u>nights</u> <u>weared</u> armor that protected them <u>well</u> from weapons.
          A   **B**   **C**
   However, horsemen who <u>fell</u> into the mud might drown. <u>No error</u>
                    D   **E**

8. In some swamps <u>gases</u> <u>raise</u> up from <u>rotting</u> plants and catch fire, <u>causing</u> a
                  A   **B**   **C**   **D**
ghostly light. <u>No error</u>
           E

9. Why is a little red schoolhouse red? In the <u>Northeast,</u> where the custom of
                                          A
painting <u>schoolhouses</u> red <u>began</u>, red paint was <u>more cheaper</u> than any other
             B   **C**   **D**
color. <u>No error</u>
       E

10. Someone <u>who</u> doesn't sweat at all "<u>sweats</u> like a pig," because pigs don't
           A   **B**
<u>sweat. In</u> fact they have to <u>lay</u> around in mud to keep their skin moist and to
   C   **D**
stay cool. <u>No error</u>
         E

11. A <u>camels'</u> split lip helps it pick <u>leaves</u> and also spit with amazing accuracy when
    A   **B**
<u>it's</u> <u>annoyed, many</u> surprised zoo visitors have suddenly discovered that the
 C   **D**
animal has this talent. <u>No error</u>
                E

12. How can you tell a duck from a <u>goose</u>? <u>Geese</u> don't <u>never</u> dive, and ducks can't
                      A   **B**   **C**
walk very <u>well</u>. <u>No error</u>
        D   **E**

13. In his books Mark Twain <u>done</u> a <u>real</u> good job of showing how Americans
                  A   **B**
<u>live. He</u> was funny <u>too</u>. <u>No error</u>
  C   **D**   **E**

14. When the moon is bright after a rain, you might see something similar to a
<u>rainbow; however</u>, you can see <u>rainbows</u> in daylight more <u>easily</u> because the
     A   **B**   **C**
sun is <u>brighter</u> than the moon. <u>No error</u>
   D   **E**

15. All sturgeon are <u>large, but</u> the <u>largest</u> of <u>these</u> kind of fish is the beluga, which
              A   **B**   **C**
can <u>weigh</u> more than 2,500 pounds. <u>No error</u>
   D   **E**

Sketch Book

A teacher can open the door, but the pupil must go through by himself.

CHINESE PROVERB

Whoever lies down with a dog will get up with fleas.

HEBREW PROVERB

Three may keep a secret if two of them are dead.

BENJAMIN FRANKLIN

When the mouse laughs at the cat, there is a hole nearby.

AFRICAN PROVERB

If you want the hen's eggs, you must put up with her cackling.

ENGLISH PROVERB

If you don't like worms, don't be an early bird.

JUNIOR-HIGH STUDENT'S PROVERB

- You have probably heard many sayings like these. Now it's your turn to think up some proverbs of your own. They can be serious or silly.

- Do you think proverbs always speak the truth? Choose a proverb you agree with or one you disagree with. Then explain why you feel the way you do.

- What advice do you have for students just entering junior high school? Give some suggestions for how to avoid the pitfalls of junior-high life.

Using Compound and Complex Sentences

- **Compound Sentences**

- **Complex Sentences**

- **Types of Subordinate Clauses**

People who live in glass houses shouldn't throw stones.
ENGLISH PROVERB

A proverb is a saying that packs a great deal of meaning into one sentence. There may be times when you want to pack a lot of meaning into your sentences too. The way you structure your sentences can help you combine ideas or expand on them.

In this workshop you will learn to express yourself more completely and to add variety and richness to your writing by using compound and complex sentences.

Using Compound and
Complex Sentences   **555**

COMPOUND SENTENCES

> A **compound sentence** consists of two or more simple
> sentences joined together.

Sometimes two simple sentences are so closely related in thought that you can join them together. You can join them by using a coordinating conjunction—*and, but,* or *or.* Two or more simple sentences joined together are called a **compound sentence.**

> The site is prehistoric. Archaeologists are studying it.
> The site is prehistoric, **and** archaeologists are studying it.

Compound sentences are useful, but they must be written carefully. Two sentences should be combined to form one sentence only if the ideas they express are closely related. If the ideas are not closely related, the resulting sentence may not make sense.

Incorrect   The mound is old, and Bradley likes archaeology.
Correct   The mound is old, and it contains ancient pottery.

Punctuating Compound Sentences

When you write a compound sentence, use a comma before the conjunction. The comma tells your reader where to pause. Without a comma, compound sentences can be quite confusing.

Confusing   Jan studies the fragment and her assistant takes
                  notes. (Did Jan study her assistant?)
Better   Jan studies the fragment, **and** her assistant takes
                  notes.

The first sentence might cause someone reading quickly to think that Jan studies both the fragment and her assistant. The comma prevents this confusion.

Sometimes you can join the parts of a compound sentence with a semicolon (;) rather than with a comma and a conjunction.

> The dwelling had partly collapsed; many stones had tumbled
>   from the walls.
> The site had been abandoned; no one knows why.

Writing
TIP

Compound sentences can give your writing variety and interest. Notice the compound sentences Margaret Poynter uses in "Krakatoa: The Greatest of Them All," pages 94–95 to describe the volcano's eruption.

Never join simple sentences with a comma alone or a run-on sentence will result. A comma is not powerful enough to hold the sentences together. Inserting a semicolon will correct the run-on error.

Incorrect	The stone tool was ancient, we did not know its use.
Correct	The stone tool was ancient, **and** we did not know its use.
Correct	The stone tool was ancient; we did not know its use.

Two Ways to Join Simple Sentences

1. Join them with a comma and the conjunction *and, but,* or *or.* Place the comma before the conjunction.
2. Join them with a semicolon without using a conjunction. Place the semicolon at the end of the first sentence.

Compound Sentences and Compound Verbs

A simple sentence with a compound verb looks and sounds like a compound sentence. Here are two reasons to learn to tell them apart:

1. Compound verbs are not separated by commas.
2. Sometimes you can improve your writing by changing a compound sentence to a simple sentence with a compound verb.

Notice that the compound sentence below has two subjects and two verbs. The simple sentence has one subject and two verbs.

Compound Sentence	Prehistoric *people built* forts, and *they created* burial mounds.
Simple Sentence	Prehistoric *people built* forts and *created* burial mounds.

Often both subjects of a compound sentence refer to the same person or thing. Then you can make your writing more concise by changing the sentence to a simple sentence with a compound verb.

Sentence Diagraming For information on diagraming compound sentences, see page 693.

Calvin and Hobbes
by Bill Watterson

Using Compound and
Complex Sentences **557**

Practice Your Skills

A. CONCEPT CHECK

Compound Sentences   Identify each of the following sentences as a *Compound Sentence,* a *Simple Sentence with Compound Verb,* or a *Run-on Sentence.*

1. You can pass an ancient mound, and you may not even notice it.
2. Mounds look natural, they often seem like enormous hills.
3. One covers many acres and is bigger than an Egyptian pyramid.
4. Mounds were built by Native Americans, some are well known.
5. Once thousands of mounds existed; now many are gone.
6. Some of these earthworks were built thousands of years ago, but others were constructed less than three hundred years ago.
7. Ancient people built them for burial purposes, or they used them as fortresses.
8. One mound covers fifteen acres and is one hundred feet high.
9. People call it Monk's Mound, it is near Cahokia, Illinois.
10. Great Serpent Mound in Ohio is curved and is 1,254 feet long.

B. REVISION SKILL

Sentence Combining   Join the following sentence pairs to make compound sentences. Two of the pairs are not related and should not be joined. Use correct punctuation and appropriate conjunctions. Use semicolons at least two times.

11. There are many mysterious monuments in the world. Some of the most mysterious are in the deserts of Peru in South America.
12. Vast figures have been drawn on the ground. They are known as the Nazca Lines.
13. Many are geometric shapes. Others are shaped like animals.
14. From ground level, the shapes cannot be seen. In fact, their existence was unknown for centuries.
15. The lines were not easily noticeable. Perhaps they were natural lines on the ground and nothing more.
16. The figures can be recognized only from an airplane. Native Americans created the drawings centuries ago.
17. Why were the drawings made? There are many theories.
18. Some people see a calendar in the lines other people disagree.
19. The calendar theory could explain some of the drawings. It cannot explain all of them.
20. No theory seems adequate. The drawings remain a mystery.

This Nazca drawing of a spider can be recognized only from the air.

C. PROOFREADING SKILL

Correcting Errors in Compound Sentences   Proofread the following paragraph, correcting errors in grammar, capitalization, punctuation, and spelling. Pay particular attention to improperly punctuated compound sentences. (10 errors)

On a remote mountain in the Big horn Mountains of wyoming is a mysterious rock circle. Is called the Big Horn Medicine Wheel. The circle is eighty feet in diameter, it has twenty-eight spokes. The spokes start at the center of the circle and they extend to the outer ring. In the middle is a pile of rocks it is called a *cairn*. The circle could be 200 years old. It could be 2,000 years old. No one knows how old it is and no one is sure about its purpose, either. Perhaps it was the sight of a religious ceramony. It may have been an astronomical calender.

FOR MORE PRACTICE
See page 571.

CHECK ✔ POINT
MIXED REVIEW • PAGES 556–559

Writing Theme
Team Mascots

Some of the following sentences are compound sentences, and others are simple sentences with compound verbs. Identify each as a *Compound Sentence* or a *Simple Sentence*.

1. Baseball, basketball, and football games are great fun, and part of the fun is watching the crazy antics of the mascots.
2. You know the kind; all the professional sports teams have them.
3. The San Diego Padres' Chicken was not the first mascot, but it was the first totally crazy one.
4. The Chicken appeared in 1974 and was an instant hit.
5. Soon fans everywhere enjoyed and applauded these crazy mascots.
6. A mascot is not just a comic; he or she is also a cheerleader.
7. Fans can get bored, but they always laugh at the mascot.
8. A mascot's job can be fun, but it requires a strong person.
9. A costume can weigh forty pounds and can be tight and heavy.
10. The mascot wears it on the hottest days, and that takes stamina.
11. A baseball mascot slides into bases and jumps into the stands.
12. Some basketball mascots jump on trampolines and do wild dunks.
13. Fans love the action, but the mascot suffers from the heat.
14. A mascot can lose four or five pounds during a game and may not be able to wear the costume more than twenty minutes at a time.
15. The work is hard, but few mascots would give up the applause.

Using Compound and
Complex Sentences   **559**

COMPLEX SENTENCES

> A **complex sentence** is a sentence that contains one *main clause* and one or more *subordinate clauses.*

To understand what a complex sentence is, you need to know about clauses. A **clause** is a group of words that contains a verb and its subject. There are two types of clauses—main clauses and subordinate clauses.

Main Clauses

A clause that can stand as a sentence by itself is a **main clause.** A compound sentence contains two or more main clauses, because it contains two or more simple sentences. Each of these simple sentences is a main clause.

> Computers store information, and they solve math problems.

In the example above, *Computers store information* and *they solve math problems* are both main clauses. They are also simple sentences. Main clauses are sometimes called **independent clauses.**

Subordinate Clauses

Some clauses do not express a complete thought, so they cannot stand by themselves. These clauses are called **subordinate clauses.** Read these examples:

If technology will improve	When robots can do the work
While electronics will work	After the system is complete

None of these clauses express a complete thought. Each one is a sentence fragment that leaves you wondering *then what?* Now cover the first word in each of these clauses. What happens? Each clause now expresses a complete thought.

The words *if, when, while,* and *after* are important. They *subordinate* the groups of words they introduce and are called **subordinating conjunctions.** They introduce subordinate clauses.

Words frequently used as subordinating conjunctions are listed in the box below.

Words Often Used as Subordinating Conjunctions			
after	because	so that	whatever
although	before	than	when
as	if	though	whenever
as if	in order that	till	where
as long as	provided	unless	wherever
as though	since	until	while

Now you have the information you need to understand complex sentences. A **complex sentence** is a sentence that contains one main clause and one or more subordinate clauses.

Main Clause	Subordinate Clause
The robot began operating	before we were out of bed.
Its battery needs recharging	so that it can work tonight.

Avoiding Sentence Fragments

When a subordinate clause is used by itself, as if it were a sentence, it is a **sentence fragment**. A subordinate clause must be joined to a main clause to form a sentence.

Fragment   When the power failed.
Complex Sentence When the power failed, the computer
                    stopped.

Practice Your Skills

A. CONCEPT CHECK

Subordinate Clauses   Write the subordinate clauses from the following sentences. Underline the subject of each subordinate clause once and the verb twice.

1. Before you know it, your flat television picture may be gone.
2. The image looks flat because it is two-dimensional.
3. The image would look more realistic if it were three-dimensional.

4. That 3-D image is not far off, since technology is changing.
5. Televisions will use holograms so that the images look real.
6. Holograms are available today, although they are not very common.
7. If you have ever seen a bank card, perhaps you have seen a hologram.
8. You can see a 3-D picture on the card when you look closely.
9. Unless problems develop, holographic television should be available in the near future.
10. Until it is, we will have to depend on today's technology.

B. CONCEPT CHECK

Kinds of Sentences   Read each sentence and identify as *Simple, Compound,* or *Complex.*

11. Most people associate robots with science fiction, but today robots are found in everyday life.
12. A robot is programmed like a computer.
13. A robot can move and do work, and some robots can even sense changes in their environment.
14. When it senses a change, the robot will respond.
15. Room thermostats are actually a kind of robot.
16. Whenever the temperature in a room falls below a certain point, the thermostat responds by turning on the heat.
17. The automatic-pilot system of an airplane is a robot and can control the plane from takeoff to landing.
18. Industrial robots are used wherever the work required is too hazardous for a person.
19. They can pick up very hot pieces of metal or work in a room that is filled with harmful gases.
20. Robots have not been in existence for very long, but they will become more and more common.

C. APPLICATION IN WRITING

Combining Sentences   Writers use subordinate clauses to avoid the monotony and choppiness that is created by writing too many simple sentences. Subordinate clauses also help make relationships among ideas clearer. Combine each pair of sentences on the next page into one complex sentence by changing one of the simple sentences into a subordinate clause.

EXAMPLE   Cars will have guidance systems. They can travel
           faster and be safer. (Use *so that*.)

           Cars will have guidance systems so that they can
           travel faster and be safer.

21. Imagine your daily routine in 2001. You drive to work. (Use *as*.)

22. You reach a new thoroughfare. You push a button on the dashboard of your car. (Use *when*.)

23. Then you take your hands off the steering wheel. You lean back and relax. (Use *as*.)

24. The car accelerates on its own. It angles into the traffic. (Use *while*.)

25. Six closely bunched cars approach at one hundred miles per hour on your left. They are going to pass. (Use *as though*.)

26. A gap opens in the line of traffic. Your car smoothly slips into line. (Use *when*.)

27. You have experienced this before. You do not pay attention to the car's maneuvering. (Use *since*.)

28. This scenario seems fantastic. It is not far from reality. (Use *although*.)

29. Car manufacturers and highway departments are developing smart cars and highways. Travel can be faster and safer. (Use *so that*.)

30. Research is proceeding quickly. Actual implementation of such a smart system is still a few years away. (Use *though*.)

31. A few systems are already being tested. The most useful systems can be identified. (Use *in order that*.)

32. The system is in place. Automobiles will drive themselves. (Use *after*.)

33. They will travel at high speeds. Cars will be bunched closely together in convoys. (Use *although*.)

34. Traffic congestion and accidents will be reduced. Human error will be removed from driving. (Use *since*.)

35. The systems work well. Roadways will be able to carry much more traffic. (Use *as long as*.)

Powerful dashboard computers and holographic displays may enable "smart cars" of the future to whisk you to your destination with little or no effort from you.

FOR MORE PRACTICE
See pages 571–572.

Using Compound and
Complex Sentences   **563**

Subordinate clauses may be used in sentences as adjectives, adverbs, and nouns. Such clauses are called **adjective clauses, adverb clauses,** and **noun clauses.**

Complex sentences can be used to add variety to your writing. They can also make your writing more interesting by adding details.

Original The old sailor told us about a hidden treasure.

Revised The old sailor, **who knew many legends,** told us about a hidden treasure.

A subordinate clause can act as an adjective, an adverb, or a noun in a complex sentence.

Adjective Clauses

An **adjective** is a word that modifies a noun or a pronoun. An **adjective phrase** is a phrase that acts as an adjective. An **adjective clause** is a subordinate clause that acts as an adjective. Remember, a clause has a subject and a verb; a phrase has neither.

Adjective The sailor told a *pirate* legend.

Adjective Phrase The sailor told a legend *about pirates.*

Adjective Clause The sailor told a legend *that involved pirates.*

An adjective clause usually comes immediately after the word it modifies, as in the following examples:

People still search for the treasure *that the pirate hid.*

Blackbeard was the pirate *who stole the treasure.*

The treasure, *which was buried,* has never been found.

Relative Pronouns and Adjective Clauses

Adjective clauses may begin with a subordinating conjunction or with the word *who, whom, whose, that,* or *which.* These words relate the subordinate clause to the word it modifies in the main clause. When used this way, *who, whom, whose, that,* and *which* are called **relative pronouns.**

Relative Pronouns					
who	whom	whose	that	which	

A relative pronoun relates the adjective clause to a noun or pronoun in the main clause. It may also act as the subject, object, predicate pronoun, or object of a preposition in the clause.

This is the island *that has the secret cave.*
 (*That* is the subject of *has.*)
The map, *which you saw,* shows the way.
 (*Which* is the object of *saw.*)
The map leads to the treasure *of which we spoke.*
 (*Which* is the object of the preposition *of.*)
Jon is the one *who found the pirate's cave.*
 (*Who* is the subject of *found.*)

Put commas around adjective clauses only if they merely add additional information to a sentence.

Sentence Diagraming For information on diagraming sentences with adjective clauses, see page 695.

Practice Your Skill

A. CONCEPT CHECK

Adjective Clauses Write each adjective clause and underline the subject of the clause once and the verb twice. Write the word or words modified by the clause.

Writing Theme
Hidden Treasure

1. Have you read *Treasure Island,* which was written by Robert Louis Stevenson?
2. The island that he wrote about was based on a real place.

3. It is Cocos Island, which is off the coast of Costa Rica.
4. The island was known to pirates, who buried their gold there.
5. Captain Edward Davis and Bonito of the Bloody Sword are only two who hid treasure on the island.
6. The richest treasure is one that was hidden by Captain Thompson.
7. It was from a cathedral that Spain was trying to capture.
8. The English captain Thompson was supposed to protect the treasure and the priests who guarded it on his ship, the *Mary Dear.*
9. Instead, Thompson, whose greed overcame his duty, threw the priests overboard and hid the treasure in a cave on Cocos Island.
10. Thompson, for whom people have little pity, died without recovering the treasure.

B. REVISION SKILL

Sentence Combining   Combine each of the following sentence pairs into one complex sentence by changing one of the sentences into an adjective clause. Use the relative pronoun provided.

EXAMPLE   The Lost Dutchman gold mine was named for Jacob Waltz. He was from Holland. (Use *who.*)

The Lost Dutchman gold mine was named for Jacob Waltz, who was from Holland.

11. The Lost Dutchman gold mine is said to lie somewhere in the Superstition Mountains. They are in Arizona. (Use *which.*)
12. This mine was discovered by Don Miguel Peralta. He led several expeditions to mine the gold. (Use *who.*)
13. On an expedition in 1864, Peralta and his crew were killed by Apaches. Their lands were overrun by gold hunters. (Use *whose.*)
14. The legend of a hidden treasure was believed by two German prospectors, Jacob Waltz and Jacob Wiser. They heard of the mine from Peralta's son. (Use *who.*)
15. The two Germans went into the mountains with Peralta's son. He shared the secret of the mine's location with them. (Use *who.*)
16. The three came safely away with $70,000 in gold. That was a great deal of money in those days. (Use *which.*)
17. Waltz and Wiser could not resist going back to the mine. It had brought them such easy wealth. (Use *that.*)
18. This time, however, the sole survivor was Waltz. He fled with more gold. (Use *who.*)

19. The Apaches then filled in the mine. It had brought so many invaders into their lands. (Use *that.*)

20. Later an earthquake finished hiding the mine. It has remained the object of treasure hunters ever since. (Use *which.*)

Adverb Clauses

An **adverb** is a word that modifies a verb, an adjective, or another adverb. An **adverb phrase** is a prepositional phrase used as an adverb. An **adverb clause** is a subordinate clause used as an adverb. Adverbs, adverb phrases, and adverb clauses all modify words by telling *where, when, how,* or *to what extent.* In addition, an adverb clause may tell *why.*

Adverb	We rode the train *once.*
Adverb Phrase	We rode the train *to the Japanese fishing village.*
Adverb Clause	We rode the train *until we reached the Japanese fishing village.*

An adverb clause contains a subject and a verb, like any other clause. It is always introduced by a subordinating conjunction. (See the list of subordinating conjunctions on page 561.

Sentence Diagraming For information on diagraming sentences with adverb clauses, see page 695.

Practice Your Skills

CONCEPT CHECK

Adverb Clauses Write the adverb clauses from the following sentences. Underline the subject of each adverb clause once and the verb twice. Label the subordinating conjunction *SC.*

Writing Theme
Traveling

1. When we arrived in Tokyo, we were exhausted.
2. All we wanted was a hotel room, because we had been traveling all day.
3. We did not know what would happen, since this was our first trip.
4. Until the rest of the tour group arrived, we waited in the airport.
5. While we were waiting, we tried to spot our guide.
6. Since we were on a group tour, we would depend on our guide.

7. After the entire group arrived, our guide introduced herself.

8. She helped us change dollars for yen before we left the airport.

9. As soon as we had our baggage, we set off for the hotel.

10. The tour guide did not speak much on the bus so that we could absorb the sights around us.

Noun Clauses

A **noun clause** is a clause used as a noun. It can be used in any way that a noun is used. The following sentences show different ways of using noun clauses.

Subject	*Why she lives in the wilderness* is a mystery.
Object	She knows *that wilderness life is challenging.*
Object of Preposition	Wilderness is available to *whoever enjoys it.* (The clause is the object of the preposition *to*. Notice, however, that *whoever* functions as a subject within the clause.)
Predicate Noun	Her first winter in the wilderness was *what she expected.*

Words Often Used to Introduce Noun Clauses

that	where	who, whom
what	when	whose
how	whatever	whoever, whomever

You cannot tell the kind of clause from the word that introduces it. You can tell the kind of clause only by the way it is used in a sentence. If the clause is used as a noun, it is a noun clause. If the clause is used as a modifier, it is an adjective clause or an adverb clause.

> *Whoever built the cabin* was not home. (noun clause as subject)
> No one knew *where he went.* (noun clause as object)
> He climbed the mountain *whenever he wished.* (adverb clause)
> This is the lake *where he lives.* (adjective clause)

Sentence Diagraming For information on diagraming sentences with noun clauses, see page 695.

Practice Your Skills

A. CONCEPT CHECK

Noun Clauses   Write the noun clauses from the following sentences. Underline the subject of each noun clause once and the verb twice. Label the clause *Subject, Object, Predicate Noun,* or *Object of Preposition.*

1. What Anne LaBastille wanted was a home in the wilderness.
2. She knew that the place should be far from civilization.
3. She found what she was after on a remote mountain lake.
4. Her Black Bear Lake cabin was what she had dreamed of.
5. There were no roads to where the cabin was located.
6. Whatever neighbors she had were miles away across the lake.
7. She kept a small boat for when a trip to town was necessary.
8. LaBastille became what she called a woodswoman.
9. How LaBastille lived is the subject of her book *Woodswoman*.
10. In it, she also explains why a wilderness home appealed to her.

Writing Theme
Wilderness
Experiences

B. APPLICATION IN LITERATURE

Subordinate Clauses   Write the italicized clauses and underline the subject of each once and the verb twice. Then identify the clause as an *Adjective Clause,* an *Adverb Clause,* or a *Noun Clause.*

> **11**This June morning is hot and humid with a haze so dense I can barely see the huge hemlock tree *in which I live.* . . .
> **12***As a hot dry wind clears the air,* I can see Frightful, my peregrine falcon, sitting in front of the six-foot-in-diameter hemlock tree *that I hollowed out for a home.* . . . Sticks snap in the distance. Someone is coming. . . . I smell the musky scent of warning from my friend Baron Weasel. **13**The Baron, *who was living here when I arrived,* considers himself the real owner of the mountaintop, but *because he finds me interesting,* he lets me stay.
>
> **Jean Craighead George, *On the Far Side of the Mountain***

Anne LaBastille at her cabin in the Adirondack Mountains of New York.

C. APPLICATION IN WRITING

Writing an Explanation   Imagine that you are going to live in the wilderness. You must take everything you will need with you. Other than food, what will you take? Write a paragraph explaining what you will take and why. Use at least five subordinate clauses.

FOR MORE PRACTICE
See page 572.

Using Compound and
Complex Sentences   **569**

C H E C K ✔ P O I N T

MIXED REVIEW · PAGES 560–569

Writing Theme
Unusual Sports

A. Identify each of the following sentences as *Simple, Compound,* or *Complex.*

1. Have you heard of wallyball?
2. The game is not very old; it was invented in 1979.
3. It has a strange name, but the game might look familiar.
4. Wallyball is similar to volleyball, although it is played on a racquetball or handball court.
5. In fact, the name *wallyball* comes from *walls* and *volleyball.*
6. The net is like a volleyball net that is attached to the walls.
7. Players can bounce the ball off the walls and over the net.
8. The action is fast, because the walls keep the ball in play.
9. Since a team has fewer than four players, everyone is busy.
10. It is good exercise, and you do not have to be a great athlete.

B. Write the subordinate clause in each sentence and identify it as an *Adjective Clause,* an *Adverb Clause,* or a *Noun Clause.*

11. While the skier plodded wearily up the mountain, another skier practically flew past him up the hill!
12. What looked like a parachute pulled the skier up the mountain.
13. The parachute was really a sail that was designed for skiing.
14. The skier packed the sail away when she reached the mountaintop.
15. After the sail was put away, the skier began skiing back down.
16. This sail was invented by a man who was tired of slow trips up snow-covered mountains.
17. He knew that the skier must have complete control of the sail.
18. The skier holds lines that he or she pulls to change direction.
19. A skier who wants to slow down or stop pulls another line to open a hole in the sail.
20. The sail is a solution to what was a problem in skiing.
21. Until the sail was invented, it could take skiers many hours to reach the upper slopes of back-country mountains.
22. Now skiers can easily climb mountains that lack chairlifts.
23. In fact, what was a major difficulty has become a popular sport.
24. The sail also answers the question of how a skier can travel rapidly across frozen lakes or vast snow-covered flatlands.
25. Some adventuresome Antarctic explorers plan to use the sails when they travel to the South Pole.

A. Recognizing Compound Sentences   Write the following sentences. Underline each subject once and each verb twice. Then label each sentence *Simple* or *Compound*.

Writing Theme
Wild Horses

1. The ancestor of the horse probably originated in North America.
2. One early horse was *Eohippus,* and it lived 55 million years ago.
3. *Eohippus,* or "dawn horse," was about 15 inches tall and looked somewhat like a greyhound.
4. Horses changed over time and gradually got bigger.
5. The modern horse developed about 3 million years ago, but it was still small.
6. Early in its history, the horse lived on every continent except Australia.
7. That was fortunate, or the horse might have become extinct.
8. We do not know why, but the horse died out in America about ten thousand years ago.
9. Humans on other continents eventually tamed horses and trained them for riding.
10. People began riding horses at least five thousand years ago.

B. Recognizing Complex Sentences   Write the following sentences. Underline each subject once and each verb twice. Then label each sentence *Simple, Compound,* or *Complex.*

11. The horse first developed in North America, but it became extinct here about ten thousand years ago.
12. Then Christopher Columbus brought horses to the New World on his second voyage.
13. The population of horses increased when Spanish conquerors brought them to Mexico in the 1500s.
14. In 1519, Hernán Cortés brought sixteen horses from Cuba so that he could use them in his invasion of the Aztec Empire.
15. Later Spanish explorers brought more horses to America, where they were useful in battle and on long expeditions.
16. Because Native Americans did not have horses, the Spanish had a great advantage in war.
17. The Spanish soldiers defeated the Native Americans and took possession of their lands.
18. Without land, many Native Americans had no means of livelihood, and they were forced to work for the Spanish.

Using Compound and
Complex Sentences   **571**

19. Although these workers cared for horses, they were not allowed to ride the horses.

20. However, the Native Americans watched the Spanish landowners and soldiers, and by 1600, they had learned to train and ride horses.

21. Some of the native peoples stole horses from the Spanish and then traded the horses among their different groups.

22. Before many years had passed, Native Americans were riding and breeding horses throughout the West.

23. Some horses escaped from the Spanish and the Native Americans; they thrived on the vast grasslands.

24. Wild horses in America are most likely descendants of these Spanish horses.

25. In fact, the word *mustang* probably comes from the Spanish word *mesteño;* it means "stray animal."

C. Recognizing Clauses   Write the subordinate clauses from the following sentences. Then label each clause *Adjective Clause, Adverb Clause,* or *Noun Clause* to show what kind of clause it is.

26. When you think of wild horses, do you think about the herds in the western states?

27. Some of the most interesting wild horses that live in the United States roam the island of Assateague off the coast of Virginia.

28. Where these horses came from is a mystery.

29. Many people think that they survived the wreck of a Spanish ship several hundred years ago.

30. Part of the island, Chincoteague National Wildlife Refuge, is for the horses and other animals that live there.

31. Although the refuge is protected, the horses must still struggle for survival in a rugged land.

32. Mighty storms from the Atlantic Ocean lash the small, flat, island, whose highest point is only forty-seven feet above sea level.

33. The grazing land is what you might expect.

34. The poor land produces scraggly vegetation that is adapted to salty environments.

35. In spite of the extremely harsh conditions, the rugged horses survive because they have adapted so well to the environment.

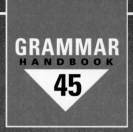

A. Recognizing Compound Sentences Write the subjects and verbs in these sentences. Label each sentence *Simple* or *Compound.*

1. The moon orbits the earth every 29½ days.
2. Early people used this cycle as a type of calendar, and they based certain decisions on it.
3. Usually, months began with the first crescent of the new moon.
4. Over the course of many days, the visible part of the moon changed shape, but it eventually returned to its starting point.
5. People identified and named four particular phases of the moon.
6. The moon calendar helped people to predict the beginning of spring and fall and, therefore, good planting and harvesting times.
7. To this day we still use the expression "harvest moon."
8. Early people established festivals based on the moon calendar, and these became the basis for some later religious holidays.
9. Moon calendars were useful, but they became inaccurate.
10. On these calendars, spring would arrive earlier and earlier every year, and spring holidays might end up in midwinter.

Writing Theme
The Moon

B. Complex Sentences Write the subordinate clause from each sentence. Underline the subject once and the verb twice.

11. Wherever people live, there are superstitions about the moon.
12. Some people watch the moon as though it affects their lives.
13. Perhaps these beliefs developed because the moon changes.
14. A crescent moon gets larger every day, as if it were growing.
15. According to folklore, living things grow as the moon grows.
16. When the moon becomes smaller, living things cease growing.
17. Therefore, if you plant a tree, plant it during the new moon.
18. Even if you do not plant trees, you should be aware of other superstitions.
19. For example, do not look at a new moon through a window, because you will have bad luck.
20. When you do that, the glass comes between you and good luck.
21. Also, never look at the moon over your left shoulder unless you are prepared for bad luck.
22. Some superstitions developed when people felt helpless about the world around them.
23. Farmers used weather signs so that they could plan their work.
24. When they saw a ring around the moon, they planned for rain.
25. Finally, do not believe any moon lore until you test it.

Using Compound and
Complex Sentences   **573**

C. Identifying Sentence Structure Label each of the following sentences *Simple, Compound,* or *Complex.*

26. Although the moon is relatively close to the earth, we did not know much about it until very recently.
27. As astronomy advances, our knowledge of the moon increases.
28. However, scientific observations have not always been accurate, and some early scientific conclusions are amusing.
29. Galileo was the first to look at the moon through a telescope.
30. He called the dark areas seas since they looked like oceans.
31. Other scientists have also drawn incorrect conclusions.
32. In 1822, F. P. Gruithuisen saw a city on the moon.
33. Although people finally gave up the idea of people on the moon, W. H. Pickering saw "insects" there as recently as 1922.
34. A reputable U.S. astronomer, Pickering saw shadows, and they seemed to move about.
35. Pickering's shadows were "insects," and they were migrating!

D. Types of Subordinate Clauses Write the subordinate clause in each sentence. Then identify the clause as an *Adjective Clause,* an *Adverb Clause,* or a *Noun Clause.*

36. One of history's great hoaxes, which are practical jokes, occurred in 1835.
37. In that year, the English astronomer Sir John Herschel was in South Africa so that he could make observations of the stars.
38. Richard Adam Locke, a journalist, wrote a series of fictitious stories about what Herschel supposedly discovered.
39. The hoax was effective because accurate news traveled slowly.
40. Locke's stories circulated before true sources disproved them.
41. His stories told about a huge telescope that could magnify the surface of the moon to an astonishing degree.
42. According to the hoax, when Herschel focused this telescope on the moon, he saw flowering plants and living beings!
43. The people, who were about four feet tall, had wings.
44. The story said that they were intelligent beings.
45. What supposedly convinced Herschel were their buildings.
46. They had what seemed to be temples with gold roofs.
47. The stories, which were widely reprinted, were very convincing.
48. The hoax ended when the newspaper confessed to the joke.
49. Herschel, who heard about the hoax much later, was amused.
50. The publicity was not what he had expected from his trip.

Revise the following analysis of a story by using the directions at the bottom of the page. Then proofread your revision, paying special attention to your use of compound and complex sentences. Also check for errors in grammar, capitalization, punctuation, and spelling.

[1]Guy de Maupassant's short story The Necklace tells of a young woman. [2]Who suffers many years for one evening of glory. [3]It is a memorable story. [4]O. Henry is often called the master of the surprise ending. [5]The story tells of a woman. [6]She borrows a necklace from a friend. [7]Unfortuately, she loses the necklace. [8]She believes the necklace is very expensive. [9]She is afraid to tell her friend about the loss. [10]Instead she buys her friend a new one. [11]She spends the next ten year's paying for it. [12]The story is written in such a way. [13]That the reader beleives the necklace is very valuable. [14]In the surprise ending, the reader learns the original necklace was fake. [15]It changes the reader's feelings about the suffering of the young woman. [16]It also changes the message of the story.

1. Delete the sentence that does not belong.

2. Rewrite sentence 3 to say that the story is memorable because it has a surprise ending.

3. Combine sentences 5 and 6, making one of them into a subordinate clause.

4. Add sentence 8 to the beginning of sentence 9 as a subordinate clause beginning with *since*.

5. Combine sentences 10 and 11 to make a compound sentence.

6. Replace the vague pronoun *it* in sentence 15 with a more precise phrase.

7. Combine sentences 15 and 16 to make a compound sentence.

Responding to Literature

Analyzing a story helps you understand the story's meaning and the techniques of the writer. (See Workshop 7.) When you revise an analysis, look to see that your reasoning is clear and that you have given enough details to support your points. Using compound and complex sentences can add clarity as well as variety to your analysis.

• What's going on in this piece of art? Describe what you see here.

Green Sliding (1980), Kim MacConnel.

• Play a form of word association by first listing all the synonyms of *run* that you can think of. Then match each synonym with a person, a group, an animal, or a thing that fits that word. For example, batters slide—a horse gallops.

• Write a letter to a pen pal in another country, explaining some family tradition. Help your friend experience the event by describing what each person or group does and how each person acts.

Understanding Subject and Verb Agreement

Beckett and Baseball (1986), Harvey Breverman.

- **Making Subjects and Verbs Agree in Number**
- **Compound Subjects**
- **Indefinite Pronouns**
- **Other Problems of Agreement**

In baseball and in life, disagreements are sometimes inevitable. In writing, however, some disagreements can be avoided—disagreements between subjects and verbs. You can reach agreement in your sentences by making sure that singular subjects are matched with singular verbs and plural subjects with plural verbs.

In this workshop you will learn ways subject-verb agreement keeps the meaning of your sentences clear.

MAKING SUBJECTS AND VERBS AGREE IN NUMBER

> The subject and the verb in a sentence must agree in **number.**

When a word refers to one thing, it is **singular.** When it refers to more than one thing, it is **plural. Number** refers to whether a word is singular or plural.

A verb must agree in number with its subject. A singular subject takes a singular verb. A plural subject takes a plural verb.

To find the subject of a sentence, first find the verb. Then ask *who* or *what* performs the action of the verb. By asking this question, you will have no trouble with agreement, even when words come between the subject and its verb.

> The tea burned my mouth. (*Burned* is the verb. What burned? Tea burned. *Tea* is the subject.)

Notice in the examples below that the third person singular form of the verbs *pour* and *sip* ends in *s.* Plural verbs, however, do not end in *s.*

Singular	The waiter *pours.*	One guest *sips.*
Plural	The waiters *pour.*	Two guests *sip.*

Interrupting Words and Phrases

Watch for phrases that occur between the verb and its subject.

> *Tables* by the door *are* empty.   *Ned,* one of the hosts, *greets* us.

The subject of the verb is never found in a prepositional phrase or an appositive. In the two sentences above, the nouns *door, one,* and *hosts* cannot be subjects.

Other phrases, such as those beginning with *with, together with, including, as well as, along with,* and *in addition to,* can also separate the subject and the verb.

> The *owner,* as well as the waiters, *is* friendly.

Amitié (1991), Mara Superior. Plural teapots are much more difficult to use than plural nouns and verbs.

Practice Your Skills

A. CONCEPT CHECK

Agreement in Number   Write the subject of each sentence. Then choose and write the correct verb.

1. Some old customs still (lives, live) on today.
2. In Britain four o'clock in the afternoon (marks, mark) more than just the time.
3. Daily at this time, many British people (stops, stop) work.
4. This break in the day (has, have) been a tradition for many years.
5. The average worker, as well as people from other walks of life, (enjoys, enjoy) the ritual of teatime.
6. A tea in some areas of England (tends, tend) to be a meal.
7. For example, workers in the country (eats, eat) hearty food.
8. Tea with hard-boiled eggs, ham, and tomatoes (satisfies, satisfy) their appetites.
9. Well-to-do persons, as well as an occasional tourist, (goes, go) to fancy London tearooms.
10. Elegant waiters in formal attire (serves, serve) tea and goodies.
11. Exotic tea, along with finger sandwiches of cucumbers, salmon, or ham, (makes, make) up a typical feast.
12. Other food, including sweet cakes, (tempts, tempt) diners.

B. REVISION SKILL

Making Subjects and Verbs Agree   Write the following sentences, correcting errors in subject-verb agreement. If a sentence has no error, write *Correct*.

13. What game does British people play with a bat?
14. Their traditional sport, cricket, share some characteristics with baseball and field hockey.
15. However, cricket's many rules, as well as unfamiliar terms and equipment, makes it difficult to understand.
16. Two goals, or wickets, marks the central playing area.
17. Eleven players are on a team.
18. A fielder on one team bowl the ball to a batsman on the other.
19. Using a long, flat bat, the batsman try to hit the ball.
20. The batsman, together with a teammate, try to score runs by dashing from wicket to wicket.
21. The fans, along with team members, cheers for a run.
22. Cricket matches sometimes are five days long.

Writing Theme
British Traditions

FOR MORE PRACTICE
See page 587.

COMPOUND SUBJECTS

> **Compound subjects** joined by *and* take a plural verb.
> When the parts of a subject are joined by *or* or *nor,* the verb agrees with the part of the subject nearer to it.

Compound subjects joined by *and* take a plural verb regardless of the number of each part. Consider these examples:

> The actor and the director *are* on the set.
> Good actors and directors *are* important in making commercials.

When the parts of a compound subject are joined by *or* or *nor,* the verb agrees with the part nearer to it. Read the following sentences:

> Either the camera or the lenses *have* broken.
> Neither the lenses nor the camera *has* been fixed.
> Either the actors or the director *has* the final script.

Practice Your Skills

A. CONCEPT CHECK

Compound Subjects Write the compound subject in each sentence. Then write the correct form of the verb in parentheses.

1. The cast and the crew members (arrives, arrive) at 5:00 a.m.
2. Actors and musicians (is, are) on the beach set within an hour.
3. Neither the director nor her assistants (has, have) arrived.
4. Time and patience (is, are) required for filming ads.
5. Often either the cameras or the weather (creates, create) problems.
6. Glare and blowing sand (stops, stop) the filming.
7. The actors and the crew (waits, wait) impatiently.
8. Neither the actors nor the actress (leaves, leave) the set.
9. Scenes and lines (is, are) rehearsed several times before the camera begins to roll.
10. Either the director or the sponsors (approves, approve) finished commercials.

B. PROOFREADING SKILL

Agreement with Compound Subjects   Rewrite this paragraph, correcting errors in grammar, capitalization, punctuation, and spelling. Pay special attention to errors in agreement. (10 errors)

> According to recent polls. Videocassette recorders (VCRs) are in more than 70 percent of all homes in the united states. Advertisors are successfully taking advantage of this market. Auto makers, stores, and even a cosmetic company has ads on videocassettes. Neither the advertisers nor the viewers thinks this kind of advertising will fail, consumers at home see them with no interferance from other commercials. Depending on your point of view, either the consumer or the advertiser benefits more from advertising on videocassettes. The possibilitys and future of this new type of advertising is unlimited. progress marches on!

C H E C K   ✔   P O I N T
MIXED REVIEW · PAGES 578–581

Write the correct form of each verb in parentheses.

FOR MORE PRACTICE
See pages 587–588.

Writing Theme
Modern Cowhands

1. A rider (ropes, rope) the largest steer in the herd.
2. Other cowhands, near the fire, (grabs, grab) a branding iron.
3. Neither the steer nor the cowhands (is, are) in the Old West.
4. This scene, along with similar ones, (occurs, occur) in Hawaii.
5. These cowhands (is, are) called *paniolos.*
6. People from Mexico (was, were) among the first to work on Hawaiian cattle ranches.
7. Either the skills or the excitement (was, were) appealing to Hawaiians, who quickly learned from the Mexicans.
8. Today many *paniolos* (works, work) on the Parker Ranch.
9. A straw hat, together with chaps and spurs, (serves, serve) as the *paniolos'* work clothes.
10. Parker Ranch, along with more than two hundred other ranches, (is, are) part of the Hawaiian cattle industry.
11. On the smaller Hawaiian islands, neither the cattle nor the industry (has, have) survived.
12. Herds on Molokai (was, were) wiped out by tuberculosis.
13. However, the *paniolos* on Hawaii still (rides, ride).
14. February and March (marks, mark) the time for rodeos.
15. Races and rodeo events (tests, test) the *paniolos'* skills.

Understanding Subject
and Verb Agreement   **581**

Some **indefinite pronouns** are singular and some are plural. A few can be either singular or plural.

Study the chart of indefinite pronouns below. Then study the examples that follow. Notice that interrupting words do not change the agreement of subject and verb in number.

Indefinite Pronouns

Singular			Plural
another	either	nobody	both
anybody	everybody	no one	few
anyone	everyone	one	many
anything	everything	somebody	several
each	neither	someone	

Singular
Everybody *has* a name.
Neither of us *is* satisfied.

Plural
Many *have* nicknames.
Both of our names *are* silly.

The words *some, all, any, none,* and *most* may be either singular or plural. They are singular when they refer to a singular word and plural when they refer to a plural word or words.

Singular
All of the *book* is factual.
Most of the *chapter* is done.

Plural
All of the *facts* are new.
Most of the *names* are real.

Practice Your Skills

A. CONCEPT CHECK

Indefinite Pronouns   Write the correct form of each verb in parentheses.

1. Anything that has a nickname (has, have) a given name.
2. Some of the cities in the United States (is, are) nicknamed.
3. Most of the nicknames (has, have) a long history.

Writing Theme
Nicknames

4. Today, however, nobody (knows, know) for sure how the cities got their names.
5. Several even (shares, share) a nickname.
6. Few of us (recognizes, recognize) Waco as the Athens of Texas.
7. However, everyone in Massachusetts probably (knows, know) Boston as the Athens of America.
8. Some of its citizens (connects, connect) this nickname with Boston's history of culture, education, and literature.
9. Another of Boston's nicknames (is, are) the Cradle of Liberty.
10. Either of these nicknames (applies, apply) to Boston today.
11. (Does, Do) many of Utah's residents know that Springfield, Utah, is the Cradle of Industry?
12. Today nobody (calls, call) Cincinnati the Paris of America.
13. Neither of Chicago's old nicknames (has, have) endured.
14. Both of these names, Phoenix City and New York of the West, (is, are) forgotten.
15. Each of the nicknames (lives, live) only as long as the people who use it.

"LIVE WITH US"

CHARMING CHERAW THE TIP TOP TOWN

Prettiest Town
IN
"DIXIE"

B. DRAFTING SKILL

Using Indefinite Pronouns   Write these sentences, using the correct present-tense form of each verb in parentheses.

16. All of the computer industry (be) expanding.
17. Undoubtedly, everybody (have) heard of Silicon Valley.
18. However, (do) anybody know about Silicon Prairie?
19. Probably no one (know) about Silicon Glen either.
20. Each of these places (be) known for its computer industry.
21. Many of the computer businesses in Texas (be) in an area near Dallas, nicknamed Silicon Prairie.
22. Some of the companies located between Glasgow and Edinburgh in Scotland (produce) silicon chips that are used in computers.
23. All of the area between these cities (be) called Silicon Glen.
24. Each of these places (remind) us that silicon is the second most abundant element in the earth's crust.
25. (Have) anyone thought to call Earth the Silicon Planet?

FOR MORE PRACTICE
See page 588.

Understanding Subject
and Verb Agreement   **583**

In sentences beginning with *here, there,* and *where,* the subject often comes after the verb. The order of words in inverted sentences does not affect the agreement of subject and verb.

With the pronouns *he, she,* and *it,* the verb *does* is used. With all other personal pronouns, *do* is used.

Agreement in Inverted Sentences

A sentence is **inverted** when the subject comes after the verb. Questions are usually in inverted order. Sometimes writers achieve a special tone by inverting the order of a sentence.

Across the room drifts the scent of roses.
Are roses really used to make perfume?

Here, There, Where   In sentences beginning with *here, there,* and *where,* the subject often comes after the verb. First find the subject to be sure the verb agrees with it in number.

Here is the laboratory.
There is the secret formula.
Where are the ingredients?

Agreement with Forms of *Do*

Does and *doesn't* are used with singular nouns and the singular pronouns *he, she,* and *it. Do* and *don't* are used with plural nouns and with the personal pronouns *I, you, we,* and *they.*

Sam *doesn't* use cologne.	I *do* like to wear perfume.
It *doesn't* appeal to him.	I *don't* wear it every day, though.
He *does* use after shave.	We *do* think you'll like this scent.
Erin *does* like the smell of musk.	You *don't* need more than a drop.
She *doesn't* wear perfume herself.	Many perfumes *do* come from France.

Practice Your Skills

A. CONCEPT CHECK

Problems of Agreement   Write the correct form of each verb.

Writing Theme
Perfume

1. Most of us probably (doesn't, don't) know what making perfume was like in ancient Rome.
2. Here (is, are) one perfume maker's description of a typical day.
3. Into the shop (comes, come) my first customer, a soldier.
4. Like all soldiers, he (does, do) need to anoint himself with perfume.
5. However, he (doesn't, don't) know much about scents.
6. He asks, "Where (is, are) the oils of tangerine and lemon made?"
7. "From my Greek friends (comes, come) those fine oils," I reply.
8. "What ingredients (does, do) the other scents contain?"
9. "Into one concoction (goes, go) jasmine and hyacinth oils."
10. "For your feet, here (is, are) a lotion called *aegyptium.*"
11. "(Does, Do) you have any ginger?" he inquires.
12. "None of the scents (smells, smell) more exquisite," he adds.
13. "Here (is, are) the best place to find ginger," I boast.
14. "Out of my own experimenting (comes, come) a new formula."
15. "Only for special clients (is, are) this scent reserved."

B. DRAFTING SKILL

Making Subjects and Verbs Agree   Complete each sentence, using a present-tense verb.

16. _____ you wear perfume or some other kind of scent?
17. There _____ great secrecy in the perfume business.
18. Where _____ the perfume makers create new scents?
19. In guarded laboratories _____ the scientists.
20. Here _____ equipment for distilling essential oils.
21. There _____ one of the scientists.
22. She _____ the extraction procedure.
23. In one perfume there _____ often one hundred ingredients.
24. From all over the world _____ exotic herbs and roots.
25. _____ one of the main ingredients flower petals?
26. Here _____ alcohols for extracting the scents.
27. What substances _____ the fragrance last?
28. One substance, ambergris, _____ as a preservative.
29. From the sperm whale _____ ambergris.
30. There _____ laws against using it, though, because the sperm whale is an endangered species.

The cartoon character Pepe Le Pew, star of the 1949 animated film *For Scent-imental Reasons.* ©1949 Warner Bros.

Understanding Subject and Verb Agreement   **585**

C. PROOFREADING SKILL

Agreement Errors   Write the following paragraph, correcting errors in grammar, capitalization, punctuation, and spelling. Pay special attention to errors in agreement. (10 errors)

You have probaly heard of Cleopatra. There has been many stories written about her beauty. Around the Johnson farmyards, though, romp another Cleopatra. Here's the facts about this unusual creature Ms. Johnson named her favorite dog after the Egyptian ruler. Where's the connection? Well, the Egyptian Cleopatra was fond of fragrence. Oils of roses, crocuses, and violets were always on her hands. Another lotion, with almonds, cinnimin, and honey, was used for her feet. The Johnsons' Cleopatra is also fond of fragrance. On her head are the scents of stinkweeds and mud. There's also skunks around the farm. Cleo don't ever leave them alone. So throughout the rooms waft the horrible scent of skunk! Cleo needs to take a lesson in "scent-sibility" from her Egyptian namesake.

FOR MORE PRACTICE
See page 588.

Writing Theme
Dinosaur Mania

C H E C K ✔ P O I N T
MIXED REVIEW • PAGES 582–586

Write the correct form of each verb in parentheses.

1. (Is, Are) dinosaurs really extinct?
2. I, for one, (doesn't, don't) think so.
3. In the human imagination still (roams, roam) the "terrible lizards."
4. There (has, have) actually been an outbreak of dinosaur mania!
5. Here (is, are) some of the evidence.
6. Everybody (has, have) probably seen a television show or a movie about dinosaurs.
7. Well, there also (exists, exist) more than two hundred books about them in print today.
8. One of the books (is, are) *Jurassic Park* by Michael Crichton.
9. (Doesn't, Don't) it keep you on the edge of your seat?
10. "Dinomania," however, (does, do) not stop there.
11. (Has, Have) any of you eaten dinosaur macaroni?
12. In the stores (is, are) T-shirts, stickers, and all kinds of other dinosaur merchandise.
13. Where (has, have) all of the dinosaur action figures gone?
14. Because of their popularity, few (remains, remain) in stores long.
15. No one (doubts, doubt) the never-ending popularity of dinosaurs.

A. Making Verbs Agree with Their Subjects   Write the correct form of each verb in parentheses.

1. This letter, along with others like it, (pleads, plead) for change.
2. An injustice to my friends the Guillotins (continues, continue).
3. Citizens of the land (uses, use) their name unjustly.
4. A new machine for beheading convicts (has, have) been created.
5. The inventor of this device (is, are) Dr. Antoine Louis.
6. The name Louisette (suits, suit) the device well.
7. However, people in France (calls, call) it the guillotine.
8. The crowds in the plaza (chants, chant) that name.
9. Dr. Guillotin, as well as his colleagues, (is, are) upset.
10. Members of Guillotin's family (feels, feel) outrage.
11. A belief in humane executions (was, were) Dr. Guillotin's reason for supporting the use of the device.
12. Speed, along with mercy, (is, are) its main feature.
13. Dr. Guillotin, with his family, (argues, argue) that the name *guillotine* is inappropriate.
14. However, calls for *la guillotine* still (rings, ring) out.
15. Supporters, including me, (wants, want) to protest this undeserved fame.

Writing Theme
Fame

B. Using Verbs with Compound Subjects   Write the correct form of each verb in parentheses.

16. The lives and experiences of famous people (sounds, sound) glamorous and satisfying.
17. Yet neither fame nor status (creates, create) happiness.
18. Therefore, many entertainers and other celebrities (chooses, choose) to share their success with others.
19. Either their talents or their money (is, are) donated to worthy causes.
20. Neither politicians nor businesspeople (has, have) more opportunities than entertainers to help the needy.
21. For example, the actor Paul Newman's food-product sales and humanitarian work (has, have) benefited many charities.
22. Newman's salad dressing and popcorn (is, are) gourmet treats that also provide food, housing, and medical care for needy people.
23. The actress Liv Ullmann (has, have) worked hard for the United Nations Children's Fund.
24. Both the rock group U2 and the singer Willie Nelson (is, are) still famous for their participation in the Farm Aid concerts.

Understanding Subject
and Verb Agreement   **587**

25. Apartheid and other injustices in South Africa (was, were) fought with money earned by Paul Simon's *Graceland* album.

26. Neither the success of this album nor his fame (has, have) been as important to Simon as achieving this humanitarian goal.

27. The comedians Robin Williams and Whoopi Goldberg (was, were) important participants in the telethon "Comic Relief."

28. Health care and other services (has, have) been made available to thousands of homeless people thanks to their efforts.

29. Our enjoyment and appreciation of these performers (grows, grow) because of their generosity.

30. For these celebrities, sharing and caring (goes, go) hand in hand.

C. Using Verbs with Indefinite Pronouns   Write the sentences, using the correct form of each verb in parentheses.

31. One of the benefits of fame (is, are) money from endorsements.

32. Some of the stars (collects, collect) millions of dollars.

33. All of the ads (sounds, sound) sincere.

34. Each (attempts, attempt) to influence people to buy a product.

35. Most of this advertising (has, have) been aimed at teenagers.

36. (Does, Do) anyone really pay attention to these ads?

37. Someone (is, are) taking celebrity endorsements seriously.

38. Most television viewers (remembers, remember) seeing them.

39. Many (claims, claim) to enjoy watching the stars.

40. Few, however, (admits, admit) that the celebrities influence their purchases.

D. Avoiding Problems of Agreement   Write the sentences, using the correct present-tense forms of the verbs in parentheses.

41. Here (be) a story from the memoirs of conductor André Previn.

42. He (do) remember it with a smile.

43. On a certain day there (be) an important meeting of film people.

44. Down the hall (come) the dog Lassie, along with her trainer.

45. So where (be) the funny parts?

46. On command, Lassie (do) her trick of shaking hands with Fred Astaire, Cyd Charisse, and all the other celebrities.

47. However, she (do) not shake hands with André Previn.

48. There (stand) the famous conductor, snubbed by a dog!

49. Here (be) proof that fame (do) not ensure good manners.

50. Somewhere in the back of Previn's mind (gnaw) this memory.

A. Agreement in Number   Write the form of the verb in parentheses that agrees with the subject in number.

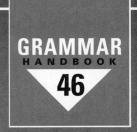

GRAMMAR
HANDBOOK
46

Writing Theme
Asian Cultures

1. Two reporters in China (has, have) written a book.
2. The book, *Chinese Lives,* (contains, contain) interviews.
3. Both authors, as well as many people they interviewed, (was, were) born in Beijing, the capital of China.
4. In one interview, a boy thirteen years of age (tells, tell) how he left home to earn a living.
5. The young boy, together with others, (works, work) as a popcorn vendor in Beijing.
6. The popcorn machines, because of their noise, (is, are) called land mines.
7. The noisy popping, as well as the boy's loud cries, (draws, draw) crowds.
8. Customers on the street (brings, bring) their own popcorn kernals to the boy.
9. The young boy with the land mine (pops, pop) them.
10. Another vendor on the street (sells, sell) tea broth.
11. His recipe, including tea and sorghum flour, (is, are) ancient.
12. A young man, but not his companions, (tries, try) the broth.
13. Most young people, unlike the older generation, (prefers, prefer) more modern beverages.
14. However, the street vendor's wares (appeals, appeal) to foreign visitors.
15. Many photographers from abroad (has, have) taken his picture.
16. These photos, as well as the vendor's memories, (fills, fill) him with great pride.
17. In another interview, a young girl, among her other remarks, (talks, talk) about going to college.
18. Only one student in twenty (passes, pass) the examination.
19. The parents of the girl (is, are) worried about her chances.
20. Her dream, more than anything else, (is, are) to write.
21. The authors of the book (gives, give) readers a look at the Chinese people in the mid-1980s.
22. The interviews in the book (precedes, precede) the events of 1989 in Tiananmen Square.
23. The leaders of China still (prohibits, prohibit) democracy.
24. The people, however, (has, have) endured hard times before.
25. This collection of interviews (lets, let) readers appreciate their difficulties and triumphs.

B. Agreement with Compound Subjects   Write the sentences, correcting any errors of agreement. If a sentence has no error, write *Correct.*

26. Social customs and behavior is different in every culture.
27. Of course, change and progress affects all cultures.
28. In Korea, for example, neither "Good morning" nor "Good evening" are a common greeting.
29. Instead, friends and acquaintances ask about each other's health.
30. Joy, anger, and sadness is never expressed openly.
31. Either a gentle smile or a touch express emotion.
32. Young men and women still respect their elders.
33. Their behavior and speech is well-mannered.
34. Winks between friends or a walk with a boyfriend or girlfriend have been frowned on in the past.
35. In the past neither chairs nor a bed were found in a Korean home.
36. In recent years some homes have added them.
37. In Korea, customs and rules about naming a child is also changing.
38. A childhood name and a lifelong name is given to each boy.
39. In the past, a girl or a woman were able to live her life without a name.
40. In modern Korea neither women nor men support this old custom, however.

C. Agreement with Indefinite Pronouns   Write the form of the verb in parentheses that agrees with the subject in number.

41. One of the most interesting Asian countries (is, are) Thailand.
42. Many of us (doesn't, don't) know that its name means "land of the free."
43. Most of the Thai people (makes, make) their living by farming.
44. In riverside villages almost everybody (lives, live) in houses built on stilts.
45. Many of the city workers (has, have) jobs in factories.
46. One of the scenic features of the capital city, Bangkok, (is, are) its canals.
47. Everything the people need (floats, float) down the river in colorful market boats.
48. Few of the favorite Thai pastimes (exists, exist) anywhere else in the world.
49. For example, (has, have) anyone ever heard of *takraw?*

50. Everyone in Thailand (knows, know) about this popular sport.
51. Each of the players (tries, try) to keep a ball in the air.
52. No one (touches, touch) the ball with his hands.
53. All of the parts of a person's body (is, are) used in Thai-style boxing, however.
54. Many people in Thailand also (plays, play) *mak ruk,* a game that is similar to chess.
55. One of the more popular activities (features, feature) ferocious fighting fish.
56. Few of the world's spectacles (dazzles, dazzle) viewers more than Thai classical dancing.
57. All of the movements, expressions, and costumes (tells, tell) a traditional story.
58. Each of the Thai meals (includes, include) rice or vegetables.
59. Several of the hot and cold salads (is, are) popular.
60. Many of the things in this country (offers, offer) visitors a special experience.

D. Other Problems of Agreement   Write the following sentences, correcting errors of agreement. If a sentence has no errors, write *Correct.*

61. There is quite a few islands in Japan.
62. South of the main island of Honshu are the island of Kyushu.
63. On this island there exist a respect for the old ways.
64. Here is an example of an old tradition.
65. People still goes to the public baths, called *onsen.*
66. Into the mineral water steps the bathers to relax.
67. At the beach of Ibusuki is found the thermal sands.
68. Here is one tourist who bathed in the hot sand.
69. She don't recommend it for everybody.
70. Don't they bury you in the black lava sand?
71. Above the sand appear only your face.
72. It don't matter if you have never tried it.
73. There is friendly people to help you.
74. Here on Kyushu is the city of Nagasaki.
75. Reminders of World War II still does exist.
76. From the top of Mount Inasa is seen the city's lights.
77. The city does look beautiful since its rebuilding.
78. Despite progress and modern developments, there are some of the old way of life still in evidence on Kyushu.

Persuasion

Presenting an argument gives you a chance to persuade others to agree with you. (See Workshop 6.) When you revise persuasive writing, make sure you support your opinions with specific details and respond to opposing viewpoints. Correct errors in subject-verb agreement that might detract from your message.

Revise the following draft of an argument by using the directions at the bottom of the page. Then proofread the argument, paying special attention to errors in subject-verb agreement. Also look for other grammatical errors as well as errors in capitalization, punctuation, and spelling.

¹Many people thinks Americans watch to much television. ²They points to studies showing that Americans spend more time watching television than doing anything else. ³Except sleeping and working. ⁴Others claims that television takes time from other worthwhile activities. ⁵However, there is benifits to television as well. ⁶One of the benefits are its ability to give people new experiences. ⁷Important govermental activities are showed on television. ⁸Important political events are showed on television. ⁹News about real-life tragedies are also presented. ¹⁰Television exposes people to a wide range of cultural events. ¹¹A Soap Opera or a Situation Comedy give people a chance to escape for a while from the problems and pressures of the world.

1. In sentence 4, explain "other worthwhile activities" by adding the phrase "such as reading, conversation, cultural events, and exercise."

2. Combine sentences 7 and 8 to make a sentence with a compound subject.

3. Add to sentence 10 some examples of cultural events presented on television.

4. Add this information after sentence 10: "Even popular entertainment programs can be worthwhile."

5. Divide the passage into two paragraphs.

Mother Tongue

Oh, to be in England
   If only 'arf a mo',
Where, when they speak of wireless,
   They mean a radio,

Where private schools are public
   And public schools are snobby
And insurance is assurance
   And a cop is called a bobby,

Where a traffic hub's a circus
   And up is down the street
And a sweater is a jumper
   And candy is a sweet,

Where a cracker is a biscuit
   And a trifle is dessert
And bloody is a cuss word
   And an ad is an advert,

Where gasoline is petrol
   And a stone is fourteen pound
And motorcars have bonnets
   And you take the Underground,

Where, holding up your trousers,
   It's braces that you use
And a truck is called a lorry
   And boots are really shoes,

Where a druggist is a chemist
   And the movies are the flicks
And you queue up on the pavement
   For a stall at three and six. . . .

There is no language barrier
   The tourist needs to dread
As long as he knows English
   From A to Z (no, zed).

Richard Armour

Sketch Book

THE
COUCH
POTATO
VIDEO GAME
CAMP

Learn to play video games better than
ever before. At the Couch Potato Video Game
Camp, you are guaranteed
- to improve your hand-eye
coordination
- to increase finger speed
and endurance
You will learn strategies for
- outwitting sorcerers,
wizards, and demons
- conquering alien invaders
We provide classes in
- understanding video game
fundamentals
- mastering advanced skills

SIGN UP
TODAY!

- What kind of camp would you like to run? Make up a brochure, telling what activities your camp would have.

- What are your hobbies? Describe one of your hobbies, telling what it is and why you like it.

- What are your goals for the next year? Make a list of things you would like to accomplish.

Using Verbals

- **Infinitives**
- **Participles**
- **Gerunds**

Is *playing* video games your favorite activity? Perhaps you prefer *collecting* stamps? Perhaps *swimming* is what you like best. The key words in these sentences are usually verbs, but here they are something else. When is a verb not a verb? When it is a verbal. Using verbals—infinitives, gerunds, and participles—gives you more flexibility in writing about actions.

In this handbook you will learn how to use verbals to add variety to your writing.

> An **infinitive** is a verbal that usually appears with the word *to* before it. *To* is called the **sign of the infinitive.**

You have learned that there are eight parts of speech: nouns, pronouns, verbs, adverbs, adjectives, prepositions, conjunctions, and interjections. In addition, the English language contains three other kinds of words: infinitives, participles, and gerunds. These words are called verbals.

A **verbal** is a word that is formed from a verb but acts as another part of speech. In this handbook section, you will study all three kinds of verbals. You will learn how they can add interest and variety to spoken and written sentences.

The infinitive is the easiest verbal to recognize. An **infinitive** is a form of a verb that usually appears after the word *to.*

to lift   to travel   to orbit   to launch

The word *to* is also used as a preposition. It is a preposition if it is followed by a noun or pronoun that is its object. It is the sign of the infinitive if a verb follows it.

People dreamed of flights *to the moon.* (prepositional phrase)
Not until the 1960s were people able *to succeed.* (infinitive)

Because infinitives are formed from verbs, they are like verbs in several ways. Infinitives can, for example, have objects. They can also be modified by adverbs. An infinitive and its objects and modifiers form an **infinitive phrase.** The italicized groups of words in the sentences below are infinitive phrases.

Astronauts tried *to master space.*
(*Space* is the direct object of the infinitive *to master.*)

Weightlessness began *to give astronauts several problems.*
(*Astronauts* is the indirect object and *problems* is the direct object of *to give.*)

Astronauts eventually learned *to maneuver successfully.*
(*Successfully* is an adverb modifying *to maneuver.*)

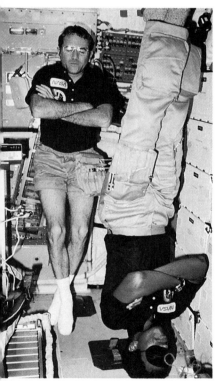

Astronauts Richard H. Truly, crew commander, and Guion S. Bluford, mission specialist, stretch out for a rest session as their space shuttle orbits Earth.

The Split Infinitive

When a modifier is placed between the word *to* and the verb in an infinitive, it is said to split the infinitive. A split infinitive sometimes sounds awkward and should usually be avoided.

Awkward   Astronauts learn to *quickly* adjust to weightlessness.
Better   Astronauts learn to adjust *quickly* to weightlessness.

Uses of Infinitives

Infinitives and infinitive phrases can be used in three ways: as nouns, as adjectives, and as adverbs. Recall that nouns are used as subjects and objects of verbs. Infinitives and infinitive phrases can be used as subjects, as direct objects, and in other ways that nouns are used.

Subject   *To move in zero gravity* is not easy. (*To move in zero gravity* is the subject of *is.*)
Direct Object   Astronauts learn *to adapt to zero gravity*. (*To adapt to zero gravity* is the object of *learn.*)

Infinitives and infinitive phrases can also be used as modifiers. If the infinitive or infinitive phrase modifies a noun or a pronoun, it is being used as an adjective. If it modifies a verb, an adjective, or an adverb, it is being used as an adverb.

Adjective   The landing on the moon was an event *to watch*. (*To watch* modifies the predicate noun *event.*)
Adverb   Pictures of the moonwalk were incredible *to see*. (*To see* modifies the predicate adjective *incredible.*)
Adverb   Millions gathered *to watch the event*. (*To watch the event* modifies the verb *gathered.*)

Practice Your Skills

A. CONCEPT CHECK

Identifying Infinitives   Write the infinitive phrases in the following sentences.

1. To travel into space was the dream of Robert Goddard.
2. This U.S. scientist began to experiment with rockets around 1908.
3. He was one of the first to take these devices seriously.

Writing **TIP**

Begin some of your sentences with infinitives and infinitive phrases instead of nouns and pronouns. Varying your sentence beginnings makes your writing livelier.

Writing Theme
Space Flight

4. His discoveries helped to make rapid progress in rocket science.
5. Goddard was able to launch rockets on high-altitude flights.
6. To send a rocket to the moon was Goddard's ultimate goal.
7. At first few other scientists bothered to listen to Goddard.
8. He was even forced to finance much of his research himself.
9. Goddard worked hard to share his vision of space flight.
10. His work made it easier for scientists to study space today.

B. DRAFTING SKILL

Using Infinitives   Write an infinitive to complete each sentence.

11. Rigorous training prepares astronauts _____ into space.
12. _____ for space missions is their chief goal.
13. Astronauts are trained to pilot a spacecraft and _____ scientific experiments in space.
14. As part of the training program, NASA invites instructors from universities _____ the astronauts various skills.
15. Space crews take classes _____ about astronomy and other subjects.
16. Astronauts also learn _____ in the harsh conditions of space.
17. Their ability _____ problems is always being tested.
18. They must know how _____ a spacecraft after it returns to the earth's atmosphere.
19. Special training prepares them _____ difficult situations and emergency landings.
20. Astronauts practice ways _____ their spacecraft in the ocean and to survive in the jungle.

C. PROOFREADING SKILL

Using Infinitives and Infinitive Phrases   Proofread the following paragraph. Then write it, correcting errors in grammar, capitalization, punctuation, and spelling. Pay particular attention to split infinitives. (7 errors)

For over twenty-five years, the Vertical Asembly Building (VAB) has stood at the John F Kennedy Space Center. Hear, people work to carefully prepare the giant rockets of the United States space program. everything from the first spacecraft to the moon to today's space shuttle has used this facility. Over seven hundred feet long and five hundred feet high. The VAB is one of the worlds' largest buildings.

FOR MORE PRACTICE
See page 606.

PARTICIPLES

A **participle** is a verbal that always acts as an adjective.

One of the principal parts of a verb is the past participle. The **past participle** is usually formed by adding *-d* or *-ed* to the present tense: *walk, walked*. The past participles of irregular verbs, however, do not follow this rule: *run, run; throw, thrown*.

Another kind of participle is called the present participle. A **present participle** is formed by adding *-ing* to the present tense of any verb: *walk, walking; hit, hitting*.

Participles may be used as parts of verb phrases: *had tossed, am throwing*. When used as verbals, however, both past and present participles always function as adjectives, modifying either nouns or pronouns. Using participles is a simple way to add information to sentences or to vary sentence beginnings.

Smiling, the batter stepped up to the plate.
(*Smiling* is a present participle modifying the noun *batter.*)

Fooled, he swung at the curve ball.
(*Fooled* is a past participle modifying *he.*)

Because participles are formed from verbs, they can have objects and be modified by adverbs. A participle and its objects and modifiers form a **participial phrase.**

Rounding third base, the runner charged toward home plate.
(*Rounding third base* is a participial phrase modifying *runner; base* is the object of the participle *rounding.*)

Especially pleased, the crowd cheered loudly.
(*Especially pleased* is a participial phrase modifying *crowd; especially* is an adverb modifying the participle *pleased.*)

A participle or participial phrase is not always at the beginning of a sentence. It should be near the noun or pronoun it modifies.

The *skilled* catcher trapped the wild pitch in his mitt.

The pitcher, *losing control,* had overthrown the ball.

Writing
TIP
Vary your sentence structure by using participial phrases in different positions. Remember to place a participial phrase near the noun or pronoun it modifies.

The fans watched the ball *sailing into the stands.*

Known as a slugger, the batter hit another home run.

Using Verbals   **599**

Practice Your Skills

A. CONCEPT CHECK

Identifying Participles   Write the participles and participial phrases in the following sentences. Then write the word each one modifies.

1. In the early days of baseball, star pitchers had a tiring job.
2. Hired by the best teams, they played almost every day.
3. Playing other positions on their off days, these players earned their pay.
4. Some pitchers truly "went the distance" for struggling teams.
5. Unprepared, the Providence, Rhode Island, team suddenly lost one of its best pitchers in the middle of the 1884 season.
6. The team, faced with the rest of the season, was in trouble.
7. Sent to the mound nearly every day, the team's other star pitcher might bow to the pressure.
8. Worried, the fans hoped that "Hoss" Radbourn would succeed.
9. Asked to do the work of two pitchers, Hoss thought he could lead the team to victory.
10. Determined, Hoss was ready for the challenge.
11. Manager Frank Bancroft, seeing no alternative, played Hoss in every game.
12. Pitching thirty-eight games in a row, Hoss beat his opponents.
13. Hoss, showing remarkable talent, won the last eighteen games of the season.
14. Continuing this streak, he won every game against the original New York Mets in the World Series.
15. Hoss's excellent record earned him an honored place in baseball's Hall of Fame.

B. DRAFTING SKILL

Sentence Combining   Combine each pair of sentences to make a sentence with a participle or participial phrase. Insert the italicized word or phrase from the second sentence into the first sentence at the place indicated by a caret.

EXAMPLE   There are many ∧ stories about the origins of team names. The stories are *interesting*.

There are many *interesting* stories about the origins of team names.

16. An old tradition ∧ is to give sports teams colorful names. The tradition is *still followed today.*

17. The San Francisco 49ers football team chose a nickname ∧. The nickname was *associated with California's history.*

18. A historical event ∧ occurred in 1849. The event was *called the Gold Rush.*

19. ∧ Treasure hunters flocked to California. They were *searching for gold.*

20. The ∧ prospectors were called the forty-niners. The prospectors were *daring.*

21. ∧ The Giants baseball team got its name by accident. The team has been *playing in San Francisco since 1957.*

22. The team ∧ was first called the Gothams. The team was *formed in New York City.*

23. In 1885, the manager ∧ proclaimed, "My big fellows! My Giants!" The manager was *impressed by a spectacular victory.*

24. The name ∧ remains. It was *based on the manager's remark.*

C. APPLICATION IN WRITING

Directions   Have you ever taught someone how to use a piece of sports equipment? Have you ever tried to explain the rules of a sport? Using sports as your topic, describe how to use or do something. Use at least two participles or participial phrases in your explanation.

FOR MORE PRACTICE
See pages 606–607.

C H E C K  P O I N T
MIXED REVIEW · PAGES 596–601

A. APPLICATION IN LITERATURE

Identify each underlined verbal in this passage by writing *Infinitive, Infinitive Phrase, Participle,* or *Participial Phrase.* If a sentence has no verbals, write *None.*

Writing Theme
Exploration

> [1]NASA simply calls it "Voyager: The Grandest Tour."
> [2]Indeed, there has been nothing like it before, nor will there ever again be anything <u>to match it</u>. . . . [3]<u>Using the gravitational pull of each planet</u> <u>to increase their speed</u>, the [two] spacecraft swooped from one marvelous world to the next. . . . [4]One by one, the mysterious objects came into view. [5]There was

spectacular Jupiter, guarded by a fiery moon; beautiful Saturn, harboring a place where life could start up; tilted Uranus, which might have been smacked by a planet-sized object; and blue Neptune, lashed by 1,200-mile-an-hour winds. . . .

[6]Voyager 2, launched from Cape Canaveral on August 20, 1977, is 3.3 billion miles from Earth, speeding along at a rate of 290 million miles a year. [7]Voyager 1, launched less than a month later, is 4.3 billion miles away, traveling at 320 million miles a year.

Ronald Kotulak, "Voyager," *The Chicago Tribune Magazine*

B. Write the verbals in the following sentences. Label each one *Infinitive, Infinitive Phrase, Participle,* or *Participial Phrase.* Write the word that each participle or participial phrase modifies.

The *Victoria,* the only ship in Ferdinand Magellan's five-ship fleet to complete the voyage around the world. Detail of a map, 1590, by Abraham Ortelius.

8. In the fall of 1519, five ships set out to reach the Far East.

9. Before that time, most ships bound for the East had sailed around Africa.

10. However, Ferdinand Magellan had studied the maps made by earlier explorers.

11. He believed that a brief voyage beyond the Americas would lead to the fabled riches of the East.

12. Convinced, Magellan set sail from Spain on a westward course.

13. This westward voyage was difficult for the ships to complete.

14. Magellan's five ships took more than a year to reach the Pacific Ocean.

15. Crossing the Pacific, the ships' crews faced starvation and disease.

16. To die at sea was a fear of many sailors.

17. In the spring of 1521, three ships finally managed to arrive in the Philippines.

18. Magellan, aiding Filipinos in a battle, was killed.

19. Reorganizing the expedition, the survivors then started their journey home.

20. One ship, carrying fewer than twenty men, returned to Spain.

21. The expedition had taken almost three years to finish.

22. It was the first expedition to sail completely around the world.

GERUNDS

A **gerund** is a verbal that is used as a noun.

A **gerund** is a verb form used as a noun. Adding *-ing* to the present tense of a verb creates a gerund. Gerunds can be used in all the ways nouns are used—as subjects, direct objects, objects of prepositions, and predicate words.

Uses of Gerunds	
Subject	*Tilting* was a popular sport in the 1400s. (*Tilting* is a gerund, the subject of *was.*)
Direct Object	The sport involved *riding.* (*Riding* is a gerund, the direct object of *involved.*)
Object of Preposition	The sport was similar to *jousting.* (*Jousting* is a gerund, the object of the preposition *to.*)

Because gerunds are formed from verbs, they can have objects and can be modified by adverbs. Because they are used as nouns, they can also be modified by adjectives and by prepositional phrases. A **gerund phrase** consists of a gerund with its objects and modifiers. Look at the following examples of gerund phrases:

Unseating a rider was the object of the sport.
   (*Unseating* is a gerund; *rider* is the object of *unseating.*)

Successfully overpowering a knight was a challenge.
   (*Overpowering* is a gerund; *successfully* is an adverb modifying *overpowering.*)

Accurate aiming contributed to the safety of the sport.
   (*Aiming* is a gerund; *accurate* is an adjective modifying *aiming.*)

A barrier, or tilt, was used for *separating contestants*.
   (*Separating* is a gerund; *contestants* is its object.)

Gerund or Participle?

Both the gerund and the present participle are created by adding *-ing* to the present tense of a verb. How can you tell whether a word is a gerund or a participle? It depends on how the word is used in a sentence. When it is used as a modifier, it is a participle. When it is used as a noun, it is a gerund.

Wearing armor shielded a knight's body.
(*Wearing armor* is a gerund phrase, the subject of *shielded.*)

Wearing armor, a knight felt safer and bolder.
(*Wearing armor* is a participial phrase modifying *knight.*)

Practice Your Skills

A. CONCEPT CHECK

Identifying Gerunds   Write the gerunds and gerund phrases in the following sentences. Label each one *Subject, Direct Object,* or *Object of Preposition.*

1. In the Middle Ages, fighting was the profession of knights.
2. However, knights were mostly interested in capturing enemies.
3. Killing an enemy in battle would mean that the knight could collect no ransom.
4. Much of a knight's life was devoted to preparing for battle.
5. A young boy in training spent his first years at home.
6. There he learned about caring for horses.
7. Later, as a page, he started handling smaller versions of weapons.
8. At fifteen or sixteen, he began acting as a servant to a knight.
9. Now called a squire, he received training as a mounted soldier.
10. Going into battle was part of a squire's duty.

B. CONCEPT CHECK

Gerund or Participle?   Write the verbals in the following sentences. Label each one *Gerund, Gerund Phrase, Participle,* or *Participial Phrase.*

11. In the 1100s, knights practiced their fighting skills in tournaments.
12. Splitting up into two sides, large numbers of knights fought mock battles.
13. Lasting all day, the battles ranged all over the countryside.

14. Losing meant that the knight either paid a ransom or lost his possessions.

15. These tournaments were famous for causing destruction and rebellions.

16. As a result, holding tournaments required the king's permission.

17. Hoping to save lives, the government and the church discouraged these events.

18. In the 1200s, jousting, or combat between two people, was introduced as an alternative to tournaments.

19. Using blunt weapons, two knights fought in an enclosed field.

20. The joust became a means of entertaining the public.

FOR MORE PRACTICE
See pages 606–607.

C H E C K ✔ P O I N T
MIXED REVIEW · PAGES 602–605

Writing Theme
Gliding

Write the verbals in the following sentences. Label each one *Gerund, Gerund Phrase, Participle,* or *Participial Phrase.* Write the word that each participle or participial phrase modifies.

1. Coasting through the air in a glider is a wonderful experience.

2. Airplanes stay aloft by using their engines for power.

3. Having no engines at all, gliders rely only on the air.

4. Airplanes tow the gliders before launching them in the air.

5. The airplanes then release the floating gliders.

6. The gliders are on their own, remaining in the air for anywhere from one to five hours.

7. Some gliders have succeeded in staying aloft for seventy hours.

8. The fascinating story of gliders began in the 1800s.

9. By the 1890s, Otto Lilienthal, a German engineer, had succeeded in making almost 2,500 glider flights.

10. Intrigued, the Wright brothers also tried gliders between 1900 and 1902.

11. Aircraft with engines soon arrived, lessening interest in gliders.

12. During World War II, developing gliders was again important.

13. Moving silently, gliders carried soldiers on surprise attacks.

14. Making a glider was also relatively easy and inexpensive.

15. To the countries fighting the war, expense was a crucial issue.

16. After the war soaring became a recreational sport.

17. By the 1970s, individuals began gliding on large kites.

18. These "hang gliders" were capable of making long flights.

19. Taking off from hillsides, their pilots floated gracefully in the air.

20. Flying like a bird has finally become a reality for people.

Writing Theme
Mountain Climbing

A. Identifying Verbals: Infinitives and Infinitive Phrases
Write the infinitives and the infinitive phrases in the following sentences.

1. To find adventure, some people climb mountains.
2. Mountain climbers are not afraid to take risks.
3. The first person to make a major climb was a French aristocrat.
4. In 1492, Antoine de Ville managed to scale Mont Aiguille near Grenoble, France.
5. To accomplish this feat took courage and skill.
6. After that climb enthusiasm for the sport began to build.
7. Among the many people to take up climbing was Leonardo da Vinci.
8. To climb in the Pennine Alps was a joy for the famous painter, sculptor, and inventor.
9. The spirit of adventure led people to try more daring climbs.
10. In time climbers strove to conquer the very highest mountains.
11. Climbers were able to reach more and more of the tallest mountain peaks.
12. Not until 1953, though, did climbers manage to conquer Mount Everest.
13. Today, there are few firsts to achieve.
14. Yet mountains still continue to lure climbers to their heights.
15. To scale mountains has become a sport for thousands of people.

B. Identifying Verbals: Participles and Participial Phrases
Write the participles and participial phrases in the following sentences. Label each one *Participle* or *Participial Phrase* and write the word it modifies.

16. The fabled conquest of the Matterhorn is one of mountain climbing's most famous tales.
17. In 1865, a group led by Edward Whymper braved this deadly peak.
18. Defying many climbers over the years, the Matterhorn had never been scaled.
19. Whymper himself had made seven attempts, failing each time.
20. Originally, Whymper had planned to climb with an experienced guide.
21. Meeting another group by chance, Whymper included them in his effort at the last minute.

22. The seven climbers ascended quickly, making steady progress.
23. Pleased with their progress, the group camped at eleven thousand feet.
24. The next day, the determined Whymper and his party reached the top.
25. Two hours later the daring group began their descent.
26. Problems developed because of an inexperienced climber, Douglas Hadow.
27. Slipping, young Hadow fell against one of the guides.
28. A rope worn from too many climbs then broke.
29. Four of the climbers fell, sliding to their death thousands of feet below.
30. Whymper's victorious climb left him haunted by its tragic results.

C. Identifying Verbals: Gerunds and Gerund Phrases Write the gerunds and gerund phrases in the following sentences. Label each one *Subject, Direct Object,* or *Object of Preposition.*

31. For years conquering Mount Everest was every climber's goal.
32. All great climbers dreamed of reaching its peak.
33. In the end a British group got credit for being the first to the top.
34. Assembling the giant expedition was Colonel John Hunt's job.
35. He started by recruiting some of the best climbers in the world.
36. Planning the climb took months of work.
37. Finally, in 1953, the moment for leaving arrived.
38. Carrying the equipment required a crew of more than three hundred porters.
39. Thirty-four local mountaineers began guiding the dangerous expedition.
40. Toward the top, teams of climbers started taking turns.
41. Getting ready for the final climb was a difficult and tense task.
42. Tom Bourdillon and R. C. Evans started climbing first.
43. They were forced back, however, after coming within three hundred feet of the summit.
44. After waiting out a heavy storm, Edmund Hillary and Tenzing Norgay then started for the top.
45. Hours later, after a risky climb, they began photographing themselves at "the top of the world."

GRAMMAR
H A N D B O O K
47

Writing Theme
Treasures from the
Sea

A. Infinitives   Write the infinitives and infinitive phrases in the following sentences.

1. To find sunken treasure is a magical dream.
2. In the 1600s, William Phips, a ship's carpenter from Boston, asked the king of England to pay for his treasure hunts.
3. Phips's arguments were strong enough to win the support of two kings.
4. To find the wreck of a well-known Spanish ship was Phips's main goal.
5. There was no reason to doubt the ship's location.
6. Everyone wanted to believe the story of its sinking in 1643.
7. According to stories, the ship continued to lie on a reef off the coast of Hispaniola.
8. Phips hoped to find a fortune in treasure.
9. After a long search, he was able to locate the ship.
10. In 1686, Phips began to bring the treasure to the surface.
11. To the delight of everyone, Phips managed to recover a fortune in gold, jewels, and silver.
12. To reward him, King James II presented Phips with seventy-five thousand dollars.
13. Later, Phips was chosen to serve as governor of the Massachusetts colony.
14. To be wealthy and powerful, however, was not in Phips's future.
15. He was unable to buy happiness and died a poor man.

B. Participles   Write the participles and participial phrases in the following sentences. Then write the word or words that each one modifies.

16. The silver fleet was an armada of Spanish ships carrying priceless treasures.
17. Each year the silver fleet brought back gold, silver, and jewels collected in the Americas.
18. Between 1713 and 1715, however, warfare interrupted the scheduled trips.
19. As a result, two years' worth of treasure accumulated, waiting for shipment to Spain.
20. The silver fleet finally sailed in July 1715, with a treasure valued at 14 million dollars.
21. Traveling in the hurricane season, the fleet ran into trouble.

22. A violent storm, striking the fleet, sank every one of the ships.
23. For centuries, tales of the destroyed fleet spread around Florida.
24. Then, in 1955, Kip Wagner, a Florida beachcomber, found a coin marked with the royal seal of Spain.
25. Wagner hunted for the missing fleet for more than three years.
26. Wagner's next find was a gold ring containing a giant diamond.
27. Searching the area by plane, Wagner found signs of the fleet.
28. Heavy equipment, removing the sand, helped in the search.
29. Divers found thousands of gold coins scattered on the ocean floor.
30. In time Wagner's group, discovering all eleven ships, uncovered more than a million dollars in treasure.

C. Gerunds   Write the verbals in the following sentences. Label each one *Gerund Phrase, Participle,* or *Participial Phrase.*

31. Gold and silver are not the only treasures found in the sea.
32. Getting energy from the sea has become even more important than extracting these precious metals.
33. Over the years people have used much of the oil found under land.
34. Now oil companies have begun taking their "black gold" from under the sea.
35. Exploring for oil takes time and money.
36. Searching for this undersea resource costs companies millions of dollars.
37. After finding oil, the companies establish giant platforms on the sea.
38. Pumping the oil to the surface, these rigs make available a natural resource with hundreds of uses.
39. Oil, of course, is not the only energy source provided by the sea.
40. Hundreds of years ago, people used water power from ocean tides for grinding wheat into flour.
41. Today, this tidal power can produce clean energy, keeping the environment safe.
42. A tidal power plant operating on France's Rance River is an example of this clean energy.
43. There, giant turbines capture the energy of the flowing water.
44. Water rushing through the turbines generates electricity.
45. In the future this electricity may prove more valuable than the gold and silver sought by treasure hunters.

Narrative and Literary Writing

Writing poetry enables you to use language to express your ideas and feelings in a uniquely personal way. (See Workshop 3.) When you revise a poem you have written, experiment with the sounds as well as the meanings of words. Try different ways of creating rhythm. For example, you can repeat a pattern of verbals.

On your paper revise the draft of a poem below. Follow the directions at the bottom of the page. Proofread your revision, paying special attention to the use of verbals. Also look for other errors in grammar, as well as errors in capitalization, punctuation, and spelling.

1 Listening for the sound of a car in the distance,
2 Looking for headlights to appear,
3 To hope for them to come,
4 Waiting . . .
5 The night is dark.
6 the shadows are my only friends.
7 Not a sound disturbs the quite.
8 Soon they will arrive.
9 Do I hear them now?
10 Will they come around the corner?
11 no, just the sound of the wind.
12 To wait is being lonely.

1. Make the words beginning the first four lines the same form by changing the infinitive in line 3 to a participle.

2. Replace the weak adjective "dark" in line 5 with a word or phrase that is more descriptive.

3. Combine the information in lines 9 and 10. Put a participial phrase beginning with "coming" into line 9.

4. Replace the vague noun "sound" in line 11 with a gerund that more precisely suggests or names a sound.

5. Make the verbals the same form in line 12 by changing the gerund phrase to an infinitive phrase.

on the LIGHT side

All in the Family

You've probably never heard the term *grubbled water.* Or *train trails.* Both are expressions created by a six-year-old on a Colorado vacation. To her, the foaming mountain rapids were grubbled. Gleaming railroad tracks stretching westward to the horizon were train trails.

"Trains," Smedley said, "and by the look of the trails, big trains."

Every family creates words, and many are both funny and useful. The following are from a collection, *Family Words,* by Paul Dickson. He loves them, he says, because they are "family traditions wrapped up in words." What words from your family can you add to his list?

Chizzly   *Chilly* plus *drizzly.* A particular kind of day.

Eardo   Condition of a dog's floppy ear when it is flipped backwards.

F.H.B.   Family Hold Back, used to let the family know that an article of food is in short supply and to hold back so that the guests will have enough.

Foiling   Peeling after sunburn.

Gummatajuma   To ride over the railroad tracks in the car, from the noise made.

Lapkin   A cloth napkin.

Musgos   Leftovers and other food that "must go."

Odoralls   Toddler's overalls.

One!   Do it now, or else. Comes from a father's "counting to three."

Pass the potatoes   Family code phrase to change the subject at the table.

Pididdle   A car with one headlight burnt out.

Show towel   One family's term for a guest towel. "Show towel" is more accurate, since guest towels are never used, even by guests.

Toad Cloth   Any dishrag that has gotten too wet and clammy to dry dishes.

Skills

Directions   One or more of the underlined sections in the following sentences may contain an error in grammar, usage, punctuation, spelling, or capitalization. Write the letter of each incorrect section. Then rewrite the section correctly. If there is no error in an item, write *E*.

> ***Example*** The <u>Pulitzer Prize</u>–winning writer N. Scott Momaday grew
>   **A**
> up on a <u>Kiowa</u> <u>reservation and</u> his books <u>show</u> his interest in
>   **B**   **C**   **D**
> the culture of Native Americans. <u>No error</u>
>   **E**
>
> ***Answer***   C—reservation, and

1. In the second century <u>B.C.</u>, Hipparchus was almost <u>exactly</u> correct in his
                  A   **B**
   estimation of the circumference of the earth. <u>It's</u> too bad there couldn't have
                                          C
   been a little conversation between Columbus and <u>him</u>. <u>No error</u>
                                     D   **E**

2. <u>Wow.</u> There <u>are</u> some squids that are not <u>quite</u> an inch long and some that are
    A   **B**   **C**
   fifty-two feet <u>long!</u> <u>No error</u>
              D   **E**

3. Highways <u>are</u> often cut through hills or <u>mountains and</u> the resulting cross
            A   **B**
   sections are wonderful <u>opportunities. To</u> view rock <u>layers</u>. <u>No error</u>
                       C   **D**   **E**

4. To show that it could be <u>done the</u> writer Thor <u>Heyerdahl, and</u> a five-person
                     A   **B**
   crew <u>sailed</u> a wood raft named *Kon-Tiki* across 4,300 miles of <u>ocean.</u> <u>No error</u>
        C   **D**   **E**

5. When light <u>passes</u> through <u>two</u> layers of air with different <u>temperatures. A</u>
            A   **B**   **C**
   mirage <u>results</u> <u>No error</u>
         D   **E**

6. Some birds are difficult to <u>identify, but</u> other birds say <u>who</u> they <u>are, pewees</u>
                     A   **B**   **C**
   and whippoorwills call out <u>their</u> own names over and over. <u>No error</u>
                       D   **E**

7. Every colony of penguins <u>include</u> a great number of <u>members. Sometimes</u>
    A B
millions of <u>them</u> large birds <u>live</u> in one rookery. <u>No error</u>
    C D E

8. Although some people <u>believe</u> that someone with epilepsy cannot live a
    A
normal <u>life the Roman</u> emperor Julius Caesar and the world conqueror
    B
<u>Alexander the Great</u> <u>was</u> both epileptics. <u>No error</u>
    C D E

9. <u>There's</u> <u>perfectly</u> preserved insects in <u>pieces</u> of amber, which is fossilized tree
    A B C
sap. Some amber pins and necklaces have <u>flies</u> in them. <u>No error</u>
    D E

10. In 1869, George Wright <u>batted</u> <u>.518, and</u> earned a salary of <u>$1,400</u>. One could
    A B C
make some interesting comparisons between Cubs player Ryne Sandberg and <u>he</u>.
    D
<u>No error</u>
    E

11. Each of the <u>two</u> <u>most serious</u> cat <u>illnesses</u> <u>are</u> preventable with a vaccine.
    A B C D
<u>No error</u>
    E

12. A supposedly crippled <u>bird, and</u> a <u>motionless</u> opossum <u>are</u> both using the
    A B C
common <u>defense</u> of trickery. <u>No error</u>
    D E

13. The row of buttons on a coat sleeve <u>seem</u> useless to <u>us, but</u> those buttons once
    A B
kept soldiers from <u>wiping</u> their noses on their sleeves. <u>Ouch!</u> <u>No error</u>
    C D E

14. <u>Leaves</u> in spring and summer <u>actually</u> <u>contains</u> all the fall <u>colors, but</u> green
    A B C D
chlorophyll masks the orange and red. <u>No error</u>
    E

15. <u>Neither</u> the liger nor the tigon <u>are</u> <u>imaginary; both</u> <u>are</u> the children of rare
    A B C D
matings between lions and tigers. <u>No error</u>
    E

Sketch Book

- If you had your own sports team, what would you name it? Play around with some interesting names.
- What is your favorite brand of clothing? Write a description of your favorite clothing and compare it to other brands.
- What do you know about your name? Where does it come from? What does it mean?

Capitalization

- **Proper Nouns and Proper Adjectives**

- **Geographical Names**

- **Organizations, History, and Time**

- **Languages, Peoples, Courses, Transportation, and Abbreviations**

- **First Words**

What's the difference between a bear and a Bear? Besides fur and shoulder pads, an important difference is capitalization. Capitalization helps readers tell these "beasts" apart in print.

In this handbook you will study the ways capitalization affects the meanings of words and sentences.

PROPER NOUNS AND PROPER ADJECTIVES

Capitalize proper nouns and proper adjectives.

A **common noun** is the name of a whole class of persons, places, things, or ideas. A **proper noun** is the name of an individual person, place, thing, or idea. A **proper adjective** is an adjective formed from a proper noun. All proper nouns and proper adjectives are capitalized.

Common Noun	Proper Noun	Proper Adjective
person	William Shakespeare	Shakespearean
country	France	French
city	Rome	Roman

There are many different types of proper nouns. The following rules and examples will help you solve problems in capitalizing proper nouns and proper adjectives.

Names and Titles of Persons

Capitalize the names of persons and also the initials or abbreviations that stand for those names.

J. M. W. Turner	**J**oseph **M**allord **W**illiam **T**urner
E. B. White	**E**lwyn **B**rooks **W**hite
Ida **B. W**ells-**B**arnett	**I**da **B**ell **W**ells-**B**arnett

Capitalize titles used with names of persons and capitalize the initials or abbreviations that stand for those titles. Capitalize the titles *Mr., Mrs., Ms.,* and *Miss.*

Mayor Diane Adare	**M**r. David Chang
Dr. T. George Bellini	**M**rs. G. H. Nelson
Lt. C. E. Morro	**M**s. Angela Ruiz

Do not capitalize titles used as common nouns.

Yesterday the **m**ayor addressed the city council.
One of the **d**octors on call is Dr. Ramirez.

Writing
TIP

Using proper nouns and adjectives helps make your meaning clear and your writing specific.

Capitalize the following titles when used alone if they refer to the current holders of the positions.

the **P**resident (of the U. S.)   the **Q**ueen (of England)

the **V**ice-**P**resident (of the U. S.)   the **P**ope

Family Relationships

Capitalize words such as *mother, father, aunt,* and *uncle* when these words are used as names.

Uncle **B**en gave **M**other a vase for her birthday.

Note that when the noun is modified by a personal pronoun, the noun is not capitalized.

My **m**other helped me make my costume for the party.

The Pronoun *I*

Capitalize the pronoun *I*.   Will **I** see you later?

Religious Names and Terms

Capitalize words referring to the Deity and to religious scriptures.

God   **A**llah   **J**esus   the **B**ible   the **K**oran

Do not capitalize the words *god* and *goddess* when they refer to mythological deities.

In Greek myths, Athena is the goddess of wisdom.

Practice Your Skills

A. CONCEPT CHECK

Proper Nouns and Proper Adjectives   Write the words that should be capitalized in each sentence.

1. My uncle, dr. carlos p. montoya, is an expert on the major religions of the world.
2. According to uncle carlos, these religions include judaism, hinduism, buddhism, confucianism, taoism, shinto, christianity, and islam.

Writing Theme
Heritage

3. jewish tradition teaches that judaism began with abraham in the Middle East.
4. The jewish religion is based on the torah, the first five books of the bible.
5. hinduism and buddhism are two religions that developed in india.
6. buddhism is based on the teachings of a prince named siddhartha gautama.
7. Two religions that developed in china are taoism, which emphasizes individual freedom, and confucianism, which is based on the teachings of confucius.
8. The oldest surviving religion of japan is shinto.
9. The christian religion derives from the teachings of jesus christ in palestine, and the islamic religion was founded in arabia by muhammad.
10. Thanks to uncle carlos, i appreciate the role of religion in the heritage of many countries.

B. APPLICATION IN LITERATURE

Correcting Proper Nouns and Adjectives   Write the following paragraphs. Correct errors in capitalization. (20 errors)

[11]"Thanksgiving is an important american holiday," poppa would say. [12]"You kids are americans, and you ought to celebrate important American holidays. [13]On thanksgiving, you eat turkey. [14]Would you want People to think you were ungrateful?" [15]Poppa came from poland, and he was very big on Holidays, and being an American. There was no arguing with him. [16]They had Turkey every year.

[17]Most of the kids in the Neighborhood had the same scene at home. [18]Some of them liked turkey, some of them didn't—but they all had it on thanksgiving. [19]They all had fathers like arthur bobowicz's Father—they came from italy, and the ukraine, and Puerto rico, and Hong kong. [20]The kids were all being raised to be americans, and everyone's Father knew that Americans eat turkey on thanksgiving.

D. Manus Pinkwater, *The Hoboken Chicken Emergency*

FOR MORE PRACTICE
See page 631.

GEOGRAPHICAL NAMES

> Capitalize major words in geographical names. Also capitalize names of sections of the United States but not compass directions.

The following are examples of geographical names:

Continents	**N**orth **A**merica, **A**sia, **E**urope
Bodies of Water	the **A**tlantic **O**cean, the **N**ile **R**iver, the **B**lack **S**ea, the **B**ay of **F**undy, the **S**uez **C**anal, **L**ake **O**ntario
Landforms	the **R**ocky **M**ountains, the **N**ullarbor **P**lain, the **K**alahari, **A**concagua, **T**ierra del **F**uego, the **V**ermilion **R**ange
Political Units	**N**ew **Y**ork **C**ity, **W**est **V**irginia, **T**hailand, the **P**rovince of **B**ritish **C**olumbia
Public Areas	**D**inosaur **N**ational **M**onument, **C**entral **P**ark, **C**herokee **N**ational **F**orest, **F**ort **M**c**H**enry, **P**oint **L**obo **S**tate **R**eserve
Roads and Highways	**I**nterstate 80, **R**oute 41, **S**tate **S**treet, **F**ifth **A**venue, **B**lue **S**tar **H**ighway

Directions and Sections

Capitalize the names of sections of the United States and proper adjectives derived from them.

Many large cities are located in the **N**ortheast.
The **S**outhwest is known for its hot, dry weather.
The **W**est has many mountain resorts.
Tornadoes sometimes sweep across the **M**idwestern prairies.

Do not capitalize directions of the compass or adjectives derived from them.

The flight **e**ast was smooth. He likes **n**orthern winters.
I drove **s**outh along the coast. The **w**estern route is scenic.

A. CONCEPT CHECK

Geographical Names   Write the words that should be capitalized in each sentence.

1. On May 29, 1953, an explorer from new zealand made history.
2. The explorer was Edmund Hillary, a mountain climber already well-known in europe and north america.
3. Hillary succeeded in reaching the top of mount everest, the highest mountain in the world.
4. According to a survey by the government of india, this mountain towers 29,028 feet.
5. It is part of the himalayas, a great mountain system that separates northern india from tibet, an area in china.
6. This system extends across southern asia, west of the great bend of the indus river and eastward to the brahmaputra river.
7. Many asian legends, including that of the Abominable Snowman, are associated with this mountain system.
8. For his climb, Hillary was knighted by the Queen of england.
9. Besides climbing mount everest, Hillary had other adventures.
10. He crossed antarctica from the pacific ocean to the South Pole.
11. In 1977, Hillary took a jet boat up the ganges river in india.
12. This river flows into the bay of bengal, in the indian ocean.
13. Hillary built schools and a hospital for the Sherpas of nepal.
14. He also established sagarmatha national park.
15. This park helped to preserve the himalayan wilderness.

B. PROOFREADING SKILL

Correct Capitalization   Write the paragraph, correcting all errors in capitalization, spelling, punctuation, and grammar. (30 errors)

As a child in the midwest, Amelia Earhart lived in Kansas, Iowa, minnesota, Missouri, and illinois. However, it was in California that she first flue an airplane. In 1928 she became the first women passanger to fly across the Atlantic ocean. Four years later she became the First Woman pilet to fly solo across the atlantic. She was also the first women to make a solo flight from new york to los angeles and back. In 1935 she became the first person. To fly from hawaii to California. She was also the first to fly solo from Los Angeles to Mexico city, then across the gulf of mexico and on to Newark, New jersey.

Two years later Amelia and her navigator, Fred Noonan, began a round-the-world Flight, flying from West to East. Leaving Lae, new guinea, they heeded for Howland island in the Pacific they disappeared without a trace.

FOR MORE PRACTICE
See page 631.

C H E C K ✔ P O I N T
MIXED REVIEW · PAGES 616–621

Writing Theme
Myths

Write the following sentences, adding capital letters where necessary. If a sentence requires no added capitalization, write *Correct*.

1. Myths are traditional stories, usually about superhuman beings.
2. These stories were passed down from one generation to the next in north america, africa, asia, and europe.
3. An american writer, t. bulfinch, became famous for his popular retelling of these stories.
4. His books introduced generations of readers to greek, roman, celtic, scandinavian, and oriental mythologies.
5. The greeks and romans used myths to help explain the world.
6. According to greek myths, thunder occurred because Zeus hurled thunderbolts from mount olympus.
7. Zeus, the supreme god, was worshiped in elevated places, including Mount Lycaeus in arcadia, mount apesas in Argolis, Mount olympus in macedonia, and mount Ida in crete.
8. Zeus was the father of heracles, one of the greatest heroes of greek mythology.
9. To complete one of his twelve labors, this son of zeus had to journey to the western edge of the ancient world.
10. poseidon ruled the waters, sometimes causing mighty storms to ravage the aegean, the ionian, or the mediterranean sea.
11. The greeks believed that winter came whenever demeter, the mother of persephone, grieved for her absent daughter.
12. Aphrodite, the goddess of love, was worshiped in greece and at mount eryx in sicily, an island off the southern tip of italy.
13. The romans, who adopted much of greek mythology, worshiped their chief god, jupiter, in a temple that graced the capitoline hill in rome.
14. Venus took the place of aphrodite, the goddess who inspired love in humans.
15. A famous statue of venus is displayed at the louvre, a french museum in paris.

ORGANIZATIONS, HISTORY, AND TIME

Capitalize the names of
- organizations
- institutions
- historical events
- documents
- periods of time
- months
- days
- holidays

Organizations and Institutions

Capitalize all the important words in the names of organizations and institutions, including their abbreviations.

Winston **P**ark **H**igh **S**chool	**P**rentice **W**omen's **H**ospital
University of **T**exas	**OAS**
Affordable **R**oofing **C**o.	**U**nited **N**ations
City of **L**ombard	**P**ark **M**iddle **S**chool

Do not capitalize such words as *school, college, church,* and *hospital* when they are not used as parts of names.

There will be a pep rally at **s**chool.
My mother is teaching two classes at the **u**niversity.
Turn left at the **c**hurch, then go right at the traffic light.

Events, Documents, and Periods of Time

Capitalize the names of historical events, documents, and periods of time.

Battle of **N**ew **O**rleans	**T**reaty of **G**hent
Civil **W**ar	**A**ge of **R**eason
Gettysburg **A**ddress	**R**econstruction

Months, Days, and Holidays

Capitalize the names of months, days, and holidays but not the names of seasons.

June	**I**ndependence **D**ay	**P**residents' **D**ay
Thursday	**M**emorial **D**ay	**a**utumn

Practice Your Skills

A. CONCEPT CHECK

Organizations, History, and Time   Write the words that should be capitalized in each sentence.

Writing Theme
Leaders in War
and Peace

1. George C. Marshall, who was born on new year's eve, 1880, made history as a soldier and a statesman.
2. After graduating from the virginia military institute, Marshall received a commission as a second lieutenant.
3. In 1918 he helped plan the final battles of world war I.
4. On september 1, 1939, world war II erupted in Europe.
5. As Chief of Staff, George C. Marshall helped make the U.S. army the greatest fighting force in history.
6. On tuesday, january 21, 1947, he was appointed Secretary of State.
7. Marshall gave an address at harvard university in late spring.
8. In this address he proposed the european recovery program.
9. This program, called the marshall plan, provided about $13 billion to help Europe rebuild after world war II.
10. Marshall, who died on october 16, 1959, is buried at arlington national cemetery.

B. REVISION SKILL

Correcting Capitalization Errors   Write the following sentences, correcting all errors in capitalization.

11. Who could have predicted that Woodrow Wilson, a former University professor, would lead the u.s. in war and peace?
12. In march 1913, president Woodrow wilson took office.
13. In the Winter of 1913, he signed the federal reserve act, which changed the banking system in the united states.
14. When he signed the declaration of war against Germany in the Spring of 1917, America entered world war I.
15. On monday, november 11, 1918, the war ended.
16. november 11 became armistice day and later veterans' day.
17. After the War, Wilson helped draw up the treaty of versailles.
18. A provision of this treaty established the league of nations, an international association to promote peace.
19. Although the Association was Wilson's idea, the United States never became a member nation.
20. Wilson left office in march 1921, with the world at peace.

FOR MORE PRACTICE
See pages 631–632.

Capitalization   **623**

LANGUAGES, PEOPLES, COURSES, TRANSPORTATION, AND ABBREVIATIONS

Capitalize the names of
- languages
- races
- nationalities
- religions
- courses
- transportation

Capitalize abbreviations:
- B.C.
- A.D.
- A.M.
- P.M.

Languages, Races, Nationalities, and Religions

Capitalize the names of languages, races, ethnic groups, nationalities, religions, and the adjectives derived from them.

Korean	**C**aucasian	**F**rench	**C**hristianity
Bantu	**H**ispanics	**N**igerian	**M**uslim

School Subjects

Do not capitalize the names of school subjects unless they are languages or unless a course name is followed by a number.

World **H**istory II   **m**athematics   **B**iology I

Ships, Trains, Aircraft, Automobiles

Capitalize the names of ships, trains, and aircraft. Capitalize brand names of automobiles.

Mayflower	*Santa Fe Chief*	*Spruce Goose*
U.S.S. Missouri	*Voyager 2*	**G**old **R**acer

Abbreviations

Capitalize the abbreviations *B.C., A.D., A.M.,* and *P.M.*

Native Americans used canoes perhaps as early as 3000 **B.C.**
Eric the Red sailed a Viking ship to Greenland in **A.D.** 982.
The plane will arrive at 10:45 **A.M.**, not 11:45 **P.M.**

Writing
TIP

Remember to place the abbreviation *A.D.* before the year and the abbreviation *B.C.* after the year.

Practice Your Skills

A. CONCEPT CHECK

Languages, Peoples, Courses, Transportation, and Abbreviations   Write the words that should be capitalized.

1. For centuries, the legend of Atlantis, an island that supposedly sank into the sea, has fascinated europeans.
2. The ancient greeks believed that the people of a large island named Atlantis once ruled the western parts of the european and african continents.
3. The tale of Atlantis first appeared in two dialogues by Plato, the *Timaeus* and the *Critias,* written in the fourth century b.c.
4. Students in philosophy I might read these dialogues, which recount the destruction of Atlantis as a result of the people's greed.
5. They might also read *The New Atlantis,* an account of an ideal state by Francis Bacon, an english writer.
6. Plato's tale may derive from accounts of volcanic eruptions that destroyed the island of Thira in 1470 b.c.
7. James Mavor, an american, tested this theory in the 1960s.
8. Aboard the research ship *chain,* Mavor sailed to the Aegean Sea to explore the sunken island of Thira.
9. This island once belonged to an ancient cretan civilization named after the legendary King Minos.
10. Mavor concluded this minoan island was the legendary Atlantis.

B. PROOFREADING SKILL

Capitalization   Rewrite this paragraph, correcting all errors in capitalization, spelling, punctuation, and grammar. (18 errors)

Late on the night of april 14, 1912, the *titanic* radioed for help. The british luxury liner, the largest Ship ever built up to that time, had struck an iceberg in the Atlantic Ocean? At 2:20 a.m. on April 15, the *titanic*, with more than fifteen hundred people still abroad, sank into the sea, survivors in lifeboats on the icy waters watched in horor. Responding to the destress call, the first rescue ship arived around 4:00 a.m. The *carpathia* picked up more than seven hundred survivors and took them to New York city. At the time of the disaster, another liner, the *californian*, was less than twenty miles away. However, no operator was on duty. To recieve the radio signal.

Writing Theme
Lost at Sea

An artist's representation of *Alvin,* a research submersible, as it explores the stern of the sunken *Titanic.*

FOR MORE PRACTICE
See page 632.

Capitalization   **625**

A. Write the words that should be capitalized in each sentence.

1. The ancient greeks originated the olympic games as part of religious festivals honoring Zeus, the ruler of the gods.
2. The first competitions were probably held in 776 b.c.
3. After the romans conquered Greece during the second century b.c., the games gradually lost their religious meaning.
4. Theodosius, a roman emperor, ended the games in a.d. 394.
5. In the 1890s, Baron Pierre de Coubertin, a french educator who was born on new year's day, organized the international olympic committee.
6. The members of this committee all spoke french or english.
7. At 2 p.m. on sunday, april 10, 1896, the marathon began.
8. A young greek shepherd won this race, earning the first gold medal for the homeland of the olympic games.
9. Jesse Owens, an african american who excelled in track and field at ohio state university, won four gold medals in 1936.
10. Because of world war II, the olympic games were canceled in 1940 and 1944.

B. Write the following sentences, adding capital letters where necessary. If a sentence needs no added capitalization, write *Correct*.

11. The french hosted the XVI olympic winter games.
12. The opening ceremonies took place in Albertville, France, on saturday, february 8, 1992.
13. One of the trains known as the tom george victor, or the tgv, brought many spectators from Paris to Albertville each day.
14. The XVI winter olympics were important for several reasons.
15. The ussr, which had won many gold medals since world war II, was no longer one nation.
16. Athletes from this former nation became the unified team.
17. Also, for the first time since 1964, german athletes marched as members of a single nation.
18. On monday, february 10, Bonnie Blair made history.
19. She became the first american woman to win a gold medal for speed skating in two different winter olympics.
20. The Olympic Games were held during both winter and summer in 1992.

The Unified Team at the opening ceremonies of the 1992 Summer Olympics in Barcelona, Spain.

Fɪʀsᴛ ᴡᴏʀᴅs

Capitalize the first word in sentences, most lines of poetry, quotations, outline entries, and the closings of letters. Capitalize the first word and all important words in the greetings of letters and in titles.

Sentences

Capitalize the first word of every sentence.

Did you see that movie about baseball?
The main character is a farmer who builds a baseball field.

Poetry

Capitalize the first word in most lines of poetry.

Sometimes in modern poetry, the lines of a poem do not begin with a capital letter. The following poem shows the traditional style for capitalization of poetry.

> **G**aily bedight,
> **A** gallant knight,
> **I**n sunshine and in shadow,
> **H**ad journeyed long,
> **S**inging a song,
> **I**n search of Eldorado.
> **Edgar Allan Poe, "Eldorado"**

Quotations

Capitalize the first word of a direct quotation.

Jennifer exclaimed, "**T**his book would make a great movie!"

Do not capitalize the first word of the second part of a divided quotation unless it starts a new sentence.

> "**I** think," replied Sasha, "**t**hat book was made into a very popular movie."
> "**Y**ou are right," said Dan. "**T**he movie was made in 1990."

Writing TIP

To add a lively touch to your writing, try using a direct quotation now and then.

Outlines

Capitalize the first word in each entry of an outline.

I. **M**otion pictures
   A. **S**tory lines
      1. **O**riginal scripts
      2. **B**ook adaptations
   B. **C**ostume design

Letters

Capitalize all the important words in the greeting of a letter.

Dear **M**s. **H**ardin: **D**ear **D**r. **M**artinez: **D**ear **M**rs. **W**ong:
Dear **M**adam: **D**ear **P**ublisher: **D**ear **A**nton,

Do not capitalize the word *or* or *and* in a greeting.

Dear **S**ir or **M**adam: **D**ear **M**r. and **M**rs. **C**ortesi:

In the closing of a letter, capitalize only the first word of the phrase.

Sincerely yours,   **Y**ours truly,

Titles

Capitalize the first word, the last word, and all important words in the titles of books, poems, short stories, articles, newspapers, magazines, plays, motion pictures, works of art, television programs, and musical compositions.

Articles (the words *a, an,* and *the*), conjunctions, and prepositions with fewer than five letters are not usually considered important words. However, note that an article, a conjunction, or a preposition used as the first or last word of a title must be capitalized.

Book	***T**he **I**sland of the **B**lue **D**olphins*
Poem	"**T**he **D**ream **K**eeper"
Story	"**T**o **B**uild a **F**ire"
Article	"**H**arnessing **N**uclear **F**usion"
Play	***T**he **S**ound of **M**usic*
Magazine	***R**eader's **D**igest*
Movie	***F**ield of **D**reams*

Writing **TIP**

The titles of books, plays, magazines and newspapers, and movies are underlined when typed or written. The titles of poems, short stories, and articles are enclosed in quotation marks.

Practice Your Skills

A. CONCEPT CHECK

First Words and Titles   Write the words that should be capitalized in the following letter.

dear cecily,

    have you seen any good movies lately? I just saw *white Fang* on videotape. it is based on the novel *White fang* by Jack London. it is about a wolf who is tamed and lives with people. "this movie," one critic said, "is dynamite entertainment." was that critic ever right!

    Mom told me that other books by Jack London have also been made into movies. According to Mom, "the movie version of *the call of the wild* is great!" I'm going to see if the movies *adventures of martin eden* and *the sea wolf* are on videotape. mom suggested that I compare the movies with the books for my report. Here is the first part of my outline:

  I. the works of Jack London
      A. the stories in his books
      B. movie adaptations

    Why don't you rent the videotape *white fang* and let me know what you think of it?

your friend,
angelo

B. PROOFREADING SKILL

Correcting Errors   Write the paragraphs, correcting all errors in capitalization, spelling, punctuation, and grammar. (18 errors)

    Lewis Carroll's classick tale *alice's adventures in wonderland* was published in 1865. in this imaginative story, Alice tries to recal a poem that she mistakenly thinks begins like this:

  how doth the little crocodile
  improve his shiny tail,

    alice then meets extraordinary characters. As she wanders through Wonderland. Suddenly, she hears her sister exclaim, "wake up, Alice dear!" it had all been a dreem!

    In 1951, Walt Disney produced an animated movie titled *alice in wonderland,* which was based on the book. since then, people of all ages have enjoyed the delightfull cartoon characters romping through Wonderland in the movie?

Writing Theme
Books into Movies

Alice, the Mad Hatter, and the White Rabbit from Walt Disney's 1951 animated version of *Alice in Wonderland.*

FOR MORE PRACTICE
See page 632.

Writing Theme
On Stage

Write each sentence, correcting all errors in capitalization.

1. According to the *Information Please almanac,* some of the most popular musicals on Broadway were adapted from other famous works.
2. In 1981 Andrew lloyd Webber set poems to music in *cats.*
3. Webber selected poems from *Old possum's Book of practical cats* by T. s. eliot.
4. Frank Rich of the *New york times* said, "the songs—and *Cats* is all songs—give each cat his or her voice."
5. The most popular song from this Musical was "memory."
6. In the musical *annie,* the most loved Song was "Tomorrow."
7. The first line from this song begins this way:
   the sun will come out tomorrow.
8. *Annie* features popular characters from *Little orphan annie,* a comic strip by harold gray.
9. The strip first appeared in the *new york Daily News* in 1924.
10. The musical *hello, Dolly!* is based on *The matchmaker,* a Play written by thornton Wilder in 1954.
11. This play is a revision of Wilder's earlier play, *the merchant of Yonkers.*
12. the Idea for *The Merchant of yonkers* came from an austrian play by Johann nestroy.
13. in alan lerner and frederick loewe's *My fair lady,* professor Henry Higgins and flower seller eliza Doolittle are the main characters.
14. *"my Fair Lady,"* Brooks atkinson said in the *New York times,* "Is the finest musical play in years."
15. It is based on george bernard Shaw's Comedy *Pygmalion* that mocks the english class system.
16. Shaw adapted the greek myth of pygmalion and galatea.
17. according to this myth, Pygmalion made a Statue of the perfect woman, galatea, which then came to Life.
18. Like *Hello, dolly!* and *my Fair Lady, Oklahoma!* is based on an earlier play, *Green grow the lilacs,* by Lynn Riggs.
19. *Oklahoma!* was the First musical on which richard rodgers and oscar hammerstein II collaborated.
20. they later wrote several more musicals together, including *south Pacific, The King and i,* and *The sound of music.*

GRAMMAR
H A N D B O O K
48

Writing Theme
The American West

A. Capitalizing Proper Nouns and Adjectives   Write the words that should be capitalized in each sentence.

1. i admire women who braved the american frontier.
2. narcissa prentiss whitman and her husband, dr. marcus whitman, were missionaries and teachers of the bible.
3. She was the first white woman to follow the oregon trail.
4. She and her husband settled in waiilatpu.
5. henrietta chamberlain king helped her husband, captain richard king, build a cattle ranch near brownsville, texas.
6. mrs. king dealt with mexican settlers and union soldiers.
7. After the captain's death, henrietta ran the king ranch alone.
8. My great-grandmother grew up in what is now wyoming.
9. She told grandpa stories about teaching in south pass city.
10. i would like to write about frontier women like her.

B. Capitalizing Geographical Names   Write the words that should be capitalized in each sentence.

11. The colorado river, one of the longest rivers in north america, is a source of fresh water in the american southwest.
12. This river flows across five states—colorado, utah, arizona, nevada, and california—and ninety miles of mexico.
13. The colorado begins at la poudre pass in the rocky mountains.
14. Snows from the tetons and the uintas melt into the river.
15. The green river, the san juan river, and the gunnison river flow into the colorado.
16. Over time, the river formed the walls of the grand canyon.
17. Each year tourists visit grand canyon national park.
18. The hoover dam on the colorado provides electricity for southern california.
19. The city of los angeles gets its water from the colorado.
20. The colorado river mouth empties into the gulf of california.

C. Capitalizing Organizations, History, and Time   Write the words that should be capitalized in each sentence.

21. The United States and Spain signed a treaty in february 1819.
22. The adams-onis treaty drew up a western boundary for the U. S.
23. The mexican war resulted from long-standing border disputes.
24. When Texas became a state in december 1845, Mexico broke off diplomatic relations with the United States.

25. On may 13, 1846, congress declared war on Mexico.
26. American and Mexican forces had clashed at the battle of palo alto.
27. On christmas day, American troops won at El Brazito.
28. The treaty of guadalupe hidalgo, signed on february 2, 1848, recognized the Rio Grande as the Mexico-Texas border.
29. As a result of the mexican war, the United States gained more than 525,000 square miles.
30. This land is known as the mexican cession.

D. Capitalizing Languages, Peoples, Courses, Transportation, and Abbreviations   Write the words that should be capitalized in each sentence.

31. american history I classes study native american cultures.
32. The hohokam were a group of north american indians.
33. They lived between 300 b.c. and a.d. 1400 in what is now Arizona.
34. This was long before Columbus's ships—the *niña,* the *pinta,* and the *santa maría*—reached the West Indies.
35. The hohokam lived together in small farming villages.
36. Sometime between 300 b.c. and a.d. 500, the hohokam built their first irrigation canal.
37. After a.d. 500, they built ball courts like those of the maya.
38. The hohokam disappeared during the early fifteenth century.
39. The hohokam may have been the ancestors of the pima indians.
40. The name may be a pima term meaning "those who have vanished."

E. Capitalizing First Words and Titles   Write the words that should be capitalized in each sentence.

41. Painter georgia O'Keeffe lived in the New Mexico desert.
42. The drawing *the maid of athens* inspired her to try painting.
43. Her high school yearbook was called the *Mortar board yearbook.*
44. it contained a rhyme about her.
45. "o is for O'Keeffe, an artist divine;
    her paintings are perfect and her drawings are fine."
46. Her paintings include *summer days* and *Ranchos church.*
47. they capture the stark beauty of the Southwest.
48. O'Keeffe said, "i found my inspirations and painted them."
49. "it's mostly a lot of nerve," she also said, "and a lot of very, very hard work."
50. In 1976 her autobiography, *Georgia o'Keeffe,* was published.

Writing Theme
International Travel

A. Rewrite the following letter, correcting the words that should be capitalized.

dear andy,

You asked me, "what is it like to live in australia?" We live in a state called the northern territory on a large sheep station, or ranch, called clonkilty. it is named after the irish village my great-grandparents came from. Have you heard of a book called *a town like alice?* It's about our nearest town, alice springs, which is one hundred kilometers away, almost in the center of australia. Alice springs began as a station on the telegraph line from adelaide in the south to darwin in the north. When we go to town, we can drive down the stuart highway, but we usually fly in our airplane, *the southern cross*. Living so far away from town, i have to attend alice springs's school of the air. That means I use a two-way radio to talk to my teacher, mrs. abruzzi, and my classmates. Last week i played beethoven's *moonlight sonata* over the radio. The whole class meets in alice springs twice a year. In may we attend the camel cup to watch the camel races, and in august we go to the henley-on-todd regatta to watch the boat races. the todd river is dry, so the boats are carried by people!

My older brother, michael, goes to essex house school in sydney, where he lives with aunt janet, my mom's sister. sydney, australia's largest city, is famous for its beautiful bay, the sydney harbour bridge, and the sydney opera house. Most australians live in cities in the southeast, like sydney and melbourne. But i love clonkilty. I like riding around the station on my horse beau, but dad says, "give me a land rover anytime!" (It's like a jeep.) i wish you could visit the australian outback. Please write and tell me more about florida.

your pal,
jamie

B. Write the words that should be capitalized in each sentence.

1. At 10:00 a.m. on september 23, 1988, michael palin walked down the stairs of the reform club in london, england.
2. palin, a british actor and writer, was about to begin circling the world as Phileas Fogg had done.
3. phileas fogg is a fictional character in a jules verne novel.

4. verne published *around the world in eighty days* in 1873 after gaining great popularity in 1870 with his science-fiction adventure, *twenty thousand leagues under the sea.*
5. In the novel, members of the reform club challenge fogg to circle the globe in eighty days.
6. in 1873, this challenge seemed absurd.
7. when palin attempted the journey in 1988, however, people could circle the earth in less than two days by airplane.
8. However, with the support of the british broadcasting company, or BBC, palin tried to re-create phileas fogg's journey.
9. like fogg, palin traveled by boat, train, and other means of transportation available in 1873.
10. unlike fogg, he was accompanied by a television crew from the bbc.
11. The bbc filmed palin's extraordinary journey for a travel documentary.
12. Palin and the film crew sailed across the english channel on the ship *horsa.*
13. Once in paris, france, Palin boarded the *orient express* for a train trip through europe.
14. After a scenic ride through austria, Palin got off the *orient express* in venice, italy.
15. There he boarded the ship *espresso egitto.*
16. The ship crossed the adriatic sea and sailed to greece, crete, and egypt.
17. As the ship approached the coast of egypt, palin thought about alexander the great.
18. Alexander, a mighty greek king, had conquered egypt around 332 b.c.
19. Palin then traveled through arabia, where many people are muslims, worshippers of allah.
20. he visited india, china, singapore, and japan.
21. he crossed the united states by train, dog sled, and balloon.
22. Palin sailed across the atlantic ocean on the ship *leda maersk.*
23. Finally, he arrived back in great britain on december 12, 1988.
24. By 4:55 p.m. of that seventy-ninth day, he once again stood in front of the reform club, just as fogg had.
25. "my journey gave me a sense of global scale," he said, "of the size and variety of this extraordinary planet."

WRITING CONNECTIONS

Elaboration, Revision, and Proofreading

Revise this portion of a report by using the directions at the bottom of the page. Then proofread your paper, paying special attention to correcting errors in capitalization. Also look for errors in grammar, punctuation, and spelling.

1Alice Walker is an important african-american Novelist, Poet, and Social Activist. **2**She is perhaps best known for her novel <u>The color purple</u>. **3**It won a pulitzer prize and an American Book Award. **4**Walker was born on febuary 9, 1944 in Eatonton, georgia. **5**She was the youngest of eight children in a family of share-croppers. **6**Growing up poor in the south was offen difficult for Walker. **7**When she was eight, she was playing with her Brothers, and a shot from one of there BB guns struck her right eye. **8**She was blinded and scar tissue covered the eye. **9**"I used to pray every night that i would wake up and somehow it would be gone." **10**Finally, when she was 14, she visited her older Brother Bill, who took her to a Hospital. **11**They operated on her eye. **12**"I was a changed person," She said.

1. Add sentence 3 to sentence 2 as a subordinate clause beginning with "which."

2. Add the explanatory words "Walker said" after the quotation in sentence 9.

3. Replace the vague pronoun "they" in sentence 11 with the more precise noun "doctors."

4. Explain the result of the operation by adding the clause "and because the scar was gone, Walker no longer felt ugly and shy" to sentence 11.

5. Divide the passage into paragraphs.

Informative Writing: Reports

Writing a report gives you a chance to explore a topic in depth. (See Workshop 8.) When you revise a report, make sure that you have presented all the information your readers will need. Also check the accuracy of your facts and make sure you have used proper capitalization.

Showers, Clearing Later in the Day

```
   !! !! !!    ! !    !
 !!!!!!!! !!!! !! !!!
 !!!!!!!!!!!!!!!!!!!!!!!!!
 !!!!!!!!!!!!!!!!!!!!!!!!!
 !!!!!!!!!!!!!!!!!!!!!!!!!!       !!!!!
   !!!!!!!! !!!!!!!!!!!
 **!!!!!!!!!!!
       !!  ! !!
       * ! * !
              .. *- ! ! ...
               *
                .

                    .


          *
          .
```

Eve Merriam

- Make your own poem or drawing using various punctuation marks.
- Write a description of a storm you experienced recently.
- Tell about a time when someone misunderstood something you said or wrote. Use dialogue as you write about this experience.

Punctuation

When do we get to cook Dad?

Lectro RANGE

Is Dad the cook or the meal? A single mark of punctuation can change the entire meaning of a sentence. Punctuation marks tell you when to pause or to stop completely. They interrupt and add emphasis. They link and they clarify.

In this handbook, you will learn how you can use punctuation to point readers toward your meaning.

ＥND MARKS

> Use a **period,** a **question mark,** or an **exclamation point** to end a sentence.

The tone of voice you use to communicate a message tells a great deal about what you are saying. Your tone may tell that your message is a complete thought, that it is a question, or that it is something about which you are very excited. When you write, punctuation marks called **end marks** do the job your tone of voice does when you speak.

End marks show where sentences end. There are three kinds of end marks: the **period,** the **question mark,** and the **exclamation point.**

The Period

Use a period at the end of a declarative sentence.

A **declarative sentence** is a sentence that makes a statement. You use it to tell something, that is, to give information.

> The Statue of Liberty is more than 150 feet tall.
> It stands on Liberty Island in New York Harbor.

Use a period at the end of an imperative sentence.

An **imperative sentence** is a sentence that makes a request or tells someone to do something. It is followed by a period except when it expresses a strong emotion. Then it is followed by an exclamation point.

> Please board the boat carefully.   Watch your step!

Use a period at the end of an indirect question.

An **indirect question** tells what someone asked, without using the person's exact words. If you use the exact words of a person's question, however, the question is a **direct question.** A direct question ends with a question mark. This question mark should always appear within the quotation marks that set off the person's exact words.

Indirect Question	The tour guide asked if anyone knew who wrote the poem on the statue's base.
Direct Question	Dominic asked, "Who wrote the poem?"

The Question Mark

Use a question mark at the end of an interrogative sentence.

An **interrogative sentence** is a sentence that asks a question.

When was the statue erected?   Who built the statue?

The Exclamation Point

Use an exclamation point at the end of an exclamatory sentence and after an interjection.

An **exclamatory sentence** is a sentence that expresses strong feeling. An **interjection** is a word or group of words that expresses strong feeling.

Exclamatory Sentence	Oh, what a beautiful statue it is!
Interjections	Fantastic! Impressive! Great view!

You may also use an exclamation point at the end of an imperative sentence that expresses strong feeling.

Stop! Get back in line!

Exclamation points can be used to add more feeling or emphasis to declarative sentences.

The observation deck of the statue is closed for repairs.
Deck closed! Danger ahead!

Practice Your Skills

CONCEPT CHECK

End Marks   In these sentences end marks are used incorrectly or are missing. Rewrite each sentence using the correct end mark.

1. Dad asked if I knew what *Liberty Enlightening the World* is?
2. I replied, "It's the Statue of Liberty, isn't it."
3. The people of France gave Lady Liberty, designed by Frédéric Auguste Bartholdi, to the United States

Glorious Lady Freedom (1985–1986), Moneca Calvert. Winner of the Great American Quilt Contest, 1986. The Museum of American Folk Art, The Scotchgard Collection of Contemporary Quilts.

4. Lady Liberty raises a torch in one hand and grasps a tablet with the date of the Declaration of Independence in the other?
5. Do you know why this majestic structure is so important
6. It symbolizes a new life for immigrants?
7. Could anything other than Lady Liberty have been such a powerful symbol!
8. For more than one hundred years, immigrants have been welcomed by the statue!
9. If you visit it, read Emma Lazarus's poem on its base! The poem is beautiful.
10. How inspiring? What a magnificent tribute it is to America.

Other Uses of the Period

Without periods, sentences would run together, and initials and titles would run into names. Abbreviations would look like words. The letters and numbers of outlines and lists would run into the words beside them. Without periods, your writing would be so confusing that no one could understand it.

Use a period after initials and after most abbreviations.

L. L. Corum	Mr. Joe Dawson, Jr.	10:00 A.M.
Sept.	Tues.	4 hr. 16 min.

Some abbreviations do not require periods. When you are not sure whether to use periods following the letters of an abbreviation, look up the abbreviation in a dictionary.

m (*meters*)   FM (*frequency modulation*)   km (*kilometers*)

TIP

Dictionaries vary in their use of periods with abbreviations. Check with your teacher about which dictionary to use.

Use a period after each number or letter that shows a division of an outline or precedes an item in a list.

Outline	List
I. Automobile racing	1. Formula One racing
A. Racing courses and tracks	2. Sports car racing
1. Road-racing course	3. Indy car racing
2. Oval track	4. Stock car racing
B. Major events	5. Drag racing
1. Le Mans	6. Super Vee racing
2. Indianapolis 500	7. Sprint car racing

Use a period between numerals representing dollars and cents and before a decimal.

$25.95   167.58   66.6%

Practice Your Skills

A. CONCEPT CHECK

Periods   Add and delete periods in these sentences.

1. How are A J Foyt, Sr, and Al Unser, Sr, alike?
2. Both have won the Indianapolis 500, or the Indy 500, four times
3. The Indy is held in Indianapolis, Ind, on Memorial Day weekend
4. The race begins promptly at 11:00 AM and lasts between 2 hr 30 min and 4 hr
5. The oval track at the speedway is 2½ (or 25) miles long
6. Drivers race for 500 miles (805 km.), often at speeds greater than 200 m.p.h.
7. Foyt and Unser now have competition from their sons, A J Foyt, Jr, and Al Unser, Jr
8. Other racers include Mario G Andretti and his son Michael
9. In 1990, Al Unser, Jr, was the highest-paid driver of Indy-style cars
10. He earned about $1,936,83300 in that year!

B. DRAFTING SKILL

Periods in an Outline   Rewrite this outline, adding and deleting periods and capitalizing the first words of the entries.

    I stock car racing.
      A type of cars
        1 late-model sedans
        2 steel bodies.

Writing Theme
Indianapolis 500

FOR MORE PRACTICE
See page 669.

Use a **comma** before the conjunction in a compound sentence and to separate items in a series.

When you speak, your pauses and the tone of your voice punctuate what you are saying. However, when you write, commas indicate your pauses and show which words belong together.

Commas in Compound Sentences

Use a comma before the conjunction that joins the clauses of a compound sentence.

Two simple sentences joined by a conjunction become a compound sentence made up of independent clauses.

> Matt photographed the event, and he sold his pictures to the newspaper.
> Most of his photographs were beautiful, but some were blurry.

A comma is not required in a very short compound sentence in which the parts are joined by *and.* However, always use a comma before the conjunctions *but* and *or.*

> Marilena photographed the event and Tony reported it.
> Marilena photographed the event, but Tony reported it.

A comma is not required before the conjunction that joins the parts of a compound verb unless there are more than two parts.

> Erin entered and won the photography contest.
> That camera focuses, flashes, and rewinds automatically.

Practice Your Skills

A. CONCEPT CHECK

Commas in Compound Sentences Rewrite the following sentences, adding and deleting commas where necessary.

1. Margaret Bourke-White had always wanted to be a biologist but she discovered photography in college.

2. She had to make a decision and it was not an easy one.
3. Would she be a biologist or would she be a photographer?
4. Bourke-White finally decided on a career in photography and she became a pioneer of the photo-essay form of journalism.
5. She organized, and published her photos in books and magazines.
6. During World War II, she became the first U.S. woman war correspondent and she photographed battle scenes.
7. Once she was on a ship that was shot at hit and sunk.
8. She survived the attack, and went on to photograph the war.
9. Her photos stunned shocked and upset many Americans.
10. The war photography helped make Bourke-White famous but it was just a small part of her award-winning work.

B. DRAFTING SKILL

Achieving Clarity with Commas   Combine each pair of sentences to form a compound sentence or verb. Add commas and appropriate conjunctions where necessary.

11. Who are *paparazzi*? What do they do?
12. *Paparazzi* are professional photographers. They earn a living by taking and selling their pictures.
13. They may be employees of newspapers. They may be freelancers.
14. Not all professional photographers are *paparazzi*. Some of them are.
15. *Paparazzi* specialize in taking pictures of well-known people. The celebrities do not pose for the pictures.
16. Many people enjoy seeing famous people in candid photos. *Paparazzi* provide such pictures.
17. *Paparazzi* follow celebrities. They photograph celebrities.
18. They take pictures. They do not ask permission to do so.
19. Celebrities may know they're being photographed. They may not.
20. *Paparazzi* stalk the celebrities. They hide near their homes.
21. Many celebrities dislike *paparazzi*. They avoid them.
22. *Paparazzi* followed Elizabeth Taylor. They photographed her.
23. Taylor didn't like the intrusion. She wanted it stopped.
24. She tried to keep her privacy. She wasn't always successful.
25. Should *paparazzi* be able to take candid pictures of celebrities? Should they be stopped?

FOR MORE PRACTICE
See page 669.

Commas in a Series

Use a comma after every item in a series except the last.

The three or more items in a series can be nouns, verbs, adjectives, adverbs, phrases, independent clauses, or other parts of a sentence.

Kristin, Kerry, and Tessa ride their bikes to school. (nouns)
Ted located, patched, and sealed the leak in his tire. (verbs)
I pedaled quickly, steadily, and calmly. (adverbs)
The racing route wound through the park, over the bridge, and onto the city streets. (prepositional phrases)
The bicycle race was over, the crowd cheered, and Terrel accepted the first-place trophy. (independent clauses)

In the examples above, a comma followed by a conjunction precedes the last item in each series. That comma is always used.

If you can use *and* between two or more adjectives that precede a noun and if you can reverse the order of the adjectives without changing the meaning, use a comma after each adjective except the last one.

That crowded, narrow path is a long, winding, bumpy trail.

If two or more adjectives preceding a noun work together to express a single idea, do not use commas between the adjectives.

Luis wants a *big red* bike and *blue racing* skates.

Use commas after the adverbs *first, second, third,* and so on, when these adverbs introduce items in a series.

There are three rules of bicycle safety: first, keep your bike repaired; second, wear a helmet; third, follow the rules of the road.

Practice Your Skills

A. CONCEPT CHECK

Commas in a Series   Write the following sentences, adding commas where needed. If a sentence is correct, write *Correct.*

1. The annual spring bicycle rally was held today.
2. Local businesses sponsored organized and monitored the event.

3. The schools the police department and the recreation center had encouraged riders of all ages to participate in the rally.
4. Riders wove in, out, and in again through the obstacle course.
5. Cyclists sped down the streets over hills and into the park.
6. To join the rally, riders first paid a small fee; second wore helmets; and third demonstrated bicycle safety procedures.
7. You joined the race you pedaled hard and you were in front.
8. You wanted to win, but so did Tanya, Julio, and Jackson.
9. They were strong eager and fast competitors.
10. Your determination, your hard training, and your new bike helped you win.

B. REVISION SKILL

Achieving Clarity   Rewrite the following paragraphs, adding commas where necessary to help make the meaning clear. Then write five sentences of your own that contain items in a series.

¹¹Did you know that several years ago a popular musical featured performers on roller skates? ¹²The dancers in *Starlight Express* skated glided and sped across the stage. ¹³They skated up down over and under elaborate stage ramps. ¹⁴Their dynamic athletic and energetic skating dazzled audiences.
¹⁵This musical health concerns and innovative roller skates have all helped to revive interest in skating. ¹⁶The new skates have wheels down the middle they glide easily and they have an interesting name—Rollerblades. ¹⁷People wear them at rinks on streets and in parks. ¹⁸Rollerblades are fun fast and dangerous. ¹⁹Beginning users should first wear kneepads and elbow pads; second practice in traffic-free areas; and third learn to brake properly. ²⁰Beginners usually find that Rollerblading is an enjoyable invigorating pastime.

C. PROOFREADING SKILL

Commas in a Series   Rewrite the following paragraph, correcting all errors in capitalization, punctuation, and spelling. (15 errors)

As a baby a toddler and a child, you had your "wheals." You rode in strollors, on tricycles, and in little red wagans. Then you got a bicycle you learned to ride it and you could get from place to place on it. In just a few years. You will, first aply for; second test for; and third recieve a learner's permit to drive a car. You are impatiently, and excitedly awating the day when you can drive.

Bicycle race at the 1992 Summer Olympics in Barcelona, Spain.

FOR MORE PRACTICE
See page 669.

COMMAS THAT SET OFF
SPECIAL ELEMENTS

> Use **commas** to set off introductory elements, interrupters, nouns of direct address, and appositives.

In speaking, you pause to indicate the presence of a special element such as an interruption. In writing, punctuation does the work of these pauses.

Special elements add specific information to a sentence, but they are not essential. Any sentence is complete without its special elements.

Commas After Introductory Elements

Use a comma to separate an introductory word, phrase, or clause from the rest of the sentence.

Nervously, I played a concerto for the audition.
After my last audition, I had practiced the concerto daily.
Because I had practiced for hours, I played the concerto
   perfectly during the audition.

If the pause after a short introductory element would be very brief, you may omit the comma. Note that it is also correct to use a comma in these instances.

At first I was unsure of my playing ability.
Finally it was my turn.

Commas with Interrupters

Use commas to set off interrupters.

An interrupter is a word or words that break, or interrupt, the flow of thought in a sentence. The commas around an interrupter indicate a pause before and after the interruption.

I didn't expect, however, to get the job.
So many people, I thought, play as well as I do.
I was chosen, nevertheless, as the new orchestra member.

Practice Your Skills

A. CONCEPT CHECK

Commas with Special Elements Rewrite the following dialogue, adding commas where necessary.

1. JOE: Our grandma I suppose is not what you would call a traditional grandmother.
2. KIM: True she doesn't stay home as some grandmothers do.
3. JOE: In fact Grandma is seldom at home.
4. KIM: You can usually find her at the health club however.
5. JOE: Since she manages it you would expect her to be there.
6. KIM: I wouldn't however expect her to teach aerobic dance classes as well.
7. JOE: You do remember I imagine that Grandma was a professional dancer when she was younger.
8. KIM: Yes I have seen pictures of her onstage.
9. JOE: I for one am proud of Grandma and her career.
10. KIM: Indeed she's a great grandmother and manager.

B. DRAFTING SKILL

Sentence Combining Rewrite these sentences to place the words in parentheses at the caret. The new material is either an introductory element or an interrupter.

11. Some dog trainers ∧ specialize in teaching dogs to help visually impaired people. (I have learned)
12. ∧A good trainer can teach a dog to guide a sightless person. (in the course of several months)
13. Not just any dog ∧ can be a guide dog. (however)
14. ∧A dog must be obedient, good-tempered, and intelligent to qualify for training. (in fact)
15. ∧Trainers like Evan Rogers begin the dogs' special training. (when the future guide dogs are a little over a year old)
16. Rogers ∧ helps a dog get used to its harness. (at first)
17. He ∧ teaches the dog to obey commands. (of course)
18. ∧Rogers teaches the dog to guide a person safely across streets. (in addition)
19. ∧He works with both the dog and its future owner. (finally)
20. A good guide dog ∧ will give its owner greater independence. (according to Rogers)

FOR MORE PRACTICE
See page 670.

Writing Theme
America at Work

Commas with Nouns of Direct Address

Use commas to set off nouns of direct address.

You often address by name the person to whom you are speaking. When you do this, you are using a **noun of direct address.** Nouns of direct address are the words you use to name the persons you address.

> Yes, Sara, members of Congress serve two-year terms.
> Sal, do you know when Clare Boothe Luce served in Congress?

Commas with Appositives

Use commas to set off most appositives.

An **appositive** is a word or group of words used directly after another word to explain it. Most appositives are nouns. Nouns used as appositives are called **nouns in apposition.** When an appositive adds extra information about the word preceding it, the appositive is set off with commas. Note the italicized phrase in the following sentences:

> Lynn Martin, *the secretary of labor,* had served in Congress.
> The legislative branch of the federal government, *or Congress,* is responsible for lawmaking.

When an appositive is necessary for understanding the meaning of a sentence, it is not set off with commas.

> The New York congresswoman Bella Abzug was known for her support of federal jobs programs.

Practice Your Skills

A. CONCEPT CHECK

Commas with Direct Address and Appositives   Rewrite the sentences. Add commas where necessary. If a sentence has no errors, write *Correct.*

1. Theo and Maria who was the first woman in Congress?
2. Jeannette Rankin a Republican from Montana was.
3. That's right Maria; she was elected to the House of Representatives the lower house of Congress in 1916.

4. That was before women had national voting rights or suffrage.
5. Congresswoman Rankin supported women's voting rights.
6. She encouraged others to support these rights too Maria
7. In 1920, Theo women gained national suffrage.
8. Rankin was a pacifist a person who doesn't believe in war.
9. As a pacifist, she voted against entering the "war to end all wars," World War I.
10. In 1918, she ran for the Senate the upper house of Congress.
11. Rankin lost the election Maria and left Congress in 1919.
12. However, Rankin returned to Congress in 1941, only months before Pearl Harbor Naval Base a U. S. base in Hawaii was attacked.
13. Franklin Roosevelt the President at the time asked Congress to declare war.
14. For a second time, Rankin still a pacifist voted against war.
15. Maria and Theo Rankin's vote reflected her beliefs about war.

B. REVISION SKILL

Commas with Appositives   The following paragraph has a choppy, abrupt writing style. Rewrite the paragraph, making the writing style smoother by combining sentences and using the underlined words as appositives. Remember to punctuate all appositives correctly.

Barbara Jordan became a member of Congress in 1973. She was a Texas Democrat. She was the first African-American woman from Texas to be elected to Congress. In 1974, Jordan was serving on the House Judiciary Committee, which was investigating the Watergate scandal. Jordan and the other committee members recommended three articles of impeachment against President Richard M. Nixon for his role in the coverup of the Watergate scandal. Articles of impeachment are charges of wrongdoing. However, Nixon resigned before the vote for impeachment reached the full House of Representatives. In 1976, Jordan was asked to give the keynote address at the Democratic National Convention. It was the opening speech. Jordan received a standing ovation for the address. She was known as a powerful and eloquent speaker. Throughout her years in Congress, Jordan promoted legislation that called for equal rights for all citizens. She continued serving in Congress until 1979.

Barbara Jordan, a former congressional representative from Texas, delivers a keynote speech at the 1992 Democratic Convention.

FOR MORE PRACTICE
See page 670.

A. Rewrite the sentences, adding end punctuation, periods, and commas where necessary.

1. Do you enjoy watching mystery shows on TV
2. If so you may have seen the show *Murder, She Wrote* in reruns
3. It stars Angela Lansbury as J B Fletcher a mystery story writer
4. In every show J B Fletcher helps the police solve a crime but the police do not always want her help
5. Some consider her a nuisance an obstacle or even a pest
6. J B however continues to search for clues and she sometimes seeks the help of Dr Seth Hazlitt one of her friends
7. She might ask him, "Seth what do you think it means"
8. The smallest clue such as a missing button smudges on a wall or a few flower petals can help her solve a mystery
9. How you might ask is she able to piece together the clues
10. J B Fletcher uses keen insightful observations and thinking to solve crimes. What a crime solver What a show

Basil Rathbone and Nigel Bruce starred as Sherlock Holmes and Dr. Watson in the 1945 film *House of Fear.*

B. Application in Literature Rewrite the following paragraph, adding end marks and commas where necessary.

[11]My sister and I you will recollect were twins and you know how subtle are the links which bind two souls so closely allied [12]It was a wild night [13]The wind was howling outside and the rain was beating and splashing against the windows [14]Suddenly amid all the hubbub of the gale there burst forth the wild scream of a terrified woman [15]I knew that it was my sister's voice [16]I sprang from my bed wrapped a shawl around me and rushed into the corridor [17]As I opened the door I seemed to hear a low whistle

**Sir Arthur Conan Doyle,
"The Adventure of the Speckled Band"**

OTHER USES OF THE COMMA

Use **commas** to set off quotations, parts of dates, parts of addresses, and parts of a letter.

Certain elements in your writing require commas to separate them from the rest of the sentence. In this section, you will learn when to use such commas.

Commas with Quotations

Use commas to set off the explanatory words of a direct quotation.

When you use the exact words of a speaker or writer, you are using a **direct quotation.**

When you quote directly, you usually include explanatory words such as *Marilena said, Karen asked,* or *Mike answered.* If the explanatory words precede the direct quotation, you place a comma after the last explanatory word. When the explanatory words follow the quotation, place a comma after the last word of the quotation and before the end quotation mark.

Timothy said, "After my injury I had to learn to walk again."
"The therapists urged me to keep trying," he continued.

When the explanatory words interrupt the quotation, the quotation is called a **divided quotation.** In a divided quotation, use commas after the last word of the first part of the quotation and after the last word in the explanatory phrase.

"After a while," he noted, "I was walking with only a cane."

The quotations you have just looked at are all direct quotations. When you rephrase the words of a speaker or writer, you are using an **indirect quotation.** You need not set these words off with commas. In most cases, however, you should credit the quotation to the original speaker or writer.

Timothy said that *the many hours of therapy had paid off because he was now able to run again.*

Practice Your Skills

A. CONCEPT CHECK

Commas with Quotations   Write the following sentences, adding and deleting commas where necessary.

1. I asked "Mom, do you know anyone who is blind?"
2. "No" Mom replied "but let me tell you about Tom Sullivan."
3. Mom continued "Tom, a singer and guitar player who performed on stage and TV, lost his sight soon after birth."
4. "At times" she said "he would be angry about being blind."
5. "He wanted to be like all other people" explained Mom.
6. "However, he learned to accept his blindness" she noted "and did not let it stop him from enjoying many activities."
7. Mom told me, that he even learned to play golf with help.
8. I asked "How do you know so much about Tom Sullivan, Mom?"
9. "Years ago, I saw him sing on TV programs" she replied.
10. She then said, that she had also read a biography about him.

B. REVISION SKILL

Sentence Variety   Write each of the following sentences as a direct quotation. Place the name of the speaker, identified in parentheses, at the position indicated by a caret. Add appropriate punctuation and explanatory words, such as *said, stated,* or *asked.*

> EXAMPLE   "Cass, when will you finish the book?" ∧ (Jeff)
> "Cass, when will you finish the book?" asked Jeff.

11. "I just finished reading the book *Alesia* by Eloise Greenfield and Alesia Revis." ∧ (Carlos)
12. ∧ "What is it about?" (Elena)
13. "It's a story about how Alesia recovered from severe injuries after she was hit by a car when she was nine years old." ∧ (Anna)
14. "That's right, ∧ and Alesia tells the story." (Carlos)
15. ∧ "At first, Alesia was completely disabled." (Anna)
16. "She had to learn to crawl first and then to walk." ∧ (Carlos)
17. ∧ "She spent years in physical therapy, exercising." (Anna)
18. ∧ "She finally learned to walk with help." (Carlos)
19. "Learning to walk again was hard work, ∧ but Alesia never gave up, and she triumphed!" (Anna)
20. "It sounds like a great story. ∧ May I borrow the book?" (Elena)

FOR MORE PRACTICE
See page 670.

Commas in Dates, Addresses, and Letters

When you are writing dates, place a comma after the day of the month.

When a date falls in the middle of the sentence, use a comma after the day of the month and another comma after the year. When only a month and year are given, no commas are necessary.

July 4, 1776   November 10, 1992   April 1865

The bill was proposed in November 1988. It wasn't until
September 15, 1991, that it became a law, however.

When referring to a geographical location, place a comma between the name of the town or city and the name of the state, district, or country. When a postal address is used in a sentence, place a comma after each part of the address.

Springfield, Illinois   Paris, France

The senator lives at 2395 Saddlebridge Drive, Houston,
Texas 77069, when she isn't in Washington.

Note that there is no comma between the name of the state and the ZIP code.

Use a comma after the greeting of a friendly letter and after the closing of a friendly or business letter.

Dear George,   Sincerely,

Practice Your Skills

CONCEPT CHECK

Commas in Dates, Addresses, and Letters   Write the following sentences, adding necessary commas and deleting unnecessary commas.

Writing Theme
Historical Places

1. Dear Allison
     I've finally arrived in Washington D.C.
2. My train left Lexington Kentucky on July 15.
3. I'm staying at 35 Wisconsin Avenue Washington D.C. 10017.
4. I've learned so much about this city. Did you know that the dome on the Capitol wasn't completed until December, 1863?

5. On May 30 1922 the Lincoln Memorial was dedicated.
6. I visited 1600 Pennsylvania Avenue Washington D.C.
7. President Adams and his family became the first residents of the White House in November 1800.
8. Did you know that on August 24 1814 the White House was burned down?
9. The rebuilt White House was formally opened in January, 1818 by President Monroe.
10.
                                    Your friend
                                    Robert

FOR MORE PRACTICE
See page 670.

Commas to Prevent Misreading

When speaking, you sometimes pause in your statements to keep your listeners from misunderstanding what you mean to say. In writing, commas prevent similar misunderstandings. Even when a comma is not strictly required, you may insert one to prevent misreading. Notice how the following sentence is unclear unless a comma is added.

When we finished packing the bags were ready.
When we finished packing, the bags were ready.

Practice Your Skills

CONCEPT CHECK

Commas for Clarity   Write the following sentences, adding commas where necessary.

Writing Theme
At the Amusement Park

1. The day before my dad suggested a trip to the local amusement park.
2. I invited Jessica and Adam invited Tim.
3. Before leaving my mom packed the car with food.
4. When we walked in the park was already crowded and noisy.
5. Screaming Jessica and I rode the roller coaster five times.
6. When the roller coaster zoomed by my dad waved to us.
7. While turning the merry-go-round played the same tune over and over.
8. Calling to Tim Adam climbed on a wooden horse.
9. After riding around and around the boys wanted to go on the Ferris wheel.
10. By the time we left the boys were too tired to walk.

Write the following letter, adding and deleting commas where necessary. As an alternative, you may write only the words before and after commas in each line.

1   May, 24 1994
2   Dear Matt
3   Saturday May 21 1994 will always be an
4   important date for me because that's the
5   day I went rock climbing for the first
6   time. After worrying my cousin Dana
7   invited me to go with her club, the
8   Alpiners. My mom just said "Have a good
9   time and be careful." My brother said
10 "You have trouble climbing the stairs!"
11 "He's just jealous" said Dana "because
12 I've never invited him to go rock climb-
13 ing!" Before leaving Dana told me to be
14 sure to wear sturdy shoes with rubber
15 soles, comfortable pants, and a long-
16 sleeved T-shirt. We met at 3115, Meadow-
17 view Drive for the drive to the cliffs in the
18 state park. At first I was scared, but while
19 climbing Dana showed me what to do.
20 Most importantly, she told me "Take your
21 time; this isn't a race, so concentrate on
22 finding good holds." I was so happy
23 when she said to me "Good job!" The
24 next climb takes place Saturday June 18
25 1994 at the same site. Not only am I
26 planning on going again, but I'm going
27 to the Alpiners' next meeting on Monday
28 June 6. Also, I think I will get some more
29 information on rock climbing by writing
30 the American Alpine Club 113 East
31 Ninetieth St. New York, New York
32 10028.
33   Love
34   Jenna

> Use a **semicolon** to separate parts of a compound sentence.
>
> Use a **colon** to introduce lists of items, to follow the greeting of a business letter, and to separate hours from minutes in time expressions.

The Semicolon

Semicolons are frequently used to punctuate compound sentences. A compound sentence is made up of two or more independent clauses.

Use a semicolon to separate the parts of a compound sentence when no conjunction is used.

Adventure travel is exciting, but it can also be dangerous.
Adventure travel is exciting; it can also be dangerous.

Note that the semicolon replaces the comma and the coordinating conjunction *but.* Conjunctions commonly replaced by semicolons are *and, but, or, for,* and *nor.*

Use a semicolon before a conjunctive adverb that joins the clauses of a compound sentence.

Conjunctive adverbs commonly used are *therefore, however, hence, so, then, moreover, nevertheless, yet, consequently,* and *besides.*

The safari takes place in May; *however,* I prefer June.

Use semicolons to separate the parts of a series when commas occur within the parts.

Like commas, semicolons are used in sentences to prevent misreading. For example, if you list a series of cities and their countries without semicolons, the list would confuse a reader.

In recent years, I have flown to Beijing, Nanjing, and Shanghai, China; Cairo and Alexandria, Egypt; Jakarta, Indonesia; and Kuala Lumpur, Malaysia.

The Colon

Use a colon to introduce a list of items.

In speaking and writing, people often use lists. Someone gives you a list of things to bring on a trip. You tell someone the list of your favorite books. You make lists to remind you to do certain things. You should introduce these lists with a colon.

> My flight bag contains the following items: my camera, ten rolls of film, batteries, a change of clothes, a guidebook, several maps, and a sweater.

Never place a colon immediately after a preposition or a verb.

Incorrect   I made sure I had: passport, credit cards, traveler's checks, and driver's license.

Correct   I made sure I had the following items: my passport, credit cards, traveler's checks, and driver's license.

Place a colon after the greeting of a business letter.

> Dear Ms. Albertson:
> Thank you for sending my ticket so quickly.

Use a colon between numerals that represent hours and minutes and between chapter and verse in a biblical reference.

> 9:00 A.M.   6:30 P.M.   Genesis 7:1–5

Practice Your Skills

A. CONCEPT CHECK

Semicolons and Colons   Write the following sentences, adding and deleting semicolons and colons where necessary. If a sentence is already correct, write *Correct*.

1. *Safari* originally meant: "having to do with a journey" in Arabic subsequently the word passed into Swahili.
2. Safaris can be hunting trips often they are sightseeing trips.
3. They are most common in these African countries Zimbabwe, Botswana, Kenya, Tanzania, and South Africa.
4. People on photographic safaris always carry two things: cameras and binoculars.

5. You go to water holes at 500 A.M.; to observe animals.
6. Around 900 P.M. is another good time to watch for animals.
7. You may see zebras, giraffes, and antelopes early, elephants later, and wild dogs and baboons still later.
8. At night you can hear the animals they may come to the camp.
9. The guide knows how to look for animals; however, anyone can learn to spot animals in the wild.
10. Antelopes, zebras, and gnus in Tanzania, giraffes in Kenya, and hyenas in Botswana live on protected reserves.

B. PROOFREADING SKILL

Using Semicolons and Colons Correctly   Write this letter, correcting all errors in grammar, capitalization, punctuation, and spelling. (25 errors)

674 Cleveland place
Metairie Louisiana, 70003
March 24 1994

Adventure Travel, inc.
1197, Powell Street
San francisco, California, 94108

Dear Sir or madam:

I recently read an article describing your company it sounded like my kind of travel agency! The article was vary informative however, i would like to know more. I am partickularly interested in traveling to the following countries Malaysia, India, and china. If you have any upcoming trips to those countries. Please send me the following information dates, departures, itineraries, preices, and restrictions. Also do you arrange trips to Myanmar. Do you have any plans to visit Nepal? Thank you for your help I look forward to heering from you soon.

Sincerely yours;
Anna Gonzalez

FOR MORE PRACTICE
See page 671.

THE HYPHEN

Use a **hyphen** to mark the division of a word at the end of a line. Use hyphens in compound numbers, nouns, and adjectives.

Use a hyphen to divide a word at the end of a line of writing.

Only words of two or more syllables may be divided at the end of a line. Words should be divided only between syllables.

> When tracing my family history, I began with my local li-brary's collection of books on genealogy.

Never divide a word of one syllable. Do not divide words to leave a single letter at the end or at the beginning of a line.

Incorrect   a-luminum   *Correct*   alu-minum

Use hyphens in compound adjectives that precede the words they modify and in certain compound nouns.

> Dr. Herbert is a world-famous authority on census records. *But:* Dr. Herbert is world famous.

> sister-in-law   great-grandson   self-knowledge

Use hyphens in compound numbers from twenty-one through ninety-nine and in fractions.

> seventy-three relatives   one-half full

Practice Your Skills

CONCEPT CHECK

Hyphens   Write the following sentences, adding hyphens where necessary.

1. My great grandparents came from Poland ninety two years ago.
2. She traveled with twenty one relatives and neighbors.
3. He came with his great uncle, who was seventy five.
4. She carried a much loved quilt made by a great aunt.
5. His prize possession was a well worn family Bible.

Writing
TIP

Do not use a hyphen between an adverb that ends in -*ly* and a participle acting as a modifier.

My great-grandmother was known for her beautifully stitched embroidery.

Writing Theme
Family History

FOR MORE PRACTICE
See page 671.

THE APOSTROPHE

> Use **apostrophes** to show possession, to form the plurals of letters and words used as words, and to show where letters are omitted in contractions.

The apostrophe is a punctuation mark that is helpful only to a reader. The apostrophe can be used to show possession, to represent the omitted letters in contractions, and to help form some plurals.

Forming Possessives and Plurals

To form the possessive of a singular noun, add an apostrophe and an *s*.

the baby's toy   Charles's coat   Maria's book

To form the possessive of a plural noun that does not end in *s*, add an apostrophe and an *s*.

children's   men's

To form the possessive of a plural noun that ends in *s*, add only an apostrophe.

visitors'   animals'

To form the possessive of an indefinite pronoun, use an apostrophe and an *s*.

everybody's   somebody's   no one's

For a listing of indefinite pronouns, see Handbook 41, "Using Pronouns," page 448.

Never use an apostrophe with a possessive pronoun.

our   yours   hers   theirs

Use an apostrophe and an *s* to form the plural of a letter or a word referred to as a word.

p's and q's   too many *thus*'s

In names of organizations and businesses, in hyphenated terms, and in cases of joint ownership, show possession in the last word only.

the chamber of commerce's brochure
my great-aunt's photograph album
Henry and Elizabeth's vacation

Forming Contractions

Use an apostrophe in a contraction.

In contractions, apostrophes replace omitted letters.

she's = she is	aren't = are not	I'm = I am
it's = it is	isn't = is not	we'll = we will
won't = will not	can't = cannot	they've = they have

If you remember the rule that an apostrophe replaces one or more omitted letters, you will be less likely to confuse *it's* with *its*. *It's* is a contraction of *it is*. *Its* is a possessive pronoun. Note that *won't* is the exception to the apostrophe rule.

Use an apostrophe to show that part of a date has been omitted.

Klondike gold rush of '96 (Klondike gold rush of 1896)
the '64 earthquake (the 1964 earthquake)

Practice Your Skills

A. CONCEPT CHECK

Apostrophes   Correctly write the words in these sentences that have incorrect or missing apostrophes.

1. Polar bear's live on Canadas and Alaskas northern coasts.
2. They cant see or hear well, but they have a keen sense of smell.
3. Theyll wait at seals dens or breathing holes in the ice.
4. Their white fur helps hide the bears when theyre hunting.
5. The pads of fur on a polar bears feet help it walk on ice.
6. Its a good climber, swimmer, and runner, even though an adult males' weight may be more than a thousand pounds.
7. Peoples fear of being attacked by the bears is unjustified.
8. In fact, the polar bears survival is threatened by hunters.

9. The worlds polar bear population is estimated to be around twenty-five thousand in *The World Book Encyclopedias'* 91 edition.

10. Its anybodys guess how many polar bears will survive in the future.

B. REVISION SKILL

Using Apostrophes Correctly   Write the following paragraph, adding apostrophes where necessary.

[11]Ive been reading about the aurora borealis, commonly called the northern lights. [12]Theyre the lights that can be seen in the night sky, particularly in Alaska. [13]They appear as green, red, and purple arcs and streaks, even shapes like zs and ss, that move and flicker. [14]The lights are one of the suns effects on the atmosphere. [15]When electrically charged particles from the sun reach the earths magnetic field, some are trapped and move toward the earths magnetic poles, releasing energy as they strike atoms and molecules in the earths atmosphere. [16]I think I used too many earth'ss in that sentence! [17]Anyway, thats the current explanation; scientists are still studying the phenomenon. [18]Im interested in less scientific explanations. [19]Some people believed that a radiant snakes dancing caused the lights; others thought the lights were spirits torches. [20]Id like to see the aurora borealis someday.

C. APPLICATION IN WRITING

Notes   Imagine that you took the following science notes in a hurry. You notice that you did not make the possessives clear. Write the notes, adding apostrophes where they are needed. Use an encyclopedia to check the facts if necessary.

<u>Notes on the North Pole</u>
Geographic North Pole—at northern end of earths axis
—located near Arctic Oceans center
—Robert Pearys expedition in 1909
—N. Uemuras solo expedition by dog sled in 1978
Magnetic North Pole—in different location
—compass needle points to this poles location
Geomagnetic North Pole—in different location—at northern end of earths geomagnetic field

FOR MORE PRACTICE
See page 672.

C H E C K ✔ P O I N T

Write these sentences, adding and deleting semicolons, colons, hyphens, and apostrophes where necessary.

1. People learned how to weave thousands of years ago however, no one is exactly sure when.
2. Early weavers materials included: grasses, palm leaves, wood strips, and twigs.
3. People first wove these objects hats, masks, mats, and baskets.
4. Dried grass baskets were used to store and carry peoples food.
5. Every culture has made baskets each has added something to make it's baskets different.
6. Decorating with shells and feathers is the Pomo Indians style.
7. Theyre considered the finest basket makers in the Americas.
8. Basket makers and cloth weavers techniques are the same.
9. Cloth weavers make these things blankets, clothes, and rugs.
10. Cloth is woven from the following materials silk, wool, cotton, and synthetic fibers, such as nylon.
11. Its anybodys guess who were the first people to weave cloth.
12. The Egyptians weaving techniques are shown in ancient paintings.
13. The Chinese first used the silkworms thread four thousand years ago.
14. About two thousand years ago, the Romans traded for wool from Britain, Gaul, and Spain: cotton from Egypt; and silk from China.
15. Seventh century Pueblos knew how to weave cotton.
16. The Navajos learned how to weave from the Pueblos subsequently, the Navajos developed their own unique blanket patterns.
17. Inca weavers fine wool cloth is still-admired today.
18. By the 1400s weaving was a well developed art in Europe too.
19. Weaving on a hand loom is an ancient craft still practiced to day in many of the worlds cultures.
20. Its also a popular handicraft many people weave as a hobby.

Writing Theme
Weaving

Hopi basketweaver Fermina Banyacya continues a family tradition of weaving with yucca leaves.

QUOTATION MARKS

> Use **quotation marks** at the beginning and the end of direct quotations and to set off titles of short works.

When you use another person's exact written or spoken words, you are using a **direct quotation.** On the other hand, when you refer to a person's words but do not quote him or her exactly, you are using an **indirect quotation.**

Use quotation marks to enclose a direct quotation. Indirect quotations need no quotation marks.

Direct Quotation	The candidate for the senate said, "Creating new jobs will be my first priority."
Indirect Quotation	The candidate for the senate said that creating new jobs would be her first priority.

Remember to place the quotation marks before the first word and after the last word of a direct quotation.

Always begin a direct quotation with a capital letter.

Senator Ruiz said, "You must believe that every vote counts."

When a direct quotation is divided by explanatory words, begin the second part of the quotation with a lowercase letter.
If the second part of the quotation is a complete sentence, the first word of this sentence is capitalized.

"Register to vote," said Liz, "**b**efore the end of the day."
"I did," said Carol. "**I**t took only a few minutes."

Place commas and periods inside quotation marks. Place semicolons and colons outside quotation marks.

"Last night**,**" said Liz, "I listened to a debate**.**"
Carol said to Liz, "One candidate was more persuasive than the others"**;** however, Liz did not agree.
These candidates were quoted in the article "Our Country's Future"**:** Senator Ruiz, Governor Henry, and Judge Wong.

Place question marks and exclamation points inside quotation marks if they belong to the quotation. Place them outside if they do not belong to the quotation.

Liz asked, "Whom are you voting for**?**"
Did Carol say, "I don't know yet"**?**
I can't believe that she said, "I don't know yet"**!**
"Don't get excited**!**" exclaimed Liz.

Use single quotation marks to enclose a title or quotation within a quotation. If the title or quotation within the quotation ends the sentence, use both the single and the double quotation marks after the last word of the sentence.

"Liz heard you say, 'Call Carol,' before you hung up."
"Liz heard you say, 'Call Carol.'"
"Carol told Liz that her favorite song was 'Memory.'"

In a quotation of more than one paragraph, use quotation marks at the beginning of each paragraph and at the end of the final paragraph.

"Being elected the first time is not difficult," said Senator Ruiz, "because voters will give you a chance.
"Being elected the second time is trickier; then you must prove that you used your chance wisely."

Practice Your Skills

CONCEPT CHECK

Quotation Marks   Write the following sentences, punctuating quotations correctly. If a sentence is correct, write *Correct*.

1. Being President is like riding a tiger, said Harry S. Truman, A man has to keep on riding or be swallowed.
2. Is it true that Jimmy Carter said, I can get up at nine and be rested, or I can get up at six and be President
3. Dwight Eisenhower said, "Always take the job, but never yourself, seriously"; that was his advice about the presidency.
4. Eisenhower also said There is one thing about being President; nobody can tell you when to sit down!
5. Joan said I read that Truman used to say The buck stops here, to show the difficulties of the President's job.

Writing Theme
Presidents on the Presidency

6. A President's hardest task, said Lyndon Johnson, is not to do what is right, but to know what is right.
7. Herbert Hoover said that the only two occasions when Americans respected the President's privacy were prayer and fishing.
8. No President, said Theodore Roosevelt, ever enjoyed the presidency as I did; that sounds like something he would say!
9. I think the President is the only person, said Jimmy Carter, Who can change the direction or attitude of our nation.
10. When he was appointed, Gerald Ford said, I guess it proves that in America anyone can be President, said Joan.

FOR MORE PRACTICE
See page 672.

Punctuating Dialogue

There is one simple rule to remember when you write dialogue: begin a new paragraph each time you quote a different speaker.

"Truman often commented on the difficulties of being President," said Alice.

Jake said, "He once compared the White House to a prison—a nice prison, of course, but still a prison."

Alice laughed at that. "That sounds like something Truman would have said."

"Yes, I have always admired his sense of humor."

Punctuating Titles

Use quotation marks to enclose the titles of poems, short stories, songs, reports, articles, and chapters of books.

Poem	"Fame"
Short Story	"Hail and Farewell"
Song	"Everything's Coming Up Roses"

Underline titles of books, plays, magazines, newspapers, television series, works of art, musical compositions, epic poems, and motion pictures. Titles that are underlined are italicized in print.

Book	Max Malone, Superstar
Magazine	People
Television Series	Entertainment Tonight
Motion Picture	The Band Wagon

Practice Your Skills

A. CONCEPT CHECK

Using Punctuation Correctly   Write these sentences, adding and deleting punctuation and underlining where necessary.

Writing Theme
Show Time!

1. All right said Ms. Kehoe, What play do you want to do for this year's Spring Festival
2. Well, last year we did a science fiction play called Return to Planet Oog said Will
3. It was based on the short story Final Frontier said Jo
4. Annie asked How about writing a mystery based on a Sherlock Holmes story, like The Red-Headed League.
5. Susan suggested We could do a musical, like Grease
6. No musicals! groaned Doug. Let's do a play, like Our Town
7. I think we should write our own play said Eric We could dramatize a book, like The Outsiders
8. Did you read the article Making People Laugh asked Will. I think we should write a series of funny skits?
9. How will you choose from so many good ideas asked Ms. Kehoe
10. I'll make a list of the ideas, said Jo and then we should do as Mr. Bell always says, and I quote Let's put it to a vote.

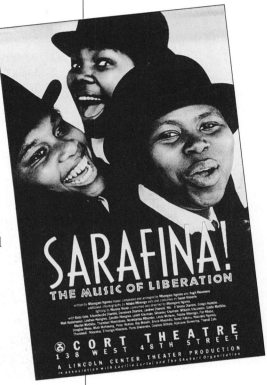

B. APPLICATION IN LITERATURE

Punctuating Dialogue   Write this dialogue, adding the correct punctuation and paragraph divisions.

[11]Mrs. Bacon I said trying to think fast remember how you said that the play was really about kids? [12]You know, Juliet thirteen, Romeo a little older? [13]That's true [14]Shakespeare isn't just for all times of the day but for all ages [15]That's the whole point I agreed [16]We thought since it's about kids and we're doing it for kids it's only fair that kids get to do it themselves [17]Right Lucy chimed in nobody knows us more than us [18]Except him I quickly said [19]Who is him said Mrs.Bacon a bit confused [20]The Bard I said edging Lucy toward the door

Avi, *Romeo and Juliet: Together (and Alive!) at Last*

FOR MORE PRACTICE
See page 672.

Write these sentences, punctuating each correctly by adding quotation marks and underlining where necessary. If a sentence is correct, write *Correct.*

1. Ken asked that the meeting of the local Eco-Watch group come to order.
2. What do we want to talk about today? he asked.
3. John said, We still haven't decided what to do for Earth Day.
4. Did you see the article called Beware, Polluters: Little Brother Is Watching in the Daily News? asked Paul.
5. It said that kids are really getting involved in environmental issues these days, he continued.
6. We could write a pamphlet, suggested Emma, that lists things people can do every day to help the environment.
7. Barbara said, The book Fifty Simple Things Kids Can Do to Save the Earth has lots of good suggestions.
8. Yes, agreed Cathy, so does the book called Save the Earth.
9. It says, Think globally, act locally. Our group is trying to do that, she pointed out.
10. Ken asked, What kinds of suggestions would we make?
11. Well, replied Cathy, Chapter 3, Water, lists things like fixing leaks, taking shorter showers, and saving rainwater.
12. She said, We need simple, helpful hints like those; the others nodded in agreement.
13. Good! said Emma. We could all collect ideas from books and articles.
14. She added, Then we can choose the ideas we think are the best.
15. It'll be a lot of work, said Paul, and there's not much time.
16. We can do it if we all work together, Emma reminded him.
17. She said, I want to be able to say, as one kid said, It makes me feel that I'm doing something for the earth.
18. All right, said Ken. Let's vote. All those in favor say Aye.
19. Everyone shouted Aye at the same time.
20. Ken said that the vote was unanimous.

A. Using End Marks   Write the following sentences, adding periods, question marks, and exclamation points where needed.

1. You know who Thomas Jefferson was, don't you
2. He was the writer of the Declaration of Independence, the third President, an inventor, and a founder of the University of Virginia
3. What a wonderful and inspired leader he was
4. He was also a person who corresponded with many people
5. He wrote hundreds of letters in his lifetime
6. About what did he write and to whom did he write
7. He wrote to friends, relatives, political leaders, and government officials
8. In a letter to Mr T J Smith, a friend's son, he wrote:
   "1 Never put off till to-morrow what you can do to-day
   2 Never trouble another for what you can do yourself
   3 Never spend your money before you have it."
9. Did Smith heed the advice We don't know
10. We do know, however, that Jefferson's letters have helped us better understand Jefferson, his times, and the American past

Writing Theme
Correspondence
Through the Ages

B. Using Commas That Separate Ideas   Write the words that should be followed by commas. If a sentence is correct, write *Correct.*

11. Newspapers magazines and news programs receive mail daily.
12. People write them with praise for their work or people write to express their views on issues of interest.
13. Some people write to editors but others write to reporters.
14. Letters to editors are written to express opinions to discuss issues or to ask for corrections.
15. Some of the letters are written by ordinary people and some are written by celebrities and political leaders.
16. Here's how to write to the media: first outline your ideas; second make your statement; and third format the letter properly.
17. Express your opinions, support them with facts, and be polite.
18. Try to write a concise informative and interesting letter.
19. Also make sure that your letter has a heading an inside address a salutation a body a closing and your signature.
20. Good letters are read enjoyed and possibly printed by editors.

C. Using Commas That Set Off Special Elements Write these sentences, adding commas where they are needed.

21. ISAAC: The history of the postal service in the United States is really interesting Carol. Do you know anything about it?

22. CAROL: Well I know that Congress issued the first U.S. postage stamps in 1847.

23. ISAAC: True; however the use of stamps wasn't required until almost ten years later.

24. JERRY: One of the more exciting developments I believe was the pony express a mail delivery system.

25. CAROL: Didn't it operate between Missouri and California Jerry?

26. JERRY: Right—riders on horses rode day and night in relays or shifts to deliver the mail.

27. ISAAC: The service lasted for about a year Carol.

28. CAROL: It's odd don't you think that the service didn't last longer.

29. ISAAC: Well the transcontinental telegraph began operating in 1861 and I believe eliminated the need for the pony express.

30. JERRY: In fact the pony express service closed just two days after the wire service or telegraph opened.

D. Using Commas in Other Ways Write the following letter, adding commas where necessary.

[31]Dear Carrie

[32]Today is April 5 1993. I never will forget this date.

[33]"We are moving to Libertyville Illinois" my parents told me this morning.

[34]"Where's Libertyville?" I asked. "I've never heard of it."

[35]Mom replied, "Libertyville is near Chicago Illinois."

[36]I have lived in Marin County California all my life and I thought that I would always live here. [37]I was really looking forward to starting high school with my friends in San Francisco California.

[38]Dad said "We will leave San Francisco in August 1993. [39]After the movers come" he continued "we'll drive east and make a few stops along the way."

[40]"We will be stopping in Phoenix Arizona" Mom explained "to visit friends and then in Des Moines Iowa to see Grandma."

[41]Carrie didn't you see two plays an opera and a baseball game when you visited Chicago in June 1991?

[42]"In Chicago are the Sears Tower the Field Museum and several sports teams" Dad reminded me "and I think you will love it."

[43]Mom told me "After we settle Carrie can visit."

[44]Once we move, you can write me at 200 Western Avenue Libertyville Illinois 60048.

[45]Your friend always
Elise

E. Using Semicolons and Colons   Write the following letter, adding semicolons and colons where necessary.

[46]Dear Mr. Samuelson

[47]I received your manuscript titled <u>The 820 A.M. Train to Milwaukee</u> however, I am afraid I must return it to you. [48]Davis and Brand, Inc., specializes in publishing the following genres poetry, short stories, essays, and critical reviews. [49]We do not publish novels. [50]Perhaps you could try submitting your work to these publishers Runsom House, Scribblers, and Carter/Hollins in New York Wattleway in Boston and Deal, Inc., in Chicago. [51]They are always looking for new authors they might be interested in reading your novel. [52]Remember, a writing career requires the following traits confidence, perseverance, and a thick skin! [53]Your local library has additional information about publishing for example, <u>Literary Market Place</u> and <u>Writer's Market</u> are valuable sources. [54]I wish you success in your writing career.

[55]Sincerely,
Claire Edison

F. Using Hyphens   Write these sentences, adding hyphens where necessary.

56. Long ago, people used hand sharpened straws or reeds as pens.
57. Later, people made finer tipped pens by using goose feathers in stead of straws or reeds.
58. Fountain pens were invented in our great grandparents' time.
59. Ballpoint pens became popular after World War II pilots dis covered they wrote well during high altitude flying.
60. Soft tip pens and rolling ball pens were invented about twenty five years ago.

G. Using Apostrophes   Write the words that need apostrophes and the words that have incorrectly placed apostrophes.

61. What would you do if you couldnt write a letter for yourself?
62. Youd find someone who could write it for you, wouldnt you?
63. If you wanted to write a letter in ancient times, youd have gotten a scribes help.
64. Some scribes made their living writing peoples letter's.
65. The churchs and the governments business also required many written documents.
66. A kings scribe would write out the kings instructions and record peoples tax payments.
67. The churchs sacred books were all written by hand.
68. In the Middle Ages, printing hadnt been developed, so scribes copies were the only books that existed.
69. These copies are important to modern historians research.
70. Theyre one of the main sources historians use to find out about the past.

H. Using Quotation Marks   Write these sentences, adding punctuation and underlining where necessary.

71. In his book Biographical Essays, Lytton Strachey said The great letter writer must be an egotist What do you think he meant by that
72. A good letter is an exercise of the ego agreed Clifton Fadiman
73. Was it Thoreau who said I have received no more than one or two letters in my life that were worth the postage
74. But Stephen Spender said A letter is like a present Lena said the same thing when she got a ten-page letter from a friend
75. Janice said I agree with Mark Van Doren, who said The letter that merely answers another letter is no letter at all
76. The lines Letters of thanks, letters from banks, / Letters of joy from girl and boy are from W. H. Auden's poem Night Mail
77. Letters are largely written to get things out of your system said John Dos Passos in his book The Fourteenth Chronicle
78. Dr. Johnson said that a short letter to a friend was an insult
79. John said, Voltaire once remarked Letters are the consolation of life.
80. The true use of a letter said James Russell Lowell is to let one know that one is remembered and valued

GRAMMAR
HANDBOOK
49

A. Using Commas and End Marks   Write these sentences, adding commas and end marks where they are needed. If a sentence is correctly punctuated, write *Correct*.

Writing Theme
Puzzles and Problems

1. Do you know who Esther Pauline Friedman Lederer and Pauline Esther Friedman Phillips are
2. They are better known as Ann Landers and Abigail Van Buren.
3. Did you know that these popular advice columnists are sisters
4. In fact they are twins
5. Since the 1950s the sisters have been writing advice columns
6. Ann began her column in 1955 and Abigail began hers in 1956.
7. Since then both have received thousands of letters
8. The letters ask for advice about problems express readers' concerns and comment on important issues
9. Of course they cannot answer all the letters they receive but they do try to answer ones that deal with common problems.
10. They do not rely only on their own knowledge however when they answer the letters.
11. They consult experts such as lawyers doctors and the clergy.
12. Their advice is usually filled with common sense, good humor, and concern for individuals.
13. At times both urge that writers seek professional help.
14. Thousands have enjoyed their columns and many have benefited from their advice
15. They have been thoughtful realistic problem solvers for years.

B. Using Commas and Semicolons   Write these sentences, adding commas and semicolons where necessary.

16. Looking up from her crossword puzzle Mom asked "Jeff do you know a three-letter word for a large African antelope?"
17. I told Mom an avid crossword-puzzle fan that the right answer was probably *gnu.*
18. My parents Ed and Cati Morini enjoy working crossword puzzles they say that doing the puzzles relaxes them.
19. Although they both work puzzles daily Mom always works the puzzles from beginning to end Dad skips around filling in blanks here and there.
20. They work the crossword puzzles in our local newspaper the *Jefferson Times* and in the paper's Sunday magazine and they also buy crossword-puzzle books.

21. One day as he worked on a puzzle Dad asked "Do you know when the first modern crossword puzzle appeared?"
22. "No Dad I don't" I replied. "In fact I never thought about it."
23. I learned that the modern crossword puzzle now a popular word game was created by Arthur Wynne.
24. "His first puzzle appeared in a New York paper the *New York World* on December 21 1913" Dad explained.
25. Since then people in the United States in Canada and all over the world have worked crossword puzzles and some people even compete in crossword-puzzle contests.

C. Using Apostrophes and Quotation Marks   Write the following sentences, adding apostrophes, underlining, quotation marks, and commas where necessary.

26. The complex patterns of mazes have long tested peoples patience and sense of humor.
27. The best-known hedge maze is at Englands Hampton Court Palace.
28. The hedge maze at Longleat House is the worlds largest.
29. Finding the center of the maze said Jill is easier than getting out again.
30. We needed the maze keepers help to get out agreed Mary.
31. People get lost all the time said the maze keeper. Weve had some in there for three hours.
32. A modern maze builder said Its not about getting lost. Its about having fun.
33. At his maze he encourages people to play tag on the paths and forget that theyre adults.
34. Its best to enter a maze with a childs sense of fun he said.
35. The turf maze at Saffron Walden is my favorite Jill said.
36. Our aunt and uncles book on tile mazes shows interesting patterns in the floors of churches and houses said Jill.
37. The good thing about tile and turf mazes explained Mary is that when youve had enough, you can just walk off.
38. Jill laughed Yes, thats not true in hedge mazes.
39. The article Garden-Variety Puzzles in the magazine European Travel & Life has wonderful pictures of different mazes.
40. You can find more information in books such as Labyrinth: Solving the Riddle of the Maze and The British Maze Guide.

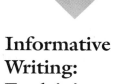

Revise the following draft of a process description, using the directions at the bottom of the page. Then proofread your work, paying particular attention to correcting punctuation errors. Also look for errors in grammar, capitalization, and spelling.

[1]Have you ever wondered how a copy machine works. [2]Electrostatic copying the most common type of copying was invented in 1938 by Chester f Carlson. [3]According to the book "Questions and Answers," Carlsons invention works like this: [4]First a flash of light projects the image of the page being copied onto a drum. [5]The drum has a light-senstive surface. [6]Which takes on an electric charge in the pattern of the image. [7]Then it is dusted with toner. [8]Toner is an inked powder. [9]Toner can be messy. [10]The powder clinged to the part's of the drum with the electric charge. [11]The powder image is transferred to the paper. [12]The paper is heated, to bake on the powder. [13]The result is a exact copy of the orignal image.

1. In sentence 2, identify Carlson by adding the appositive "an American physicist."

2. In sentence 7, replace the pronoun "it" with the more precise "the drum."

3. Add the information in sentence 8 to sentence 7 as a subordinate clause beginning with a comma and "which."

4. Delete the sentence that does not belong.

5. After sentence 10 add this missing step: "Next, a piece of paper is rolled against the drum."

6. Add "finally" to the beginning of sentence 12 to show that heating the paper is the last step of the process.

Informative Writing: Explaining *How*

Describing a process involves giving a step-by-step account of how something works or how something is done. (See Workshop 4.) When you revise this type of writing, make sure you have presented all the steps in the proper order. Using punctuation effectively can help guide your readers through the steps of the process.

Skills

Directions   One or more of the underlined sections in the following sentences may contain an error in grammar, usage, punctuation, spelling, or capitalization. Write the letter of each incorrect section. Then rewrite the section correctly. If there is no error in an item, write *E*.

> ***Example*** <u>Lester nixon</u> may need a wheelchair, but he certainly gets
>   **A**
> <u>around; he</u> has <u>visited</u> more than one hundred <u>countries</u>.
>   **B**   **C**   **D**
> <u>No error</u>
> **E**
>
> ***Answer*** A—Lester Nixon

1. There <u>is</u> a church in the Channel Islands that has room for only one <u>priest</u> and
     A   **B**
two congregation <u>members; a</u> church in <u>maine</u> is even smaller. <u>No error</u>
                   C   **D**   **E**

2. Bessie Anderson <u>won</u> a magazine contest by <u>writing</u> "He has achieved success
                 A   **B**
who has lived well, laughed <u>often and</u> loved <u>much.</u>" <u>No error</u>
                       C   **D**   **E**

3. The <u>substance vanillin</u> is really <u>smelly!</u> The odor of just <u>0.0001</u> ounce can be
        A   **B**   **C**
detected in a room the size of a football field with a roof <u>forty-five</u> feet high.
                                                D
<u>No error</u>
 E

4. While <u>growing a</u> baby cuckoo may find home a tight squeeze. The mother
        A
cuckoo <u>lays</u> an egg in the nest of another, often smaller, <u>bird and</u> leaves her
       B   **C**
child to be hatched and <u>raised</u> by a "foster parent." <u>No error</u>
                D   **E**

5. <u>Explaining</u> why she loved books, Helen Keller <u>said "They</u> talk to me without
     A   **B**
<u>embarrassment</u> or <u>awkwardness.</u>" <u>No error</u>
     C   **D**   **E**

6. When a <u>pair</u> of German officers demanded the surrender of the 101st
        A
<u>Airborne Division</u>, Anthony McAuliffe replied <u>simply,</u> <u>"Nuts"!</u> <u>No error</u>
   B   **C**   **D**   **E**

7. Victims of practical jokes prove Will <u>Rogers'</u> wisdom. <u>"Everything</u> is funny,"
   A   B

   said Rogers, <u>"As</u> long as it is happening to somebody <u>else."</u> <u>No error</u>
             C   D   E

8. The town-hall clock in <u>copenhagen, denmark,</u> took ten years to make and <u>has</u>
                        A   B

   fourteen thousand parts. <u>It's</u> accurate to within <u>one-half</u> a second in three
                            C   D

   hundred years. <u>No error</u>
                 E

9. Among the <u>earliest</u> musical instruments in history <u>are</u> simple ones such <u>as:</u> the
             A   B   C

   bell, the <u>flute and</u> the mouth bow. <u>No error</u>
           D   E

10. Observances of <u>Easter</u> and <u>Passover</u> vary from year to year; <u>Independence Day,</u>
                   A   B   C

    on the other hand, always falls on the <u>fourth of July</u>. <u>No error</u>
                                  D   E

11. Some <u>World war II</u> American radio <u>operators</u> used a code no enemy could break.
            A   B

    They were <u>navajo</u> Indians, and the code was <u>their</u> language. <u>No error</u>
              C   D   E

12. A <u>journalist</u> who dined with the <u>rev.</u> Francis Egerton <u>wrote</u> that a dozen dogs
         A   B   C

    <u>set</u> at the dinner table, each wearing a linen napkin. The dogs were well-behaved.
    D
    <u>No error</u>
       E

13. At the <u>Bingham Canyon</u> copper mine in <u>Utah, more</u> earth has been <u>taken</u> out
            A   B   C

    than was moved to make the <u>Panama Canal</u>. <u>No error</u>
                          D   E

14. Although <u>thirty-eight</u> other <u>english</u> words are pronounced the same as <u>*air,* a</u>
             A   B   C

    <u>frequent</u> reader will probably come across only two or three. <u>No error</u>
      D   E

15. Some <u>meteors</u> that fell <u>thousands</u> of years ago left craters a mile <u>wide; but</u> most
          A   B   C

    of these "shooting stars" <u>are</u> the size of a grain of sand. <u>No error</u>
                     D   E

Skills

Directions   One or more of the underlined sections in the following sentences may contain an error in grammar, usage, punctuation, spelling, or capitalization. Write the letter of each incorrect section. Then rewrite the section correctly. If there is no error in an item, write *E*.

> **Example** <u>Centipedes</u> don't really have a hundred <u>legs, they</u> have one
>   **A**   **B**
> <u>pair</u> of legs per body <u>segment and</u> have as few as 5
>   **C**   **D**
> segments or as many as 170. <u>No error</u>
>   **E**
>
> **Answer** B—legs; they *or* legs. They

1. In half the <u>world</u>, rice is a major part of the <u>diet, and</u> 90 percent of it is <u>growed</u>
            A   **B**   **C**
in <u>Asia</u>. <u>No error</u>
  D   **E**

2. At <u>angel falls</u> in <u>Venezuela,</u> thousands of gallons of water <u>falls</u> every second from
      A   **B**   **C**
a <u>height</u> of 3,212 feet. <u>No error</u>
  D   **E**

3. Did you put the correct ZIP code on that <u>package?</u> <u>Forgetting</u> to include a ZIP
                                  A   **B**
code is the <u>more</u> common error the <u>post office</u> encounters. <u>No error</u>
         C   **D**   **E**

4. Both photography and stamp collecting <u>is</u> popular <u>hobbies each</u> <u>requires</u> some
                                 A   **B**   **C**
special <u>knowledge and</u> equipment. <u>No error</u>
        D   **E**

5. About ten <u>inchs</u> of <u>snow and</u> one inch of rain <u>contain</u> the same amount of water.
           A   **B**   **C**
Therefore, to wet the earth, it must snow <u>heavy</u>. <u>No error</u>
                            D   **E**

6. Not all slave states <u>fought</u> on the side of the <u>south</u> during the Civil <u>War, four</u> of
                A   **B**   **C**
them supported the <u>Union Army</u>. <u>No error</u>
          D   **E**

7. Many <u>languages</u> have only one remaining <u>speaker, in</u> fact <u>there is</u> more than
    　　　A　　　　　　　　　　　　　　　　　B　　　　　　　　C
twenty such languages in the <u>world</u>. <u>No error</u>
    　　　　　　　　　　　　D　　　　E

8. The <u>French</u> artist Paul Cezanne painted so <u>slow</u> that he often used wax fruit as
    　　　A　　　　　　　　　　　　　　　　B
<u>models; real</u> fruit would have <u>rotted</u>. <u>No error</u>
    　　C　　　　　　　　　　　　D　　　E

9. <u>Who</u> do you think <u>of when</u> you hear, "<u>to</u> be, or not <u>to be</u>"? <u>No error</u>
    　A　　　　　　　B　　　　　　　C　　　　　　D　　　E

10. Most people <u>know</u> that the bloodhound is the <u>world's</u> best tracker, but
    　　　　　　　A　　　　　　　　　　　　　　　B
few <u>realize</u> that this dog is capable of following an <u>eight-day-old</u> trail.
    　　C　　　　　　　　　　　　　　　　　　　D
<u>No error</u>
    E

11. There <u>are</u> no <u>irregular</u> verbs in <u>Esperanto. A</u> language invented in 1887 and
    　　　A　　　B　　　　　　C
<u>spoke</u> by at least a million people. <u>No error</u>
    D　　　　　　　　　　　　　E

12. <u>Interestingly, birds</u> do not have dainty <u>appetites, most</u> of them eat close to half
    　　A　　　　　　　　　　　　　　B
<u>there</u> <u>weight</u> each day. <u>No error</u>
    C　　D　　　　　E

13. When Langston Hughes was young and <u>unknown, he</u> was helped and
    　　　　　　　　　　　　　　　A
encouraged by the famous <u>poet Vachel Lindsay</u>. Now <u>him</u> and Lindsay are
    　　　　　　　　　　B　　　　　　　　　C
<u>equally</u> famous. <u>No error</u>
    D　　　　E

14. During the <u>Summer</u> of 1982, <u>sceintists</u> at the <u>State University of New York</u>
    　　　　　A　　　　　　B　　　　　　C
recorded 15,000 lightning bolts in just one storm. Amazingly, that's not
<u>unusual!</u> <u>No error</u>
    D　　　E

15. The site of the <u>Incan</u> city of <u>Machu Picchu</u> <u>lays</u> high in the <u>Andes.</u> <u>No error</u>
    　　　　　A　　　　　B　　　C　　　　　　D　　　E

Appendix

Sharing your writing with others is an important part of being a writer. The following response techniques can help you give and receive useful feedback as you share your writing and as you read the writing of others.

Sharing

How to Use   Read your words aloud to a peer. Your only purpose is to share and to hear how your words sound. Your listeners may ask you to slow down or to read your piece again, but at this stage their only response should be to listen carefully.

When to Use   Do this when you are just exploring and you do not want criticism. Reading to a peer is also a good way to celebrate finishing a piece of writing.

Pointing

How to Use   Ask readers to tell you what they like best in your writing. Tell them to identify specific words and phrases that they especially like. Encourage readers to say why those particular words are memorable.

When to Use   Use this technique when you want to find out what is getting through to your readers or when you want some encouragement and support.

Summarizing

How to Use   Ask readers to tell you what they think are your main ideas. The idea is to have readers tell you the points that most stand out for them, not the points that they like or the ones that confuse them. Tell readers that at this stage you are not asking for an evaluation of your writing.

When to Use   Use this technique when you want to know if the main ideas or goals of your writing are clear to your readers.

Telling

How to Use   Ask readers to tell you a bit about what happened to them as they read your words. For example, did they feel surprised at any point? Did anything in the writing make them feel happy or sad? As readers describe their reactions, ask them to connect their responses to specific passages in the writing.

When to Use   Use this technique when you want to know which words and phrases and ideas are especially effective and which ones are confusing to readers.

Replying

How to Use   Discuss with your readers the ideas you used in your writing. Ask readers to give you their own ideas on your topic.

When to Use   Use this technique when you want to get some new ideas to use in your writing.

Identifying Problems

How to Use   Ask for feedback on specific features of your writing, such as the organization, the development of ideas, or the choice of words. Ask questions that require more than a yes-or-no answer, such as the following: "What parts, if any, were confusing?" "How can I improve the organization?" "Where do you like the wording, and where does it need improvement?"

When to Use   Use this technique to identify the strengths and weaknesses of your piece.

OUTLINING

An outline can help you organize information logically. In a formal outline, the key ideas are the headings of the main parts. The details are the subpoints. A **sentence outline** uses complete sentences; a **topic outline** uses words or phrases, as in this model.

Zoos

Thesis Statement: Zoos serve three main functions: educating the public, promoting research, and conserving wildlife.

I. Educating the public (Key idea)
 A. Displays (Subpoint for I)
 B. Tours
 C. Lectures
 D. Attractions for children
II. Promoting research
 A. Study of animal organisms (Subpoint for II)
 B. Study of animal behavior
III. Conserving wildlife
 A. Breeding of zoo animals (Subpoint for III)
 B. Return of animals to the wild
  1. European bison (Detail for B)
  2. Hawaiian goose
 C. Care of zoo animals
  1. Re-creation of natural habitats (Detail for C)
  2. Feeding
  3. Veterinary aid

Correct Outline Form

1. Write the title at the top of the outline.
2. Arrange Roman numerals, capital letters, and Arabic numerals as shown in the model.
3. Indent each division of the outline.
4. Do not use a single subheading. Subdivide a main heading only if it can be broken down into at least two subpoints.
5. In a topic outline, use the same form for items of the same rank. If A is a noun, then B and C should be nouns.
6. In a topic outline, begin each item with a capital letter but use no end punctuation.

Heading   These lines contain your street address; your town or city, state, and ZIP code; and the date of the letter.

Inside Address   Include the name of an individual if you know it and the name and address of the organization.

Salutation   This begins two lines below the inside address and ends with a colon. If you are writing to a specific person, use the person's name. If you do not know who will receive your letter, use a general greeting.

Body   This section should be brief, courteous, and clear. State the purpose of your letter and indicate any items that you are requesting or have enclosed.

Closing   This appears two lines below the body and is always formal. "Sincerely" and "Yours truly" are examples.

Signature   Skip four spaces below the closing, print or type your name, and write your signature in the space.

Heading   58 Eagle Road
La Crosse, Wisconsin 54601
February 10, 19––

Superintendent of Documents   Inside Address
U. S. Government Printing Office
Washington, D.C. 20402

Dear Sir or Madam: Salutation

Body   I am writing a report about solar energy. I understand that your agency has several publications on this subject.

Please send me any free pamphlets you have available about solar energy. Also please send me your free catalog Selected List of U. S. Government Documents so that I can learn about inexpensive books you may have about solar energy.

I am also interested in any bills in Congress that deal with solar energy. Can you give me any information about legislation that may be pending? I will appreciate any help you can give me.

Sincerely,   Closing
Stella Noyes   Signature
Stella Noyes

Good spelling gives your writing a professional look and impresses your audience. You can improve your spelling by applying the strategies used by successful spellers. The following guidelines and tips should help.

Good Spelling Habits

1. **Conquer your personal spelling demons.** Keep a list of the words you misspell in your writing.

2. **Pronounce words carefully.** Pronouncing words correctly can help you spell them correctly. For example, if you spell *helpfully* as *helpfly,* it might be because you are mispronouncing the word.

3. **Get into the habit of seeing the letters in a word.** Some English spellings are tricky. By looking at new or difficult words letter by letter, you will remember the spellings more easily.

4. **Create memory devices for difficult words.** For example:

   a**cq**uaint (cq)   To get a**cq**uainted, I will *seek you.*
   princi**pal** (pal)   The princi**pal** is my *pal.*
   princi**ple** (ple)   Follow this princi**ple,** *ple*ase.

5. **Proofread everything you write.** Slowly read what you've written, word for word. You might even try reading a line in reverse order. Otherwise, your eyes may play tricks on you and let you skip a misspelled word.

Guidelines for Spelling Difficult Words

1. Look at the word and say it one syllable at a time.
2. Look at the letters and say each one.
3. Write the word without looking at it.
4. Check to see whether you spelled the word correctly. If so, write the word two more times.
5. If you made a mistake, note exactly what the mistake was. Then repeat steps 3 and 4 above.

Words Ending in a Silent *e*

Before adding a suffix beginning with a vowel to a word ending in a silent *e,* drop the *e* (with some exceptions).

amaze + -ing = amazing   love + -able = lovable
create + -ed = created   nerve + -ous = nervous

Exceptions: change + -able = changeable; courage + -ous = courageous

When adding a suffix beginning with a consonant to a word ending in a silent *e,* keep the *e* (with some exceptions).

late + -ly = lately   spite + -ful = spiteful
noise + -less = noiseless   state + -ment = statement

Exceptions: true + -ly = truly; argue + -ment = argument

Words Ending in *y*

Before adding a suffix to a word that ends in *y* preceded by a consonant, change the *y* to *i.*

easy + -est = easiest   crazy + -est = craziest

However, when you add *-ing,* the *y* does not change.

worry + -ed = worried *but* worry + -ing = worrying

When adding a suffix to a word that ends in *y* and is preceded by a vowel, the *y* usually does not change.

play + -er = player   employ + -ed = employed

Words Ending in a Consonant

In one-syllable words that end in *one* consonant preceded by *one* vowel, double the final consonant before adding a suffix beginning with a vowel, such as *-ed* or *-ing.* These are sometimes called 1+1+1 words.

dip + -ed = dipper   set + -ing = setting
hop + -ed = hopped   drug + -ist = druggist

The rule does not apply to words of one syllable that end in a consonant preceded by two vowels.

feel + -ing = feeling   peel + -ed = peeled
reap + -ed = reaped   heat + -ing = heating

In words of more than one syllable, double the final consonant (1) when the word ends with one consonant preceded by one vowel and (2) when the word is accented on the last syllable.

be•gin´   per•mit´   re•fer´

In the following examples, note that in the new words formed with suffixes, the accent remains on the same syllable.

be•gin´ + -ing = be•gin´ ning
per•mit´ + -ed = per•mit´ ted

In the following examples, the accent does not remain on the same syllable; thus, the final consonant is not doubled.

re•fer´ + -ence = ref´ er•ence
con•fer´ + -ence = con´ fer•ence

Prefixes and Suffixes

When adding a prefix to a word, do not change the spelling of the base word.

dis- + approve = disapprove   re- + build = rebuild
ir- + regular = irregular   mis- + spell = misspell

When adding -ly to a word ending in l, keep both l's. When adding -ness to a word ending in n, keep both n's.

careful + -ly = carefully   sudden + -ness = suddenness
final + -ly = finally   thin + -ness = thinness

Special Spelling Problems

Only one English word ends in -sede: *supersede.* Three words end in -ceed: *exceed, proceed,* and *succeed.* All other verbs ending in the sound -seed are spelled with -cede.

concede   precede   recede   secede

In words with *ie* and *ei* when the sound is long *e* (ē), the word is spelled *ie* except after *c* (with some exceptions).

i before *e*	thief	relieve	piece	field	grieve	pier
except after *c*	conceit	perceive	ceiling	receive	receipt
Exceptions:	either	neither	weird	leisure	seize

Improving Your
Spelling   **687**

U SING THE RIGHT WORD

Good writers master words that are easy to misuse and misspell. Study the following words, noting how their meanings differ.

accept, except   *Accept* means "to agree to something" or "to receive something willingly." *Except* usually means "not including."

Did the teacher *accept* your report?
Everyone smiled for the photographer *except* Jody.

all ready, already   *All ready* means "all are ready" or "completely prepared." *Already* means "previously."

The students were *all ready* for the field trip.
We had *already* pitched our tent before it started raining.

all right   *All right* is the correct spelling. *Alright* is nonstandard and should not be used.

a lot   *A lot* may be used in informal writing. *Alot* is incorrect.

borrow, lend   *Borrow* means "to receive something on loan." *Lend* means "to give out temporarily."

Please *lend* me your book.
He *borrowed* five dollars from his sister.

bring, take   *Bring* refers to movement toward or with. *Take* refers to movement away from.

I'll *bring* you a glass of water.
Please *take* these books back to the library.

capital, capitol, the Capitol   *Capital* means "excellent," "most serious," or "most important." It also means "seat of government." *Capitol* is a "building in which a state legislature meets." *The Capitol* is "the building in Washington, D.C., in which the U.S. Congress meets."

Proper nouns begin with *capital* letters.
Is Madison the *capital* of Wisconsin?
Protestors rallied at the state *capitol.*
A subway connects the Senate and the House in *the Capitol.*

choose, chose *Choose* is a verb that means "to decide or prefer." *Chose* is the past tense form of *choose*.

He had to *choose* between taking art or band.
She *chose* to write for the school newspaper.

desert, dessert *Des′ ert* means "a dry, sandy, barren region." *De sert′* means "to abandon." *Des sert′* is a sweet, such as cake.

The Sahara in North Africa is the world's largest *desert*.
The night guard did not *desert* his post.
Alison's favorite *dessert* is chocolate cake.

farther, further *Farther* refers to distance. *Further* refers to something additional.

We traveled two hundred miles *farther* that afternoon.
This idea needs *further* discussion.

fewer, less *Fewer* refers to numbers of things that can be counted. *Less* refers to amount, degree, or value.

Fewer than ten students camped out.
We made *less* money this year on the walkathon than last year.

good, well *Good* is always an adjective. *Well* is usually an adverb that modifies an action verb. *Well* can also be an adjective meaning "in good health."

Dana felt *good* when she finished painting her room.
Angela ran *well* in yesterday's race.
I felt *well* when I left my house.

its, it's *Its* is a possessive pronoun. *It's* is a contraction for *it is* or *it has*.

Sanibel Island is known for *its* beautiful beaches.
It's great weather for a picnic.

lay, lie *Lay* is a verb that means "to place." It takes a direct object. *Lie* is a verb that means "to be in a certain place." *Lie* never takes a direct object.

The carpenter will *lay* the planks on the bench.
My cat likes to *lie* under the bed.

lead, led *Lead* can be a noun that means "a heavy metal" or a verb that means "to show the way." *Led* is the past tense form of the verb.

> *Lead* is used in nuclear reactors.
> Raul always *leads* his team onto the field.
> She *led* the class as president of the student council.

learn, teach *Learn* means "to gain knowledge." *Teach* means "to instruct."

> Enrique is *learning* about galaxies and black holes in space.
> Marva *teaches* astronomy at a college in the city.

loan, lone *Loan* refers to "something given for temporary use." *Lone* refers to "the condition of being by oneself, alone."

> I gave that shirt to Max as a gift, not a *loan*.
> The *lone* plant in our yard turned out to be a scraggly weed.

lose, loose *Lose* means "to mislay or suffer the loss of something." *Loose* means "free" or "not fastened."

> That tire will *lose* air unless you patch it.
> My little brother has three *loose* teeth.

of Use *have*, not *of*, in phrases such as *could have, should have,* and *must have*.

> He could *have* passed if he had studied for the test.

principal, principle *Principal* means "of chief or central importance" and refers to the head of a school. *Principle* is a "basic truth, standard, or rule of behavior."

> Lack of customers is the *principal* reason for closing the store.
> The *principal* of our school awarded the trophy.
> One of my *principles* is to be honest with others.

quiet, quite *Quiet* refers to "freedom from noise or disturbance." *Quite* means "truly" or "almost completely."

> Observers must be *quiet* during the recording session.
> We were *quite* worried about the results of the test.

raise, rise   *Raise* means "to lift" or "to make something go up." It takes a direct object. *Rise* means "to go upward." It does not take a direct object.

> The maintenance workers *raise* the flag each morning.
> The city's population is expected to *rise* steadily.

set, sit   *Set* means "to place" and takes a direct object. *Sit* means "to occupy a seat or a place" and does not take a direct object.

> He *set* the box down outside the shed.
> We *sit* in the last row of the upper balcony at every concert.

stationary, stationery   *Stationary* means "fixed or unmoving." *Stationery* means "fine paper for writing letters."

> The wheel pivots, but the seat is *stationary.*
> Rex wrote on special *stationery* imprinted with his name.

than, then   *Than* is used to introduce the second part of a comparison. *Then* means "next in order."

> Ramon is stronger *than* Mark.
> Cut the grass and *then* trim the hedges.

their, there, they're   *Their* means "belonging to them." *There* means "in that place." *They're* is the contraction for they are.

> All the campers returned to *their* cabins.
> I keep my card collection *there* in those folders.
> Because Lisa and Beth run daily, *they're* on the track team.

whose, who's   *Whose* is the possessive form of who. *Who's* is a contraction for *who is* or *who has.*

> *Whose* parents will drive us to the movies?
> *Who's* going to the recycling center?

your, you're   *Your* is the possessive form of you. *You're* is a contraction for *you are.*

> What was *your* record in the fifty-yard dash?
> *You're* one of the winners of the essay contest.

SENTENCE DIAGRAMING

A sentence diagram is a drawing that shows how the parts of a sentence are related to each other. Use these models as guides.

Subjects and Verbs

Diagram subjects and verbs as you see here. Capitalize words capitalized in the sentence. Do not use punctuation except for abbreviations.

Spring arrived.

| Spring | arrived |

Interrogative and Imperative Sentences

In an interrogative sentence, the subject often comes after the verb. In diagraming, place the subject before the verb.

Did Carlos win?

| Carlos | Did win |

In an imperative sentence, the subject is usually not stated but is understood to be *you*. In diagraming, place the understood subject *you* before the verb. Enclose *you* in parentheses.

Wait. | (you) | Wait   Stop! | (you) | Stop

Direct and Indirect Objects

Write a direct object after a verb. Draw a short vertical line between them. Write an indirect object on the horizontal part of an angled line below the verb.

We sent him letters.

| We | sent | letters |
               \ him

Predicate Words

Write predicate words—nouns, pronouns, or adjectives—after a slanted line following the verb.

Gary felt lonesome.

| Gary | felt \ lonesome

Modifiers

Write adjectives and adverbs on slanted lines below the words they modify.

The lanky pitcher threw wildly.

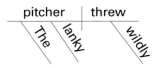

Sentences with Compound Parts

Split the line for the compound part. Draw a broken line for the conjunction.

She and I argued.
(Compound Subject)

People clapped and cheered.
(Compound Verb)

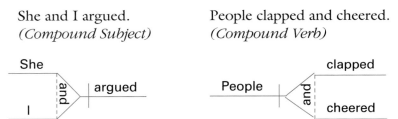

Prepositional Phrases

Draw an angled line below the word modified. Write the preposition on the slanted part and its object on the horizontal part. Put any modifiers on slanted lines below the object.

We heard footsteps
in the attic.

Infinitives and Infinitive Phrases

Draw an angled line. Write the word *to* on the slanted part and the verb on the horizontal part. Put the angled line on a bridge (⋀) at the place where the infinitive is used in the sentence.

To err is human.
(Infinitive used as subject)

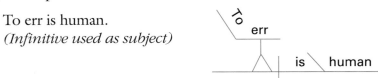

Participles and Participial Phrases

Write a participle on an angled line below the word it modifies. If a participle has a direct object, write the direct object after the participle and draw a vertical line between them. Put modifiers on slanted lines below the words they modify.

Opening the box,
he held his breath.

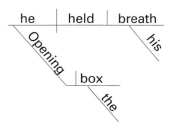

Gerunds and Gerund Phrases

Write a gerund on a step (⌐). Put the step on a bridge and place it where the gerund is used in the sentence. If a gerund has a direct object or modifiers, diagram them as shown.

Kitt enjoys riding a frisky pony.
(Gerund phrase used as direct object)

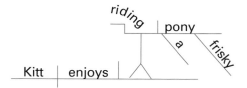

Compound Sentences

Show one simple sentence above another. Join them with a broken line and a step for the conjunction, as shown here.

The boys explored the cave, but they found no treasure.

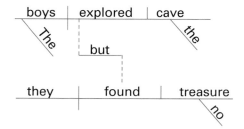

Complex Sentences

To diagram a complex sentence, determine the function of the subordinate clause.

Diagram an **adjective clause** on a line drawn below the line for the main clause. Draw a broken line from the word that introduces the adjective clause to the word it modified in the main clause.

Kareem is the student who won the contest.

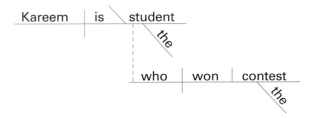

Diagram an **adverb clause** on a line below the line for the main clause. Write the subordinating conjunction on a broken line that connects the adverb clause to the word it modifies.

As we boarded the bus, we noticed a stranger.

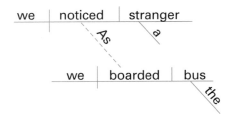

Diagram a **noun clause** on a bridge at the place where the clause is used in the sentence. Write the word that introduces the noun clause on a horizontal line above the clause.

That she would win was certain.
(Noun clause used as subject)

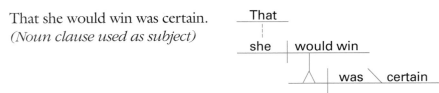

ADJECTIVE a word that modifies a noun or pronoun: *old* fence.

ADVERB a word that modifies a verb, an adjective, or another adverb; in "She sang well," *well* is an adverb modifying *sang.*

ARGUMENT speaking or writing that takes a position or states an opinion and gives evidence or reasons to support it; an argument often takes into account other points of view.

AUDIENCE your readers or listeners.

BRAINSTORMING a way of finding ideas that involves listing them without stopping to judge them.

CAUSE AND EFFECT a strategy for analyzing a subject that involves examining the reasons for actions or the results of specific actions.

CLASSIFICATION a way of organizing ideas by grouping them according to certain characteristics.

CLICHÉ an overused expression, such as "quiet as a mouse."

CLUSTER a kind of map made up of circled groupings of related details.

COHERENCE a paragraph has coherence when its sentences flow logically from one to the next; a composition has coherence when its paragraphs are connected logically.

COMPARISON AND CONTRAST a way of grouping ideas or things by showing their similarities and differences.

COMPLEX SENTENCE a sentence that contains one independent clause and one or more subordinate clauses.

CONJUNCTION a word or pair of words that connects other words or groups of words: Maya *and* Amy traveled.

CONNOTATION the ideas and feelings associated with a word as opposed to the dictionary definition of the word.

DENOTATION the dictionary definition of a word.

DIALECT   a form of a language that has a distinctive pronunciation, vocabulary, and word order.

DIALOGUE   spoken conversation; the conversation in novels, stories, plays, poems, or essays.

ELABORATION   the support or development of a main idea with facts, statistics, sensory details, incidents, examples, or quotations.

FIGURATIVE LANGUAGE   the imaginative and poetic use of words; writing that contains such figures of speech as similes, metaphors, and personifications.

FREEWRITING   a way of exploring ideas, thoughts, or feelings that involves writing freely—without stopping or otherwise limiting the flow of ideas—for a specific length of time.

GRAPHIC DEVICE   a visual presentation of details; graphic devices include charts, graphs, outlines, clusters, and idea trees.

IDEA TREE   a graphic device in which main ideas are written on "branches" and details related to them are noted on "twigs."

INTERJECTION   a word or phrase used to express strong feeling.

LEARNING LOG   a kind of journal specifically for recording and reflecting on what you have learned and for noting problems and questions to which you want to find answers.

METAPHOR   a figure of speech that makes a comparison without using the word *like* or *as;* "all the world's a stage" is a metaphor.

NONSEXIST LANGUAGE   language that includes both men and women when making reference to a role or group that comprises people of both sexes; "A medic uses his or her skills to save lives" and "Medics use their skills to save lives" are two nonsexist ways of expressing the same idea.

NOUN   a word that names a person, a place, a thing, or an idea.

PARAPHRASE   a restatement in your own words that keeps the ideas, the tone, and the general length of an original passage.

PEER RESPONSE   suggestions and comments on a piece of writing provided by peers, or classmates.

PLAGIARISM   the dishonest act of presenting someone else's words or ideas as if they were your own.

POINT OF VIEW   the angle from which a story is told, such as first-, third-, or second-person point of view.

PORTFOLIO   a container (usually a folder) for notes on work in progress, drafts and revisions, finished pieces, and peer responses.

PREPOSITION   a word that relates its object to some other word in the sentence; in "Marta moved to Detroit," *to* is a preposition.

PRONOUN   a word that is used to replace a noun or another pronoun; in "She called him at home," *she* and *him* are pronouns.

SENSORY DETAILS   words that express the way something looks, sounds, smells, tastes, or feels.

SIMILE   a figure of speech that uses the word *like* or *as* to make a comparison; "trees like pencil strikes" is a simile.

SPATIAL ORDER   organization in which details are arranged in the order that they appear in space, such as from left to right.

SUMMARY   a brief restatement in your own words of the main idea of a passage; supporting details are not included in a summary.

THESIS STATEMENT   a one-to-two-sentence statement of the main idea or purpose of a piece of writing.

TOPIC SENTENCE   a sentence that expresses the main idea of a paragraph.

TRANSITION   a connecting word or phrase that clarifies relationships between details, sentences, or paragraphs.

UNITY   A paragraph has unity if all its sentences support the same main idea or purpose; a composition has unity if all its paragraphs support the overall goal.

VERB   a word that expresses an action, a condition, or a state of being; in "Juan scored a touchdown," *scored* is a verb.

WRITING VOICE   the personality of the writer that comes across in the writing through word choice and sentence structure.

INDEX

A

A.D., 624
A.M., 624
Abbreviations
   capitalization of, 624
   notetaking and, 341
   periods with, 640
accept, except, 688
Action verbs, 474, 516
   in descriptive writing, 60
Active reading, 343–44
Active verbs, 489
Addresses
   commas in, 653
   in letters, 684
Adjective clauses, 564–65
   diagraming, 695
Adjective phrases, 540, 564
Adjective suffixes, 335
Adjectives, 507–10, 696
   adverbs confused with, 514
   adverbs modifying, 511
   articles, 510
   commas between, 644
   comparative forms, 518–20
   compound, 659
   diagraming, 693
   good and *well,* 516
   infinitives as, 597
   loaded language, 148
   predicate, 400, 507, 515–16
   pronouns as, 508
   proper, 507, 616
Adverb clauses, 567
   diagraming, 695
Adverb phrases, 540, 567
Adverbs, 511–12, 696
   adjectives confused with, 514
   with adjectives or other adverbs, 511
   commas after introductory, 644
   comparative forms, 522–23
   conjunctive, 656
   diagraming, 693
   direct objects confused with, 397
   forming, 512
   good and *well,* 516
   infinitives as, 597
   predicate adjectives and, 515–16
   prepositions confused with, 538
   with verbs, 511
Agreement
   pronoun–antecedent, 456
   subject–verb, 448, 577–92
Alliteration, 321

all ready, already, 688
all right, 688
Almanacs, 357
a lot, 688
Analysis frames, 260
Analyzing a story, 163–77
   drafting, 172–74
   prewriting, 170–72
   proofreading, 176
   publishing and presenting, 176–77
   reflecting, 177
   revising, 174–75
and, in stringy sentences, 298
Antecedents, 456
Apostrophes, 425, 660–61
Appositives, 311–12
   commas with, 648
   subject–verb agreement and, 578
Argument, 137–49, 696
   drafting, 144–45
   prewriting, 142–44
   proofreading, 148
   publishing and presenting, 149
   reflecting, 149
   revising, 146–47
Articles (*a, an, the*), 510
Assessment. *See* Evaluation, standards for;
   Peer response; Skills assessment
Assessment, writing for, 155–58
   drafting, 157–58
   prewriting, 156–57
   reviewing, 158
Assonance, 321
Atlases, 357
Audience, 4, 59, 88, 109, 234–35, 696
   for consumer report, 131
   language level and, 315
   for social action letter, 153
   word choice and, 314
Autobiographical incident, 27–39
   drafting, 34–35
   exploring topics for, 32–33
   prewriting, 32–33
   proofreading, 38
   publishing and presenting, 38–39
   reflecting, 39
   revising, 36–37
Autobiography, in library, 353

B

B.C., 624
Bandwagon appeal, 338
Bar graphs, 350

Superlative forms, 126
  adjectives, 518–20
  adverbs, 522–23
Support, for arguments, 144
  for analyzing a story, 174
  for position in social action letter, 154
Syllables, hyphens between, 659
Symbols
  evaluating, 365
  notetaking and, 341
Synonyms, coherence and, 276–77

T

take, bring, 688
teach, learn, 493, 690
Tense, using same, 57
Tenses, 483–84
Test questions
  analogy, 374
  antonym, 373
  completion, 370
  essay, 371
  fill–in–the–blank, 370
  grammar, usage, and mechanics, 373
  matching, 369
  multiple choice, 370
  reading comprehension, 372
  short–answer, 370
  synonym, 373
  true–false, 369
  vocabulary, 373
  see also Assessment, writing for
Test taking, 368–75
  classroom tests, 368–71
  standardized tests, 372–74
than, then, 691
that, using for sentence combining, 311
their, there, they're, 691
them, problems with, 460
them, those, 525
Theme, literary analysis and, 172, 173
there
  problems with, 525
  sentences beginning with, 391, 584
Thesis statement, 200, 683, 698
Third–person point of view, 322–23
those, problems with, 460
Time lines, 36, 108
Time order. *See* Chronological order
Titles (personal), capitalization of, 616
Titles (of written works)
  capitalization of, 628
  quotation marks with, 666

  underlining for, 176, 666
to, sign of the infinitive, 596
Topic outlines, 683
Topics
  focusing, 224–26
  see also Ideas for writing
Topic sentences, 34, 248–49, 698
  unity and, 269–70
Transitions, 274–76, 698
  in argument, 146
  chart of, 274
  chronological order and, 240–241
  comparison and contrast, 125
  demonstrative pronouns as, 450
  in informative writing, 102
  punctuation and, 104
  spatial order and, 242
  test answers and, 157
Transitive verbs, 396, 489

U

Underlining, with titles, 176, 666
Unity, 268–71, 698
  descriptive writing and, 270
  main idea and, 268–69
  narrative writing and, 270
  in paragraphs, 244–45, 250
  topic sentences and, 269–70

V

Variety, in sentences, 46–47, 68–69, 302–303
Vehicles, capitalization of, 624
Venn diagrams, 121, 231
Verbals, 595–610
  gerunds, 603–604
  infinitives, 596–97
  participles, 599
Verb phrases, 389, 476
Verbs, 389, 473–503, 698
  action, 60, 474, 516
  active, 489
  compound, 68–69, 403, 557, 693
  defined, 474
  diagraming, 692, 693
  helping, 389, 476
  intransitive, 396
  irregular, 67
  linking, 400–401, 474, 507, 516
  main, 389, 476
  passive, 489
  perfect tenses, 484

ACKNOWLEDGMENTS

Sources of Quoted Materials

22: Ashley K. Kuhlman and Northwestern University Center for Talent Development Summer Program: For "Dear Omoni" by Ashley Kuhlman; copyright © 1990 by Ashley Kuhlman. Reprinted by permission of the author. **26:** Liveright Publishing Corp.: For "to be nobody-but-yourself" by E. E. Cummings, from "A Poet's Advice to Students," from *A Miscellany* by E. E. Cummings, edited by George C. Firmage with the permission of Liveright Publishing Corporation; copyright 1955 by E. E. Cummings. Copyright © 1965 by Marion Morehouse Cummings. Copyright © 1958, 1965 by George James Firmage. **40:** Warner/Chappell Music, Inc.: For lyrics of "The Circle Game" by Joni Mitchell; copyright 1966 & 1974 Siquomb Publishing Corp. All rights reserved. Used by permission. **51:** The New York Times Company: For excerpts from "The Days of a Scavenger amid the Rubble" by Deborah Sontag, from *The New York Times*, September 1, 1992; copyright © 1992 by The New York Times Company. Reprinted by permission. **70:** Little, Brown & Company: For "Further Reflection on Parsley," from *Verses from 1929 On* by Ogden Nash; copyright 1942 by Ogden Nash. Reprinted by permission of Little, Brown & Company. For "Song to My Mother's Macaroni and Cheese" and "Song Against Broccoli," from *One Fell Soup* by Roy Blount, Jr.; copyright © 1976 by Roy Blount, Jr. By permission of Little, Brown & Company. **72:** T. D. Allen: For "Celebration" by Alonzo Lopez, from *The Whispering Wind*, Doubleday, 1972. Used by permission of the author. **73:** Farrar, Straus & Giroux, Inc.: For "The Drum," from *Spin a Soft Black Song* by Nikki Giovanni; copyright © 1971 by Nikki Giovanni. University Press of New England: For "The Base Stealer" by Robert Francis, from *The Orb Weaver;* copyright 1948 by Robert Francis. Wesleyan University Press by permission of University Press of New England. **84:** Tom Musca/Green Light Productions: For excerpts from the script *Stand and Deliver* by Tom Musca and Ramon Menendez; copyright © 1988 by Tom Musca and Ramon Menendez. **94:** Margaret Poynter: For excerpts from "Krakatoa, the Greatest of Them All" by Margaret Poynter, from *Cricket*, June 1985 issue. By permission of the author. **106:** HarperCollins Publishers: For edited text excerpts from *Mummies Made in Egypt* by Aliki; copyright © 1979 by Aliki Brandenberg. Reprinted by permission of HarperCollins Publishers. **111:** Macmillan Publishing Company: For six sniglets from *Sniglets* by Rich Hall and

Friends; copyright © 1984 by Not the Network Company, Inc. Reprinted with the permission of Collier Books, an imprint of Macmillan Publishing Company. For two sniglets from *More Sniglets* by Rich Hall and Friends; copyright © 1985 by Not the Network Company, Inc. Reprinted with the permission of Collier Books, an imprint of Macmillan Publishing Company. **116:** The Time Inc. Magazine Company: For an excerpt from "A Land of Staggering Proportions" by Steve Petranek, Brad Darrach, and Ann Hollister, from *Life Magazine;* copyright © 1991, The Time Inc. Magazine Company. Reprinted with permission. **128:** Consumers Union: For "Why Is Everybody Eating Frozen Yogurt?" published in the August/September 1991 issue of *Zillions;* copyright © 1991 by Consumers Union of United States, Inc., Yonkers, NY 10703. Reprinted by permission from *Zillions,* August/September 1991. **138:** Scholastic, Inc.: For excerpts from "Privacy and Teens" by Lauren Tarshis, from *Update,* September 2l, 1990; copyright © 1990 by Scholastic, Inc. Used with permission. **164:** Pat MacEnulty: For an excerpt from "Dancing for Poppa" by Pat MacEnulty, from *American Way,* November 1991. By permission of the author. **178:** HarperCollins Publishers: For excerpts from "Why Monkeys Live in Trees," from *African Folk Tales* by Jessie Alford Nunn; copyright © 1969 by Jessie Alford Nunn. Reprinted by permission of HarperCollins Publishers. **206:** John Hawkins & Associates, Inc.: For "My Furthest-Back Person" by Alex Haley, published in *The New York Times Magazine,* July 16, 1972; copyright © 1972 by Alex Haley. Reprinted by permission of John Hawkins & Associates, Inc. **272:** Washington Journalism Review: For excerpts from "Take 2" by Carl Sessions Stepp, from *Washington Journalism Review,* issues 12/90, 4/91, 10/9l, and 10/90. Reprinted by permission of Washington Journalism Review. **345:** Deborah Hopkinson: For excerpts from "The Girls' Doll Festival" by Deborah Hopkinson, from *Cricket,* August 1992 issue. Reprinted by permission of the author. **593:** The New Yorker Magazine, Inc.: For "Mother Tongue" by Richard Armour, from *The New Yorker,* May 26, 1956; copyright © 1956, 1974 The New Yorker Magazine, Inc. Reprinted by permission. **611:** Addison-Wesley Publishing Company: For excerpts from *Family Words* by Paul Dickson; copyright © 1988 by Paul Dickson. Reprinted with permission of Addison-Wesley Publishing Company.

The authors and editors have made every effort to trace the ownership of all copyrighted selections found in this book and to make full acknowledgment for their use.

Illustration & Photography Credits

Commissioned Illustrations: Ray Ameijide: **94-95;** Al Brandtner: **206-207;** Rondi Collette: **258;** Eddie Corkery: **164-167;** David Cunningham: **564;** Joe Fournier: **128-129, 233;** Roz Hosier: *graphics* **153;** Mary Jones: **26, 283, 417;** Tim Jonke: **138-139;** Linda Kelen: **220, 618;** Jared D. Lee: **3, 4, 7, 8, 314, 342;** Peg Magovern: **637;** Eric Masi: **92, 119 *l* , 320, 380, 504, 524, 638;** Beth Morrison: *graphics* **294;** Richard Murdock: **147, 324, 336 *t*, 338;** Steve Musgrave: **136,** *graphics* **637;** Lance Paladino: **72-73;** Kevin Pope: **67, 183, 111, 267, 367, 433, 593, 611;** Precision Graphics, Inc.: **45 *t* ;** Ruben Ramos: **40-41;** Jesse Reisch: **178-179;** John Rodgers: **211 *t* ;** Richard Shanks: **36, 133 *t* , 142, 149 *t*, 504;** Troy Thomas: **331;** Russell Thurston: **28-29, 116-117;** Robert Voigts: **70, 84-85, 108, 228, 229, 230, 231, 272, 336 *b* , 341, 349, 350, 351, 415, 416, 423, 483, 554, 594, 603, 614;** Amy Wasserman: **360;** Cheryl Winser (*handcoloring*): **45 *b*, 133, 292, 300, 381.**

Assignment Photography: John Morrison: **12-13, 22-23, 30-31, 52-53, 62 *t*, 74-75, 77, 81, 83, 96-97, 118-119, 140-141, 149 *b* , 152, 168-169, 188-189, 190-191, 192-193, 376, 418, 434;** Art Wise: **ii.**

Art and Photography: xxii: Photography © Jack Parsons; **13:** Ashley Kuhlman; **24:** From the Collection of Nancy Berliner and Zeng Xiaojun. Copyright Nancy Berliner; **28-29:** Family photographs courtesy of Dr. Leo F. Buscaglia, Ph.D.; **33:** © David Barnes; **39:** © David Barnes; **43:** © G. Kalt/Allstock; **44:** © Obremski/The Image Bank; **45:** UPI/Bettmann; **48:** Illustration from *The Mysteries of Harris Burdick* by Chris Van Allsburg. Copyright © 1985 by Chris Van Allsburg. Reprinted by permission of Houghton Mifflin Company. All rights reserved; **50-51:** © Porter Gifford/Gamma-Liaison; **55:** © Superstock; **58:** © Lawrence Migdale; **61:** © Lawrence Migdale; **62:** *b* Gerry Ellis/The Wildlife Collection; **62-63:** *border* © Gerry Ellis/The Wildlife Collection; **63:** © 1990 Boyd Norton; **65:** © Keiji Terakoshi/The Image Bank; **66:** *t* © John Terence Turner/FPG; *b* *After the Alaskan Oil Spill*, by Sigrid Holmwood, age 11. Courtesy The National Exhibition of Children's Art, London; **87-88:** © Mitzi Trumbo/Shooting Star; **89:** *t* © James Marsh; *b* © Martha Swope; **97:** ©

Peter Miller/Photo Researchers, Inc.; **98:** © Bruce Davidson/Magnum Photos, Inc.; **102:** © David Robinson; **106-107:** Field Museum of Natural History, Chicago, Neg# A111057C; **107:** The Oriental Institute, Chicago; **110:** *t* Field Museum of Natural History, Chicago/Illustration by Carl Kock; *b* © Laurence Hughes/The Image Bank; **114:** © George Rodriguez/Shooting Star; **116-117:** United States Geological Survey, public domain; **117:** ESA/Science Photo Library/Photo Researchers, Inc.; **119:** *r* © Ron Kimball; **121:** © Bob Torrez/TSW; **122:** © Ron Kimball; **124:** © John Terence-Turner/FPG; **127:** Copyright William Wegman, Courtesy Pace/MacGill Gallery, New York; **131:** © 1990 G.A.S./PhotoBank, Inc.; **132:** Photograph from "Why is Everybody Eating Frozen Yogurt?" Copyright 1991 by Consumers Union of U.S., Inc., Yonkers, NY 10703-1057. Reprinted by permission from *Zillions*. August/September 1991; **133:** *c* © 1992 The Andy Warhol Foundation for the Visual Arts, Inc.; *b* From the Collections of Henry Ford Museum and Greenfield Village; **149:** *b* Courtesy Thro Dough Studios, Toronto; **150-151:** © Jim Sloane; **152:** T-Shirt Courtesy Citizen Alert; **153:** © Jim Sloane; **159:** *t* © 1988 Middleton/Liittschwager; *c* Illustration by Guy Billout, reprinted with permission of A.C. Nielsen Company; *b* Courtesy The Mill Valley Film Festival; **162:** © Brian Seed/TSW; **170:** © Comstock; **172:** © Superstock; **177:** © Theo Westenberger; **181:** © Peter Kuper; **182:** *t* Photofest, New York; *b* Photography Courtesy Perls Galleries, NY; **186:** © Robert McCall; **188:** *t* Cahokia Mounds State Historic Site; *b* Courtesy Illinois Historic Preservation Agency/Photograph by Terry Farmer; **189:** Courtesy Cahokia Mounds State Historic Site; **193:** © T. Linke/Superstock; **194:** Courtesy National Park Service/ Photography courtesy Detroit Institute of Arts; **195:** Courtesy National Museum of the American Indian/Smithsonian Institution, NEG # 18/9306; **201:** Gilcrease Museum, Tulsa, OK; **203:** Gilcrease Museum, Tulsa, OK; **204:** Ohio State Historical Society; **209:** © Dan Krovatin; **210:** Design and Art: George Tscherny; **211:** *cl* Ralph Brunke; *cr* The "T" ball, manufactured in England and used extensively in America in the 1930s and 1940s is from the Archives of the National Soccer Hall of Fame, Oneonta, NY/ Photograph by Ed Clough; *b* © Alain Choisnet/The Image Bank; **214:** © Faith Ringgold, Collection of Marilyn Lanfear; **217:** The Carson Collection; **219:** The Art Institute of Chicago, Friends of American Art Collection, 1942.51; **223:** © Jill Freedman; **224:** Copyright William Wegman, Courtesy Pace/MacGill Gallery, New York; **227:** © Andrew Shachat; **236:** © Doron Ben-Ami/The Image Bank; **243:** © Chip Simons; **247:** Photography Courtesy

United States Geological Survey; **248:** © Lupus; **251:** © Richard Kolar/Animals, Animals; **253:** The Hayden Collection, Courtesy Museum of Fine Arts, Boston; **254:** © Shooting Star; **261:** © Ormond Gigli/The Stock Market; **269:** Courtesy Cirque du Soleil/Photography © Al Seib; **271:** Curt Teich Postcard Archive, Lake County (IL) Museum; **278:** © 1989 Wendell Minor; **285:** © Clayton Fogle/Allstock; **289:** AP/Wide World Photos; **292:** Photograph Courtesy Myrt and John Deambrogio, Queensland, Australia; **294:** © Paul Natkin/ Photo Reserve Inc.; **295:** © 1983 Ron Scherl/The Bettmann Archive; **299:** © 1992 The Andy Warhol Foundation for the Visual Arts, Inc.; **300:** UPI/The Bettmann Archive; **302:** © Paul Natkin/Photo Reserve Inc.; **307:** © Kevin Horan; **311:** © William Caxton/ Archive Photos; **317:** © Chip Simons; **322:** BOUND & GAGGED comic strip series by Dana Summers. Reprinted by permission: Tribune Media Services; **328:** MOTHER GOOSE & GRIMM comic strip series by Mike Peters. Reprinted by permission: Tribune Media Services; **329:** © Erich Lessing/Art Resource, NY; **345:** From the Collection of Charlene Lopez/ Photography Courtesy Pat Smith; **346:** © Jon Conrad; **352:** "Discover the Americas" poster © 1991 American Library Association. Design: Belinoff & Bagley, Albuquerque, NM. Used by permission; **354:** Courtesy California State Library, California Section; **365:** Photograph Courtesy Michelin Tire Corporation; **366:** © Gilles Bussignac/ Gamma-Liaison; **372:** © Andrew Stawicki; **376:** Permanent Collection of the Mexican Fine Arts Center Museum, Chicago, 1992.165, Candelabro, Oscar Soteno, polychrome ceramic and wire, 1992, 19" x 17 3/4 x 7 1/2, Museum Purchase Fund; **381:** © Springer/Bettmann Film Archive; **385:** © Pat Crowe/Animals, Animals; **390:** Montana Historical Society, Helena; **393:** NASA; **395:** Illustration from *Just A Dream* by Chris Van Allsburg. Copyright © 1990 by Chris Van Allsburg. Reprinted by permission of Houghton Mifflin Company. All rights reserved; **399:** The Carson Collection; **402:** © Derek Berwin/The Image Bank; **418:** CLUE ® is a registered trademark of Waddingtons Games Ltd. Used with permission of Parker Brothers, the exclusive licensee; **424:** Photograph from *Trevor's Place: The Story Of The Boy Who Brings Hope To The Homeless* by Frank and Janet Ferrell with Edward Wakin. Copyright © 1985 Frank and Janet Ferrell. Afterword copyright © 1985 by Rebecca J. Laird. Reprinted by permission of HarperCollins Publishers; **435:** © Dilip Mehta/Contact Press Images; **437:** © Eric Hansen; **441:** © Superstock; **442:** © Mel Horst; **447:** The Far Side cartoon by Gary Larson is reprinted by permission of Chronicle Features, San Francisco, CA; **451:** Private Collection, oil on canvas, 26 x

40 inches. Fractional Gift to The Fine Arts Museums of San Francisco, CA; **455:** *t* © 1990 Rob Nelson/Black Star; *b* © David Madison/ Duomo; **458:** © Spencer Grant/ PhotoBank, Inc.; **461:** © Martha Cooper/ Peter Arnold, Inc.; **472:** © Bill Dekay/ Nawrocki Stock Photo, Inc.; **473:** © 1993 The Estate of Keith Haring/Courtesy Fotofolio, New York; **477:** © Ken Biggs/ TSW; **481-482:** American Red Cross; **486:** Photography Courtesy Yale University Art Gallery, Gift of Duncan Phillips, B.A. 1908; **488:** © William R. Sallaz/Duomo; **492:** © Geoffrey Moss; **495:** The Granger Collection, New York; **505:** © Mark W. Richards; **506:** *l* Giraudon/Art Resource, NY; *r* Vincent Van Gogh Foundation/Van Gogh Museum, Amsterdam; **507:** Art Resource, NY/Van Gogh Museum, Amsterdam; **509:** Collection, The Museum of Modern Art, New York. Oil on canvas, 29 x 36 1/4. Acquired through the Lillie P. Bliss Bequest; **514:** © John Running; **515:** Photograph © 1987 Jack Parsons; **519:** © Jane Burton/Bruce Coleman Limited; **528:** The Library of Congress; **534-535:** © John Margolies/Esto. All rights reserved; **536:** © Tom Sanders/Adventure Photo; **540:** © Spencer Grant/Photobank, Inc.; **545:** Photo by Alma Walters Compton, Denver Public Library, Western History Department; **555:** © Eric Meola/The Image Bank; **558:** © Jean-Claude Carton/Bruce Coleman, Inc.; **563:** © George Haling/Photo Researchers, Inc.; **569:** © Anne La Bastille; **576:** Courtesy of the Holly Solomon Gallery, New York; **577:** Collection of Dr. and Mrs. Paul Chapnick/Photography Courtesy of the New York State Museum; **578:** Photography by Geoff O'Connell, Courtesy of Ferrin Gallery, Northampton, MA; **583:** Curt Teich Post Card Archive, Lake County (IL) Museum; **585:** Still Courtesy of Warner Bros.; **595:** © Chip Simons; **596:** NASA; **602:** The Granger Collection, New York; **615:** © Darrell Gulin/Allstock; **625:** © Ken Marschall; **626:** © Steven E. Sutton/Duomo; **629:** © Shooting Star; **640:** Collection of the Museum of American Folk Art, New York, 1986.14.1; **645:** © William D. Adams/FPG; **649:** © Tom Sobolik/Black Star; **650:** Photofest, New York; **655:** © Uli Wiesmeier/Adventure Photo; **658:** © Jeff Foott/Tom Stack & Associates; **663:** © 1987 Jack Parsons; **667:** Poster Courtesy Triton Gallery, NY; **668:** © Richard A. Goldberg/Stockworks.

Cover
Ryan Roessler